PROGRAMMING
in RPG IV

4th Edition

**Bryan Meyers
and Jim Buck**

Programming in RPG IV, 4th Edition
Bryan Meyers and Jim Buck

First Edition
First MC Press Printing—June 2010

MC Press Online, LLC, offers excellent discounts on this book when ordered in quantity for bulk purchases or special sales, which may include custom covers and content particular to your business, training goals, marketing focus, and branding interest.

MC Press Online, LLC
Corporate Offices: 3695 W. Quail Heights Court, Boise, ID 83703-3861 USA
Sales and Customer Service: (208) 629-7275 ext. 500; service@mcpressonline.com
Permissions and Bulk/Special Orders: mcbooks@mcpressonline.com
www.mcpressonline.com • www.mc-store.com

ISBN: 978-1-58347-355-9   WB201407

For Judy Yaeger, an RPG Classic.

Acknowledgments

More so than most new editions, this edition of Programming in RPG IV seemed more like writing an entirely new book than updating an existing one. Without the help of the following individuals, this edition would not have been possible. At MC Press, Merrikay Lee streamlined the transition to our new publisher, assuring the book's continuing availability. Katie Tipton provided her signature careful editing of the manuscript; Jan Fonda transformed hundreds of pages of text into a handsome layout; and Nathan Martin designed the new cover art. The following Gateway Technical College graduates provided their programming and editing skills to produce the database, programming examples, and other ancillary materials for instructors: Nick Arndt, Joe Upright, Chris Anderson, and Michele Oksa.

Table of Contents at a Glance

Table of Contents

[*Italic type* indicates a sidebar.]

Preface

RPG IV, the version of the RPG language that participates in IBM's Integrated Language Environment (ILE), represents a dramatic step forward in RPG's evolution. RPG IV diverges from its predecessor, RPG III, in significant ways. However, to encourage adoption of the new ILE RPG/400 compiler and to prevent a nightmare for those programmers faced with maintaining older RPG programs, IBM made this latest release largely "backward-compatible" with older versions of RPG. Programs written before 1995 can easily be converted to RPG IV and subsequently modified, without the need for complete program rewrites. Although such backward-compatibility is a practical solution for language developers, it means that the language must retain some components that, in fact, the new features make obsolete.

Writing a textbook about a new version of a language, then, presents authors with a difficult decision: How much emphasis should be given to those features that, although still available in the language, really represent an outmoded approach to programming? Giving obsolete syntax equal importance with the language's more modern features might inappropriately encourage students to write outdated code; at the very least, equal coverage can unnecessarily complicate the learning process. On the other hand, ignoring those obsolete features completely would give students an incomplete understanding of the language and would ill prepare them for program-maintenance tasks. With the introduction of the free-format specification, the challenge becomes even more problematic than before. The free-format syntax represents a much more dramatic departure from traditional columnar RPG than did previous releases.

This textbook tries to solve the dilemma by initially presenting students with the most suitable, modern techniques that RPG IV offers for solving typical programming problems. As RPG IV matures and its use becomes widespread, it's important that students be presented with the language in its most current form, using the style and techniques that will serve them for the long term. Thus, the bulk of the book features the appropriate methods and strategies that contemporary programmers use, relegating much of the older styles, operations, and fixed-format techniques to Appendix E. When students tackle maintenance tasks on older RPG programs (maybe even RPG III or RPG II programs), they will be able to refer to the information in Appendix E for help.

Programming in RPG IV tries to bridge the gap between academia and the business world by presenting all the facets of RPG IV needed by a professional programmer. The material is introduced incrementally, and the book is organized so that students quickly begin writing complete—although simple—programs. Each successive chapter introduces additional information about RPG IV syntax and fundamental programming methods, so that students become increasingly proficient at developing RPG IV programs—programs that grow in complexity as students progress through the book.

Each chapter includes a brief overview, which orients students to the material contained in the chapter, and a chapter summary, which reviews the chapter's major points. The end-of-chapter sections include discussion/review questions, exercises, and programming assignments designed to help students develop their analytical and problem-solving skills, as well as their proficiency with RPG IV syntax.

The programming assignments at the end of each chapter are arranged roughly in order of difficulty, so that instructors can assign programs appropriate to their time schedules and their students' abilities. Although none of the program solutions are long by commercial standards, some of the necessary algorithms are quite difficult; the assignments require time and effort on the part of the students to develop correct solutions. Unfortunately, there is no "easy road" to becoming a good programmer, nor can students learn to deal with program complexity by merely reading or talking about it. Programming, as much as any other activity we know, is truly a matter of "learning by doing." Those students interested in becoming IT professionals must recognize that they have chosen a rewarding—but demanding and challenging—profession, and they need to realize that they must be willing to work hard to succeed in this profession.

To give students experience developing application systems, rather than programming in a vacuum, most of the programming assignments relate to three fictitious companies and their application needs (described in Appendix F). By working on these assignments, students should gain a sense of how a company's data files are repeatedly used by numerous applications for different, related purposes.

The structure and order of this edition of *Programming in RPG IV* have dramatically changed from previous editions. The new sequence of topics is the result of actual experience using the existing materials in both corporate training and academic institutional environments. We think you'll find the new order and the new topics work better than previous editions to methodically introduce students to RPG IV. This edition also places much more emphasis on the Integrated Language Environment than did previous editions and better covers the important topics of procedures and binding. The material uses Version 5 Release 4 as a baseline and is current at that release and later.

Appendices A and B are intended to be reference material not only for students, but also for working RPG IV programmers. Appendix A serves as a reference digest of RPG specifications, keywords, and miscellaneous entries. Appendix B suggests style guidelines for writing programs that will be easy to read, understand, and maintain.

Although a complete introduction to using the System i is beyond the scope of this text, Appendix C introduces students to working on the system using Programming Development Manager (PDM) as well as WebSphere Development Studio Client (WDSc). This appendix also acquaints students with PDM's Source Entry Utility (SEU) and WDSc's LPEX editor. Appendix D provides some insights into program testing and debugging, often bewildering processes for beginning programmers.

This text strives toward a coding style that represents the current state of RPG IV syntax, but it's likely that RPG IV programmers will be called upon to maintain existing RPG programs that are based on older features. To help students understand these programs, Appendix E covers older, now obsolete, RPG IV syntax as well as RPG III and RPG II.

Depending on the length of the school term and the pace of the course, some instructors may choose to present this material over two terms. An instructor's manual is available to those instructors adopting this text for classroom use. The manual provides answers to the review questions and solutions to the exercises. The manual also includes a CD with the data files needed for the programming assignments, the source code for the solutions to the programming assignments, and copies of the output produced by the solutions.

Chapter 1

Introduction to Programming and RPG

Chapter Overview
This chapter introduces you to RPG and describes its history and evolution from punched cards to a modern business programming language. It also explains general programming and computer-related concepts that you need to know as you begin to program in RPG IV.

Programming
Computer programming involves writing instructions that tell a computer exactly how to process, or manipulate, data. No matter how complex a computer application may be, its actions are ultimately directed by individual lines of code that operate on input information and generate a result. When those individual instructions are organized and grouped together, they typically represent a step-by-step process that will result in a specific product, such as a sales report. It is the job of a computer programmer to design, organize, write, and test those individual lines of code, creating a working computer program as the end result.

The computer is a binary device, with electronic components that can depict only two states: on and off, or flow of current and no flow of current. To represent those states, computers internally store and manipulate instructions (and data) as patterns of **bits**, or **binary digits,** with values of 1 or 0. Programmers originally were forced to write computer instructions as strings of 1s and 0s, using machine language. Humans, however, do not function as well at this low-representation level. Fortunately, advances in computer science soon led to the development of **high-level languages (HLLs).**

A high-level language allows a programmer to write computer instructions in a format and syntax that is more easily recognizable than long strings of 1s and 0s. This HLL **source code** is stored in a file on the computer. But before the computer can actually execute the instructions, they must be translated into the bit patterns that the computer can recognize. The computer itself can accomplish this translation using a special program called a **compiler.** A compiler reads the source code and translates it into machine language that the computer can understand.

History of RPG
IBM introduced the **Report Program Generator (RPG)** programming language in the early 1960s. RPG was one of the first high-level languages. It filled a niche for providing quick solutions to a common business task: generating reports needed within the business. RPG was unique among computer languages in several respects.

RPG is a **procedural language.** Procedural languages typically require that you explicitly code each processing step or instruction, in the correct sequence, to define the procedure or process necessary for the computer to produce the end result. Unlike other procedural languages, RPG did not require the programmer to detail each processing step. Instead, the language included a fixed logic cycle that automatically executed the normal read–calculate–write process found in most report programs.

The RPG programmer's job was to describe accurately the files, record layouts, calculations, and output desired for a specific program. RPG required that these descriptive specifications appear in a specific designated sequence within a program and that entries within each specification line appear in fixed locations, or columns. The programmer typically coded these specifications onto paper hole-punch cards, a deck of which formed the source code for a program. The RPG compiler read that card deck and, through its logic cycle, supplied the needed missing steps to provide a standard machine language program for the computer to execute.

Another unique characteristic of RPG was its use of a special class of built-in variables called **indicators**. These variables, many of which simply had numbers for names, were predefined to the computer and could have only one of two values: '1' or '0' (corresponding to "on" or "off"). The indicators could be set on or off in one part of the program; their status could then be referenced in another part of the program to determine what processing was to occur.

RPG II

By the late 1960s, RPG had gained popularity, especially in small and midsized data-processing departments. Programmers were stretching the language beyond its original intended use and using RPG for complex computations and complicated file updating as well as for report generation.

Accordingly, IBM introduced an enhanced version of the language—RPG II—when it released its System/3 computer. Other computer vendors observed the popularity of RPG and developed RPG II compilers for their minicomputers—but for the most part, RPG remained a language associated with IBM installations.

RPG III

During the 1970s, several trends in data processing became apparent. First, as computers became less expensive and more powerful and as operating systems became more sophisticated, interest in interactive programs began to mushroom. In **interactive applications**, a user interacts directly with the computer through a terminal or workstation to control the actions of a computer program as it is running. Previously, programs had involved only **batch processing**, in which the computer processes a "batch" of data (typically representing business transactions) without user intervention.

A second emerging trend was a growing interest in a database approach to data management. With a database approach, programmers define data independently of programs, using a database design tool, such as **Structured Query Language (SQL)**. The files storing the data are rigorously designed and organized to minimize redundancy and to facilitate accessing data stored in separate files. Any program can use these database files without having to explicitly define the details of the data within the program itself.

Finally, a third trend during that decade was an increasing concern with program design. This trend resulted in a methodology called **structured design**. As companies' libraries of developed programs continued to grow, the need to revise those programs to fit evolving business needs grew as well. It became apparent that computer professionals had paid too little attention to the initial design of programs. Poorly designed programs were causing inefficiencies in program maintenance. Experts attributed much of this inefficiency to "spaghetti code"—that is, to programs that included undisciplined, haphazard transfer of control from one part of a program to another.

Advocates of structured design recommended restricting indiscriminate flow of control within a program and using only those operations that kept tight controls on that flow. With this emphasis on structured design, concepts of modular programming and code reusability also began to emerge.

IBM addressed all these trends when it introduced the System/38 minicomputer in 1979. This computer's architecture was unique in that the design of the computer and its operating system featured a built-in database, and the S/38 required data files to be predefined at a system level before a program could reference or use those files. This requirement alone forced IBM to release a new version of RPG to allow external file definition. IBM called this new version RPG III.

At this time, IBM also made several other major changes to RPG. First, it added features that made it easier for programmers to develop interactive applications. Second, to address the issues of structured design, IBM included structured operations for looping and decision logic. Finally, to support modular code and reusability, IBM revamped the language to include the capability to perform calls to other programs and to pass data between programs.

RPG/400

In 1988, IBM announced its successor computer to the S/38: the Application System/400, or AS/400. With the new computer came a new version of RPG: RPG/400.

Despite its new name, RPG/400 was really just a compiler that read the existing RPG III syntax and had a few added operations and enhancements. Following RPG/400's initial release, IBM periodically added additional features to the language, but these changes, too, were relatively minor.

RPG IV

Meanwhile, a growing number of critics accused that RPG was difficult to understand because of its short data names, abbreviated operation codes, and rigidly fixed format. The critics contended that the language was showing its age in its limited choice of data types (e.g., no direct support for date data types), its inability to handle multidimensional arrays, and its patchwork approach to data definition.

To address some of these criticisms, in 1994, concurrent with the release of V3R1 of the AS/400's operating system (called OS/400), IBM introduced a version of RPG sufficiently unlike earlier versions that it warranted a change in name: RPG IV. In addition to trying to address the criticisms previously mentioned, IBM included RPG as part of its newly introduced **Integrated Language Environment (ILE)**, a programming model that allows program modules to be first compiled and then bound together into executable programs. This change supported the growing interest in developing reusable units of code and improving system performance. Moreover, it let programmers develop a program using modules written in different computer languages and then bind these modules into a single program.

RPG IV (also commonly known as ILE RPG/400) relaxes many of the strict fixed-format requirements imposed by previous RPG versions, allowing free-format expressions and keyword notation in its specifications. Data naming limits have been extended, and many other artificial limits have been effectively removed from the language. In addition, RPG IV adds several new organizational constructs, including a central data definition specification and procedure prototyping, which lets many program modules efficiently share information with each other. RPG IV borrows many of the best features of other programming languages and incorporates those features into its own new syntax.

IBM has rebranded the AS/400 several times over its lifetime to conform to current marketing strategies. It has been known by various combinations of AS/400, eServer, iSeries, and System i. The **OS/400 operating system** has also been rebranded as **i5/OS**, which is the name we will use in this text. Despite the system's various names, though, the RPG IV syntax remains intact.

Recent releases of RPG IV have focused on enabling the RPG IV architecture to coexist with Internet-based applications and objected-oriented languages, including Java. Modern e-business applications usually incorporate several hardware platforms (most notably, Intel-based computers) and software standards. As RPG IV evolves, it strives to maintain compatibility with these platforms and standards.

These changes have quieted—but not suppressed—RPG's critics. However, given the large base of existing RPG applications and IBM's present willingness to support RPG, it is likely that the language will continue to evolve and will remain the primary language for application development on i5/OS for many years to come.

If you compared RPG programs written 20 years ago with those written by RPG professionals today, you would be struck by their great design differences. These differences are not due solely to the use of operations unavailable in the past, although the new operations enabled the changes. The biggest change is that RPG, originally a language that emphasized specification instead of procedure, has been transformed by programming practices into a largely free-format procedural language. Today's programmers virtually ignore RPG's **fixed logic cycle**—the feature that made the language unique in the 1960s. And most modern programmers use RPG's indicators only in those instances in which the language absolutely requires their use.

Learning the RPG Language

Many RPG texts start by instructing students in RPG II and introduce RPG III or RPG IV only after thoroughly indoctrinating the students in the fixed logic cycle and the use of indicators. This book begins by teaching RPG as today's programmers use it. Only after you have mastered modern RPG will you become familiar with features of the language that were common in the past.

You may wonder why (if RPG programming has changed so much) you, as a student, even need to bother to learn features of the older versions of RPG. The reason is simple: For better or worse, most companies still use some programs that were written ten or more years ago. Because your first job in the computer profession probably will involve maintenance programming, you no doubt will be working with some programs based on RPG III or even RPG II. You will therefore need to understand the features of these language versions so that you can modify such programs when you encounter them. Appendix E points out the important differences between RPG II, RPG III, and RPG IV that you will need to know to complete your understanding of this language.

The newest releases of the RPG IV compiler allow **free-format** specifications for certain portions of the program. Free-format specifications bring with them many advantages, including improved readability, improved reliability, the ability to indent code, and a similarity to other languages you may already know. In this book, you'll generally find free-format illustrations. Because free format is a relatively new feature of RPG IV, however, it's likely that you will encounter many older fixed-format RPG IV programs. Appendix E describes fixed-format syntax. While the free-format version is generally preferred, your organization's standards will dictate which alternative you will use.

Now that you have an understanding of RPG's evolution, we can turn to some basic programming concepts that you need to know before you begin to learn RPG IV programming.

Note
Though this book refers to the System i hardware throughout, most RPG IV concepts also apply to older AS/400 and iSeries hardware. The i5/OS operating system concepts also apply to the operating system under its old name, OS/400.

Program Variables

Computer programs would be of little value if you needed a different program each time you wanted to change the values of the data to be processed. For example, imagine you are developing a payroll program, and one processing step is to multiply hours worked by pay rate. If you had to rewrite this step to explicitly state the number of hours worked and the hourly pay rate for each employee, you would be better off calculating wages by hand or with a calculator. The power and value of computer programming rests in the concept of variables.

A **program variable** is a named data item within a program that represents a location in the memory of the computer that can store data. When a programming instruction involves the manipulation of a variable, the computer checks the value stored at that memory location and uses that value in the calculation. Thus, you can tell the computer to take the value stored in variable Hours, multiply that by the value stored in variable Rate, and store the answer in variable GrossPay. If Hours contained 35 and Rate 6, GrossPay would become 210. If Hours contained 40 and Rate 5, GrossPay would become 200. In a program you might represent this process using variable names in this expression:

```
GrossPay = Hours * Rate;
```

RPG has traditionally used the term **field** rather than **variable**. Modern usage tends to restrict the term **field** to those variables defined within a database file and uses **variable** for other data items defined in the program; however, the terms are generally interchangeable. RPG is a strictly typed language—it requires you to define all variables by naming them, assigning each one a fixed length that determines the amount of memory allocated for storing the variable's values and declaring what type of data (character, numeric, date, etc.) the variable will contain. A program variable's name has meaning only within the context of the program where it is defined, even if it is a field in a database file. You will learn the methods RPG IV uses to define variables and the data types it allows in subsequent chapters of this book.

Objects, Data Files, and the Data Hierarchy

An important i5/OS architectural concept is that of **objects**. Almost every named entity is an object; every object is categorized by type. The object type identifies the purpose of the object and how it is used by the computer. Some common object types are

- Libraries, which are containers for other objects
- Files, which hold formatted data records
- Programs, which contain executable machine instructions
- Commands, which are shortcuts to executing programs
- Data areas, which are spaces used to store brief, unformatted information
- User profiles, which contain user IDs, passwords, and authorization and configuration information

RPG programs typically center on processing sets of data in files stored on disk or removable storage. Like other objects, files are stored within libraries. There are two major types of database files: physical files and logical files. A **physical file** contains physical data; a **logical file** contains a customized view of the data in a physical file. Logical files do not contain actual data records. Instead, they provide sorting and selection criteria for processing the records in the physical file. Logical files are typically maintained *dynamically*. That means that if you change a record in a physical file, the view of that data will change in every logical file related to the physical file. In other words, if you change a record in a logical file, the physical record in the related physical file will also change. RPG does not distinguish between physical files and logical files; it uses the same coding and techniques to process either one.

Generally, the information in a physical file falls into one of two conceptual categories: *transaction* or *master*. Files containing details of transactions—generated during the course of a day's business—are **transaction files**. Transaction files might contain individual sales transactions, orders, hours worked, journal entries, or similar information. Once you have processed a transaction file, you typically have no further use for it except for archival purposes.

In contrast, most companies have sets of data that are of long-term importance to the company. These files, called **master files**, contain vital information about customers, products, accounts, and so on. Although you may update or change master files, companies regard master files as permanent files of data. The i5/OS database does not specifically identify files as master files or transaction files; instead, it stores all the data in physical files within libraries in arrival sequence order. Your RPG application determines how you will use the data in the file.

Files, Records, and Fields

All files are organized into a data hierarchy of file/record/field. A **file** is a collection of data about a given kind of entity or object. For example, a business might have a customer master file that contains information about its customers. In the i5/OS architecture, a file is a distinct object you can create, move, copy, rename, delete, save, and restore as a unit.

A file, in turn, is broken down into **records** that contain data about one specific instance of the entity. Data about customer number 20 would be stored in a record within the customer file; data about customer number 321 would be stored in a separate record but within that same file.

Finally, each record contains several discrete pieces of data about each entity instance. For example, a customer record might contain the customer's account number, last name, first name, street address, city, state, zip code, phone number, date of last order, credit limit, and so on. Each of these items is a **field**. A field generally represents the smallest unit of data that we want to manipulate within a program. Figure 1.1 (*opposite*) illustrates this data hierarchy.

All records within a file usually contain the same fields of data. The file's **record format**, or record layout, describes the fields within a record; most files have only one record format. Because you define these fields to be fixed in length, if an alphanumeric value—for example, a person's last name—is shorter than the space allocated for it, blanks (or spaces) occupy the unused positions to the right of the value. If a numeric value is smaller than the space allocated for it, the system stores zeros in the unused positions. If quantity on hand, for example, is six positions long and has a value of 24, the value is stored in the file as 000024. Note that numeric values are stored as "pure" numbers—without dollar signs, commas, or decimal points. If a numeric field includes decimal places, it will be described with a total length, *including* the decimal places. For example, a numeric field described as three digits long with two decimal places could contain a value up to 9.99, which it would store as 999.

Rarely, a file may contain different record types, with different fields, each with its own distinct format. In this case, each record usually contains a code field whose value signals which format the record represents. Figure 1.2 (*opposite*) illustrates a data file with multiple record formats, with the format being determined by the Record Code field.

Figure 1.1
Example of the Data Hierarchy

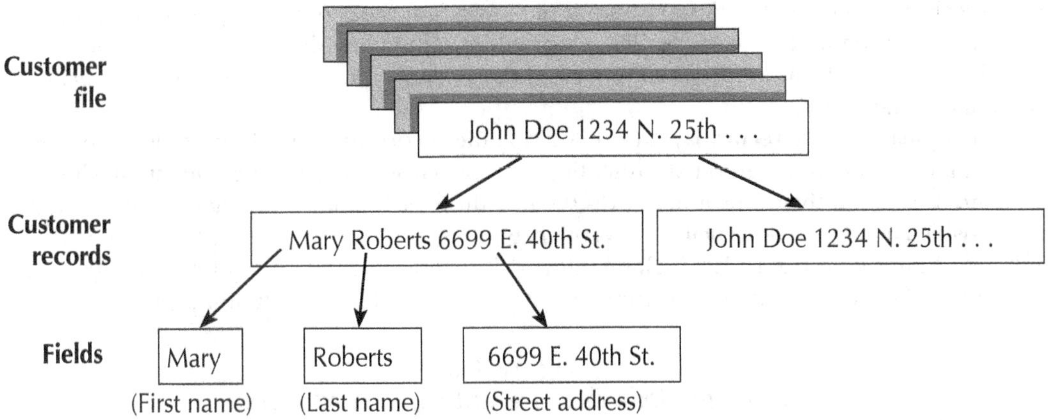

Customer file

John Doe 1234 N. 25th . . .

Customer records

Mary Roberts 6699 E. 40th St.

John Doe 1234 N. 25th . . .

Fields

Mary	Roberts	6699 E. 40th St.
(First name)	(Last name)	(Street address)

Figure 1.2
Order File with Multiple Record Formats

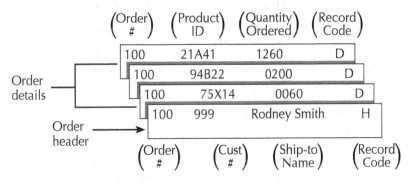

	(Order #)	(Product ID)	(Quantity Ordered)	(Record Code)
	100	21A41	1260	D
	100	94B22	0200	D
	100	75X14	0060	D
	100	999	Rodney Smith	H

Order details

Order header

(Order #) (Cust #) (Ship-to Name) (Record Code)

Note
Modern database design techniques discourage using files with multiple record formats, preferring instead to separate different record formats into separate files. The i5/OS database requires that a physical file (i.e., a file that contains data) have but one—and only one—record format.

Programming Specifications

In many installations, programmers work from specifications given to them by systems analysts. These specifications detail the desired output of a program, the required input, and a general statement of the required processing. The programmer must then develop the instructions needed to generate the appropriate output from the given input, ensuring that the correct data manipulations take place.

Analysts may provide **record layouts** to describe the record formats of input files to be used by a program. One common method of presenting a record layout—called **length notation**—lists fields in the order in which they appear and gives the length of each field. The other common method—called **positional notation**—explicitly shows the beginning and ending positions of each field. These methods, illustrated in Figure 1.3, include information about the data type of each field as well as the number of decimal positions for numeric data. Generally, length notation is preferred.

Figure 1.3

Alternate Methods of Describing Record Layouts

Item Number	Description	Quantity on Hand (0 decimals)	Unit Cost (2 decimals)	Vendor Code	Reorder Point (0 decimals)	Last Order Date
1 5	6 25	26 34	35 39	40 42	43 51	52 61

	Length Notation		
Field	**Data Type**	**Length**	**Decimal Positions**
Item Number	Alphanumeric	5	–
Description	Alphanumeric	20	–
Quantity on Hand	Numeric	9	0
Unit Cost	Numeric	5	2
Vendor Code	Alphanumeric	3	–
Reorder Point	Numeric	9	0
Last Order Date	Date	10	–

	Positional Notation		
Field	**Data Type**	**Positions**	**Decimal Positions**
Item Number	Alphanumeric	1-5	–
Description	Alphanumeric	6-25	–
Quantity on Hand	Numeric	26-34	0
Unit Cost	Numeric	35-39	2
Vendor Code	Alphanumeric	40-42	–
Reorder Point	Numeric	43-51	0
Last Order Date	Date	52-61	–

The Printer Spacing Chart

When the desired output includes a report, programmers may use a **printer spacing chart** (or an online development tool) to design the details of the desired report layout. The position of lines within the chart indicates the desired line spacing for the report. The printer spacing chart shows all constants (report headings or titles, column headings, and so on) that the report should include and where on the report they should appear. Printer spacing charts generally represent variable information using Xs, with each X representing one character of data.

We often want numeric data presented with special formats to facilitate comprehension. The printer spacing chart can depict the desired formatting, or **output editing**. Although there is no single accepted convention for indicating desired output editing, programmers generally recognize the notation presented in this chapter section (and used throughout this book). Commas, decimal points, and other insertion characters included within the Xs signal that these characters are to appear in the printed output.

A zero within the Xs signals that **zero suppression** is desired. Zero suppression means simply that leading, nonsignificant zeros are not printed. Thus, 000123 would be printed as bbb123 (where b = blank) if zero suppression were in effect. The location of the 0 within the Xs indicates the extent to which blanks, rather than leading zeros, are to be printed. X0XX signals "suppress up to and including the hundreds place but no farther." With this format, 0001 should be printed as bb01. A zero at the end of the format—for example, XXX0—signals that zero suppression should continue to the rightmost digit; with this format, a value of 0000 should be printed as all blanks.

Currency symbols (typically, dollar signs) can appear two ways in output: as fixed or as floating symbols. A **fixed dollar sign** is positioned in a set column of the output, regardless of the number of significant digits in the number following the sign. A **floating dollar sign** is printed next to the leftmost significant digit of the number—its position varies, or floats, depending on the value of the number with which it is associated. In a printer spacing chart, you can denote a fixed dollar sign by adding a single dollar sign to the immediate left of the Xs representing a numeric field. To signal a floating dollar sign, use two dollar signs, one at the far left of the Xs and the other in place of the zero-suppression character.

PSC notation	Meaning
$XXXX.XX	Fixed dollar sign, no zero suppression, no comma
$X,XX0.XX	Fixed dollar sign, zero suppress to units place, insert commas
X,XX.XX	Floating dollar sign, zero suppress to units place, insert commas
XX0	No dollar sign or decimal; complete zero suppression

Printer spacing charts also indicate how the analyst wants negative numeric values to be printed. A single hyphen (-) at the left signals a fixed negative sign. Two hyphens, one to the left and one in place of a zero, indicate a floating negative sign. A single hyphen or the characters CR to the right of the Xs signal a fixed, trailing negative sign or credit notation.

PSC notation	Meaning
XXX	No sign to be displayed
–XX0	Fixed sign, complete zero suppression
–XX–.XX	Floating sign, zero suppress to units place
XX0.XX–	Zero suppress, trailing negative sign
XX0.XXCR	Zero suppress, indicate negative value with CR

Figure 1.4 shows a printer spacing chart that includes headings, lines of detailed information, departmental subtotals, and a grand total. Note that the chart indicates that slashes should be inserted within the date and that asterisks are to appear to the right of totals.

Figure 1.4
Sample Printer Spacing Chart

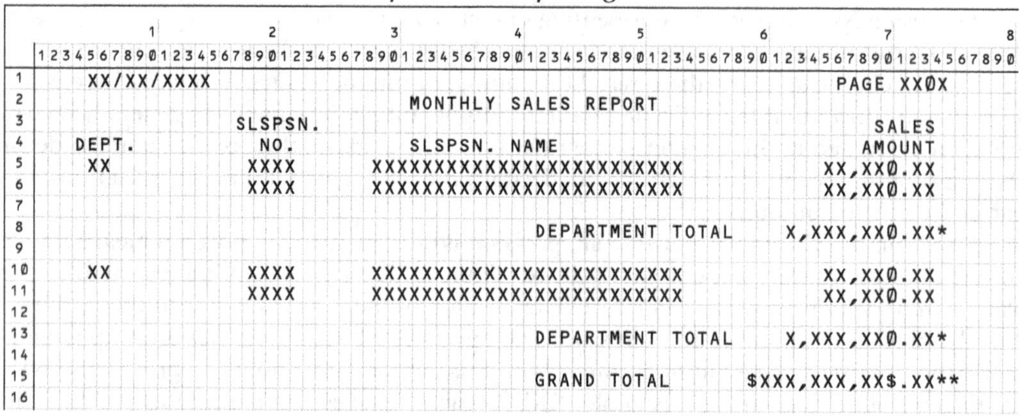

```
            1         2         3         4         5         6         7         8
   1234567890123456789012345678901234567890123456789012345678901234567890123456789 0
 1  XX/XX/XXXX                                                      PAGE XXØX
 2                                    MONTHLY SALES REPORT
 3                 SLSPSN.                                              SALES
 4  DEPT.          NO.            SLSPSN. NAME                         AMOUNT
 5    XX           XXXX           XXXXXXXXXXXXXXXXXXXXXXXXX           XX,XXØ.XX
 6                 XXXX           XXXXXXXXXXXXXXXXXXXXXXXXX           XX,XXØ.XX
 7
 8                                            DEPARTMENT TOTAL    X,XXX,XXØ.XX*
 9
10    XX           XXXX           XXXXXXXXXXXXXXXXXXXXXXXXX           XX,XXØ.XX
11                 XXXX           XXXXXXXXXXXXXXXXXXXXXXXXX           XX,XXØ.XX
12
13                                            DEPARTMENT TOTAL    X,XXX,XXØ.XX*
14
15                                               GRAND TOTAL    $XXX,XXX,XX$.XX**
16
```

The Program Development Cycle

The programmer's job is to develop a solution to a data processing problem represented by the program specifications. To achieve this solution, the programmer generally uses a method called the **program development cycle**. This cycle, which summarizes the sequence of activities required in programming, can be described as follows:

- Define the problem.
- Design the solution.
- Write/code the program.
- Compile and bind the program.
- Test and debug the program.
- Document the program.
- Maintain the program.

The cycle starts with **problem definition**. It should be obvious that unless you understand the problem as described in the programming specifications, you have little chance of coming up with a correct solution.

Once you understand the problem, you need to design a solution to the problem. **Program design** requires working out the process, or **algorithm**, to reach the solution to the problem before expressing it in a given programming language. Formal design tools—such as program **flowcharts**, Warnier-Orr diagrams, or **pseudocode**—can help clarify and illustrate program logic. Some programmers develop their own methods of sketching out a program solution.

Regardless of the method used, the importance of designing a solution *before* writing the program cannot be overemphasized. Developing a correct, well-structured design for a program represents the challenge of programming—this is the stage where most of your thinking should take place. Time spent at the design stage results in time saved fixing problems later in the cycle.

Writing the program involves translating the design into a program using a particular programming language. This stage is often called *coding*. Beginning programmers may find this task difficult because they are unfamiliar with the rules of the language. Once you have mastered the syntax of a language, however, coding becomes almost a mechanical process that requires relatively little thought. The challenge of programming lies in design. Years ago, coding consisted of keypunching program statements onto cards; today, most program entry is done interactively on a terminal, using a system utility called an **editor**. Many tools, called **integrated development environments (IDEs)**, exist to help with this step of the program development cycle. For i5/OS, the two most common IDEs are called **Programming Development Manager (PDM)** and **WebSphere Development Studio Client (WDSc)**. PDM includes an editor called **Source Entry Utility** (SEU); WDSc's editor is called Live Parsing Extensible Editor (**LPEX**). A special type of physical file, the **source physical file**, is specifically formatted to hold program source statements. When you use an editor to code a program, you are typically changing records in the source physical file.

Once you have coded your program and stored it as source code, you must *compile and bind* it to translate the RPG source code into machine language and prepare it for execution. The compiler will translate the source code, and the binding process will copy the compiled code into a program object (in a library), which the computer can then execute. The compile and bind step is two distinct processes, but for many programs you can combine the steps with a single command to the computer.

Testing the program is required to determine the existence of syntax or logic errors in your solution. **Syntax errors** are errors in your use of the rules of the language. The computer flags these errors either as you enter the statements or later when the compiler tries to translate your statements into machine language. **Logic errors** are errors of design; it is up to you, as the programmer, to detect such errors through rigorous program testing by running the program with sets of test data and carefully checking the accuracy of the program's output. **Debugging** means discovering and correcting any errors. Testing should continue until you are convinced that the program is working correctly.

Program documentation provides material useful for understanding, using, or changing the program. Some documentation—such as system and program flow charts, user manuals, or operator instructions—is referred to as **external documentation**. **Internal documentation** refers to comments included within the code itself. Such comments make the program more understandable to other programmers. Although documentation appears as one of the final stages in the program development cycle, documentation is best developed as you progress through the stages of the cycle. For example, it is easiest to provide comments within a program as you are actually entering the program rather than waiting until the program is completely tested and running.

Program maintenance is the process of making changes once the program is actually being used, or in production. Estimates are that up to 70 percent of a programmer's time is spent modifying existing programs. The need for maintenance may arise from a "bug" discovered in the program or from changing user needs. Because maintenance is a way of life, any program you develop should be designed with ease of future maintenance in mind. This means, among other things, that your code's logic and organization should be clear, the variable names well chosen, and the internal comments appropriate and sufficient.

Program Entry and Testing

To complete the program entry and testing stages, you need to eliminate all program errors. As we've indicated, these errors fall into two general classes: syntax errors and logic errors. Syntax errors represent violations of the rules of the language itself; they are detected and corrected relatively easily. Logic errors are errors in your program that cause the program to produce incorrect results; these problems are detected by extensively testing the program with sets of test data and correcting any program statements that are causing incorrect processing.

You typically enter a program by interacting with the system's editor. Your program statements are called **source code**. The set of statements for one program module constitutes a **source member** (often called a **compile unit**) on the System i.

The editor will detect some syntax errors as you enter your program and will let you correct them immediately. Other syntax errors become apparent when you attempt to **compile** your program. Compiling means translating the source code into machine language, or **object code**. A program called a compiler accomplishes this translation, provided you have not violated any rules of RPG IV in writing your program. An i5/OS command, **CRTRPGMOD (Create RPG Module)**, executes the RPG IV compiler. If syntax errors prevent the translation from being completed, the compiler provides you with a list of the syntax errors it encountered. All such errors need to be fixed before you can progress to the next stage of testing.

If your program is free of syntax errors, the compiler creates a **program module object**. You must, in turn, **bind** the module (with other modules, if appropriate) to produce an executable program that can be run on the System i. The **CRTPGM (Create Program)** command accomplishes this binding step. If your source code represents an entire program in one module, the **CRTBNDRPG (Create Bound RPG Program)** command lets you combine compiling and binding into a single step.

Once you have successfully compiled and bound your program, you need to run it with test data to determine whether it is working correctly. Note that the computer executes the bound program object (i.e., the translated version of your program). Errors discovered at this stage require you to back up, make changes to the program using the editor, and then recompile the program and bind it again before additional testing. Figure 1.5 (*opposite*) illustrates this iterative process.

If you forget to recompile and rebind your program after making changes to the source code, the computer will run your old version of the program because you have not created a new object incorporating those changes.

Figure 1.5
Steps Required to Enter, Test, and Debug a Program

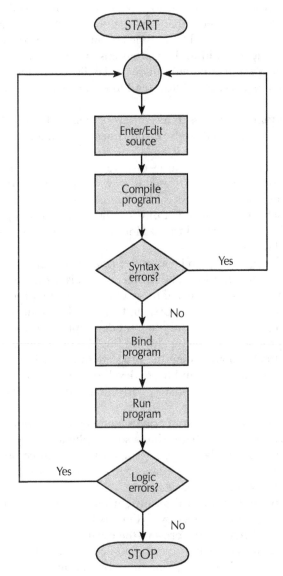

Chapter Summary

Report Program Generator, or RPG, is a high-level programming language introduced by IBM in the early 1960s to provide an easy way to produce commonly needed business reports. Since introducing RPG, IBM has added enhancements to expand the language's functionality. Programmers originally used RPG's fixed logic cycle and built-in indicators to minimize the need for explicit procedural instructions within their programs. As processing requirements have grown more complex and concerns about program understandability have increased, programmers have moved away from the fixed logic cycle and now tend to explicitly include all processing instructions within their programs.

Variables enable programs to process different sets of data. RPG provides this flexibility through fixed-length named fields that generally represent character or numeric data (although other types of data are supported).

The i5/OS object architecture uses libraries to store named entities for specific purposes. A prominent type of object is the file, which is used to store data records. Data is typically organized in a hierarchy of files, records, and fields. Physical files contain actual data records, while logical files are used for sorting and selecting records in a physical file. Relatively temporary data files that often need to be processed only once are called transaction files, while files of data of lasting importance to the company are called master files.

The process of developing a program is often described as the program development cycle. The cycle begins with problem definition. The problem often is presented through programming specifications, which include record layouts of files to be used by the program, printer spacing charts that describe the layout of desired reports, and an overview of needed processing.

In addition to defining the problem, the program development cycle includes designing the solution, writing the program, compiling and binding the program, testing and debugging, documenting, and—eventually—maintaining the program once it is in production. Too often, programmers short-cut the design stage and try to develop their logic as they write the program. This approach often leads to programs that are poorly designed or full of errors that must be corrected.

You enter an RPG IV program as source code using an editor provided for that purpose. The program is stored as a source member within a source physical file on the system. Because computers actually execute machine language instructions, your source program needs to be translated into an object program of machine language before the computer can run it. A special program called a compiler performs this translation.

As part of its translation, the compiler flags any entries in your source program that it cannot understand. These kinds of errors are called syntax errors because they are caused by your misuse of the rules of the language. Syntax errors prevent the creation of an object program.

Once your source code has successfully been compiled, you need to bind the resulting module into an executable program and then test the program by running it with input data. You must correct any logic errors in the program that are preventing the program from working correctly to produce the desired results. Each time you use the editor to correct a problem in your program, you must recompile the source member and bind the module again before running it to incorporate the changes into the executable program.

Key Terms

algorithm
batch processing
bind
bits (binary digits)
compile
compile unit
compiler
CRTBNDRPG (Create Bound RPG Program)
CRTPGM (Create Program)
CRTRPGMOD (Create RPG Module)
debugging
editor
external documentation
field
file
fixed dollar sign
fixed logic cycle
floating dollar sign
flowcharts
free-format specifications
high-level languages (HLLs)
i5/OS
indicators
integrated development environment (IDE)
Integrated Language Environment (ILE)
interactive applications
internal documentation
length notation
Live Parsing Extensible Editor (LPEX)
logic errors
logical file

master files
object code
objects
output editing
physical file
positional notation
printer spacing chart (PSC)
problem definition
procedural language
program design
program development cycle
program maintenance
program module object
program variable
Programming Development Manager (PDM)
pseudocode
record format
record layouts
records
Report Program Generator (RPG)
source code
Source Entry Utility (SEU)
source member
source physical file
structured design
Structured Query Language (SQL)
syntax errors
transaction files
variable
WebSphere Development Studio Client (WDSc)
zero suppression

Discussion/Review Questions

1. What was the original purpose of RPG?
2. What is an indicator?
3. What trends emerged in the 1970s to influence the enhancements included in RPG III?
4. What criticisms influenced IBM's enhancements to RPG in RPG IV? What computer industry developments have contributed to the evolution of RPG IV?
5. Do you think that a programming language that requires revisions over time is poorly designed in the first place? Why or why not?
6. Give an example of a syntax error and a logic error in your native language (e.g., English).
7. Would it make sense to describe a person's complete address (street address, city, state, and zip code) as one field? Why or why not?
8. Would you define each letter in a person's last name as a separate field? Why or why not?
9. Keeping in mind the fact that all records within a file generally have the same, fixed number of fields, how do you think your school handles the problem of storing information about what courses you've taken?
10. Differentiate between source code and object code.
11. How many times do you need to compile a program?
12. Would you build a house without a blueprint? Is this a good analogy to writing a program without first designing it? Why or why not?
13. Explain why the Integrated Language Environment is important to RPG programmers.
14. Why is it important to use external documentation such as flowcharts in developing your programs?
15. Why is it important for students of RPG to learn about the older versions of RPG?
16. Why is the fixed logic cycle not used in RPG today?

Exercises

1. Develop a list of data fields you think your school might store in its student master file. Then, design a record layout for this file that includes the length needed for each field, an indication of the data type (character or numeric), and the number of decimal positions of numeric fields.

2. Research the history and development of the System i. How has this system and its software changed over the years?

3. For each printer spacing chart notation in the table below, show how the data value associated with the notation should appear when printed.

	PSC notation	Data value	
a.	XXXXX	98100	98100
b.	XXXXX	01254	01254
c.	XX,XX0	31331	31,331
d.	XX,XX0	00010	___10
e.	XX,XX0	01000	_1000
f.	XX,XX0	00000	_____
g.	$XX,X0X	00872	$__872
h.	XX,XX	00298	_$,298
i.	XX,XX	00000	__,__$
j.	–XX,X–X	–07254	–7254
k.	–XX,X–X	00451	451
l.	XX,X0XDB	–00923	
m.	XX,XX0–	–91486	–9486
n.	XX,XX0–	00000	–

1) ENAME Char   10   0
   MI   Char   1   0
   LNAME Char   15

   STUID Num   7   0
   GPA   Num   3   2
   STRYR Num   4 . 0

Chapter 2

Getting Started

Chapter Overview

This chapter introduces you to RPG IV specifications. You'll learn how to write a
simple file read/write program using a procedural approach. You'll also learn how to
include comments within your programs as documentation. Finally, you'll see how
RPG's techniques of output editing let you control the appearance of values on reports.

RPG IV Specifications

RPG IV programs consist of different kinds of lines, called specifications. Each type of specification
has a particular purpose. The specification types are

- Header (Control) specifications—provide default options for the source
- File specifications—identify the files a program will use
- Definition specifications—define variables and other data items the program will use
- Input specifications—describe the record layout for program-described input files
- Calculation specifications—detail the procedure the program will perform
- Output specifications—describe the program output (results)
- Procedure boundary specifications—segment the source into units of work, called
  procedures

Not every program requires every kind of specification. Most of the specification types require
a different identifier, or form type, which must appear in position 6 of each program line. A
File specification line of code, for example, must include an F in position 6; for this reason, File
specifications are commonly called F-specs.

Specifications that you use must appear in a specific order, or sequence, within your source
code, with all program lines that represent the same kind of specification grouped together. Figure
2.1 illustrates the order in which the specifications are grouped.

Figure 2.1
Order of Specifications in an RPG Program

```
H . . . . . . . . . . . . Header (control) specifications
F . . . . . . . . . . . . File specifications
D . . . . . . . . . . . . Definition specifications
I . . . . . . . . . . . . Input specifications
C . . . . . . . . . . . . Calculation specifications
O . . . . . . . . . . . . Output specifications
P . . . . . . . . . . . . Procedure boundary
D . . . . . . . . . . . .         Definition specifications for procedure
C . . . . . . . . . . . .         Calculation specifications for procedure
P . . . . . . . . . . . . Procedure boundary
```

Most RPG IV specifications require fixed-position entries in at least part of the specification. **Fixed position**, or **fixed format**, means that the location of an entry within a program line is critical to the entry's interpretation by the RPG IV compiler. The editor you use to enter your source code can provide you with prompts to facilitate making your entries in the proper location. (Appendix C provides more information about editors.)

Most specifications also support a **free-form** area of the specification, where you can code keywords and values with little or no regard to their specific location within the free-form portion of the specification.

The code samples in this book use two (or more) ruler lines to help you determine where to make your entries. The first ruler line indicates column position; the following line (or lines) contains "prompts" similar to those given by an editor. Most editors also provide a similar ruler line near the top of the editing window. These ruler lines should not appear in your source code; they are provided to help you understand where entries should appear.

Tip

As you begin to work with RPG specifications, don't be overwhelmed by what appear to be hundreds of entries with multiple options. Fortunately, many entries are optional, and you will use them only for complex processing or to achieve specific effects. This book introduces these entries gradually, initially showing you just those entries needed to write simple programs. As your mastery of the language grows, you will learn how to use additional specification entries that may be required for more complex programs.

When you begin writing your first program, you will notice that an entry does not always take up all the positions allocated for it within a specification. When that happens, a good rule of thumb is that alphabetic entries start at the leftmost position of the allocated space, with unused positions to the right, while numeric entries are usually right-adjusted, with unused positions to the left.

RPG Specifications for a Sample Program

Let's start with the minimal entries needed to procedurally code a simple read/write program. To help you understand how to write such a program, we will walk through writing an RPG IV program to solve the following problem.

We have a file—Customers—with records laid out as follows:

Field	Data Type	Length	Decimal Positions
Account Identifier	Alphanumeric	4	-
Salesperson	Alphanumeric	4	-
Customer Name	Alphanumeric	35	-
Customer Address	Alphanumeric	35	-
City	Alphanumeric	21	-
State/Province	Alphanumeric	2	-
Postal Code	Alphanumeric	10	-
Foreign Country	Alphanumeric	20	-
Date of Last Sale	Date (*mm/dd/yyyy*)	10	-
Year-to-Date Sales	Numeric	11	2

You want to produce a report laid out as follows:

```
          1         2         3         4         5         6         7         8         9
 1234567890123456789012345678901234567890123456789012345678901234567890123456789012345678901234567890
 1
 2 YTD SALES REPORT                                        DATE XX/XX/XXXX      PAGE XXX0
 3
 4 ACCT  SALES                                                  YTD         DATE OF
 5  ID   PERSON  CUSTOMER                                      SALES       LAST SALE
 6
 7 XXXX  XXXX    XXXXXXXXXXXXXXXXXXXXXXXXXXXXXXXXXXXXX   XXX,XXX,XX0.XX   XX/XX/XXXX
 8 XXXX  XXXX    XXXXXXXXXXXXXXXXXXXXXXXXXXXXXXXXXXXXX   XXX,XXX,XX0.XX   XX/XX/XXXX
 9
10
11
12
13
14
15
```

When you compare the desired output with the input record layout, you can see that all the output fields are present on the input records. No data transformation, data generation, or arithmetic calculation needs to take place within the program. Not all of the input fields are used in the report, but their locations in the input record layout will need to be considered when we are coding the RPG program. The required processing consists of reading each record from the input file, writing that data to the report with appropriate headings, and formatting the variable data.

Control Specifications

Although our sample program doesn't include them, **Control specifications** (sometimes called Header specifications, or H-specs) may be useful to control an RPG program's behavior. Control specifications provide the following functions:

- default formats (e.g., date formats) for the program
- changes to normal processing modes (e.g., changing the internal method the program uses to evaluate expressions)
- special options to use when compiling the program
- language enhancements that affect the entire program

Control specifications require an H in position 6. The remaining positions, 7–80, consist of reserved **keywords**, which have special values and meanings associated with them. There are no strict positional requirements for the keywords; they may appear in any order and in any position 7–80. The following header shows the layout of a Control specification:

```
*.. 1 ...+... 2 ...+... 3 ...+... 4 ...+... 5 ...+... 6 ...+... 7 ...+... 8
HKeywords+++++++++++++++++++++++++++++++++++++++++++++++++++++++++++++++++++++
```

In the following example, Control specification keywords dictate the date and time formats to be used:

```
*.. 1 ...+... 2 ...+... 3 ...+... 4 ...+... 5 ...+... 6 ...+... 7 ...+... 8
HKeywords+++++++++++++++++++++++++++++++++++++++++++++++++++++++++++++++++++++
H Datfmt(*USA) Timfmt(*HMS)
```

A Control specification can include more than one keyword (with at least one space between them), and a program can have multiple Control specifications. Appendix A includes a complete list of Control specification keywords and their usage. Not all programs require Control specifications, but if they are present, Control specifications must appear as the first specifications in a program.

File Description Specifications

Our introductory RPG IV program will begin with File description specifications (also known by the shorter names **File specifications** and **F-specs**). All File specifications include an F in position 6. File specifications describe the files our program uses and define how the files will be used within the program. Each file used by a program requires its own File specification line. In our illustrative problem, the file Customers contains the data we want to process.

The output of our program is a printed report. Although you usually think of a report as hard copy rather than as a file per se, in RPG we produce a report through a printer file. Our introductory program will use a system-supplied printer file, Qprint, as the destination file for our report lines. This file then resides as a spooled file in an output queue, where it will wait until we release it to the printer. Your instructor will tell you which printer file to use in your programs and explain how to work with spooled files in the output queue.

You must code one File specification for each file the program uses. Although you can describe the files in any order, it is customary to describe the input file first. The following header shows the layout of a File specification. Note that in addition to column positions, the layout includes prompts to help you remember where to insert required entries.

```
*.. 1 ...+... 2 ...+... 3 ...+... 4 ...+... 5 ...+... 6 ...+... 7 ...+... 8
FFilename++IPEASFRLen+LKLen+AIDevice+.Keywords+++++++++++++++++++++++++++++++
```

The completed File specifications for our program are shown below. We'll explain in detail each of the necessary entries for our sample program, and in subsequent chapters we will explain the entries not described here. (Appendix A includes a complete summary of all the RPG IV specifications.)

```
*.. 1 ...+... 2 ...+... 3 ...+... 4 ...+... 5 ...+... 6 ...+... 7 ...+... 8
FFilename++IPEASFRLen+LKLen+AIDevice+.Keywords+++++++++++++++++++++++++++++++
FCustomers IF   F 152        Disk
FQprint    O    F 132        Printer Oflind(*Inof)
```

RPG IV lets you use both uppercase and lowercase alphabetic characters, but the language is not **case sensitive**. Thus, any lowercase letter you use within a file or variable name will be interpreted as its uppercase equivalent by the compiler. To aid in the program's readability, many programmers use **title case**, wherein each word in the source code is capitalized.

File Name (Positions 7–16)

First, in positions 7–16 (labeled *Filename++* on the ruler line), you enter the name of the file. In RPG IV, file names can be a maximum of 10 characters long. They must begin with an alphabetic character or the special character $, #, or @; the remaining characters may be alphabetic characters, numbers, or any of the four special characters _, #, $, and @. A file name cannot contain blanks embedded within the permissible characters.

Our practice problem input file is called Customers. The report file is Qprint. Note that you code file names like other alphabetic entries: beginning in the leftmost position allowed for that entry—in this case, position 7. Simply leave blank any unneeded positions to the right of the name.

File Type (Position 17)

Position 17 (labeled *I* on the ruler line) specifies the type of file or how the file will be used by the program. The two types we will work with in this program are input (type I) and output (type O). An **input file** contains data to be read by the program; an **output file** is the destination for writing output results from the program. In our example, Customers is an input file, and Qprint is an output file.

File Designation (Position 18; Input Files Only)

Every input file requires a file designation entry (position 18, labeled *P*). File designation refers to the way the program will access, or retrieve, the data in the file. In our example, we are going to retrieve data by explicitly reading records within our program rather than by using the built-in retrieval of RPG's fixed logic cycle. In RPG terminology, that makes the input file **full procedural**, so F is the appropriate entry for position 18. Since this designation applies only to input files, we'll leave it blank for the Qprint specification line.

File Format (Position 22)

The next required entry is file format. An F in position 22 (labeled *F*) stands for fixed format, which means that file records will be described within this program and that each record has the same fixed length. Although it is preferable to describe files externally using OS/400's built-in database facilities, for simplicity's sake we will start with program-described files and progress to externally described files in the next chapter. Because our files will be program described, an F is appropriate for both files of our sample program. All files, regardless of type, require an entry for file format.

Record Length (Positions 23–27)

You need to define the record length for each program-described file. Data file records can be of any length from 1 to 32,766 bytes; it is important that you code the correct value for this specification. When we add up the lengths of all the fields in Customers, we come up with a length of 152 bytes, so we enter 152 in positions 23–27. Note that record length is right-adjusted within the positions allocated for this entry. This is typical of most RPG IV entries that require a numeric value.

Most printers support a line of 132 characters. As a result, records of printer files (which correspond to lines of report output) are usually 132 positions long. Accordingly, output file Qprint is assigned a record length of 132 on its File specification.

Device (Positions 36–42)

The Device entry indicates the device associated with a file. Database files are stored on disk; accordingly, Disk is the appropriate device entry for the Customers file. The device associated with printer files is Printer. You enter these device names, left-adjusted, in positions 36–42 (labeled *Device+*).

Keywords (Positions 44–80)

The Keywords area of the File specification gives you an opportunity to amplify and specialize the basic file description in the positional area (positions 6–43) of the F-spec. RPG allows a number of reserved keywords (listed in Appendix A) in this area of the specification. Typically, they are coded with one or more values (**arguments**) in parentheses immediately following the keyword itself. You can code more than one keyword on a specification line in positions 44–80 without being too concerned about any other positional requirements. Most RPG programmers, however, prefer to limit their code to one keyword per line; if a specification requires more than one keyword, you can simply continue coding them in the Keywords area on subsequent F-spec lines.

Our sample program will use only one keyword: Oflind (Overflow indicator). **Overflow** is the name given to the condition that occurs when a printed report reaches the bottom of a page. Usually, when overflow occurs you will want to eject the printer to the next page and print a new set of heading lines before printing the next detail line. Your program can automatically detect overflow through the use of a reserved variable called an **overflow indicator**. The overflow indicators provided by RPG are called OA, OB, OC, OD, OE, OF, OG, and OV; you would code these indicators as *INOA, *INOB, and so on. The Oflind keyword associates one of these indicators with a printer device file—if that file signals overflow, the file's overflow indicator will be automatically set to *On. You can then test that indicator just before printing a detail line to determine whether or not you want to print headings first. In our sample, we name indicator OF as the overflow indicator for Qprint by coding Oflind(*Inof) in the Keywords area of the appropriate F-spec.

No other File specification entries are required to describe the files used by our sample program. In this introductory explanation, we've skipped over some of the entries that are not needed in this program; we'll cover them later. The completed File specifications for the program are shown again below.

```
*.. 1 ...+... 2 ...+... 3 ...+... 4 ...+... 5 ...+... 6 ...+... 7 ...+... 8
FFilename++IPEASFRLen+LKLen+AIDevice+.Keywords++++++++++++++++++++++++++++++++
FCustomers IF   F  152        Disk
FQprint    O    F  132        Printer Oflind(*Inof)
```

Input Specifications

Input specifications, identified by an I in position 6, come after the File specifications in our introductory program. **Input specifications** (I-specs) describe the records within program-described input files and define the fields within those records. Every program-described input file defined on the File specifications must be represented by a set of Input specification lines.

Input specifications use two types of lines:

- **Record identification entries,** which describe the input records at a general level
- **Field description entries,** which describe the specific fields within the records

Together, these two types of lines describe the structure of the record layout for each program-described input file in the program. Each record identification line must precede the field entries for that record. The general layout for these two kinds of Input specifications is shown below.

```
*.. 1 ...+... 2 ...+... 3 ...+... 4 ...+... 5 ...+... 6 ...+... 7 ...+... 8
IFilename++SqNORiPos1+NCCPos2+NCCPos3+NCC.................................
I......................Fmt+SPFrom+To+++DcField++++++++++L1M1FrP1MnZr......
```

The I-specs for our introductory program are shown here. We'll explain in detail those entries required by our sample program.

```
*.. 1 ...+... 2 ...+... 3 ...+... 4 ...+... 5 ...+... 6 ...+... 7 ...+... 8
IFilename++SqNORiPos1+NCCPos2+NCCPos3+NCC.................................
I......................Fmt+SPFrom+To+++DcField++++++++++L1M1FrP1MnZr......
ICustomers NS
I                             1    4   Accountid
I                             5    8   Salesperson
I                             9   43   Name
I                            44   78   Address
I                            79   99   City
I                           100  101   State
I                           102  111   Postalcode
I                           112  131   Country
I                    *USA D  132  141   Lastsaledate
I                           142  152   2Ytdsales
```

Record Identification Entries

Record identification lines describe the input records at a general level. Each line takes the following form:

```
*.. 1 ...+... 2 ...+... 3 ...+... 4 ...+... 5 ...+... 6 ...+... 7 ...+... 8
IFilename++SqNORiPos1+NCCPos2+NCCPos3+NCC.................................
```

File Name (Positions 7–16)

A record identification line must contain the name of the input file in positions 7–16 (labeled *Filename++* on the specification line). This name must match the entry on the File specification—in our case, Customers. The file name is a left-adjusted entry.

Sequence (Positions 17–18)

The next required record identification entry is Sequence, in positions 17–18 (labeled *Sq*). This entry signals whether the system should check the order of records in the file as the records are read during program execution. **Sequence checking** is relevant only when a file contains multiple record formats (that is, records with different field layouts). When sequence checking is not appropriate (which is usually the case), code any two alphabetic characters in positions 17–18 to signal that sequence checking is not required. Many programmers use NS to signal "no sequence." Because the Customers file contains a single record format, we enter NS in positions 17–18.

The complete record identification specification is illustrated below.

```
*.. 1 ...+... 2 ...+... 3 ...+... 4 ...+... 5 ...+... 6 ...+... 7 ...+... 8
IFilename++SqNORiPos1+NCCPos2+NCCPos3+NCC.................................
ICustomers NS
```

Note

Note that with the specification coded as shown, the compiler will issue a warning that a record identification indicator is missing from the line. Although record identification indicators are relevant in fixed logic processing (discussed in Appendix E), they are not used in modern RPG programming. Simply ignore the compiler warning; it will not prevent your program from being compiled successfully.

Field Description Entries

Field description entries immediately follow the record identification entry. You define each field within the record by giving the field a valid name, specifying its length, and declaring its data type. Although you can define the fields of a record in any order, convention dictates that fields be described in order from the beginning of the record to the record's end.

Each field description entry takes the following form:

```
*.. 1 ...+... 2 ...+... 3 ...+... 4 ...+... 5 ...+... 6 ...+... 7 ...+... 8
I.......................Fmt+SPFrom+To+++DcField++++++++L1M1FrP1MnZr......
```

Field Location (Positions 37–46)

You define a field's length by specifying the beginning position and the ending position of the field within the input record. Length notation is not allowed. The beginning position is coded as the "from" location (positions 37–41 of the Input specifications, labeled *From+*); the ending position is the "to" location (positions 42–46, labeled *To+++*). If the field is 1 byte long, the from and to entries will be identical because the field begins and ends in the same location of the record.

Character fields may be up to 65,535 bytes long. Numeric fields may be up to 63 digits long. The length of native dates depends on their format but may be up to 10 bytes long. The beginning and ending positions are right-adjusted within the positions allocated for these entries. You do not need to enter leading, nonsignificant zeros.

Decimal Positions (Position 47–48)

Numeric fields require a decimal position entry in positions 47–48 (labeled *Dc*) indicating the number of decimal positions to the right of the decimal point. In RPG IV, a field must be numeric to be used in arithmetic calculations or to be edited for output, so it is important to *not* overlook the decimal position entry. If a numeric field represents whole numbers, the appropriate entry for its decimal positions is 0 (zero). Numeric fields can contain up to 63 positions to the right of the decimal point. Remember that the total length of the numeric field *includes* any decimal places (but not the decimal point itself or comma separators).

To define a field as a **character field**, simply leave the decimal position entry blank. Date fields (with a *D* in position 36) are also coded with a blank in the decimal position entry. Chapter 4 provides a more complete discussion of RPG IV data types.

Field Name (Positions 49–62)

The last required entry for a field description specification is a name for the field being described. This name, entered left-adjusted in positions 49–62 (labeled *Field*+++++++++) must adhere to the rules for valid field names in RPG IV. Within a record, a valid field name

- Uses letters, digits, or the special characters _, #, @, and $
- Does not begin with a digit or an underscore
- Does not include embedded blanks

In addition, a field name generally is 14 characters long or less. This is a practical limit, imposed by the fixed-format nature of the input specification.

The alphabetic characters can be either uppercase or lowercase or a combination (mixed case). RPG IV does not distinguish between letters on the basis of their case, but using a combination of upper- and lowercase characters—for example, capitalizing each word in the source code—makes your field names easier for others to understand.

> **Tip**
> Although RPG allows them, you should avoid the use of special characters $, #, and @ in RPG names. These special characters may not exist in all the languages or the character sets your program may use to compile. If the language or character set cannot recognize the character, the compiler will not be able to successfully translate the code. You should also avoid the underscore (_) in an RPG name; it's a "noisy" character and doesn't significantly aid the readability of your program.

Although not an RPG IV requirement, it is good programming practice to choose field names that reflect the data they represent by making full use of the 14-character limit for names. For example, "Loannumber" is far superior to "X" for the name of a field that will store loan numbers. Choosing good field names can prevent your accidental use of the wrong field as you write your program and can help clarify your program's processing to others who may have to modify the program.

Data Attributes (Positions 31–34)

RPG most commonly uses positions 31–34 to specify a format for date or time fields. RPG supports native date and time data types to enable date calculations and manipulation—important factors in modern business processing. We'll discuss dates and date formats in more detail in Chapter 7. The entry *USA in positions 31–34 of an I-spec indicates that the field Lastsaledate is in *mm/dd/yyyy* format, including the slash (/) separator characters. Since the other fields in the record layout are not date fields, this entry for those fields is left blank.

Data Type (Position 36)

For most alphanumeric (character) or numeric fields, you may leave position 36 blank. But for fields that represent other types of data, you must make an entry in position 36 to tell the compiler the external data type of the field. In our sample program, the D entry in this position indicates that the field Lastsaledate is a native date. The other fields in the record layout are character or numeric fields and do not require an entry here. Chapter 4 provides a more complete discussion of RPG data types.

Note

Native date fields are *not* the same as numeric fields that may be used to store date information. A native date field is stored in a special format that the computer will implicitly recognize as a date. Numeric fields require specific arithmetic or conversion coding to treat them as dates. We'll cover more about native dates in Chapter 7.

You'll recall that not all the fields in the Customers file will appear on our desired report. If a program does not use all the fields coded in the Input specifications, the compiler will issue a warning, but this is not necessarily an error condition that will prevent a successful compile. You can omit the unused fields from the I-specs, but the remaining entries must reflect their correct position in the record layout. To review, the field description entries of the Input specifications for our sample program are shown below. Unused fields have been omitted.

```
*.. 1 ...+... 2 ...+... 3 ...+... 4 ...+... 5 ...+... 6 ...+... 7 ...+... 8
IFilename++SqNORiPos1+NCCPos2+NCCPos3+NCC.....................................
I.......................Fmt+SPFrom+To+++DcField+++++++++L1M1FrP1MnZr......
ICustomers NS
I                                1    4  Accountid
I                                5    8  Salesperson
I                                9   43  Name
I                       *USA D  132  141  Lastsaledate
I                              142  152 2Ytdsales
```

In these Input specifications, we define field Ytdsales as numeric by including a decimal position entry in positions 47–48. Lastsaledate is a native date (with a D in position 36). The remaining fields are character fields.

Output Specifications

Calculation specifications follow immediately after Input specifications in RPG programs. We, however, will discuss **Output specifications** next because their required entries parallel those required on Input specifications in many ways. Every program-described output file named on the File specifications needs a set of Output specifications that provide details about the required output. All Output specification lines require an O in position 6.

Output specifications, like Input specifications, include two kinds of lines: record identification lines, which deal with the output at the record level; and field description lines, which describe the content of a given output record. When the output is a report rather than a data file, "record" roughly translates to "report line." Most reports include several different report-line formats; each needs definition on the Output specifications.

To refresh your memory, our output file, Qprint, is to contain a weekly sales report, formatted as shown in the printer spacing chart on page 21.

Our report includes four kinds of lines, or **record formats**. Three of the lines are headings, which should appear at the top of the report page, while the fourth is a **detail line** of variable information. The term "detail line" means that one line is to be printed for each record in an input file. The line contains detailed information about the data records being processed.

The following RPG IV code shows the complete Output specifications to produce the report described above. You should refer to this code again as you read about the required Output specification entries.

```
*.. 1 ...+... 2 ...+... 3 ...+... 4 ...+... 5 ...+... 6 ...+... 7 ...+... 8
OFilename++DF..N01N02N03Excnam++++B++A++Sb+Sa+..............................
O...............N01N02N03Field+++++++++YB.End++PConstant/editword/DTformat++
OQprint     E            Headings      2  2
O                                              16 'YTD SALES REPORT'
O                                              56 'DATE'
O                        *Date         Y       67
O                                              74 'PAGE'
O                        Page          Z       79

O          E            Headings      1
O                                               4 'ACCT'
O                                              11 'SALES'
O                                              65 'YTD'
O                                              78 'DATE OF'

O          E            Headings      2
O                                               3 'ID'
O                                              12 'PERSON'
O                                              22 'CUSTOMER'
O                                              66 'SALES'
O                                              79 'LAST SALE'

O          E            Detail        1
O                        Acountid              4
O                        Salesperson          11
O                        Name                 49
O                        Ytdsales      1      66
O                        Lastsaledate         79
```

Record Identification Entries

Output specifications require a record identification entry for each different line of the report. Each of these lines represents a record format and must be followed with detailed information about what that record format (or report line) contains. Because our report has four types of lines to describe, we have four record format descriptions in our Output specifications.

The header that follows illustrates the layout for record identification entries. The following discussions refer to this layout.

```
*.. 1 ...+... 2 ...+... 3 ...+... 4 ...+... 5 ...+... 6 ...+... 7 ...+... 8
OFilename++DF..NØ1NØ2NØ3Excnam++++B++A++Sb+Sa+.........................
```

File Name (Positions 7–16)

The first record identification entry requires a file name entry in positions 7–16 (labeled *Filename*++). This file name serves to associate the record being described with the output file described on the File specifications. Thus Qprint, our output file, appears as the file name entered on the first record identification line of the Output specifications above. Although the Output specifications include four record format descriptions, because each describes a format to be written to the same file (Qprint), you do not have to repeat the file name entry on subsequent record identification entry lines.

Type (Position 17)

Each record format description requires an entry in position 17 (labeled *D*) to indicate the type of line being described. In this context, "type" refers to the way RPG IV is to handle printing the line. Because we will be using procedural techniques to generate the report instead of relying on RPG's fixed logic cycle, all the record format lines are **Exception lines**. As a consequence, we enter an *E* in position 17 of each record format line.

Exception Name (Position 30–39)

In RPG IV, it is common practice to provide a name in positions 30–39 (labeled *Excnam*++++) for each exception line. Although not required, such names let you control printing without the use of indicators. By using **exception names**, you can easily refer to lines to be printed from within your Calculation specifications.

Moreover, you can assign the same name to lines that need to be printed as a group at the same time. Because our report has three lines that should be printed together at the top of the page, we have given each the name Headings. The fourth line, which will contain the variable information from our data file, is identified as Detail. Note that Headings and Detail are arbitrarily assigned names, not RPG-reserved terms. Exception names follow the same rules of naming as field names (up to 10 characters long), and they are left-adjusted within positions 30–39.

Space and Skip Entries (Positions 40–51)

One more set of entries is needed to complete the record format line definitions. These entries describe the vertical alignment of a given line within a report page or relative to other report lines. Two kinds of entries control this vertical alignment: **Space entries** and **Skip entries**. Each variant offers "before" and "after" options.

It is important to understand the differences between Space entries and Skip entries. Space entries specify vertical printer positioning *relative to the current line*. Space is analogous to the carriage return on a typewriter or the Enter key on a computer. Each Space is the equivalent of hitting the Return (or Enter) key. Space before (positions 40–42, labeled *B*++) is like hitting the Return key before you type a line; Space after (positions 43–45, labeled *A*++) is like hitting Return after you type a line.

The same record format line can include both a Space before and a Space after entry. If both the Space before and the Space after entries are left blank within a record format description, the system defaults to Space 1 after printing—the equivalent of single-spacing. If you have either a Space before or a Space after entry explicitly coded and the other entry is blank, the blank entry defaults to 0. The maximum value you can specify for any Space entry is 255.

In contrast to Space entries, Skip entries instruct the printer to "skip to" the designated line on a page. Skip entries specify an *absolute vertical position on the page*. Skip 3 before printing causes the printer to advance to the third line on a page before printing; Skip 20 after printing causes the printer to advance to the 20th line on the page after printing a line. If the printer is already past that position on a given page, a Skip entry causes the paper to advance to the designated position on the next page. Most often, you will have a Skip before entry only for the first heading line of a report. Programmers most often use Skip entries to advance to the top of each new report page. Skip entries are also useful when you are printing information on a preprinted form, such as a check or an invoice.

You code any Skip before entry in positions 46–48 (labeled *Sb*+); Skip after entries are made in positions 49–51 (labeled *Sa*+). If you do not code any Skip entries, the system assumes that you do not want any skipping to occur. The maximum value you can specify for any Skip entry is 255.

The following record format lines show the spacing and skipping entries for our sample program:

```
*.. 1 ...+... 2 ...+... 3 ...+... 4 ...+... 5 ...+... 6 ...+... 7 ...+... 8
OFilename++DF..NØ1NØ2NØ3Excnam++++B++A++Sb+Sa+.............................
OQprint    E           Headings     2  2
...
O          E           Headings     1
...
O          E           Headings     2
...
O          E           Detail       1
```

Because we want the first heading of our report to print on the second line of a page, we code a Skip 2 before entry in positions 46–48 of the record format line describing that line. The Space 2 after entry (positions 43–45) for that same heading line will advance the printer head to the correct position for the second Headings line—that is, line 4.

The second Headings line, with its Space 1 after entry, positions the printer head for the third Headings line, which in turn, with its Space 2 after entry, positions the printer head for the first Detail line of data to print. Because the report-detail lines are to be single spaced, exception line Detail contains a Space 1 after entry.

Field Description Entries

Each record format line of the Output specifications is followed by field description entries that describe the contents of the line. Each field description specification

- Identifies an item to appear on the line
- Indicates where the item is to appear horizontally on the line
- Specifies any special output formatting for that item

The **field-level** items to be printed will be either a variable (field) or a constant (literal). Field-level items to be included within a record format may be entered in any order, although by convention programmers enter them in the order in which they are to appear in the output. The code below illustrates the layout for these field description entries.

```
*.. 1 ...+... 2 ...+... 3 ...+... 4 ...+... 5 ...+... 6 ...+... 7 ...+... 8
O..............N01N02N03Field+++++++++YB.End++PConstant/editword/DTformat++
```

Field Name (Positions 30–43)

The name of each field whose value is to appear as part of the output record is coded in positions 30–43 (labeled *Field+++++++++*). Any field appearing as part of the Output specifications must have been defined earlier in the program.

In our sample program, most of the fields to be printed are part of the Detail record format. These are the same fields—Accountid, Salesperson, Name, Ytdsales, and Lastsaledate—that we defined as part of our input record (though not necessarily in the same order as they appear in the record layout). When we include these field names in the output, each time our program processes a successive record from the input file, each Detail line printed will contain the data values present in those fields of the input record.

In addition to the input fields, two RPG IV reserved words that function as built-in, predefined fields appear as part of the report headings. In the first Headings line defined on page 29, notice the field name **Page**. RPG supplies this field to automatically provide the correct page numbers for a report. Page, a four-digit numeric field, has an initial value of 1; this value is automatically incremented by 1 each time the report begins a new page.

The **Date* field, which also appears as part of the first Headings line, is another RPG IV **reserved word**. *Date, an 8-digit numeric field, stores the current date, typically in *mmddyyyy* format. Any time your program needs to access the date on which the program is running, you can simply use *Date as a field. RPG IV also stores a 6-digit version of the date in reserved word *Udate*. Reserved words **Day*, *Uday*, **Month*, *Umonth*, **Year* (4 digits), and *Uyear* (2 digits) let you individually access the day, month, and year portions of the current date. Note that these reserved words refer to numeric fields, not native dates; the RPG program will treat them as numbers.

Constants (Positions 53–80)

In addition to fields, whose values change through the course of a program's execution, Output specifications typically contain **constants**, or **literals**—characters that do *not* change and instead represent the actual values that are to appear on the report. You enter each constant, enclosed within apostrophes ('), in positions 53–80 (labeled *Constant/editword/DTformat++*) of the Output specifications. The apostrophe on the left of the code should appear in position 53; in other words, you enter constants left-adjusted within positions 53–80. A constant cannot appear on the same Output specification line as a field; each needs its own line.

In our sample program, the first heading is to contain the word PAGE as well as the page number. Accordingly, we code PAGE as a constant within the first Heading line. Also, part of this first heading is the title—YTD SALES REPORT. Although several words make up this constant, you enter the group of words as a single constant, enclosed in apostrophes; the spaces between the words form part of the constant.

The second and third report lines, or record formats, consist of column headings for the report. These, too, are handled as constants, with the appropriate values entered in positions 53–80.

Notice that in the sample program, the column heading lines are broken up into conveniently sized logical units and that each unit is then coded as a separate constant.

Note also that you can ignore blank, or unused, positions in output lines unless they appear within a string of characters that you want to handle as a single constant (e.g., 'DATE OF' or 'LAST SALE').

End Position in Output Record (Positions 47–51)

You denote where a field or constant appears horizontally within a line by coding its **end position**— that is, the position of its last, or rightmost, character—within the line. To specify an end position, enter a numeric value that is right-adjusted within positions 47–51 (labeled *End++*); this represents the actual position desired for the rightmost character of the field or constant.

For example, because we want the E in constant PAGE to appear in column 74 of the first heading line of our sample report, we code a 74 in positions 50–51 of the specification entry for the constant PAGE. The printer spacing chart indicates that the rightmost digit of the page number should appear in column 79 of the report line. Accordingly, 79 is the specified end position for field PAGE within its Output specification line.

Our Output specifications include an end position for each field or constant that is part of our report. If you omit an end position for a field or constant, that item is output immediately adjacent to the previous item, with no blanks separating the items.

You can also optionally specify the placement of a field or constant relative to the end position of the previously defined field. To use this alternative method, you put a plus sign (+) in position 47 and a right-adjusted numeric value in the remaining positions. The value tells how many blanks you want between the end of the previous field and the beginning position of the current field. The listing below illustrates how you would code the Detail line of our report using this relative notation.

```
*.. 1 ...+... 2 ...+... 3 ...+... 4 ...+... 5 ...+... 6 ...+... 7 ...+... 8
OFilename++DF..N01N02N03Excnam++++B++A++Sb+Sa+..........................
O.............N01N02N03Field+++++++++YB.End++PConstant/editword/DTformat++
O           E           Detail           1
O                       Acountid                 4
O                       Salesperson       +      3
O                       Name              +      3
O                       Ytdsales        1 +      3
O                       Lastsaledate      +      3
```

The above code will end field Accountid in position 4 and put three blanks between the end of Accountid and the start of Salesperson, three blanks between the end of Salesperson and the start of Name, and so on.

Edit Codes (Position 44)

Three of the fields appearing in the output—Page, *Date, and Ytdsales—have an entry in position 44, **Edit codes** (labeled *Y*). An edit code formats numeric values to make them more readable. The Z edit code associated with Page suppresses leading zeros when printing the value; so if Page shows a value of 0001, it will print as 1.

The Y edit code associated with *Date inserts slashes within the printed number. Thus, if *Date has a value of 12202009, it will be printed as 12/20/2009. Note that edit codes apply to numeric fields only. Lastsaledate, which is a native date field—not a number—already has separator characters as part of its value, so it does not require an edit code.

Edit code 1 causes commas and a decimal point to be inserted within the printed value of Ytdsales, and it signals that if the Ytdsales value is 0, the zero balance should appear on the report rather than being completely suppressed. RPG IV includes a large selection of editing alternatives to let you print or display values using a format most appropriate to your needs. A detailed discussion of these editing features appears at the end of this chapter.

Output Continuation Lines

Although they are not appropriate for our current report, output **continuation lines** introduced in RPG IV let you code long constants as a single entry that spans more than one specification line. The layout for the continuation form of the Output specification is as follows:

```
*.. 1 ...+... 2 ...+... 3 ...+... 4 ...+... 5 ...+... 6 ...+... 7 ...+... 8
O.................................................Constant/Editword-continues+
```

Assume, for example, that you're defining a report that is to be captioned "ACME EXPLOSIVES SALES REPORT"— a constant too long to fit on one specification line. You can code this caption as a single constant on two (or more) specification lines by using the continuation feature. (Of course, you could also break the constant into two or more constants and then just code each constant on its own output line.)

To use the continuation feature, you code the end position for the entire constant on the first line—here, we use 90—together with some portion of the constant; then, signal that the constant is continued by terminating the entry on the first line with a hyphen (-) or a plus sign (+). A hyphen signals that the continuation resumes with the *first position* (i.e., position 53) of the continued constant on the next line, while a plus signals that the continuation resumes with the *first nonblank character* encountered in the continued constant on the next line.

The following code illustrates this output feature. Notice that you use an apostrophe only at the very beginning and the very end of the continued constant, rather than needing a set of apostrophes on each line.

```
*.. 1 ...+... 2 ...+... 3 ...+... 4 ...+... 5 ...+... 6 ...+... 7 ...+... 8
O..............N01N02N03Field+++++++++YB.End++PConstant/editword/DTformat++
O.................................................Constant/Editword-continues+
   // The two examples below would produce the same output because of the
   // use of the + and -.
O                                          90 'ACME EXPLOSIVES SALES +
O                                                                 REPORT'

O                                          90 'ACME EXPLOSIVES SALES -
O                                             REPORT'
```

Calculation Specifications

We have now defined the files to be used by our application, the format of the input records to be processed, and the desired output of the application. All we need to complete our program is a description of the processing steps required to obtain the input and write the report. We use **Calculation specifications** to describe these processing steps.

Before coding Calculation specifications, you need to develop the logic required to produce the desired output. In general, you would complete this stage of the program-development cycle—designing the solution—before doing any program coding, but we delayed program design to introduce you to some of the RPG IV specifications and give you a taste of the language.

We can sketch out the required processing of our program using **pseudocode**. Pseudocode is simply stylized English that details the underlying logic needed for a program. Although no single standard exists for formatting pseudocode, it consists of key control words and indentation to show the scope of control of the logic structures. It is always a good idea to work out the design of your program before actually coding it in RPG IV (or in any other language). Pseudocode is language independent and lets you focus on what needs to be done rather than on the specific syntax requirements of a programming language.

Our program exemplifies a simple read/write program in which we want to read a record, write a line on the report, and repeat the process until no more records exist in the file (a condition called **end-of-file**). This kind of application is termed **batch processing** because once the program begins, a "batch" of data, accumulated in a file, directs its execution. Batch programs can be run unattended because they do not require control or instructions from a user.

The logic required by our read/write program is quite simple:

Correct algorithm

Print headings
Read a record
While there are more records
    Print headings if necessary
    Write a detail line
    Read the next record
Endwhile
End program

Note that *While* indicates a repeated process, or loop. Within the loop, the processing requirements for a single record—in this case, simply writing a report line—are detailed and then the next record is read. Because we want to print report headings just once at the beginning of the report rather than once for each record, that step is listed at the beginning of the pseudocode *outside* the loop.

You may wonder why the pseudocode contains two read statements. Why can't there be just a single read, as in the first step within the While loop below?

Incorrect algorithm

Print headings
While there are more records
    Read the next record
    Print headings if necessary
    Write a detail line
Endwhile
End program

The preceding algorithm would work fine as long as each read operation retrieved a data record from the file. The problem is that eventually the system will try to read an input record and fail because there are no more records in the file to read. Once a program has reached end-of-file, it should not attempt to process any more input data. The incorrect algorithm above would inappropriately write a detail line after reaching end-of-file.

The correct algorithm places the read statement as the last step within the While loop so that as soon as end-of-file is detected, no further writing will occur. However, if that were the only read, our algorithm would try to write the first detail line before reading any data. That's why the algorithm also requires an initial read (often called a **priming read**) just before the While loop to "prime" the processing cycle.

After you have designed the program, it is a simple matter to express that logic in a programming language—that is, once you have learned the language's syntax. The following free-format Calculation specifications show the correct algorithm expressed in RPG IV. Notice the specifications' striking similarity to the pseudocode we sketched out earlier.

```
*.. 1 ...+... 2 ...+... 3 ...+... 4 ...+... 5 ...+... 6 ...+... 7 ...+... 8
/Free
   Except Headings;
   Read Customers;

   Dow Not %Eof(Customers);

     If *Inof;
       Except Headings;
       Eval *Inof = *Off;
     Endif;

     Except Detail;
     Read Customers;
   Enddo;

   Eval *Inlr = *On;
   Return;
/End-Free
```

Calculation specifications specify the processing that needs to be done. Free-format Calculation specifications are specified between /Free and /End-free instructions. These instructions, called **compiler directives**, direct the RPG IV compiler to use free-format syntax rules for any of the instructions within the block of code between the directives. The /Free and /End-free directives must be coded exactly as shown, beginning with a slash (/) character in position 7.

The instructions within the /FREE block usually begin with an operation that specifies an action to be taken. RPG IV supports a number of reserved words to identify valid operations. Many of these operations are followed by **operand values**, which RPG calls **factors**, to provide the compiler with the details necessary to perform an operation; other operation codes (Dow, If, and Eval in our example) are followed by expressions that the program will evaluate. Finally, each free-format Calculation specification must end with a semicolon (;).

Spacing is not usually critical in a free-format Calculation specification. You may code the specification in any position from 8 to 80; positions 6 and 7 *must* be blank. You may also indent operations to clarify the flow of the program.

RPG IV Operations

The RPG program executes the Calculation specifications sequentially (from beginning to end) unless the computer encounters an operation that redirects flow of control. Our program uses eight operations: Eval, Except, Read, Dow, Enddo, If, Endif, and Return. Let's look at the specific operations used within the calculations of our program. The intent here is to provide you with sufficient information to understand our basic program and to write similar programs. Several of the operations described in the following section are discussed in more detail in subsequent chapters of this book.

Except (Calculation Time Output)

An **Except** operation directs the program to output one or more E lines from the Output specifications. If no factor is coded with Except, the operation causes the system to output all unnamed E lines. In general, however, RPG programmers name their E lines and use the Except operation with an E-line name to state explicitly which line or lines are to be involved in the output operation. In the sample program, the first Except operation specifies Headings as the name of the group of E-lines to print. As a result, the three heading lines of our report will be printed. Later on, a second Except also prints heading lines if overflow has been reached. A third Except specifies Detail. When the program executes this line of code, our exception line named *Detail* will be printed, using the values of the fields from the currently retrieved Customers record.

Read (Read Sequentially)

Read is an input operation that instructs the computer to retrieve the next sequential record from the named input file—in this case, our Customers file. To use the Read operation with a file, you must have defined that file as input-capable on the File specifications.

Dow (Do While)

The **Dow** operation establishes a loop in RPG IV. An Enddo operation signals the end of the loop. Note that this Dow and Enddo correspond to the While and Endwhile statements in our pseudocode. The Dow operation repeatedly executes the block of code in the loop as long as the condition associated with the Dow operation is true. Because our program's Dow condition is preceded by the word *Not*, this line reads "Do while the end-of-file condition is not true." It is the direct equivalent of the pseudocode statement "While there are more records" because the end-of-file condition will come on only when our Read operation runs out of records.

The *%Eof* entry in this statement is an RPG IV built-in function that returns a true ('1' or *ON) or false ('0' or *OFF) value to indicate whether the file operation encountered end-of-file. **Built-in functions** (sometimes called *BIFs*) perform specific operations and then return a value to the expression in which they are coded. Most built-in functions allow you to enter values called *arguments* in parentheses immediately following the built-in function to govern the function. In this case, %Eof(Customers) means that we want our program to check the end-of-file condition specifically for the Customers file.

Enddo (End Do Group)

The **Enddo** operation serves to mark the end of the scope of a Do operation, such as Dow. All the program statements between the Dow operation and its associated Enddo are repeated as long as the Dow condition is true.

If

RPG's primary decision operation is the **If** operation. If the relationship expressed in the conditional expression coded with the If operation is true, all the calculations between the If and its associated Endif operation are executed; if the relationship is not true, those statements are bypassed. By coding

```
If *Inof = *On;
```

or simply

```
If *Inof;
```

we are telling the program that it should execute the following lines of code only if the overflow indicator *OF* is on:

```
Except Headings;
Eval *Inof = *Off;
```

Endif (End If Group)

The **Endif** operation marks the end of the scope of an If operation. All the program statements between the If operation and its associated Endif are executed as long as the If condition is true.

Tip

It is common practice to indent blocks of code that appear between Dow or If and their associated Enddo or Endif operations. By indenting the blocks, you can easily see which code is associated with the Dow or If operation. Don't overdo it, though. Indenting a couple of spaces is enough.

Eval (Evaluate Expression)

Eval is an operation used to assign a value to a variable. In the sample program, by coding

```
Eval *Inof = *Off;
```

we are assigning the value *Off to the overflow indicator OF (coded as *Inof). We do this after printing the heading lines, so that the program will know that it is no longer necessary to print the headings until indicator OF is once again set to *On automatically.

Later in the program, we use the line

```
Eval *Inlr = *On;
```

to assign the value *On to a special reserved indicator variable called **Last Record** (coded as ***Inlr**, read as **indicator LR**). *Inlr (commonly referred to as LR) performs a special function within RPG IV. If LR is on when the program ends, it signals the computer to close the files and free the memory associated with the program. If LR is not on, the program continues to tie up some of the system's resources even though the program is no longer running.

In most cases, specifying Eval is optional in a free-format Calculation specification; you can simply code the assignment expression without explicitly coding the Eval operation. Eval is included in this example to provide easy comparison with the fixed-format code—where it is required—but it could have been left out in the free-format C-spec.

Return (Return to Caller)

The **Return** operation returns control to the program that called it—either the computer's operating system or perhaps another program. Program execution stops when a Return is encountered. Although your program will end correctly without this instruction—provided you have turned on LR—including it is a good practice. Return clearly signals the endpoint of your program and lets the program become part of an application system of called programs. Chapter 12 deals in detail with called programs.

Fixed-Format Calculations

You may wonder why the free-format section of code is called *Calculation specifications*. Earlier versions of RPG IV (before Version 5) did not support free-format specifications. Instead, this function was handled by a fixed-format specification, which had a C in column 6. These specifications were called Calculation specifications (C-specs). Though modern RPG programming style encourages free format, this section of code is still commonly called Calculation specifications—even though the C in column 6 is no longer used.

The following shows the fixed-format C-specs equivalent to our free-format code.

```
*.. 1 ...+... 2 ...+... 3 ...+... 4 ...+... 5 ...+... 6 ...+... 7 ...+... 8
CLØN01Factor1+++++++Opcode(E)+Factor2+++++++Result++++++++Len++D+HiLoEq....
CLØN01Factor1+++++++Opcode(E)+Extended-factor2+++++++++++++++++++++++++++++++
C                   Except    Headings
C                   Read      Customers
C                   Dow       Not %Eof(Customers)
C                   If        *Inof
C                   Except    Headings
C                   Eval      *Inof = *Off
C                   Endif
C                   Except    Detail
C                   Read      Customers
C                   Enddo
C                   Eval      *Inlr = *On
C                   Return
```

Fixed-format Calculation specifications do not require the /Free and /End-free directives. Instead, each line requires a C in position 6. Each Calculation specification contains an operation entered in positions 26–35 (labeled *Opcode(E)+*). Depending on the operation, specifications may also include a value in Factor 1 (positions 12–25), Factor 2 (positions 36–49), the Result field (positions 50–63), or the extended Factor 2 field (positions 36–80). Indicators associated with operations may also appear in positions 71–76. Fixed-format Calculation specifications do not require a semicolon delimiter at the end of the line. Appendix E covers fixed-format Calculation specifications in more detail.

Internal Documentation

You might think that once you have a program written and running, you are done with it forever and can move forward and develop new programs. Actually, about 70 percent of all programming is maintenance programming rather than new application development. Maintenance programming involves modifying existing programs to fix problems, address changing business needs, or satisfy user requests for modifications.

Because of the high probability that any program you write will be revised sometime in the future—either by yourself or by some other programmer in your company—it is your responsibility to make your program as understandable as possible to facilitate these future revisions. RPG programmers use several techniques to document their programs.

Program Overview

Most companies require overview documentation at the beginning of each program. This documentation, coded as a block of comments, states the function or purpose of the program, the program's author, the date when the program was written, and any special instructions or peculiarities of the program that those working with it should know.

If the program is revised, entries detailing the revisions—including the date of the revisions and their author—are usually added to that initial documentation. If a program uses several indicators, many programmers will provide an indicator "dictionary" as part of their initial set of comments to state the function or role of each indicator used within the program.

Comments

Another good way to help others understand what your program does is to include explanatory documentation internal to your program through the use of **comment lines**. RPG IV comments begin with **double slashes** (//) entered anywhere within positions 8–80. In free-format specifications, these comments can make up an entire line or a portion of the line. Once the compiler encounters the // characters, it will ignore the rest of the line, treating the remainder as a comment. Using // to specify comments is not limited to free-format specifications; you can enter comment lines anywhere in the program. In fixed-format specifications, the comments make up an entire line (positions 7–80); the line must begin with // characters and cannot include any compilable code.

Comments exist within the program at a source-code level only; they are for the benefit of programmers who may have to work with the program later. You should include comments throughout your program as needed to help explain specific processing steps that are not obvious. In adding such comments, you should assume that anyone looking at your program has at least a basic proficiency with RPG IV; your documentation should help clarify your program to such a person. Documenting trivial, obvious aspects of your program is a waste of time. On the other hand, failing to document difficult-to-grasp processing can cost others valuable time. Inaccurate documentation is worse than no documentation at all because it supplies false clues that may mislead the person responsible for program modification.

Appropriately documenting a program is an important learned skill. If you are uncertain about what to document, ask yourself, "What would I want to know about this program if I were looking at it for the first time?"

Fixed-Format Comments

In addition to the preferred // comment notation, fixed-format RPG statements allow an older alternative: asterisk comments. In fixed-format RPG IV syntax, an asterisk (*) in position 7 of any line—regardless of the specification type—designates that line as a comment; you can enter any documentation, in any form that you like, within the remaining portion of the line.

Free-format specifications do not allow asterisk comments. This book uses // comments exclusively. All the specification forms also include a comment area in positions 81–100 so that you can easily add a short comment to any line of code.

Blank Lines

In addition to the use of comments, many programmers find that a program's structure is easier to understand when blank lines are used to break the code into logical units. To facilitate using blank lines within your code, RPG IV treats two types of lines as blank: first, any line that is completely blank between positions 6 and 80 can appear anywhere within your program. Second, if position 6 contains a valid specification type and positions 7–80 are blank, the line is treated as a blank line; however, the line must be located in that portion of the program appropriate for its designated specification type.

The Completed Program

Our completed sample RPG IV program is shown below. Note that the order of the program statements is File, Input, Calculations, and Output. RPG requires this order. Also note that you can use blank comment lines or lines of asterisks to visually break the program into logical units and that using lowercase lettering within internal documentation helps it stand out from program code.

```
*.. 1 ...+... 2 ...+... 3 ...+... 4 ...+... 5 ...+... 6 ...+... 7 ...+... 8
 // -----------------------------------------------------------------
 // This program produces a year-to-date sales report. The report data
 // comes directly from input file Customers.
 //     Date Written:  12/15/2006
 // -----------------------------------------------------------------

FCustomers IF   F  152        Disk
FQprint    O    F  132        Printer Oflind(*Inof)

ICustomers NS
I                                    1     4  Accountid
I                                    5     8  Salesperson
I                                    9    43  Name
I                          *USA D  132   141  Lastsaledate
I                                  142   152 2Ytdsales

 /Free

    Except Headings;
    Read Customers;

    Dow Not %Eof(Customers);

      If *Inof;
        Except Headings;
        *Inof = *Off;
      Endif;

      Except Detail;
      Read Customers;
    Enddo;

    *Inlr = *On;
    Return;

 /End-Free
```

continued...

continued...

```
OQprint     E           Headings        2  2
O                                           16 'YTD SALES REPORT'
O                                           56 'DATE'
O                       *Date           Y   67
O                                           74 'PAGE'
O                       Page            Z   79

O           E           Headings        1
O                                            4 'ACCT'
O                                           11 'SALES'
O                                           65 'YTD'
O                                           78 'DATE OF'

O           E           Headings        2
O                                            3 'ID'
O                                           12 'PERSON'
O                                           22 'CUSTOMER'
O                                           66 'SALES'
O                                           79 'LAST SALE'

O           E           Detail          1
O                       Accountid            4
O                       Salesperson         11
O                       Name                49
O                       Ytdsales        1   66
O                       Lastsaledate        79
```

To create this program, you would use an editor to enter the RPG IV code into a source member with an SEU member type of RPGLE. Once the source member contains all the required code, then you would compile the source using the CRTBNDRPG (Create Bound RPG Program) command to compile the source and create the program. Once the program is successfully created, you would execute it, using the CALL command.

Now that you have seen how to write a complete RPG IV program, we can return to the concept of output editing to learn RPG IV's editing features in greater detail.

Output Editing

Output editing refers to formatting output values by suppressing leading zeros and adding special characters—such as decimal points, commas, and dollar signs—to make the values easier for people looking at the output to comprehend. RPG IV allows numeric fields (but not character fields) to be edited as part of the Output specifications. You often will use editing to obtain the output format requested in a printer spacing chart.

Editing is used in part because of the way numbers are stored in the computer. For example, if Amount—a field six bytes long with two decimal positions—is assigned the value 31.24, the computer stores that value as 003124. Although the computer keeps track of the decimal position, a decimal point is not actually stored as part of the numeric value. If you were to specify that Amount be printed without editing, the number would be printed as 003124; the nonsignificant zeros would appear, and there would be no indication of where the decimal point should be.

Edit Codes

To make it easier to specify the most commonly needed kinds of editing, RPG IV includes several built-in edit codes you can use to indicate how you want a field's value to be printed. You associate an edit code with a field by entering the code in position 44 of the Output specification containing that field. All commonly used edit codes automatically result in **zero suppression**—that is, printing blanks in place of nonsignificant leading zeros—because that is a standard desired format.

Editing Numbers

Some editing decisions vary with the application. Do you want numbers to be printed with commas (or other appropriate grouping separator for your region) inserted? How do you want to handle negative values—ignore them and omit any sign, print CR immediately after a negative value, print a floating minus sign (-) after the value, or print a floating negative sign to the left of the value? And if a field has a value of zero, do you want to print a zero or leave that spot on the report blank? A set of 16 edit codes—1 through 4, A through D, and J through Q—cover all combinations of these three options: commas, sign handling, and zero balances. The following table details the effects of the 16 codes (in the shaded area).

Options and Edit Codes

Print commas	Print zero balance	No sign	CR	Right -	Floating -
Yes	Yes	1	A	J	N
Yes	No	2	B	K	O
No	Yes	3	C	L	P
No	No	4	D	M	Q

Thus, if you want commas, zero balances to print, and a floating negative sign, you would use edit code N; if you did not want commas or any sign but did want zero balances to print, you would use edit code 3.

To give you a clearer understanding of the effects of each of these edit codes, the following table demonstrates how various values would appear when printed with each of the edit codes. The position of the decimal place in the values is indicated by a caret (^). Notice that if you use edit codes 1–4 with a field containing a negative value, the field will be printed like a positive number.

Edit code	1234^56	1234^56-	0234^56-	0000^00	000000^
1	1,234.56	1,234.56	234.56	.00	.00
2	1,234.56	1,234.56	234.56		
3	1234.56	1234.56	234.56	.00	.00
4	1234.56	1234.56	234.56		
A	1,234.56	1,234.56CR	234.56CR	.00	.00
B	1,234.56	1,234.56CR	234.56CR		
C	1234.56	1234.56CR	234.56CR	.00	.00
D	1234.56	1234.56CR	234.56CR		
J	1,234.56	1,234.56-	234.56-	.00	.00

continued...

continued...

Edit code	Value				
	1234^56	1234^56-	0234^56-	0000^00	000000^
K	1,234.56	1,234.56-	234.56-		
L	1234.56	1234.56-	234.56-	.00	.00
M	1234.56	1234.56-	234.56-		
N	1,234.56	-1,234.56	-234.56	.00	.00
O	1,234.56	-1,234.56	-234.56		
P	1234.56	-1234.56	-234.56	.00	.00
Q	1234.56	-1234.56	-234.56		

RPG provides three additional useful edit codes: X, Y, and Z. Edit code *Y* results in slashes being printed as part of a date. For example, if you run your program on December 11, 2009, the reserved field *Date will contain 12112009. If edited with edit code Y, this date will be printed as 12/11/2009. Although edit code Y is normally used to edit dates, you can also use it with any field for which slash insertion is appropriate.

Edit code Z simply zero suppresses leading nonsignificant zeros. Z does *not* enable the printing of a decimal point or a negative sign, so if a field contained a value of -234.56, the Z edit code would cause the field to be printed as 23456. The use of Z is usually limited to whole number fields.

With one exception, all the edit codes suppress leading zeros. Edit code X, however, retains them. For this reason, the X edit code is useful when you want to convert a numeric value to a character string and retain the leading zeros.

Currency Output Editing
You occasionally will want dollar signs (or other local currency symbols) to be printed as part of your report. As we mentioned in Chapter 1, you can position dollar signs in a fixed column of the report or you can place them just to the left of the first significant digit of the values with which they are associated. This latter type of dollar sign is called a *floating dollar sign*.

Fixed currency symbol	Floating currency symbol
$ 12.34	$12.34
$5,432.10	$5,432.10
$ .00	$.00

In general, you want to use a dollar sign in addition to one of the editing codes. To specify a floating dollar sign, code '$' (apostrophes included) in the constant/edit word positions (columns 53–80) of the Output specifications *on the same line* as the field and its edit code. To specify a fixed dollar sign, code '$' as a constant *on its own line* with its own end position.

You can use one additional feature along with edit codes. An asterisk coded in the constant/edit word position on the same line as the field and edit code specifies that insignificant leading zeros be replaced by asterisks rather than simply being suppressed. This feature is called **asterisk fill** or sometimes **check protection** because its most common use is in printing checks—to prevent tampering with a check's face value. For example, a check worth $12.15 might include the amount written as $****12.15.

The following examples illustrate how to code the various currency output options.

```
*.. 1 ...+... 2 ...+... 3 ...+... 4 ...+... 5 ...+... 6 ...+... 7 ...+... 8
O..............N01N02N03Field+++++++++YB.End++PConstant/editword/DTformat++
   // The following line illustrates a floating dollar sign.
O                       Amount        1    65 '$'
   // The next two lines illustrate a fixed dollar sign.
O                                          56 '$'
O                       Amount        1    65
   // The following line illustrates asterisk fill.
O                       Amount        1    65 '*'
   // The next two lines combine a fixed dollar sign with asterisk fill.
O                                          56 '$'
O                       Amount        1    65 '*'
```

Edit Words

You would think that given the variety of edit codes built into RPG IV, you would be able to find a code to fit your every need. Unfortunately, that is not the case. Social Security and telephone numbers represent good examples of values that we are used to seeing in a format that an edit code cannot supply. RPG IV includes an alternative to edit codes, called **edit words**, that can help in this kind of situation.

You code an edit word in the constant/edit word portion of the Output specifications on the same line as the field with which it is to be used. Note that because they perform the same function, edit words and edit codes are never used together for the same field. An edit word supplies a template into which a number is inserted. The template is enclosed with apostrophes. Within the template, a blank position indicates where a digit should appear, while a 0 indicates how far zero suppression should take place. With no zero in the edit word, the default is to zero suppress to the first significant digit.

You can use any character—including commas—as an insertion character within the template. The insertion characters will be printed in the specified place as long as they are to the right of a significant digit. A dollar sign at the left of the edit word signals a fixed dollar sign; a dollar sign adjacent to a zero denotes a floating dollar sign. To indicate a blank as an insertion character, use an ampersand (&).

Examine the table below to see how edit words work.

Raw value	Edit word	Printed result
999999999	' - - '	999-99-9999
999999999	' & & '	999 99 9999
1234123412	'0( ) - '	(123)412-3412
00012^14	' $0. '	$12.14
00012^14	'$ 0. '	$ 12.14
00012^14	' *0. '	***12.14
05678^90	'$, 0. '	$ 5,678.90
05678^90-	' , $0. CR'	$5,678.90CR
05678^90-	' , $0. -'	$5,678.90-
05678^90	' , **DOLLARS* *CENTS'	*5,678*DOLLARS*90*CENTS

You can duplicate the effects of any edit code with an edit word. In general, RPG programmers use edit words only when there is no edit code that provides the format they want for their output.

Chapter Summary

RPG IV programs are written as fixed-format or free-format specifications. Different specification forms convey different kinds of information to the RPG IV compiler, which translates the program into machine language.

File specifications contain descriptions of all files used within a program. Input specifications provide detailed information about each program-described input file used by a program. There are two kinds of Input specification lines: one that contains record identification entries to generally describe a record format within a file, and one that contains field identification entries to define the fields of the record. Each field is described on a separate line.

Calculation specifications center on operations, or processing steps, to be accomplished by the computer. Each Calculation specification includes an RPG IV operation either by coding it explicitly (or, in the case of the Eval operation, implicitly) in an expression. Depending on the specific operation, it may also include additional entries. The computer executes operations in the order specified on the Calculation specifications unless the computer encounters an operation that specifically alters this flow of control.

Output specifications provide details about each program-described output file. You use two kinds of Output specification lines: a record identification line to describe an output record format at a general level and field description lines to describe each field or constant that appears as part of a record format. When the output is a report, you need a record identification line and corresponding field-identification entries for each kind of line to appear on the report.

An important part of programming is documenting the program. Comment lines—signaled by double slashes (//) in nearly any position of a specification line—can appear anywhere within a program. Most comments are coded on a separate line, but in free-format specifications, they may be included on the same line as executable RPG statements but positioned after the RPG statements. The RPG IV compiler ignores such comments.

Within your code, you can insert completely blank lines and lines that are blank except for the specification type to visually break the code into sections.

It is customary to edit printed numeric values. RPG IV supplies ready-made edit codes for common editing requirements and lets you create special editing formats by using edit words.

The following table summarizes the operation codes and built-in functions discussed in this chapter. Optional entries are shown within curly braces ({}).

Function or operation	Description	Syntax
Dow	Do while	Dow *logical-expression*
Enddo Endif	End a structured group	End*xx*
%Eof	End of file	%Eof{(*file-name*)}
Eval	Evaluate expression	{Eval} *result = expression*
Except	Calculation time output	Except {*name*}
If	If	If *logical-expression*
Read	Read a record	Read *file-name*
Return	Return to caller	Return

Key Terms

arguments
asterisk fill
batch processing
built-in functions
Calculation specifications
case sensitive
character field
check protection
comment lines
compiler directives
constants
continuation lines
Control specifications
detail line
double slashes (//)
Dow (Do While)
edit code
edit words
end position
Enddo (End Do Group)
Endif
end-of-file
Eval
Except
exception lines
exception names
factors
field-level
field description entries
File specifications/F-specs
fixed format

fixed position
free form
full procedural
If
indicator
*Inlr
Input specifications
keywords
Last Record
literals
native date fields
numeric fields
operand values
output editing
output file
Output specifications
overflow
overflow indicator
Page
priming read
pseudocode
Read
record formats
record identification entries
reserved word
Return
sequence checking
Skip entries
Space entries
title case
zero suppression

Discussion/Review Questions

1. What is a fixed-format language? Can you give an example of a free-format language? Which form offers the most advantages?

2. Why do reports generated by RPG IV programs need to appear on File specifications?

3. Why don't you need to enter a File Designation for output files?

X	1STQTR	#3
ABC	QTY-OH	CustNo
@end	SALES	$AMT
_YTD_Sales	CUST#	Day1
YR END	YR_END	Yearend
InvoiceNumber	avg.sales	cusTnbR

4. Which of the following are invalid RPG IV variable names? Why?

5. What is an indicator? What specific methods of turning on indicators were introduced in this chapter? How can you use indicators to control processing? What alternative RPG IV feature can be used to reduce or eliminate indicators in a program?

6. Describe the difference between a Skip entry and a Space entry on the Output specifications.

7. How could you obtain five blank lines between detail lines of a report?

8. What is the advantage of giving the same name to several exception lines of output?

9. What are some fields that are automatically provided by RPG IV for your use?

10. Why do you often need two read statements within a program?

11. What is the correct order of specifications within an RPG IV program?

12. What is the purpose of each kind of RPG IV specification introduced in this chapter?

13. What is LR? Why is it used?

14. What is maintenance programming? And what programming techniques can you adopt to facilitate it?

15. Why does RPG IV include both edit codes and edit words? What exceptions are there to the rule that an edit code and an edit word or constant should never appear together on the same Output specification line?

16. What are the programming implications of the fact that RPG IV is not case sensitive?

17. Describe internal and external documentation. Why is there so much importance placed on correctly documenting a program?

18. Research Control specifications. What are some of the advantages of using them? Are there disadvantages?

Exercises

1. A Customer listing program uses data from file Customers to generate a report that reflects all the data in the file. The record layout of file Customers follows:

Description	Positions	(Decimal positions)	Notes
Customer number	1–5	(0)	—
Customer name	6–25	—	—
Last order date	26–33	—	mmddyyyy
Balance owed	34–43	(2)	—

Write the File specifications for this program.

2. Given the above problem definition, write the Input specifications.

3. Write the pseudocode to produce the report.

4. Design a report for the application in Exercise 1, using the printer spacing chart notation of Chapter 1.

5. Develop Output specifications based on your printer spacing chart from Exercise 4 and the File specifications of Exercise 1.

Programming Assignments

All five of the programming assignments below center on a single company, CompuSell. CompuSell is a mail-order company specializing in computers and computer supplies. Appendix F provides a description of the company and the record layouts of its data files.

1. CompuSell would like you to write a program to produce a listing of all its customers. Use data file CSCSTP, the customer master file for CompuSell, as your input file. The listing should exactly match the format described in the following printer spacing chart.

Note: the grid has been split to allow the report to be formatted for the textbook.

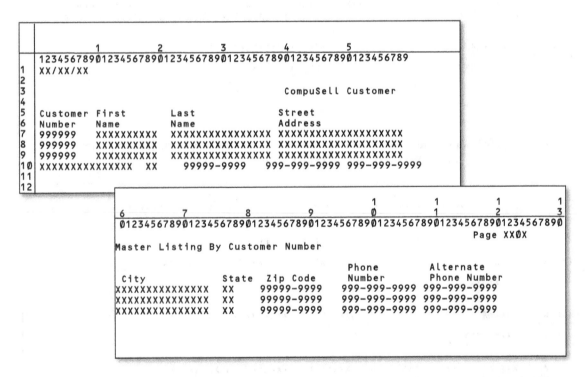

2. CompuSell wants an inventory listing, formatted as shown in the following printer spacing chart. Write the program to produce this report, exactly matching the printer spacing chart specifications. The input file is CSINVP; its record layout is given in Appendix F.

```
          1         2         3         4         5         6         7         8         9         1
                                                                                                    0
 1234567890123456789012345678901234567890123456789012345678901234567890123456789012345678901234567890
1   XX/XX/XX                   Compusell Inventory Listing                          Page XXØX
2
3 Prod.                            Weight    Qty. on     Average      Current     Selling
4 Num.        Description          lbs. Ozs. Hand         Cost         Cost        Price
5
6 XXXXX   XXXXXXXXXXXXXXXXXXXXXXXX  XØ   XX    XXØX       X,XXØ.XX     X,XXØ.XX    $X,XX$.XX
7 XXXXX   XXXXXXXXXXXXXXXXXXXXXXXX  XØ   XX    XXØX       X,XXØ.XX     X,XXØ.XX    $X,XX$.XX
8
```

3. CompuSell wants to send out two separate mailings to each of its customers contained in file CSCSTP (see Appendix F for the record layout). Accordingly, the company asks you to write a label-printing program that will print two-across labels. Each of the labels reading across should represent the same customer. The printer will be loaded with continuous label stock when this program is run. Each label is five print lines long. The desired format for the labels is shown below. Note that the information in the parentheses is included to let you know what should appear on the label; it should not appear within your output.

```
         1         2         3         4         5         6         7         8         9        10
1234567890123456789012345678901234567890123456789012345678901234567890123456789012345678901234567890
1   XXXXXXXXX XXXXXXXXXXXXXX          XXXXXXXXX XXXXXXXXXXXXXX      (first, last name)
2   XXXXXXXXXXXXXXXXXXXX              XXXXXXXXXXXXXXXXXXXX          (street address)
3   XXXXXXXXXXXXXXX  XX XXXXX-XXXX    XXXXXXXXXXXXXX  XX XXXXX-XXXX (city, state, zip)
4
5
6   XXXXXXXXX XXXXXXXXXXXXXX          XXXXXXXXX XXXXXXXXXXXXXX
7   XXXXXXXXXXXXXXXXXXXX              XXXXXXXXXXXXXXXXXXXX
8   XXXXXXXXXXXXXXX  XX XXXXX-XXXX    XXXXXXXXXXXXXX  XX XXXXX-XXXX
9
10
11
12
```

4. CompuSell wants a telephone and address listing of all its suppliers. Write a program to produce this listing. Your input file, CSSUPP, is described in Appendix F.

```
         1         2         3         4         5         6         7         8         9        10
1234567890123456789012345678901234567890123456789012345678901234567890123456789012345678901234567890
1     Compusell Supplier List as of XX/XX/XX              Page XXØX
2
3     Name/Address                  Phone            Contact Person
4
5  XXXXXXXXXXXXXXXXXXXXXXXXXX    (XXX) XXX-XXXX    XXXXXXXXXXXXXXXXXXXXXXXXXXXXXX
6  XXXXXXXXXXXXXXXXXXXX
7  XXXXXXXXXXXXXXX XX XXXXX-XXXX
8
9
10 XXXXXXXXXXXXXXXXXXXXXXXXXX    (XXX) XXX-XXXX    XXXXXXXXXXXXXXXXXXXXXXXXXXXXXX
11 XXXXXXXXXXXXXXXXXXXX
12 XXXXXXXXXXXXXXX XX XXXXX-XXXX
13
14
15 XXXXXXXXXXXXXXXXXXXXXXXXXX    (XXX) XXX-XXXX    XXXXXXXXXXXXXXXXXXXXXXXXXXXXXX
16 XXXXXXXXXXXXXXXXXXXX
17 XXXXXXXXXXXXXXX XX XXXXX-XXXX
18
```

5. CompuSell wants a listing of all its employees. Write a program to produce this listing. Your input file, CSSEMP, is described in Appendix F.

```
         1         2         3         4         5         6         7         8         9        10
1234567890123456789012345678901234567890123456789012345678901234567890123456789012345678901234567890
1 XX/XX/XX                                                                              Page XXØX
2
3                       CompuSell Employee Listing By Employee Number
4  Employee First        Last          Street                                            Phone
5  Number   Name         Name          Address            City           St  Zip Code    Number
6  999999   XXXXXXXXX    XXXXXXXXXXXXXX XXXXXXXXXXXXXXXXXX XXXXXXXXXXXXXX XX  99999-9999  999-999-9999
7  999999   XXXXXXXXX    XXXXXXXXXXXXXX XXXXXXXXXXXXXXXXXX XXXXXXXXXXXXXX XX  99999-9999  999-999-9999
8  999999   XXXXXXXXX    XXXXXXXXXXXXXX XXXXXXXXXXXXXXXXXX XXXXXXXXXXXXXX XX  99999-9999  999-999-9999
9
10
11
```

Chapter 3

Externally Described Files

Chapter Overview

In this chapter, you will learn how i5/OS handles database files. The chapter explains the differences between physical and logical files and discusses field reference files. You will be introduced to the System i data types and the storage implications of numeric, date, and character data types. The chapter covers how to use DDS to define database files at a system level and how to access these definitions from within RPG IV programs. You will also learn about externally described printer files.

The i5/OS Approach to Database Files

The i5/OS operating system is unique in the way it handles data. Unlike other systems, which require additional, costly software to provide them with database capabilities, i5/OS was designed with database applications in mind, so the database is tightly integrated into the operating system. The operating system automatically treats all data files as part of a large relational database system. One consequence of this approach is that all data files need to be defined to the system independently of application programs. Even those applications that on the surface seem to be "creating" files are actually creating records and storing them in a file that must have been defined to i5/OS before program execution.

These files may be defined to the system at a record level (i.e., not broken down into individual fields) or at a field level. If you define a file only to the record level, any RPG IV program that uses that file must subdivide that record into the appropriate fields in the Input or Output specifications; this type of file is called a **program-described file** because the field descriptions are explicitly coded in the RPG IV programs that will use the file. On the other hand, if you define the file to the field level—outside the programs that will use it—you do not need to code those field definitions within the programs that use the file; the definitions will be brought into the program when you compile it. This type of file is called an **externally described file** because the field definitions are external to the programs that use the file; the field definitions are a part of the file object itself. RPG IV programmers almost universally prefer externally described files over program-described files.

Externally described files can reduce the need for duplication of data (**redundancy**) across files, following well-established database-design principles. Externally described files impose standardization among programmers and across applications because all programs using a given file use the same field definitions and names. Externally described files also increase programmer efficiency and reduce errors because programmers don't need to duplicate the file definition effort each time they need to use a file within a program.

Externally described files simplify system maintenance. For example, if it is necessary to add a field to a record layout or to change a field's definition (e.g., expand postal code to ten characters), these changes need to be made in only one place (in the external file definition) rather than in every program that uses that file. Simply recompiling the programs that use the file will let them use the new layout—in many cases without any changes to their coding—and under certain conditions, even recompiling is not necessary.

Physical and Logical Files

i5/OS lets you define two kinds of database files: physical files and logical files. **Physical files** actually store data records in arrival sequence—that is, the order in which they are written to the file. If you define a physical file at a field level and one or more of those fields is designated as a **key field**, you can subsequently access records stored in that file in either **key sequence** or **arrival sequence** (first-in, first-out). If you do not define a key field, access is limited to arrival sequence.

Logical files describe how data appears to be stored in the database. Logical files do not actually contain data records. Instead, they store **access paths**, or pointers, to records in physical files. A logical file is always based on one or more physical files. The three most common uses for a logical file are to provide these capabilities:

- Sorting the records in a physical file
- Selecting certain records from a physical file
- Selecting certain fields from a physical file's record layout

A common use for a logical file is to provide an alternative order for accessing the records in a physical file based on values of key fields. In this case, the logical file will have one or more fields designated as key fields—but different key fields from the ones that may be defined in the physical file. Consider the following example, which shows records of an employee master physical file and two logical files based on the physical file. Employee number is the key field to the physical file. One of the logical files is keyed on a **composite**, or **concatenation**, of last name and first name, while the other has postal code as the key field. The example shows the order in which the records would appear to an application program for each file if you stipulated **sequential retrieval** by key.

Physical file EMPLOYEES (keyed on employee number)

Emp. no.	Last name	First name	Dept.	Salary	Street	City	State	Postal code	Hire date
111111111	Jones	Mary	MKT	54000	123 W. 45th	Decatur	MI	49065	1977-07-01
222222222	Smith	Sam	ACT	61500	4422 N. Oak	Paw Paw	MI	49045	1985-04-01
333333333	Adams	Arnold	MKT	34950	1120 W. Main	Kalamazoo	MI	49008	1993-08-12
444444444	Houston	Wanda	MIS	29500	290 S. State	Kalamazoo	MI	49007	2006-04-23
555555555	Jacobs	David	ACT	43275	9911 S. 88th	Mattawan	MI	49069	2002-07-01
666666666	Salinger	Carol	MIS	38500	1300 Maple Lk.	Paw Paw	MI	49065	2005-05-30
777777777	Riley	Thomas	MKT	24600	8824 E. Drake	Kalamazoo	MI	49008	2006-12-19

Logical file EMPLOYEES1 (keyed on last name and first name)

Emp. no.	Last name	First name	Dept.	Salary	Street	City	State	Postal code	Hire date
333333333	Adams	Arnold	MKT	34950	1120 W. Main	Kalamazoo	MI	49008	1993-08-12
444444444	Houston	Wanda	MIS	29500	290 S. State	Kalamazoo	MI	49007	2006-04-23
555555555	Jacobs	David	ACT	43275	9911 S. 88th	Mattawan	MI	49069	2002-07-01
111111111	Jones	Mary	MKT	54000	123 W. 45th	Decatur	MI	49065	1977-07-01
777777777	Riley	Thomas	MKT	24600	8824 E. Drake	Kalamazoo	MI	49008	2006-12-19
666666666	Salinger	Carol	MIS	38500	1300 Maple Lk.	Paw Paw	MI	49065	2005-05-30
222222222	Smith	Sam	ACT	61500	4422 N. Oak	Paw Paw	MI	49045	1985-04-01

Logical file EMPLOYEES2 (keyed on postal code)

Emp. no.	Last name	First name	Dept.	Salary	Street	City	State	Postal code	Hire date
444444444	Houston	Wanda	MIS	29500	290 S. State	Kalamazoo	MI	49007	2006-04-23
333333333	Adams	Arnold	MKT	34950	1120 W. Main	Kalamazoo	MI	49008	1993-08-12
777777777	Riley	Thomas	MKT	24600	8824 E. Drake	Kalamazoo	MI	49008	2006-12-19
222222222	Smith	Sam	ACT	61500	4422 N. Oak	Paw Paw	MI	49045	1985-04-01
111111111	Jones	Mary	MKT	54000	123 W. 45th	Decatur	MI	49065	1977-07-01
666666666	Salinger	Carol	MIS	38500	1300 Maple Lk.	Paw Paw	MI	49065	2005-05-30
555555555	Jacobs	David	ACT	43275	9911 S. 88th	Mattawan	MI	49069	2002-07-01

You might use the first logical file to produce an employee listing in alphabetic order, while the second logical file could be used to print mailing labels for employees, ordered by postal code. Although the actual data records are stored only in the physical file (remember that the logical files store only access paths to records), programs can use logical files just as though the logical files themselves contained the data. In fact, there is no difference in the way you code the file descriptions in your RPG IV program.

Another common use for a logical file is to select certain records (a **subset**) from a physical file. Depending on which fields are specified and which are named as keys, the apparent data content and processing order of a logical file may vary greatly from those of the physical file (or files) underlying it. Using our Employees physical-file example above, we might have a logical file that contains a subset of the actual records in the physical file—for example, only the employees in Marketing:

Logical file EMPLOYEES3 (keyed on employee number, select MKT department)

Emp. no.	Last name	First name	Dept.	Salary	Street	City	State	Postal code	Hire date
111111111	Jones	Mary	MKT	54000	123 W. 45th	Decatur	MI	49065	1977-07-01
333333333	Adams	Arnold	MKT	34950	1120 W. Main	Kalamazoo	MI	49008	1993-08-12
777777777	Riley	Thomas	MKT	24600	8824 E. Drake	Kalamazoo	MI	49008	2006-12-19

While the physical file Employees contains all the possible records, if a program processes those records in Employees3, that program will have access only to those employees in Marketing.

Logical-file records do not need to include all the fields present in the physical records on which they are based; which fields appear within a logical file depend on the logical file's definition. Again using our Employees physical-file example, we might have a logical file that omits the salary information from the employee records while another omits the name and address information. Both of these examples also omit the hire date:

Logical file EMPLOYEES4 (keyed on employee number)

Emp. no.	Last name	First name	Dept.	Street	City	State	Postal code
111111111	Jones	Mary	MKT	123 W. 45th	Decatur	MI	49065
222222222	Smith	Sam	ACT	4422 N. Oak	Paw Paw	MI	49045
333333333	Adams	Arnold	MKT	1120 W. Main	Kalamazoo	MI	49008
444444444	Houston	Wanda	MIS	290 S. State	Kalamazoo	MI	49007
555555555	Jacobs	David	ACT	9911 S. 88th	Mattawan	MI	49069
666666666	Salinger	Carol	MIS	1300 Maple Lk.	Paw Paw	MI	49065
777777777	Riley	Thomas	MKT	8824 E. Drake	Kalamazoo	MI	49008

Logical file EMPLOYEES5 (keyed on employee number)

Emp.no.	Dept.	Salary
111111111	MKT	54000
222222222	ACT	61500
333333333	MKT	34950
444444444	MIS	29500
555555555	ACT	43275
666666666	MIS	38500
777777777	MKT	24600

i5/OS Database and SQL

You may be familiar with **Structured Query Language** (SQL), an industry-standard language for defining, accessing, and manipulating database records. The i5/OS operating system does support SQL as well as DDS (described in this chapter). While the i5/OS database principles and DDS predate SQL, there are many correlating concepts between the two, and there are corresponding terms.

The computer stores all objects (programs, files, and so on) in special container objects called **libraries**; SQL calls a library a **collection**. i5/OS stores data in physical files, which may or may not be keyed; the SQL term for a physical file is a **table**. The i5/OS database supports logical files to provide alternative views of physical files, possibly with different record layouts than the physical files on which they are based; the SQL term for an unkeyed logical file is a **view**. A keyed logical file can be used by SQL to improve the performance of certain SQL statements; SQL calls this an **index**. Finally, SQL uses the term **rows** for the records in a file and **columns** for the fields in a record layout.

SQL syntax is divided into three major areas: **Data Definition Language** (**DDL**) for creating database files, **Data Manipulation Language** (**DML**) for accessing those files, and **SQL programming statements**, which SQL uses to create programs and to embed SQL statements into other languages, such as RPG.

RPG IV can process tables, views, and indexes that were originally created by SQL. SQL can access physical files and logical files that were originally created using DDS. A complete discussion of SQL goes beyond the scope of this text.

Programs that use these logical files would have access only to the information in the logical record formats. Using i5/OS security techniques, we can secure the various physical and logical files to ensure that only authorized personnel and programs would have access to sensitive information.

Introduction to DDS

The procedure for creating database file definitions is similar to that of creating an RPG IV program. The first step is to use an editor—such as Source Entry Utility (SEU) or the WDSc LPEX editor—to create a source member of definition statements. Most installations use a file named *QDDSSRC* to store members representing externally described files. The source type of a physical-file member is PF; the type of a logical-file member is LF. SEU automatically provides prompts appropriate to the member type you specify.

Data Description Specifications (**DDS**) comprise a fixed-format language that you can use to code the source definitions for physical and logical database files as well as for display and printer files. The format for DDS definitions resembles RPG specifications—and for a good reason: DDS file definitions were closely modeled after RPG. All DDS lines include an A in position 6. An asterisk (*) in position 7 of a DDS source line signals a comment line. You can use comment lines throughout the file definition. Minimally, you should include a few comment lines at the beginning of each file definition to identify the nature of the file.

In addition to comment lines, DDS includes record format descriptions, which name each **record layout** (**format**) within the file; field definition lines, which describe fields within records; and perhaps key specifications, which designate the fields that are to serve as keys to the file. The particular nature of these specifications depends on whether you are defining a physical file or a logical file.

DDS extensively uses a variety of keywords, each with a special meaning. Some **keywords**, which apply to the file as a whole, are called **file-level keywords**; some apply to a specific record format within the file and are called **record-level keywords**; and some, which are associated only with a specific field, are called **field-level keywords**.

Although all externally-defined files share those general features mentioned above, the details of a DDS definition depend on the type of file you are defining. Accordingly, let's first look at using DDS to define physical files.

Physical Files

A physical file's source statements define the data contents the file will have. Physical files can contain only one record format. That means that every record within a physical file must have an identical record layout. The record format is signaled by an R in position 17 (labeled *T* for Type), and you enter a name for the record format in positions 19–28 (*Name++++++*).

Following the record format specification, you must enter lines to define each field the record contains. Following the field definitions, you optionally can designate a key for the file. A K in position 17 denotes a key field. If you list a key field, its contents determine a sequence in which you can retrieve records from the file. The following example shows the DDS code for an employee master file named Employees.

```
*.. 1 ...+... 2 ...+... 3 ...+... 4 ...+... 5 ...+... 6 ...+... 7 ...+... 8
A..........T.Name++++++RLen++TDcB......Keywords+++++++++++++++++++++++++++++++
 * Employee master physical file EMPLOYEES
A                                   UNIQUE
A          R EMPREC
A            EMPNBR         9S 0     TEXT('Employee number')
A            LASTNAME      15A       TEXT('Last name')
A            FIRSTNAME     10A       TEXT('First name')
A            DEPT           3A       TEXT('Department')
A            SALARY         6P 0     TEXT('Annual salary')
A            STREET        15A       TEXT('Street address')
A            CITY          15A       TEXT('City')
A            STATE          2A       TEXT('State or province')
A            POSTCODE      10A       TEXT('Postal code')
A            HIREDATE       L        TEXT('Hire date')
A          K EMPNBR
```

Let's look at the details of this definition. First, **UNIQUE** is a file-level keyword. (All file-level keywords appear at the beginning of the DDS, before any record format specification line.) UNIQUE stipulates that the file cannot contain records with duplicate key values. When you include this keyword, attempts to write a record to the file with a key value identical to a record already in the file will cause the system to generate an error message. Use of UNIQUE is optional; without its use, the system permits records with duplicate key values.

The record format line is next. Note the R in position 17 and the **format name**, EMPREC, left justified in positions 19–28. DDS allows record format names (and field names, for that matter) up to ten characters long. These names must begin with an alphabetic character (A–Z, @, $, or #). The remaining characters can be any of the alphabetic characters, any of the digits 0–9, or the underscore character (_). Unlike RPG IV, DDS source code cannot contain lowercase alphabetic characters, so all record format and field names in DDS source are entered as uppercase.

You define the fields of a record on successive lines below the record format line. The field name begins in position 19. Next, you specify the length of the field, right adjusted in positions 30–34 (*Len++*). As in RPG IV, any numeric-field definition must include a decimal entry (*Dc*, positions 36–37) to indicate how many decimal places the field includes. You use position 35 to specify the data type, a concept we'll explore in detail in the next section.

Following the definition of all the fields to appear within the record, you can designate one or more fields as the record key by coding a K in position 17 and specifying the name of the key field in positions 19–28. In the example, EMPNBR is named as the key field of the file. Notice that you must define the key field as part of the record before naming it in the K specification.

If you list more than one key line, you are specifying a composite, or concatenated, key. For a **composite key**, list the key fields in order from major to minor. Note that fields need not be adjacent to each other within the record to be key components.

The TEXT keyword entries are optional ways to provide documentation. In the example, TEXT is used with each field to explain what the field represents. You must enclose text comments with apostrophes (' ') and surround them with parentheses. Although text comments are not required, it makes good sense to include them, especially if your field names are somewhat cryptic. TEXT also can appear as a record-level keyword to document the record format.

Programmers new to DDS are sometimes confused by the fact that the name of the file is not included within the DDS (except, perhaps, within a comment line). The file name is determined when you actually compile the DDS; by default the name of the source member becomes the name of the compiled object or database file.

Data Types and Data Storage

As we mentioned a few paragraphs ago, you must assign a **data type** to each field in a physical file. The data type assigned to a field determines how the field's values are stored, how much storage the field occupies, and what kinds of operations can be performed on the field when it is used within a program.

From the previous chapter, you are already familiar with three general types of data: character, numeric, and date. To denote that a field is to contain **character** (or alphanumeric) data, you code an A for its type; if you leave the type entry blank and also leave the decimal position entry blank, the system assumes that the data type of the field is character.

Storing Numeric Data

Numeric fields, signaled by nonblank decimal position entries, are a little more complicated. DDS supports four numeric data types:

- Zoned decimal (type S)
- Packed decimal (type P)
- Binary (type B)
- Floating point (type F)

RPG IV does not differentiate among numeric data types in determining what kinds of operations you can perform on a field or what kinds of output editing are possible. However, the data type of a numeric field—zoned decimal, packed decimal, binary, or floating point—determines how that field is represented and stored within the database. If you leave the type entry blank for a numeric field, the system defaults to the packed decimal data type for the field.

To understand the various data representations, you must first understand how the computer stores data. You probably know that any numeric value can be converted from its familiar decimal, or base 10, value to a corresponding value in binary, or base 2, notation. The computer stores all data in this binary format, with all data represented as a combination of 1s and 0s. At first glance, then, data representation should be a simple matter of converting values from one base to another. However, many characters and values that we want to represent to the computer are not numbers— letters of the alphabet, for example, or special characters, such as $ and {.

IBM developed a coding scheme to allow any data character—whether numeric or non-numeric—to be represented to the computer. This coding scheme, based on the English alphabet, is called Extended Binary Coded Decimal Interchange Code, or **EBCDIC**, generally pronounced "*eb-si-dik*." EBCDIC assigns a unique eight-bit binary pattern to each representable character. Capital A, for example, is 11000001 in EBCDIC, while the digit 1 is represented as 11110001. The leftmost four bits are often called zone or **high-order bits**, while the rightmost four bits are digit or **low-order bits**. Because eight bits constitute a byte, it takes one byte of storage to store each character in EBCDIC. i5/OS stores all non-numeric, or character, data values this way—one byte represents one character.

Numbers can be handled slightly differently. The following table shows the EBCDIC codes for the digits 0 through 9.

Digit	EBCDIC
0	11110000
1	11110001
2	11110010
3	11110011
4	11110100
5	11110101
6	11110110
7	11110111
8	11111000
9	11111001

The first thing you should notice is that the high-order bits (zone) of all digits are identical: 1111. This means that the zone portion is redundant for numeric data—that is, if the system already knows the data is numeric, it knows that the zones of the data are all 1s. Two forms of numeric data storage take advantage of this redundancy.

The first form—**zoned** (or signed) **decimal**—takes a full byte to store each digit of a numeric value *except* that the zone of the rightmost digit is used to store the sign of the data: 1111 represents a plus sign (+), while 1101 represents a negative sign (–). Zoned decimal representation, then, is almost identical to character representation except that the sign is represented as part of the rightmost digit's byte.

The second form of numeric representation—**packed decimal**—takes greater advantage of the redundancy built into digit representation by simply not bothering to store the zones of numbers. Data in packed format takes just over half the amount of storage it would take to store the same number in zoned decimal format. In packed format, only the digit, or low-order, bits of a number are stored, with the sign of the number represented by an additional four bits. These sign bits always occupy the rightmost four bit positions of a packed decimal value.

Study the following table to understand the differences in data representation between these two formats. Each group of eight bits represents one byte. Notice the location of the signs (in **bold** type) in both representations and the elimination of the zone bits in the packed format. The zoned decimal number uses three bytes to store the value, while the packed format uses only two.

Value to represent	Zoned decimal	Packed decimal
+136	11110001 11110011 **1111**0110	00010011 0110**1111**
–136	11110001 11110011 **1101**0110	00010011 0110**1101**

Instead of reading long strings of 1s and 0s, most programmers find it easier to represent byte values using **hexadecimal** (base 16) **notation** for the high- and low-order bits according to the following table:

Digit	Hexadecimal
0	0000
1	0001
2	0010
3	0011
4	0100
5	0101
6	0110
7	0111
8	1000
9	1001
A	1010
B	1011
C	1100
D	1101
E	1110
F	1111

The following table illustrates the difference between zoned and packed decimal representation, using hexadecimal notation (the sign is in **bold**):

Value to represent	Zoned decimal	Packed decimal
+136	F1 F3 **F6**	13 6**F**
−136	F1 F3 **D6**	13 6**D**

As you can see, the numeric value begins to appear more clearly in both zoned and packed decimal representations when we use hexadecimal notation—with the sign being represented by an F for positive numbers and a D for negative numbers. Occasionally, to make the illustration even more clear, the high-order bits are shown above the low-order bits, as in the following table:

Value to represent	Zoned decimal	Packed decimal
+136	F F **F** 1 3 6	1 6 3 **F**
−136	F F **D** 1 3 6	1 6 3 **D**

Two forms remain for representing numbers: **binary** format (type B) and **floating point** format (type F). Binary format dispenses completely with EBCDIC and stores a number as its direct binary equivalent. This format can result in the greatest savings in storage. A two-byte binary number can represent up to four digits, and a four-byte binary number can represent up to nine digits. Floating point format, sometimes called scientific notation, represents numeric values using powers of ten in a character string notation that makes it easy to represent a large range of numeric values; in floating point format, the number 136 would be represented by the string +1.360000000000000E+002.

Some system programs use binary numbers (or integers, which are closely related to binary numbers)—and, rarely, floating point—but most business programming can be accomplished with zoned or packed decimal formats. Although some programmers prefer to define numeric fields as zoned decimal (type S)—because it's easier to print or view the raw data in the file when the data is stored in this format—the computer works more efficiently with numbers stored in packed decimal format.

The length of the entry you give a field in DDS represents the number of digit positions in the value to be represented, but the number of bytes of storage it will take to actually store the value may vary given the data type. Packed fields take $(n + 1)/2$ bytes of storage (rounded to the nearest whole byte), where n is the number of digit positions in the data value. The formula derives from the fact that in packed format, the sign and each digit require half a byte of storage. You need to round up to the nearest whole byte because data storage is allocated in byte-sized units. A number eight positions long would have a length of 5 if stored in packed format. So would a number nine positions long. Because it takes the same amount of storage, many programming experts recommend that you always define packed numeric fields with an odd number of digit positions. For zoned decimal format, storage length corresponds exactly to digit positions in the value to be stored—eight digits, eight bytes. An eight-digit number would have a storage length of 4 if binary were the type specified for it.

Storing Dates

DDS supports a unique data type for dealing with dates. The **native date data type** (L) represents dates in a format that the computer can easily recognize, process, and manipulate as dates without requiring any special coding in an RPG program. You may remember from Chapter 2 that we used a date field in our sample program and that it was coded with a D in the Input specifications. While RPG IV uses a D to designate native date fields, DDS uses an L in position 35 to represent the same data type.

When defining a date, you do not need to specify a length because the system determines the length automatically. A separator character—usually a slash (/), hyphen (-), or period (.)—is an intrinsic part of the date. The computer stores dates in a special compact encoded format, but it always shows them to you in a user-friendly format. By default, dates are shown to you in a format set by the International Standards Organization; this ***ISO** format is ten bytes long in *yyyy-mm-dd* format. This display format can be changed using the Datfmt keyword in DDS.

Native date fields are *not* the same as numeric fields that may be used to store date information. A native date field is stored in a special format that the computer will automatically recognize as a date. Numeric fields require specific arithmetic or conversion coding to be treated as dates. We'll cover more about native dates in Chapter 7.

DDS recognizes other data types besides A, S, P, B, F, and L; RPG IV recognizes still other data types as well. We will look at the additional RPG IV data types in Chapter 4. For now, we'll limit our scope to the character, numeric, and date types presented above so that we can turn our attention to logical files.

EBCDIC, ASCII, and Unicode

All computers use some kind of an encoding system to represent characters as bit patterns, but not all systems use EBCDIC, which is unique to some IBM systems. Many operating systems use an encoding system called **ASCII** (American Standard Code for Information Interchange), generally pronounced "*as*-kee."

EBCDIC was developed separately from ASCII; consequently, the bit patterns in ASCII are not the same as those found in EBCDIC. For example, the letter A in EBCDIC is represented by a hexadecimal C1, but in ASCII it is a hexadecimal 41. In addition, the two schemes use different **collating sequences**; that is, they do not sort all the characters in the same sequence. In EBCDIC, lowercase characters sort before uppercase characters, and letters sort before numbers: for example, a, b, c, ... A, B, C, ... 7, 8, 9. In ASCII, the opposite is true: 1, 2, 3, ... A, B, C, ... x, y, z. The following table shows some commonly used characters and their encoding for each system (in EBCDIC sequence).

Character	EBCDIC Bits	Hex	ASCII Bits	Hex	Character	EBCDIC Bits	Hex	ASCII Bits	Hex	Character	EBCDIC Bits	Hex	ASCII Bits	Hex
	0100 0000	40	0010 0000	20	u	1010 0100	A4	0111 0101	75	P	1101 0111	D7	0101 0000	50
a	1000 0001	81	0110 0001	61	v	1010 0101	A5	0111 0110	76	Q	1101 1000	D8	0101 0001	51
b	1000 0010	82	0110 0010	62	w	1010 0110	A6	0111 0111	77	R	1101 1001	D9	0101 0010	52
c	1000 0011	83	0110 0011	63	x	1010 0111	A7	0111 1000	78	S	1110 0010	E2	0101 0011	53
d	1000 0100	84	0110 0100	64	y	1010 1000	A8	0111 1001	79	T	1110 0011	E3	0101 0100	54
e	1000 0101	85	0110 0101	65	z	1010 1001	A9	0111 1010	7A	U	1110 0100	E4	0101 0101	55
f	1000 0110	86	0110 0110	66	A	1100 0001	C1	0100 0001	41	V	1110 0101	E5	0101 0110	56
g	1000 0111	87	0110 0111	67	B	1100 0010	C2	0100 0010	42	W	1110 0110	E6	0101 0111	57
h	1000 1000	88	0110 1000	68	C	1100 0011	C3	0100 0011	43	X	1110 0111	E7	0101 1000	58
i	1000 1001	89	0110 1001	69	D	1100 0100	C4	0100 0100	44	Y	1110 1000	E8	0101 1001	59
j	1001 0001	91	0110 1010	6A	E	1100 0101	C5	0100 0101	45	Z	1110 1001	E9	0101 1010	5A
k	1001 0010	92	0110 1011	6B	F	1100 0110	C6	0100 0110	46	0	1111 0000	F0	0011 0000	30
l	1001 0011	93	0110 1100	6C	G	1100 0111	C7	0100 0111	47	1	1111 0001	F1	0011 0001	31
m	1001 0100	94	0110 1101	6D	H	1100 1000	C8	0100 1000	48	2	1111 0010	F2	0011 0010	32
n	1001 0101	95	0110 1110	6E	I	1100 1001	C9	0100 1001	49	3	1111 0011	F3	0011 0011	33
o	1001 0110	96	0110 1111	6F	J	1101 0001	D1	0100 1010	4A	4	1111 0100	F4	0011 0100	34
p	1001 0111	97	0111 0000	70	K	1101 0010	D2	0100 1011	4B	5	1111 0101	F5	0011 0101	35
q	1001 1000	98	0111 0001	71	L	1101 0011	D3	0100 1100	4C	6	1111 0110	F6	0011 0110	36
r	1001 1001	99	0111 0010	72	M	1101 0100	D4	0100 1101	4D	7	1111 0111	F7	0011 0111	37
s	1010 0010	A2	0111 0011	73	N	1101 0101	D5	0100 1110	4E	8	1111 1000	F8	0011 1000	38
t	1010 0011	A3	0111 0100	74	O	1101 0110	D6	0100 1111	4F	9	1111 1001	F9	0011 1001	39

Recently, extended versions of ASCII, called **Unicode** and **UCS** (Universal Character Set), have also become widely accepted. These newer character sets, which extend beyond the English alphabet, have a much wider array of characters available than either ASCII or EBCDIC because they generally use double-byte sequences instead of the single-byte eight-bit sequences that ASCII and EBCDIC employ.

The i5/OS operating system includes processor instructions that give it the capability to translate data among EBCDIC, ASCII, Unicode, and UCS. The system also supports other double-byte character sets commonly used in Asian countries, such as China or Japan.

Logical Files

Although in theory you could "get by" using only physical files to define your data, you are just scratching the surface of i5/OS database capabilities until you begin to use logical files.

As we discussed in the introduction of this chapter, logical files define access paths to data actually stored in physical files. You can use a logical file to restrict user views to a subset of fields contained in a physical file, to change the retrieval order of records from a file (by changing the designated key field), or to combine data stored in two or more separate physical files into one logical file. Although the data actually is stored in physical files, once you have defined logical files to the system you can refer to these logical files in RPG IV programs as though the logical files themselves actually contained records. The advantage of using logical files is that they can provide alternative ways to look at data, including different orders of record access, without redundantly storing the actual data on the system.

Simple Logical Files

A logical file based on a single physical file is called a **simple logical file**. The method of defining simple logical files is similar to that of defining physical files. You first specify a record format, follow that with a list of fields (optional), and follow *that* with one or more (optional) key fields. Because logical files provide views of physical files, you must include the keyword **PFILE** beginning in position 45 of the Keywords area on the record format line, followed—in parentheses—by the name of the physical file on which the logical record format is based.

The easiest way to code a simple logical file is to use the same record format name within the logical file as the record format name in the physical file on which the logical file is based. With this method, the system assumes the record layouts of the files are identical. As a result, you do not need to include fields within your logical record description. However, you can still designate one or more fields as a key, and this key does not have to match the key of the physical file. The following example shows a logical file based on the employee master file called *Employees*:

```
*.. 1 ...+... 2 ...+... 3 ...+... 4 ...+... 5 ...+... 6 ...+... 7 ...+... 8
A..........T.Name++++++RLen++TDcB......Keywords++++++++++++++++++++++++++++++++
 * Logical file EMPLOYEES1, keyed on last name, first name
A          R EMPREC                    PFILE(EMPLOYEES)
A          K LASTNAME
A          K FIRSTNAME
```

Notice that there are no field-level entries in this DDS. With this definition, all the fields defined within the physical file are included within the logical file. Because the logical file is keyed on last name, then first name, keyed sequential access of this logical file will retrieve the employee records in alphabetic order by last name, then first name. This kind of logical file definition is widely used to change the retrieval order of records in a file. Its effects are identical to that of physically sorting file records into a different order but without the system overhead that a physical sort requires.

If you want to restrict the logical file so that it includes only some of the fields from the physical file, give the logical file a record format name different from that of the record format name in the physical file; then list only those fields to be included in the logical file. Again, you may designate one or more of these fields to serve as the key to the file.

```
*.. 1 ...+... 2 ...+... 3 ...+... 4 ...+... 5 ...+... 6 ...+... 7 ...+... 8
A..........T.Name++++++RLen++TDcB......Keywords++++++++++++++++++++++++++++++
 * Logical file EMPLOYEES4, keyed on employee number.
 * Only those fields listed are accessible through the logical file.
A          R EMPREC4                   PFILE(EMPLOYEES)
A            EMPNBR
A            LASTNAME
A            FIRSTNAME
A            DEPT
A            STREET
A            CITY
A            STATE
A            POSTCODE
A          K EMPNBR

*.. 1 ...+... 2 ...+... 3 ...+... 4 ...+... 5 ...+... 6 ...+... 7 ...+... 8
A..........T.Name++++++RLen++TDcB......Keywords++++++++++++++++++++++++++++++
 * Logical file EMPLOYEES5, keyed on employee number.
 * Only those fields listed are accessible through the logical file.
A          R EMPREC5                   PFILE(EMPLOYEES)
A            EMPNBR
A            DEPT
A            SALARY
A          K EMPNBR
```

These DDS specifications would be used to define the logical files shown earlier. Notice that you do not need to specify length, type, and decimal positions for the fields in a logical file; these field attributes are already given in the physical file on which the logical file is based.

Record Selection/Omission

You can define logical files to exclude certain records contained in the physical file or to include only a subset of the records contained in the physical file by using **Omit** or **Select specifications**. You can use this feature only if the logical file contains a key specification. Your specifications base the record exclusion or inclusion on actual data values present in selected fields of the physical file records.

For example, assume you want to include only the MKT department in the salary report. You simply designate department as a select field (S in position 17); then, in position 45, provide the basis for the selection. One way to do this is with the VALUES keyword. If the field type is character, you must enclose each value with apostrophes. In this case, we want the logical file to include records where the DEPT field has a value of MKT:

```
*.. 1 ...+... 2 ...+... 3 ...+... 4 ...+... 5 ...+... 6 ...+... 7 ...+... 8
A..........T.Name++++++RLen++TDcB......Keywords++++++++++++++++++++++++++++++
 * Logical file EMPLOYEES3, keyed on employee number.
 * Only MKT employees are included in the file.
A          R EMPREC                    PFILE(EMPLOYEES)
A          K EMPNBR
A          S DEPT                       VALUES('MKT')
```

The field used for selection—DEPT—must exist in the record format for both the physical file and the logical file.

For the limited database shown in the chapter, you could also accomplish the definition of this logical file by omitting the values you do not want. Change the S in position 17 of the select/omit field to an O and specify MIS and ACT as values. In that case, the logical file would omit the MIS and ACT departments. In our example, only MKT, the remaining department, would be included:

```
*.. 1 ...+... 2 ...+... 3 ...+... 4 ...+... 5 ...+... 6 ...+... 7 ...+... 8
A..........T.Name++++++RLen++TDcB......Keywords+++++++++++++++++++++++++++++++
 * Logical file EMPLOYEES3, keyed on employee number.
 * Only MKT employees are included in the file.
A          R EMPREC                PFILE(EMPLOYEES)
A          K EMPNBR
A          O DEPT                   VALUES('MIS' 'ACT')
```

Besides VALUES, two additional keywords let you specify the basis of record inclusion or exclusion: RANGE and COMP. Keyword RANGE followed by parentheses containing two values lets you specify the beginning value and the ending value of a range of values on which the selection or omission is to be based. In the following example, only employees with salaries between 20,000 and 50,000 (inclusive) will be included in the logical file:

```
*.. 1 ...+... 2 ...+... 3 ...+... 4 ...+... 5 ...+... 6 ...+... 7 ...+... 8
A..........T.Name++++++RLen++TDcB......Keywords+++++++++++++++++++++++++++++++
 * Logical file EMPLOYEES6, selecting specified records based on a
 * range of postal codes
A          R EMPREC6               PFILE(EMPLOYEES)
A            EMPNBR
A            LASTNAME
A            FIRSTNAME
A            SALARY
A          K EMPNBR
A          S SALARY                RANGE(20000 50000)
```

With keyword COMP, you can specify a comparison between a field's value and a single given value to serve as the basis of selection or omission. You specify the nature of the comparison by using one of eight relational operators:

- EQ (equal to)
- NE (not equal to)
- LT (less than)
- NL (not less than)
- GT (greater than)
- NG (not greater than)
- LE (less than or equal to)
- GE (greater than or equal to)

To use this feature, enter field-level keyword COMP; follow the keyword with parentheses containing first the relational operator and then a literal indicating the comparison value.

The following example shows yet another way to accomplish the task of selecting only those employees from the MKT department:

```
*.. 1 ...+... 2 ...+... 3 ...+... 4 ...+... 5 ...+... 6 ...+... 7 ...+... 8
A..........T.Name++++++RLen++TDcB......Keywords+++++++++++++++++++++++++++++
 * Logical file EMPLOYEES3, keyed on employee number.
 * Only MKT employees are included in the file.
A           R EMPREC                    PFILE(EMPLOYEES)
A           K EMPNBR
A           S DEPT                       COMP(EQ 'MKT')
```

You can designate multiple select and/or omit fields, set up alternate criteria using ORs (O in position 7), or list multiple criteria using ANDs (A in position 7) so that several specifications must hold true for record inclusion or exclusion to occur.

DDS offers many other database capabilities beyond the physical and logical file constructs that we've discussed here. Variants on logical files, for instance, can be much more complex than the simple examples we've illustrated. For example, you can create logical files based on two or more physical files with multiple record formats—with each format based on a different physical file. The logical file then gives the appearance that the physical files have been merged together. Another feature—**join logical files**—joins fields from different physical files into a single record using a matching field common to the physical files on which to base the join. The logical file then appears as if the data exists in one file with one format when, in reality, it has been brought together from several different physical files. You can, however, accomplish many of these same results in an RPG IV program without using complex logical files. Most programmers prefer to stick with simple logical files and avoid the more complex constructs. In addition to the keywords used in this chapter, the DDS supports several dozen other keywords used with data file definition. For additional details about these capabilities, see IBM's *Programming DDS for Physical and Logical Files*.

Creating Database Files

The first step in actually creating a physical or logical file is to enter the DDS statements into a source member using an editor. As we mentioned, it is standard practice to use source file QDDSSRC to store database source members. Also recall that the source type for physical file is PF; LF is the source type for logical file.

Here is the DDS for the Customers file that we used in our sample program in Chapter 2:

```
*.. 1 ...+... 2 ...+... 3 ...+... 4 ...+... 5 ...+... 6 ...+... 7 ...+... 8
A..........T.Name++++++RLen++TDcB......Keywords+++++++++++++++++++++++++++++
 * Physical file CUSTOMERS
A           R CUSTREC
A             ACCOUNTID     4A        TEXT('Account identifier')
A             SALESPERS     4A        TEXT('Salesperson')
A             NAME         35A        TEXT('Customer name')
A             ADDRESS      35A        TEXT('Customer address')
A             CITY         21A        TEXT('Customer city')
A             STATE         2A        TEXT('Customer state')
A             POSTALCODE   10A        TEXT('Postal code')
A             COUNTRY      20A        TEXT('Foreign country')
A             LASTSALEDT    L         TEXT('Date of last sale')
A                                     DATFMT(*USA)
A             YTDSALES     11S 2      TEXT('Year-to-date sales')
A           K ACCOUNTID
```

The DDS for this file represents a few minor changes from the one shown in Chapter 2. The layout has been named Custrec to conform to the requirement that an externally described file have a named format. A couple of field names (Salespers and Lastsaledt) have been shortened to accommodate DDS's limit of ten-character field names. We have also added a key field, Accountid, so that we may process this file in account order. Notice the Datfmt keyword associated with the Lastsaledt field; as was the case in Chapter 2, the field is in *USA format (*mm/dd/yyyy*).

Once you've entered your DDS code, you must compile it to create the file as an object on the system. If you are working from Programming Development Manager (PDM) or WebSphere Development Studio Client (WDSc), follow the same procedure to compile a database object that you use to create a program module object. If you compile by directly entering a command at a command line, rather than by working through menus or other tools, the appropriate commands are **CRTPF (Create Physical File)** and **CRTLF (Create Logical File)**.

If the system encounters syntax errors while trying to create your file, you will receive a message indicating that the creation was not successful. Otherwise, the system will tell you that the job was completed normally and that the database object now exists. Once the file object exists, you can use it to store data. You can enter data into physical files by using system utilities, such as **Data File Utility (DFU)** or **iSeries Navigator**, by writing values to the file through a program, by copying records to the file from another file, or by using SQL statements.

Caution
You must create a physical file before you can create logical files based on that physical file; failure to do so will result in error messages.

If you want to change the definition of a physical file after you have created a logical file based on that definition, you must first delete the logical file, then recreate it after the physical file has changed. Also, you must delete all the logical files associated with a physical file before you can delete the physical file.

You should be aware of one additional caveat: If you want to change a physical file's definition after you have stored data in the file, *deleting the file deletes the data in the file as well.* You can avoid such data loss by using the *CHGPF (Change Physical File)* command; your instructor can provide you with this information, should you need it.

RPG IV Programming with Externally Defined Files

Now that you understand how to define and create files on the System i, you will find that it is simple to refer to these external definitions within your programs. Basically, all you need to do is make a few minor changes to your File specifications and eliminate your Input specifications.

On the File specifications in position 22, instead of an F for fixed format, code an E for externally defined. Next, omit a record length entry—the system will supply that information automatically based on the external definition. Last, if the file is keyed and you want to access records in keyed order, code a K in position 34. Omitting the K results in record retrieval based on arrival sequence (i.e., the order in which the records were originally written to the file). The following code illustrates a File specification for an externally described file.

```
*.. 1 ...+... 2 ...+... 3 ...+... 4 ...+... 5 ...+... 6 ...+... 7 ...+...
FFilename++IPEASFRLen+LKLen+AIDevice+.Keywords+++++++++++++++++++++++++++++
FCustomers IF   E          K Disk
```

Customers is a physical file. If you wanted to use a logical file, you would enter the logical file name; the remaining entries would be identical to those shown for the physical file. At a program level, no distinction is made between physical and logical files.

If your input file is externally described, you do not need to code Input specifications for the file. When you compile your program, the system will copy the file's definition into your source listing where the Input specifications would normally appear. Obviously then, when you use external definition, the file must exist before your program can be compiled successfully.

Less obviously, if you change the definition of a physical or logical file after you have compiled a program that uses that file, you must recompile the program before the system will let the program be run. This feature, called **level checking**, prevents you from running a program based on an obsolete or inaccurate definition of a database file.

Calculation and Output specifications can use any fields defined as part of the externally described input file just as though the fields were defined internally as part of the Input specifications. You also can externally describe database files used as output; in that case, Output specifications are unnecessary, and writing to the file can take place directly from your calculations. Chapter 10 explores this concept in detail.

Externally Described Printer Files

In addition to allowing the external definition of database files, RPG IV lets you define reports externally. Externally describing printer files offers many of the same benefits as externally describing database files. In particular, this method lets you change a report format without changing the source code of the program that produces the report—a wise approach to application maintenance. In addition, if you externally define printer files, you can use a system utility, such as **Report Layout Utility (RLU)** or **Code Designer**, to help you design the layout of the report visually on your workstation; you don't need to use paper and printer spacing chart forms. The utility then generates the DDS required to describe the report so you don't have to do the "grunt work" of figuring out line position and spacing entries. (The details of using these utilities fall outside the scope of this text; those persons interested in developing printer files using this method should consult the appropriate IBM manuals.)

You use DDS to define printer files in a source file, the same as you do for database files. The source members of printer files, like those of database files, are generally stored in QDDSSRC; a printer file's type, however, is PRTF.

Once you have entered the source code using an editor or another utility, you compile the source to create a printer file object. The compiler command for printer files is **CRTPRTF (Create Printer File)**. Once the object exists, it can receive output from a program for printing. The DDS code for a printer file is analogous to that of a database file, except that its focus is the definition of record formats of information to be sent to a printer. A record format in a printer file represents one or more printed lines on the report. Printer files, like logical files, can contain multiple record formats, each defining a different set of output lines. The DDS can also include keyword entries at the file level, the record level, and/or the field level to define the position and/or appearance of the output.

To illustrate how you would externally define a printer file, let's reconsider the sales report from Chapter 2. Recall that the desired report includes headings and detail lines. The printer spacing chart for the report is reproduced on page 67. The RPG IV program in Chapter 2 defined two exception lines, grouped as Headings and Detail to generate this output. These exception lines were defined in the program's Output specifications. You would follow much the same construction to externally describe this report in DDS.

```
          1         2         3         4         5         6         7         8         9
 123456789012345678901234567890123456789012345678901234567890123456789012345678901234567890
 1
 2|YTD SALES REPORT                                      DATE XX/XX/XXXX    PAGE XXX0
 3
 4|ACCT  SALES                                                    YTD       DATE OF
 5| ID   PERSON  CUSTOMER                                        SALES     LAST SALE
 6
 7|XXXX  XXXX    XXXXXXXXXXXXXXXXXXXXXXXXXXXXXXXXXXXX    XXX,XXX,XX0.XX   XX/XX/XXXX
 8|XXXX  XXXX    XXXXXXXXXXXXXXXXXXXXXXXXXXXXXXXXXXXX    XXX,XXX,XX0.XX   XX/XX/XXXX
 9
10
11
12
13
14
15
```

The following code shows the DDS for the sales report. First, you must define one record format for each line or group of lines to be printed in a single output operation. Then, for each of those record formats, you need to specify what fields and/or literals are to be printed as part of that format, what vertical line spacing each format should follow, where the variable or constant data should appear horizontally on a line, and what editing (if any) should be associated with the numeric fields.

```
*.. 1 ...+... 2 ...+... 3 ...+... 4 ...+... 5 ...+... 6 ...+... 7 ...+... 8
AAN01N02N03T.Name++++++RLen++TDcBLinPosFunctions+++++++++++++++++++++++++++++
 * Printer file YTDSLSRPT, externally describing the sales report
A                                       REF(CUSTOMERS)
A           R HEADINGS                  SKIPB(2)
A                                       1'YTD SALES REPORT'
A                                       53'DATE'
A                                       58DATE
A                                         EDTCDE(Y)
A                                       71'PAGE'
A                                       76PAGNBR
A                                         EDTCDE(Z)
A                                         SPACEA(2)
 *
A                                       1'ACCT'
A                                       7'SALES'
A                                       63'YTD'
A                                       72'DATE OF'
A                                         SPACEA(1)
 *
A                                       2'ID'
A                                       7'PERSON'
A                                       15'CUSTOMER'
A                                       62'SALES'
A                                       71'LAST SALE'
A                                         SPACEA(2)
 *
A           R DETAIL                    SPACEA(1)
A             ACCOUNTID R               1
A             SALESPERS R               8
A             NAME      R               15
A             YTDSALES  R               53EDTCDE(1)
A             LASTSALEDTR               70
```

You must begin each record format definition with an R in position 17, followed by the name of the format in positions 19–28. Next, for each record format, you need to define all the information that is to be printed as part of that format. Specify fields in positions 19–28, just as for database files. Constants and literals are coded in positions 45–80 and must be enclosed in apostrophes.

You also need to specify where each piece of information is to appear horizontally on the line. Use positions 42–44 for this purpose. DDS, unlike RPG IV, specifies the field's or constant's *beginning* position (where it starts within the line), rather than its ending position. Thus, in our example, because YTD SALES REPORT begins in column 1 of the first heading, you code 1 in positions 43–44 of the DDS line for that constant; the corresponding O-spec in Chapter 2 specified an ending position of 16.

DDS handles the system date and the report page numbers a little bit differently than RPG IV. RPG IV includes built-in variables *Date and Page, which supply the system date and page number, respectively. In DDS, you access the same information through the keywords DATE and PAGNBR. As shown in the example, you enter these keywords on their own lines in DDS.

To define each field within the DDS, we would normally provide its length in positions 30–34 and, for numeric fields, the number of decimal positions in positions 36–37; blanks in the decimal position columns signal a character field. This is similar to the way we defined the field length and data type for database fields.

This report, however, uses database fields in the Detail format that we have already defined in the Customers file (Accountid, Salespers, Name, Ytdsales, and Lastsaledt). Rather than redefining these fields in our report (causing extra work, and risking coding errors), we can simply refer to the corresponding fields already defined in the Customers file. The REF file-level keyword at the top of the DDS names the Customers file as one that we want to use as a reference for some of the field definitions in this DDS. Then, instead of coding a length, data type, and decimal positions for each of the fields, we simply code an R in position 29 for each field. When the computer compiles the printer file, it will copy the attributes of these fields from the Customers file.

If you do not specify an R in position 29, you must explicitly code the field attributes, and the field's attributes must be consistent throughout the program. This means that Accountid, for example, must be defined as a four-byte character field everywhere in the program, or a compile error will occur. Using the field reference function will help avoid this problem.

Editing and Line Positioning in DDS

The same edit codes and edit words available in RPG IV to change the appearance of numeric output are available within DDS. However, you indicate desired editing through the use of keywords **EDTCDE** or **EDTWRD**, followed by the appropriate edit code or word enclosed within parentheses. In our example, Date will be printed with slashes as a result of the EDTCDE(Y) entry, while Page will use EDTCDE(Z) to accomplish zero suppression. The field Ytdsales will be printed with commas and zero balances because of keyword EDTCDE(1). In our example, we restricted the keywords to one per line, but multiple keywords can appear on the same code line separated by at least one space.

We could code a DATFMT keyword for the Lastsaledt field to ensure that the date will be printed in *mm/dd/yyyy* format. But it is not needed here, because the field reference function (R in position 29) mentioned earlier will copy the date format from the Customers file, where DATFMT(*USA) is specified. If we wanted to print a different format, we could specify it here, though.

The easiest way to specify vertical line positioning on a page in DDS is to use four keywords:

- SPACEA
- SPACEB
- SKIPA
- SKIPB

The meaning of these keywords—space after or before and skip after or before—corresponds exactly to the meaning of these terms in RPG IV. You designate the number of lines to space (for SPACEA or SPACEB) or the line to skip to (for SKIPA and SKIPB) within parentheses after the keyword. You can use these keywords at the record level or at the field level. If you want line positioning to change within a record format, you use the appropriate keyword at a field level; if line positioning is to change for the record format as a whole, use the keyword at the record level.

In our example, because we want the Headings to begin on the second line of each new page, we use the keyword entry SKIPB(2) at the record format level (that is, on the line containing the Headings R entry or a line immediately following that entry and before any field or constant entry). But recall that record format Headings contains information about three heading lines for our report, and we want to position the second line two lines below the first. In the DDS, the SPACEA(2) keyword entry immediately following the EDTCDE keyword entry associated with PAGNBR produces the desired line spacing; immediately after the page number is printed, the paper is advanced two lines. Printing would then continue with the constant 'ACCT'. Following the constant 'DATE OF' we also specified SPACEA(1) so that the report could continue with the constant 'ID' on the next line. Finally, we used SPACEA(2) with 'LAST SALE' to leave a blank line after the last heading line. The Detail lines are singled spaced, as indicated by the SPACEA(1) keyword at the Detail record level.

Other optional features of externally described printer files (e.g., changing fonts, printing bar codes, using indicators, defining fields by reference) are beyond the scope of this text. But with this introduction, you should be able to use DDS to externally describe most common types of printed output.

Externally Described Printer Files and RPG

How does external definition of printed output affect an RPG IV program? First, in the File specification entry for the report file, include the actual name of the printer file, rather than the generic output file Qprint. In addition, change the file format entry (position 22) to E—for externally described. Last, omit any entry for record length.

Overflow indicators *INOA through *INOG and *INOV are not valid for externally described files. You can use numbered indicators (*IN01-*IN99) or named indicators (which we will discuss in Chapter 4). For now, in our example we'll use *IN99 for overflow. The following example shows a File specification for an externally described printer file.

```
*.. 1 ...+... 2 ...+... 3 ...+... 4 ...+... 5 ...+... 6 ...+... 7 ...+... 8
FFilename++IPEASFRLen+LKLen+AIDevice+.Keywords+++++++++++++++++++++++++++++++
FYtdslsrpt O    E              Printer Oflind(*In99)
```

The externally described printer file eliminates the need for Output specifications in your program. How then do you direct the computer to print at the appropriate times as it executes the program? Instead of using the Except operation, which references only lines defined on Output specifications, you use the **Write operation**, specifying the name of the appropriate record format of your printer file in Factor 2:

```
Write Headings;
```

Putting It All Together

Now that you have seen how database files and printer files can be externally described and you have a sense of how this approach to file definition affects RPG IV programs, we can rewrite our introductory program from Chapter 2 to take full advantage of externally described files.

We have already developed the DDS for the Customers file and the Ytdslsrpt printer file. Before these files can be used, we must compile them to create the actual objects. Use the CRTPF (Create Physical File) command to compile Customers, and the CRTPRTF (Create Printer File) command to compile Ytdslsrpt. The Customers file will initially be empty; you would need to put actual data records into the file before it could meaningfully be used as input.

With those files externally described, our RPG IV program becomes considerably shorter. In addition, we can now make changes to our report layout or to our data file definition without having to change the RPG IV program, except possibly to recompile it.

```
*.. 1 ...+... 2 ...+... 3 ...+... 4 ...+... 5 ...+... 6 ...+... 7 ...+... 8
  // ---------------------------------
  // This program produces a year-to-date sales report. The report data
  // comes directly from input file Customers.
  //      Date Written:  12/20/2006
  //
  // Indicator usage: 99 = Printer overflow
  // ---------------------------------

FCustomers IF   E           K Disk
FYtdslsrpt O    E             Printer Oflind(*In99)

 /Free

    Write Headings;
    Read Customers;

    Dow Not %Eof(Customers);

      If *In99;
        Write Headings;
        *In99 = *Off;
      Endif;

      Write Detail;
      Read Customers;
    Enddo;

    *Inlr = *On;
    Return;

 /End-Free
```

Note the changes in the File specifications to use externally described files. Because these files are externally described, we no longer need Input or Output specifications. Also, we use *In99 in the place of *Inof to indicate overflow. Finally, instead of using the Except operation to send output to the printer, we use the Write operation.

DDS provides features for defining externally described files that go far beyond what we have covered in this chapter. We'll use more features later, but now you should have a basic understanding of how DDS and externally described files interact with an RPG IV program.

Using a Field Reference File

Elsewhere in this chapter, we discuss the use of the REF keyword to take advantage of DDS's ability to copy field definitions from one file to another. You can use this ability to create a physical file that serves as a centralized **data dictionary** of fields used within an application system. Such a physical file is called a **field reference file**. You never actually use this kind of file for data storage; its sole purpose is to provide field definitions for use in subsequent physical file creation. Once you have created a field reference file, you can define the fields that comprise your physical files simply by referring to the definitions contained in the field reference file.

Instead of defining each field within a physical database file, you can first create a physical file containing the definitions of all the fields that application will need to store. The following code illustrates an example of a field reference file from a student records application:

```
*.. 1 ...+... 2 ...+... 3 ...+... 4 ...+... 5 ...+... 6 ...+... 7 ...+... 8
A..........T.Name++++++RLen++TDcB......Keywords+++++++++++++++++++++++++++++++
 * Field reference file STUDREF for the student records system
A          R RECORD
A            STUD_NO       9S 0       TEXT('Student Number')
A            LNAME         20A        TEXT('Last Name')
A            FNAME         10A        TEXT('First Name')
A            MAJOR         6A         TEXT('Major')
A            ADM_DTE       6S 0       TEXT('Date Admitted')
A            CRSE_ID       6A         TEXT('Course Identifier')
A            SEMESTER      3A         TEXT('Semester Taken')
A            GRADE         2A         TEXT('Grade Received')
```

Once you have created the reference file, you can create physical database files whose field definitions are obtained from the reference file. To use this feature, simply include in your physical file the file-level keyword REF, with the name of the field reference file in parentheses. You can then define any field in this physical file whose definition already exists in the reference file by simply coding an R in position 29 (labeled *R* for Reference) and omitting the length, type, decimal entry, and relevant keyword information for that field. The two physical files that follow illustrate the use of the field reference file to supply field definitions.

```
*.. 1 ...+... 2 ...+... 3 ...+... 4 ...+... 5 ...+... 6 ...+... 7 ...+... 8
A..........T.Name++++++RLen++TDcB......Keywords+++++++++++++++++++++++++++++++
 * Physical file definition for student master file STUDMAST
A                                     REF(STUDREF)
A          R STUDREC
A            STUD_NO    R
A            LNAME      R
A            FNAME      R
A            MAJOR      R
A            ADM_DTE    R
A          K STUD_NO
```

continued...

> ## Using a Field Reference File...*continued*
>
> ```
> *.. 1 ...+... 2 ...+... 3 ...+... 4 ...+... 5 ...+... 6 ...+... 7 ...+... 8
> A..........T.Name++++++RLen++TDcB......Keywords+++++++++++++++++++++++++++++++
>  * Physical file definition of student courses taken, file STUDCRSE
> A                                       REF(STUDREF)
> A          R CRSEREC
> A            STUD_NO    R
> A            CRSE_ID    R
> A            SEMESTER   R
> A            GRADE      R
> A          K STUD_NO
> A          K CRSE_ID
> ```
>
> Field reference files can enforce a uniformity and consistency throughout an application system that facilitates program development and maintenance. Using such files, however, requires a thoughtful, structured approach to application system development because your data needs should be determined before any file creation or application development.
>
> A crucial application system development step is determining the file structure for the system. What data fields will you need to store? What physical and logical files will you need? How do you determine what fields belong in what files? Whole books have been written on the subject of relational database design. Although this topic is beyond the scope of this book, every professional programmer should have a solid understanding of relational database design.
>
> As systems become complex and the number of files used in a system grows, it becomes increasingly important for an organization's developers to have file naming conventions that provide some information about the function and type of each file. Although working with a maximum of ten-character file names imposes some restrictions on your ability to assign good file names, many installations use an agreed-upon mnemonic prefix to denote the system within which the file was designed to be used and use a short alphabetic mnemonic code—often related to the key of the file—to uniquely identify each file within the system. Some companies also use a suffix of P, L, or F to denote whether the file is a physical, logical, or field reference file and use a number to differentiate between similar files.

Chapter Summary

i5/OS defines data files independently of your programs. Such files, defined through DDS statements, exist as objects on the system and can be used by any program as externally described files. Physical files contain data records, while logical files provide access paths, or pointers, to the physical file records. A logical file is always associated with one or more physical files. Both physical and logical files can contain a key that lets you retrieve records based on the key's value. The key can consist of one or several data fields.

A physical file can contain only a single record format or type. Logical files can contain multiple record formats, based on records from two or more physical files. Logical file record formats may or may not include all the fields from their associated physical file. Logical files can also specify records to be selected for inclusion or omitted from inclusion based on data values of the records in the physical file on which the logical file is based.

DDS requires you to specify the type of data to be stored within fields. Three data classes the System i recognizes are character (or alphanumeric), numeric, and date. Character fields occupy one byte for each character in the field.

The two most common numeric data formats are zoned decimal and packed decimal. Zoned decimal is easiest to view but takes up the most room on disk. Packed decimal eliminates redundant high-order bits in storing digit values. Both zoned decimal and packed decimal formats use EBCDIC representation.

DDS supports a unique data type that makes date processing relatively easy. Native date fields are not the same as numeric fields that may be used to store date information. The computer always presents native date fields in a familiar format, complete with separator characters. The default format, *yyyy-mm-dd*, is set by the International Standards Organization; you can use the Datfmt keyword in to change it.

Before you can compile an RPG program that uses externally described files, the files must exist as compiled objects. To create externally described files, you must first store DDS specifications in a source member, then compile the source. The command for compiling physical file (PF) source is CRTPF (Create Physical File); for logical file (LF) source, use CRTLF (Create Logical File). To compile an externally described printer file (PRTF) source member, the command is CRTPRTF (Create Printer File).

Externally described files offer several advantages over program-described files. For example, you can change the file format without changing the program. Using externally described files will shorten your program's code and eliminate redundant code across an entire application. Externally described files will enforce naming standards. If you use externally described files to define report formats, you can use utilities, such as RLU or Code Designer, to design the reports and generate the DDS.

Key Terms

access paths
arrival sequence
ASCII
binary data type
character data type
CHGPF (Change Physical File)
Code Designer
collating sequence
collection
columns
composite
composite key
concatenation
CRTLF (Create Logical File)
CRTPF (Create Physical File)
CRTPRTF (Create Printer File)
Data Definition Language
    (DDL)
Data Description Specifications
    (DDS)
data dictionary
Data File Utility (DFU)
Data Manipulation Language
    (DML)
data type

EBCDIC
EDTCDE
EDTWRD
externally described file
field reference file
field-level keywords
file-level keywords
floating point data type
format
format name
hexadecimal notation
high-order bits
index
iSeries Navigator
*ISO format
join logical files
key field
key sequence
keywords
level checking
libraries
logical files
low-order bits
native date data type
Omit specifications

packed decimal data type
PFILE
physical files
program-described file
record layout
record-level keywords
redundancy
Report Layout Utility (RLU)
rows
Select specifications
sequential retrieval
simple logical file
SQL programming statements
Structured Query Language
    (SQL)
subset
table
UCS
Unicode
UNIQUE
view
Write operation
zoned decimal data type

Discussion/Review Questions

1. Explain the advantages of externally describing database files. Do externally described printer files share the same advantages?

2. Explain the difference between a logical file and a physical file.

3. What does concatenation mean? What is a concatenated key?

4. What are the advantages of logical files? Why not just create lots of physical files to store records in different orders or to present different combinations of data fields?

5. How does the system know whether you intend a keyword to be a file level, record level, or field-level keyword?

6. Why might you use UNIQUE as a keyword in a physical file?

7. Express the following values in zoned decimal and packed decimal format:

   +362

   –51024

8. How many bytes will it take to store the number 389,241,111 in zoned decimal? In packed decimal? In binary?

9. Provide several practical examples of using logical files.

10. Explain the differences among keywords COMP, RANGE, and VALUES.

11. If Select and Omit specifications were not available in logical file definitions, how could you produce a report that included only the employees of the ACT and MIS departments and excluded other employees?

12. What is a join logical file?

13. Explain the difference between arrival sequence and key sequence of sequential record retrieval.

14. Assume you wanted to write a program that used an externally described logical file that was based on a physical file. What order would you use to create the three objects required to execute the program? Why?

15. Some programmers argue that standards in file and field naming and the use of features such as field reference files reduce their opportunities to be creative and should not be enforced. How would you respond to these people?

16. Research the differences between RLU (Report Layout Utility) and Code Designer. Describe the advantages of one over the other.

17. Explain the difference between SKIPA, SKIPB, SPACEA, and SPACEB.

18. What are the advantages of storing dates in the native date data type format rather than the traditional numeric field?

19. What is the purpose of the PFILE keyword in a logical file?

20. What are the advantages of using field reference files? Are there any disadvantages?

Exercises

1. A library wants a database file to store book title; author's last name, first name, and middle initial; catalog number; publisher; date published; number of pages; and number of copies owned. Code a physical file definition to store this data after determining what you believe

to be the appropriate fields and the length and type for each field. Consider what the key field (if any) should be and whether use of keyword UNIQUE is appropriate.

2. The library wants to be able to access the catalog information described in Exercise 1 based on author's last name, first name, and middle initial. Among other things, staff members want to be able to print out listings by author so that all books by the same author appear together. Define a logical file that enables this kind of access.

3. The library also wants to store a description of each book. Because the books' descriptions vary greatly in length, from a few words to a long paragraph, the person designing the library's database has suggested storing the descriptions in a separate physical file, in which each record contains the catalog number, a description line number, and 40 characters of description. Define this physical file. How would you define the keys for this file?

4. Define a field reference file for the library based on the data requirements of Exercises 1 and 3, and then rewrite the physical file definitions to take advantage of the field reference file.

5. The library has decided that it is also necessary to store the first date each book was purchased in the file described in Exercise 1 above. What steps are required to add this field to the file? How will this affect the logical files that you have created? Is is possible for you to "lose" the data that you have collected?

Programming Assignments

Note
The following assignments all involve producing reports that either can be defined as part of your RPG IV program or can be described externally; your instructor will tell you which technique to use.

1. Create Database Assignment One
   a. Create a physical file for Wexler University's student master file (file WUSTDP, in Appendix F). Key this file on student number (SSN), and specify that keys be unique.
   b. Enter records in the file, following your instructor's directions.
   c. Create a logical file over WUSTDP with last name and first name as a concatenated key.
   d. Create a logical file over WUSTDP with student number as the key.

2. Design a report for Wexler University that provides a listing of student information. Include student number, first and last name, credits earned, major, date admitted, and grade point average in your report layout.
   a. Write a program to produce the report to show students listed in order by student number.

```
            1         2         3         4         5         6         7         8         9         1
                                                                                                      0
   1234567890123456789012345678901234567890123456789012345678901234567890123456789012345678901234567890
 1 XX/XX/XX                                  Wexler University                                  Page XXX
 2                          Student Information By Social Security Number
 3                 Student    First         Last                          Admit
 4                 Number     Name          Name            Credits Major Date          G.P.A.
 5                 999-99-9999 XXXXXXXXXX XXXXXXXXXXXXXX      999    XXX   99/99/9999     9.99
 6                 999-99-9999 XXXXXXXXXX XXXXXXXXXXXXXX      999    XXX   99/99/9999     9.99
 7                 999-99-9999 XXXXXXXXXX XXXXXXXXXXXXXX      999    XXX   99/99/9999     9.99
 8                 999-99-9999 XXXXXXXXXX XXXXXXXXXXXXXX      999    XXX   99/99/9999     9.99
 9                 999-99-9999 XXXXXXXXXX XXXXXXXXXXXXXX      999    XXX   99/99/9999     9.99
10                 999-99-9999 XXXXXXXXXX XXXXXXXXXXXXXX      999    XXX   99/99/9999     9.99
11
```

b. Modify your program from Part 2a to use a new logical file as the input file. The resulting report should list the students in alphabetical order by last name, by first name.

```
          1         2         3         4         5         6         7         8         9         10
 123456789012345678901234567890123456789012345678901234567890123456789012345678901234567890
1 XX/XX/XX                              Wexler University                                   Page
2 XXX
3                         Student Information By Lastname By Firstname
4              Student    First       Last                          Admit
5              Number     Name        Name          Credits  Major  Date          G.P.A.
6              999-99-9999 XXXXXXXXXX XXXXXXXXXXXXXXX   999    XXX    99/99/9999    9.99
7              999-99-9999 XXXXXXXXXX XXXXXXXXXXXXXXX   999    XXX    99/99/9999    9.99
8              999-99-9999 XXXXXXXXXX XXXXXXXXXXXXXXX   999    XXX    99/99/9999    9.99
9              999-99-9999 XXXXXXXXXX XXXXXXXXXXXXXXX   999    XXX    99/99/9999    9.99
10             999-99-9999 XXXXXXXXXX XXXXXXXXXXXXXXX   999    XXX    99/99/9999    9.99
11             999-99-9999 XXXXXXXXXX XXXXXXXXXXXXXXX   999    XXX    99/99/9999    9.99
12
```

3. Create Database Assignment Two

  a. Create a physical file for CompuSell's customer master file (file CSCSTP in Appendix F). Key the file on customer number, and specify that keys be unique.

  b. Enter records in the file, following your instructor's directions.

  c. Create a logical file over CompuSell's customer master file (file CSCSTP in Appendix F) keyed by customer number.

  d. Create a logical file over the customer file keyed on last name and, within last name, by first name.

  e. Create a file over the customer file, this time keyed on balance due and selecting only those customers with a balance greater than zero.

4. Write a program using the logical file you created in 3c as input to produce the following report. All the customers should be listed, in order of customer number.

```
          1         2         3         4         5         6         7         8         9         10
 123456789012345678901234567890123456789012345678901234567890123456789012345678901234567890
1 XX/XX/XX                          CompuSell Company                                  Page 9999
2                      Customer Information in Customer Number Order
3         Customer   First        Last                                Last Order   Balance
4         Number     Name         Name          City           State  Date         Due
5         999999     XXXXXXXXXX XXXXXXXXXXXXXX XXXXXXXXXXXXXX XX      99/99/9999   $9999.99
6         999999     XXXXXXXXXX XXXXXXXXXXXXXX XXXXXXXXXXXXXX XX      99/99/9999   $9999.99
7         999999     XXXXXXXXXX XXXXXXXXXXXXXX XXXXXXXXXXXXXX XX      99/99/9999   $9999.99
8         999999     XXXXXXXXXX XXXXXXXXXXXXXX XXXXXXXXXXXXXX XX      99/99/9999   $9999.99
9         999999     XXXXXXXXXX XXXXXXXXXXXXXX XXXXXXXXXXXXXX XX      99/99/9999   $9999.99
10        999999     XXXXXXXXXX XXXXXXXXXXXXXX XXXXXXXXXXXXXX XX      99/99/9999   $9999.99
11        999999     XXXXXXXXXX XXXXXXXXXXXXXX XXXXXXXXXXXXXX XX      99/99/9999   $9999.99
12
```

a. Write a program to use the file you created in Part 3d as the input file. The report should now list customers in name order.

	1		2		3		4		5		6		7		8		9	1 0
	1234567890	1234567890	1234567890	1234567890	1234567890	1234567890	1234567890	1234567890	1234567890

```
 1 XX/XX/XX                           CompuSell Company                                    Page 9999
 2                     Customer Information By Lastname By Firstname
 3       First        Last             Customer                        Last Order  Balance
 4       Name         Name             Number   City           State   Date       Due
 5       XXXXXXXXXX   XXXXXXXXXXXXXXX   999999   XXXXXXXXXXXXXX  XX      99/99/9999 $99999.99
 6       XXXXXXXXXX   XXXXXXXXXXXXXXX   999999   XXXXXXXXXXXXXX  XX      99/99/9999 $99999.99
 7       XXXXXXXXXX   XXXXXXXXXXXXXXX   999999   XXXXXXXXXXXXXX  XX      99/99/9999 $99999.99
 8       XXXXXXXXXX   XXXXXXXXXXXXXXX   999999   XXXXXXXXXXXXXX  XX      99/99/9999 $99999.99
 9       XXXXXXXXXX   XXXXXXXXXXXXXXX   999999   XXXXXXXXXXXXXX  XX      99/99/9999 $99999.99
10       XXXXXXXXXX   XXXXXXXXXXXXXXX   999999   XXXXXXXXXXXXXX  XX      99/99/9999 $99999.99
11       XXXXXXXXXX   XXXXXXXXXXXXXXX   999999   XXXXXXXXXXXXXX  XX      99/99/9999 $99999.99
12
```

b. Modify your program from Part 4a to use the file you created in Part 3e as the input file. The report should now list customers in balance owed order and include only those customers who owe the company money.

```
 1 XX/XX/XX                                   CompuSell Company                            Page 9999
 2                        Customer Listed in Balance Due order
 3        Balance     Customer  First       Last                                Last Order
 4        Due         Number    Name        Name            City        State   Date
 5        $9,999.99   999999    XXXXXXXXXX  XXXXXXXXXXXXXXX  XXXXXXXXXXXX XX     99/99/9999
 6        $9,999.99   999999    XXXXXXXXXX  XXXXXXXXXXXXXXX  XXXXXXXXXXXX XX     99/99/9999
 7        $9,999.99   999999    XXXXXXXXXX  XXXXXXXXXXXXXXX  XXXXXXXXXXXX XX     99/99/9999
 8        $9,999.99   999999    XXXXXXXXXX  XXXXXXXXXXXXXXX  XXXXXXXXXXXX XX     99/99/9999
 9        $9,999.99   999999    XXXXXXXXXX  XXXXXXXXXXXXXXX  XXXXXXXXXXXX XX     99/99/9999
10        $9,999.99   999999    XXXXXXXXXX  XXXXXXXXXXXXXXX  XXXXXXXXXXXX XX     99/99/9999
11        $9,999.99   999999    XXXXXXXXXX  XXXXXXXXXXXXXXX  XXXXXXXXXXXX XX     99/99/9999
12
```

5. Create Database Assignment Three

   a. Create a physical file for Wexler University's student master file (file WUSTDP, in Appendix F). Key this file on student number, and specify that keys be unique.

   b. Create a physical file for Wexler University's department file (WUDPTP, in Appendix F), keyed on department code.

   c. Enter records in both files, following your instructor's directions.

6. Create a logical file over the Wexler Student Master file (WUSTDP) and the Wexler Department file (WUDPTP) keyed by department. Hint: You will have to use control break logic. You may assume that the student major has been validated, so there will never be a student who does not belong within an existing department. However, there may be departments that do not currently have students enrolled in their programs. In that case, print the message shown in the printer spacing chart.

```
          1         2         3         4         5         6         7         8         9         10
 1234567890123456789012345678901234567890123456789012345678901234567890123456789012345678901234567890
 1 XX/XX/XX                              Wexler University                                 Page 9999
 2                              Department Listing of Students
 3 Department
 4    Student    First      Last                        Admit
 5    Number     Name       Name        Credits  Major  Date          G.P.A.
 6 XXXXXXXXXXXXXXXXXXXXXXXXXXXXX
 7    999-99-9999 XXXXXXXXXX XXXXXXXXXXXXXXX    999     XXX    99/99/9999  9.99
 8    999-99-9999 XXXXXXXXXX XXXXXXXXXXXXXXX    999     XXX    99/99/9999  9.99
 9    999-99-9999 XXXXXXXXXX XXXXXXXXXXXXXXX    999     XXX    99/99/9999  9.99
10    999-99-9999 XXXXXXXXXX XXXXXXXXXXXXXXX    999     XXX    99/99/9999  9.99
11 XXXXXXXXXXXXXXXXXXXXXXXXXXXXX
12    (No Majors at this time)
13 XXXXXXXXXXXXXXXXXXXXXXXXXXXXX
14    999-99-9999 XXXXXXXXXX XXXXXXXXXXXXXXX    999     XXX    99/99/9999  9.99
15    999-99-9999 XXXXXXXXXX XXXXXXXXXXXXXXX    999     XXX    99/99/9999  9.99
16
```

Chapter 4

Defining Data with Definition Specifications

 Chapter Overview

Now that you can write simple read/write programs in RPG IV, you will learn how to define work fields, data structures, and other data items your program might need to perform its tasks. RPG IV supports a rich set of data types; in this chapter, you'll discover which ones are appropriate for most business programming. You will also learn how to set the initial value for a data item and how to distinguish among program variables, literals, and constants.

Introducing Definition Specifications

RPG IV requires you to define all variables used in your program by giving them valid names, specifying their lengths and data types, and, for numeric variables, designating the number of decimal positions they are to have.

At this point, you should have a good understanding of how to use RPG's Input specifications to define fields that will receive values from records of a data file. The programs you have worked with so far simply wrote those field values to reports. Typically, however, program requirements include manipulating input data in other ways and storing the resulting values in preparation for output.

To enable this kind of processing, you need to identify to the computer the additional variables and other data items used to store such results. RPG provides **Definition specifications** to define to your program those data items that do not originate as fields in a file's record layout. Definition specifications (D-specs) are used to define these types of data items:

- Standalone variables
- Named constants
- Data structures
- Prototypes
- Procedure interfaces

In this chapter, we'll explain how to define standalone variables, named constants, and data structures; in Chapters 12 and 13 we'll cover prototypes and procedure interfaces. The following shows the general layout of the Definition specification:

```
*.. 1 ...+... 2 ...+... 3 ...+... 4 ...+... 5 ...+... 6 ...+... 7 ...+... 8
DName++++++++++ETDsFrom+++To/Len+IDc.Keywords+++++++++++++++++++++++++++++++
```

The Definition specification is identified by a D in position 6. If your program uses Definition specifications, they must follow the File specifications and precede any Input specifications. The main purpose of Definition specifications is to define data items your program may need in addition to file input and output fields; variables defined in Definition specifications are not typically defined in data files. Because Definition specifications concentrate data definition into a single group of consecutive statements near the beginning of your program, they facilitate later program maintenance.

Defining Standalone Variables

Standalone variables (sometimes called work fields) are so called because these variables are not part of a database record or any other kind of data structure. They "stand alone" in the program, without depending upon any other kind of data item. A typical use for a standalone variable might be as a counter, to count the number of transactions being processed; or as an intermediate variable, to temporarily hold a value for later processing; or as an accumulator, to keep running track of year-to-date sales amounts; or as an indicator, to represent whether or not a condition is true. The value stored in a standalone variable might change often while the program is running.

Here are a few examples of definitions for standalone variables:

```
*.. 1 ...+... 2 ...+... 3 ...+... 4 ...+... 5 ...+... 6 ...+... 7 ...+... 8
DName++++++++++ETDsFrom+++To/Len+IDc.Keywords+++++++++++++++++++++++++++++++
 // Variable Totaldue defined on a Definition specification as a standalone
 // variable seven positions long with two decimal positions
D Totaldue        S              7 2

 // Variable Citystatezip defined as a character variable 40 positions long
D Citystatezip    S             40

 // Variable Yeartodatetotalsales defined as a number 11 digits with two
 // decimal positions
D Yeartodatetotalsales...
D                 S             11 2

 // Variable Counter define as an unsigned integer
D Counter         S             10U 0

 // Variable Basedate defined as a native date
D Basedate        S               D

 // Variable Taxexempt defined as an indicator
D Taxexempt       S               N
```

Data Item Name (Positions 7–21)

To define a standalone variable, you first name the variable anywhere within positions 7–21 (*Name+++++++++++*) of the line. The name need not begin in position 7; in fact, to aid readability, many programmers always leave position 7 blank to separate the data item name from the D in column 6. The data item name must begin with an alphabetic character or the special character $, #, or @; the remaining characters may be alphabetic characters, numbers, or any of the four special characters _, #, $, and @. A data item name cannot contain blanks embedded within the permissible characters.

Data item names are typically restricted to 15 characters (10 if they must be used in an externally described printer file), but they may be up to 4,096 characters long. If the name won't fit in positions 7–21, you can use an ellipsis (...; actually three periods across three positions) as a special continuation character to allow a longer name. On the following line(s), you can simply continue the definition. The ellipsis can appear at the end of the variable name, or within the name if necessary. In the above examples, the Yeartodatetotalsales variable illustrates the use of the ellipsis to accommodate a long variable name.

Definition Type (Positions 24–25)
Definition specifications use positions 24–25 (*Ds*) to indicate what type of a data item the line is defining. For a standalone variable, enter an S (for standalone) left-adjusted in these positions. Later, we'll cover the other entries for other definition types.

Length (Positions 33–39)
Enter the length of the variable right-adjusted in positions 33–39 (To/Len+). **Standalone variables** defined as character data can be from 1 to 65,535 bytes long; numeric variables can be from 1 to 63 digits long.

Decimal Positions (Positions 41–42)
For numeric variables, positions 41–42 (*Dc*) indicate the number of decimal positions, right-adjusted. A number can include up to 63 decimal positions. A decimal position entry signals to the system that the variable is numeric; the system generally interprets blanks in positions 41–42 to mean that the variable is of character data type. The default data representation for numeric standalone variables is packed representation. All numeric variables can store negative values without special specification. Recall, however, that negative values will be printed without a sign unless you use an appropriate edit code with the variable on output.

Data Type (Position 40)
Position 40 (*I*) is used to indicate what data type RPG uses to internally store a variable. For most character and numeric variables, you may leave position 40 blank. If you leave the Data Type and the Decimal Positions entries blank, RPG will assume that the variable is a character (alphanumeric) variable; if you leave position 40 blank but do make an entry in the Decimal Positions space, RPG will default to a packed decimal standalone variable.

So far, we've discussed only numeric, character, and date data in general terms; these are the three basic classes of data used in most business processing. RPG IV actually supports several variations of these data classes, along with a few others that have special uses. You can specify any of the following data types when you are describing a data item in Definition specifications, using a code to signal the data type.

Data class	Data type	RPG code
Character	Character	A
Numeric	Zoned decimal	S
	Packed decimal	P
	Signed integer	I
	Unsigned integer	U
	Binary	B
	Floating point	F
Date	Date	D
	Time	T
	Timestamp	Z
Boolean	Indicator	N
DBCS	Graphic	G
	Unicode	C
Object	Object/class	O
Pointer	Pointer	*

To define a standalone variable with a specific data type, you can simply include the code in column 40 of the Definition specification. If the variable is a character variable, you need not code a data type in column 40; the system generally interprets blanks in positions 41–42 to mean that the variable is of character data type.

```
*.. 1 ...+... 2 ...+... 3 ...+... 4 ...+... 5 ...+... 6 ...+... 7 ...+... 8
DName++++++++++ETDsFrom+++To/Len+IDc.Keywords+++++++++++++++++++++++++++++++
 // The following definitions are equivalent for a character variable
D Citystatezip   S             40A
D Citystatezip   S             40
```

Numeric Data Types

Six data types deal with numbers; the differences among these data types are primarily in the way the computer stores the data. The two most common numeric types are **zoned decimal** and **packed decimal**. Recall that for a zoned decimal number, each digit of a numeric value requires a full byte of storage; the number's sign is stored within the rightmost digit. Packed decimal numbers, on the other hand, use a compressed storage format, wherein each digit and the sign require only one half byte (four bits) of storage; in packed format, for example, a five-digit number would occupy three bytes of storage (five half bytes for the digits and one half byte for the sign). Although it's not required, packed decimal variables usually have an odd number of digits, to fully use every full byte allocated for them.

To define a specific numeric data type in a Definition specification, include the appropriate code in column 40. For standalone variables, you usually need not code a data type. Simply enter the number of decimal positions right-adjusted in positions 41–42 (*Dc*); a decimal position entry signals to the system that the variable is numeric. For a standalone variable, RPG IV will define the variable using the packed decimal format, which will usually be appropriate. Notice in the following examples that you code the number of digits in the standalone variable, not the number of bytes.

```
*.. 1 ...+... 2 ...+... 3 ...+... 4 ...+... 5 ...+... 6 ...+... 7 ...+... 8
DName++++++++++ETDsFrom+++To/Len+IDc.Keywords+++++++++++++++++++++++++++++++
 // The following definitions are equivalent for a packed decimal number
D Totaldue          S              7P 2
D Totaldue          S              7  2

 // To force zoned decimal representation, code the data type in column 40
D Totaldue          S              7S 2
```

Integers require even less memory than the decimal data types do. RPG can use these data types to store whole numbers. For example, integers can store five-digit numeric values in just two bytes or store ten-digit values in just four bytes. Unsigned integers are coded with a U in position 40, while signed integers are coded with an I. Integers can be 3, 5, 10, or 20 digits long and should always be defined with zero decimal positions.

```
*.. 1 ...+... 2 ...+... 3 ...+... 4 ...+... 5 ...+... 6 ...+... 7 ...+... 8
DName++++++++++ETDsFrom+++To/Len+IDc.Keywords+++++++++++++++++++++++++++++++
 // Variable Reccount is an unsigned long (10 digit) integer
D Reccount          S             10U 0

 // Variable Updown is a signed short (5 digit) integer
D Updown            S              5I 0
```

The range of values allowed for an integer depends upon its length; signed integers (type I) support half the range of unsigned integers (type U) in the same amount of storage. The following table illustrates the valid integer definitions:

Data type	Size (bytes)	Length (digits)	Range of values
I	1	3	-128 to 127
	2	5	-32,768 to 32,767
	4	10	-2,147,483,648 to 2,147,483,647
	8	20	-9,223,372,036,854,775,808 to 9,223,372,036,854,775,807
U	1	3	0 to 255
	2	5	0 to 65,535
	4	10	0 to 4,294,967,295
	8	20	0 to 18,446,744,073,709,551,615

Binary numbers (type B), which are rarely used, use two bytes to store any whole number that is one to four digits long, or four bytes to store whole numbers from one to nine digits long. Integers are generally the preferred alternative to binary numbers.

Floating point format (type F), sometimes called scientific notation, represents numeric values using powers of ten in a character string notation that makes it easy to represent a large range of numeric values; in floating point format, the number 136 would be represented by the string +1.3600000E+002 (in algebraic terms, $+1.36 \times 10^2$). The leftmost portion of the string is called the mantissa, while the portion following the E is called the exponent. Floating point format uses four bytes to store a 14-character value (eight-digit mantissa) or eight bytes to store a 23-character value (16-digit mantissa). Unlike the other formats, floating point is defined with a byte length instead of the number of digits; decimal positions are left blank:

```
*.. 1 ...+... 2 ...+... 3 ...+... 4 ...+... 5 ...+... 6 ...+... 7 ...+... 8
DName++++++++++ETDsFrom+++To/Len+IDc.Keywords+++++++++++++++++++++++++++++++
 // Variable Float is an eight byte floating point number
D Float          S              8F
```

Which numeric representation should you use? Typically, you'll use packed decimal format for numbers that include more than zero decimal positions and for those that might hold values longer than 19 digits. Zoned decimal might also be appropriate in either of these situations, but packed decimal numbers will perform better in arithmetic operations than will zoned decimal numbers. If there are no decimal positions, and if the possible values will fit within 19 digits, you should use integers or unsigned integers. Reserve floating point numbers for those variables that will need to hold very small and/or very large values that the other formats cannot accommodate; you should not use floating point when you need to ensure a specific decimal precision.

Note

Remember to use editing when you are printing or displaying a number. If you write a number without editing, the sign will not print separately; instead, the last digit of the number will include the sign. For example, a zoned decimal value of –123.45 will appear as 1234N.

Date, Time, and Timestamp

Three data types deal with date- and time-related information: **date**, **time**, and **timestamp**. Dates and times are fairly self-explanatory. A timestamp is a combination of a date and a time. Each of these data types has specific requirements and capabilities, which we discuss later. RPG supports these data types in calendar-related operations using specialized built-in functions, which we also discuss later.

To define standalone variables with the date/time data types, you specify a D (for dates), T (for times), or Z (for timestamps) in column 40. You do not specify a length or number of decimal positions; the system determines the length automatically.

```
*.. 1 ...+... 2 ...+... 3 ...+... 4 ...+... 5 ...+... 6 ...+... 7 ...+... 8
DName++++++++++ETDsFrom+++To/Len+IDc.Keywords+++++++++++++++++++++++++++++++
 // Variable Enrolldate is a date variable
D Enrolldate     S              D

 // Variable Starttime is a time variable
D Starttime      S              T

 // Variable TransTime is a timestamp variable
D Transtime      S              Z
```

Indicator Data Type

RPG IV also supports an **indicator data type**, which many other computer languages refer to as a **Boolean data type**. An indicator variable is a single-byte variable that can contain only two logical values: '1' or '0'. You can also refer to these values using the figurative constants *ON and *OFF, respectively. Indicator data is usually used within an RPG IV program to signal a true/false condition.

To code an indicator variable, you type N for the data type in column 40. You do not need to code a length; the system will create a single-byte variable.

```
*.. 1 ...+... 2 ...+... 3 ...+... 4 ...+... 5 ...+... 6 ...+... 7 ...+... 8
DName++++++++++ETDsFrom+++To/Len+IDc.Keywords++++++++++++++++++++++++++++++++
 // Variable Inputerror is an indicator
D Inputerror      S                 N

 // Variable Endofpage is an indicator
D Endofpage       S                 N
```

The remaining data types listed in the table on page 82 are seldom used in normal business processing. The DBCS (Double Byte Character Set) data types define and manipulate data in which two bytes represent a single graphic character or an extended-character-set character in multinational applications or Internet applications. Object definitions help RPG IV programs coexist with other object-oriented languages, such as Java. Pointers let you dynamically access storage for data items and/or procedures associated with the pointers. We discuss many of these data types in more detail later in this text.

Once you've defined a standalone variable in a Definition specification, you can assign it a value, use it with operations, or print it—just like an input field. Before you learn how to assign values to standalone variables, you need to understand three other kinds of data constructs: numeric literals, character literals, and figurative constants. You can use these constructs in Definition specifications to assign initial values to a data item; you can also use literals and constants with operations in Calculation specifications.

Numeric Literals

A **numeric literal** is a number; its value remains fixed throughout the program (unlike a variable, whose value can change throughout the program). The literal may include a decimal point and/or a sign. If the numeric literal includes a sign, the sign must be the leftmost character of the literal. If the numeric literal does not include a sign, the computer assumes that the literal represents a positive number.

Other than a decimal point and a sign, the literal may include only the digits 0 through 9. You should never use blanks, dollar signs, percent signs, or commas (unless the comma is used as a decimal separator) in numeric literals. Numeric literals are not enclosed in apostrophes ('). The numeric value can be as long as 63 digits, with up to 63 decimal positions. Some examples of valid numeric literals follow.

–401230.12

0.0715

102

1

+3

–1

3.1416

.123456789

Numeric literals can also be in floating point format, using a one– to 16–digit mantissa and an exponent from –308 to +3008.

+1.36E+002

0E0

1e1

Character Literals

Often, you will want to work with character values as well with as numeric values. RPG IV lets you use **character literals** in D-specs and C-specs when working with character values. Like numeric literals, character literals maintain a constant value during the execution of the program. To indicate that a value is a character literal (and not a variable name) simply enclose it within apostrophes. There is no restriction on what characters can make up the literal; any character that you can represent via the keyboard—including a blank—is acceptable. Character literals can be up to 1,024 bytes long. Some examples of character literals follow:

'John Doe'

'Abc   246   #18w'

'321444'

'45%'

Note
You cannot use a character literal — one enclosed within apostrophes — with an arithmetic operation even if all the characters of the literal are digits. Numeric literals do not use apostrophes.

Typed Literals

In addition to numeric and character literals, you can express other data values, such as dates and times, using **typed literals**. To code a typed literal, enclose the value within apostrophes, but precede it with a data type code to indicate which data type the literal represents. To refer to a value of January 1, 2008, for example, you'd code D'2008-01-01' as the literal. Other common data type codes for literals are T (for times), Z (for timestamps), and X (for hexadecimal literals). Here are more examples of typed literals:

Data type	Typed literal
Date	D'2008-03-15'
Time	T'08.56.20'
Timestamp	Z'2008-03-15-08.56.20.000000'
Hexadecimal	X'F0F0F0'

Figurative Constants

RPG IV includes a special set of reserved words called **figurative constants**. Figurative constants are implied literals that can be used without a specified length. Figurative constants assume the length and decimal positions of the variables with which they are associated. Some of RPG's figurative constants are

*Blank (or *Blanks)

*Zero (or *Zeros)

*Off

*On

*Hival

*Loval

*All

*Null

RPG IV lets you assign *Blank or *Blanks to cause a character variable to be filled with blanks. Assigning *Zero or *Zeros to both numeric and character variables fills the variables with 0s.

Figurative constants *Off and *On represent '0' and '1' character values. *Off is the equivalent of '0', while *On equates to '1'. Although you can use *Off and *On with any character variable of any length, programmers most often use *Off and *On to change the value of an RPG IV indicator or to compare an indicator's value.

Assigning *Hival fills a variable with the highest possible collating value appropriate to its data type. Setting a character variable to *Hival sets all the bytes to hexadecimal FF (all bits on). For a numeric variable, *Hival is the maximum positive value allowed for the data representation; for example, for a packed, zoned, or binary numeric variable, *Hival is all 9s and a plus sign (+). Assigning *Loval fills a variable with the lowest possible collating value appropriate to its data type — hexadecimal 00 (all bits off) for character variables or a minimum negative value for numeric variables. Programmers often assign *Hival or *Loval to a variable to ensure that the variable's value is the maximum or minimum possible value.

Assigning figurative constant *All immediately followed by one or more characters within apostrophes, causes the string within the apostrophes to be cyclically repeated through the entire length of the result variable. For example, assigning *All'Z' to a character variable will fill the variable with Zs, while assigning *All'7' to a numeric variable will fill the variable with 7s.

The constant *Null represents a null value; *Null is usually used to represent the absence of any value—not even blanks or zeros. Usually RPG IV uses *Null only in unusual situations, which we'll discuss later in the text.

Assigning Initial Values to Data

In addition to defining data items, such as standalone variables, in Definition specifications, you can assign an **initial value** to those data items. If the data item is a variable, its value can change during the execution of the program, but its initial value is the one the variable contains when the program starts.

To initialize (i.e., assign an initial value to) a standalone variable, you specify the value using the Inz (Initialize) keyword in the variable's definition. The initial value is indicated using a literal or, in some cases, a figurative constant.

```
*.. 1 ...+... 2 ...+... 3 ...+... 4 ...+... 5 ...+... 6 ...+... 7 ...+... 8
DName+++++++++ETDsFrom+++To/Len+IDc.Keywords+++++++++++++++++++++++++++++++++
 // Variable Maxlimit defined as numeric seven positions long with two
 // decimal positions and an initial value. Both of these definitions
 // are equivalent.
D Maxlimit        S              7 2 Inz(10500.00)
D Maxlimit        S              7 2 Inz(10500)

 // Variable Compname defined as a 40 character field, with an
 // initial value
D Compname        S             40   Inz('Kay Elmnop Enterprises')

 // Variable Highlimit defined as numeric, seven positions long with
 // two decimal positions and an initial value of 99999.99. Both of
 // these definitions are equivalent.
D Highlimit       S              7 2 Inz(99999.99)
D Highlimit       S              7 2 Inz(*Hival)

 // Variable Check defined as a 9 character field, with an initial value
 // of all bits off. Both of these definitions are equivalent.
D Check           S              9   Inz(X'000000000000000000')
D Check           S              9   Inz(*Loval)

 // Variable Basedate defined as a native date, with an initial value of
 // 30 December 1899
D Basedate        S              D   Inz(D'1899-12-30')

 // Variable Today defined as a native date, with an initial value of
 // the current system date
D Today           S              D   Inz(*Sys)

 // Variable Username defined as a character field, ten bytes long,
 // initialized with the name of the current user profile
D Username        S             10   Inz(*User)
```

There are some special reserved values that you can use to initialize date-related definitions. To initialize a date field to the **job date** (the same as *Date in our previous examples), you can code Inz(*Job) in the keyword area of the field's definition. You can also initialize a date, time, or timestamp field to the current system date at runtime by coding Inz(*Sys). What's the difference between the job date and the system date? You can think of the job date as being an "as of" date which is assigned to a job when you run a program; it may or may not be the actual date that the program is running. The system date, on the other hand, is always the current date.

One other useful initialization value, *User, can be used with character fields if they are at least ten bytes long. Coding Inz(*User) for a character field assigns the name of the current user profile to the character field. We'll cover other initial values later in this text, as the need arises.

You should know that it is not always necessary to assign an initial value to a data item. RPG will automatically initialize data items to default values when the program starts unless you use the **Inz keyword** to initialize the variable. The default values are typically blanks for character variables and zeros for numeric variables. If the default values are sufficient, you need not initialize the data item.

```
*.. 1 ...+... 2 ...+... 3 ...+... 4 ...+... 5 ...+... 6 ...+... 7 ...+... 8
DName++++++++++ETDsFrom+++To/Len+IDc.Keywords+++++++++++++++++++++++++++++++
 // The following definitions for Totaldue would result in identical
 // initial values
D Totaldue        S              7  2 Inz(0)
D Totaldue        S              7  2 Inz(*Zeros)
D Totaldue        S              7  2 Inz
D Totaldue        S              7  2

 // The following definitions for Title would result in identical
 // initial values
D Title           S             25    Inz(' ')
D Title           S             25    Inz(*Blanks)
D Title           S             25    Inz
D Title           S             25
```

Remember that the Inz keyword assigns only the initial value for a variable. In subsequent chapters, we discuss how you can assign new values to a variable once a program is running.

Defining Constants

You are already familiar with the concept of a literal. In addition to using Definition specifications to define standalone variables, RPG IV lets you associate a data name with a literal so that you can reference the literal by its name throughout your program. The resulting **named constant** differs from a standalone variable in three respects:

- Its value never changes during processing.
- It is defined with no specified length.
- Its type is automatically determined by its value.

You define a named constant in the Definition specifications by entering its name anywhere in positions 7–21 (*Name+++++++++++*); the name must follow the rules governing variable names. The letter C, for constant, must appear in position 24 (*Ds*) of the specification. You enter the value of the constant in the Keywords area, positions 44–80. Enter numeric constant values with a decimal separator or sign if appropriate, but never with thousands separators (commas). Enclose character constant values within apostrophes. Constants of other data types should follow the rules indicated earlier for typed literals.

```
*.. 1 ...+... 2 ...+... 3 ...+... 4 ...+... 5 ...+... 6 ...+... 7 ...+... 8
DName++++++++++ETDsFrom+++To/L+++IDc.Keywords+++++++++++++++++++++++++++++++
// Examples of valid named constants
D Fica            C                   Const(.0765)

D Pi              C                   3.142

D Exvicepres      C                   'John Adams'

D Longestword     C                   'floccinaucinihilipilification'

D Sentence        C                   'This long constant has -
D                                      blanks where you would expect them-
D                                       to appear in a sentence.'

D Phoneedit       C                   '(   )   -    '

D Indday          C                   D'1776-07-04'
```

Note
You may occasionally see the value for a named constant coded within parentheses following the Const keyword (as in the Fica example, above); this notation is valid but optional, and most programmers prefer simply to code the value without the Const keyword.

A named constant can be at most 1,024 bytes long; a numeric constant can contain up to 63 digits with up to 63 decimal positions. To enter a named constant too long to fit on a single line, continue the value into the Keywords area (positions 44–80) of one or more Definition specification continuation lines. A hyphen (-) at the end of a line to be continued indicates that the constant continues in the first position of the Keywords area of the continuation line. A plus sign (+) signals that the constant resumes with the first nonblank character in the continuation line.

Once you've defined a named constant, you can use it in calculations appropriate to its type. The value of a named constant is fixed; you cannot change it during the course of program execution.

Named constants let you define constants in one place near the beginning of your program rather than coding them as literals throughout your calculations. This practice is a standard of good programming because it facilitates maintenance programming. If a value, such as FICA rate, needs to be changed, it is much easier and less error-prone to locate the named constant and change its value in that one place rather than have to search through an entire program looking for every calculation in which the literal value .0765 occurs.

You can also use a named constant as the initial value for a variable. You cannot initialize a variable to the value of another variable, but you can initialize a variable to the value of a named constant, as the following example shows.

```
*.. 1 ...+... 2 ...+... 3 ...+... 4 ...+... 5 ...+... 6 ...+... 7 ...+... 8
DName+++++++++++ETDsFrom+++To/L+++IDc.Keywords++++++++++++++++++++++++++++++++
D Fica             C                   Const(.0765)

 // Taxrate will have an initial value of .0765000
D Taxrate          S              7  7 Inz(Fica)
```

Tip
Always use a named constant instead of a literal in your program, unless the use of the literal is obvious. Using named constants will make your programs much easier to read, understand, and maintain than if you use literals. For example, it's easier to immediately understand the use of the term Fica than the literal .0765; it's also easier to change the program later if the law changes.

One exception to this rule might be the use of the literals '1' and '0', which have generally accepted meanings of *On and *Off, respectively.

Defining Data Structures

In addition to standalone variables and named constants, you can define data structures using Definition specifications. **Data structures** are simply a means of organizing multiple variables within a single section of contiguous portions of memory. Data structures can give you flexibility in your handling of data by letting you group variables into a logical structure, subdivide variables into **subfields**, and redefine variables with different data types or names. An RPG program can process the entire data structure as a unit or process its subfields individually.

The data structure definition has two parts:

- The data structure definition itself (sometimes called the data structure header)
- The definition(s) for the subfield(s) within the data structure

DS, coded in positions 24–25 (*Ds*), signals the beginning of a data structure. You also may enter a name for the data structure in positions 7–21 (*Name*+++++++++++); this name entry is optional, but it is required if you plan to refer to the data structure as a whole elsewhere in your program.

Data structure names follow the same rules as variable names. Although you can enter the length of the entire data structure in positions 33–39 (To/L+++) of the DS header line, this entry is optional. If you omit it, the system derives the length of the structure as a whole from the lengths of its subfields. The maximum length for a named data structure is 65,535 bytes; the maximum for an unnamed data structure is 9,999,999.

Defining Data Structure Subfields

The lines to describe subfields composing the data structure follow the DS header line. You define each subfield entry by giving it a name (in positions 7–21). The name can float (be indented) within its prescribed positions to make the hierarchical layout of the data structure easily visible.

For each subfield, you must specify its location within the data structure as a whole. Two methods exist for specifying the location, and consequently the length of a subfield. The first method, called **positional notation** (or sometimes, absolute notation), involves using positions 26–32 (From+++) and positions 33–39 (To/L+++) to indicate the beginning and ending byte positions of the subfield within the data structure. This method closely mimics the notation that Input specifications use to indicate the location of fields in a record layout. The second method, **length notation**, leaves positions 26–32 blank and records the subfield's length in positions 33–39. The system will organize each subfield adjacent to the previously defined subfield within the data structure.

Most programmers prefer length notation because it is cleaner, more descriptive, and easier to modify than positional notation. The following code demonstrates these alternative methods.

```
*.. 1 ...+... 2 ...+... 3 ...+... 4 ...+... 5 ...+... 6 ...+... 7 ...+... 8
DName++++++++++ETDsFrom+++To/L+++IDc.Keywords+++++++++++++++++++++++++++++++
 // Defining subfields of a data structure using positional notation
D Optname        DS
D   SubfieldA              1      3 0
D   SubfieldB              4      8 2
D   SubfieldC              9     13P 2
D   SubfieldD             14     17U 0
D   SubfieldE             18     27
D   SubfieldF             28     37D
```

continued...

continued...

```
// Defining the same structure using length notation
D Optname          DS
D   SubfieldA                      3  0
D   SubfieldB                      5  2
D   SubfieldC                      9P 2
D   SubfieldD                     10U 0
D   SubfieldE                     10
D   SubfieldF                      D
```

Regardless of the method you use, numeric subfields require a decimal position entry in positions 41–42 (*Dc*), as shown above. Code the data type of the subfield in position 40 (*I*), just as you did for standalone variables. As you'd expect, if the type is blank, the default is character (type A) for subfields without a decimal position entry; for numeric subfields (those with a decimal position entry), however, the default data type is zoned decimal (type S)—not packed decimal (type P) as it was for standalone variables.

It's worth pointing out that when you use positional notation to denote numeric data structure subfields, the From and To positions represent the number of bytes that the subfield occupies. When you use length notation, the Length represents the number of digits. This difference becomes important if the data structure includes packed decimal, integer, unsigned, or binary subfields.

Occasionally, your program will encounter a data structure that will not use all the locations in the data structure and will skip over those unneeded locations. Usually, this will only occur with data structures that are predefined by an application or by IBM. If you describe the data structure using positional notation, you can skip over locations by providing proper From and To positions in the D-specs. If you are using length notation, you can skip over unused areas of the data structure by simply coding the number of bytes you want to skip in positions 33–39 and leaving the subfield name and data attributes blank:

```
*.. 1 ...+... 2 ...+... 3 ...+... 4 ...+... 5 ...+... 6 ...+... 7 ...+... 8
DName++++++++++ETDsFrom+++To/L+++IDc.Keywords++++++++++++++++++++++++++++++++
 // Skipping subfields using positional notation
D Phone          DS
D   Areacode              1     3  0
D   Localnbr              7    10  0

 // Skipping subfields using length notation
D Phone          DS
D   Areacode                     3  0
D                                3
D   Localnbr                     4  0
```

In both of these equivalent examples, there are three unused bytes between the two subfields in the data structure.

Once you have defined the data structure subfields, you can initialize them, if necessary, using the Inz keyword. The Inz keyword initializes entire data structures or data structure subfields. If you code Inz (with no value following it) on the data structure header, the program will initialize all the subfields in the data structure with initial values appropriate to the subfields' data types. If you do not code Inz on the data structure header, the entire data structure, including all its subfields, will be initialized with blanks—unless you code individual Inz keywords for specific subfields.

Initialization of Data Structures

Data structures are considered character fields regardless of the data type of their subfields; as a result, they will contain blanks at the start of your program unless you explicitly initialize their subfields. You initialize a data structure globally when you include the Inz keyword in the data structure header line; this use of Inz causes all subfields in the entire data structure to be automatically initialized.

For program-described data structures, specifying Inz on the data structure header line causes all the subfields to be initialized to the default value appropriate for their data types (e.g., all numeric subfields are set to zero, all character fields to spaces):

```
*.. 1 ...+... 2 ...+... 3 ...+... 4 ...+... 5 ...+... 6 ...+... 7 ...+... 8
DName+++++++++++ETDsFrom+++To/L+++IDc.Keywords+++++++++++++++++++++++++++++++
D Optname          DS                    Inz
D   SubfieldA                    3 0
D   SubfieldB                   10U 0
D   SubfieldC                   10
```

In this example, SubfieldAand SubfieldB would be initialized to zero; Subfield C would be blank. Without the Inz keyword, all the subfields would be initially blank. The program would end abnormally if you tried to perform arithmetic operations on SubfieldA or SubfieldB without first initializing them.

As an alternative, you can initialize specific subfields of a data structure by including the Inz keyword as part of their definitions. If you want to initialize the subfield to a value other than the default, you can include the desired value within parentheses following Inz. You can express this value as a literal or a named constant, but it must fit the data type of the subfield; moreover, it cannot be longer than the subfield or have more decimal positions than the subfield (if the type is numeric).

```
*.. 1 ...+... 2 ...+... 3 ...+... 4 ...+... 5 ...+... 6 ...+... 7 ...+... 8
DName+++++++++++ETDsFrom+++To/L+++IDc.Keywords+++++++++++++++++++++++++++++++
D Optname          DS
D   SubfieldA                    3 0 Inz
D   SubfieldB                   10U 0 Inz(1)
D   SubfieldC                   10
```

In this example SubfieldA would initially be zero; SubfieldB would be 1; SubfieldC would be blank.

Overlapping Subfields

The locations of subfields within a data structure can overlap, and the same position within a data structure can fall within the location of several subfields. When using positional notation to define subfields, such overlapping is clearly indicated by the From and To position entries.

As an illustration of the concept of overlapping, or defining subfields within subfields, assume your program contains variables Firstname (15 bytes) and Phone (10 digits). The program needs to work with just the initial of the first name and with the area code, exchange, and local portions of the phone number as separate data items. Data structures let you easily access the data that way:

```
*.. 1 ...+... 2 ...+... 3 ...+... 4 ...+... 5 ...+... 6 ...+... 7 ...+... 8
DName++++++++++ETDsFrom+++To/L+++IDc.Keywords++++++++++++++++++++++++++++++
 // Data structures to "split up" input fields into subfields
D                 DS
D Firstname              1    15
D   Initial              1     1

D                 DS
D Phone                  1    10 0
D   Areacode             1     3 0
D   Exchange             4     6 0
D   Localnbr             7    10 0
```

In the above code, subfield Initial will contain the first letter of the value of Firstname, and the phone number of Phone will be broken into three pieces accessible through subfields Areacode, Exchange, and Localnbr. Because Areacode, Exchange, and Localnbr share common space with Phone in the data structure, if your program changes the value of any one subfield, that change will be reflected in the overlapping subfield(s).

If you want to use length notation to describe the above data definition, you need a way to indicate that Initial is supposed to be a part of Firstname rather than a subfield adjacent to it. RPG IV includes the **Overlay** keyword to supplement length notation for this purpose. The format of the keyword is

```
OVERLAY(name{:position})
```

Overlay indicates that the subfield overlays the storage of *name*, starting in the position within *name* indicated by *position*. Note that {*:position*} indicates that the position entry is optional; if you omit the entry, Overlay defaults to the first position of *name*. RPG IV also supports the special value ***Next** with the Overlay keyword; specifying Overlay(*name:**Next) instead of a position begins a subfield at the next available position of the overlaid field.

The following code reworks our example using length notation and Overlay.

```
*.. 1 ...+... 2 ...+... 3 ...+... 4 ...+... 5 ...+... 6 ...+... 7 ...+... 8
DName++++++++++ETDsFrom+++To/L+++IDc.Keywords++++++++++++++++++++++++++++++
D                 DS
D Firstname                   15
D   Initial                    1    Overlay(Firstname)

 // Using Overlay with a position specified
D                 DS
D Phone                       10 0
D   Areacode                   3 0 Overlay(Phone)
D   Exchange                   3 0 Overlay(Phone:4)
D   Localnbr                   4 0 Overlay(Phone:7)

 // Using Overlay with *Next
D                 DS
D Phone                       10 0
D   Areacode                   3 0 Overlay(Phone)
D   Exchange                   3 0 Overlay(Phone:*Next)
D   Localnbr                   4 0 Overlay(Phone:*Next)
```

When you use the Overlay keyword, the data name within the parentheses must be a subfield already defined within the current data structure or the name of the current data structure itself; the subfield being defined must be completely contained within the subfield or data structure it overlays.

If a subfield name appears in one or more Overlay keywords, it may not be necessary to define a data type or length for the subfield. In the following example, the compiler will assume that Phone is a character field, ten bytes long (the sum of the lengths of Areacode, Exchange, and Localnbr).

```
*.. 1 ...+... 2 ...+... 3 ...+... 4 ...+... 5 ...+... 6 ...+... 7 ...+... 8
DName++++++++++ETDsFrom+++To/L+++IDc.Keywords+++++++++++++++++++++++++++++++
D                 DS
D Phone
D   Areacode                     3  0 Overlay(Phone)
D   Exchange                     3  0 Overlay(Phone:4)
D   Localnbr                     4  0 Overlay(Phone:7)
```

In this combination, the assumed data type is always character and its length is always the sum of the overlapping subfields. Most programmers prefer to explicitly code the data attributes of all the subfields.

You can use Overlay to redefine subfields in a data structure with different names and/or data types. In the following example, subfield Basedate is a native date, but Basechar is a character subfield. Both subfields occupy the same location in the data structure; if your program changes the value of one subfield, it also changes the value of the other one.

```
*.. 1 ...+... 2 ...+... 3 ...+... 4 ...+... 5 ...+... 6 ...+... 7 ...+... 8
DName++++++++++ETDsFrom+++To/L+++IDc.Keywords+++++++++++++++++++++++++++++++
D                 DS
D Basedate                        D
D Basechar                      10   Overlay(Basedate)
```

Externally Described Data Structures

The data structures we discussed up to now are program-described data structures. The entire data structure description (i.e., all the subfields) is described in the program's Definition specifications. RPG IV also supports externally described data structures, in a manner similar to the way it handles externally described data files. The subfields in an externally described data structure follow the layout of an existing file; the subfields in the data structure have the same names, locations, and data attributes as the record format. Externally described data structures might be useful when you want to use a data structure in several different programs, when your company's standards dictate the use of specific data structures, or when you need a data structure to mimic the layout of an existing file's record format.

Recall, from Chapter 3, the DDS for our example Employees file:

```
*.. 1 ...+... 2 ...+... 3 ...+... 4 ...+... 5 ...+... 6 ...+... 7 ...+... 8
A..........T.Name++++++RLen++TDcB......Keywords+++++++++++++++++++++++++++++
 * Employee master physical file EMPLOYEES
A                                       UNIQUE
A          R EMPREC
A            EMPNBR        9S Ø         TEXT('Employee number')
A            LASTNAME     15A           TEXT('Last name')
A            FIRSTNAME    10A           TEXT('First name')
A            DEPT          3A           TEXT('Department')
A            SALARY        6P Ø         TEXT('Annual salary')
A            STREET       15A           TEXT('Street address')
A            CITY         15A           TEXT('City')
A            STATE         2A           TEXT('State or province')
A            POSTCODE     10A           TEXT('Postal code')
A            HIREDATE      L            TEXT('Hire date')
A          K EMPNBR
```

Here's an example of an externally described data structure based on that file's layout:

```
*.. 1 ...+... 2 ...+... 3 ...+... 4 ...+... 5 ...+... 6 ...+... 7 ...+... 8
DName++++++++++ETDsFrom+++To/L+++IDc.Keywords+++++++++++++++++++++++++++++++
 // Defining an externally described data structure, based on Employees
D Employees     E DS
```

Typically, an externally described data structure will be named in positions 7–21, and often the name will be the same as the file upon which the data structure is based. Coding E in position 22 (*E*) tells the compiler that this data structure is externally described. DS, coded in positions 24–25, of course, signals the beginning of the data structure. Because the compiler will automatically acquire the subfields from the Employees file, it is not necessary to code any subfields for the data structure; all the fields in the file will become subfields in the data structure.

If the name of the data structure does not match the name of the file upon which it is based, the data structure definition will require the **Extname** (External name) keyword to explicitly name the file:

```
*.. 1 ...+... 2 ...+... 3 ...+... 4 ...+... 5 ...+... 6 ...+... 7 ...+... 8
DName++++++++++ETDsFrom+++To/L+++IDc.Keywords+++++++++++++++++++++++++++++++
 // Defining an externally described data structure, based on Employees
D Empds         E DS                  Extname(Employees)
```

You can code additional program-described subfields following the data structure header and you can use Overlay if you want to describe subfields that overlap existing subfields in the data structure.

To initialize an externally described data structure, specify Inz(*Extdft):

```
*.. 1 ...+... 2 ...+... 3 ...+... 4 ...+... 5 ...+... 6 ...+... 7 ...+... 8
DName++++++++++ETDsFrom+++To/L+++IDc.Keywords+++++++++++++++++++++++++++++++
D Empds         E DS                  Extname(Employees)
D                                     Inz(*Extdft)
```

The subfields will be initialized to their default values as specified in the DDS for the externally described data structure. You can override the external default for one or more subfields by listing them with their own Inz keyword.

Qualified Data Structures

Normally, an RPG program can refer to the individual subfields in a data structure by their simple names. Those names must be unique; that is, you cannot normally have multiple data structures with identically named subfields. A **qualified data structure** lets you ignore that rule. When you include the Qualified keyword on a data structure header line, you create a qualified data structure.

The Qualified keyword indicates to the compiler that you will refer to the subfields in the data structure by their qualified name — that is, the data structure name followed by a period (.) and the subfield name. If the Qualified keyword is not used, you will refer to the subfields by their simple name, and that name must be unique. Qualified data structures may be program-described or externally described, and they must be named data structures. The following examples illustrate how you would define qualified data structures:

```
*.. 1 ...+... 2 ...+... 3 ...+... 4 ...+... 5 ...+... 6 ...+... 7 ...+... 8
DName+++++++++++ETDsFrom+++To/L+++IDc.Keywords+++++++++++++++++++++++++++++++
D Customer        DS                      Qualified
D   Name                          35
D   State                          2
D   Postcode                      10
D   Phone                         10
D   Creditlimit                   11  2

D Vendor          DS                      Qualified
D   Name                          35
D   Address                       35
D   City                          21
D   State                          2
D   Postcode                      10
D   Phone                         10  0
```

In these examples, the RPG program must refer to subfields Customer.Name or Vendor.Name to refer to the Name subfield in either the Customer data structure or the Vendor data structure. Notice that the subfields can have identical names even if they don't have identical data attributes; in the above examples, Customer.Phone is an alphanumeric field while Vendor.Phone is a zoned decimal number. The data structures need not have identical subfields, and the subfields need not be in the same order in each data structure. You can use qualified subfield names almost anywhere in the program that will allow a variable name.

Tip
Use qualified data structures extensively to help document the origins of a data structure subfield. They are especially useful in large, complex programs and in those programs that employ many modular programming devices, such as subroutines and procedures (discussed later).

Using Like, Likeds, and Likerec

Several Definition specification keywords let you define data structures, data structure subfields, and standalone variables that "inherit" certain characteristics of other data items in the program. RPG uses the **Like, Likeds,** and **Likerec keywords** to define a new data item like an already defined "parent" data item.

The Like keyword defines a standalone variable or data structure subfield that takes on the length and the data type of another data item. When you define a data item with the Like keyword, the data type, decimal positions, and, usually, the length are left blank because the compiler will retrieve those attributes from the referenced parent. Here are some examples of using Like:

```
*.. 1 ...+... 2 ...+... 3 ...+... 4 ...+... 5 ...+... 6 ...+... 7 ...+... 8
DName++++++++++ETDsFrom+++To/L+++IDc.Keywords++++++++++++++++++++++++++++++++
 // Variables Firstname and Lastname are both character fields,
 // 20 bytes long
D Firstname       S             20
D Lastname        S                           Like(Firstname)

 // Variables Statetax and Fedtax are both zoned numeric fields, with
 // 7 digits and 7 decimals
D Statetax        S              7S 7
D Fedtax          S                           Like(Statetax)

 // Data structure Customer is a data structure, totaling 70 bytes.
 // Variable Label is a character standalone variable, 70 bytes long.
D Customer        DS
D   Name                                      Like(Lastname)
D   Address                    35
D   City                       21
D                               1
D   State                       2
D                               1
D   Postcode                   10

D Label           S                           Like(Customer)
```

In these examples, the newly defined data item uses the existing parent data item (another stand-alone variable, data structure, or data structure subfield) as a reference when assigning a data type, length, and number of decimal positions (if any). You can also adjust the size of the new character or numeric data item, based on the parent, by including an entry in the length positions (33–39) along with a plus sign (+) to add length or a minus sign (-) to subtract length.

```
*.. 1 ...+... 2 ...+... 3 ...+... 4 ...+... 5 ...+... 6 ...+... 7 ...+... 8
DName++++++++++ETDsFrom+++To/L+++IDc.Keywords++++++++++++++++++++++++++++++++
 // Variables Name and Longname are both character fields.
 // Name is 20 bytes long, Longname is 35 bytes long.
D Name            S             20
D Longname        S            +15           Like(Firstname)

 // Variable Unitsales is a packed decimal number, 9 digits, 2 decimals.
 // Variable Totalsales is a packed decimal number, 11 digits, 2 decimals.
D Unitsales       S              9 2
D Totalsales      S             +2            Like(Unitsales)
```

The Like keyword is useful in documenting data dependencies in your program and in ensuring the reliability of future program maintenance. In the above example, if Unitsales ever needs to be lengthened to, say, 13 digits, the RPG compiler will then automatically define Totalsales as 15 digits without any additional coding.

Use another keyword, Likeds (Like Data Structure), to define one data structure (or a data structure subfield) to be like another data structure, with the same subfields:

```
*.. 1 ...+... 2 ...+... 3 ...+... 4 ...+... 5 ...+... 6 ...+... 7 ...+... 8
DName++++++++++ETDsFrom+++To/L+++IDc.Keywords+++++++++++++++++++++++++++++++++
 // Data structure Vendor will have the same subfield structure as
 // data structure Customer
D Customer       DS                   Qualified
D   Name                    35
D   Address                 35
D   City                    21
D                            1
D   State                    2
D                            1
D   Postalcode              10
D   Origdate                     D   Inz(*Sys)

D Vendor         DS                   Likeds(Customer)
```

The subfields in the new data item will be identical to the parent data structure. The new data structure is implicitly qualified, even if the parent data structure is not qualified; this means that you must refer to the subfields in the new data structure by their qualified name (Vendor.Name, Vendor.Address, so on) even though you do not explicitly code the Qualified keyword. In the above example, we have also qualified the Customer data structure, for the sake of consistency.

In the above example, subfield Vendor.Origdate will not be automatically initialized to the current system date, even though Customer.Origdate is coded with the Inz keyword. The Like and Likeds keywords cause only the data attributes of the parent to be copied, not its values. We could, however, initialize a data structure with the same values as its parent by adding a special Inz value:

```
*.. 1 ...+... 2 ...+... 3 ...+... 4 ...+... 5 ...+... 6 ...+... 7 ...+... 8
DName++++++++++ETDsFrom+++To/L+++IDc.Keywords+++++++++++++++++++++++++++++++++
D Vendor         DS                   Likeds(Customer)
D                                     Inz(*Likeds)
```

Coding Inz(*Likeds) causes all the subfields in the new data structure to be initialized with the same values as the parent's initial values.

Similar to Likeds, the Likerec (Like Record Format) keyword defines a data structure (or a subfield) to be like a record format defined in the File specifications of the program. In the following example, both data structures, Before and After, have the same layout as the Custrec format in the Customers file (described in Chapter 3):

```
*.. 1 ...+... 2 ...+... 3 ...+... 4 ...+... 5 ...+... 6 ...+... 7 ...+... 8
FFilename++IPEASFRLen+LKLen+AIDevice+.Keywords+++++++++++++++++++++++++++++++
DName++++++++++ETDsFrom+++To/L+++IDc.Keywords+++++++++++++++++++++++++++++++++
FCustomers IF   E           K Disk

D Before          DS                  Likerec(Custrec)

D After           DS                  Likerec(Custrec)
```

Data structures using Likerec are similar to externally described data structures, but Likerec must refer to a record format that exists in a file described in File specifications. Data structures defined with Likerec are implicitly qualified, so this program would refer to Before.Address, After.Address, and so on.

An additional Likerec feature (also available with externally described data structures) allows you to restrict the subfields in the data structure to the key fields only. The following example uses the Employees1 logical file (from Chapter 3) to define a data structure that consists of two subfields, Empkeys.Lastname and Empkeys.Firstname—the two key fields from the record format:

```
*.. 1 ...+... 2 ...+... 3 ...+... 4 ...+... 5 ...+... 6 ...+... 7 ...+... 8
FFilename++IPEASFRLen+LKLen+AIDevice+.Keywords+++++++++++++++++++++++++++++++
DName++++++++++ETDsFrom+++To/L+++IDc.Keywords+++++++++++++++++++++++++++++++++
FEmployees1IF   E           K Disk

D Empkeys         DS                  Likerec(Emprec:*Keys)
```

Specifying the figurative constant *Keys as the second argument for the Likerec keyword restricts the data structure to using only the key field definitions from the record format.

Using Definitions in a Program

In this chapter, we've discussed how to define data items to your program using Definition specifications. To help you understand how you might use some of these definitions, we've added a few lines to the completed program from Chapter 3. This modified program produces an enhanced sales report that counts the number of sales made and calculates the total of all the sales on the report.

Before we can modify the program, we'll need to make some changes to the DDS for the printed report to accommodate the new data. The following DDS adds a Totals line to the Ytdslsrpt file, adds a couple of variables to the heading lines to hold the current system date and user profile, and makes a few other minor changes as well:

```
*.. 1 ...+... 2 ...+... 3 ...+... 4 ...+... 5 ...+... 6 ...+... 7 ...+... 8
AAN01N02N03T.Name++++++RLen++TDpBLinPosFunctions++++++++++++++++++++++++++++++
 * Printer file YTDSLSRPT, externally describing the sales report
A                                     REF(CUSTOMERS)
A          R HEADINGS                 SKIPB(2)
A                                    1'YTD Sales Report'
A                                   53'Date'
A            TODAY         L         58DATFMT(*USA)
A                                   71'Page'
A                                   76PAGNBR
A                                     EDTCDE(Z)
```

continued...

continued...

```
A                                          SPACEA(1)
 *
A                                          1'Printed By'
A              USERNAME        10         12SPACEA(2)
 *
A                                          1'Acct'
A                                          7'Sales'
A                                         63'YTD'
A                                         72'Date of'
A                                          SPACEA(1)
 *
A                                          2'ID'
A                                          7'Person'
A                                         15'Customer'
A                                         62'Sales'
A                                         71'Last Sale'
A                                          SPACEA(2)
 *
A         R DETAIL                          SPACEA(1)
A           ACCOUNTID  R                    1
A           SALESPERS  R                    8
A           NAME       R                   15
A           YTDSALES   R                   53EDTCDE(1)
A           LASTSALEDTR                    70
 *
A         R TOTALS                          SPACEB(1)
A           COUNT          7  0             7EDTCDE(Z)
A                                          17'Customers'
A           TOTALSALES    13  2            53EDTCDE(1)
A                                          59'* Total'
```

Once we have made the DDS changes and recompiled the printer file, we can make the required changes to the RPG program and recompile it.

```
*.. 1 ...+... 2 ...+... 3 ...+... 4 ...+... 5 ...+... 6 ...+... 7 ...+... 8
  // --------------------------------------------------------
  // This program produces a year-to-date sales report. The report data
  // comes directly from input file Customers.
  //     Date Written:  01/02/2007
  //
  // --------------------------------------------------------

  // ----------------------------- Files
FCustomers IF   E           K Disk
FYtdslsrpt O    E             Printer Oflind(Endofpage)

  // ----------------------- Standalone variables
D Endofpage       S             N   Inz(*On)
D Today           S             D   Inz(*Sys)
D Username        S            10   Inz(*User)
```

continued...

continued...

```
/Free

  // --------------------------- Main routine
  Read Customers;

  Dow Not %Eof(Customers);
    Count = Count + 1;
    Totalsales = Totalsales + Ytdsales;

    If Endofpage;
      Write Headings;
      Endofpage = *Off;
    Endif;

    Write Detail;
    Read Customers;
  Enddo;

  // ----------------------- End of program routine
  If Endofpage;
    Write Headings;
    Endofpage = *Off;
  Endif;

  Write Totals;
  *Inlr = *On;
  Return;

/End-Free
```

The F-spec for the printer file now refers to a named variable, Endofpage, as the overflow indicator instead of *In99, as it was in Chapter 3. Most programmers prefer named indicators instead of number indicators because they are more explanatory and less error prone. The first definition in the D-specs describes Endofpage as an indicator (type N) and gives it an initial value of *On. The indicator is initially *On so that headings will be printed on the first page, when the first Customers record is read. Because Endofpage is an indicator variable—sometimes called a logical variable—we can test whether it is *On or *Off with a simple logical test:

```
If Endofpage;
```

or

```
If Not Endofpage;
```

Note how much easier it is to read the expression with a carefully named indicator instead of a numbered one with no special significance.

The Today and Username variables are used by the printer file and are defined in the DDS for the externally described printer file. Ordinarily, because these variables are already defined in the DDS, we would not need to redefine them in the RPG code. But, by defining these variables in the RPG program, we can easily give them their desired initial values by coding the Inz keyword with their definitions. Because these variables are defined in two places (the DDS code and the RPG code), we need to be careful that the definitions in both places exactly match.

The Count and Totalsales variables are also defined in the DDS for the printer file, and we don't need to redefine them in the RPG program. But we can use those variables in calculations. The assignment expression

```
Count = Count + 1;
```

increments the current value of the Count variable by 1 each time it is processed. The assignment expression

```
Totalsales = Totalsales + Ytdsales;
```

adds the Ytdsales value for each record to the current value of Totalsales, thus keeping a running tally of the Totalsales amount for the final printed line. Before the program ends, it writes a Totals line to the printer file; this line includes the record count and the total sales amount.

The example program does not require the use of named constants or data structures. We'll cover those definitions later in this text, as they are needed.

Chapter Summary

RPG IV requires you to define all the variables your program will use, naming the variables and describing their data attributes (data type, length, and number of decimal positions, if any). Some fields are described within files, using DDS or Input specifications, while Definition specifications describe standalone variables that are not part of a database file. Definition specifications also define named constants and data structures to your program. Definition specifications enhance program organization by concentrating all data definition into a group of statements near the beginning of the program.

Once you've defined a standalone variable in a Definition specification, you can assign it a value, use it with operations, or print it. RPG IV supports more than a dozen specific data types, which you can specify in Definition specifications using a code in column 40. If you don't specify a code, RPG IV defaults to either character data or numeric data, depending on whether you specify a number of decimal positions. For standalone variables, numeric variables default to packed decimal; for data structures, numeric variables default to zoned decimal. The other most common numeric data types are signed and unsigned integers. Other common data types include date-related data (date, time, and timestamp) and indicator data, which has a value of *On or *Off.

You can use the Inz keyword with numeric literals, character literals, or figurative constants to assign initial values to a standalone variable. Literals and constants do not change during the processing of an RPG IV program. You do not enclose numeric literals within apostrophes; apostrophes signal to the computer the presence of a character literal, which cannot participate in arithmetic operations. Typed literals let you express other data values, such as dates or hexadecimal values. Figurative constants are built-in literals with specified values. The length of a figurative constant automatically adjusts to match the length of the variable with which the constant is used. Figurative constants include *Blank, *Blanks, *Hival, *Loval, *Zero, *Zeros, *All, *Off, *On, and *Null.

Definition specifications let you define named constants as well as standalone variables. This feature lets you refer to a constant by name instead of having to code the constant as a literal. The value of a named constant never changes during processing. In addition to numeric and character constants, you can define constants with other data values, such as dates and times, using typed literals.

Data structures, also defined with Definition specifications, organize multiple variables within a single section of contiguous portions of memory. Data structures let you subdivide fields into subfields and redefine fields with different data types or names. You can use either absolute notation or length notation to indicate the length and position of a subfield within a data structure. Most programmers prefer length notation, without a From position specified. The Overlay keyword lets you overlap fields within a data structure.

Data structures can be program-described or externally described. Qualified data structures help document the origins of a subfield by requiring that the program refer to the subfields by their qualified name. Qualified data structures also allow the program to have multiple data structures with identically named subfields.

The Like, Likeds, and Likerec keywords let you define data structures, data structure subfields, and standalone variables that inherit their data attributes from parent data items defined elsewhere in the program. These keywords document data dependencies within the program and simplify program maintenance.

Organizing Definition Specifications

Definition specifications impose some organization on your program by concentrating all the definitions in one physical area of the program. But you can further organize the program by coding D-specs in a predictable, consistent order. Generally, the order of Definition specifications is not critical to a successful compile—consistency is more important—but grouping definitions in the following order will simplify organization and maintenance (prototypes and procedure interfaces are discussed in Chapters 12 and 13):

- Main procedure prototype
- Procedure interface
- Other prototypes
- Named constants
- Data structures
- Standalone variables

Within each group of definitions, further organize the definitions in alphabetic order. You might find it useful to include a comment line at the top of each group of definitions, as a header, following the example program shown in this chapter.

Key Terms

binary numbers

Boolean data type

character literals

data structures

date

Definition specifications

Extname (External name)

figurative constants

floating point format

indicator data type

initial value

integers

Inz keyword

job date

left-adjusted

length notation

Like, Likeds and Likerec keywords

named constant

*Next

numeric literal

Overlay

packed decimal

positional notation

qualified data structure

right-adjusted

standalone variables

subfields

time

timestamp

typed literals

zoned decimal

Discussion/Review Questions

1. What is the main purpose of Definition specifications?
2. Why would you not use Definition specifications to describe file input?
3. What is a named constant?
4. What are the advantages of using named constants in a program?
5. Compare and contrast literals, named constants, and figurative constants.
6. What is the main difference between a constant and a variable?
7. When is it important to assign an initial value to a data item?
8. Which data types would be appropriate for storing money-related data? Why?
9. When would you use an indicator data type?
10. What kinds of capabilities can you gain by using data structures?
11. What is a figurative constant? What are possible uses for figurative constants? How does figurative constant *ALL work?
12. List five uses for subfields in data structures.
13. What are the advantages of using an externally described data structure?

Exercises

1. Code the following standalone variables using Definition specifications:
   - Total sales, with 11 digits precision
   - Product description, 30 bytes long
   - Sales tax rate percent
   - Transaction date

   Use variable names, lengths, and data types appropriate to the variables' use.

2. Code the following values as named constants:
   - A commission rate of 2.5 percent
   - The company name "Acme Explosives Company"
   - The FICA cut-off income of $76,400
   - An edit word for editing Social Security numbers
   - The date January 1, 2000

3. Code a data structure for organizing information to be printed on a label. The subfields should include name, Social Security number, phone number, two address lines, city, state/province, postal code, and country. Variable names and lengths should be appropriate to the variables' use.

4. Using the data structure you created in Exercise 3; redefine the Social Security number and phone number using the Overlay keyword.

5. Code two qualified data structures (Student and Employee). Each of these data structures will have the same named fields: ID, Firstname, Lastname, Streetaddress, City, State, Phonenumber, and Socialsecuritynumber. The Social Security number and phone number should be redefined using the Overlay keyword.

6. How would you reference the area code in the Student data structure from Exercise 5?

Programming Assignments

1. Modify the CompuSell customer listing program from Chapter 2 (Programming Assignment 1) to include two total lines at the end of the report: the Count of all customers and the total Balance Due. The total balance due should appear in line below the balance due column in the rest of the report. Use standalone variables to store the count and the total.

```
                    1         2         3         4         5         6         7         8         9         1
                                                                                                             0
   1234567890123456789012345678901234567890123456789012345678901234567890123456789012345678901234567890
 1 XX/XX/XX                                                                                    Page XXØX
 2                        CompuSell Customer Listing By Customer Last Name
 3
 4
 5 Employee First        Last           Street
 6 Number   Name         Name           Address          City             State Zip Code     Due
 7 999999   XXXXXXXXXX   XXXXXXXXXXXXXX XXXXXXXXXXXXXX   XXXXXXXXXXXXXX    XX    99999-9999    9,999.99
 8 999999   XXXXXXXXXX   XXXXXXXXXXXXXX XXXXXXXXXXXXXX   XXXXXXXXXXXXXX    XX    99999-9999    9,999.99
 9 999999   XXXXXXXXXX   XXXXXXXXXXXXXX XXXXXXXXXXXXXX   XXXXXXXXXXXXXX    XX    99999-9999    9,999.99
10                                                                     Total Balance Due $999,999.99
11                                                                     Total Customers Processed 9999
12
```

2. CompuSell's Marketing Department wants a list of suppliers. This report should be in State then City order. This will require you to create a logical file over the CSSUPP file, and you will have to use control break logic. Use a data structure to redefine the Telephone number. The Marketing department also wants to know the total number of Suppliers in each state.

```
                    1         2         3         4         5         6         7         8         9         1
                                                                                                             0
   1234567890123456789012345678901234567890123456789012345678901234567890123456789012345678901234567890
 1 XX/XX/XX                                                                                    Page XXØX
 2                        CompuSell Supplier Listing By State By City
 3
 4 Supplier Supplier                     Contact
 5 Code     Name                         Name                              City                   Phone
 6 State XX
 7 999999   XXXXXXXXXXXXXXXXXXXX         XXXXXXXXXXXXXXXXXXXXXXXXXXXXXX     XXXXXXXXXXXXXXXXXXXX   999-999-9999
 8 999999   XXXXXXXXXXXXXXXXXXXX         XXXXXXXXXXXXXXXXXXXXXXXXXXXXXX     XXXXXXXXXXXXXXXXXXXX   999-999-9999
 9 999999   XXXXXXXXXXXXXXXXXXXX         XXXXXXXXXXXXXXXXXXXXXXXXXXXXXX     XXXXXXXXXXXXXXXXXXXX   999-999-9999
10                                                                      Total Suppliers 999
11 State XX
12 999999   XXXXXXXXXXXXXXXXXXXX         XXXXXXXXXXXXXXXXXXXXXXXXXXXXXX     XXXXXXXXXXXXXXXXXXXX   999-999-9999
```

3. CompuSell's Accounting department wants an inventory report by Supplier ID (SUPCOD) by Part Number (PRODNO). This will require a logical file built over the CSINVP file, and you will have to use control break logic. Totals required for this report are total average cost and number of parts in inventory. This report also requires a total quantity of parts on hand (QTYOH) and the total average cost (AVGCST) of inventory.

```
              1         2         3         4         5         6         7         8         9        10
    12345678901234567890123456789012345678901234567890123456789012345678901234567890123456789012345678901234567890
 1  XX/XX/XX                                                                              Page XXØX
 2                CompuSell Inventory Listing By Supplier By Part Number
 3
 4  Product                               Selling   Current  Average  Quantity  Average
 5  Number   Description                  Price     Cost     Cost     On Hand   Cost Extended
 6
 7  Supplier ID XXX
 8  999999   XXXXXXXXXXXXXXXXXXXXXXXXXX   9999.99   9999.99  9999.99  9999      999999.99
 9  999999   XXXXXXXXXXXXXXXXXXXXXXXXXX   9999.99   9999.99  9999.99  9999      999999.99
10  999999   XXXXXXXXXXXXXXXXXXXXXXXXXX   9999.99   9999.99  9999.99  9999      999999.99
11  Total Part Numbers          999
12  Supplier ID XXX
13  999999   XXXXXXXXXXXXXXXXXXXXXXXXXX   9999.99   9999.99  9999.99 9999       999999.99
14
15  Total Part Numbers        99999
16  Total Quantity On Hand    999999
17  Total Average Cost     $999,999.99
```

4. CompuSell's Accounting department wants an order report by Order Number (ORDNBR). This will require a logical file built over the CSCSTP and CSORDP files. The Date Ordered field is stored in *yyyymmdd* and should be printed in *mm/dd/yyyy* format. The total amount of all orders and the total number of orders should be printed. The format should exactly match the grid below.

```
              1         2         3         4         5         6         7         8
    12345678901234567890123456789012345678901234567890123456789012345678901234567890123
 1  XX/XX/XX                                                              Page XXXX
 2                    CompuSell Order Listing By Order Number
 3
 4  Order    Customer  Customer                     Phone        Order      Order
 5  Number   Number    First Name Last Name         Number       Date       Total
 6  999999   999999    XXXXXXXXXX XXXXXXXXXXXXXXX    999-999-9999 mm/dd/yyyy 9999.99
 7  999999   999999    XXXXXXXXXX XXXXXXXXXXXXXXX    999-999-9999 mm/dd/yyyy 9999.99
 8  999999   999999    XXXXXXXXXX XXXXXXXXXXXXXXX    999-999-9999 mm/dd/yyyy 9999.99
 9
10  Total Number of Orders 9999
11  Total Amount of Orders $999,999.00
12
```

Chapter 5

Using Arithmetic Operations and Functions

 ## Chapter Overview

Now that you can write simple read/write programs in RPG IV, you're ready to learn how to perform arithmetic calculations in your programs. You will learn how to express calculations using free-form expressions and appropriate operation codes. You'll also be introduced to some of RPG's built-in functions that facilitate going beyond the traditional addition, subtraction, multiplication, and division functions used by basic arithmetic. In addition, you will learn how to determine the correct size for fields that store the results of arithmetic operations and how to round calculations to avoid truncation.

Simple Numeric Assignment

RPG IV's **assignment operation** is Eval (Evaluate Expression). Assigning a value to a field simply means giving the field a value. In previous chapters, we used the Eval operation to evaluate simple assignment expressions. Eval always works in conjunction with an assignment expression, which consists of a result (target) variable, followed by the assignment operator (=), followed by an expression. An Eval statement says, in effect, "Evaluate the expression to the right of the equal sign (=) and store its value in the result variable to the left of the equal sign." The Eval statement appears in the Calculation specifications of the program. The general format for an Eval statement is shown below.

```
Eval result = expression;
```

Explicitly coding the Eval operation in free-format calculations is optional, unless you need to use a special feature, such as rounding (discussed later). You can simply code the assignment expression, and the RPG IV compiler will assume that it should use Eval to make the assignment. In this book, the examples will not explicitly code the Eval operation unless it is required.

The following examples demonstrate how to use Eval for simple numeric assignment. In each case, the numeric field that appears to the left of the equal sign receives the value that appears to the right of the sign. The value to the right may be a field, literal, or named constant, but it must already be defined as numeric. You cannot define the result field within the Eval statement; it must be defined elsewhere in the program (e.g., in a Definition specification).

```
/Free
    Counter = 0;              // Initialize a counter
    Taxrate = .045;          // Assign a value > 0
    Absolutezero = -273.16;  // Assign a value < 0
    Amtowed = Balancedue;    // Assign a field value
/End-Free
```

Assigning Values with Figurative Constants

RPG IV lets you assign figurative constant *Zero (or *Zeros) to numeric variables to fill the variables with zeros. You can also assign the special values ***Hival** and ***Loval** to numeric variables. For a numeric variable, *Hival is the maximum positive value allowed for the data representation; for example, for a packed or zoned decimal variable, *Hival is all 9s and a plus sign (+). Assigning *Loval fills a numeric variable with the minimum possible value; for example, for a packed or zoned decimal variable, *Loval is all 9s and a minus sign (–). Different numeric representations will have different values for *Hival and *Loval. To find the possible range of values for integers and unsigned integers, see the table in Chapter 4.

```
/Free
   Totalsales = *Zeros;
   Count = *Loval;
/End-Free
```

Using Eval for Arithmetic

In the previous sections, we saw how to use Eval for simple numeric assignment. The Eval operation also provides a flexible and powerful method for assigning numeric fields the results of simple or complex arithmetic calculations in a single step. The expression for evaluation can contain the **arithmetic operators** + (addition), – (subtraction), * (multiplication), / (division), and ** (**exponentiation**, or raising a value to a power), as well as parentheses, relational symbols (e.g., <, >), logical operators (e.g., AND, OR), and built-in functions (discussed later in this chapter).

A single expression can contain as many arithmetic operators, numeric literals, and numeric fields as needed to accomplish a desired calculation.

```
/Free
   // Examples of calculations using the Eval operation
   Withhold = Fica + Statetax + Fedtax;
   Netpay = Grosspay - Withhold;
   Grossprofit = Cost * .6 * Qtysold;
   Avgamount = Totamount / Counter;
   Numsquared = Number ** 2;
/End-Free
```

All values used in the arithmetic expression to the right of the equal sign must, of course, be numeric fields, literals, or constants. One other restriction arises when you use division in an expression. Remember that division by zero is mathematically impossible. A runtime error occurs if, at the time of the division, the divisor (the part of an expression immediately to the right of the division sign) evaluates to zero.

When the arithmetic expression contains more than one operator, the computer uses the **rules of precedence** from mathematics to determine the order in which to perform the operations. Exponentiation has the highest precedence, followed by multiplication and division, and then addition and subtraction. When an expression contains operations of equal precedence, the system executes them in order from left to right. You can use parentheses to change the order in which the computer executes these operations; operations within parentheses are performed before any operations outside the parentheses.

```
/Free
    // In this example, the multiplication will occur before the
    // subtraction (because of operator precedence rules)
    Answer = A * B - 1;

    // In this example, the parentheses cause the subtraction to take place
    // before the multiplication
    Answer = A * (B - 1);
/End-Free
```

The expression can include as many (or as few) blanks between fields, literals, and operations as you like to make the expression readable and easy to understand. If it is necessary, you can simply continue the expression anywhere on subsequent lines and then end it with a semicolon (;) when the expression is finished. The following code illustrates the use of a continuation line with the Eval operation.

```
/Free
    Pay = Hourlyrate * 40 +
          1.5 * Hourlyrate * (Hoursworked - 40);
 /End-Free
```

In this example, the plus sign (+) in the expression is an addition operator, not a continuation character; no special character is usually necessary to continue an expression.

Those of you who have studied algebra recognize the similarity between assignment expressions and algebraic equations. Don't be misled by this similarity, however. An algebraic equation asserts equality; an assignment expression instructs the computer to perform the calculation to the right of the equal sign and then assign the result to the field left of the equal sign. In algebra, the equation $x = x + 1$ is a logical impossibility; within an Eval operation, $x = x + 1$ is a perfectly legitimate instruction that tells the computer to take the value of field x, add 1 to it, and store the result in field x.

In fact, this form of assignment expression is frequently used in RPG IV programming for counting and accumulating. For example, to count the number of customers in a file, you would increment a counter field (i.e., add 1 to it) each time you processed a customer record. Or, to accumulate employees' salaries, you would add each salary to a field representing the grand total of the salaries.

```
/Free
    Counter = Counter + 1;                    // Increment a counter
    Grandtotal = Grandtotal + Empsalary;      // Accumulate a total
/End-Free
```

You can also decrement a counter or decrease the value of an accumulator by using subtraction:

```
/Free
    Countdown = Countdown - 1;
    Inventory = Inventory - Orderqty;
/End-Free
```

For these types of expressions, which use the result variable as the first operand in the expression, RPG offers several **compound arithmetic/assignment operators**: +=, -=, *=, /=, and **-. These operators allow you to code this common type of expression in a more concise manner. They perform the requested arithmetic function, using the result variable as the first operand of the operation. For example, with +=, the expression is added to the result variable; the following expressions are equivalent to the ones shown earlier:

```
/Free
   Counter += 1;
   Grandtotal += Empsalary;
   Countdown -= 1;
   Inventory -= Orderqty;
/End-Free
```

When you use these compound assignment operators with complex expressions, the entire expression is evaluated as a unit before the operator is processed. You can think of the entire concise expression as being enclosed in parentheses. The following expressions are equivalent:

```
/Free
   Totalsale += Price + Price * Taxrate;
   Totalsale = Totalsale + (Price + Price * Taxrate);
/End-Free
```

Of course, you can also explicitly code parentheses in the concise expression, if appropriate. To simplify your code and prevent possible errors, most programmers restrict the use of the compound assignment operators to simple expressions.

Numeric Overflow, Truncation, and Field Sizes

With all arithmetic operations, one of your jobs as a programmer is to determine appropriate length and decimal position entries for result fields. It is important to allow sufficient room; otherwise, if a calculation produces an answer too big to store in the result field, a numeric overflow error or truncation will occur.

The computer stores the result of any arithmetic expression in the result field based on decimal position alignment. If the value to be stored is too large for the result field, overflow or truncation occurs, resulting in a runtime error or a loss of digits. If the overflow occurs on the left side (high-order digits portion) of the result, a **numeric overflow error** occurs. A numeric overflow error is a runtime error, which means your program will stop and display an error message to which the operator must respond. **Truncation** occurs when the loss of digits is from the right end (the decimal portions) of the result field. Overflow or truncation occurs only when the answer has more digits (left or right of the decimal) than the result. If the answer has fewer digits, the system simply zero fills the unneeded positions.

Overflow and truncation are important to understand because if they occur during a program's execution, the program may simply continue to run without issuing a warning that digits have been lost, or the program may end abnormally (abend). Losing 1/1000 of a dollar may not be the end of the world (although on a large run, it could add up), but losing $10,000 would probably cause your company some distress. Furthermore, program abends reflect poorly on the programmer.

In RPG IV, all arithmetic expressions automatically—and without warning—truncate extra decimal positions (**low-order truncation**) to fit the value in the result variable's decimal positions. **High-order overflow** generates a runtime error that causes the program to end abnormally.

How do you determine the size of a result field to ensure that truncation or abends do not inadvertently happen? Eval keeps track of any intermediate results that occur during the evaluation of its expression, maintaining full precision internally (up to limits imposed by numeric data types) until the expression is completely evaluated and ready to be stored in the result field. However, you must analyze the expression—that is, consider the operations it performs and whether or not it occurs within a loop—to estimate the size needed for the final result. Fortunately, some guidelines exist for result variable definition to help you ensure that your result variables are large enough to store the calculated answers. The following sections present some guidelines for determining variable sizes of results occurring from two values and an operation. When in doubt, you can always manually perform some representative calculations that mirror what you want the computer to do to guide you in this matter.

Sizing Results for Addition

To avoid numeric overflow when adding two values, you should define the result field with *one more* position *left of the decimal* than the larger of the addends' integer digit positions. Positions to the right of the decimal in the result field should equal the larger of the decimal positions of the addends. For example, if you're adding two fields, one defined as length 3 with two decimal positions (i.e., one to the left and two to the right of the decimal) and one defined as length 6 with three decimal positions (i.e., three to the left, three to the right of the decimal), your result field should be defined as length 7 with three decimal positions (four to the left, three to the right). To see why this rule eliminates the possibility of numeric overflow, simply do the addition with the largest possible values the addends can contain and you will understand its basis:

```
    999.999
  +   9.99
  = 1009.989
```

When you are using addition to count or accumulate, the value of the result keeps getting larger and larger each time the calculation is performed (for example, when accumulating individuals' calculated gross pay figures to generate a grand total gross pay). In this case, to determine the necessary size of the result variable, you need to have an approximate idea of how many times the calculation will be performed (i.e., how many employees you will process). Once you have this estimate, follow the rule for multiplication, given below.

Sizing Results for Subtraction

To eliminate the chance of numeric overflow with subtraction, follow the rule given for addition. This advice may seem strange at first, until you realize that you must provide for the possibility of subtracting a negative number, which essentially turns the problem into one of addition.

Thus, to avoid numeric overflow when subtracting two values, define the result variable to have one more digit position to the left of the decimal position than the larger of the high-order positions of the two values. And define the result variable to have the same number of decimal positions as the larger of the number of decimal positions of the two values.

Sizing Results for Multiplication

When multiplying, to determine the needed number of digit positions in a result variable, add the number of positions to the left of the decimal positions of the two multipliers and use the resulting value to determine the number of high-order digits in the result. The sum of the number of positions to the right of the decimal in the multipliers represents the number of positions your result variable must have to the right of the decimal.

For example, if you were multiplying 999.99 by 99.99, your result field would require five places to the left of the decimal and four to the right to store the answer without overflow. In RPG IV, this would mean a variable nine positions long, with four decimal positions:

```
    999.99
  *  99.99
  = 99989.0001
```

Sizing Results for Division

When dividing by a value of 1 or greater, the maximum required positions, to the left of the decimal in the result, is the number of high-order decimal positions in the dividend (the value *being* divided). To understand this point, recognize that dividing any value by 1 yields the original value; dividing by any value greater than 1 will yield a value smaller than the original value.

When dividing by values less than 1, computing the number of digit positions in the result becomes a more complicated process; the smaller the divisor, the more significant positions needed in the result variable. If you are working with divisors less than 1, your safest approach is to hand calculate with some representative values to get a sense of the size needed to store your answer.

Because few divisions work out evenly, there is no way to guarantee you will provide enough decimal positions to avoid low-order truncation. In general, you choose the number of decimal positions for the result variable based on the degree of significance, or accuracy, that the calculation warrants. Because most business data processing deals with calculations involving dollars and cents, it usually makes sense to carry out intermediate calculations with the maximum needed or the maximum allowable number of decimal positions (whichever is smaller) and then to reduce that to two decimal positions in the final calculation.

Rounding

When you store a value in a result variable that has fewer decimal positions than the calculated answer, common business practice dictates that you should always round your answer rather than let the system truncate it. Rounding is sometimes called **half adjusting** because of the technique computers use to accomplish this feat. The computer adds half the value of your rightmost desired decimal position to the digit immediately to the right of that decimal position before storing the answer in the result field. Because the value added is half the value of the least-significant digit position of your result, the term "half adjust" came into being.

For example, assume the computer has calculated an answer of 3.14156 that you want to store, in rounded form, in a result field defined as length 4 with three decimal positions. The computer will add 0.0005 to the answer (i.e., 1/2 of 0.001, the lowest decimal position you are retaining in your result), yielding 3.14206. It then stores this value in the result field, truncated to three decimal positions, as 3.142. If you had defined the result as length 3 with two decimal positions, the computer would add 0.005 (1/2 of 0.01) to 3.14156, yielding 3.14656, and store that answer in the result as 3.14.

Fortunately, even if you don't completely understand how the computer rounds, the method RPG IV uses to specify that rounding should take place is simple: You just enter an H (for half adjust) within parentheses immediately following the operation code of the calculation whose result you want rounded. RPG IV calls this entry an **operation extender**, because it extends the function that the operation would normally perform. The following examples show the use of the (H) operation extender.

```
/Free
  // Sample calculations specifying that the result should be rounded
    Eval(H) Interest = Rate * Loanamt;
    Eval(H) Avgamount = Totamount / Counter;
    Eval(H) Yards = Sqyards **.5;
/End-Free
```

Note that you must include the (H) in every calculation line where you want rounding to occur, even if those calculations use the same result field. The compiler will *not* warn you if you inadvertently omit an extender. Note also, that you must explicitly code the Eval operation if you are going to use the (H) extender.

```
/Free
  // In the below calcs, rounding is specified in each calculation
  // that is to result in a rounded value for interest
    Eval(H) Interest = Loanamt * Stdrate;
    Eval(H) Interest = Altamt * Primerate;
/End-Free
```

Although you most often need to round when multiplying or dividing, you can also specify rounding for addition and subtraction operations, as well as for multiplication and division. Recognize that you do not always need to round when multiplying. For example, consider the following expression:

```
Inventoryvalue = Qtyonhand * Unitprice;
```

If Qtyonhand is an integer (whole number) and Unitprice is stored as dollars and cents (e.g., length 4 with two decimal positions), the resulting answer will never have more than two decimal positions, so you do *not* need to round the answer to store it in Inventoryvalue, defined as length 6 with two decimal positions.

Caution

Sometimes, out of either uncertainty or laziness, programmers decide to play it safe by rounding all arithmetic operations, regardless of whether the rounding is needed. Avoid this practice. The RPG IV compiler will issue a warning message about unnecessary half adjusting, performance may suffer, and rounding when uncalled for reflects poorly on your programming skills and/or style.

Improving Eval Precision

After accounting for all issues involving operator precedence, the Eval operation evaluates complex expressions from left to right, automatically allocating memory for any intermediate values the operation may need to evaluate an expression. These intermediate numeric values are limited in size to 63 total digits, including digits to the right of the decimal. Eval uses rules similar to those discussed above to avoid size overflow within these intermediate values. In some complex expressions, or with some large operands, Eval may be forced to truncate low-order decimal positions from an intermediate result in order to fit the intermediate field into 63 total digits. This truncation may affect the precision of Eval's results.

To ensure the best accuracy when using Eval, you should instruct RPG that no intermediate value should have fewer decimal places than the end result. This instruction, called the **result decimal positions rule** for evaluating expressions, is *not* the rule RPG uses by default. There are two ways to invoke this rule:

- Using the **Expropts Control specification keyword**
- Using the (R) operation code extender

Typically, you will want to make the result decimal positions rule the default method within an RPG program by including the following Control specification keyword at the beginning of each program:

```
*.. 1 ...+... 2 ...+... 3 ...+... 4 ...+... 5 ...+... 6 ...+... 7 ...+... 8
HKeywords++++++++++++++++++++++++++++++++++++++++++++++++++++++++++++++++++++
H Expropts(*Resdecpos)
```

When you include this keyword value, the RPG program will use the result decimal positions rule as its default method for evaluating all expressions; using this rule will help ensure adequate decimal precision throughout the program. If you do not include this Control specification—or if you specify Expropts(*Maxdigits)—the program will use its own default rule, called the **maximum digits rule**, which may cause incorrect results for complex expressions.

If you want a single Eval operation to evaluate an expression with a different rule than you specified in the Control specifications, you can override the rule with an operation code extender. Specifying Eval(R) will force Eval to use the result decimal positions rule; Eval(M) will force the maximum digits rule. Note that you can combine several operation code extenders within the parentheses after the operation; in the following case, not only do we ensure Eval precision, but we also round (half adjust) the result.

```
Eval(HR) Pay = Hourlyrate * 40 + 1.5 * Hourlyrate * (Hoursworked - 40);
```

Note that the half adjusting will occur only once, after the entire expression is evaluated. Using the (H) extender will not cause the intermediate results (i.e., the individual parts of the expression) to be rounded.

Using Built-in Functions

RPG IV supports many **built-in functions (BIFs)** that you use in conjunction with free-form expressions. These provide new functions that aren't available by coding simple expressions. Built-in functions always begin with a percent sign (%). You typically code built-in functions within free-format expressions in the program. You've already seen how to use the %Eof built-in function to return the end-of-file condition to a program. In addition to returning file operation results, BIFs can simplify complex calculations, perform string operations and perform data type conversion. In this chapter, we'll examine some functions that you can use in arithmetic calculations.

%Abs (Absolute Value)

The %Abs (Absolute value) built-in function calculates the absolute value of a numeric expression (or a numeric field or literal). This BIF essentially removes the sign from an expression's result. You specify the expression within parentheses immediately following the %Abs notation in the expression:

```
/Free
    // In this example, Transtotal will be positive regardless of whether
    // the expression results in a positive or a negative number.
    Transtotal = %Abs(Debits - Credits);
/End-Free
```

%Div (Divide)

The %Div (Divide) built-in function performs integer division of two numbers (literals, fields, or expressions). The two numbers are passed as arguments, within parentheses and separated by a colon (:), immediately following the %Div notation. The arguments must be numeric values with no decimal places. The result of the division is always also numeric with no decimal places. The division operator (/), on the other hand, performs precise division, including decimal places in the quotient if the result field is defined with decimal places.

```
/Free
   // Convert total minutes to hours by dividing total minutes by 60.
   // Hours is accurate to the number of decimal places defined for it.
   Hours = Minutes/60;

   // The %Div BIF will return only the integer portion of Hours,
   // regardless of how many decimal places are defined for it.
   Hours = %Div(Minutes:60);
/End-Free
```

%Rem (Remainder)

The %Rem (Remainder) built-in function returns the remainder (sometimes called the *modulus*) when dividing two numbers (literals, fields, or expressions). The two numbers are passed as two arguments immediately following the %Rem notation. Although %Rem is often used with the %Div function, it is not necessary to actually perform the division operation in order to get the remainder.

```
/Free
   // Convert total minutes to hours and minutes by dividing total minutes
   // by 60 to get hours and then returning the remainder as Minutes.
   Hours = %Div(Minutes:60);
   Minutes = %Rem(Minutes:60);
/End-Free
```

%Sqrt (Square Root)

The %Sqrt (Square Root) function returns the square root of a numeric expression. The expression is included in parentheses immediately following the %Sqrt notation. The %Sqrt function returns a value that is accurate to the number of decimal places defined for the result; you may use the (H) extender with Eval if you want to round the result.

```
Hypotenuse = %Sqrt(Length**2 + Width**2);
```

Data Conversion Functions

RPG is a **strictly typed language**. This means that all the operands in an expression must be of compatible data types; the program cannot mix numeric data and character variables in the same expression, even if the character variables include only numbers. Several built-in functions convert character expressions to numeric formats or force numeric expressions into a specific numeric size. These conversion functions are

- %Dec (Convert to packed decimal format)
- %Dech (Convert to packed decimal format with half adjust)
- %Int (Convert to signed integer format)
- %Inth (Convert to signed integer format with half adjust)

- %Uns (Convert to unsigned integer format)
- %Unsh (Convert to unsigned integer format with half adjust)
- %Float (Convert to floating point format)

The %Dec (Convert to packed decimal format) function converts the result of a numeric, character, or date expression to a packed decimal format of the precision you specify. The numeric expression is coded as the first parameter within parentheses following %Dec. The next two parameters indicate the number of digits and the number of decimal positions in the result.

```
/Free
   Result = %Dec(Hours*Rate : 7 : 2);

   // This formula calculates a monthly payment, converting it to a
   // 13-digit packed number with two decimal places
   Payment = %Dec(Principal * (((Interest / 12) *
                  (1 + (Interest / 12)) ** Months) /
                  (((1 + (Interest / 12)) ** Months) - 1))
                  : 13 : 2);
/End-Free
```

A related function, %Dech (Convert to packed decimal format with half adjust), performs the same data conversion but half adjusts the result. This feature is useful when you want to round individual components of a complex expression. Recall that when you code the (H) extender for Eval, the half adjusting occurs only once, after the entire expression is evaluated. Using the (H) extender will not cause the intermediate results to be rounded, but by using %Dech, you can round just a portion of the expression.

```
/Free
   // This formula calculates total pay, by first calculating regular pay
   // and overtime pay, rounding each component (accurate to 11 digits
   // with two decimal places), then adding them together
   Pay = %Dech(Hourlyrate * 40 : 11 :2) +
         %Dech(1.5 * Hourlyrate * (Hoursworked - 40) : 11 : 2);

   // This formula calculates a monthly payment, rounding the result,
   // returning a 13-digit packed number with two decimal places
   Payment = %Dech(Principal * (((Interest / 12) *
                   (1 + (Interest / 12)) ** Months) /
                   (((1 + (Interest / 12)) ** Months) - 1))
                   : 13 : 2);
/End-Free
```

The integer-related functions perform functions similar to %Dec but return integer (signed or unsigned) results:

```
/Free
   // Find the area of a circle as a rounded whole number
   Result = %Inth(3.14159 * Radius**2);

   // Truncate the decimal positions from a packed number,
   // to allow it to be used an an array element (no rounding)
   X = %Uns(Hrsworked);
/End-Free
```

You can also use any of the conversion functions to convert character expressions to numeric representation. This feature is useful when you need to use a character variable's value within an arithmetic expression. The character value must, of course, ultimately be numeric information; it can include a sign (either preceding or following the numbers) and a decimal point, as well as blanks anywhere in the data. Floating point numeric data is allowed only when using the %Float function to convert a character value to floating point format. The following code illustrates some examples of using these functions to convert character data:

```
*.. 1 ...+... 2 ...+... 3 ...+... 4 ...+... 5 ...+... 6 ...+... 7 ...+... 8
DName+++++++++++ETDsFrom+++To/Len+IDc.Keywords+++++++++++++++++++++++++++++++
D Char1           S             11     Inz('123.456789-')
D Char2           S             11     Inz(' + 9 . 876 ')
D Char3           S             11     Inz(' - 3.14 e-1')
D Result          S              9 5

 /Free
    Result = %Dec(Char1:5:2);             // Result = -123.45000
    Result = %Dech(Char2:5:2);            // Result =    9.88000
    Result = %Dech(Char2:5:2) / 3;        // Result =    3.29333
    Result = %Int(Char2:5:2);             // Result =    9.00000
    Result = %Inth(Char2:5:2);            // Result =   10.00000
    Result = %Uns(Char1:5:2);             // Result =  123.00000
    Result = %Float(Char3);               // Result =    0.31400
 /End-Free
```

RPG IV supports many other built-in functions, and you'll learn about those functions throughout the text. Now, though, you know the key information about how to use built-in functions in your RPG IV program. BIFs always begin with a % sign. They are coded within free-form expressions. If you need to pass arguments to a BIF, pass them within parentheses immediately following the name of the BIF, and separate multiple arguments with colon separators:

```
%function(argument1:argument2:...)
```

Chapter Summary

RPG IV provides the Eval operation with standard arithmetic operators to use for computations. Eval can express complex arithmetic calculations in a single, free-form expression that can continue over several lines, if necessary. Such expressions can include the arithmetic operators +, –, *, /, and **; parentheses; numeric fields; and numeric literals. You can use numeric fields, numeric literals and figurative constants in arithmetic calculations.

You may usually forego explicitly coding the Eval operation; simply code the assignment expression instead. To improve Eval's precision in complex expressions and/or with large operands, you should always specify keyword Expropts(*Resdecpos) in the program's Control specifications.

Calculations often involve creating new fields to store the results of the calculations. You must define these new fields by specifying their data type, length, and number of decimal positions (if numeric) within Definition specifications. The size of result fields should be large enough to avoid numeric overflow and truncation. If the result of an arithmetic operation contains more decimal positions than you want to store, you should round the calculation.

RPG IV supports many built-in functions to simplify complex calculations and perform data type conversion. BIFs always begin with a % sign. They are coded within free-form expressions.

To pass values to a built-in function, enclose the values within parentheses immediately following the name of the BIF; separate multiple values with colon separators.

The following table summarizes the operation codes and built-in functions discussed in this chapter. Optional entries are shown within curly braces ({}):

Function or operation	Description	Syntax
%Abs	Absolute value	%Abs(*numeric-expression*)
%Dec %Dech	Convert to packed decimal format (with optional half adjust)	%Dec(*expression* {: *precision* : *decimals*}) %Dech(*expression* : *precision* : *decimals*)
%Div	Integer division	%Div(*dividend* : *divisor*)
Eval	Evaluate expression	{Eval{(hmr)}} *assignment-expression*
%Float	Convert to floating point format	%Float(*expression*)
%Int %Inth	Convert to integer format (with optional half adjust)	%Int(*expression*) %Inth(*expression*)
%Rem	Integer remainder	%Rem(*dividend* : *divisor*)
%Sqrt	Square root	%Sqrt(*numeric-expression*)
%Uns %Unsh	Convert to unsigned integer format (with optional half adjust)	%Uns(*expression*) %Unsh(*expression*)

Key Terms

arithmetic operators
assignment operation
built-in functions (BIFs)
compound arithmetic/assignment operators
conversion functions
exponentiation
Expropts Control specification keyword
half adjusting
High-order overflow
*Hival
low-order truncation
*Loval
maximum digits rule
numeric overflow error
operation extender
result decimal positions rule
rules of precedence
strictly typed language
truncation

Discussion/Review Questions

1. Why do you think RPG IV has relatively limited mathematical capabilities?
2. What is the difference between assigning a value to a field using the INZ keyword in Definition specifications and assigning a value to a field in Calculation specifications?
3. Why does it make sense that the result of a Calculation specification or a free-form expression cannot be a literal?
4. What two mathematical impossibilities will result in a program error if your program tries to execute them?
5. Summarize the rules of thumb for determining how large to define result fields for arithmetic operations.
6. When should you round an arithmetic operation?
7. Name three uses for operation code extenders.
8. Would it be better to set Eval precision rules to use the result decimal positions rule using a Control specification keyword or an Eval operation code extender? Why?
9. Give three examples using data conversion functions in RPG IV.
10. What are some of the advantages of using built-in functions (BIFs)?
11. Why is it important for a programmer to understand how RPG IV handles rounding?
12. How do you invoke the Expropts keyword? What effect does it have on the program?

Exercises

1. Write the calculations to discount field OldPrice (six digits, two decimal positions) by 10 percent to yield NewPrice.
2. Write the calculations to convert a temperature in Fahrenheit to Centigrade, using the following formula:

   $C = F(F - 32) / 9$

   Assume F and C are three positions each with zero decimal positions.
3. Write the calculations to convert a measurement taken in inches (field Inches, five positions with zero decimal positions) into the same measurement expressed as yards, feet, and inches.
4. Code the calculations needed to determine the cost of wall-to-wall carpeting for a room. Field RmLength (three positions, one decimal) contains the room length in feet; field RmWidth (also three positions, one decimal) contains the room's width in feet; and field CostPerYard (four positions, two decimals) contains the cost per yard of the selected carpet.
5. Write the calculations to determine the Economic Order Quantity (*EOQ*), using the formula

   EOQ = square root of (2*DO* / *C*)

   where D (five positions, zero decimals) represents annual demand for product; O (five positions, two decimals) represents costs to place one order; and C (six positions, two decimals) represents carrying costs.

Programming Assignments

1. Wexler University wants a program that will produce a student grade report. Input file WUEXAMP (described in Appendix F) contains information about students in a class and five exam grades for each student.

   The program should calculate an average exam grade for each student. The school also wants to know the average exam grade for the class as a whole (i.e., the average of the averages). The desired report layout is shown below. Notice that just the initial of each student's first name is to be printed with the last name.

```
          1         2         3         4         5         6         7         8
 1234567890123456789012345678901234567890123456789012345678901234567890
1    XX/XX/XX            WEXLER U. STUDENT GRADE REPORT        PAGE XXØX
2
3                                      EXAM EXAM EXAM EXAM EXAM  AVG.
4 STUDENT NO.          NAME             1    2    3    4    5   GRADE
5
6 XXX-XX-XXXX      X. XXXXXXXXXXXXXXX   XØX  XØX  XØX  XØX  XØX  XØX
7 XXX-XX-XXXX      X. XXXXXXXXXXXXXXX   XØX  XØX  XØX  XØX  XØX  XØX
8 XXX-XX-XXXX      X. XXXXXXXXXXXXXXX   XØX  XØX  XØX  XØX  XØX  XØX
9
10                                           CLASS AVERAGE  XØX
11
```

2. CompuSell, the mail-order company, extends financing to some of its preferred customers. All financing is done for 12 months at a fixed rate of 14 percent. The company charges interest on the total amount financed, rather than on the unpaid balance remaining after each successive payment. Accordingly, the monthly payment is determined by calculating the interest due on the unpaid balance, adding the interest to the unpaid balance, and dividing that sum by 12.

   Write a program for CompuSell that will calculate monthly charges for each customer in the input file CSCFINP, described in Appendix F. The format of the desired report is shown below. Note that purchase date is to be printed using the format *dd-mm* and that the report requires a count of customers in the file.

```
          1         2         3         4         5         6         7         8
 1234567890123456789012345678901234567890123456789012345678901234567890
1    XX/XX/XX               COMPUSELL FINANCE REPORT           PAGE XXØX
2
3    CUST.     PURCHASE    PURCHASE     DOWN        BALANCE      MONTHLY
4    NUM.      AMOUNT      DATE         PAYMENT     OWED         PAYMENT
5
6    XXXXXX    X,XXØ.XX    ØX-XX        X,XXØ.XX    X,XXØ.XX     X,XXØ.XX
7    XXXXXX    X,XXØ.XX    ØX-XX        X,XXØ.XX    X,XXØ.XX     X,XXØ.XX
8
9                         TOTALS       $XXX,XX$.XX $XXX,XX$.XX  $XXX,XX$.XX
10
11   NUMBER OF CUSTOMERS PROCESSED XXØ
12
```

3. CompuSell has traditionally extended financing to its customers as shown in Programming Exercise 2. The new Chief Financial Officer has decided that CompuSell will now calculate interest on the unpaid balance remaining each month and the minimum payment must equal $100.00 or 15 percent of the remaining balance.

   The balance remaining each month will be multiplied by the interest rate (12 percent) and divided by 12. This interest will then be added to the remaining balance, and the monthly payment will be subtracted, thus leaving a new remaining balance for the following month's calculation. This will be a detail report showing each month's payment due, interest for the month, and the remaining balance.

   The program will use a logical file built over CSCSTP and CSCFINP, described in Appendix F; when the customer number changes, the report should move to the next page.

```
         1         2         3         4         5         6         7         8         9         1
                                                                                                   0
   1234567890123456789012345678901234567890123456789012345678901234567890123456789012345678901234567890
 1 xx/xx/xx                                                                        Page XXØX
 2                        CompuSell Customer Listing By Customer Last Name
 3
 4 Custome   First        Last             Phone         Purchase Down      Balance  Monthly  Monthly
 5 Number    Name         Name             Number        Amount   Payment   Due      Interest Payment
 6 999999    XXXXXXXXXX   XXXXXXXXXXXXXXX  999-999-9999  9,999.99 9,999.99  9,999.99 9,999.99 9,999.99
 7                                                                          9,999.99 9,999.99 9,999.99
 8                                                                          9,999.99 9,999.99 9,999.99
 9 999999    XXXXXXXXXX   XXXXXXXXXXXXXXX  999-999-9999  9,999.99 9,999.99  9,999.99 9,999.99 9,999.99
10                                                                          9,999.99 9,999.99 9,999.99
11                                                                          9,999.99 9,999.99 9,999.99
12
13
```

4. Wexler University wants a program to generate a payroll register for its hourly employees. Appendix F describes the input file for this program, WUHRLYP. The file contains information about regular and overtime hours worked and pay rate for hourly employees.

   The school pays time and a half for overtime hours. Gross pay is the sum of regular and overtime pay. Net pay is gross pay less deductions for taxes and FICA. Eighteen percent federal tax is withheld; 5 percent state tax, and 7.51 percent for FICA.

   The format of the desired payroll register is shown below. Note that just the initial of the first name is to be printed as part of each employee's name.

```
         1         2         3         4         5         6         7         8         9         1
                                                                                                   0
   1234567890123456789012345678901234567890123456789012345678901234567890123456789012345678901234567890
 1       PAGE XXØX                                                               XX/XX/XX
 2
 3                            WEXLER U. PAYROLL REGISTER
 4
 5                                    GROSS        FEDERAL       STATE                         NET
 6      SOC. SEC.      NAME            PAY           TAX          TAX        FICA              PAY
 7
 8   XXX-XX-XXXX   X. XXXXXXXXXXXXXX   X,XXØ.XX     X,XXØ.XX     XXØ.XX     XXØ.XX           X,XXØ.XX
 9   XXX-XX-XXXX   X. XXXXXXXXXXXXXX   X,XXØ.XX     X,XXØ.XX     XXØ.XX     XXØ.XX           X,XXØ.XX
10
11                  GRAND TOTALS     $XXX,XX$.XX  $XXX,XX$.XX  $XX,XX$.XX $XX,XX$.XX       $XXX,XX$.XX
12
13
14
15
16
17
```

5. Ida Lapeer, Interior Decorator, wants a program that will estimate material costs for interior painting jobs based on data in file BIDS, described in Appendix F. Coverage per gallon represents the number of square feet of surface area that can be painted by one gallon. All room measurements were taken in terms of feet and inches (e.g., 14'10"). The percent figure given for windows and doors represents Ida's estimate of wall surface that will not need paint because of doors and windows. In calculating costs, include the cost of painting the ceiling as well as all four walls of the room.

Calculate final needed coverage to the nearest square foot and gallons needed to the nearest 1/100th of a gallon. Paint cost should be based on that figure. Ida has found that 5 percent of her paint costs represents a good estimate of other miscellaneous job costs, such as masking tape, brushes and rollers, and so on.

Your program should produce the report depicted in the following printer spacing chart.

```
          1         2         3         4         5         6         7         8         9        10
 1234567890123456789012345678901234567890123456789012345678901234567890123456789012345678901234567890
 1    XX/XX/XX                   IDA LAPEER MATERIAL COST ESTIMATES
 2
 3  JOB        PAINT       COST      COVERAGE    SQ. FEET   GALLONS     ----- ESTIMATED COSTS -----
 4  NO.        CODE     PER GAL.    PER GAL.     TO COVER   NEEDED    PAINT        MISC.       TOTAL
 5
 6  XXXX     XX-XXX      XØ.XX       XØX          X,XØX      XØ.XX   X,XXØ.XX     XXØ.XX    XX,XXØ.XX
 7  XXXX     XX-XXX      XØ.XX       XØX          X,XØX      XØ.XX   X,XXØ.XX     XXØ.XX    XX,XXØ.XX
 8
 9
10
```

Chapter 6

Processing Character Data

Chapter Overview

Most business programming centers around numeric information and arithmetic processes. But character data also plays a large part in many applications. In this chapter, you'll learn how to process, manipulate, combine, and inspect character-based information using expressions. You'll become familiar with the rich set of built-in functions that RPG IV uses with character data. You'll also learn how to convert numeric data to character data so that you can use numeric data with character processing.

Simple Character Assignment

In the previous chapter, we used the Eval operation to evaluate arithmetic expressions. Now that you know how to use Eval to assign values to numeric fields using expressions, let's look at how to assign values to character fields. As you might guess, Eval easily handles this task as a simple assignment expression (recall that explicitly coding Eval is optional):

```
Email = 'jdoe@mydomain.com';
```

Just as in numeric assignment operations, the value to be assigned (in this case, a character literal) appears to the right of the equal sign, and the receiving field appears to the left. If the literal is too long to fit on one line, or if you need to continue a long literal to another line to meet a style guideline, use a continuation character (+ or -) to signal to the computer that the literal continues on the next line:

```
*.. 1 ...+... 2 ...+... 3 ...+... 4 ...+... 5 ...+... 6 ...+... 7 ...+... 8
 /Free
    Disclaimer = 'This report contains proprietary and confidential +
                               information, and is for internal use only.'
 /End-Free
```

Remember that when you use the + continuation character, the continuation starts with the first nonblank character in the subsequent line; a - directs the continuation to begin with whatever appears in position 8 of the subsequent line, even if that position is blank. The entire literal must be enclosed within a single pair of apostrophes (').

The Eval operation performs the assignment by transferring the literal character by character, starting with the leftmost character. If the result variable that receives the literal is defined to be longer than the character literal, Eval pads the variable with blanks (i.e., it fills the unused positions at the right end of the variable with blanks). If the result variable is too small to store the literal, Eval truncates the extra rightmost characters, without warning or error.

```
*.. 1 ...+... 2 ...+... 3 ...+... 4 ...+... 5 ...+... 6 ...+... 7 ...+... 8
DName+++++++++++ETDsFrom+++To/Len+IDc.Keywords++++++++++++++++++++++++++++++++
D Char1           S              7
D Char2           S             12
D Char3           S             12    Inz('mnopqrstuvwx')
D Char4           S              4

 /Free
    Char1 = 'ABCDEFG';     // Char 1 now contains 'ABCDEFG'
    Char2 = 'ABCDEFG';     // Char 2 now contains 'ABCDEFG     '
    Char3 = 'ABCDEFG';     // Char 3 now contains 'ABCDEFG     '
    Char4 = 'ABCDEFG';     // Char 3 now contains 'ABCD'
 /End-Free
```

Notice that if the result variable is longer than the character literal, the result will be padded with blanks even if it already contains other data, as the above example shows for the Char3 variable.

You can also use Eval to assign the contents of one character field to another. The same rules apply regarding padding and truncation.

```
*.. 1 ...+... 2 ...+... 3 ...+... 4 ...+... 5 ...+... 6 ...+... 7 ...+... 8
DName+++++++++++ETDsFrom+++To/Len+IDc.Keywords++++++++++++++++++++++++++++++++
D Coursename      S              5    Inz('CS365')
D Padcourse       S             10
D Prefix          S              2

 /Free
    Padcourse = Coursename;    // Padcourse now contains 'CS365     '
    Prefix = Coursename;       // Prefix now contains 'CS'
 /End-Free
```

Using the Evalr Operation

The **Eval operation** assigns values by transferring the result of the character expression character by character, starting with the leftmost character, right-padding the result with blanks if necessary. A related operation, **Evalr (Evaluate expression, right adjust)**, works with character assignment when you want to right adjust the result. Evalr assigns the character value starting with the *rightmost* character. If the result variable that receives the value is defined to be longer than the character value, Evalr *left pads* the variable with blanks (i.e., it fills the unused positions at the left end of the variable with blanks). Evalr does not work with numeric expressions, and unlike Eval, it must be explicitly coded in the program. To see how Evalr works, compare the following code with the previous character assignment examples:

```
*.. 1 ...+... 2 ...+... 3 ...+... 4 ...+... 5 ...+... 6 ...+... 7 ...+... 8
DName+++++++++++ETDsFrom+++To/Len+IDc.Keywords++++++++++++++++++++++++++++++
D Char1           S              7
D Char2           S             12
D Char3           S             12    Inz('mnopqrstuvwx')
D Char4           S              4

 /Free
    Evalr Char1 = 'ABCDEFG';     // Char 1 now contains 'ABCDEFG'
    Evalr Char2 = 'ABCDEFG';     // Char 2 now contains '     ABCDEFG'
    Evalr Char3 = 'ABCDEFG';     // Char 3 now contains '     ABCDEFG'
    Evalr Char4 = 'ABCDEFG';     // Char 3 now contains 'DEFG'
 /End-Free
```

Using the Eval-corr Operation

The **Eval-corr (Assign corresponding subfields) operation** is a specialized version of Eval used with data structures. Eval-corr assigns subfields of one data structure to the corresponding subfields of another data structure in a single operation. To be included in an Eval-corr operation, the subfield names must be identical in both data structures and must have compatible data attributes. Their subfields need not be in the same order or have identical data attributes, but they must be compatible; that is, Eval-corr will not assign a numeric subfield in one data structure to an identically named character subfield in another data structure. Eval-corr is used with an assignment expression:

```
Eval-corr target = source;
```

Both the *target* and the *source* must be data structures. At least one of the data structures must be a qualified data structure (discussed in Chapter 4); otherwise it would not be possible for them to have identically named subfields.

You may find Eval-corr a useful shortcut when your program is processing data structures. Consider the following example:

```
*.. 1 ...+... 2 ...+... 3 ...+... 4 ...+... 5 ...+... 6 ...+... 7 ...+... 8
DName++++++++++ETDsFrom+++To/L+++IDc.Keywords+++++++++++++++++++++++++++++++
D Customer         DS                      Qualified
D   Identifier                   5 0
D   Name                        30
D   State                        2
D   Zipcode                     10
D   Phone                       10
D   Creditlimit                 11 2

D Vendor           DS                      Qualified
D   Identifier                   5U 0
D   Name                        35
D   Address                     35
D   City                        21
D   State                        2
D   Postcode                    10
D   Phone                       10 0

/Free
   Eval-corr Customer = Vendor;
/End-free
```

The single Eval-corr operation is equivalent to the following expressions:

- Customer.Identifier = Vendor.Identifier;
- Customer.Name = Vendor.name;
- Customer.State = Vendor.State;

The following table describes how Eval-corr processes each of the subfields:

Vendor (source)	Customer (target)	Action
Identifier	Identifier	Subfield assigned; both subfields are numeric, even though they are different data types.
Name	Name	Subfield assigned, with truncation.
Address	—	No target subfield; subfield ignored.
City	—	No target subfield; subfield ignored.
State	State	Subfield assigned.
Postcode	Zipcode	Different subfield names; subfields ignored.
Phone	Phone	Incompatible data types; subfields ignored.
—	Creditlimit	No source subfield; subfield ignored.

Each subfield's assignment follows the same rules as the Eval operation (e.g., character fields are left-adjusted, numeric subfields are aligned at the decimal). Data is assigned in the order of the subfields in the source data structure; if any subfields in the target data structure use the Overlay keyword, later assignment may overwrite earlier assignments.

Assigning Values with Figurative Constants

RPG IV lets you assign **figurative constant** *Blank (or *Blanks) to **character variables** to fill the variables with blanks. You can also assign the special value *Zero (or *Zeros) to fill character variables with zeros. *Hival and *Loval are also valid with character variables; *Hival is all bits on (X'FF') and *Loval is all bits off (X'00').

Assigning figurative constant *All immediately followed by one or more characters within apostrophes (') causes the string within the apostrophes to be cyclically repeated through the entire length of the result field. A related figurative constant, *Allx, works the same as *All, except that you can specify hexadecimal character strings.

```
*.. 1 ...+... 2 ...+... 3 ...+... 4 ...+... 5 ...+... 6 ...+... 7 ...+... 8
DName++++++++++ETDsFrom+++To/Len+IDc.Keywords+++++++++++++++++++++++++++++++
D Char            S              9
D Underline       S             80

/Free
   Char = *Blanks;          // Char is now blank
   Char = *Zeros;           // Char is now '000000000'
   Char = *Hival;           // Char is now filled with X'FF' characters
   Char = *Loval;           // Char is now filled with X'00' characters
   Char = *All'Z';          // Char is now 'ZZZZZZZZZ'
   Char = *All'Abc';        // Char is now 'AbcAbcAbc'
   Char = *Allx'E9'         // Char is now 'ZZZZZZZZZ' (X'E9' = Z)
   Char = *Allx'C18283'     // Char is now 'AbcAbcAbc' (X'C18283' = Abc)
   Underline = *All'-'      // Underline is now 80 hyphens
/End-Free
```

Figurative constants *Off and *On represent character '0' and character '1', respectively. Although you can use *Off and *On with any character variable of any length, programmers most often use these constants to assign a value to an RPG IV indicator or to compare with an indicator's value. We've used *On and *Off previously in this text with Eval to set indicators on or off.

Concatenating Character Values

In the previous sections, we saw how to use Eval and Evalr for simple character assignment. These operations also provide a flexible and powerful method for joining character values together; this process is called **concatenation**. Use the + operator to concatenate two or more character values—which may be variables, literals, or constants—and assign the resulting new character value to a variable. A single **concatenation expression** can contain as many + operators and character operands as needed to accomplish a desired concatenation. The following examples demonstrate how to use + to concatenate strings.

```
*.. 1 ...+... 2 ...+... 3 ...+... 4 ...+... 5 ...+... 6 ...+... 7 ...+... 8
DName+++++++++++ETDsFrom+++To/Len+IDc.Keywords+++++++++++++++++++++++++++++++
D Greeting        S             12
D Fullname        S             16
D Fullname2       S             25
D Firstname       S              5     Inz('Susan')
D Firstname2      S             10     Inz('Susan')
D Midinitial      S              1     Inz('B')
D Lastname        S              7     Inz('Anthony')
D Lastname2       S             10     Inz('Anthony')

 /Free
    Greeting = 'Hello ' + 'World';  // Greeting now contains 'Hello World '

    Fullname = Firstname + ' ' + Midinitial + '. ' + Lastname;
                                   // Fullname now contains 'Susan B. Anthony'

    Fullname2 = Firstname2 + ' ' + Midinitial + '. ' + Lastname2;
                        // Fullname2 now contains 'Susan      B. Anthony     '
 /End-Free
```

Notice in the last example that the new character value (Fullname2) retains all the blanks that were in the individual concatenated variables. Later, we'll discuss two techniques for eliminating such unneeded blanks.

If the concatenated string is smaller than the result variable to which it is assigned, Eval right pads the result variable with blanks. If the concatenated string is too large to fit in the result variable to which it is assigned, truncation occurs from the right end of the string. Evalr will left pad the result in this case and will truncate from the left.

```
*.. 1 ...+... 2 ...+... 3 ...+... 4 ...+... 5 ...+... 6 ...+... 7 ...+... 8
DName+++++++++++ETDsFrom+++To/Len+IDc.Keywords+++++++++++++++++++++++++++++++
D Firstname       S              5     Inz('John')
D Lastname        S             12     Inz('Jackson III')
D Longname        S             25
D Shortname       S             10

 /Free
    Longname = Firstname + Lastname;
                // Longname contains 'John Jackson III         '
                // with blanks appearing in its unused rightmost positions

    Shortname = Firstname + Lastname;
                // Shortname contains 'John Jacks'
                // because it can store only 10 characters.

    Evalr Longname = Firstname + Lastname;
                // Longname contains '         John Jackson III '

    Evalr Shortname = Firstname + Lastname;
                // Shortname contains 'ckson III '
 /End-Free
```

All values used in the concatenation expression must, of course, be character variables, literals, or constants. You cannot use numeric values anywhere in the expression. The system executes the concatenation operations from left to right in the expression. There are no operator precedence issues to remember, since the only allowed operator is the + concatenation operator.

If it is necessary, you can simply continue the expression anywhere on subsequent lines, and then end it with a semicolon (;) when the expression is finished. The following code illustrates the use of a continuation line when concatenating character values. This expression concatenates a character literal with a variable and then appends another literal on the end of the character string:

```
/Free
    Disclaimer = 'This report is proprietary and confidential, for ' +
                 Companyname + ' internal use only.'
/End-Free
```

In this example, the plus signs (+) in the expression are **concatenation operators**, not **continuation characters**; no continuation characters are necessary unless you must continue a literal, as shown earlier in this chapter.

Using Built-in Functions with Character Data

In the previous chapter we discussed a number of built-in functions (BIFs) that RPG IV uses to simplify arithmetic expressions and convert data to numeric data. RPG IV also supports many built-in functions that you can use in conjunction with **character expressions**. These provide new functions that aren't available by coding simple concatenation.

%Trim (Trim Blanks at Edges)

The **%Trim (Trim blanks at edges) function** returns a character value after removing all leading and trailing blanks. There are three variations on the %Trim function: %Trim itself, %Triml, and %Trimr. %Trim removes both leading and trailing blanks; %Triml will remove leading blanks only, while %Trimr will remove trailing blanks only. The end result any of the %Trim functions is a **variable-length** character value; that is, it has no defined fixed length.

```
%Trim('    New York    ') results in a value of 'New York'
%Triml('    New York    ') results in a value of 'New York    '
%Trimr('    New York    ') results in a value of '    New York'
```

Notice that the %Trim function will remove only the blanks at the edges of the character value, not those inside the value; so the above %Trim functions retain the blank inside 'New York' when trimming the blanks.

The %Trim functions are useful when you want to concatenate fixed-length character fields, which may contain blanks that you want to ignore in the final result. You can include the %Trim functions inside the concatenation expression, to substitute the variable-length character value in the expression. The following example illustrates concatenation with and without the %Trim function:

```
*.. 1 ...+... 2 ...+... 3 ...+... 4 ...+... 5 ...+... 6 ...+... 7 ...+... 8
DName++++++++++ETDsFrom+++To/Len+IDc.Keywords++++++++++++++++++++++++++++++++
D Fullname        S             25
D Firstname       S             10      Inz('Susan')
D Midinitial      S              1      Inz('B')
D Lastname        S             10      Inz('Anthony')
D Lastname2       S             10      Inz('  Anthony ')

 /Free
    Fullname = Firstname + ' ' + Midinitial + '. ' + Lastname;
                       // Fullname now contains 'Susan      B. Anthony    '

    Fullname = %Trim(Firstname) + ' ' + Midinitial + '. ' + Lastname;
                       // Fullname now contains 'Susan B. Anthony         '

    Fullname = Firstname + ' ' + Midinitial + '. ' + Lastname2;
                       // Fullname now contains 'Susan      B.   Anthony  '

    Fullname = %Trim(Firstname) + ' ' + Midinitial + '. ' + Lastname2;
                       // Fullname now contains 'Susan B.    Anthony      '

    Fullname = %Trim(Firstname) + ' ' + Midinitial + '. ' +
               %Trim(Lastname2);
                       // Fullname now contains 'Susan B. Anthony         '

 /End-Free
```

Typically, you'll use the %Trim functions to remove blanks from a string, but you can also trim leading and/or trailing characters other than blanks. By coding one any of the %Trim functions with a second argument that lists one or more characters to be trimmed, you can trim those characters from the edges of a character string.

```
*.. 1 ...+... 2 ...+... 3 ...+... 4 ...+... 5 ...+... 6 ...+... 7 ...+... 8
DName++++++++++ETDsFrom+++To/Len+IDc.Keywords++++++++++++++++++++++++++++++++
D Checkword       S             25      Inz('$*****7,654.32***')
D Result          S             20

 /Free
    Result = Checkword;        // Result is now '$*****7,654.32***    '

    Result = %Trim(Checkword:'*');
                           // Result is now '$*****7,654.32***    '
                           // Checkword contains leading $ and trailing
                           // blanks, but no edge asterisks.

    Result = %Trim(Checkword:'$*');
                           // Result is now '7,654.32***          '
                           // Checkword contains trailing blanks,
                           // so trailing asterisks are not trimmed.

    Result = %Trim(Checkword:'$* ');
                           // Result is now '7,654.32             '
                           // Edge $ * and blanks are all trimmed.
 /End-Free
```

%Subst (Get or Set Substring) Function

The **%Subst (Get or set substring) function** extracts a **substring**, or portion, of a character string. You code two or three arguments in parentheses immediately following the %Subst function:

- The string from which the extraction is to occur
- The position within that string where the substring is to start
- Optionally, the length of the substring

If you omit the third argument, the substring will include all the bytes from the starting position to the final, rightmost byte of the string. Thus, the format of the substring function is

```
%Subst(String:Start{:Length})
```

As shown above, you use colon separators between arguments. You can represent the starting position and the optional length using numeric variables, constants, or expressions that evaluate to integers greater than zero. If the length is too big given the starting position (i.e., the substring would extend beyond the end of the string), a runtime error will occur. The following examples illustrate how to get a portion of a larger character string:

```
*.. 1 ...+... 2 ...+... 3 ...+... 4 ...+... 5 ...+... 6 ...+... 7 ...+... 8
DName+++++++++++ETDsFrom+++To/Len+IDc.Keywords+++++++++++++++++++++++++++++++
D Areacode        S              3
D Exchange        S              3
D Extension       S              4
D Longexten       S              7
D Phone           S             10     Inz('9705551212')

 /Free
    Areacode = %Subst(Phone:1:3);      // Areacode now contains '970'
    Exchange = %Subst(Phone:4:3);      // Exchange now contains '555'
    Extension = %Subst(Phone:7);       // Extension now contains '1212'
    Longexten = %Subst(Phone:7);       // Extension now contains '1212   '
 /End-Free
```

Like the other built-in functions we've discussed, %Subst can be used to return a value needed within a calculation, as shown in the above examples. Unlike most other functions, you can also use %Subst as the target (or result) of an assignment operation to change the value of a designated substring. For this use, the designated string must be a variable that can be assigned a value; a constant, for example, would be inappropriate. The following examples illustrate this use of %Subst.

```
*.. 1 ...+... 2 ...+... 3 ...+... 4 ...+... 5 ...+... 6 ...+... 7 ...+... 8
DName++++++++++ETDsFrom+++To/Len+IDc.Keywords+++++++++++++++++++++++++++++++
D Areacode        S              3       Inz('406')
D Phone           S             10       Inz('9705551212')
D Phone2          S             10       Inz('9516547531')

/Free
  %Subst(Phone:1:3) = '613';          // Phone now contains '6135551212'
  %Subst(Phone:1:3) = Areacode;       // Phone now contains '4065551212'
  %Subst(Phone:4:3) = %Subst(Phone2:4:3);
                                       // Phone now contains '4066541212'

/End-Free
```

%Replace (Replace Character String)

The **%Replace (Replace character string) function** changes a character string value by replacing existing characters with new values. The format for the %Replace function is

```
%Replace(newstring:oldstring{:start{:length}})
```

The first argument—which can be a character variable, literal, or expression—supplies the replacement string to be inserted into the original character string, which is the second argument— a character variable.

You can optionally specify a starting position; if you omit this third argument, the replacement will occur at the beginning of the original character variable. The fourth argument is also optional; it specifies how many characters to replace. If you omit the fourth argument, the number of characters will be the same as the length of the replacement string. You can also specify that you want to insert a new value, without replacing any existing characters, by specifying 0 as the fourth argument. The third and fourth optional arguments can be numeric variables, literals, or expressions.

The following examples use the %Replace function:

```
*.. 1 ...+... 2 ...+... 3 ...+... 4 ...+... 5 ...+... 6 ...+... 7 ...+... 8
DName++++++++++ETDsFrom+++To/Len+IDc.Keywords+++++++++++++++++++++++++++++++
D Areacode        S              3       Inz('406')
D Extension       S              3       Inz('690')
D Phone           S             10       Inz('9705551212')

D First           S              5       Inz('John')
D Initial         S              1       Inz('J')
D Middle          S              7       Inz(' Quincy')
D Name            S             17       Inz('B. Adams')

/Free
  Phone = %Replace('613':Phone);       // Phone now contains '6135551212'
  Phone = %Replace(Areacode:Phone);    // Phone now contains '4065551212'
  Phone = %Replace(Extension:Phone:4); // Phone now contains '4066901212'

  Name = %Replace(Initial:Name); // Name now contains 'J. Adams          '
  Name = %Replace(First:Name:1:2);
                                 // Name now contains 'John Adams         '
  Name = %Replace(Middle:Name:5:0);
                                 // Name now contains 'John Quincy Adams'
/End-Free
```

%Xlate (Translate) Function

The **%Xlate (Translate) function** lets you **translate**, or convert, characters within a string to other characters. It takes the form

`%Xlate(from:to:string{:start})`

The first two arguments serve as translation tables; the first one provides the characters that should be translated, and the second one specifies which characters they should be translated to. The third argument names a character variable containing the source string—it may also be a character literal. If you do not specify a starting location (fourth argument), the conversion starts at the first position of the source string. The function returns a translated version of the source string, which you can use in an assignment expression.

The "from" string and the "to" string must have the same number of characters, with the characters ordered so that each character in the "from" string has a corresponding character in the "to" string. The translation strings can be variables, literals, or named constants. During the %Xlate function processing, any character in the source string found in the "from" string is converted to the corresponding character in the "to" string. If a source string character does not appear in the "from" string, that character is unchanged in the return value.

If this sounds confusing, looking at some examples should help clarify how the %Xlate function works. The following examples convert uppercase letters to lowercase letters and vice versa; this kind of translation is the most frequent application of %Xlate. The translation tables are defined through named constants Uppercase and Lowercase.

```
*.. 1 ...+... 2 ...+... 3 ...+... 4 ...+... 5 ...+... 6 ...+... 7 ...+... 8
DName+++++++++++ETDsFrom+++To/L+++IDc.Keywords++++++++++++++++++++++++++++++++
D Lowercase       C                   'abcdefghijklmnopqrstuvwxyz'
D Uppercase       C                   'ABCDEFGHIJKLMNOPQRSTUVWXYZ'

D Fielda          S              9     Inz('abc123ABC')
D Lastname        S             15     Inz('BYRNE-SMITH')
D Name            S             15

D Amount          S             11 2
D Checkword       S             17     Inz('$*****7,654.32***')
D Result          S             17

 /Free
    Name = %Xlate(Uppercase:Lowercase:Lastname);
                              // Name now contains 'byrne-smith    '
    Name = %Xlate(Uppercase:Lowercase:Lastname:2);
                              // Name now contains 'Byrne-smith    '
    Name = %Xlate(' ':'*':Name);      // Name now contains 'Byrne-smith****'
    Fielda = %Xlate(Lowercase:Uppercase:FieldA);
                              // Fielda now contains 'ABC123ABC'

    Checkword = %Xlate('$*,':'   ':Checkword);
                              // Checkword now contains '      7 654.32  '
    Amount = %Dec(Checkword:11:2);   // Amount = 7654.32
 /End-Free
```

The last two statements in the above examples illustrate the use of %Xlate to strip non-numeric characters from a character variable, Checkword, and then convert the result to a packed decimal number, using the **%Dec function**. We could then use the number in arithmetic expressions. We could also have combined the two functions into a single statement to get the same result:

```
Amount = %Dec(%Xlate('$*,':'    ':Checkword) : 11 : 2);
```

In this example, the %Xlate function (shown in bold print) is embedded as the first argument to the %Dec function. While this single statement illustrates the fact that you can include complex expressions as the arguments for many functions, you'll want to carefully weigh the brevity of this style against its readability.

Examining Character Content

Three built-in functions let your program inspect the content of a character string to see if it contains one or more characters. These functions are

- %Scan (Scan string)
- %Check (Check characters)
- %Checkr (Check reverse)

%SCAN (Scan String)

The **%Scan (Scan string) function** looks for a character or a string of characters within a character string—usually a variable, but it could also be a literal or named constant. The direction of the %Scan is left to right. %Scan takes the form

```
%Scan(search-arg:string{:start})
```

%Scan searches the string for the search argument, beginning with the starting position (or beginning at the first position, if you don't specify the third argument). %Scan is case sensitive; that is, 'A' is not the same as 'a'. If the string you are looking for includes blanks—whether leading, trailing, or embedded—the blanks are considered part of the pattern to find. Similarly, blanks within the searched string are not ignored. The function returns an unsigned integer value that represents the next position of the search argument in the source string; if the search argument is not found, the function returns a zero. You can include %Scan anywhere in the program where an unsigned integer expression is allowed.

The following examples illustrate some typical uses for %Scan:

```
*.. 1 ...+... 2 ...+... 3 ...+... 4 ...+... 5 ...+... 6 ...+... 7 ...+... 8
DName+++++++++++ETDsFrom+++To/L+++IDc.Keywords+++++++++++++++++++++++++++++++
D Lowercase       C                     'abcdefghijklmnopqrstuvwxyz'
D Uppercase       C                     'ABCDEFGHIJKLMNOPQRSTUVWXYZ'

D Position        S              5U 0

D Fielda          S               3     Inz('XY ')
D Fieldb          S              10     Inz('QRSTUVWXYZ')
D Fieldc          S              10     Inz('XY TUVWXY ')

D Fullname        S              20     Inz('Doe/John')
 /Free
    Position = %Scan(Fielda:Fieldb); // Position = 0, because 'XY ' (with a
                                      // trailing blank) is not in Fieldb
    Position = %Scan(%Trim(Fielda):Fieldb);     // Position = 8

    Position = %Scan(Fielda:Fieldc);            // Position = 1
    Position = %Scan(Fielda:Fieldc:2);          // Position = 8

    Position = %Scan('/':Fullname);             // Position = 4
    Position = %Scan('John':Fullname);          // Position = 5

    Position = %Scan('JOHN':Fullname);          // Position = 0
    Position = %Scan('JOHN' : %Xlate(Lowercase:Uppercase:Fullname));
                                                // Position = 5
 /End-Free
```

The %Scan function is useful for inspecting text data. You could use it, for example, to scan addresses to locate all businesses or customers residing on the same street. Text retrieval software uses operations like %Scan to index text based on the presence of keywords within the text.

%Check (Check Characters) and %Checkr (Check Reverse)

The **%Check (Check characters) function** inspects a character string, checking whether or not it contains *only* the characters designated in a compare string. The first argument contains a compare string, and the second one contains the string to inspect. By coding a third argument you can also optionally specify a starting point for the inspection. The format of the %Check function is

%Check(*comparator*:*string*{:*start*})

%Check is used to verify the characters in a string. If all the characters in the string also appear in the compare string, then %Check returns a zero. If there is a mismatch—that is, if there are any characters in the string that do *not* appear in the compare string—then %Check will return an unsigned integer value that represents the leftmost position that does not match the characters in the compare string.

While both %Check and %Scan are used to examine character strings, there is a significant difference between the two functions. %Scan looks for the presence of the entire search argument within the string and returns the location of its occurrence; %Check verifies that each character in the string is among the valid characters in the compare string. If there is a mismatch, %Check returns the location of the mismatch; otherwise, %Check returns a zero.

The compare string, represented in a character variable, literal, or named constant, contains a list of valid characters. The base string contains the character variable, literal, or named constant value you want checked against characters in the compare string. If %Check returns a nonzero number, that number is the first position in the string that contains a character not in the compare string.

In the following example, the %Check function verifies that the Checkword variable contains only digits, blanks, or a decimal point. If any other characters are found, %Check will return the position of the first invalid character; otherwise it will return a zero.

```
*.. 1 ...+... 2 ...+... 3 ...+... 4 ...+... 5 ...+... 6 ...+... 7 ...+... 8
DName++++++++++ETDsFrom+++To/Len+IDc.Keywords+++++++++++++++++++++++++++++++
D Checkword       S             25     Inz('    7,654.32')
D Position        S              5U 0

 /Free
    Position = %Check(' .0123456789':Checkword);      // Position = 8

    %Subst(Checkword:Position:1) = *Blank;      // Put a blank in position 8
    Position = %Check(' .0123456789':Checkword);      // Position = 0
 /End-free
```

In the preceding examples we coded the compare string as a literal; we could have also placed the compare string in a variable or named constant:

```
*.. 1 ...+... 2 ...+... 3 ...+... 4 ...+... 5 ...+... 6 ...+... 7 ...+... 8
DName++++++++++ETDsFrom+++To/Len+IDc.Keywords+++++++++++++++++++++++++++++++
D Numbers         C                     ' .0123456789'

D Checkword       S             25     Inz('    7,654.32')
D Position        S              5U 0

 /Free
    Position = %Check(Numbers:Checkword);      // Position = 8

    %Subst(Checkword:Position:1) = *Blank;      // Put a blank in position 8
    Position = %Check(Numbers:Checkword);      // Position = 0
 /End-free
```

The **%Checkr (Check reverse) function** works exactly like %Check, except that it checks the string from right to left, rather than from left to right. You can use this operation to locate the rightmost invalid character in a string or to determine the length of a string of nonblank characters in a field.

```
*.. 1 ...+... 2 ...+... 3 ...+... 4 ...+... 5 ...+... 6 ...+... 7 ...+... 8
DName++++++++++ETDsFrom+++To/Len+IDc.Keywords+++++++++++++++++++++++++++++++
D Name            S             25     Inz('Jones')
D Length          S              5U 0

 /Free
    Length = %Checkr(' ':Name);      // Length = 5
 /End-Free
```

Data Conversion Functions

Recall that RPG is a strictly typed language. This means that all the operands in a character expression must be of a character data type; the program cannot mix numeric data and character variables in the same expression. Several built-in functions convert numeric expressions to character formats and will even edit those numeric expressions using the edit codes and edit words we discussed in Chapter 2. These functions are

- %Char (Convert to character data)
- %Editc (Edit with an edit code)
- %Editw (Edit with an edit word)
- %Editflt (Convert to floating point external representation)
- %Str (Get or set null terminated string)

The %Editflt and %Str functions are rarely used in business programming, but the remaining three functions are useful when you need to convert a numeric value to a character string.

%Char (Convert to Character Data)

The **%Char (Convert to character data) function** converts the result of a numeric variable, literal, named constant, or expression to a character value. The %Char function is especially useful when you need to include numeric data in a string expression, perhaps to concatenate a numeric value and a character string. All of the operands in a string expression must be in character format, so %Char is necessary to perform the conversion.

```
*.. 1 ...+... 2 ...+... 3 ...+... 4 ...+... 5 ...+... 6 ...+... 7 ...+... 8
DName++++++++++ETDsFrom+++To/L+++IDc.Keywords++++++++++++++++++++++++++++++++

D Message         S             45
D Points          S             10U 0 Inz(50273)
D Balance         S              9 2 Inz(-9876.54)

 /Free
   Message = 'You have earned ' + %Char(Points) + ' Frequent Flier Miles.'
         // Message = 'You have earned 50273 Frequent Flier Miles. '

   Message = 'Your account balance is ' + %Char(Balance);
         // Message = 'Your account balance is -9876.54            '
 /End-Free
```

%Char always removes all leading zeros from the result. If the numeric value includes decimal places, %Char will include a decimal point at its proper alignment. If the value is negative, %Char will return a character result with a leading sign.

%Editc (Edit with an Edit Code)

The %Char function provides only rudimentary editing when it returns a character value, removing leading zeros and adding a decimal point and sign, if necessary. But as we saw in Chapter 2, RPG provides a rich set of editing functions through the use of edit codes. The **%Editc (Edit with an edit code) function** not only converts a number to a character value but assigns one of those edit codes to the numeric value before converting it, optionally adding a currency symbol or asterisk leading fill (*****). The format for the %Editc function is

```
%Editc(number:editcode{:extension})
```

The first argument is the numeric variable, literal, named constant, or expression that you want to convert. Next, enter the desired edit code as the second argument; the edit code is typically a literal enclosed in apostrophes ('), but it can also be a named constant. %Editc supports all the edit codes described in Chapter 2.

The optional third %Editc argument adds a currency symbol or asterisk fill to the edited value. For example

```
%Editc(-0012.34:'J':*Astfill)
```

would return a character value of '***12.34-'. If you want to include a floating currency symbol in the edited value, you might code

```
%Editc(0012.34:'J':*Cursym)
```

This code would return a character value of ' $12.34 '. %Editc will use the program's default currency symbol unless you code another character. For example

```
%Editc(0012.34:'J':'C')
```

would return a value of '   C12.34 '.

The %Editc result may include leading and/or trailing blanks and will always return the same length string for a given variable, regardless of its value; to eliminate the leading and/or trailing blanks, use the %Trim function. The following examples illustrate the use of the %Editc function:

```
*.. 1 ...+... 2 ...+... 3 ...+... 4 ...+... 5 ...+... 6 ...+... 7 ...+... 8
DName++++++++++ETDsFrom+++To/L+++IDc.Keywords+++++++++++++++++++++++++++++++

D Message          S             45
D Balance          S              9  2 Inz(9876.54)
D Zerobalance      S              9  2

 /Free
    Message = 'Your account balance is ' + %Editc(Balance:'J':*Cursym);
             // Message = 'Your account balance is    $9,876.54          '
    Message = 'Your account balance is ' +
                              %Trim( %Editc(Balance:'J':*Cursym) );
             // Message = 'Your account balance is $9,876.54             '

    Message = 'Your account balance is ' + %Editc(Zerobalance:'J':*Cursym);
             // Message = 'Your account balance is         $.00          '
    Message = 'Your account balance is ' +
                              %Trim( %Editc(Zerobalance:'J':*Cursym) );
             // Message = 'Your account balance is $.00                  '
 /End-Free
```

Recall from Chapter 2 that all but one of the edit codes remove leading zeros from the edited result. If you want to retain the leading zeros in the character value, you'd use the X edit code, which retains the zeros. The X edit code does not reveal the decimal point or an explicit sign; for negative numbers, the sign is embedded in the high order of the last digit. The following examples illustrate the difference in the results between the %Char and %Editc functions:

```
*.. 1 ...+... 2 ...+... 3 ...+... 4 ...+... 5 ...+... 6 ...+... 7 ...+... 8
DName++++++++++ETDsFrom+++To/L+++IDc.Keywords++++++++++++++++++++++++++++++++
D Char            S              15

D Number1         S               9 0 Inz(98765)
D Number2         S               9 2 Inz(-98765.42)

 /Free
    Char = %Char(Number1);          Char now contains '98765          '
    Char = %Editc(Number1:'X');     Char now contains '000098765      '

    Char = %Char(Number2);          Char now contains '-98765.42      '
    Char = %Editc(Number2:'X');     Char now contains '00987654K      '
 /End-free
```

%Editw (Edit with an Edit Word)

When a simple edit code won't do, the **%Editw** (**Edit with an edit word**) **function** will apply an edit word to a numeric value while it converts the number to a character string. %Editw uses the same rules for creating an edit word that we discussed in Chapter 2. The edit word must be a literal or named constant. The %Editw function takes the form

```
%Editw(number:editword)
```

The following code illustrates some examples of using the %Editw function:

```
*.. 1 ...+... 2 ...+... 3 ...+... 4 ...+... 5 ...+... 6 ...+... 7 ...+... 8
DName++++++++++ETDsFrom+++To/Len+IDc.Keywords++++++++++++++++++++++++++++++++
D Edita           C                 '   ,   , **DOLLARS* *CENTS'
D Editp           C                 '0(   )   -      '
D Editt           C                 '   -   -      '

D Char            S              30

D Amount          S              11 2 Inz(12345.67)
D Phone           S              10 0 Inz(8005551212)
D Taxid           S               9 0 Inz(987654321)
 /Free
    Char = %Editw(Amount:Edita);
                      // Char now contains '*****12,345*DOLLARS*67*CENTS '
    Char = %Editw(Phone:Editp);
                      // Char now contains ' (800)555-1212           '
    Char = %Editw(Taxid:Editt);
                      // Char now contains '987-65-4321              '
    Char = %Editw(Taxid:'   &   &    ');
                      // Char now contains '987 65 4321              '
 /End-Free
```

Using Variable-Length Character Variables

All of the character variables that we've discussed so far have been **fixed-length** character variables, with a specific declared length. RPG IV also supports **variable-length** character fields. Like a fixed-length variable, a variable-length character variable has a **declared length**, which is its maximum length. But variable-length character variables also have a **current length,** which is generally dependent upon the value of the variable and which can change while the program is running.

To define a variable-length character variable in Definition specifications, use the Varying keyword (or use the Like keyword to inherit the properties of an existing variable-length character variable). The variable cannot be a numeric data type. The length of the variable (in positions 33–39) is its declared length (i.e., its maximum length). The data item can be a standalone variable or a data structure subfield. When you define a "varying" data item, the system allocates enough memory for the entire declared length *plus two bytes*. The computer used the leftmost two bytes internally to store the current length of the variable; you usually never see these two bytes, and you need not bother with them when processing the character value in the variable.

Note

For variable-length data structure subfields entered with positional notation, the from/to positions must account for the additional two bytes. If the subfields are entered with length notation, the length entry does not include the additional two bytes.

You can initialize a variable-length character variable with the Inz keyword. The initial current length, then, is the length of the initial value. The remaining allocated storage beyond the initial value is initialized to blanks, but these blanks are not part of the variable's value.

When you use a variable-length character variable in a character string operation, such as concatenation, you may not need to use the %Trim functions to get the results you want. Using "varying" data items can thereby improve the performance of your program as well as its readability. Compare the following examples:

```
*.. 1 ...+... 2 ...+... 3 ...+... 4 ...+... 5 ...+... 6 ...+... 7 ...+... 8
DName++++++++++ETDsFrom+++To/Len+IDc.Keywords+++++++++++++++++++++++++++++++
D Fullname       S             25

D First          S             10      Inz('Susan')
D Last           S             10      Inz('Anthony')

D Firstvar       S             10      Varying
D                                      Inz('Susan')

 /Free
    // The following lines give equivalent results.
    Fullname = %Trim(First) + ' ' + Last;
    Fullname = Firstvar + ' ' + Last;
 /End-Free
```

Many built-in functions — most of those that return character values — return variable-length character values.

Determining Data Properties

Several functions could informally be described as "self examination" functions. These functions let your program determine the properties of a variable, constant, or expression. Among these functions:

- %Size (Byte size)
- %Len (Get/set length)
- %Decpos (Number of decimal positions)

%Size (Byte Size)

The **%Size (Byte size) function** returns the number of bytes occupied by a variable or constant. When you use %Size to determine the length of a packed decimal or integer data item, it returns the number of bytes used to store the data item, not the number of digits. %Size always returns the declared byte size, regardless of the current value of the variable. For variable-length character variables, %Size returns the declared length plus two bytes. The following examples demonstrate how to determine %Size.

```
*.. 1 ...+... 2 ...+... 3 ...+... 4 ...+... 5 ...+... 6 ...+... 7 ...+... 8
DName++++++++++ETDsFrom+++To/L+++IDc.Keywords+++++++++++++++++++++++++++++++
D Bytes           S              5U 0
D Company         S              5S 0
D Salary          S              9  0 Inz(48600)

D Name            S             25    Inz('John Doe')
D Namevar         S             25    Varying
D                                     Inz('Al Fredo')

 /Free
    Bytes = %Size(Bytes);      // Bytes = 2  (integer)
    Bytes = %Size(Company);    // Bytes = 5  (zoned decimal)
    Bytes = %Size(Salary);     // Bytes = 5  (packed decimal)
    Bytes = %Size(Name);       // Bytes = 25
    Bytes = %Size(Namevar);    // Bytes = 27 (declared size + 2)
 /End-Free
```

%LEN (Get/Set Length)

The **%Len (Get/set length) function** returns the number of digits or characters in a variable, constant, or expression. %Len is especially useful with character expressions, to determine the number of significant characters in the value of the expression. For fixed-length character fields, %Len returns the declared length of the field, but for variable-length character values, %Len returns the current length of the variable or expression, which is dependent upon its value.

For numeric expressions, %Len returns the precision of the expression, not necessarily the number of significant digits in the calculated value of the expression. If you use %Len to find the decimal precision of an arithmetic expression, the system will return a length that is consistent with the sizing rules we discussed in Chapter 5. For all other data types, %Len returns the number of bytes, giving the same result as the %Size function. Here are some examples of the %Len function:

continued...

Determining Data Properties...*Continued*

```
*.. 1 ...+... 2 ...+... 3 ...+... 4 ...+... 5 ...+... 6 ...+... 7 ...+... 8
DName++++++++++ETDsFrom+++To/L+++IDc.Keywords+++++++++++++++++++++++++++++++
D Length          S              5U 0

D Company         S              5S 0
D Salary          S              9  2 Inz(48600.00)
D Tenure          S              3  0

D Firstname       S             10   Varying
D                                     Inz('Frieda')
D Lastname        S             10   Varying
D                                     Inz('Slaves')
D Name            S             25   Inz('John Doe')
D Namevar         S             25   Varying
D                                     Inz('Al Fredo')

 /Free
    Length = %Len(Length);              // Length = 5  (integer)
    Length = %Len(Company);             // Length = 5  (zoned decimal)
    Length = %Len(Salary);              // Length = 9  (packed decimal)
    Length = %Len(Salary * Tenure);     // Length = 12

    Length = %Len(Name);                // Length = 25
    Length = %Len( %Trim(Name) );       // Length = 8

    Length = %Size(Namevar);            // Length = 27 (declared size +2)
    Length = %Len(Namevar);             // Length = 8  (current length)

    Length = %Len(Firstname + ' ' + Lastname)
                                        // Length = 13

    Name = '';
    Length = %Len(Name);                // Length = 0
 /End-Free
```

The %Len function is typically used to get the length of an expression, but it can also be used to set the current length of a variable-length character field. By coding the %Len function to the left of the assignment operator (=), you can set the current length of the variable. By changing the current length of the variable, you also change the contents of the variable.

```
*.. 1 ...+... 2 ...+... 3 ...+... 4 ...+... 5 ...+... 6 ...+... 7 ...+... 8
DName++++++++++ETDsFrom+++To/L+++IDc.Keywords+++++++++++++++++++++++++++++++
D Length          S              5U 0

D Name            S             25   Varying
D                                     Inz('John Doe')

 /Free
    Length = %Len(Name);                // Length = 8  (current length)
    %Len(Name) = 4;                     // Name = 'John'
 /End-Free
```

continued...

Determining Data Properties...*Continued*

%Decpos (Number of Decimal Positions)

The **%Decpos** (**Number of decimal positions**) **function** returns the number of decimal positions in a numeric variable or expression. %Decpos is sometimes used with the %Len function to examine a data item or expression.

```
*.. 1 ...+... 2 ...+... 3 ...+... 4 ...+... 5 ...+... 6 ...+... 7 ...+... 8
DName++++++++++ETDsFrom+++To/L+++IDc.Keywords+++++++++++++++++++++++++++++++
D Decimals        S              5U 0
D Digits          S              5U 0
D Salary          S              9P 2 Inz(48600)

 /FREE
    Digits = %Len(Salary);          // Digits = 9
    Decimals = %Decpos(Salary);     // Decimals = 2
 /END-FREE
```

Chapter Summary

As RPG IV's single general-purpose assignment operation, Eval supports expressions with character values as well as numeric values. The expressions can range from a simple assignment expression to more complex concatenation expressions.

For character expressions, Eval left adjusts the result and pads to the right with blanks if necessary; Evalr, on the other hand, right adjusts the result and pads to the left with blanks. You can use character fields, character literals, and figurative constants in character string expressions.

Eval-corr is a specialized variation of Eval used with data structures, to assign subfields of one data structure to the corresponding subfields of another data structure. The corresponding subfields must have the same name and compatible data type for Eval-corr to process them.

RPG IV supports a rich set of built-in functions to simplify the processing of character strings. These functions can manipulate character strings, inspect their content and convert other data types to character data. The following table summarizes the operation codes and built-in functions discussed in this chapter. Optional entries are shown within curly braces ({}):

Function or operation	Description	Syntax
%Char	Convert to character data	%Char(*expression* {: *format*})
%Check	Check characters	%Check(*compare-string* : *base-string* {: *start*})
%Checkr	Check characters (reversed)	%Checkr(*compare-string* : *base-string* {: *start*})
%Decpos	Number of decimal positions	%Decpos(*numeric-expression*)
%Editc	Edit with an edit code	%Editc(*numeric-expression* : *edit-code* {: *fill*})
%Editw	Edit with an edit word	%Editw(*numeric-expression* : *edit-word*)
Eval	Evaluate expression	{Eval{(mr)}} *assignment-statement*
Evalr	Evaluate expression, right adjust	Evalr{(mr)} *assignment-statement*
Eval-corr	Assign corresponding subfields from one data structure to another	Eval-corr{(hmr)} *target = source*
%Len	Get or set length	%Len(*expression*)
%Replace	Replace character string	%Replace(*replacement* : *source* {:*start* {: *length*}})
%Scan	Scan string	%Scan(*search-arg* : *source* {: *start*})
%Size	Byte size	%Size(*data-item* {: *all*})
%Subst	Get or set substring	%Subst(*string* : *start* : *length*)
%Trim %Triml %Trimr	Trim characters at edges	%Trimx(*string* {: *characters*})
%Xlate	Translate	%Xlate(*from* : *to* : *string* {: *start*})

While fixed-length character variables always have the same declared length, variable-length data items have both a declared maximum length and a current length, which can change while the program is running, depending upon the value of the data item. Variable length character variables can simplify the coding and improve the performance of complex string operations.

Key Terms

character variables
character expressions
concatenation
concatenation expression
concatenation operators
continuation characters
current length
declared length
Eval operation
Evalr operation
Eval-corr operation
figurative constant
fixed-length
substring
translate

variable-length
%Char function
%Check function
%Checkr function
%Dec function
%Decpos function
%Editc function
%Editw function
%Len function
%Replace function
%Scan function
%Size function
%Subst function
%Trim function
%Xlate function

Discussion/Review Questions

1. Why would an RPG programmer need to convert character data (Example: JOHN SMITH) to upper and lower case (Example: John Smith)?
2. Explain the differences in the Eval and Evalr functions. Give an example of why these two functions are needed.
3. Describe the difference between the "+" and "-" continuation characters.
4. When concatenating strings, you need to avoid truncation. How would the programmer avoid truncation?
5. Are there circumstances where a programmer might intentionally truncate data? Please explain.
6. Explain the difference between the Eval and Evalr operations.
7. Explain how the %Trim, %Trimr, and %Triml functions work.
8. What "rules" apply to using the %Xlate function?
9. Explain the difference between the %Replace and %Xlate functions.
10. Under what circumstances would you use %Scan instead of %Check?
11. Explain the two techniques for removing unneeded blanks when concatenating strings.
12. Give three examples where you would use the following functions:
    - %Len function
    - %Size function
    - %Decpos function
    - %Scan function
    - %Check function
13. Give two examples of where Eval-corr would be useful when processing data structures.
14. Given the following two data structures, would you be able to use the Eval-corr operation? If not, explain the changes needed to allow the use of this function.

```
*.. 1 ...+... 2 ...+... 3 ...+... 4 ...+... 5 ...+... 6 ...+... 7 ...+... 8
DName++++++++++ETDsFrom+++To/L+++IDc.Keywords+++++++++++++++++++++++++++++++++
D Student          DS
D   StudentID                      5  0
D   Name                          30
D   State                          2
D   Zipcode                        9  0
D   Phone                         10
D   Creditlimit                   11  2

D Graduate         DS
D   GradID                         5U 0
D   Name                          35
D   Address                       35
D   City                          21
D   State                          2
D   Postcd                        10
D   Phone                         10  0
```

Exercises

The following exercises should be coded using the functions described in this chapter.

1. Write the code to convert the following data.

Before	After
JOHN SMITH	John Smith
SUSAN B. ANTHONY	Susan B. Anthony
GEORGE DAVID	David George
James Thomas Wells	J. T. WELLS

2. Write the code to convert the following data.

Before	After
2625643158	262-564-3158
262-564-3158	2625643158513465262
2625643158 513465262	985-58-9234 985-85-9234

3. Write the code to convert the following data.

Before	After
2625643158	506-564-3158
2625643158	262-999-3158
John Adams	John T. Adams

4.   Write the code to convert the following data.

Before	After
JAMES CARTER THOMAS	James Thomas Carter
200 WEST STREET KENOSHA WI 53142	200 West Street Kenosha WI, 53142
Alice Susan Simmons	A. S. Simmons
938-58-7843	938-66-7843

Programming Assignments

1.   GTC's accounting department wants a Customer report, sorted by the customer's phone number, which shows the following customer information. This report requires that all text fields in the Customer Master file (GTCSTP) be in shown in proper case. Write a program to convert and concatenate the CFNAME and CLNAME fields (Example: Amy Grashuis) and the CSTRET, CCITY, CSTAT, and CZIP fields (Example: 1212 35th St., Swamp Hollar, MI 49061-0000). The CURBIL, AMTOWE, and PAYDAT fields will be formatted as shown. Use the functions discussed in this chapter.

Field name	Current contents	After conversion
CPHONE	6162235255	(616) 223-5255
CFNAME	AMY	Amy
CLNAME	GRASHUIS	Grashuis
CSTRET	1212 35TH ST.	1212 35th St.
CCITY	SWAMP HOLLAR	Swamp Hollar
CSTAT	MI	MI
CZIP	49061	49061-0000
CURBILL	20.17	$**20.17
AMTOWE	36.03	$**36.03
PAYDAT	19980617	06-17-1998

```
         1         2         3         4         5         6         7         8         9
1234567890123456789012345678901234567890123456789012345678901234567890123456789012345678901
 1 XX/XX/XX                                                              Page XXØX
 2              GTC Customer Listing By Phone Number
 3
 4 Customer Phone Number: (999) 999-9999
 5 Name: XXXXXXXXXXXXXXXXXXXXXXXXXXXX
 6 Address: XXXXXXXXXXXXXXXXXXXXXXXXXXXXXXXXXXXXXXXXXXXXXXXXXX
 7 Current Bill: $***99.99    Amount Owed: $***99.99    Pay Date:  99-99-9999
 8
 9 Customer Phone Number: (999) 999-9999
10 Name: XXXXXXXXXXXXXXXXXXXXXXXXXXXX
11 Address: XXXXXXXXXXXXXXXXXXXXXXXXXXXXXXXXXXXXXXXXXXXXXXXXXX
12 Current Bill: $***99.99    Amount Owed: $***99.99    Pay Date:  99-99-9999
13
```

2. GTC's Customer Service Department wants a report showing customer calls sorted by the customer's last name, then first name, and the call information sorted by call date. This will require you to write the following report. Using the file GTCSTP, convert and concatenate fields CFNAME and CLNAME (Example: Amy Grashuis) and fields CSTRET, CCITY, CSTAT, and CZIP (Example: 1212 35th St., Swamp Hollar, MI 49061-0000). The file GTCLSP will be used to print the call information; the formatting requirements are below. Use the functions discussed in this chapter.

Field name	Current contents	After conversion
CPHONE	6162235255	(616) 223-5255
CFNAME	AMY	Amy
CLNAME	GRASHUIS	Grashuis
CSTRET	1212 35TH ST.	1212 35th St.
CCITY	SWAMP HOLLAR	Swamp Hollar
CSTAT	MI	MI
CZIP	49061	49061-0000
PHCALLED	9052470880	905-247-0880
CALDAT	19981225	12-25-1998
CALLEN	25	*25
CALTIM	2345	23:45
CALCST	5.83	$**5.83

```
            1         2         3         4         5         6         7         8         9
   1234567890123456789012345678901234567890123456789012345678901234567890123456789012345678901
 1 XX/XX/XX                                                              Page XX0X
 2              GTC Customer Listing By Last Name By First Name
 3                 Customer Detail By Phone Number Called
 4
 5 Name: XXXXXXXXXXXXXXXXXXXXXXXXXXXX
 6 Address: XXXXXXXXXXXXXXXXXXXXXXXXXXXXXXXXXXXXXXXXXXXXXXX
 7 Customer Phone Number: (999) 999-9999
 8 Current Bill: $***99.99     Amount Owed: $***99.99     Pay Date:  99-99-9999
 9
10 Call Information
11 Number               Date              Call      Call      Call
12 Called                    Called            Length  Time   Cost
13 999-999-9999    99-99-9999    *99        99:99   $**9.99
14 999-999-9999    99-99-9999    *99        99:99   $**9.99
15 999-999-9999    99-99-9999    *99        99:99   $**9.99
16
17 Name: XXXXXXXXXXXXXXXXXXXXXXXXXXXX
18 Address: XXXXXXXXXXXXXXXXXXXXXXXXXXXXXXXXXXXXXXXXXXXXXXX
19 Customer Phone Number: (999) 999-9999
20 Current Bill: $***99.99     Amount Owed: $***99.99     Pay Date:  99-99-9999
21
22 Call Information
23 Number               Date              Call      Call      Call
24 Called                    Called            Length  Time   Cost
25 999-999-9999    99-99-9999    *99        99:99   $**9.99
```

3. CompuSell wants a report sorted by CUSTNO that will convert and concatenate the fields CFNAME and CLNAME (Example: Abdul Halim Nariza) and fields CSTREET, CCITY, CSTATE, and CZIP (Example: 5652 N. 46th St., Kalamazoo, MI 49008-0000). Write a program that will read the CSCSTP file and output the following fields to the Report. The date format will change, and the BALDUE field will be padded with (*). Use the functions discussed in this chapter.

Field name	Current contents	After conversion
CUSTNO	100001	10-0001
CLNAME	NARIZA	Nariza
CFNAME	ABDUL HALIM	Abdul Halim
CSTREET	5652 N. 46TH ST.	5652 N. 46th St.
CCITY	KALAMAZOO	Kalamazoo
CSTATE	MI	MI
CZIP	490080000	49008-0000
CPHONE	6161254115	(616) 125-4115
ORDDAT	1211997	19971211
BALDUE	0	******.**

```
          1         2         3         4         5         6         7         8         9
 1234567890123456789012345678901234567890123456789012345678901234567890123456789012345678901
 1 XX/XX/XX                                                            Page XX0X
 2                CompuSell Customer Report
 3
 4 Name: XXXXXXXXXXXXXXXXXXXXXXXXXXXX
 5 Address: XXXXXXXXXXXXXXXXXXXXXXXXXXXXXXXXXXXXXXXXXXXXXXXXXX
 6 Customer Phone Number: (999) 999-9999
 7 Order Date: yyyymmdd       Balance Due: *999.99
 8
 9 Name: XXXXXXXXXXXXXXXXXXXXXXXXXXXX
10 Address: XXXXXXXXXXXXXXXXXXXXXXXXXXXXXXXXXXXXXXXXXXXXXXXXXX
11 Customer Phone Number: (999) 999-9999
12 Order Date: yyyymmdd       Balance Due: *999.99
13
14
15
16
```

4. Wexler University's new dean of instruction wants a report of all instructors hired between 1980 and 1990. This information should be sorted by department, and, within department, by instructor last name, then first name. The report should produce a count of the instructors in each department. The following fields from file WUINSTP will be converted for this report. Use the functions discussed in this chapter.

Field name	Current contents	After conversion
INSTNO	287142981	287142981
IFNAME	JOHN	John
ILNAME	WILDER	Wilder
HIRDAT	19950314	1995-03-14
STREET	6834 W. OAKLAND AVE.	6834 W. Oakland Ave.
CITY	KALAMAZOO	Kalamazoo
STATE	MI	MI
ZIP	490080000	49008-0000
SALARY	61540.00	$*61540.00

```
          1         2         3         4         5         6         7         8         9         1
                                                                                                    0
 1234567890123456789012345678901234567890123456789012345678901234567890123456789012345678901234567890
 1  XX/XX/XX                           Wexler University                                  Page      1
 2                              Instructors Hired Between
 3                                   9999 AND 9999
 4 Dept Instr#     Hire Date  Last Name, First      Address          City, State     Zipcode    Salary
 5 XXX  999999999 9999-99-99 XXXXXXXXXXXXXXXXXXX XXXXXXXXXXXXXXX XXXXXXXXXXXXX 99999-9999 $*99999.99
 6             Number of Instructors in DEPT       99
 7 XXX  999999999 9999-99-99 XXXXXXXXXXXXXXXXXXX XXXXXXXXXXXXXXX XXXXXXXXXXXXX 99999-9999 $*99999.99
 8 XXX  999999999 9999-99-99 XXXXXXXXXXXXXXXXXXX XXXXXXXXXXXXXXX XXXXXXXXXXXXX 99999-9999 $*99999.99
 9             Number of Instructors in DEPT       99
10             Total Number of Instructors        99
11
```

5. Wexler University's Registration department wants a student report sorted by the student last name, then first name. This report should convert the following fields from file WUSTDP and concatenate fields SFNAME, SMNAME, and SLNAME (Example: Patricia Eileen Smith) and fields STREET, CITY, STATE, and ZIP (Example: 647 18th St., Detroit, MI 48932-1102). Use the functions discussed in this chapter.

Field name	Current contents	After conversion
STUSSN	154488932	154-48-8932
SFNAME	PATRICIA	Patricia
SLNAME	SMITH	Smith
SMNAME	EILEEN	Eileen
STREET	647 18TH ST.	647 18th St
CITY	DETROIT	Detroit
STATE	MI	MI
ZIP	489321102	48932-1102
PHONE	3138473283	313-847-3283

```
          1         2         3         4         5         6         7         8         9
 12345678901234567890123456789012345678901234567890123456789012345678901234567890123456789012345678901
 1 XX/XX/XX            Wexler University Registration Report              Page 99
 2
 3 Student No.      Student Information
 4 999-99-9999      XXXXXXXXXXXXXXXXXXXXXXXXXXXXXX
 5                  XXXXXXXXXXXXXXXXXXXXXXXXXXXXXXXXXXXXXXXX
 6                  999-999-9999
 7
 8 Student No.      Student Information
 9 999-99-9999      XXXXXXXXXXXXXXXXXXXXXXXXXXXXXX
10                  XXXXXXXXXXXXXXXXXXXXXXXXXXXXXXXXXXXXXXXX
11                  999-999-9999
12
```

Chapter 7

Working with Dates

Chapter Overview

This chapter covers the native date-related data types. You'll learn how to define dates and how their format affects processing. You'll discover how to use several built-in functions to easily perform date arithmetic. You'll also learn how to convert among date, character, and numeric data types and how to process "legacy dates," which are defined as numeric or character data.

Defining Date-Related Data

RPG IV supports three native data types that can be used to store and process values related to dates. The three date types are

- Date (data type D)
- Time (data type T)
- Timestamp (date type Z)

Dates and **times** are self-evident data types used to store values associated with the calendar and the clock. A **timestamp** is a combination of a date and a time, carried out to microseconds precision (.000001 seconds). In general, RPG IV applies the same principles and rules to all three data types; when this book refers to dates, we'll intend that the same concept applies to times and timestamps as well, unless we indicate otherwise.

Caution
Be sure that you do not confuse the date, time, and timestamp data types with numeric or character variables that may be used to represent date-related data. Because the native date data types are a fairly recent development in the RPG world, many applications still use numeric or character variables to deal with date-related data. With these "legacy" date variables, it is up to the RPG program to provide any special processing required to validate or process them as if they were dates, times, or timestamps.

Defining Dates in Input Specifications

You can define dates as fields in program-described files, in externally described files, or as data items in Definition specifications. In Chapter 2, we illustrated how to use Input specifications to define a date for a program-described file:

```
*.. 1 ...+... 2 ...+... 3 ...+... 4 ...+... 5 ...+... 6 ...+... 7 ...+... 8
IFilename++SqNORiPos1+NCCPos2+NCCPos3+NCC..........................................
I.....................Fmt+SPFrom+To+++DcField++++++++L1M1FrP1MnZr......
ICustomers NS
I                                  1    4  Accountid
I                                  5    8  Salesperson
I                                  9   43  Name
I                                 44   78  Address
I                                 79   99  City
I                                100  101  State
I                                102  111  Postalcode
I                                112  131  Country
I                        *USA D  132  141  Lastsaledate
I                                142  152 2Ytdsales
```

In this example, the Lastsaledate field is a date field, as indicated by the D in position 36. The entry *USA in positions 31-34 indicates that Lastsaledate is in *mm/dd/yyyy* format, including the slash (/) **separator characters** (we'll discuss date formats in a moment). The Field Location entries (positions 37-46) represent the location of the field within the record format. The length of that location must correspond to the formatted length of the field. In this case, Lastsaledate occupies 10 bytes in the record format, bytes 132-141. Dates occupy 6, 8, or 10 bytes, depending upon their format; times (type T) occupy 8 bytes, and timestamps (type Z) occupy 26 bytes. Since the concept of a decimal point does not apply to native dates, positions 47-48 are left blank.

Defining Dates Using DDS

You can also define dates, times, and timestamps in externally described files, using DDS or SQL, and then use those files in an RPG IV program. Here is the DDS for the Customers file that we used as an example in Chapter 3:

```
*.. 1 ...+... 2 ...+... 3 ...+... 4 ...+... 5 ...+... 6 ...+... 7 ...+... 8
A..........T.Name++++++RLen++TDcB......Keywords++++++++++++++++++++++++++++++++
 * Physical file CUSTOMERS
A          R CUSTREC
A            ACCOUNTID    4A        TEXT('Account identifier')
A            SALESPERS    4A        TEXT('Salesperson')
A            NAME        35A        TEXT('Customer name')
A            ADDRESS     35A        TEXT('Customer address')
A            CITY        21A        TEXT('Customer city')
A            STATE        2A        TEXT('Customer state')
A            POSTALCODE  10A        TEXT('Postal code')
A            COUNTRY     20A        TEXT('Foreign country')
A            LASTSALEDT   L         TEXT('Date of last sale')
A                                   DATFMT(*USA)
A            YTDSALES    11S 2      TEXT('Year-to-date sales')
A          K ACCOUNTID
```

Lastsaledt is the date field in this example. Recall that DDS uses data type L in position 35 to define a native date; times used data type T, and timestamps are coded with data type Z. The digits (positions 30–34) and decimal positions (positions 36–37) entries are left blank. Notice the **Datfmt** keyword; as was the case in Chapter 3, the field is in *USA format (*mm/dd/yyyy*). To specify a format for time data, you'd use the corresponding **Timfmt** keyword; timestamps do not support a formatting keyword.

Defining Dates Using Definition Specifications

Standalone variables and data structure subfields can also be dates, times, or timestamps. Here are some examples:

```
*.. 1 ...+... 2 ...+... 3 ...+... 4 ...+... 5 ...+... 6 ...+... 7 ...+... 8
DName++++++++++ETDsFrom+++To/Len+IDc.Keywords+++++++++++++++++++++++++++++++
 // Variable Enrolldate is a date variable
D Enrolldate     S             D

 // Variable Starttime is a time variable
D Starttime      S             T

 // Variable TransTime is a timestamp variable
D Transtime      S             Z

 // Subfield Birthdate is a date
D Personnel      DS
D   Birthdate                  D
D   Birthyear               4  0 Overlay(Birthdate)
D   Birthmonth              2  0 Overlay(Birthmonth:6)
D   Birthday                2  0 Overlay(Birthdate:9)
```

Recall that D-specs uses position 40 to indicate the data type: D for dates, T for times, Z for timestamps. The digits (positions 33-39) and decimal positions (positions 41-42) entries are left blank. Like DDS, D-specs also support Datfmt and Timfmt keywords. If the data item is a data structure subfield, you can also use the Overlay keyword, discussed in Chapter 4, to redefine subfields or portions of subfields, as shown in the above example.

Understanding Date Formats

Each of the date-related data types has a preset size and format, and each has a **default display format** (*ISO), based on the International Standards Organization **(ISO) standards**. The default display format for dates is a 10-byte-long field with format *yyyy-mm-dd*. Time (T) has a default length of 8 bytes, with format *hh.mm.ss*. The default display format for timestamp (Z) has a length of 26 bytes, with format *yyyy-mm-dd-hh.mm.ss.mmmmmm*.

The date and time (but not the timestamp) data types allow alternate display formats to the defaults. Date, for instance, supports eight different formats, and time supports five different formats. The following tables list the valid **date and time formats**.

Date format	Description	Format	Valid separators	Edited field length	Example
*ISO	International Standards Organization	yyyy-mm-dd	-	10	2007-12-31
*USA	IBM US Standard	mm/dd/yyyy	/	10	12/31/2007
*EUR	IBM European Standard	dd.mm.yyyy	.	10	31.12.2007
*JIS	Japanese Industrial Standard	yyyy-mm-dd	-	10	2007-12-31
*YMD	Year/month/day	yy/mm/dd	/ - , . &(blank)	8	07/12/31
*MDY	Month/day/year	mm/dd/yy	/ - , . &(blank)	8	12/31/07
*DMY	Day/month/year	dd/mm/yy	/ - , . &(blank)	8	31/12/07
*JUL	Julian	yy/ddd	/ - , . &(blank)	6	07/365

Time format	Description	Format	Valid separators	Example
*ISO	International Standards Organization	hh.mm.ss	.	19.30.00
*USA	IBM US Standard	hh:mm xM	:	07:30 PM
*EUR	IBM European Standard	hh.mm.ss	.	19.30.00
*JIS	Japanese Industrial Standard	hh:mm:ss	:	19:30:00
*HMS	Hours:minutes:seconds	hh:mm:ss	: , . &(blank)	19:30:00

To specify an alternate format for a date field, you use keyword Datfmt on the Definition specification with the desired format code; for time fields, use keyword Timfmt and the desired format code. You can also change the default display format of date and time fields for a program as a whole by specifying the Datfmt and/or Timfmt keyword within the Control specifications (or in a File specification to indicate a default format for date/time fields within a program-described file).

Each display format includes a default separator character. For example, the separator character for the *ISO date format is the hyphen (-). The separator character is an intrinsic part of the format. Several of the formats let you change the separator character. For example, acceptable separator characters for the * DMY and *MDY date formats are the hyphen, the slash (/), the period (.), the comma (,), and the ampersand (&), which is displayed as a blank. Acceptable separator characters for the *HMS time format are the colon (:), the period, the comma, and the ampersand for blank. To change from the default separator, simply insert the separator character you want to use after the format code (e.g., *MDY- or *HMS&). The following code illustrates how to define standalone date variables with various formats (some using the default display formats and others specifying alternate formats).

```
*.. 1 ...+... 2 ...+... 3 ...+... 4 ...+... 5 ...+... 6 ...+... 7 ...+... 8
DName++++++++++ETDsFrom+++To/L+++IDc.Keywords+++++++++++++++++++++++++++++++
   // Define a date field in default format (*Iso): e.g., 2008-03-15.
D Todaysdate      S               D
   // Define a date field, *Ymd format, default separator (/): 08/03/15.
D Duedatea        S               D    Datfmt(*Ymd)
   // Define a date field, *Ymd format, alternate separator (.): 08.03.15.
D Duedateb        S               D    Datfmt(*Ymd.)

   // Define a time field in default format (*Iso):  e.g., 14.45.24.
D Timea           S               T
   // Define a time field in *Usa format: 2:45 PM.
D Timeb           S               T    Timfmt(*Usa)
   // Define a time field, *Hms format, blank separator: 14 45 24.
D Timec           S               T    Timfmt(*Hms&)

   //Define a timestamp field: e.g., 1995-03-15-06.15.37.000000.
D Timestmp        S               Z
```

Simple Date Assignment

In previous chapters, we used the Eval operation to evaluate numeric and character expressions. As you might guess, RPG IV also uses Eval with dates. To assign a value to a date, time, or timestamp variable, you code a simple assignment expression (recall that explicitly coding Eval is optional):

```
DName++++++++++ETDsFrom+++To/Len+IDc.Keywords+++++++++++++++++++++++++++++++
D Enrolldate      S               D
D Today           S               D    Inz(*Sys)

 /Free
    Enrolldate = Today;  // Enrolldate now contains the current system date
 /End-Free
```

This example assigns the value in one date variable to another date variable. Just as in previous assignment operations, the value to be assigned appears to the right of the equal sign, and the receiving variable appears to the left. The two date variables must both be compatible; that is, you cannot directly assign a number to a date. But the two dates need not both be in the same format, nor do they need to both use the same separator characters.

The above example uses the Inz D-specification keyword, discussed in Chapter 4, to initialize Today to the current system date. Inz(*Sys) also works to initialize times and timestamps to their current value when the program starts. To initialize a date field to the job date, you can code Inz(*Job) in the keyword area of the field's definition.

You can also use a simple assignment expression to assign a date or a time to the relevant portion of a timestamp. The following examples assign a date and time to a timestamp.

```
DName++++++++++ETDsFrom+++To/Len+IDc.Keywords+++++++++++++++++++++++++++++
D Kdate          S               D   Inz(D'1963-11-22')
D Ktime          S               T   Inz(T'12.34.56')
D Kstamp         S               Z

 /Free
            // Kstamp has an initial value of Z'0001-01-01-00.00.00.000000'
    Kstamp = Kdate;
            // Kstamp now contains Z'1963-11-22-00.00.00.000000'
    Kstamp = Ktime;
            // Kstamp now contains Z'1963-11-22-12.34.56.000000'
 /End-Free
```

Using Typed Literals

In addition to date variables, you can also assign literal values to date, time, and timestamp values by using typed literals. To code a typed literal, enclose the value within apostrophes, but precede it with a data type code to indicate which data type the literal represents. To refer to a value of January 1, 2008, for example, you'd code D'2008-01-01' as the literal. Other data type codes for date-related typed literals are T (for times) and Z (for timestamps). Here are some examples of typed literals for dates, times, and timestamps:

Data type	Typed literal
Date	D'2008-03-15'
Time	T'08.56.20'
Timestamp	Z'2008-03-15-08.56.20.000000' or Z'2008-03-15-08.56.20'

Here's an example of using a typed literal for simple assignment:

```
Enrolldate = D'2008-12-31';
```

The format of the date or time in the typed literal may vary from one program to another. The default format is *ISO. But if you've coded a Datfmt (or Timfmt) keyword in the Control specification to specify a default date (or time) format for the program, the format of the typed literal must match the format you code in the Control specification. Study this example:

```
HKeywords++++++++++++++++++++++++++++++++++++++++++++++++++++++++++++++++++
DName++++++++++ETDsFrom+++To/Len+IDc.Keywords+++++++++++++++++++++++++++++
H Datfmt(*Usa)

D Enrolldate     S               D   Datfmt(*Iso)

 /Free
    Enrolldate = D'12/31/2008';          // Enrolldate now contains 2008-12-31
 /End-Free
```

Here, we've coded the Datfmt keyword in the Control specification to indicate that the default date format for the program is *USA format. Therefore the typed literal must show the desired date in *USA format—even though the result field, Enrolldate, is in *ISO format, as indicated in its definition. Leading and trailing zeros are required for all date, time, and timestamp typed literals.

Unlike date and time typed literals, timestamp literals must always be in the same format, regardless of any formatting keywords elsewhere in the program. The microseconds portion of a timestamp literal is optional; if you omit it, the microseconds portion of the timestamp will be padded with zeros.

Assigning Values with Figurative Constants

In addition to the previously discussed options, RPG IV lets you assign the values of named constants or figurative constants ***Hival** and ***Loval** to dates, times, and timestamps (or use constants for initial values). *Hival and *Loval can have different values, though, depending upon which format a date is using. The formats that allow four-digit years can store any value from January 1, 0001, to December 31, 9999 — while dates in the two-digit year formats are restricted to a 100-year window from January 1, 1940, to December 31, 2039. The following table shows the allowable range of values for each of the date and time formats. In each case, *Loval is also the default value for that format.

Date	Format	*Loval	*Hival
*ISO	yyyy-mm-dd	0001-01-01	9999-12-31
*USA	mm/dd/yyyy	01/01/0001	12/31/9999
*EUR	dd.mm.yyyy	01.01.0001	31.12.9999
*JIS	yyyy-mm-dd	0001-01-01	9999-12-31
*YMD	yy/mm/dd	40/01/01	39/12/31
*MDY	mm/dd/yy	01/01/40	12/31/39
*DMY	dd/mm/yy	01/01/40	31/12/39
*JUL	yy/ddd	40/001	39/365

Time	Format	*Loval	*Hival
*ISO	hh.mm.ss	00.00.00	24.00.00
*USA	hh:mm xM	00:00 AM	12:00 AM
*EUR	hh.mm.ss	00.00.00	24.00.00
*JIS	hh:mm:ss	00:00:00	24:00:00
*HMS	hh:mm:ss	00:00:00	24:00:00

When you are assigning values to a date variable, you must be careful to be sure the value will fit into the format that the date variable is using. For example, the following assignment would generate an error.

```
DName++++++++++ETDsFrom+++To/Len+IDc.Keywords+++++++++++++++++++++++++++++
D Birthdate        S              D    Datfmt(*Mdy)

 /Free
    Birthdate = D'1928-07-21';                // RNQ0112 error: Invalid date
 /End-Free
```

While July 21, 1928, is indeed a valid date, it will not fit into the 100-year window imposed by the *MDY format. Consequently, an error occurs.

Tip
To avoid runtime errors when dealing with dates, you should always use one of the four-digit year formats.

Simple Date Arithmetic

In Chapter 5, we saw how to use Eval for simple numeric assignment. The Eval operation also provides a flexible and powerful method for easily performing date arithmetic using free-format expressions. Typically a date expression will include the arithmetic operators + (addition) and —(subtraction), as well as one or more functions that RPG IV uses to convert a numeric value to a special internal data type called a **duration**. Duration is the term RPG uses to describe a unit of time between two dates, times, or timestamps. RPG IV recognizes seven durations and provides seven corresponding functions:

- **%Years**, for dates or timestamps
- **%Months**, for dates or timestamps
- **%Days**, for dates or timestamps
- **%Hours**, for times or timestamps
- **%Minutes**, for times or timestamps
- **%Seconds**, for times or timestamps
- **%Mseconds** (microseconds), for times or timestamps

Each of these functions converts a number into a duration that can be added to (or subtracted from) a date, time, or timestamp in a familiar expression.

```
DName+++++++++++ETDsFrom+++To/Len+IDc.Keywords++++++++++++++++++++++++++++++
D Terms           S              5U 0
D Duedate         S              D
D Invoicedate     S              D
D Endfeb          S              D    Inz(D'2008-02-29')
D Endjan          S              D    Inz(D'2009-01-31')
D Min             S              5U 0 Inz(60)
D Monthago        S              D    Inz(*Sys)

 /Free
    Duedate = Invoicedate + %Days(30);     // Add 30 days to Invoicedate
    Duedate = Invoicedate + %Days(Terms);
                                // Add Terms value (as days) to invoice date

    Endtime = Starttime + %Minutes(Min);   // Add 60 minutes to Starttime

    // The following two lines are equivalent
    Monthago = Monthago - %Months(1);      // Subtract 1 month from Monthago
    Monthago -= %Months(1);

    // The following lines illustrate leap year effects
    // and the irreversibility of some date calculations
    Endfeb += %Years(1);                   // Endfeb = D'2009-02-28'
    Endfeb -= %Years(1);                   // Now, Endfeb = D'2008-02-28'
    Endjan = Endjan + %Months(1) - %Months(1);
                                           // Endmar = D'2009-01-28'
 /End-Free
```

If addition or subtraction would result in an invalid date, an expression will use the end of the month instead. Because of the vagaries of the calendar, addition or subtraction involving the 29th, 30th, or 31st of the month may not be reversible, as the last two examples show. The duration function must logically match the data type of the expression's result variable. For example, you cannot add a %Minutes duration if the expression's result is a date, but you can add %Minutes to a time or timestamp.

By adding a time to a date, you can assign the resulting value to a timestamp. The following example is similar to the simple assignment expression shown earlier but accomplishes the same end with a single expression.

```
DName+++++++++++ETDsFrom+++To/Len+IDc.Keywords++++++++++++++++++++++++++++++
D Kdate           S              D    Inz(D'1963-11-22')
D Ktime           S              T    Inz(T'12.34.56')
D Kstamp          S              Z

 /Free
            // Kstamp has an initial value of Z'0001-01-01-00.00.00.000000'
    Kstamp = Kdate + Ktime;
            // Kstamp now contains Z'1963-11-22-12.34.56.000000'
 /End-Free
```

Using Built-in Functions with Dates

In addition to the duration functions, RPG includes two functions that let you perform date processing that cannot be done with simple arithmetic-like expressions:

- %Diff, to find the difference between two dates, times, or timestamps
- %Subdt, to extract a portion of a date, time, or timestamp

%Diff (Difference)

The **%Diff (Difference) function** calculates the duration between two date/time values. The first two arguments must be data items of compatible types; the third argument represents the duration code that corresponds to the duration unit you want to determine. The general format is

```
%Diff(date1:date2:duration)
```

The result is a number, rounded down, with any remainder discarded. You can use the %Diff function to find the duration between

- Two dates
- Two times
- Two timestamps
- A date and the date portion of a timestamp
- A time and the time portion of a timestamp

The third argument must be a special value that corresponds to one of the seven durations:

- *Years (or *Y), for dates or timestamps
- *Months (or *M), for dates or timestamps
- *Days (or *D), for dates or timestamps
- *Hours (or *H), for times or timestamps
- *Minutes (or *Mn), for times or timestamps
- *Seconds (or *S), for times or timestamps
- *Mseconds (or *Ms), for timestamps

%Diff calculates the difference by subtracting the second argument from the first. The following examples show the use of the %Diff function.

```
*.. 1 ...+... 2 ...+... 3 ...+... 4 ...+... 5 ...+... 6 ...+... 7 ...+... 8
DName++++++++++ETDsFrom+++To/Len+IDc.Keywords+++++++++++++++++++++++++++++++
D Basedate       C                       D'1899-12-30'

D Age            S              5U 0
D Birthdate      S              D
D Endtime        S              Z
D Fracthours     S             15  5
D Message        S             80
D Starttime      S              Z
D Today          S              D   Inz(*Sys)
D Weeks          S              5U 0

 /Free
   Age = %Diff(Today:Birthdate:*Years);         // Calculate age in years

   // The following two lines are equivalent
   Message = 'You are currently ' + %Char(Age) + ' years old.';
   Message = 'You are currently ' + %Char( %Diff(Today:BirthDate:*Years) )
             + ' years old.';

   Weeks = Diff(Today:Basedate:*Days) / 7;
                                       // Calculate difference in weeks

   Eval(h) Fracthours = %Diff(Endtime:Starttime:*Seconds) / 3600;
                    // Calculate fractional hours between two timestamps
 /End-Free
```

%Subdt (Extract from Date/Time/Timestamp)

The **%Subdt (Extract from date/time/timestamp) function** "substrings" a date; that is, it extracts a portion of a date, time, or timestamp data item. The first argument is the date, time, or timestamp variable; it is followed by a special value that specifies the portion of the value you want to extract—one of the same special values used by the %Diff function. The result is numeric.

```
*.. 1 ...+... 2 ...+... 3 ...+... 4 ...+... 5 ...+... 6 ...+... 7 ...+... 8
DName++++++++++ETDsFrom+++To/Len+IDc.Keywords+++++++++++++++++++++++++++++++
D Birthdate      S              D
D Day            S              5U 0
D Month          S              5U 0
D Year           S              5U 0

D Jdate          S              D   Datfmt(*Jul)
D                                   Inz(D'2009-02-10')
                    // Jdate is displayed in Julian format as 09/041
```

continued...

continued...

```
/Free
   Year = %Subdt(Birthdate:*Years);      // Extract year from Birthdate
   Month = %Subdt(Birthdate:*Months);    // Extract month from Birthdate
   Day = %Subdt(Birthdate:*Days);        // Extract day from Birthdate

   Year = %Subdt(Jdate:*Years);          // Year = 2009
   Month = %Subdt(Jdate:*Months);        // Month = 02
   Day = %Subdt(Jdate:*Days);            // Day = 10

/End-Free
```

The %Subdt function always treats the *Days code as the day of the month (even for *JUL format dates) and always returns a four-digit year when you specify the *Years code.

Data Conversion Functions

All the operands in a date expression must be a date data type or a duration subtype; the program cannot directly mix date values with numeric or character data in the same expression. The duration functions discussed earlier convert a numeric expression to a duration subtype, so it can be used in a date expression. Several other functions convert numeric and character expressions to dates, times, and timestamps; still others convert date-related data back to character and numeric values. These functions are

- %Date (Convert to date)
- %Time (Convert to time)
- %Timestamp (Convert to timestamp)
- %Char (Convert to character)
- %Dec (Convert to decimal)

%Date (Convert to Date)

The primary use for the **%Date** (**Convert to date**) **function** is to convert a numeric or character value to a date data type. The value to convert can be a variable, literal, constant, or expression. The format of the **%Date function** is

```
%Date({value{:format}})
```

The first argument is the value that you want to convert. The second argument is the date format of the value to be converted—that is, if the value were already a date, this is the format that it would be using. If you omit the second argument, %Date will use the program's default format, usually *ISO (unless the Control specification Datfmt keyword indicates otherwise).

Recall that the date separator character is an integral part of the date. The conversion function must account for the separator. If the character value contains a separator character other than the format's default, you can include a separator character with the format designation; if the character value contains no separators; code a zero (0) following the format to indicate no separators. When converting numeric values, you need not account for a separator, since numeric values would not allow a separator. Here are some examples of using %Date to convert data.

```
*.. 1 ...+... 2 ...+... 3 ...+... 4 ...+... 5 ...+... 6 ...+... 7 ...+... 8
DName++++++++++ETDsFrom+++To/Len+IDc.Keywords++++++++++++++++++++++++++++++++
D Mydate          S              D
D Char            S             10        Inz('02/12/2009')
D Char2           S              6        Inz('031310')
D Num             S              8 0       Inz(20110414)
D Numjde          S              7 0       Inz(1110812)

D Month           S              2 0       Inz(5)
D Day             S              2 0       Inz(15)
D Year            S              4 0       Inz(2012)

 /Free
    Mydate = %Date(Char:*Usa);        // Mydate now contains D'2009-02-12'
    Mydate = %Date(Char2:*Mdy0);      // Mydate now contains D'2010-03-13'
    Mydate = %Date(Num);              // Mydate now contains D'2011-04-14'
    Mydate = %Date(Numjde:*Cymd);     // Mydate now contains D'2011-08-12'

    Mydate = %Date( ((Year*10000) + (Month*100) + Day) );
                                      // Mydate now contains D'2012-05-15'
 /End-Free
```

%Date always returns its result in *ISO format, regardless of the format of the value to be converted. If you omit the first argument, %Date will return the current system date:

```
*.. 1 ...+... 2 ...+... 3 ...+... 4 ...+... 5 ...+... 6 ...+... 7 ...+... 8
DName++++++++++ETDsFrom+++To/Len+IDc.Keywords++++++++++++++++++++++++++++++++
D Today           S              D

 /Free
    Today = %Date();        // Today now contains the current system date
 /End-Free
```

The first argument can also be a timestamp, allowing you to move the date portion of a timestamp into a date variable. Or the first argument can be the IBM-reserved word *Date or Udate to assign the current job date to a variable. *Date and Udate refer to the same value, except that *Date includes a four-digit year, while Udate includes only a two-digit year. For any of these cases—a timestamp, *Date, or Udate—you do not code a second argument, because the computer already knows the format.

```
*.. 1 ...+... 2 ...+... 3 ...+... 4 ...+... 5 ...+... 6 ...+... 7 ...+... 8
DName++++++++++ETDsFrom+++To/Len+IDc.Keywords++++++++++++++++++++++++++++++++
D Asof            S              D

 /Free
    Asof = %Date(*Date);        // Asof now contains the current job date
 /End-Free
```

The %Date function accepts a number of additional external formats that RPG IV supports for backward compatibility with legacy applications. These are not valid internal date formats, but they can be used when you want to convert character or numeric data that represents dates.

External format	Description	Format	Valid separators	Edited field length	Example
*CYMD	Century/year/month/day	cyy/mm/dd	/ - , . &(blank)	9	107/12/31
*CMDY	Century/month/day/year	cmm/dd/yy	/ - , . &(blank)	9	112/31/07
*CDMY	Century/day/month/year	cdd/mm/yy	/ - , . &(blank)	9	131/12/07
*LONGJUL	Long Julian	yyyy/ddd	/ - , . &(blank)	8	2007/365
*JOBRUN	(Format and separators are determined at runtime, using the job's attributes. Valid only for two-digit year formats.)				

In the above table the "century" portion of the date (illustrated with a "c" in the format column) is indicated by a single digit 0–9, with 0 representing 1900–1999, 1 representing 2000–2099, and so on, up to 9, which represents 2800–2899. So, in *CYMD format, the numeric value 1071231 represents December 31, 2007. The following code illustrates the use of these external formats.

```
*.. 1 ...+... 2 ...+... 3 ...+... 4 ...+... 5 ...+... 6 ...+... 7 ...+... 8
DName++++++++++ETDsFrom+++To/Len+IDc.Keywords+++++++++++++++++++++++++++++++
D Mydate          S               D
D Char            S               9       Inz('109/02/12')
D Num             S               7 0     Inz(0991231)
D Num2            S               7 0     Inz(2011040)

 /Free
    Mydate = %Date(Char:*Cymd);       // Mydate now contains D'2009-02-12'
    Mydate = %Date(Num:*Cymd);        // Mydate now contains D'1999-12-31'
    Mydate = %Date(Num2:*Longjul);    // Mydate now contains D'2011-02-09'
 /End-Free
```

%Time (Convert to Time)

The **%Time (Convert to time) function** is similar to %Date and uses many of the same principles. It will convert a numeric or character value to a time data type. The value to convert can be a variable, literal, constant, or expression. The format of the %Time function is

`%Time({value{:format}})`

The first argument is the value that you want to convert. The second argument is the time format of the value to be converted; if you omit the second argument, %Time will use the program's default format, usually *ISO (unless the Control specification Timfmt keyword indicates otherwise).

As with dates, the time separator character is an integral part of the value, and the conversion function must account for it. If the character value contains a separator character other than the format's default, you can include a separator character with the format designation; if the character value contains no separators, code a zero (0) following the format to indicate no separators. When converting numeric values, you need not account for a separator, since numeric values would not allow a separator. Some examples of using %Time to convert data follow.

```
*.. 1 ...+... 2 ...+... 3 ...+... 4 ...+... 5 ...+... 6 ...+... 7 ...+... 8
DName+++++++++++ETDsFrom+++To/Len+IDc.Keywords++++++++++++++++++++++++++++++++
D Mytime          S                    T
D Char            S              10        Inz('12:34 PM')
D Char2           S               6        Inz('134500')
D Num             S               8  0     Inz(145600)

 /Free
    Mytime = %Time(Char:*Usa);        // Mytime now contains T'12.34.00'
    Mytime = %Time(Char2:*Hms0);      // Mytime now contains T'13.45.00'
    Mytime = %Time(Num);              // Mytime now contains T'14.56.00'
 /End-Free
```

%Time always returns its result in *ISO format, regardless of the format of the value to be converted. If you omit the first argument, %Time will return the current system time:

```
*.. 1 ...+... 2 ...+... 3 ...+... 4 ...+... 5 ...+... 6 ...+... 7 ...+... 8
DName+++++++++++ETDsFrom+++To/Len+IDc.Keywords++++++++++++++++++++++++++++++++
D Mytime          S                    T

 /Free
    Mytime = %Time();        // Mytime now contains the current system time
 /End-Free
```

The first argument can also be a timestamp, allowing you to move the time portion of a timestamp into a time variable. In this case, you do not code a second argument, because the computer already knows the format.

%Timestamp (Convert to Timestamp)

As you might expect, the **%Timestamp (Convert to timestamp) function** converts the value of a character or numeric expression—or a date expression—to a timestamp data type. The function takes the form

```
%Timestamp({value{:format}})
```

The first argument is the value that you want to convert. The second argument is used only with character expressions and is one of two special values: *ISO or *ISO0 (if there are no separators). No other formats are allowed. Here are some examples of using %Timestamp:

```
*.. 1 ...+... 2 ...+... 3 ...+... 4 ...+... 5 ...+... 6 ...+... 7 ...+... 8
DName+++++++++++ETDsFrom+++To/Len+IDc.Keywords++++++++++++++++++++++++++++++++
D Mystamp         S                    Z
D Char            S              20        Inz('19631122123456789012')
D Num             S              20        Inz(19991231235959999999)

 /Free
    Mystamp = %Timestamp(Char:*Iso0);
                      // Mystamp now contains Z'1963-11-22-12.34.56.789012'
    Mystamp = %Timestamp(Num);
                      // Mystamp now contains Z'1999-12-31-23.59.59.999999'
 /End-Free
```

If you omit the arguments, %Timestamp will return the current system date and time in timestamp format:

```
*.. 1 ...+... 2 ...+... 3 ...+... 4 ...+... 5 ...+... 6 ...+... 7 ...+... 8
DName+++++++++++ETDsFrom+++To/Len+IDc.Keywords+++++++++++++++++++++++++++++++
D Now             S               Z

 /Free
    Now = %Timestamp();          // Now contains the current system date/time
 /End-Free
```

The first argument can also be a date, allowing you to move the date into the date portion of a timestamp variable. In this case, you do not code a second argument, because the computer already knows the format.

Note

Before you can use %Date, %Time, or %Timestamp to convert character or numeric data, you should ensure that the "legacy" format indeed contains a valid value for the target data type. The Test operation, discussed in Chapter 14, can be used to test the value. If you try to convert an invalid value, a runtime error (probably RNQ0112) will occur.

%Char (Convert to Character Data)

Previously, we've used the **%Char (Convert to character data) function** to convert the result of a numeric variable, literal, named constant, or expression to a character value. %Char also works to convert dates, times, and timestamps to character data. The %Char function may be useful when you want to perform date-related processing, but a legacy database requires that the data be stored in character format. When you use the %Char function to convert dates, times, or timestamps, it takes the form

%Char(*value: format*)

The first argument contains the date/time/timestamp expression to be converted. The second argument contains the format that the character result will represent. You can use any of the date or time formats discussed previously (including the additional external formats for dates). The result will include separator characters unless you code a zero (0) after the format. Leading zeros are retained in the character result. Here are some examples of using %Char to convert dates:

```
*.. 1 ...+... 2 ...+... 3 ...+... 4 ...+... 5 ...+... 6 ...+... 7 ...+... 8
DName+++++++++++ETDsFrom+++To/L+++IDc.Keywords+++++++++++++++++++++++++++++++

D Message         S              30

D Expire          S               D   Inz(D'2014-08-12')

  /Free
     Message = 'Offer expires ' + %Char(Expire:*Usa) + '.';
                         // Message = 'Offer expires 08/12/2014.       '
```

continued...

continued...

```
Message = 'It is ' + %Char( %Time() :*Usa) + ' on ' +
          %Char( %Date() :*Usa) + '.';
                    // Message contains current time and date, e.g.,
                    // 'It is 12:34 PM on 08/12/2008. '
/End-Free
```

%Dec (Convert to Decimal Data)

Previously, we used the **%Dec (Convert to decimal data) function** to convert character expressions to decimal format. But the %Dec function also works with dates, times, and timestamps, to convert them to numeric packed decimal format. Legacy databases most commonly use numeric formats to store date values, and the %Dec function is useful to convert native dates back to numeric formats for storage in the database. When you use the %Dec function to convert dates, times, or timestamps, it takes the form

```
%Dec(value{:format})
```

The first argument contains the date/time/timestamp expression to be converted. Unlike character conversion, the numeric result will not include separator characters.

The second argument contains the format that the numeric result will represent. You can use most of the date or time formats discussed previously (including the additional external formats for dates)—except *USA when you are converting a time. The %Dec function allows you to omit the second parameter—the format. If you do, the function will use the format of the date, time, or timestamp for the numeric result. If the time format is *USA, though, you must specify another format. Here are some examples of using %Dec to convert dates:

```
*.. 1 ...+... 2 ...+... 3 ...+... 4 ...+... 5 ...+... 6 ...+... 7 ...+... 8
DName++++++++++ETDsFrom+++To/L+++IDc.Keywords+++++++++++++++++++++++++++++++

D Expiredate      S             D    Inz(D'2011-06-30')
D                                     Datfmt(*Usa)
D Jobtime         S             T    Inz(T'14.25.48')

D Nbrdate         S           8 0
D Nbrhms          S           6 0
D Nbrjde          S           7 0
D Nbrjulian       S           5 0

 /Free
    Nbrdate = %Dec(Expiredate);            // Nbrdate = 06302011
    Nbrdate = %Dec(Expiredate:*Iso);       // Nbrdate = 20110630
    Nbrjulian = %Dec(Expiredate:*Jul);     // Nbrjulian = 11181
    Nbrjde = %Dec(Expiredate:*Cymd);       // Nbrjde = 1110630

    Nbrhms = %Dec(Jobtime:*Iso);           // Nbrhms = 142548
 /End-Free
```

Chapter Summary

RPG IV uses the native date (type D), time (type T), and timestamp (type Z) data types to support date-related business processing. The term "date data" covers all three data types. You can define data items as date data in DDS (for externally described files), Definition specifications, and Input specifications.

Although the system stores date data in a compact internal format, RPG IV supports a number of presentation formats. The default format is *ISO. Each format has a default separator character, which is an integral part of the format, but which can be overridden. Four-digit year formats support any date from the year 1 through 9999, but two-digit year formats can only contain values from 1940 until 2039.

The Eval operation is used to assign values to date data and, in conjunction with duration-related functions, to perform date arithmetic. To code date-related literals, you must use a typed literal, such as D'2008-03-15'.

RPG IV provides many functions to simplify the processing of date data. The following table summarizes the operation codes and functions discussed in this chapter:

Function or operation	Description	Syntax
%Char	Convert to character data	%Char(*expression* {: *format*})
%Date	Convert to date	%Date({*expression* {: *format*}})
%Days	Number of days	%Days(*number*)
%Dec	Convert to packed decimal	%Dec(*date-expression* {: *format*})
%Diff	Difference between two dates/times/timestamps	%Diff(*date1* : *date2* : *duration-code*)
Eval	Evaluate expression	{Eval{(mr)}} *assignment-statement*
%Hours	Number of hours	%Hours(*number*)
%Minutes	Number of minutes	%Minutes(*number*)
%Months	Number of months	%Months(*number*)
%Mseconds	Number of microseconds	%Mseconds(*number*)
%Seconds	Number of seconds	%Seconds(*number*)
%Subdt	Subset of a date, time, or timestamp	%Subdt(*date* : *duration-code*)
%Time	Convert to time	%Time({*expression* {: *format*}})
%Timestamp	Convert to timestamp	%Timestamp({*expression* {: *Iso* | *Iso0*}})
%Years	Number of years	%Years(*number*)

Key Terms

dates

date and time formats

Datfmt

default display format

duration data type

(ISO) standards

separator characters

times

Timfmt

Timestamp

%Char function

%Date function

%Days function

%Dec function

%Diff function

%Hours function

%Minutes function

%Months function

%Mseconds function

%Seconds function

%Subdt function

%Time function

%Timestamp function

%Years function

*Hival

*Loval

Discussion/Review Questions

1. Explain the advantages of using native date, time, and timestamps. What difficulties has this caused the RPG programmer?

2. When assigning values to date variables, what should the programmer be careful of?

3. When using a Control specification to set a default date or time format, what is always true of typed literals?

4. When working with date expressions, can you mix date values with numeric or character data in the same expression?

5. Why would the %Date, %Time, and %Timestamp functions be important to today's RPG programmer?

6. %Date always returns a date in what format? Can this be changed?

7. Why would today's RPG programmer need the %Char and %Dec functions?

8. What date restrictions are placed on date fields that use two-digit formats?

9. What is the range of dates that can be stored in a four-digit native date field?

10. Explain the "irreversibility" of adding/subtracting dates that was described in this chapter.

Exercises

```
*.. 1 ...+... 2 ...+... 3 ...+... 4 ...+... 5 ...+... 6 ...+... 7 ...+... 8
DName++++++++++ETDsFrom+++To/L+++IDc.Keywords++++++++++++++++++++++++++++++++

D Birthdate      S               D   Inz(D'1951-12-10')
D                                    Datfmt(*Usa)
D Startdate      S               D   Inz(D'1999-12-31')
D                                    Datfmt(*Usa)
D Enddate        S               D   Inz(D'2001-01-01')
D                                    Datfmt(*Usa)
D Currentdate    S               D   Inz(*sys)
D                                    Datfmt(*Usa)
D Jobstartdate   S               D   Inz(*job)
D                                    Datfmt(*Usa)
D Midnight       S               T   Inz(T'24.00.00')
D Birthtime      S               T   Inz(T'06.45.15')
D Jobstarttime   S               T   Inz(T'06.15.32')
D Jobendtime     S               T   Inz(T'13.10.55')
```

1. Given the D-specs above, write the code for this and the following exercises. Be sure to define a variable to hold the result.

   - The number of days between Birthdate and Currentdate.
   - The number of years between Startdate and Currentdate.
   - The number of hours between Startdate and Enddate.
   - The number of minutes between Birthdate and Currentdate.
   - Add 20 years to Birthdate.
   - Add 30 months to Currentdate.
   - Add six hours to Jobstarttime.
   - Subtract eight hours from Midnight.

2. Using Birthdate and Birthtime, write the code to produce the Timestamp below.

   - Birthstamp will contain Z'1951-12-10-06.45.15.000000 '.

3. Given the Timestamp Z'2005-12-10-06.45.15.000000', write the code to break this value into a native date (Startdate) and a native time (Starttime).

Programming Assignments

1. Wexler University's Human Resources Department wants an instructor report that shows the number of years each instructor has worked for the university and the number of years until each is eligible for retirement. The instructor is eligible for retirement after being employed for 20 years. The report should be in instructor name order; this will require a logical file. File WUINSTP contains the instructor records.

   - HIRDAT will be converted to a native date field in *USA format.
   - The retirement date will be calculated based on the report job date.
   - The Years Before Retirement will be a numeric field based on the report job date.
   - The IFNAME and ILNAME fields should be printed as one field.
   - The total numbers of instructors will be printed.

```
          1         2         3         4         5         6         7         8         9
 1234567890123456789012345678901234567890123456789012345678901234567890123456789012345678 90
1 XX/XX/XXXX        Wexler University Instructor Retirement Report       Page XXX0
2
3         Instructor  Instructor                Date        Eligible      Years Before
4         Number      Name                      Hired       Retire Date   Retirement
5
6         XXX-XX-XXX  XXXXXXXXXXXXXXXXXXXXXX  99/99/9999  99/99/9999    99
7         XXX-XX-XXX  XXXXXXXXXXXXXXXXXXXXXX  99/99/9999  99/99/9999    99
8         XXX-XX-XXX  XXXXXXXXXXXXXXXXXXXXXX  99/99/9999  99/99/9999    99
9
10 Total Instructors 999
11
12
```

2. CompuSell's Sales Department wants a report based on the Customer Master file (CSCSTP) that shows the number of days since a customer has placed an order. This report should be printed in customer name order and will require a logical file. Following is a list of requirements.

   - ORDDAT will be converted to a native date in *ISO format.
   - ORDDAT will be subtracted from the job date, and the duration will be displayed on the report as "Days In System."
   - CFNAME and CLNAME will be printed as one field on the report.
   - The zip code will be formatted as a text field.
   - The total number of customers will be printed.

```
          1         2         3         4         5         6         7         8         9         0
 12345678901234567890123456789012345678901234567890123456789012345678901234567890123456789012345678 90
1 XX/XX/XXXX                        Compusell Order Aging Report                        Page XXX0
2
3 Customer    Customer                      Street              State Zip        Order      Days
4 Number      Name                          Address                   Code       Date       In System
5
6 999999      XXXXXXXXXXXXXXXXXXXXXXXXXX    XXXXXXXXXXXXXXXX    XX    XXXXX-XXXX yyyy-mm-dd 9999
7 999999      XXXXXXXXXXXXXXXXXXXXXXXXXX    XXXXXXXXXXXXXXXX    XX    XXXXX-XXXX yyyy-mm-dd 9999
8 999999      XXXXXXXXXXXXXXXXXXXXXXXXXX    XXXXXXXXXXXXXXXX    XX    XXXXX-XXXX yyyy-mm-dd 9999
9
10 Total Customers 999
11
12
```

3. GTC's Customer Service Department wants a report showing customer calls. This report will be based on the Customer Master file (GTCSTP) and the Calls Transaction file (GTCLSP) and will only include customers that have made calls. The report will be printed in customer name order; this will require a logical file. Following is a list of requirements.

- PAYDAT field will be converted to a native date field in *USA format.
- CALDAT field will be converted to a native date field in *USA format.
- CALTIM field will be converted to a native time field in *ISO format.
- CALLEN will be added to the converted CALTIM field, and a call end time will be displayed on the report.
- CFNAME and CLNAME will be printed as one field on the report.
- The total number of customers will be printed.

```
           1         2         3         4         5         6         7         8         9
  1234567890123456789012345678901234567890123456789012345678901234567890123456789012345678901234567890
 1 XX/XX/XXXX              GTC Customer Call Report                           Page XXX0
 2
 3 Customer         Customer                      Call          Call        Call
 4 Phone Number     Name                          Start Time    Length      End Time
 5
 6 XXX-XXX-XXXX     XXXXXXXXXXXXXXXXXXXXXXXXXXX    hh:mm:ss      9999        hh:mm:ss
 7 XXX-XXX-XXXX     XXXXXXXXXXXXXXXXXXXXXXXXXXX    hh:mm:ss      9999        hh:mm:ss
 8 XXX-XXX-XXXX     XXXXXXXXXXXXXXXXXXXXXXXXXXX    hh:mm:ss      9999        hh:mm:ss
 9
10 Total Customers 999
11
12
```

4. GTC's Accounting Department would like a customer payment report. This report will be based on the Customer Master file (GTCSTP) and the Payments Transaction file (GTCPAYP) and will be printed in customer name order; this will require a logical file. Following is a list of requirements.

- PAYDAT field will be converted to a native date field in *USA format.
- DATRCV field will be converted to a native date field in *USA format.
- The days between the PAYDAT and the DATRCV will be calculated and displayed on the report.
- CFNAME and CLNAME will be printed as one field on the report.
- The total numbers of customers will be printed.

```
           1         2         3         4         5         6         7         8         9
  1234567890123456789012345678901234567890123456789012345678901234567890123456789012345678901234567890
 1 XX/XX/XXXX              GTC Customer Payment Report                        PAGE XXX0
 2
 3 Customer         Customer                      Customer      Customer    Processing
 4 Phone Number     Name                          Pay Date      Rcv. Date   Days
 5
 6 XXX-XXX-XXXX     XXXXXXXXXXXXXXXXXXXXXXXXXXX    99/99/9999    99/99/9999  9,999
 7 XXX-XXX-XXXX     XXXXXXXXXXXXXXXXXXXXXXXXXXX    99/99/9999    99/99/9999  9,999
 8 XXX-XXX-XXXX     XXXXXXXXXXXXXXXXXXXXXXXXXXX    99/99/9999    99/99/9999  9,999
 9
10                                                Total Customers 999
11
12
```

5. CompuSell's Shipping Department wants a report that shows the number of days since an order was placed and the quantity ordered. This report will use a logical file based on the Orders file (CSORDP), Order/Products file (CSORDPRP), and Inventory Master file (CSINVP). The report will be printed in Order Number order. Following is a list of requirements.

- The ODATE field will be converted to a native date in *ISO format.
- The number of days will be calculated using the job date.
- The total number of orders will be printed on the report.

```
            1         2         3         4         5         6         7         8         9
   1234567890123456789012345678901234567890123456789012345678901234567890123456789012345678901234567890
 1 XX/XX/XXXX              Compusell Outstanding Order Aging Report                    Page XXX0
 2
 3 Order      Customer  Product  Product                        Order      Quantity Days
 4 Number     Number    Number   Description                    Date       Ordered  Outstanding
 5
 6 99999      999999    999999   XXXXXXXXXXXXXXXXXXXXXXXXXXX     yyyy/mm/dd 9,999    9,999
 7 99999      999999    999999   XXXXXXXXXXXXXXXXXXXXXXXXXXX     yyyy/mm/dd 9,999    9,999
 8 99999      999999    999999   XXXXXXXXXXXXXXXXXXXXXXXXXXX     yyyy/mm/dd 9,999    9,999
 9
10                                                                          Total Orders 9,999
11
12
```

Chapter 8

Controlling Program Workflow

 ## Chapter Overview

This chapter focuses on program design and introduces you to RPG IV operations that let you write well-designed programs using a top down, structured approach. Loops, decision logic, and subroutines receive special attention. The chapter applies these design principles by teaching you how to code control break problems.

Structured Design

You typically can solve programming problems in many different ways, each of which might produce correct output. Correct output, although an important goal, should not be the programmer's only goal. Producing code that is readable and easily changed is also important to programmers who are concerned with quality.

Changes in user requirements and processing errors discovered as programs are used dictate that programmers spend a lot of their time maintaining existing programs rather than developing new code. A well-designed, well-documented program facilitates such maintenance; a poorly designed program can be a maintenance nightmare.

Structured design is a widely accepted development methodology to facilitate quality program design. One important aspect of structured design is limiting control structures within your program to three basic logic structures:

- Sequence
- Selection (also called decision)
- Iteration (also called repetition or looping)

Sequence lets you instruct the computer to execute operations serially. **Selection** lets you establish alternate paths of instructions within a program; which alternate path the program executes depends on the results of a test or condition within the program. And **iteration** permits instructions within the program to be repeated until a condition is met or is no longer met.

Sequential control flow is inherent in RPG IV (and other programming languages) by default. The order in which you describe operations on the Calculation specifications determines the order in which the computer executes them. The computer begins with the first instruction and then continues to execute the program statements in their order of occurrence unless it encounters an operation that explicitly transfers control to a different location within the program.

To diverge from a sequential flow of control your program must use an explicit operation code that will invoke the desired control structure. The operation codes that invoke selection (decision) structures are

- If, Else, Elseif (Else If)
- Select, When, Other (Otherwise)

The operation codes that invoke iteration (repetition) structures are

- Dow (Do While)
- Dou (Do Until)
- For

Each of these control structures has a single entry point and a single exit point. Together, the structures can serve as basic building blocks to express the complex logic required to solve complicated programming problems while maintaining the tight control over program flow that facilitates program maintenance.

Relational Comparisons

Decision and iteration operations involve testing a condition to determine the appropriate course of action. This testing involves a **relational comparison** between two values. To express the comparison, RPG IV supports six **relational symbols** that are used with decision and iteration operations:

- \> (Greater than)
- \>= (Greater than or equal to)
- = (Equal to)
- <= (Less than or equal to)
- < (Less than)
- <> (Not equal to)

The way the computer evaluates whether a comparison is true depends on the data type of the items being compared. If you are comparing two numeric values (whether variables, literals, constants, or expressions), the system compares them based on algebraic values, aligned at the decimal point. The length and number of decimal positions in the items being compared do not affect the outcome of the comparison. For example, 2.25 is equal to 00002.250000, while 00000002.12345 is smaller than 9. A positive value is always larger than a negative value. Only the algebraic values of the data items themselves determine the result of a relational comparison between numeric fields.

You can also perform relational tests between character values. This kind of comparison takes place somewhat differently from numeric comparisons. When you compare two character values, the system performs a character-by-character comparison, moving from left to right, until it finds an unmatched pair or finishes checking. When it encounters a character difference, the difference is interpreted in terms of the **EBCDIC** collating sequence, discussed in Chapter 3. In EBCDIC, A is less than B, B less than C, and so on; lowercase letters are "smaller" than uppercase letters; letters are smaller than digits; and a blank is smaller than any other displayable character.

If you are comparing two character items of unequal sizes, the system pads the smaller item with blanks to the right before making the comparison. To understand character comparisons, consider the examples below. (In the examples, ƀ represents a blank within the data item.)

- ART is less than BART
- ARTHUR equals ARTHURƀƀƀƀ
- ARTƀƀƀƀ is less than ARTHUR
- Al is less than AL
- 123 is greater than ABC

In addition to numeric and character values, you can perform relational tests against dates, times, and timestamps. If you are comparing two date-related values (whether variables, literals, constants, or expressions), the system compares them based on their relative occurrence on the calendar or the clock; that is, earlier dates are considered to be less than later dates. The dates or times being compared need not be in the same format; the system will accurately compare them, regardless of format.

You can use indicators in relational comparisons, provided you preface the indicator with *In. You can compare one indicator with another (in which case you're trying to determine whether their values are the same), or you can compare an indicator with the figurative constants *On and *Off (or the character literals '1' and '0'), which represent the only possible values an indicator may assume.

RPG IV does not let you compare incompatible data types in the same expression. For example, you cannot compare a numeric data item with a character data item, or a date with a time. You can, however, use functions, discussed in previous chapters, to convert data items among the various data types for comparison purposes.

Selection Operations

Now that you understand how RPG IV makes relational comparisons, you can learn how to use the relational operators with those RPG IV operations that determine flow of program control. First we'll look at the options for sending control to alternate statements within a program: **selection (decision) operations.**

IF (If)

RPG's primary decision operator is If. The general format of the If operation is

```
If conditional_expression;
 ...
Endif;
```

The conditional expression must be true or false. If the conditional expression is true, all the calculations between the If statement and its corresponding Endif are executed. If the relationship is not true, those statements are bypassed. The If group has a single entry point (the If statement) and a single exit point (the Endif statement).

For example, if you wanted to count all senior citizens, you could write the following lines:

```
If Age >= 65;
   Count += 1;
Endif;
```

This code can be read, "If Age is greater than or equal to 65, then increment Count by 1." The comparison need not be limited to simple variables or literals; it can also include expressions. Assuming Today and Birthdate are defined as date variables, the following statements would accomplish the same end as the previous example.

```
If %Diff(Today:Birthdate:*Years) >= 65;
  Count += 1;
Endif;
```

This code can be read, "If the difference between Today and Birthdate (in years) is greater than or equal to 65, then increment Count by 1."

Sometimes, you want to execute a series of instructions based on multiple tests or conditions. RPG IV includes the binary operators And and Or to allow such multiple conditions. When you use And to set up a compound condition, *both* relationships must be true for the If to be evaluated as true:

```
If Age >= 65 And Status = 'R';
  Count += 1;
Endif;
```

When you use Or to connect two relational tests, the If is evaluated to true if one or the other (or both) of the conditions is true:

```
If Age >= 65 Or Status = 'R';
  Count += 1;
Endif;
```

You can combine And and Or to create more complex conditional tests. Note that And is evaluated before Or. However, you can use parentheses to change the order of evaluation; parentheses are always evaluated first. If a conditional expression requires more room than a single specification offers, you can extend the expression to additional lines.

To illustrate how And and Or are evaluated and to demonstrate the use of parentheses, consider the following scenario. A company wants to print a list of employees eligible for early retirement. Only salaried employees are eligible (code = 'S'); moreover, they must have worked more than 15 years for the company or be 55 (or more) years old. The following code shows an incorrect way and a correct way to express these conditions.

Incorrect:

```
// The code below would select any employee who was salaried and had
// worked more than 15 years; it also would incorrectly include any
// employee at least 55 years old, whether or not (s)he was salaried.

If Salarycode = 'S' And Yrsworked > 15 Or Age >= 55;
  ...
Endif;
```

Correct:

```
// The parentheses in the code below cause the correct selection of
// employees who are salaried and who have either worked more than 15
// years or are at least 55 years old.

If Salarycode = 'S' And (Yrsworked > 15 Or Age >= 55);
  ...
Endif;
```

You can combine And and Or with other operations to form extremely complicated conditional tests. In these cases, order of precedence causes And and Or to be evaluated last, after any other operations, unless you use parentheses to change the order of precedence. The following code illustrates some complex If statements.

```
// In the sample below, the order in which the operations would be
// performed is as follows: first, multiplication (W*X); next, addition
// (A + B); next, AND; and last, the two ORs, moving from left to right

If A + B > 85 And X = 10 Or W*X <> G Or *In90 = *On;
   ...
Endif;

// The sample below includes parentheses that change the order of
// evaluation. Now, the multiplication (W*X) is done first; next, the
// second OR is evaluated; next, the first OR; next, the addition;
// and last, the AND.

If A + B > 85 And (X = 10 Or (W*X <> G Or *In90 = *On));
   ...
Endif;
```

Caution

Although such logic is permitted in RPG IV, building conditions of such complexity leads to programs that are difficult to understand. You should avoid the practice if at all possible.

You can also include an Else operation within an If group to set up an alternate path of instructions to be executed should the If condition be false. For example, if you were asked to calculate pay and wanted to pay time and a half for any hours over 40, you could code the following:

```
If Hours <= 40;
  Eval(H) Totalpay = Hours * Payrate;
Else;
  Eval(H) Totalpay = 40 * Payrate + (Hours - 40) * Payrate * 1.5;
Endif;
```

In this example, the first Eval statement would be executed if Hours is less than or equal to 40; otherwise, the second Eval statement would be processed. Only one Else operation is allowed in an If group. The Else operation does not require a corresponding exit point; all the statements are considered to be part of the same If group.

The flowchart in Figure 8.1 illustrates the basic structure of the If group.

Figure 8.1
Flowchart Illustrating If Group

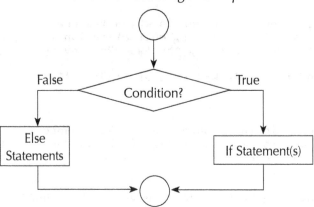

Nested If Groups and Elseif

You can also nest If groups. That is, you can build If groups within other If groups, with or without Else operations. Each If requires an Endif in the appropriate spot to indicate the end point of that If group's influence. The following example illustrates nested If logic in RPG IV.

```
// This code uses IF and Eval to assign values to LifeExpect based on
// age and sex.

If Age >= 65;
  If Sex = 'F';
    Lifeexpect = 84;
  Else;
    Lifeexpect = 79;
  Endif;
Else;
  If Sex = 'F';
    Lifeexpect = 81;
  Else;
    Lifeexpect = 78;
  Endif;
Endif;
```

The flowchart in Figure 8.2 illustrates the basic structure of a nested If group.

Figure 8.2
Flowchart Illustrating Nested If

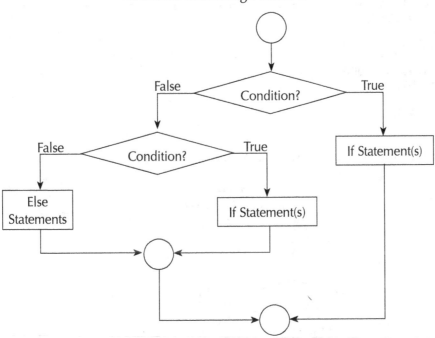

Sometimes, a program's logic requires that nesting take place only on the Else branches of the decision structure. The following example of assigning commission rates typifies this kind of construct, sometimes called **case logic**.

```
// If Used To Assign Commission Rates Based On Sales Level
If Sales <= 5000;
  Rate = .005;
Else;
  If Sales <= 10000;
    Rate = .0075;
  Else;
    If Sales <= 20000;
      Rate = .01;
    Else;
      Rate = .015;
    Endif;
  Endif;
Endif;
```

In the above examples, each If statement requires its own corresponding Endif statement, resulting in a series of Endif statements to close individual nesting levels. As an alternative, the Elseif operation combines Else and If operations and requires only a single Endif at the end of the code block.

The following example uses Elseif to simplify the nesting levels:

```
// If Used To Assign Commission Rates Based On Sales Level
If Sales <= 5000;
  Rate = .005;
Elseif Sales <= 10000;
  Rate = .0075;
Elseif Sales <= 20000;
  Rate = .01;
Else;
  Rate = .015;
Endif;
```

Figure 8.3 illustrates the basic structure of the Elseif operation.

Figure 8.3
Flowchart Illustrating Elseif

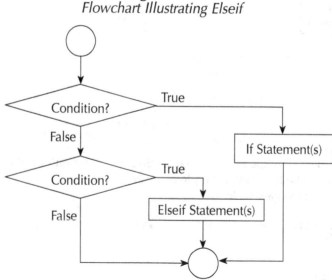

Notice in the examples presented so far in this chapter that the free-form syntax lets you indent code to make the logical groupings of conditions and the resulting actions more apparent.

Select (Conditionally Select Operations)

Although you can express even the most complex programming decisions with a series of If, Else, and Elseif operations, nested If groups can be difficult to set up and hard for others to interpret. To overcome this problem, RPG IV uses the Select (Conditionally Select Operations) operation to let you simplify the coding of case logic.

The Select operation appears on a line alone to identify the start of a Select group. The Select operation is followed by one or more When lines, each of which specifies a condition to be tested. Each When is followed by one or more calculations to be performed when that condition is met. When the program is executed, it checks the When conditions sequentially, starting with the first. As soon as it encounters a true condition, the computer executes the operation (or operations) following that When statement and then sends control to the end of the Select group, signaled by an Endsl operation.

The following code uses Select to express the same logic for determining sales commission rates shown previously with nested If groups.

```
// Using Select/When to assign a value to rate based on level of sales
Select;
  When Sales <= 5000;
    Rate = .005;
  When Sales <= 10000;
    Rate = .0075;
  When Sales <= 20000;
    Rate = .01;
  Other;
    Rate = .015;
Endsl;
```

Notice in this example that the Other operation code means "in all other cases." Other, if used, should be the final "catch-all" condition listed. When a Select group includes an Other operation, the computer will always perform one of the sets of calculations. When a Select group is composed only of When conditions, none of the operations within the Select group will be performed if none of the conditions are met.

Although not illustrated in the example above, just as in If operations, multiple operations can follow each When line—as many operations as are needed to accomplish the desired processing on that branch of the Select group. You also can couple the When conditions with And and Or to create compound selection criteria, which can continue on multiple specification lines if needed.

The flowchart in Figure 8.4 illustrates the basic structure of a Select group.

Figure 8.4
Flowchart Illustrating Select

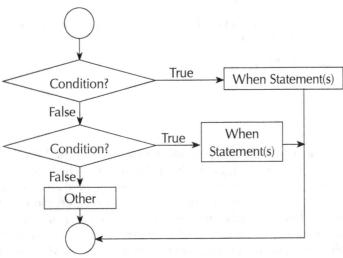

Iteration Operations

The third logical construct of structured programming is iteration. Iteration lets your program repeat a series of instructions—a common necessity in programming. In batch processing, for example, you want to execute a series of instructions repeatedly, once for every record in a transaction file. You have already used one RPG IV operation that enables iteration, or looping: Dow.

Dow (Do While)

The Dow (Do While) operation establishes a loop based on a conditional test expression. All the operations coded between this operator and its corresponding end statement (Enddo) are repeated as long as the condition specified in the relational test remains true.

You have already used Dow to repeat processing while an end of file condition remains off. You can use Dow for other kinds of repetition as well. Assume you want to add all the numbers between 1 and 100. You can use Dow to easily accomplish this summation, as shown in the following code.

```
*.. 1 ...+... 2 ...+... 3 ...+... 4 ...+... 5 ...+... 6 ...+... 7 ...+... 8
DName++++++++++ETDsFrom+++To/Len+IDc.Keywords+++++++++++++++++++++++++++++++++
D Number          S              5U Ø
D Sum             S              5U Ø

 /Free
    // This routine adds all the numbers from 1 to 100.
    Dow Number < 100;              // Loop while Number is less than 100.
      Number += 1;                 // Increment Number by 1.
      Sum += Number;               // Add Number to accumulator Sum.
    Enddo;
 /End-Free
```

Like RPG IV's decision operations, the Dow operation lets you use And and Or to form compound conditions to control the looping:

```
// Any processing specified within the loop would be repeated as long
// as both indicators 90 and 99 remain off.

Dow Not *In90 And Not *In99;
  ...
Enddo;
```

Dou (Do Until)

Dou (Do Until) is a structured iteration operation very similar to Dow. Like Dow, Dou includes a conditional test expression. However, two major differences exist between the two operations. First, a Dow operation repeats *while* the specified condition *remains* true, whereas a Dou operation repeats *until* the condition *becomes* true. Second, a Dow is a **leading decision loop**, which means the conditional expression is tested *before* the instructions within the loop are executed for the first time. If the condition is false, the computer completely bypasses the instructions within the loop. A Dou, in contrast, is a **trailing decision loop**; because the condition is tested *after* the instructions within the loop have been executed, the instructions will always be executed at least once. In contrast, instructions within a Dow loop may not be executed at all.

Figure 8.5 presents flowcharts of Do While and Do Until operations to illustrate their differences.

Figure 8.5
Do While vs. Do Until Loops

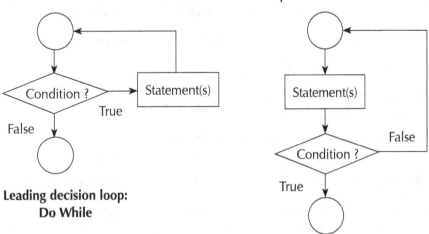

**Leading decision loop:
Do While**

**Trailing decision loop:
Do Until**

Dow and Dou are often equally suited to setting up a looping structure. For instance, you could use a Dou to solve the "add the numbers" problem illustrated earlier with Dow; all you'd need to change is the operation and the relational test. The following code illustrates how to solve this problem using Dou.

```
*.. 1 ...+... 2 ...+... 3 ...+... 4 ...+... 5 ...+... 6 ...+... 7 ...+... 8
DName++++++++++ETDsFrom+++To/Len+IDc.Keywords++++++++++++++++++++++++++++++++
D Number          S              5U 0
D Sum             S              5U 0

 /Free
    // This routine adds all the numbers from 1 to 100.
    Dou Number = 100;            // Loop until Number equals 100.
      Number += 1;               // Increment Number by 1.
      Sum += Number;             // Add Number to accumulator Sum.
    Enddo;
 /End-Free
```

For

Often, as in the previous example, you want a loop to be executed a specific number of times. To implement this kind of logic with Dou or Dow, you need to define a field to serve as a counter. Each time through the loop, you *explicitly* increment the counter as part of your loop instructions and check the counter's value after each repetition to determine whether another iteration is needed.

RPG IV offers an operation designed specifically for count-controlled loops: For. As with Dow and Dou, an end operator, Endfor, signals the end of a For group. Unlike those operations, the For operation *automatically* increments its counter to ensure the repetition occurs the desired number of times.

The format of the For operation is a little more complicated than that of Dow or Dou because For provides more options and defaults. The general layout of a For loop is shown below.

```
For counter = start_value To limit_value By increment_value;
```

In general, the For operation lets you specify four things:

- A variable to serve as the counter
- The starting value of the counter
- The limiting value of the counter for looping to continue
- The amount to be added to the counter at the end of each repetition of the loop

Although RPG IV gives you the option to specify these four values, you also can omit any of them except the counter field.

The counter variable must be defined as a numeric variable (preferably an integer) with zero decimal positions. You can omit the initial value for the counter; if you do, the counter will begin with the same value it had before the program entered the For loop.

In the To clause, specify a whole numeric variable, constant, or literal as a limit value. If your limit value is a variable, its value determines the number of repetitions. You can also omit the To clause; if you do, the loop will continue indefinitely until the program processes a Leave operation, which we will discuss shortly.

In the By clause, specify a whole numeric variable, constant, or literal as the increment value. If your increment value is a variable, its value determines the increment value. You can also omit the By clause. If you do, RPG IV will assume an increment value of 1; that is, it will add 1 to the value of the counter at the start of each additional pass through the loop.

The following examples illustrate the For loop:

```
For Idx = 1 To 50;     // Processing in this loop would be done 50 times
  ...
Endfor;

// The number of repetitions of this loop depends on the value of Iter
For Idx = 1 To Iter;
  ...
Endfor;

// This loop will repeat until the program encounters a leave operation
For Idx = 1;
  ...
  If *Inlr;
    Leave;
  Endif;
Endfor;
```

The following code shows the "add the numbers" problem implemented using For.

```
*.. 1 ...+... 2 ...+... 3 ...+... 4 ...+... 5 ...+... 6 ...+... 7 ...+... 8
DName++++++++++ETDsFrom+++To/Len+IDc.Keywords+++++++++++++++++++++++++++++++
D Number          S              5U 0
D Sum             S              5U 0

 /Free
    // This routine adds all the numbers from 1 to 100.
    For Number = 1 To 100;           // Loop until Number equals 100.
      Sum += Number;                 // Add Number to accumulator Sum.
    Endfor;
 /End-Free
```

A For loop is a leading decision loop, which means the value of the counter is tested against the limit value before the instructions within the loop are executed for the first time. If the counter has not exceeded the limit value, the instructions will be processed repeatedly until the counter exceeds the limit. In the above example, after the loop is done processing, Number will have a value of 101.

The For operation affords us great flexibility in changing the starting value and increment value. For example, we can easily change our sample solution to add all the even numbers from 1 to 100 if we set Number's starting value to 2 and the increment value to 2, as follows:

```
*.. 1 ...+... 2 ...+... 3 ...+... 4 ...+... 5 ...+... 6 ...+... 7 ...+... 8
DName++++++++++ETDsFrom+++To/Len+IDc.Keywords+++++++++++++++++++++++++++++++
D Number          S              5U 0
D Sum             S              5U 0

 /Free
    // This routine will add all the even numbers from 2 to 100 using For.
    // Start Number at 2 and loop until it exceeds 100.
    For Number = 2 To 100 By 2;
      Sum += Number;
    Endfor;
 /End-Free
```

In the unlikely event that you need to decrement a counter instead of incrementing it, the For operation offers a variation that works in reverse, using a Downto clause instead of To:

```
*.. 1 ...+... 2 ...+... 3 ...+... 4 ...+... 5 ...+... 6 ...+... 7 ...+... 8
DName++++++++++ETDsFrom+++To/Len+IDc.Keywords+++++++++++++++++++++++++++++++
D Number          S              5U 0
D Sum             S              5U 0

 /Free
    // This routine will add all the even numbers from 100 to 2 using For.
    // Start Number at 100; loop (decrementing by 2) until it goes below 2.
    For Number = 100 Downto 2 By 2;
      Sum += Number;
    Endfor;
 /End-Free
```

Loops and Early Exits

You sometimes may want to skip the remaining instructions within a loop to begin the next iteration or cycle. In other cases, you may want to exit the loop completely before the repetition is terminated by the relational comparison. Two RPG IV operations, Iter (Iterate) and Leave, give you these capabilities.

When the computer encounters an Iter operation, control skips past the remaining instructions in the loop and causes the next repetition to begin. Leave terminates the looping process completely and sends control to the statement immediately following the loop's End statement. You can use either or both of these statements with all the iterative operations (Dow, Dou, and For) — but not with the selection operations (If, Select, and so on).

Assume, for example, you are processing a file of customer records and printing a report line for those customers whose balance due exceeds zero. If amount due equals zero, you simply want to cycle around and read the next record from the file. The following code illustrates a solution that uses Leave and Iter.

```
// This routine processes all records in Custfile and prints a detail
// line for those customers whose Amountdue is not equal to 0.
Dow Not %Eof;
  Read Custfile;
  Select;
    When %Eof;
      Leave;              // If %Eof, pass control to Enddo
    When Amountdue = 0;
      Iter;               // If Amountdue is zero, pass control to Dow
    Other;
      Except Detail;
  Endsl;
Enddo;
```

Top Down Design

Up to now, this chapter has concentrated on structured design. A second design concept, "top down" methodology, usually goes hand in hand with a structured approach. **Top down design** means developing your program solution starting with a broad "outline" and then successively breaking the big pieces into smaller and smaller units. This technique is sometimes called **hierarchical decomposition**.

Hierarchical decomposition is the method your English teacher recommended for writing research papers: Work out an outline, starting with your main topics; then subdivide these into subtopics, and so on, until you have decomposed to a level of sufficient detail to allow you to write the paper (or in programming terms, the individual instructions of your program).

Top down design lets you handle problems of great complexity by permitting you to initially ignore the detailed requirements of processing. Top down design works in tandem with **modular program development**, which advocates that your program be structured into logical units, or modules. In top down design, the first, or upper level, design modules that you develop chiefly concern controlling flow to and from the lower level modules you develop later.

Each module should be as independent of the others as possible, and the statements within a module should work together to perform a single function. Structural decomposition gives you a way to deal with complexity; when used with a modular approach, structural decomposition results in programs of functionally cohesive subroutines that are easier to maintain later.

RPG IV supports three major constructs to deal with top down design and modular development:

- Subroutines
- Called programs (discussed in Chapter 12)
- Procedures (discussed in Chapter 13)

Defining Subroutines

A **subroutine** is a block of code, inside a program, with an identifiable beginning and end. It is a set of operations coded elsewhere within the calculations and invoked as a unit by referring to the subroutine's name. After performing the subroutine, the program returns control to the statement immediately following the one that invoked the routine.

A subroutine is coded between Begsr (Begin subroutine) and Endsr (End subroutine) operations. The first line contains the Begsr operation and name of the subroutine. The lines of code constituting the executable portion of the subroutine follow. The last line of a subroutine contains the Endsr operation to signal the end of that subroutine. The following code shows the skeleton of a subroutine.

```
Begsr Subroutine_Name;
  ...
Endsr;
```

Subroutines are coded as the last entries on the Calculation specifications, following all other calculations. The order in which you list the subroutines does not matter, although many programmers prefer to specify them in alphabetical order for easy reference. A program can have an unlimited number of subroutines; each must have a unique name, based on the same rules that apply to RPG IV fields.

The Exsr (Execute Subroutine) Operation

To send control to a subroutine for execution, you use the Exsr (Execute Subroutine) operation. Enter the name of the subroutine to be performed, as shown below.

```
Exsr Calctax;      // Exsr causes control to drop to subroutine Calctax.
// Control returns here when the subroutine finishes.
  .
  .
  .

// Subroutines appear at the end of the Calculation specifications.
Begsr Calctax;
  Eval(H) Fica =  Gross * .0751;
  Eval(H) Statetax = Gross * .045;
  If Gross > 5000;
    Eval(H) Fedtax = Gross * .31;
  Else;
    Eval(H) Fedtax = Gross * .25;
  Endif;
Endsr;
```

When the computer encounters an Exsr operation, control drops to the named subroutine. Upon completion of the subroutine, control returns to the operation immediately following the calculation that invoked the subroutine. The fact that control returns to a predictable location makes it possible to maintain tight control of program flow using Exsr.

Subroutines cannot contain other subroutines. They may execute other subroutines, but a subroutine should never execute itself. This latter coding technique, called **recursion**, is not permitted for subroutines.

Control Break Logic

To demonstrate how top down, structured design can be used to help develop an easily maintained program, let's apply the techniques we have discussed to solve a common business programming problem: generating a report that includes subtotals.

Assume you have a file of sales records. Each record contains a salesperson's identification number, department, the amount of a given sale, and the date of the sale. A given salesperson may have many records in the file—depending on how successful a salesperson he or she is—and the data file is keyed by salesperson, so that all the records for a given salesperson can be processed together. Here's the DDS for the Salesfile:

```
*.. 1 ...+... 2 ...+... 3 ...+... 4 ...+... 5 ...+... 6 ...+... 7 ...+... 8
A..........T.Name++++++RLen++TDcB......Keywords+++++++++++++++++++++++++++++++
 * Physical file SALESFILE
A           R SALESREC
A             SALESPRSN       4A         TEXT('Salesperson')
A             DEPT            3A         TEXT('Department')
A             SALESAMT        7S 2       TEXT('Sale amount')
A             SALEDATE        L          TEXT('Sale date')
A           K SALESPRSN
```

You've been asked to write a program that will include the details of each sales transaction and a subtotal of each salesperson's sales. The following printer spacing chart and DDS show the desired report format.

```
                    1         2         3         4         5
     1234567890123456789012345678901234567890123456789 0
 1  XX/XX/XXXX     SALES REPORT    PAGE XXX0
 2
 3       SLSPSN              AMOUNT
 4
 5       XXXX            XX,XX0.XX
 6       XXXX            XX,XX0.XX
 7
 8  * TOTAL          X,XXX,XX0.XX
 9
10       XXXX            XX,XX0.XX
11       XXXX            XX,XX0.XX
12
13  * TOTAL          X,XXX,XX0.XX
14
15  ** GRAND TOTAL XXX,XXX,XX0.XX
16
```

```
*.. 1 ...+... 2 ...+... 3 ...+... 4 ...+... 5 ...+... 6 ...+... 7 ...+... 8
AANØ1NØ2NØ3T.Name++++++RLen++TDpBLinPosFunctions+++++++++++++++++++++++++++++

  * Printer file SALESRPT, externally describing the sales report
A                                       REF(SALESFILE)
A             R HEADINGS                SKIPB(1)
A                                       1DATE
A                                       EDTCDE(Y)
A                                       14'SALES REPORT'
A                                       29'PAGE'
A                                       34PAGNBR
A                                       SPACEA(2)
  *
A                                       7'SLSPSN'
A                                       24'AMOUNT'
A                                       SPACEA(2)
  *
A             R DETAILLINE              SPACEA(1)
A               SALESPRSN R             8
A               SALESAMT  R             21EDTCDE(1)
  *
A             R BREAKLINE               SPACEB(1)
A                                       2'* TOTAL'
A               SLSPTOTAL     9   2     18EDTCDE(1)
A                                       SPACEA(2)
  *
A             R TOTALINE                SPACEB(1)
A                                       1'** GRAND TOTAL'
A               GRANDTOTAL   11   2     16EDTCDE(1)
```

This kind of problem is often referred to as a **control break problem**, because the solution involves checking the input records for a change, or "break," in the value of a control field. That occurrence signals the need for a subtotal and triggers special processing associated with printing the subtotal and preparing for the next control group.

Because the computer has only one record in memory at a time, to determine when a change in the control variable's value has occurred, you need to define a standalone work variable to hold the current value of the control field. Each time a record is read, its control field's value can then be compared with the work variable; a comparison revealing that the two values are no longer equal signals that the first record of a new group has just been read. Before continuing with the detail processing of that record, it is necessary to "break" away from detail processing and complete any processing required by such a change. Typically, this processing entails printing a subtotal line, rolling over an accumulator, zeroing out the accumulator, and storing the new control field value in the work field.

With that overview of control break logic, let's develop the pseudocode for the calculations required by the program, using a top down design strategy.

Execute Initialization routine
While not end of file
  If Salesperson changes
    Execute Slspbreak routine
  Endif
  Execute Detail Process routine
  Read next record
Endwhile
Execute Termination routine
End program

The above pseudocode works out the "mainline" logic of the program. Notice that at several spots in the pseudocode, Execute statements indicate that a number of processing steps need to be performed, but the details are not yet spelled out. This is the essence of top down design.

Once you determine that the mainline logic is correct, you can develop the logic of the additional modules, or routines:

Initialization routine
Read first record
Set up hold area
Print headings
End Initialization routine

Slspbreak routine
Print salesperson line
Add salesperson's total to grand total
Zero out salesperson's total
Move new value to hold area
End Slspbreak routine

Detail Process Routine
If page overflow
  Print headings
Endif
Print detail line
Accumulate sales in salesperson's total
End Detail Process Routine

Termination routine
Execute Slspbreak routine
Print grand total
End Termination routine

The processing in routine Slspbreak is representative of control break logic in general. Notice that Slspbreak is invoked from within the Termination routine. The break routine needs to be executed one last time to print the very last salesperson's subtotal line before printing the grand total.

The complete RPG IV program, including the calculations reflecting the logic expressed in the pseudocode, is shown in the following example.

```
*.. 1 ...+... 2 ...+... 3 ...+... 4 ...+... 5 ...+... 6 ...+... 7 ...+... 8
 // *************************************************************
 //   This program produces a sales report that lists subtotals  *
 //   for each salesperson.                                       *
 // *************************************************************

FSalesfile IF   E           K Disk
FSalesrpt  O    E             Printer Oflind(Endofpage)

D Endofpage       S              1N    Inz(*On)
D Holdslsp        S                    Like(Salesprsn)

 /Free
 // *********************************************************
 // Mainline Logic.
 // *********************************************************

    Exsr Initial;

    Dow Not %Eof(Salesfile);
      If Holdslsp <> Salesprsn;
        Exsr Slspbreak;
      Endif;

      Exsr Detailproc;
      Read Salesfile;
    Enddo;

    Exsr Terminate;
    *Inlr = *On;
    Return;

 // *********************************************************
 // Subroutine Detailproc ... executed for each input record.
 // *********************************************************
    Begsr Detailproc;
      Exsr Overflow;
      Write Detailline;
      Slsptotal += Salesamt;          // Slsptotal defined in Salesrpt DDS
    Endsr;

 // *********************************************************
 // Subroutine Initial ... to read first record, set up hold,
 // and print first page headings.
 // *********************************************************
```

continued...

continued...

```
      Begsr Initial;
       Read Salesfile;
       Holdslsp = Salesprsn;
       Exsr Overflow;
      Endsr;

   // **********************************************************
   //  Subroutine Overflow ... print headings when necessary
   //
   // **********************************************************
     Begsr;
       If Endofpage;
         Write Headings;
         Endofpage = *Off;
       Endif;
     Endsr;


   // **********************************************************
   //  Subroutine Slspbreak ... done when salesperson changes;
   //  print subtotal, roll over accumulator, zero out accumulator,
   //  and reset hold.
   // **********************************************************
     Begsr Slspbreak;
       Exsr Overflow;
       Write Breakline;
       Grandtotal += Slsptotal;          // Grandtotal defined in Salesrpt DDS
       Slsptotal = 0;
       Holdslsp = Salesprsn;
     Endsr;


   // **********************************************************
   //  Subroutine Terminate ... done at end-of-file; execute
   //  slspbreak one last time and print grand-total line.
   // **********************************************************
     Begsr Terminate;
       Exsr Slspbreak;
       Exsr Overflow;
       Write Totalline;
     Endsr;

  /End-Free
```

Notice in this program that just before each line is printed, the program executes the Overflow subroutine, to ensure that heading lines will be printed whenever the **overflow indicator** (called Endofpage in this example) is on. Also notice that it was not necessary to explicitly define fields Slsptotal and Grandtotal in the program, since those fields were already defined in the DDS for the printer file.

Multiple-Level Control Break Logic

Programmers often face coding solutions to multiple-level control break problems, in which two or more different control fields of the input file are to be associated with subtotal lines. For example, our sample problem could have specified a need for department subtotals in addition to the salesperson subtotals. If the input file were ordered by department, and within department by salesperson, producing the desired report would take little additional programming effort because the logic of multiple-level control break problems follows directly from that of a single-level problem.

To code a multiple-level control break program, set up a standalone work variable for each control field to hold the value of the group being processed. Code a separate break subroutine for each level; typically, the same processing steps take place in each kind of break (e.g., printing a subtotal line, rolling over an accumulator, zeroing out the accumulator, and moving the new control field value into the work variable), but using variables appropriate to that level.

Then, before the detail processing of each record, check each control field to see whether its value has changed, checking from major (biggest grouping) to minor (smallest grouping). If a break has occurred, execute the appropriate break subroutines, starting with the minor (smallest grouping) and finishing with the break routine that corresponds to the control field that triggered the break processing.

The following pseudocode illustrates the logic of a two-level control break problem.

Mainline logic for two-level control break
```
Execute Initialization routine
While not end of file
    If change in Department
        Execute Slspbreak routine
        Execute Deptbreak routine
    Else
        If change in Salesperson
            Execute Slspbreak routine
        Endif
    Endif
    Execute Detail process routine
    Read next record
Endwhile
Execute Termination routine
End program
```

Initialization routine
```
Read first record
Set up hold areas for department and salesperson
Print headings
End Initialization routine
```

Slspbreak routine
```
Print salesperson line
Add salesperson's total to department's total
Zero out salesperson's total
Move new salesperson to salesperson hold area
End Slspbreak routine
```

Deptbreak routine
Print department line
Add department's total to grand total
Zero out department's total
Move new department to department hold area
End Deptbreak routine

Detail Process routine
If page overflow
    Print headings
Endif
Print detail line
Add sales to salesperson's total
End Detail Process routine

Termination routine
Execute Slspbreak routine
Execute Deptbreak routine
Print grand total
End Termination routine

Notice especially the order in which the pseudocode checks for changes in the control fields, the order in which it executes the break subroutines, and the parallels between the Slspbreak and Deptbreak routines. Once you understand the logic of a two-level break problem, you can write a program with any number of level breaks because the required processing steps can be exactly modeled on those required for a two-level control break.

Chapter Summary

The goal for this chapter has been to give you a basic understanding of structured design and how it is often used with a top down, modular approach to program development. Structured program design means developing your program logic with flow of control tightly managed, by using structured operations. Top down methodology requires you to approach designing your program hierarchically, working out its broad logic first—concentrating primarily on flow of control—and later attending to the detailed processing requirements. Both design concepts encourage a modular approach to programming, in which you design your program around subroutines of statements that form functionally cohesive units of code.

RPG IV provides structured operations If and Select/When to implement decision logic and structured operations Dow, Dou, and For to implement looping logic. These operations let you express the conditional test associated with the operation as a free-form logical expression. All the structured operations mentioned above have a single entry point and a single exit point that help maintain tight flow of control within a program.

RPG IV uses the subroutine as one vehicle to accommodate top down design. A subroutine is a block of code, inside a program, that can be invoked by name. After performing the subroutine, the program returns control to the statement immediately following the one that invoked the routine.

Control break logic involves checking input records for a change in the value of one or more control fields, usually for the purpose of printing subtotals or grouping input records into subcategories.

The following table summarizes the operation codes discussed in this chapter:

Function or operation	Description	Syntax
Begsr	Begin a subroutine	Begsr *subroutine-name*
Dou	Do until	Dou{(mr)} *logical-expression*
Dow	Do while	Dow{(mr)} *logical-expression*
Else	Else	Else
Elseif	Else if	Elseif{(mr)} *logical-expression*
Enddo Endfor Endif Endsl	End a structured group	End*xx*
Endsr	End of subroutine	Endsr
Exsr	Invoke subroutine	Exsr *subroutine-name*
For	For	For{(mr)} *counter* {= *start*} {By *increment*} {To | Downto *limit*}
If	If	If{(mr)} *logical-expression*
Iter	Reiterate a Do/For group	Iter
Leave	Leave a Do/For group	Leave
Other	Otherwise select	Other
Select	Begin a select group	Select
When	When true then select	When{(mr)} *logical-expression*

Key Terms

case logic
control break problem
EBCDIC
hierarchical decomposition
iteration
leading decision loop
modular program development
overflow indicator
recursion

relational comparison
relational symbols
selection
selection (decision) operations
sequence
structured design
subroutine
top down design
trailing decision loop

Discussion/Review Questions

1. Characterize structured design.
2. If RPG IV did not include a relational symbol or code to check for "not equal," in what alternate way could you express the following logic in RPG IV? "If balance due < > 0, execute the calculation routine."
3. What does "tight" flow of control mean?
4. Describe how RPG IV compares numeric values.
5. Describe how RPG IV compares character values.
6. RPG has a Select operation. Can you always avoid writing nested If statements? Explain your answer.
7. What's the difference between And and Or? Give an example of each.
8. How would you decide whether to use Select or Cas*xx*?
9. Why does RPG IV need looping operations other than For?
10. Why are both Dow and Dou essential from a logical standpoint? Give an example of using both operations.
11. Describe how Iter and Leave work. Would they be considered structured options? Explain.
12. Characterize a control break problem.
13. In control break processing, why is a "hold" or work field needed to store the value of the control field?
14. Can you think of an alternative way to handle page advance other than referencing an overflow indicator?

Exercises

1. Use If to code the calculations needed to determine property tax based on a property's value, stored in Value (six positions, zero decimal positions). Use the information in the table below as the basis for your calculations:

Property value	Property tax
$0–$50,000	1% of value
$50,001–$75,000	$50 plus 2% of value
$75,001–$100,000	$70 plus 2.5% of value
over $100,000	$100 plus 3% of value

2. Solve the problem described in Exercise 1 using operation Select.

3. Write a routine to determine traffic fines based on the values of two input fields: Mphover (miles over speed limit) and Nbroffense (number of offenses). Fines are to be determined as follows:

MPH over limit	Fine
1–10	$25
11–20	$40
21–30	$70
over 30	$100

If the speeder is a first-time offender, there is no additional fine. However, second-time offenders are fined an additional $25 if they are no more than 20 miles over the limit and an additional $50 if they are more than 20 miles over the limit. Third-time offenders are fined an additional $50 if they are no more than 20 miles over the limit and an additional $100 if they are going more than 20 miles over the limit.

4. Use For to write the calculations needed to obtain the squares, cubes, and square roots of all numbers from 1 to 50.

5. Write three routines, each using a different structured operator that checks an update code stored in the variable Code and sends control to one of three different subroutines (AddSR, ChangeSR, and DeleteSR), depending on whether the code is A, C, or D (Add, Change, or Delete records). Invalid codes should cause subroutine ErrorSR to be executed.

6. Write a Dow and a Dou that executes while the value of the variable Index is less than 100. This construct will execute a subroutine Printline each time through the construct and also increment the variable Index.

Programming Assignments

1. Wexler University wants a summary report of its student population that shows how many in-district, out-of-district, and international students there are at the freshman, sophomore, junior, senior, and graduate levels. The input file for this program is the school's student master file, WUSTDP. Appendix F provides the record layout for this file. The records in the file are ordered by student (Social Security) number.

   Note that district code is a code field where I = in-district, O = out-of-district, and F = international student status. The classification field differentiates G (graduate) from U (undergraduate) students. The school subdivides undergraduates based on earned credits: Students with fewer than 30 credits are freshmen; those with 30–59 credits are sophomores; those with 60–89 credits are juniors; and those with 90 or more credits are seniors.

   The school wants the summary report to be formatted as shown in the following printer spacing chart.

```
            1         2         3         4         5         6         7         8
   1234567890123456789012345678901234567890123456789012345678901234567890123456789 0
 1 XX/XX/XXXX                         Wexler University                   Page XXX0
 2                          Student Population Summary Report
 3
 4                                   Student Residency
 5     Classification      In-District    Out-Of-District    International     Total
 6     --------------      -----------    ---------------    -------------     -----
 7        Freshman            X,X0X            X,X0X             X,X0X        XX,X0X
 8        Sophomores          X,X0X            X,X0X             X,X0X        XX,X0X
 9        Juniors             X,X0X            X,X0X             X,X0X        XX,X0X
10        Seniors             X,X0X            X,X0X             X,X0X        XX,X0X
11
12        Total              XX,X0X           XX,X0X            XX,X0X       XXX,X0X
13
```

2. Wexler University needs a report to determine how equitable its faculty salaries are across sexes. Because salaries vary with academic rank and length of employment, the school wants average salaries broken down by rank, as well as by sex, and would also like average-length-of-employment figures. Appendix F describes the input file, WUINSTP. The desired report is shown below.

```
            1         2         3         4         5         6         7         8
   1234567890123456789012345678901234567890123456789012345678901234567890123456789 0
 1 XX/XX/XXXX                         Wexler University                   Page XXX0
 2                          Faculty Salary Report
 3
 4                    Average Salaries and Length of Employment
 5                          Male                            Female
 6  Rank         Average Salary  Years    N      Average Salary  Years    N
 7  ----------   --------------------------      --------------------------
 8 Instructor    XXX,XXX,XX0.XX    0X    (0X)    XXX,XXX,XX0.XX    0X    (0X)
 9 Assistant     XXX,XXX,XX0.XX    0X    (0X)    XXX,XXX,XX0.XX    0X    (0X)
10 Associate     XXX,XXX,XX0.XX    0X    (0X)    XXX,XXX,XX0.XX    0X    (0X)
11 Professor     XXX,XXX,XX0.XX    0X    (0X)    XXX,XXX,XX0.XX    0X    (0X)
12
13 Overall
14 Average       XXX,XXX,XX0.XX    0X    (0X)    XXX,XXX,XX0.XX    0X    (0X)
15
16 Total Instructors X0X
17
```

3. The municipal water company needs a program that will calculate monthly water charges. The rates for city residents are

$0.035 per unit for the first 500 units.
$0.030 per unit for the next 500 units.
$0.027 per unit for all units beyond 1,000.

In addition, there is a service fee of $10.00 per month for all customers, regardless of usage. Water users who are not residents of the city pay 1.5 times the total bill.

An input file, MWC001P, described in Appendix F, contains customer information and old and new meter readings. Determine usage from the old and new meter readings. Note that the meters are like car odometers — when they reach their maximum value (9999), the next unit's usage causes them to read 0000. You must take this feature into account in your calculations. You may assume that no one will ever use more than 9,999 units of water per month. This report will require the totals shown on the grid below.

Output should appear as shown on the following printer spacing chart.

```
              1         2         3         4         5         6         7         8         9
    1234567890123456789012345678901234567890123456789012345678901234567890123456789012345678901234567890
 1  XX/XX/XXXX                    City of Kenosha, Wisconsin                      Page XXXØ
 2                                Monthly Water Billing Report
 3
 4  Customer                               Res.     Old    New    Current      Current
 5  Number       Customer Name             Code    Meter  Meter   Usage         Bill
 6
 7  XXXXX        XXXXXXXXXXXXXXXXXXXXXXXXX    X     XXXX   XXXX    X,XØX       X,XXØ.XX
 8  XXXXX        XXXXXXXXXXXXXXXXXXXXXXXXX    X     XXXX   XXXX    X,XØX       X,XXØ.XX
 9                                                                -------    -----------
10  Total Customers XØX                                 Totals   XXX,XØX    $XXX,XXX.ØØ
11
```

4. ACME manufacturing company wants you to write a payroll program. Each record in the input file, ACP001, described in Appendix F, represents one day's work for an employee. Records are accumulated for a week, so there will be several records per employee. Records in the file are ordered by Social Security number. The company uses both an hourly rate and a piece rate to pay its employees. Everyone gets $5.50 per hour worked. In addition, if a person produces 0–500 units during the week, he or she receives 25 cents per unit; if he or she produces 501–1,000 units, he or she receives 30 cents per unit; if more than 1,000 units, 40 cents per unit. After using these figures to calculate gross pay, you must subtract a 4.6 percent state tax and a 15 percent federal tax from gross pay to obtain net pay.

Your program should generate the report illustrated in the following printer spacing chart.

```
          1         2         3         4         5         6         7         8         9         1
          0
 12345678901234567890123456789012345678901234567890123456789012345678901234567890123456789012345678901234567890
 1 XX/XX/XXXX                              ACME Industries Weekly Payroll Report                        PAGE XXX0
 2
 3 Social          Employee                Hrs  Units    Piece      Hourly     Gross      State   Fed    Net
 4 Security        Name                    Wrk  Produced Rate Pay   Pay        Pay        Tax     Tax    Pay
 5
 6 XXX-XX-XXXX     XXXXXXXXXXXXXXXXXXXXX 0X   X,X0X    X,XX0.XX   X,XX0.XX   X,XX0.XX   XX0.XX  XX0.XX X,XX0.XX
 7 XXX-XX-XXXX     XXXXXXXXXXXXXXXXXXXXX 0X   X,X0X    X,XX0.XX   X,XX0.XX   X,XX0.XX   XX0.XX  XX0.XX X,XX0.XX
 8 XXX-XX-XXXX     XXXXXXXXXXXXXXXXXXXXX 0X   X,X0X    X,XX0.XX   X,XX0.XX   X,XX0.XX   XX0.XX  XX0.XX X,XX0.XX
 9
10 Average Gross Pay: $X,XX0.XX
11 Average Piece Rate Pay: X,XX0.XX
12 Average Units Per Employee: X,XX0
13 Average Units Per Hour: X,X0X
14
```

5. Wexler University's faculty members run a credit union. They want you to write a program to calculate monthly payments for loan applicants. The monthly payment is to be calculated using the formula shown below. Note that *I* represents monthly interest rate and *N* represents number of months for the loan. Also note that the *N* in the formula is an exponent, not a multiplier. The formula to be used in calculating payment amount is:

$$\text{Payment} = \text{LoanAmt} * (I * (1 + I)^N) / ((1 + I)^N - 1)$$

Records in input file, WULOANP, described in Appendix F, contain information about the loan amounts, interest rates, and length of loan. This will require you to create a logical file over WUINSTP and WULOANP sorted by Applicant Name. Generate a report formatted as follows:

```
          1         2         3         4         5         6         7         8         9
 1234567890123456789012345678901234567890123456789012345678901234567890123456789012345678901234567890
 1 XX/XX/XXXX            Wexler University Faculty Credit Union          PAGE XXX0
 2                           New Loan Application Report
 3
 4 Loan        Applicant                        Loan       Annual      Number    Monthly
 5 Number      Name                             Amount     Interest    Of        Payment
 6                                                         Rate        Months
 7
 8 XXXXX       XXXXXXXXXXXXXXXXXXXXXXXXXX        XX,XX0.XX  X0.XX%      X0X       XX,XX0.XX
 9 XXXXX       XXXXXXXXXXXXXXXXXXXXXXXXXX        XX,XX0.XX  X0.XX%      X0X       XX,XX0.XX
10 XXXXX       XXXXXXXXXXXXXXXXXXXXXXXXXX        XX,XX0.XX  X0.XX%      X0X       XX,XX0.XX
11
12             Total Loan Amounts               X,XXX,XX0.XX
13             Total Monthly Payments           X,XXX,XX0.XX
14             Total Number of Applicants          X0X
15
```

Chapter 9

Using Arrays and Tables

Chapter Overview

In this chapter, you will learn how to process arrays and tables, which are data structures that can simplify repetitive processing of similar data. This chapter discusses how to define arrays and tables, populate them with data, and access that data. You'll also learn the differences between arrays and tables and when to use which construct.

Representing Tables of Data

In common usage, a table is a collection of data organized into columns and rows. Similar kinds of data are stored within a column, and the data elements within a row of the table are related, or "belong" together. Typically, the data elements in the first column of a table are organized sequentially in ascending order to facilitate finding an item. Once you find the item you want in column 1, you then read across the row to extract the data related to that item.

The following three-column table, for example, would let you look up a U.S. state code to extract the name and sales tax rate of the state associated with that state code. (Note that the full table would include 50 codes and their corresponding names and tax rates, not just the six shown.)

State code	State name	Tax rate
AK	Alaska	.00000
AL	Alabama	.04000
AR	Arkansas	.06000
AZ	Arizona	.05600
CA	California	.06250
...	...	...
WY	Wyoming	.04000

RPG IV provides two data constructs that you can use to represent such collections of data: arrays and tables. Arrays and tables are both collections of data items (elements) with the same data attributes (data type, size, format, and number of decimal positions, if numeric). Originally, RPG included only tables; IBM added arrays to the language later to allow greater flexibility than tables could offer.

Although tables and arrays have several similarities, the capabilities of arrays go beyond those of tables. In fact, most RPG programmers no longer use tables; they prefer to use arrays for any solution that requires addressing multiple data values with a single field name. In this chapter, we'll discuss arrays first and then look at tables.

Arrays

An **array** is a grouping of data that contains multiple elements, all defined with a common name. The major difference between an RPG IV array and the tables as we are used to thinking about them is that a typical RPG IV array represents only a single column of data. The table data shown earlier might be represented in a program by three arrays:

Abbrev

AK	AL	AR	AZ	CA	. . .	WY

State

Alaska	Alabama	Arkansas	Arizona	California	. . .	Wyoming

Taxrate

.00000	.04000	.06000	.05600	.06250	. . .	.04000

A program can refer to an individual element in an array by the element's ordinal position—using State(3) to refer to Arkansas, for example—or it can refer to the entire array by name (e.g., State).

An array can be a grouping of simple data items (i.e., standalone variables or data structure subfields) or it can be a grouping of identical data structures. If the array elements are simple data items, they will all have the same data type, with the same length and (if the elements are numeric) number of decimal positions. In the Abbrev array, the state codes are all two-byte-long character data; the state names in the State array, however, have different lengths. To use the names in an RPG IV array, you would have to determine the length of the longest state name (South Carolina and North Carolina both have 14 characters) and pad the names of the other states with trailing blanks to make them all 14 characters long.

You define arrays in Definition specifications; the required entries are the same as those required for other data items, but with several keywords added to support arrays. You enter the array name anywhere in positions 7–21 (*Name+++++++++++*) of the Definition specifications; the name cannot begin with TAB. Typically, a simple array is defined as a standalone variable, so you would code an S left-adjusted in positions 24-25 (*Ds*); unlike other standalone variables we have worked with, however, an array stores multiple values, called **elements**. You must indicate the length of each array element right-adjusted in positions 33–39 (*To/L++*) of the specification line, along with the number of decimal positions within each element (for numeric data) in positions 41–42 (*Dc*). To indicate how many elements the array contains, you must include the Dim (Dimension) keyword in positions 44–80, specifying the number of table elements within parentheses after the keyword.

Let's look at how we could define the three arrays shown above.

```
*.. 1 ...+... 2 ...+... 3 ...+... 4 ...+... 5 ...+... 6 ...+... 7 ...+... 8
DName++++++++++ETDsFrom+++To/L+++IDc.Keywords+++++++++++++++++++++++++++++++
D Abbrev          S              2    Dim(50)
D State           S             14    Dim(50)
D Taxrate         S              5 5  Dim(50)
```

These definitions define three arrays, Abbrev, State, and Taxrate, with 50 elements each (as indicated by the Dim keyword). Each element of State is a two-byte character field; each element of State is a 14-byte character field; while each element of Taxrate is a five-digit packed decimal number with five decimal places. The arrays are standalone variables and are not necessarily related to each other.

Thus far, we have defined the structure of the arrays, but we have not provided any values for the individual elements of the arrays. There are three types of arrays, depending upon the method you use to provide values to the array elements:

- Runtime arrays
- Compile time arrays
- Preruntime arrays

Runtime Arrays

If you code no further specifications beyond the definitions shown above, you are defining a **runtime array**. The runtime array is so called because you load it with values during the course of program execution (i.e., at runtime); its values can also change while the program is running. You can assign initial values to a runtime array by assigning values during the Calculation specifications, as the following code illustrates.

```
*.. 1 ...+... 2 ...+... 3 ...+... 4 ...+... 5 ...+... 6 ...+... 7 ...+... 8
DName+++++++++++ETDsFrom+++To/L+++IDc.Keywords+++++++++++++++++++++++++++++
D Taxrate         S              5 5 Dim(50)

   /Free
      Taxrate(2) = .04;
      Taxrate(3) = .06;
      Taxrate(4) = .056;
      Taxrate(5) = .0625;
      ...
      Taxrate(50) = .04;
   /End-free
```

If you do not initialize an array, its initial elemental values will be compatible with its data type—blanks for character arrays, zeros for numeric arrays, and so on.

Runtime arrays are useful for storing related values that will be used in calculations during the course of the execution of the program. For example, it would be easier to define and process a single Monthlysales array as a standalone variable in a program instead of 12 individual standalone variables to hold monthly sales totals:

```
*.. 1 ...+... 2 ...+... 3 ...+... 4 ...+... 5 ...+... 6 ...+... 7 ...+... 8
DName+++++++++++ETDsFrom+++To/L+++IDc.Keywords+++++++++++++++++++++++++++++
D Monthlysales   S             11 2 Dim(12)
```

Compile Time Arrays

A **compile time array** obtains its data from the program's source code; the data is bound to the array when you compile the program. The array data must be entered at the very end of the program, following the last program entries (most often the last Output specification).

RPG IV uses what is called a ****Ctdata record** as a delimiter (or separator line) to explicitly identify the array whose data follows. To code this delimiter, place an asterisk (*) in positions 1 and 2 of a line following the last line of program code; in positions 3–8, enter Ctdata (for compile time data); leave position 9 blank; and, starting in position 10, enter the name of the array whose data follows.

The actual array data follows this separator line. How you enter the data at this point is up to you. You could code one element per line, two per line, three per line, and so on. In our example, because each state code is two bytes long, we could code all 50 state codes in two lines of 25 states each if we wanted to do so. The only stipulations are

- The values must begin in the first position of each line (unlike most RPG specifications, which begin in position 6 of each line).

- They must be entered in the order in which you want them to appear in the table.

- Multiple entries per line must be entered contiguously (without spaces separating them).

- You must be consistent in the number of entries you put on each line.

The array element coding would look like this:

```
...+... 1 ...+... 2 ...+... 3 ...+... 4 ...+... 5 ...+... 6 ...+... 7 ...+... 8
**CTDATA Abbrev
AKALARAZCACOCTDEFLGAHIIAIDILINKSKYLAMAMDMEMIMNMOMS
MTNCNDNENHNJNMNVNYOHOKORPARISCSDTNTXUTVAVTWAWIWVWY
```

If the number of entries per line is not an even multiple of the number of total array entries, the odd number of entries goes on the last line. For example, assume that you decide to enter 16 state codes on one line. There would be three lines of 16 codes, with a final fourth line containing only two codes. The coding would look like this:

```
...+... 1 ...+... 2 ...+... 3 ...+... 4 ...+... 5 ...+... 6 ...+... 7 ...+... 8
**CTDATA Abbrev
AKALARAZCACOCTDEFLGAHIIAIDILINKS
KYLAMAMDMEMIMNMOMSMTNCNDNENHNJNM
NVNYOHOKORPARISCSDTNTXUTVAVTWAWI
WVWY
```

The definition for a compile time array requires a Ctdata (Compile time data) keyword to signal that the array's compile time data appears at the end of the program. In addition, you may need to use the Perrcd (Per record) keyword to indicate how the data values are entered in the source. Each program line in your source member is a record in the source file. Accordingly, if you have entered 25 state codes per line, there are 25 table entries per record; if you have entered 16 state codes per line, there would be 16 array entries per record. Including the Perrcd keyword, with the number of array entries per record (or code line) indicated within parentheses after the keyword, lets the system correctly obtain the data to load within the array. If you omit keyword Perrcd for a compile time array, the system assumes you have entered the data with only one entry per record. The size of a single entry is limited to 100 bytes, and each one must be contained in a single source record.

The following code shows the Definition specification for the Abbrev array as a compile time array with 16 entries per record.

```
*.. 1 ...+... 2 ...+... 3 ...+... 4 ...+... 5 ...+... 6 ...+... 7 ...+... 8
DName+++++++++++ETDsFrom+++To/L+++IDc.Keywords+++++++++++++++++++++++++++++++
D Abbrev          S              2    Dim(50)
D                                     Ctdata Perrcd(16)
```

The array data for a compile time array is loaded into the array when you compile the program, and its elements will have the same initial values each time you call the program anew. During its execution a program can change the values of the array elements, but those changes will not be retained when the program ends with *Inlr on.

Compile time arrays are useful for relatively small arrays whose data is not likely to change over time. If the array data changes frequently, a programmer would have to go back to the source program, change the compile time data at the end of the program, and recompile the program each time the data needed updating. You should avoid this practice, because each time you use an editor to change your source code, you run the risk of inadvertently introducing errors into the program.

Preruntime Arrays

An alternate way to handle data values required by an array is to store the data in a database file that is loaded into the array each time the program is run. This kind of array is called a **preruntime array**, because RPG IV automatically retrieves all the array data from the file before the program's procedural processing begins.

The Definition specification for a preruntime array varies slightly from that of a compile time array. Instead of using the Ctdata keyword, preruntime arrays require you to include the Fromfile (From file) keyword, specifying the name of the file containing the array data. The value indicated with the Perrcd keyword should indicate how many array elements are coded per record within the array file; if only one value appears per record, you can omit the Perrcd keyword.

```
*.. 1 ...+... 2 ...+... 3 ...+... 4 ...+... 5 ...+... 6 ...+... 7 ...+... 8
DName+++++++++++ETDsFrom+++To/L+++IDc.Keywords+++++++++++++++++++++++++++++++
D Abbrev          S              2    Dim(50)
D                                     Fromfile(States)
```

Because the data for a preruntime array is obtained from a file, you must include a definition of this file within the File specifications of the program that uses the array. The File specification for a file that contains array data differs somewhat from that of other files with which you have worked. The file type (position 17) is I (Input) because the program reads the data, but the file's designation (position 18) is T (Table); this entry directs the system to read all the data into an array automatically at the program's start. The array input file for a preruntime array must be program-described; code an F (for fixed format) in position 22 and include the appropriate record length in positions 23–27. The file must be processed sequentially (key access is not allowed).

```
*.. 1 ...+... 2 ...+... 3 ...+... 4 ...+... 5 ...+... 6 ...+... 7 ...+... 8
FFilename++IPEASFRLen+LKlen+AIDevice+.Keywords+++++++++++++++++++++++++++++
FStates    IT  F   2        Disk
```

If you want to write the array back to a file at the end of program execution—perhaps because your program has changed some of the array values and you want to update the file to reflect these changed values—you need to include the Tofile (To file) keyword as part of the array's Definition specification, specifying the name of the target file. If the Fromfile is different from the Tofile, you would need an additional File specification defining the Tofile as an output file. If the table data is to be written back to the same file from which it was initially read, the file type should be C (for combined):

```
*.. 1 ...+... 2 ...+... 3 ...+... 4 ...+... 5 ...+... 6 ...+... 7 ...+... 8
FFilename++IPEASFRLen+LKlen+AIDevice+.Keywords+++++++++++++++++++++++++++++
DName++++++++++ETDsFrom+++To/L+++IDc.Keywords+++++++++++++++++++++++++++++
  // Table file of 50 state codes, with one code per record;
  // records to be rewritten at end of processing
FStates    CT  F   2        Disk

  // Preruntime array of 50 state codes, entered one per record;
  // table file to be rewritten at end of processing
D Abbrev         S            2     Dim(50)
D                                   Fromfile(States) Tofile(States)
```

Runtime Arrays and Data Structures

It is common for programmers to want to define some fields within an input record as an array to facilitate coding repetitive operations. Although you cannot directly define fields as array elements within an externally described file, you can use a data structure to let you redefine separately defined input fields into elements of a single runtime array. Remember that an array can be a data structure subfield, or an entire data structure, as well as a standalone variable.

Assume you have a file of sales records from all of a company's sales staff. Each record contains a salesperson's identification number and that person's total sales for each month during the past year—12 sales figures in all. Each sales figure is 11 digits long, with two decimal positions. Because you plan to redefine the sales figures as an array, you have defined Sales as one large character field, as shown in the following DDS specifications.

```
*.. 1 ...+... 2 ...+... 3 ...+... 4 ...+... 5 ...+... 6 ...+... 7 ...+... 8
A..........T.Name++++++RLen++TDpB......Functions+++++++++++++++++++++++++++
 * Externally described file SalesFile with 12 sales figures defined as
 * a single field
A          R Salesrec
A            Slsnbr        5A        Text('Salesperson Number')
A            Sales       132A        Text('Twelve Months Sales')
```

You are writing a program that uses file SalesFile as input, and you want to refer to the 12 sales figures within each record as elements of an array. To do this, you must include within the program's Definition specifications a data structure definition that references the sales input field and redefines it as an array. The following specifications illustrate such a data structure.

```
*.. 1 ...+... 2 ...+... 3 ...+... 4 ...+... 5 ...+... 6 ...+... 7 ...+... 8
DName+++++++++++ETDsFrom+++To/L+++IDc.Keywords+++++++++++++++++++++++++++++++
D                       DS
D Sales                          132
D  Salesarray                     11  2 Dim(12) Overlay(Sales)
```

The DS entry in positions 24–25 of the first line declares that what follows is a data structure definition (unnamed, in this case). The second line says that the character field Sales (from file SalesFile) occupies the first 132 bytes of the data structure. The third line defines Salesarray as an array of 12 zoned decimal elements, each with two decimal positions. Salesarray represents an **overlay**, or a redefinition of the Sales field, breaking the Sales field down into 12 array elements, each 11 bytes long; as a result Salesarray also occupies bytes 1–132 of the data structure.

An alternate way to externally describe the sales file is to define each month's sales figure separately, as the following DDS shows.

```
*.. 1 ...+... 2 ...+... 3 ...+... 4 ...+... 5 ...+... 6 ...+... 7 ...+... 8
A..........T.Name++++++RLen++TDpB......Functions++++++++++++++++++++++++++++++
 * Externally described file SalesFile
A          R Salesrec
A            Slsnbr        5A          Text('Salesperson Number')
A            Sales01      11S 2        Text('January Sales')
A            Sales02      11S 2        Text('February Sales')
A            Sales03      11S 2        Text('March Sales')
A            Sales04      11S 2        Text('April Sales')
A            Sales05      11S 2        Text('May Sales')
A            Sales06      11S 2        Text('June Sales')
A            Sales07      11S 2        Text('July Sales')
A            Sales08      11S 2        Text('August Sales')
A            Sales09      11S 2        Text('September Sales')
A            Sales10      11S 2        Text('October Sales')
A            Sales11      11S 2        Text('November Sales')
A            Sales12      11S 2        Text('December Sales')
```

Given the above file definition, you must slightly change the data structure to manipulate the sales figures as array elements:

```
*.. 1 ...+... 2 ...+... 3 ...+... 4 ...+... 5 ...+... 6 ...+... 7 ...+... 8
DName+++++++++++ETDsFrom+++To/L+++IDc.Keywords+++++++++++++++++++++++++++++++
D Sales           DS
D   Sales01                    11  2
D   Sales02                    11  2
D   Sales03                    11  2
D   Sales04                    11  2
D   Sales05                    11  2
D   Sales06                    11  2
D   Sales07                    11  2
D   Sales08                    11  2
D   Sales09                    11  2
D   Sales10                    11  2
D   Sales11                    11  2
D   Sales12                    11  2
D   Salesarray                 11  2  Dim(12)
D                                     Overlay(Sales)
```

In the above data structure, each month's sales amount is defined as a successive 11-byte area within the data structure; array Salesarray, overlaying the entire 132-byte Sales data structure, redefines the 12 sales figures as its 12 elements.

With either method of defining the input file and its associated data structure, each time you read a record from SalesFile, the 12 sales figures from that record will be stored in array Salesarray. When a new input record is read, the sales figures from that record replace the previous contents of the array. Thus, the contents of Salesarray change as the program is running, and that's the reason why we call Salesarray a runtime array.

You can also use data structure overlays to provide initial values to a runtime array whose data does not come from a file. This technique provides the same end result as coding a compile time array but does not require additional keywords, nor does it require that you separate the array definition from the array data:

```
*.. 1 ...+... 2 ...+... 3 ...+... 4 ...+... 5 ...+... 6 ...+... 7 ...+... 8
DName+++++++++++ETDsFrom+++To/L+++IDc.Keywords+++++++++++++++++++++++++++++++
D Days            DS
D                              9     Inz('Sunday')
D                              9     Inz('Monday')
D                              9     Inz('Tuesday')
D                              9     Inz('Wednesday')
D                              9     Inz('Thursday')
D                              9     Inz('Friday')
D                              9     Inz('Saturday')
D   Daynames                   9     Dim(7)
D                                    Overlay(Days)
```

This example initializes the first 63 bytes of the Days data structure with values that correspond to the names of the days of the week. Notice that you don't need to name each data structure subfield if you will not use the name elsewhere in the program; the Inz keyword will provide the correct initial value for each nine-byte section of the data structure. Then, the Daynames subfield is an array with seven elements, each nine bytes long; Daynames overlays the Days data structure, so its elemental values will be the days of the week. Compare the above runtime array with the following compile time array, which defines the same structure:

```
...+... 1 ...+... 2 ...+... 3 ...+... 4 ...+... 5 ...+... 6 ...+... 7 ...+... 8
    DName++++++++++ETDsFrom+++To/L+++IDc.Keywords++++++++++++++++++++++++++++++
    D Daynames       S              9    Dim(7)
    D                                    Ctdata Perrcd(7)

...

**Ctdata Daynames
Sunday   Monday   Tuesday  WednesdayThursday Friday   Saturday
```

In the latter example, the array definition may be separated from the array data by many pages of other code, and may be more prone to coding errors than the simpler definition in the earlier example. In a modular programming environment, it is useful to be able to keep all the related parts of a construct close together in the actual code; for this reason, many RPG programmers prefer the earlier example over the latter one.

Defining Related Arrays

In RPG IV an array corresponds to one column of information. If you wanted to represent the information in the tables illustrated at the beginning of this chapter, you would have to define three separate arrays:

```
*.. 1 ...+... 2 ...+... 3 ...+... 4 ...+... 5 ...+... 6 ...+... 7 ...+... 8
DName++++++++++ETDsFrom+++To/L+++IDc.Keywords++++++++++++++++++++++++++++++
D Abbrev        S              2    Dim(50)
D State         S             14    Dim(50)
D Taxrate       S              5  5 Dim(50)
```

If the arrays are compile time or preruntime arrays, however, you may find it convenient to load the data for two arrays in **alternating format** by defining one of the arrays with the Alt (Alternating format) keyword. For example, you could define the Abbrev and State arrays as a pairs of related arrays with the following definitions:

```
*.. 1 ...+... 2 ...+... 3 ...+... 4 ...+... 5 ...+... 6 ...+... 7 ...+... 8
DName++++++++++ETDsFrom+++To/L+++IDc.Keywords++++++++++++++++++++++++++++++
D Abbrev        S              2    Dim(50)
D                                   Ctdata
D State         S             14    Dim(50)
D                                   Alt(Abbrev)
```

In this definition, Abbrev is the main array. State is the alternate array, related to Abbrev by the Alt keyword. The main array must be a compile time array or a preruntime array; both arrays must include the Dim keyword; the alternate array cannot use the Ctdata, Perrcd, Fromfile or Tofile keywords. The array data is coded at the end of the program's source (or in a file for a preruntime array) in alternating format:

```
**CTDATA Abbrev
AKAlaska
ALAlabama
ARArkansas
AZArizona
CACalifornia
...
WYWyoming
```

Note that because the Perrcd keyword has been omitted from the Abbrev array's definition, the number of entries per record defaults to 1; so, only one pair of entries is coded on each line. If the data had been laid out so that several pairs of data were entered on the same line, the Perrcd keyword would have been required.

The keywords on the main array definition control how the arrays' elements are loaded when the program starts. The program will use the compile time data (or the Fromfile data) to initialize *both* arrays in alternating order—Abbrev ... State ... Abbrev ... State ... and so on—with the end result being that the pair of arrays will be loaded with the related information. The Alt keyword allows you to pair only two arrays.

Using Dim(%Elem) and Dim(%Size)

The **%Elem** (**Number of elements**) **function** returns the number of elements in an array (or a table, discussed later). The %Elem function can be used with the Dim keyword in an array definition to make the dimension of the array dependent upon the dimension of another array:

```
*.. 1 ...+... 2 ...+... 3 ...+... 4 ...+... 5 ...+... 6 ...+... 7 ...+... 8
DName++++++++++ETDsFrom+++To/L+++IDc.Keywords++++++++++++++++++++++++++++++++
D Abbrev          S                   2     Dim(50)
D State           S                  14     Dim(%Elem(Abbrev))
D Taxrate         S                   5 5   Dim(%Elem(Abbrev))
```

These definitions describe three arrays: Abbrev, State, and Taxrate. The Abbrev array has 50 elements. The State and Taxrate arrays also have 50 elements each, because their definitions use the %Elem function to say, "This array has the same number of elements as the Abbrev array." The State and Taxrate arrays "inherit" the dimension of the Abbrev array.

The %Elem function can also be used to control the number of times that a loop will be processed, by coding it with the iterative structured operations, such as Dow, Dou, or For:

```
For Count = 1 to %Elem(State);
      // If State has 50 elements, this code will be executed 50 times.
Endfor;
```

Once the program is compiled, the %Elem value will not change at runtime.

Earlier, we discussed the **%Size** (**Size in bytes**) **function**, which returns the byte size of another data element in an RPG program. You can use the %Size function in a similar manner to the %Elem function if you want an array's dimension to be dependent upon another variable's byte size:

```
*.. 1 ...+... 2 ...+... 3 ...+... 4 ...+... 5 ...+... 6 ...+... 7 ...+... 8
DName++++++++++ETDsFrom+++To/L+++IDc.Keywords++++++++++++++++++++++++++++++++
D Custname        S                  35
D Custarray       S                   1     Dim(%Size(Custname)

 /Free
    For Count = 1 to %Size(Custname);    // Or %Elem(Custarray)
                                   // This code will be executed 35 times.
    Endfor;
 /End-Free
```

This code would define Custarray with 35 elements, because Custname is 35 bytes long, and would execute the For loop 35 times.

Many programmers prefer this coding technique over "hard coding" the dimension of the dependent arrays. By using the %Elem or %Size function, they document the dependency. They also ensure that any future changes to the dimension of the "parent" array will be automatically passed down to the "children" when the program is recompiled.

Arrays and Indexing

You can directly reference and manipulate *individual* elements of an array using an **index**, or element number. To indicate an array element in RPG IV, you use the array name followed by a set of parentheses that contains the location number of the element within the array. The index numbering starts with 1. Thus, Salesarray(3) means the third element in the array Salesarray; Taxarray(10) is the tenth element in the array Taxarray. When you use an array name *without* an index, the system infers that you want to reference or manipulate the entire array—that is, *all* its elements.

The index that you use to reference an element of an array does not have to be a numeric literal. Instead, you can use a variable as an index, provided you have defined the variable as numeric with zero decimal positions. If the index is a variable, the current value of that variable determines which element of the array is referenced. Thus, if Index has a value of 3, Taxarray(Index) is the third element of Taxarray; if Index's value is 10, Taxarray(Index) is the tenth element of the array.

The array index may also be an expression, as long as it evaluates to a positive numeric value with no decimal places. If your program refers to an array using an index with a value that is negative, zero, or greater than the number of elements defined for the array, a runtime error—an array index error—will occur.

Calculations with Arrays

You can use any of RPG IV's arithmetic or assignment operations with arrays or their elements. If you just reference individual elements in your calculations, the effects are the same as if you were using fields:

```
// Add the values of two elements and store result in a third element.
Array(12) = Array(6) + Array(3);

// Divide the third element of array Array by 60, storing the quotient
// in Quotients(3) and the remainder in Remainders(3).
Quotients(3) = %Div(Array(3):60);
Remainders(3) = %Rem(Array(3):60);
```

You can also use entire arrays, rather than just individual elements of the arrays, in calculations. In this case, the expression's target entry must always be an array name. If all the factors involved in the operation are arrays, the operation is performed successively on corresponding elements of the arrays until the array with the fewest number of elements has been completely processed.

```
// Multiply corresponding elements of Array_A and Array_B,
// storing the products in Array_C.
Eval(H) Array_C = Array_A * Array_B;

// Assign the values of Array_B to Array_A.
Array_A = Array_B;

// Take the square root of each element of Array_A and store the result
// in the corresponding element of Array_B.
Array_B = %Sqrt(Array_A);
```

When you combine nonarray values and arrays in calculations, the operation works with corresponding elements of the arrays, along with the nonarray values in each case, and continues until all the elements in the shortest array have been processed:

```
// Calculate gross pay for employees that work overtime; arrays Rate and
// Hours contain employee values; array GPay stores results.
Gpay = 40 * Rate + ( (Hours-40) * 1.5 * Rate);

// Store 'ABCDE' in each element of array Array_A
Array_A = 'ABCDE';
```

%Lookup (Look up an Array Element)

You can use one of the **%Lookup (Look up an array element) functions** to search an array for a specific elemental value. The %Lookup functions take the following form:

```
%Lookupxx(search-argument : array {:start {:elements}} )
```

Typically, you'll have a value—either a field from an input file or a program variable—that you want to find in the array; this value is the search argument, the first argument in the %Lookup function. Next, you specify the name of the array that you want to search. The search argument must match the data type of the array that you want to search—for example, if the array has numeric elements, the search argument must be numeric—but it need not have the same length or number of decimal positions.

%Lookup will return a number representing the array index of the element that matches the search argument. If no element in the array matches the value of the search argument, %Lookup will return a zero. There are five variations of %Lookup functions, each representing a different type of match:

- **%Lookup** searches for an exact match.
- **%Lookuplt** searches for an element that is closest to, but less than, the search argument.
- **%Lookuple** searches for an exact match, or for an element that is closest to, but less than, the search argument.
- **%Lookupge** searches for an exact match, or for an element that is closest to, but greater than, the search argument.
- **%Lookupgt** searches for an element that is closest to, but greater than, the search argument.

The most common usage is a simple %Lookup (exact match).

If you simply want to know whether a value exists as an element in an array, but you don't need to access the element or know its location within the array, you can compare the %Lookup result to zero. In the following example, the %Lookup simply indicates whether or not an array element exists that matches Value:

```
If %Lookup(Value:Array) > 0;
  Exsr Valuefound;
Else;
  Exsr Notfound;
Endif;
```

If, on the other hand, you want to know not only whether a value exists in the array but also its location in the array, you need to use an index variable in an assignment expression. The following %Lookup, if successful, assigns index I the value that points to the array element whose value matches Value. If the lookup is unsuccessful, I will be zero:

```
I = %Lookup(Value:Array);
If I > 0;
  Exsr Valuefound;
Else;
  Exsr Notfound;
Endif;
```

If the index is greater than zero following the lookup, it means that the value was found in the array. Moreover, index I's value points to the location of the array element that has the same value as Value. Thus, if the third element of Array had the same value as Value, the value of index I would be 3 after the %Lookup. To process that element, you could refer to it as Array(I).

If you specify a third (numeric) argument, the search will begin at that element of the array; otherwise the search will start at the first element. If you specify a fourth (numeric) argument, the search will continue for that number of elements; otherwise the search will continue to the end of the array.

To understand how you might use the %Lookup functions to extract data from an array, let's reconsider the three-column table of state codes, state names, and sales tax rates we discussed earlier in this chapter. Let's assume that the three columns of data are entered successively into our program as three individual arrays: Abbrev, State, and Taxrate. With a single %Lookup function to search the primary array (Abbrev), you can find the appropriate index to use with all three arrays. Consider the code shown opposite (for ease of illustration, we'll use runtime arrays overlaying data structures, but you could use any of the array loading methods).

If Statecode had a value of 'CA' the %Lookup function would assign a value of 5 to the variable I. We can then reuse that index with any of the related arrays to point to the corresponding element in each additional "column" (Taxrate and State in this example). If Salesamount had a value of 53.99, Taxdue would be 3.37, and Statename would be 'California' after processing this code. If Statecode were 'BD' then I would be 0, Taxdue would be 0, and Statename would be '*Error*' because BD is not in the Abbrev array.

```
*.. 1 ...+... 2 ...+... 3 ...+... 4 ...+... 5 ...+... 6 ...+... 7 ...+... 8
DName++++++++++ETDsFrom+++To/L+++IDc.Keywords+++++++++++++++++++++++++++++++
   // ------------------------- Data structures
D Abbreviations    DS
D                             30     Inz('AKALARAZCACOCTDEFLGAHIIAIDILIN')
D                             30     Inz('KSKYLAMAMDMEMIMNMOMSMTNCNDNENH')
D                             30     Inz('NJNMNVNYOHOKORPARISCSDTNTXUTVA')
D                             10     Inz('VTWAWIWVWY')
D    Abbrev           2       Dim(50)
D                             Overlay(Abbreviations)

D Names            DS
D                             14     Inz('Alaska')
D                             14     Inz('Alabama')
D                             14     Inz('Arkansas')
D                             14     Inz('Arizona')
D                             14     Inz('California')
...                           ...    ...
D                             14     Inz('Wyoming')
D    State           14      Dim(50)
D                             Overlay(Names)

D Rates            DS
D                           5 5 Inz(0)
D                           5 5 Inz(.04)
D                           5 5 Inz(.06)
D                           5 5 Inz(.056)
D                           5 5 Inz(.0625)
...                         ...    ...
D                           5 5 Inz(.04)
D    Taxrate         5 5 Dim(50)
D                             Overlay(Rates)

   // ------------------------- Standalone variables
D I                S          5U 0
D Saleamount       S         11 2
D Statecode        S          2
D Statename        S         14
D Taxdue           S         11 2

 /Free
    I = %Lookup(Statecode:Abbrev);
    If I > 0;
       Eval(H) Taxdue = Saleamount * Taxrate(I);
       Statename = State(I);
    Else;
       Taxdue = 0;
       Statename = '*Error*';
    Endif;
 /End-Free
```

Using Unequal Searches

To understand when you might use one of the unequal %Lookup functions, consider the following table of shipping charges:

Package weight	Shipping charge
0–1	2.50
2–5	4.25
6–10	7.50
11–20	9.00
21–40	12.00
41–70	16.00

You would use this table to look up a package weight to determine the shipping charges for the package. Unlike the previous examples, in this table the weight column entries represent a range of values rather than discrete values.

How should these values be represented, and how should the %Lookup be performed? One solution is to represent this data as two arrays, storing only the upper end of the range of weights in one array and the charges is another, as follows:

```
*.. 1 ...+... 2 ...+... 3 ...+... 4 ...+... 5 ...+... 6 ...+... 7 ...+... 8
DName+++++++++++ETDsFrom+++To/L+++IDc.Keywords+++++++++++++++++++++++++++++++
    // ---------------------------- Data structures
D Weightdata      DS
D                                3   0 Inz(1)
D                                3   0 Inz(5)
D                                3   0 Inz(10)
D                                3   0 Inz(20)
D                                3   0 Inz(40)
D                                3   0 Inz(70)
D   Weight                       3   0 Dim(6)
D                                      Ascend
D                                      Overlay(Weightdata)

D Chargedata      DS
D                                5   2 Inz(2.50)
D                                5   2 Inz(4.25)
D                                5   2 Inz(7.50)
D                                5   2 Inz(9.00)
D                                5   2 Inz(12.00)
D                                5   2 Inz(16.00)
D   Charge                       5   2 Dim(6)
D                                      Overlay(Chargedata)

    // ---------------------------- Standalone variables
D I               S              5U   0
D Pkgcharge       S              5    2
D Pkgweight       S              3    0
D Totalcharge     S              5    2
```

continued...

continued...

```
/Free
   I = %Lookupge(Pkgweight:Weight);
   If I > 0;
      Totalcharge = Pkgcharge + Charge(I);
   Else;
      Exsr Cannotship;
   Endif;
/End-Free
```

The above Definition specifications define Weight and Charge as arrays of six elements each. Of course, these arrays could have been defined as compile time or preruntime arrays, possibly in alternating format. The unequal %Lookup functions require a sequence entry in the array definition, so the Weight arrays uses the Ascend keyword to indicate that the data is in ascending order. The lookup statement above translates to "Find the first weight that is greater than or equal to the package weight." If the search is successful, the function will return a positive number to the index I, which you can then use with the Charge array to find the correct shipping charge. Because the maximum table weight is 70, failure of the search indicates an input weight over the 70-pound limit; in such cases, the program executes an error routine to indicate that the package cannot be shipped.

Sorta (Sort an Array)

As mentioned, the unequal %Lookup functions require a sequence entry in the array definition. The Ascend and Descend keywords describe the sequence of the data in the array. If the array is in ascending order, for example, elements in the array start with the lowest collating value and go to the highest; elements with duplicate values are allowed. Compile time arrays and preruntime arrays are checked for the correct sequence when their data is loaded; if an array is out of sequence when it is loaded, an error occurs. The program does not recheck an array's sequence once its data is loaded; if a program changes an element's value, that value may cause the array to be out of sequence. RPG does not enforce sequence checking for runtime arrays, even with the Ascend or Descend keyword.

Sorta (**Sort an Array**) is a simple but useful operation that rearranges the values of the elements of an array into ascending or descending sequence. The order used depends on the sequence keyword specified within the array's definition. If the definition includes neither keyword, the Sorta operation sorts the values in ascending sequence, the default order. The specification for this operation includes just the operation and the name of the array to be sorted in the following example, assume Array_A is array of five numeric elements:

Operation: `Sorta Array_A;`

Array_A contains

Before	10	92	33	85	12
After	10	12	33	85	92

If you have specified a sequence entry for an array definition, you should always sort the array before performing a %Lookup function—even an equal %Lookup. If you do not, the %Lookup results will be unpredictable and may be incorrect. *Unsequenced* arrays need not be sorted in order for an equal %Lookup to work properly.

Note
The %Lookup function uses a technique called a binary search to improve performance for sequenced arrays. For those arrays defined without a sequence entry, %Lookup will perform a sequential search of the elements.

%Xfoot (Sum the Elements of an Array)

The **%Xfoot (Sum the elements of an array) function**—called "crossfoot"—sums the elements of a numeric array. The function's only argument contains the name of the array whose elements are to be added together; use an assignment expression to name the field where the answer is to be stored. If you half adjust this operation, the rounding takes place just before the final answer is stored.

Crossfooting is a term used in accounting to sum across a row of figures to develop a total for that row. The %Xfoot function is very useful in such applications, provided the figures to be added are array elements. The following example will sum the elements of array Array_A, storing the answer in field Total:

```
Eval(H) Total = %Xfoot(Array_A);
```

%Subarr (Set/Get Portion of an Array)

The **%Subarr (Set/get portion of an array) function** returns a subset of an array, similar to the way the **%Subst function** returns a section of a character string. The %Subarr function takes the following form:

```
%Subarr(array:start {:elements})
```

The first argument is the array that you want to subset; the second argument tells %Subarr where (i.e., which element of the array) to begin the subset; this value must be a positive whole number less than or equal to the number of elements in the array.

If you specify a third argument, it represents the number of elements to include in the subset. It must be a positive whole number less than or equal to the remaining number of elements, beginning with the starting element (indicated by the second argument).

Generally, you can use %Subarr in any expression that would allow an unindexed array. If it is used as the result of an expression, %Subarr will change (i.e., set) the specified elements in an array; on the right side of the expression, %Subarr gets the specified elements from an array so that they can be assigned to another array. %Subarr can also be used with the Sorta operation and the %Xfoot function to sort or crossfoot a subset of an array. %Subarr respects the element boundaries of the arrays involved in the expression.

To illustrate the use of the %Subarr function, consider the following definitions:

```
*.. 1 ...+... 2 ...+... 3 ...+... 4 ...+... 5 ...+... 6 ...+... 7 ...+... 8
DName++++++++++ETDsFrom+++To/L+++IDc.Keywords++++++++++++++++++++++++++++++++
D A_data          DS
D                               12    Inz('abcdefghijkl')
D   Array_A                      3    Dim(4)
D                                     Overlay(A_data)

D B_data          DS
D                               10    Inz('mnopqrstuv')
D   Array_B                      2    Dim(5)
D                                     Overlay(B_data)

D C_data          DS
D                               10    Inz('abcdefghij')
D   Array_C                      2    Dim(5)
D                                     Overlay(C_data)
```

The following tables illustrate the effects of different array expressions, including several using the %Subarr function.

Example 1

Expression: `Array_A = Array_B;`

Array_A contains

Before	abc	def	ghi	jkl
After	mnƀ	opƀ	qrƀ	stƀ

In this example, because Array_B has more elements (5) than Array_A, only the first four elements of Array_A are assigned to the corresponding elements of Array_B. Array_A elements are padded with blanks (represented by ƀ). Equivalent expressions would be:

```
Array_A(1) = Array_B(1);
Array_A(2) = Array_B(2);
Array_A(3) = Array_B(3);
Array_A(4) = Array_B(4);
```

Example 2

Expression: `Array_B = Array_A;`

Array_B contains

Before	mn	op	qr	st	uv
After	ab	de	gh	jk	uv

In this example, because Array_A has fewer elements (4) than Array_B, only the first four elements of Array_B are affected by the expression. Array_A elements are truncated in Array_B. Equivalent expressions would be:

```
Array_B(1) = Array_A(1);
Array_B(2) = Array_A(2);
Array_B(3) = Array_A(3);
Array_B(4) = Array_A(4);
```

Example 3

Expression: Array_B = Array_C;

Array_B contains

Before	mn	op	qr	st	uv
After	ab	cd	ef	gh	ij

In this example, Array_B and Array_C have identical properties. Equivalent expressions would be:

```
Array_B(1) = Array_C(1);
Array_B(2) = Array_C(2);
Array_B(3) = Array_C(3);
Array_B(4) = Array_C(4);
Array_B(5) = Array_C(5);
```

Example 4

Expression: `Array_B = %Subarr(Array_A:2:3);`

Array_B contains

Before	mn	op	qr	st	uv
After	de	gh	jk	st	uv

In this example, the three elements of Array_A beginning with the second element, are assigned to Array_B. Array_A elements are truncated in Array_B. The fourth and fifth elements of Array_B are unaffected. Equivalent expressions would be:

```
Array_B(1) = Array_A(2);
Array_B(2) = Array_A(3);
Array_B(3) = Array_A(4);
```

Example 5

Expression: `Array_B = %Subarr(Array_C:2:3);`

Array_B contains

Before	mn	op	qr	st	uv
After	cd	ef	gh	st	uv

In this example, the three elements of Array_C beginning with the second element, are assigned to Array_B. The fourth and fifth elements of Array_B are unaffected. Equivalent expressions would be:

```
Array_B(1) = Array_C(2);
Array_B(2) = Array_C(3);
Array_B(3) = Array_C(4);
```

Example 5

Expression: `%Subarr(Array_B:3) = Array_A;`

Array_B contains

Before	mn	op	qr	st	uv
After	mn	op	ab	de	gh

In this example, the elements of Array_A are assigned to Array_B beginning with the third element of Array_B. Array_A elements are truncated in Array_B. Only the first three elements of Array_A are assigned to Array_B, because Array_B runs out of elements before the complete Array_A can be assigned. Equivalent expressions would be:

```
Array_B(3) = Array_A(1);
Array_B(4) = Array_A(2);
Array_B(5) = Array_A(3);
```

Example 6

Expression: `%Subarr(Array_B:3) = Array_C;`

Array_B contains

Before	mn	op	qr	st	uv
After	mn	op	ab	cd	ef

In this example, the elements of Array_C are assigned to Array_B beginning with the third element of Array_B. Only the first three elements of Array_C are assigned to Array_B, because Array_B runs out of elements before the complete Array_C can be assigned. Equivalent expressions would be:

```
Array_B(3) = Array_C(1);
Array_B(4) = Array_C(2);
Array_B(5) = Array_C(3);
```

Example 7

Expression: `%Subarr(Array_B:3) = %Subarr(Array_A:3);`

Array_B contains

Before	mn	op	qr	st	uv
After	mn	op	gh	jk	uv

In this example, the third and fourth elements of Array_A are assigned to the third and fourth elements of Array_B. Array_A elements are truncated in Array_B. The expression skips the first and second elements of Array_B; the fifth element is also unaffected because Array_A runs out of elements. Equivalent expressions would be:

```
Array_B(3) = Array_A(3);
Array_B(4) = Array_A(4);
```

Example 8

Expression: `%Subarr(Array_B:2) = %Subarr(Array_C:3:2);`

Array_B contains

Before	mn	op	qr	st	uv
After	mn	ef	gh	st	uv

In this example, the third and fourth elements of Array_C are assigned to the second and third elements of Array_B. The remaining elements of Array_B are unaffected. Equivalent expressions would be:

```
Array_B(2) = Array_C(3);
Array_B(3) = Array_C(4);
```

Array Data Structures and Multidimensional Arrays

Recall that a typical RPG IV array represents only a single column of data. Recall also that an array can be a data structure subfield or a data structure itself. An **array data structure** is a data structure defined with the Dim keyword. By defining an array as a subfield within an array data structure, a program can effectively define a two-dimensional array. Consider the following Definition specifications:

```
*.. 1 ...+... 2 ...+... 3 ...+... 4 ...+... 5 ...+... 6 ...+... 7 ...+... 8
DName++++++++++ETDsFrom+++To/L+++IDc.Keywords+++++++++++++++++++++++++++++++
D Galaxy          DS                    Dim(8)
D                                       Qualified
D  Sector                      1        Dim(8)
```

Conceptually, this definition would create a structure that you could visualize with rows and columns:

	Sector(1)	Sector(2)	Sector(3)	Sector(4)	Sector(5)	Sector(6)	Sector(7)	Sector(8)
Galaxy(1)								
Galaxy(2)								
Galaxy(3)								
Galaxy(4)								
Galaxy(5)								
Galaxy(6)								
Galaxy(7)								
Galaxy(8)								

Array data structures must be runtime arrays (Ctdata, Perrcd, Fromfile, and Tofile keywords are not allowed) and must include the Qualified keyword, discussed in Chapter 4. This keyword forces the program to refer to the data structure's subfields using qualified names—that is, the data structure name followed by a period (.) and the subfield name. When the qualified data structure is an array data structure, the qualified name must include an index. For example, in the above definition you'd code Galaxy(3).Sector(6) to refer to the sixth element of Sector in the third element of Galaxy; Galaxy(3).Sector would refer to the entire Sector array in the third element of Galaxy; Galaxy.Sector, without an index entry for Galaxy, would not be allowed. The index can be a whole numeric literal, constant, or expression.

If a subfield in a data structure uses the Likeds keyword, discussed in Chapter 4, to "inherit" the characteristics of another data structure—and if that data structure includes array subfields—the inherited subfields will also be arrays. You can use this feature to add even more dimensions to an array data structure, as the following definition illustrates:

```
*.. 1 ...+... 2 ...+... 3 ...+... 4 ...+... 5 ...+... 6 ...+... 7 ...+... 8
DName++++++++++ETDsFrom+++To/L+++IDc.Keywords+++++++++++++++++++++++++++++++
D X               DS
D  C                           1        Dim(8)

D A               DS                    Dim(8)
D                                       Qualified
D  B                                    Dim(8)
D                                       Likeds(X)
```

In this definition, subfield B is an array within the array data structure A. Because subfield B uses the Likeds keyword with data structure X as its "parent," it will consist of subfield C, which is also an array. To refer to the fourth element of C, within the third element of B, within the second element of A, you'd code A(2).B(3).C(4); to refer to the entire C array within the third element of B, within the second element of A, you'd code A(2).B(3).C. In the case of a complex data structure such as this, you can omit the index only for the rightmost array.

 Caution
If a data item uses the Like or Likeds keyword to "inherit" the data attributes of a standalone variable or a data structure, it will not copy the Dim keyword—or any other array-related keywords—from the "parent." (The only situation in which the "child" will use the Dim keyword from a parent is the one described in the previous paragraph, in which the child inherits the Dim keyword from the parent's subfield.) The child must explicitly include the Dim keyword if it is to be an array. You could, however, code the Dim keyword with the %Elem function to define a child array with the same number of elements as its parent:

```
*.. 1 ...+... 2 ...+... 3 ...+... 4 ...+... 5 ...+... 6 ...+... 7 ...+... 8
DName++++++++++ETDsFrom+++To/L+++IDc.Keywords+++++++++++++++++++++++++++++++
D Parent          S              2    Dim(50)
D Child           S                   Like(Parent)
D                                     Dim(%ELem(Parent))
```

Array data structures may be useful when you need to store multiple layers and dimensions of related data, but you cannot use the %Lookup or the %Xfoot function—or the Sorta operation—with array data structures. These functions work only with "pure" arrays, not data structures. The "rightmost" array in a complex data structure, however, *can* use %Lookup, %Xfoot, or Sorta, because it is not a data structure, but a pure array subfield:

```
I = %Lookup( '1' : A(2).B(3).C );
```

This code would look for a 1 in the C array, within the third element of the B array, within the second element of the A array. A successful search would return the first index within the C array that contains a 1; an unsuccessful search would yield a 0.

Overlaying Arrays

Some of the arrays in this chapter use the Overlay keyword to define an array over simple data structure subfields. You can also use the Overlay keyword to overlay one array over another.

```
*.. 1 ...+... 2 ...+... 3 ...+... 4 ...+... 5 ...+... 6 ...+... 7 ...+... 8
DName++++++++++ETDsFrom+++To/L+++IDc.Keywords+++++++++++++++++++++++++++++++
D                 DS
D   Statedata           21      Dim(50)
D     Abbrev             2      Overlay(Statedata)
D     State             14      Overlay(Statedata:3)
D     Taxrate            5    5 Overlay(Statedata:17)
```

These definitions describe a base array, Statedata, and three overlay arrays: Abbrev, Name, and Taxrate. Even though the overlay arrays do not use the Dim keyword, they each have 50 elements ("inherited" from the Statedata array), and an RPG IV program can treat them as arrays. For example, the following code from an earlier example would work:

```
I = %Lookup(Statecode:Abbrev);
If I > 0;
   Eval(H) Taxdue = Saleamount * Taxrate(I);
   Statename = State(I);
Else;
   Taxdue = 0;
   Statename = '*Error*';
Endif;
```

You can also use the Sorta operation to sort the base array using one of the overlay arrays to determine the sort order. For example, the following code would sort the Statedata array (as well as each of the overlay arrays) in Taxrate order:

```
Sorta Taxrate;
```

You could also use the Inz keyword to provide initial data to an array defined using this technique:

```
*.. 1 ...+... 2 ...+... 3 ...+... 4 ...+... 5 ...+... 6 ...+... 7 ...+... 8
DName++++++++++ETDsFrom+++To/L+++IDc.Keywords+++++++++++++++++++++++++++++++
D   Stateinfo       DS
D                           21      Inz('AKAlaska         00000')
D                           21      Inz('ALAlabama        04000')
D                           21      Inz('ARArkansas       06000')
D                           21      Inz('AZArizona        05600')
D                           21      Inz('CACalifornia     06250')
...                              ...    ...
D                           21      Inz('WYWyoming        04000')
D   Statedata               21      Dim(50)
D                                   Overlay(Stateinfo)
D     Abbrev                 2      Overlay(Statedata)
D     State                 14      Overlay(Statedata:3)
D     Taxrate                5    5 Overlay(Statedata:17)
```

Using Arrays

Now that you understand how to define arrays and how to use them in different calculations or special array operations, you are ready to see how arrays can simplify or expedite solutions to different kinds of programming problems. The ability to index an array with a variable or an expression, rather than a literal, adds tremendous flexibility to your ability to manipulate arrays and makes arrays the preferred structure to handle problems requiring identical processing of similar data items.

Recall, for example, the SalesFile file we described earlier, in which each record contained a salesperson's number and 12 monthly sales totals for that salesperson:

```
*.. 1 ...+... 2 ...+... 3 ...+... 4 ...+... 5 ...+... 6 ...+... 7 ...+... 8
A..........T.Name++++++RLen++TDpB......Functions++++++++++++++++++++++++++++
 * Externally described file SalesFile
A            R SALESREC
A              SLSNBR        5A         TEXT('Salesperson Number')
A              JANSALES     10S 2       TEXT('January Sales')
A              FEBSALES     10S 2       TEXT('February Sales')
A              MARSALES     10S 2       TEXT('March Sales')
A              APRSALES     10S 2       TEXT('April Sales')
A              MAYSALES     10S 2       TEXT('May Sales')
A              JUNSALES     10S 2       TEXT('June Sales')
A              JULSALES     10S 2       TEXT('July Sales')
A              AUGSALES     10S 2       TEXT('August Sales')
A              SEPSALES     10S 2       TEXT('September Sales')
A              OCTSALES     10S 2       TEXT('October Sales')
A              NOVSALES     10S 2       TEXT('November Sales')
A              DECSALES     10S 2       TEXT('December Sales')
```

Assume that this file is to be used in a program to help a company determine the end-of-year bonuses to be paid to the sales force. The bonuses are determined on a monthly basis by the salesperson's sales for that month; any time the monthly sales exceeds $50,000, the bonus for that month is one-half percent of the sales; otherwise, there is no bonus for that month. The company wants to calculate the total annual bonus for each salesperson but also print the individual monthly bonuses. The printer spacing chart on the next page shows the desired report.

To program a solution without using arrays would require writing a set of calculations that would be replicated 12 times, each time with a different set of fields representing each of the 12 months. With sales for different salespersons handled as elements of an array and with another array to store the salesperson's bonus for each of the 12 months, you can considerably shorten the calculations.

First, recall that we can define the 12 monthly sales figures as elements of an array by using a data structure. The Definition specifications that follow illustrate the data structure as well as define an additional array, Bonus, and some standalone work fields that we require for our solution.

```
                    1         2         3         4         5         6         7         8         9         1
                                                                                                              0
   1234567890123456789012345678901234567890123456789012345678901234567890123456789012345678901234567890
 1         XX/XX/XX
 2                                                        ANNUAL SALES BONUS REPORT
 3
 4 SLSPSN      JAN.      FEB.      MAR.      APR.      MAY      JUNE      JULY      AUG.
 5 XXXXX    XXX,XX0   XXX,XX0   XXX,XX0   XXX,XX0   XXX,XX0   XXX,XX0   XXX,XX0   XXX,XX0
 6 XXXXX    XXX,XX0   XXX,XX0   XXX,XX0   XXX,XX0   XXX,XX0   XXX,XX0   XXX,XX0   XXX,XX0
 7 XXXXX    XXX,XX0   XXX,XX0   XXX,XX0   XXX,XX0   XXX,XX0   XXX,XX0   XXX,XX0   XXX,XX0
 8 XXXXX    XXX,XX0   XXX,XX0   XXX,XX0   XXX,XX0   XXX,XX0   XXX,XX0   XXX,XX0   XXX,XX0
 9
10
```

```
                    1         2         3         4         5         6         7         8         9         1
                                                                                                              0
   1234567890123456789012345678901234567890123456789012345678901234567890123456789012345678901234567890
 1         PAGE XX
 2
 3
 4   SEPT.      OCT.      NOV.      DEC.       TOTAL
 5   XXX,XX0   XXX,XX0   XXX,XX0   XXX,XX0   XX,XXX,XX0
 6   XXX,XX0   XXX,XX0   XXX,XX0   XXX,XX0   XX,XXX,XX0
 7   XXX,XX0   XXX,XX0   XXX,XX0   XXX,XX0   XX,XXX,XX0
 8   XXX,XX0   XXX,XX0   XXX,XX0   XXX,XX0   XX,XXX,XX0
 9
10         GRAND TOTAL  $XX,XXX,XXX,XX$
11
12
```

```
*.. 1 ...+... 2 ...+... 3 ...+... 4 ...+... 5 ...+... 6 ...+... 7 ...+... 8
DName++++++++++ETDsFrom+++To/L+++IDc.Keywords++++++++++++++++++++++++++++++++
  // ------------------------------- Sales array
D Sales           DS
D  Jansales                     11  2
D  Febsales                     11  2
D  Marsales                     11  2
D  Aprsales                     11  2
D  Maysales                     11  2
D  Junsales                     11  2
D  Julsales                     11  2
D  Augsales                     11  2
D  Sepsales                     11  2
D  Octsales                     11  2
D  Novsales                     11  2
D  Decsales                     11  2
D  Salesarray                   11  2 Dim(12)
D                                      Overlay(Sales)

  // ------------------------- Array for bonuses
D Bonus           S              6S 0 DIM(%Elem(Salesarray))

  // ------------------------- Standalone work fields
D GrandTotal      S             11  0
D TotBonus        S              9  0
D I               S              3U 0
```

Given the above array definitions, the calculations for solving our problem are relatively short:

```
// Specifications for calculating and printing bonuses for all
// salespersons in Salesfile
Grandtotal = 0;
Write Headings;
Read Salesfile;

Dow Not %Eof(Salesfile);
  For I = 1 To %Elem(Salesarray);
    If Salesarray(I) > 50000;
      Eval(H) Bonus(I) = Salesarray(I) * .005;
    Else;
      Eval Bonus(I) = 0;
    Endif;
  Endfor;

  Totbonus = %Xfoot(Bonus);
  Grandtotal = Grandtotal + Totbonus;

  If Endofpage;
    Write Headings;
    Endofpage = *Off;
  Endif;

  Write Detail;
  Read Salesfile;
Enddo;

Write Totalline;
*Inlr = *On;
Return;
```

The beauty of handling data with arrays and variable indexes, as this example shows, is that if there were 1,200 sales figures for each salesperson, instead of 12, the calculations to determine bonuses and totals would be no longer; the only required change would be to increase the number of elements in Salesarray (and to increase the lengths of the work fields to avoid truncation).

Note

When you want to print an array in an externally described printer file, you will typically list each element of the array as an individual field—DDS does not support coding an array index.

When you specify an array name to be printed as part of an Output specification (for a program-described printer file), all the elements appear, separated by two blanks, with the last element ending in the ending position specified for the array. Any editing associated with the array applies to each element. Depending on the printer spacing chart you are following, you may be able to use this shortcut; the alternative is to list each element of the array individually, with an index, and give each its own ending position.

Tables

A **table** is a data construct similar to an array, in that it contains multiple elements all defined with a common name. As with an array, each element within a table must be the same data type, with the same length and (if the elements are numeric) number of decimal positions.

You define tables in Definition specifications; the required entries are the same as those required for arrays. In fact, only two definition differences exist between tables and arrays:

- Tables must be loaded at compile time or preruntime (runtime tables are not allowed).

- Table names must begin with TAB (case is not significant).

The following definitions describe two compile time tables, Tababbrev and Tabstate. These tables are similar to the arrays we described earlier in the chapter:

```
*.. 1 ...+... 2 ...+... 3 ...+... 4 ...+... 5 ...+... 6 ...+... 7 ...+... 8
DName++++++++++ETDsFrom+++To/L+++IDc.Keywords+++++++++++++++++++++++++++++++++
D Tababbrev       S              2    Dim(50)
D                                     Ctdata Perrcd(25)
D Tabstate        S             14    Dim(50)
D                                     Ctdata

**CTDATA Tababbrev
AKALARAZCACOCTDEFLGAHIIAIDILINKSKYLAMAMDMEMIMNMOMS
MTNCNDNENHNJNMNVNYOHOKORPARISCSDTNTXUTVAVTWAWIWVWY
**CTDATA Tabstate
Alaska
Alabama
Arkansas
Arizona
California
...
Wyoming
```

You could also define these related tables in alternating format:

```
*.. 1 ...+... 2 ...+... 3 ...+... 4 ...+... 5 ...+... 6 ...+... 7 ...+... 8
DName++++++++++ETDsFrom+++To/L+++IDc.Keywords+++++++++++++++++++++++++++++++++
D Tababbrev       S              2    Dim(50)
D                                     Ctdata
D Tabstate        S             14    Dim(50)
D                                     Alt(Tababbrev)

**CTDATA Tababbrev
AKAlaska
ALAlabama
ARArkansas
AZArizona
CACalifornia
...
WYWyoming
```

Table Lookups

Tables are used for one primary purpose: to look up data values. The major difference between arrays and tables lies in the way RPG searches their elements. Only one element of a table is active at a time. You cannot specify an index for a table; instead you simply refer to the currently active element by using the table's name. Instead of using the %Lookup function to search a table, you use one of the %Tlookup (Look up a Table Element) functions. The %Tlookup function is coded using this format:

```
%Tlookupxx(search-argument :table {:alternate-table} )
```

The search argument is the first argument in the %Tlookup function. Next, you specify the name of the table that you want to search. The search argument must match the data type of the table that you want to search—e.g., if the table has numeric elements, the search argument must be numeric—but it need not have the same length or number of decimal positions.

%Tlookup will return an *On condition (not a number) if it finds a table element that matches the search argument. If no element in the table matches the value of the search argument, %Tlookup will return an *Off condition. There are five variations of %Tlookup functions, each representing a different type of match:

- **%Tlookup** searches for an exact match.
- **%Tlookuplt** searches for an element that is closest to, but less than, the search argument.
- **%Tlookuple** searches for an exact match, or for an element that is closest to, but less than, the search argument.
- **%Tlookupge** searches for an exact match, or for an element that is closest to, but greater than, the search argument.
- **%Tlookupgt** searches for an element that is closest to, but greater than, the search argument.

The most common usage is a simple %Tlookup (exact match). The following %Tlookup indicates whether or not a table element exists that matches Value:

```
If %Tlookup(Value:Table)= *On;
  Exsr Valuefound;
Else;
  Exsr Notfound;
Endif;
```

Because %Tlookup returns a logical value (*On or *Off), you could code the above example more simply, just like an indicator:

```
If %Tlookup(Value:Table);          // Successful search
```

or

```
If Not %Tlookup(Value:Table);      // Unsuccessful search
```

When %Tlookup is successful, in addition to returning the value *On, an internal pointer is positioned at the matching table value. You can then refer to that element of the table by simply using the table's name. If the search is not successful, %Tlookup returns the value *Off, and does not reposition the table pointer.

Consider the following code:

```
*.. 1 ...+... 2 ...+... 3 ...+... 4 ...+... 5 ...+... 6 ...+... 7 ...+... 8
DName++++++++++ETDsFrom+++To/L+++IDc.Keywords++++++++++++++++++++++++++++++
D Statecode       S               2
D X               S               2

D Tababbrev       S               2       Dim(50)
D                                         Ctdata Perrcd(25)

  /Free
     If %Tlookup(Statecode:Tababbrev);
       X = Tababbrev;
     Else;
       X = '**';
     Endif;
  /End-Free
```

```
**CTDATA Tababbrev
AKALARAZCACOCTDEFLGAHIIAIDILINKSKYLAMAMDMEMIMNMOMS
MTNCNDNENHNJNMNVNYOHOKORPARISCSDTNTXUTVAVTWAWIWVWY
```

A **table lookup** involving a single table is useful to validate the value of an input field. In the above code, if Statecode had a value of 'CA' the %Tlookup function would return an *On value (i.e., the If condition would be true), and the internal table pointer would point to CA in the Tababbrev table. In the next line, X would be assigned a value of 'CA' because that would be the value of the current element in the table. If Statecode were 'BD' then %Tlookup would return an *Off value because BD is not in the table; X would have a value of '**'. The pointer would not be repositioned, and the previous element would remain the current element (before the first successful %Tlookup, the first table element is the current element). Good programming practice suggests you should always provide for the possibility of unsuccessful lookups within your code.

Using Related Tables

You can also reposition a second table with a single %Tlookup function, by naming the second table as the third argument in the %Tlookup function. Only one lookup is performed, against the primary table; but if the primary lookup is successful, %Tlookup will also set the internal pointer for the secondary table. In the following example, which uses the tables defined earlier, a successful code search causes the internal pointer to be positioned in Tabstate at the name that corresponds to the matched code in Tababbrev.

```
If %Tlookup(Codein:Tababbrev:Tabstate);
   Statename = Tabstate;
Else;
   Statename = '*Error*';
Endif;
```

The result is that Tabstate contains the desired state name, and you can print or display Tabstate or use it in any other operation for which you need the appropriate state name. If the search of Tababbrev is not successful, Tabstate will contain the state name from the last successful lookup; in that case, this example would assign a value of '*Error*' to Statename.

The %Tlookup function lets you name only a primary table and a single secondary table. If you need to set additional secondary tables based on the primary lookup, you will need to execute multiple %Tlookup functions, as the following example illustrates:

```
*.. 1 ...+... 2 ...+... 3 ...+... 4 ...+... 5 ...+... 6 ...+... 7 ...+... 8
DName++++++++++ETDsFrom+++To/L+++IDc.Keywords++++++++++++++++++++++++++++++++
D Tababbrev       S               2    Dim(50) Ctdata
D Tabstate        S              14    Dim(%Elem(Tababbrev))
D                                      Alt(Tababbrev)
D Tabrate         S               5 5 Dim(%Elem(Tababbrev)) Ctdata

  /Free
    If %Tlookup(Codein:Tababbrev:Tabstate);
       And %Tlookup(Codein:Tababbrev:Tabrate);
      Statename = Tabstate;
      Eval(H) Taxdue = Amount * Tabrate;
    Else;
      Exsr Badcode;
    Endif;
  /End-Free

**CTDATA Tababbrev
AKAlaska
ALAlabama
ARArkansas
AZArizona
CACalifornia
...
WYWyoming
**CTDATA Tabrate
00000
04000
06000
05600
06250
...
04000
```

This example presents the Tababbrev and Tabstate data in alternating format, but they could be presented as separate tables or as **preruntime tables** instead. We used two %Tlookup functions against Tababbrev; if these searches are successful, the internal pointers for all three tables will be set to the appropriate elements.

Range Tables

Recall the example earlier in this chapter that used an unequal %Lookup function to determine shipping charges based upon package weight. The following example illustrates how you could perform the same function with tables instead of arrays:

```
*.. 1 ...+... 2 ...+... 3 ...+... 4 ...+... 5 ...+... 6 ...+... 7 ...+... 8
DName++++++++++ETDsFrom+++To/L+++IDc.Keywords+++++++++++++++++++++++++++++++
D Tabweight       S              3 0 Dim(6)
D                                    Ctdata Ascend
D Tabcharge       S              5 2 Dim(%Elem(Tabweight))
D                                    Alt(Tabweight)

   // ------------------------ Standalone variables
D Pkgcharge       S              5 2
D Pkgweight       S              3 0
D Totalcharge     S              5 2

  /Free
     If %Lookupge(Pkgweight:Tabweight:Tabcharge);
       Totalcharge = Pkgcharge + Tabcharge;
     Else;
       Exsr Cannotship;
     Endif;
  /End-Free

**CTDATA Tabweight
00100250
00500425
01000750
02000900
04001200
07001600
```

Changing Table Values

Tables are generally used for extracting values. It is possible, however, to change table values during program execution. Anytime you specify a table name as the result of a mathematical or an assignment operation, the value of the entry where the table is currently positioned will be changed. Failing to understand this fact can sometimes lead to inadvertent program errors.

For example, consider the shipping weight problem. Assume that in the program you want to add and print either the appropriate shipping charge or, for packages weighing more than 70 pounds, to add and print 0 to indicate that the package can't be shipped. The following incorrect solution may tempt you, but it may inadvertently change random values in Tabcharge to 0:

```
If Not %Tlookupge(Weightin:Tabweight:Tabcharge);
  Tabcharge = 0;
Endif;
Totalcharge = Pkgcharge + Tabcharge;
```

The result of the above code would be that each time a package weighing more than 70 pounds is processed, the TabCharge value of the most recently successful lookup would be set to 0. The next time a package of that lower weight was processed, its shipping charge would incorrectly be extracted as 0. Before changing a table value, be sure that you have first executed a successful %Tlookup operation to position the table correctly.

If the table data came from a file and you want to store the table with its revised values back in the file at the end of processing, you can accomplish this task quite simply with a few changes to the File and Definition specifications. First, designate the table file as a combined file rather than an input file. Then, include the file name with keywords Fromfile and Tofile on the Definition specification. These two changes will cause the (changed) table values to be written back to the file upon program completion.

Chapter Summary

You can use both arrays and tables to store sets of similar elements in RPG IV. The two constructs have several similarities, but arrays are generally more flexible than tables. Both constructs are defined in Definition specifications, with a Dim keyword to indicate how many elements are in the array or table.

You can explicitly reference an individual array element by using an index, or you can manipulate the array as a whole by using the array name without an index. You can use a numeric literal or field as an index to point to a specific array element.

Arrays can be standalone variables, data structure subfields or array data structures. Array data structures can be used to simulate multidimensional arrays. You can load arrays at compile time, from data hard coded at the end of the source program; or at preruntime, from data contained in a table file; or during runtime, from values contained in input records or as the result of calculations.

The %Lookup function will search an array for a specific value, returning a number representing the index of the found value. %Lookup typically searches for equal matches but can also find unequal matches. The Sorta operation will sort an array into ascending or descending sequence, depending upon the sequence specified in the array definition. The %Xfoot function will sum all the elements of a numeric array. The %Subarr function allows you to process a subset of an array instead of the entire array.

A table is defined as a standalone variable whose name begins with TAB and whose definition includes the Dim keyword. Tables must be loaded at compile time or preruntime. Only one element of a table is active at a time. This is the current element, set when the %Tlookup function successfully finds a specific value in the table. No index is necessary to refer to the current element of a table; referring to the table itself indicates the current element of the table. The %Tlookup function can also set a secondary table as the result of the successful search of a primary table. The following table summarizes the functions and operation codes discussed in this chapter:

Function or operation	Description	Syntax
%Elem	Number of elements in an array, table, or multiple occurrence data structure	%Elem(*data-item*)
%Lookup %Lookuplt %Lookuple %Lookupge %Lookupgt	Look up element in an array	%Lookup*xx*(*search-argument* : *array* {: *start* {: *elements*}})
%Size	Size	%Size(*data-item* {: *All*})
Sorta	Sort array	Sorta *array-name*
%Subarr	Get or set portion of an array	%Subarr(*array-name* : *start* {:*elements*})
%Tlookup %Tlookuplt %Tlookuple %Tlookupge %Tlookupgt	Look up element in a table	%Tlookup*xx*(*search-argument* : *table* {: *alternate-table*})
%Xfoot	Sum array expression elements	%Xfoot(*array-expression*)

Key Terms

alternating format
array
array data structure
compile time array
compile time tables
crossfooting
**Ctdata record
elements
index
overlay
preruntime array
preruntime tables
runtime array
Sorta operation
table
table lookup

%Elem function
%Lookup function
%Lookuple function
%Lookuplt function
%Lookupge function
%Lookupgt function
%Size function
%Subarr function
%Subst function
%Tlookup function
%Tlookup function
%Tlookuple function
%Tlookuplt function
%Tlookupge function
%Tlookupgt function
%Xfoot function

Discussion/Review Questions

1. If you wanted to describe the telephone book as a table in RPG IV, how many tables would you define?

2. If a program uses tables, what additional specification form is required and where should these specifications appear in your program?

3. What is the difference between the "number of entries per table" and "number of entries per record" entries on the Definition specifications?

4. What factors would you use to determine whether to hard-code a table or store the table data in a disk file?

5. What are the two techniques that can be used to define tables of more than two columns? What are the advantages and disadvantages of each technique?

6. What is a "range" table? Give an example of one.

7. When would you need to use keyword Fromfile as part of a table or array definition on the Definition specifications?

8. What are RPG IV's requirements for naming tables and arrays? What practical considerations add additional constraints to array names?

9. What do the terms compile time, preruntime, and runtime refer to when used to describe tables or arrays?

10. Give four ways that arrays can obtain data values.

11. What is the difference between using a table name and an array name (without an index) in a calculation (i.e., what data is being represented)?

12. How are the effects of standard arithmetic operations dependent upon whether array elements or arrays are entered as factors in the calculations?

13. What RPG IV operations are used only with arrays? What does each do?

14. Describe appropriate uses for tables and arrays. How would you decide which (if either) to use in a given application?

Exercises

1. You are writing an application to process orders. Records include the date ordered in *yymmdd* format, but you want to print the name of the month ordered rather than the number of the month.

   a. Show how you would hard-code data for a two-column table relating month number to month name.

   b. Code the Definition Specifications for these compile-time tables, matching the definitions to the way in which you've laid out your data.

   c. Write the calculations needed to look up OrdMonth (*order-month*) in one table to extract the appropriate month name.

2. Modify your work in Exercise 1 by using arrays, rather than tables. Don't require your program to do more work than needed. (Hint: Can you think of a way to obtain the correct month name without performing a lookup?)

3. An input file contains records of sales. Each record represents one week of sales, with seven sales figures, each 10 with two decimal positions, in positions 21–90 of the input record. Code the Definition, Input, and portion of the Calculation specifications needed to generate a weekly sales total and also to separately accumulate sales for each day of the week as input to the file is processed.

4. Assume the IRS wants you to use the following table to determine how much salary to withhold for federal taxes:

	Tax rate	
If weekly salary is	Single	Married
0–$150	.18	.15
$151–$250	.25	.18
$251–$500	.28	.25
$501–$1,000	.31	.28
over $1,000	.33	.31

5. Hard-code this information so it can be handled with RPG IV tables.

6. Define the Definition specifications to reflect your hard-coding.

7. Write the calculations needed to assign the proper value to field Rate based on Salary (salary) and Marital status (marital status: S = single, M = married) of an employee's input record.

8. Modify your code as would be needed if the table data were stored in a table file, rather than hard-coded.

Programming Assignments

1. Wexler University wants a program that will produce a student grade report and assign final grades. An input file, WUEXAMP (Appendix F), contains student records with five exam grades per student. The program will need to calculate an average exam grade for each student. The school also wants to know class averages for each exam and for the course as a whole. The program should also assign final grades based on the following criteria:

Average grade	Final grade
93–100	A
88–92	B+
83–87	B
75–82	C+
70–74	C
65–69	D+
60–64	D
<60	F

The desired report layout is shown below. Note that the students' first and last names are to be printed as one field.

```
           1         2         3         4         5         6         7         8         9
  1234567890123456789012345678901234567890123456789012345678901234567890123456789012345678901234567890
 1 XX/XX/XX                  Wexler University Student Grade Report            PAGE XXØX
 2
 3                                        Exam Exam Exam Exam Exam  Average Final
 4  Student ID.   Student Name              1    2    3    4    5   Grade   Grade
 5
 6 XXX-XX-XXXX   XXXXXXXXXXXXXXXXXXXXXXXXXXX XØX  XØX  XØX  XØX  XØX   XØX    XX
 7 XXX-XX-XXXX   XXXXXXXXXXXXXXXXXXXXXXXXXXX XØX  XØX  XØX  XØX  XØX   XØX    XX
 8 XXX-XX-XXXX   XXXXXXXXXXXXXXXXXXXXXXXXXXX XØX  XØX  XØX  XØX  XØX   XØX    XX
 9
10               Class Average:             XØX  XØX  XØX  XØX  XØX   XØX
11
```

2. Wexler University wants you to write a program to score student tests. Each test is a 50-question, multiple-choice test. (Possible answers for each question are A, B, C, D, and E.) Student responses are scanned and stored in database file WUTSTP. Appendix F describes the format of these records; each record includes information about the course, the test, the student, and the student's test responses. The file is keyed on course ID, test number, and section number. An answer key to each test is prepared and stored in database file WUKEYP (Appendix F); this file is keyed on course ID and test number.

   The field TESTDATE is a native date field and is set up to be null capable. Processing this file will require you to include the H-spec "H ALWNULL(*USRCTL)" to avoid warnings. H-specs were covered in Chapter 5.

   a. There will be several sets of tests, possibly from different sections and different courses, in file WUTSTP. The same key may be used to grade different sections' tests, provided the test number and course ID of the key record of file WUKEYP match those of the records to be graded.

   b. You want to grade every record in WUTSTP; there may be keys in WUKEYP that don't match any of the current batches of tests, but there should not be any student test that does not have a corresponding key in WUKEYP.

   c. Start each new section and/or each new test on a new page with all headings. If a section takes more than one page, repeat all headings on successive pages.

d. Note that an average grade for each section is required.

e. You will need to access the Student Master file (WUSTDP) to get the students' name, and the students' name will be printed as one field on the report.

f. Use arrays to do the scoring. Then use a compile-time table to assign letter grades. The table should reflect the following scale:

Score	Letter grade
<= 29	F
30–34	D
35–39	C
40–44	B
45–50	A

g. Update the field TESTDATE with the system date when this program processes.

h. Update the GRADE field with the letter grade when this program processes.

Prepare the report using the following grid:

```
              1         2         3         4         5         6         7         8         9
    12345678901234567890123456789012345678901234567890123456789012345678901234567890123456789 0
 1  XX/XX/XXXX              Wexler University Student Grade Report              PAGE XXX0
 2
 3  Course ID:  XXXXXX    Test:  XXXX
 4
 5  Section:  XXXXXX   Instructor: XXXXXXXXXXXXXX
 6
 7  Student ID    Student Name               Test  Score       Letter Grade
 8  XXX-XX-XXXX   XXXXXXXXXXXXXXXXXXXXXXXXX    0X                  X
 9  XXX-XX-XXXX   XXXXXXXXXXXXXXXXXXXXXXXXX    0X                  X
10  XXX-XX-XXXX   XXXXXXXXXXXXXXXXXXXXXXXXX    0X                  X
11
12                        Section Average     0X
13
14
15
```

3. GTC, a local telephone company, wants you to write a program to calculate costs of calls as part of a billing system. A calls transaction file, GTCLSP (described in Appendix F), is generated automatically as part of the company's switching system. Call data accumulates in this file during the course of the month. At the end of the month, the file is first used with this program and then used to print bills before being cleared for the next month's accumulation of call data. Note that the file includes a cost-of-call field, but the value for that field will be supplied by this program when it updates each record. When the record is read initially, this field contains zeros.

Each record contains the cost for the first minute and the per-minute charge for each additional minute for calls made to that area code/exchange. This file should be loaded into a table that can be used to look up the appropriate charges for each call in the calls file.

a. Cost of calls depends on the area code and exchange of the number called, and the time and day of the week the call was placed.

b. Base daytime rates for all area codes and exchanges are contained in a rates file, GTCRATP (Appendix F). This file should be loaded as a preruntime table.

c. Time of the call and the day of the week (Sun – Sat) affect the cost based on the following discount table. Notice that the time of call in the calls file is based on a 24-hour clock, such that 2:15 p.m. would be stored as 1415.

d. The date field CALDAT is stored as a numeric field. You will need to convert this field to a native date field to determine the day of the week.

e. The table below should be incorporated into a hard-coded table so it can be used for lookups during processing. The percents are discounts to the standard costs contained in the rate file.

Hours	Mon–Fri	Sat	Sun
8:00 a.m.–4:59 p.m.	0%	60%	60%
5:00 p.m.–10:59 p.m.	35%	60%	35%
11:00 p.m.–7:59 a.m.	60%	60%	60%

Use the following grid:

```
         1         2         3         4         5         6         7         8         9         10
1234567890123456789012345678901234567890123456789012345678901234567890123456789012345678901234567890
1 XX/XX/XXXX                  GTC Customer Call Cost Report              Page XXX0
2
3 Customer           Customer
4 Phone Number       Name
5 XXX-XXX-XXXX       XXXXXXXXXXXXXXXXXXXXXXXXXXXX
6
7 Number        City           Call      Call     Start    Call     End       Rate  Call     Discount Total
8 Called        Called         Date      Day      Time     Length   Time      Min   Cost     Rate     Cost
9
10 XXX-XXX-XXXX XXXXXXXXXXXXXX XX/XX/XX XXXXXXXX hh:mm:ss 9999 hh:mm:ss X0X XXX.XX X0% XX0X.0X
11 XXX-XXX-XXXX XXXXXXXXXXXXXX XX/XX/XX XXXXXXXX hh:mm:ss 9999 hh:mm:ss X0X XXX.XX X0% XX0X.0X
12 XXX-XXX-XXXX XXXXXXXXXXXXXX XX/XX/XX XXXXXXXX hh:mm:ss 9999 hh:mm:ss X0X XXX.XX X0% XX0X.0X
13 XXX-XXX-XXXX XXXXXXXXXXXXXX XX/XX/XX XXXXXXXX hh:mm:ss 9999 hh:mm:ss X0X XXX.XX X0% XX0X.0X
14
15 Total Calls X0X                                                                    $X,X0X.0X
16
17
18 Total Customers 999                                                  Total Cost  $X0X,X0X.0X
19
```

4. Wexler University's Payroll department wants a history report showing the monthly income of its instructors; this report will be by instructor ID and year. This information is stored in a history file (WUINPAY) described in Appendix F; each record includes the wage information for each instructor for a specific year in one field (PMNTHS). This 84-byte character field is composed of 12 sections where each month's wages is contained in seven bytes. This field should be processed as an array.

Note: The Grid has been split to allow the report to be formatted for the textbook.

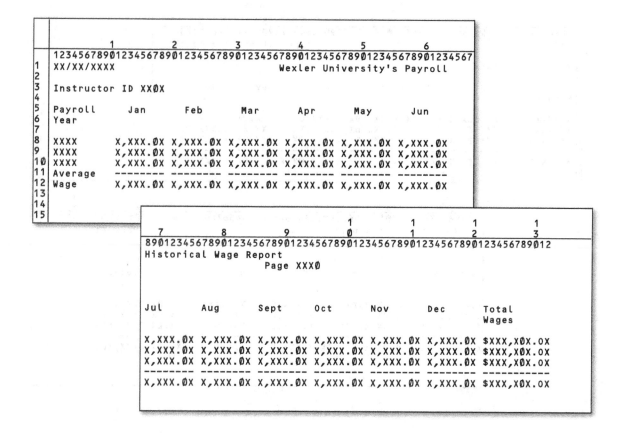

```
                   1         2         3         4         5         6
         1234567890123456789012345678901234567890123456789012345678901234567
1        XX/XX/XXXX                            Wexler University's Payroll
2
3        Instructor ID XXØX
4
5        Payroll      Jan       Feb       Mar       Apr       May       Jun
6        Year
7
8        XXXX         X,XXX.ØX  X,XXX.ØX  X,XXX.ØX  X,XXX.ØX  X,XXX.ØX  X,XXX.ØX
9        XXXX         X,XXX.ØX  X,XXX.ØX  X,XXX.ØX  X,XXX.ØX  X,XXX.ØX  X,XXX.ØX
10       XXXX         X,XXX.ØX  X,XXX.ØX  X,XXX.ØX  X,XXX.ØX  X,XXX.ØX  X,XXX.ØX
11       Average      --------  --------  --------  --------  --------  --------
12       Wage         X,XXX.ØX  X,XXX.ØX  X,XXX.ØX  X,XXX.ØX  X,XXX.ØX  X,XXX.ØX
13
14
15
```

```
                               1         1         1         1
          7         8         9         Ø         1         2         3
         8901234567890123456789012345678901234567890123456789012345678901234567
         Historical Wage Report
                     Page XXXØ


         Jul       Aug       Sept      Oct       Nov       Dec       Total
                                                                     Wages

         X,XXX.ØX  X,XXX.ØX  X,XXX.ØX  X,XXX.ØX  X,XXX.ØX  X,XXX.ØX  $XXX,XØX.OX
         X,XXX.ØX  X,XXX.ØX  X,XXX.ØX  X,XXX.ØX  X,XXX.ØX  X,XXX.ØX  $XXX,XØX.OX
         X,XXX.ØX  X,XXX.ØX  X,XXX.ØX  X,XXX.ØX  X,XXX.ØX  X,XXX.ØX  $XXX,XØX.OX
         --------  --------  --------  --------  --------  --------  -----------
         X,XXX.ØX  X,XXX.ØX  X,XXX.ØX  X,XXX.ØX  X,XXX.ØX  X,XXX.ØX  $XXX,XØX.OX
```

5. CompuSell's Accounting department wants a report showing the monthly sales of merchandise. The information is printed by year by part number with average sales per month totals. This information is stored in a History file called CSCHST. Appendix F describes the format of these records; each record includes the sales information for a specific part for a specific year in twelve fields.

Note: The Grid has been split to allow the report to be formatted for the textbook.

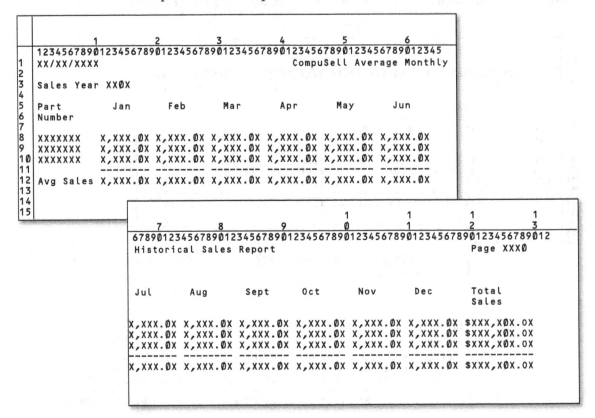

Chapter 10

Accessing and Updating Database Files

Chapter Overview

This chapter introduces you to RPG IV's operations for reading, writing, and updating records. You will learn both sequential and random file access techniques. The chapter also discusses file maintenance—adding, deleting, and changing records in a file—and record locking considerations in update procedures.

Operations for Input Files

File access refers to how records can be retrieved, or read, from an input file. RPG IV offers several alternative operations for accessing data from full procedural database files. Several of these operations are appropriate for sequential processing; you can use others for random access processing.

Sequential Access

In **sequential access**, records are retrieved in either key order, if the file is keyed and it is so noted in column 34 on the File specifications, or in arrival—first-in first-out (FIFO)—order for nonkeyed files. Reading generally starts with the first record in the file, with each subsequent read operation retrieving the next record in the file until eventually you reach end of file. This kind of sequential access is especially suited for batch processing.

RPG IV includes several file input/output (I/O) operations that provide variations on sequential record access. Some of these operations control where in the file sequential reading will next occur; others determine the nature of the reading itself. These operations are:

- Read (Read a record)
- Setll (Set lower limit)
- Setgt (Set greater than)
- Reade (Read equal key)
- Readp (Read prior record)
- Readpe (Read prior equal)

Read (Read a Record)

As you know, the **Read (Read a Record) operation** retrieves records sequentially from a full procedural file. The general format of the Read operation is

```
Read filename {data-structure};
```

A required file name argument designates which file the Read accesses. When the Read operation finds no additional records to read, it will set the value of the **%Eof (End of file) function** to *On. You should test the %Eof value after each Read operation. When you code the %Eof function, you should name a specific file in parentheses after the function; if you omit the file name, the %Eof function refers to the most recent file operation. The following example demonstrates the use of Read and %Eof.

```
/Free
   Read Custmast;
   If %Eof(Custmast);
     // End of file processing goes here
   Endif;
/End-Free
```

For externally described files, the file argument can actually be a record format name rather than a file name. However, if the Read encounters a record format different from that named by the Read operation—as could be the case when the input file is a logical file with multiple formats—the operation ends in error. We'll discuss how to detect and handle such errors in Chapter 14.

You can specify an additional argument for the Read operation to name a data structure to receive the record data. When you name a **result data structure**, the Read operation will transfer data directly from the record to the data structure, which may improve the program's performance and give you direct control over how your program interprets the data. The following example demonstrates the use of a result data structure:

```
*.. 1 ...+... 2 ...+... 3 ...+... 4 ...+... 5 ...+... 6 ...+... 7 ...+... 8
FFilename++IPEASFRlen+LKlen+AIDevice+.Keywords++++++++++++++++++++++++++++++
DName++++++++++ETDsFrom+++To/Len+IDc.Keywords++++++++++++++++++++++++++++++++
FCustmast  IF   E            Disk

D Customer       DS                    Likerec(Custrec)

 /Free
    Read Custmast Customer;
    If %Eof(Custmast);
      // End of file processing goes here
    Endif;
 /End-Free
```

If the Read operation is accessing an externally described file, the result data structure must use the Likerec keyword or the Extname keyword to exactly match the record format's input fields; for program-described files, the data structure's length must be the same length as the file's record length in the File specifications. In the above example, a successful Read operation transfers record data from the Custmast file directly into the Customer data structure, which reflects the layout of the Custrec record format in file Custmast.

If the Read operation successfully accesses a record, it positions the file at the next sequential record to be read. If the %Eof condition for a file is on, you cannot read any further records from that file unless you reposition the file, perhaps using the Setll or Setgt operations, discussed next.

Setll (Set Lower Limit)

The **Setll (Set Lower Limit) operation** provides flexibility related to where sequential reading occurs within a file. Setll lets you begin sequential processing at a record other than the first one in the file. It also can be used to reposition the file, for example, once end of file has been reached. The general format of a Setll operation is

```
Setll search-argument filename;
```

Setll positions a full procedural file at the first record whose key (or relative record number in the file) is greater than or equal to the value specified in the search argument. The search argument can be a literal, variable name, figurative constant, or composite key (we describe composite keys later in this chapter). The second operand can be a file name or record format name (if the file is externally described).

You can use the **%Found** and %Equal functions with Setll. %Found is turned on if there is a record in the file that has a key equal to or greater than the value in the search argument. The **%Equal** function is turned on if a record is found whose key exactly matches the search argument.

The Setll operation does not actually retrieve a record; it simply positions the file to determine which record the next sequential read will access. An unsuccessful Setll causes the file to be positioned at end of file.

Setll has two common uses in RPG IV programming. The first is to reposition the file to the beginning during processing by using figurative constant *Loval as the search argument. The next sequential read operation then retrieves the first record in the file:

```
/Free
   Setll *Loval Custmast;
   Read Custmast;                          // Read first record in file
/End-Free
```

The second common use of Setll is to position the file to the first record of a group of records with identical key values in preparation for processing that group of records. (We discuss details of this use when we cover the Reade operation.)

You also can use Setll to determine whether a record exists in a file without actually reading the record. If you simply need to check for the presence of a record with a given key without accessing the data contained in the record, using Setll is more efficient than doing a Read operation:

```
/Free
   Setll Custin Custmast;
   If %Equal(Custmast);
     Exsr Validcust;
   Else;
     Exsr Invalidcust;
   Endif;
/End-Free
```

Setgt (Set Greater Than)

The **Setgt (Set Greater Than) operation** works similarly to Setll. The primary difference is that this operation positions the file to a record whose key value is greater than the value of the search argument, rather than greater than or equal to the value of the search argument. The general form of the Setgt operation is

```
Setgt search-argument filename;
```

As with the Setll operation, the search argument can be a variable, literal, figurative constant, or composite key; the second operand can be a file name or (for an externally described file) a record format name. You can test the %Found function, which is turned on if the positioning is successful, or code Not %Found to detect unsuccessful positioning (in which case the file would be positioned at end of file). The %Equal function does not apply to Setgt.

```
/Free
   Setgt Custin Custmast;
   If %Found(Custmast);
       Exsr Success;
     Other;
       Exsr Valuetoohi;
   Endsl;
/End-Free
```

Following a successful Setgt operation, the file is positioned so that the next record to be read will be the record whose key is greater than the search argument. Setgt can also be used with figurative constant *Hival to position a file to end of file in preparation for a Readp operation (discussed later). Remember that a Setgt, like a Setll, merely positions the file; it does not actually retrieve a record from the database.

Reade (Read Equal Key)

The **Reade (Read Equal Key) operation** sequentially reads the next record in a full procedural file if the key of that record matches the search argument value. If the record's key does not match, or if the file is at end of file, the %Eof function is turned on. The Reade operation follows the general form

```
Reade search-argument filename {data-structure} ;
```

The search argument can be a variable, literal, figurative constant, or composite key. The second operand can be the file name or (for externally described files) the record format name. You can specify an optional third argument for the Reade operation to name a result data structure to receive the data.

Programmers use the Reade operation within a loop to identically process sets of records with duplicate keys in a file. Programmers often precede the first Reade with a Setll operation to position the file initially, in preparation for processing those records with keys identical to the value specified by the Setll.

Assume, for example, that you want to list all orders received on a specific date and that the order file is keyed on date. Further assume that field Indate stores the date whose orders are to be printed. The following processing would be appropriate.

```
/Free
// Code to list all orders placed on Indate
   Setll Indate Orders;
   If %Equal(Orders);
      Reade Indate Orders;
      Dow Not %Eof(Orders);
         Write Orderline;
         Reade Indate Orders;
      Enddo;
   Else;
      Exsr Noorders;
   Endif;
/End-Free
```

This code uses the value of Indate to position the Orders file to a key value that matches that of Indate. If a match exists, the %Equal function is turned on, and the program does an initial Reade of the file and then sets up a loop with a Dow operation; within the loop, the program writes an order line and then reads the next equal record. The loop is continued as long as the Reade is successful. If the initial Setll fails to find any order for Indate (signaled by %Equal being off), flow bypasses the loop, drops down to the Else, and then executes the Noorders subroutine.

Readp (Read Prior Record) and Readpe (Read Prior Equal)

The **Readp (Read Prior Record)** and **Readpe (Read Prior Equal) operations** are sequential reading operations that have their parallels in Read and Reade, respectively. The only difference between Readp and Read, and between Readpe and Reade, is directionality; the "prior" read operations move "backwards" through the file. These operations follow the general format

```
Readp filename {data-structure};
```

```
Readpe search-argument filename {data-structure};
```

Like Reade, Readpe requires a search argument entry; both prior read operations also require a file name or a record format name. Both operations also support a result data structure.

Like Read and Reade, both Readp and Readpe support the %Eof function. This function is turned on at *beginning of file* (not end of file) for Readp or when the key of the prior sequential record does not match the search argument value for Readpe.

The concept of "backwards" sequential access is relatively easy to grasp; it is harder to visualize why such processing might be desired. To get a sense of when these operations might be appropriate, let's consider an example.

Imagine the following scenario. As part of an order processing application, a program is to assign order numbers sequentially. Each day the program is run, the number assigned to the first order number is to be one larger than the number of the last order processed the previous day. Assume also that the order file is keyed on order number. The following code will determine the appropriate starting value for the day's orders.

```
/Free
 // Code using Setgt and Readp to determine the next order number to use.
 // Orders file is keyed on field Ordernbr.
   Setgt *Hival Orders;
   Readp Orders;
   If Not %Eof(Orders);
     Ordernbr += 1;
   Else;
     Ordnbr = 1;
   Endif;
/End-Free
```

In this code, Setgt positions the file at end of file. The Readp operation retrieves the last record in the file (i.e., the record with the highest order number). Adding 1 to Ordernbr, then, gives you the value for the first new order of the day. If %Eof is turned on, it indicates that you are at beginning of file, which means no records exist in the order file; in this case, Ordnbr will be 1.

In general, you might use the prior read operations any time you want to process files in descending key order because ordinarily i5/OS organizes keyed files in sequence by ascending key value.

Random Access

All the operations we've discussed so far in this chapter deal with retrieving database records sequentially. Often, however, you want to be able to read a specific record, determined by its key value, without having to read through the file sequentially to reach that record. This kind of access is called **random access.** Random access lets you "reach into" a file and extract just the record you want. RPG IV supports random access of full procedural database files through the Chain operation.

Chain (Random Retrieval from a File)

The **Chain (Random Retrieval from a File) operation** requires a search argument—a variable, literal, figurative constant, or composite key—that contains the key value of the record to be randomly read. The second operand is also required; it contains the name of the file (or record format) from which the record is to be randomly retrieved. A third, optional, operand can name a result data structure to receive the record. The Chain operation uses the general format

```
Chain search-argument filename {data-structure};
```

The %Found function is turned on if the random retrieval is successful—that is, if a record in the file matches the specified search argument.

```
/Free
   Chain Custnbr Custmaster;
   If %Found(Custmaster);
     Exsr Validcust;
   Else;
     Exsr Nocust;
   Endif;
/End-Free
```

In the example shown above, Custnbr contains the key value of the Custmaster record you want to read. If the Chain finds a record, the program executes subroutine Validcust; if the record is not found, the program executes subroutine Nocust. If the file contains records with duplicate keys, such that more than one record would qualify as a match, the system retrieves the first record that matches.

If the Chain successfully retrieves a record (signaled by the %Found function), the system reads the data into the program and then positions the file to the record immediately following the retrieved record. Accordingly, issuing a Read or Reade to the file following a successful Chain results in sequentially accessing the file starting with the record immediately following the retrieved record. Because of this feature, you can use the Chain operation to position the file in a manner similar to Setll. The primary difference between these two approaches is that a successful Chain actually reads a record, whereas a successful Setll merely repositions the file without retrieving a record.

If a Chain operation does not find a record, you cannot follow it with a sequential read operation without first successfully repositioning the file with another Chain, Setll, or Setgt operation. You can, however, follow it with subsequent Chain operations; Chain will not set the %Eof function on.

Using Composite Keys

As we discussed in Chapter 3, both physical and logical files can have keys based on more than one field. This kind of key is called a **composite key** or a **concatenated key**. The existence of composite keys raises a puzzling question: What can you use as a search argument for Chain, Setll, Reade, and so on when the records in the file you are trying to access are keyed on more than one field value?

The operation codes that support a composite key (Chain, Delete, Reade, Readpe, Setgt, and Setll) let you simply code a list of values in place of the key operand for the operation code. To understand how this feature works, assume you have a database file of student grades, Studgrades, which contains one record per student per course taken. The file is keyed on Student number, Semester, and Course number. Here is the DDS for the file:

```
*.. 1 ...+... 2 ...+... 3 ...+... 4 ...+... 5 ...+... 6 ...+... 7 ...+... 8
A..........T.Name++++++RLen++TDcB......Keywords++++++++++++++++++++++++++++++
 * Student Grades physical file STUDGRADES
A                                       UNIQUE
A          R STUDREC
A            STUDNBR      9S 0           TEXT('Student number')
A            SEMESTER     5S 0           TEXT('Semester (YYYY#)')
A            COURSENBR    7A             TEXT('Course number')
A            GRADE        2A             TEXT('Grade')
A            GPAHOURS     5P 3           TEXT('GPA Hours')
A
A          K STUDNBR
A          K SEMESTER
A          K COURSENBR
```

You are writing a program that requires you to randomly access the StudGrades file to retrieve a grade that a given student received in a given class. To retrieve a record using a composite key, you can list the values that make up the composite key in parentheses, separated by colons:

```
Chain (Studnbr:Semester:Coursenbr) Studgrades;
```

The order in which the values are listed determines the order in which they are combined to form the composite key. The variable names can have, but do not need to have, the same names as those of the file records' composite key. In fact, the values need not be variables; they can be literals, constants, or even expressions. However, each value's base type must match the corresponding key field in the file; that is, numeric values for numeric key fields, character values for character key fields, and so on. The compiler will perform any required conversion using the same rules that the Eval operation uses to assign values.

The following example shows how you might use expressions and literals in the list of keys:

```
Chain (Studnbr : %Char(*Year * 10 + 2) : 'SPAN312' ) Studgrades;
```

In this example, the semester is calculated in an expression (using the *Year special value), then converted to a character value and used as the second key value. The third key value ('SPAN312') is a character literal.

Partial Composite Keys

Composite keys offer an additional feature that makes processing groups of logically associated records relatively simple. Let's use the previous example, but this time, instead of wanting information about a grade for one course for one student, assume you want to be able to access all the records in Studgrades for a particular student for a given semester, perhaps to print out his or her grades earned that semester. The following code accomplishes the desired processing.

```
/Free
   Chain (Studnbr:Semester) Studgrades;
   If %Found(Studgrades);
     Dow Not %Eof(Studgrades);
       Exsr Printgrade;
       Reade (Studnbr:Semester) Studgrades;
     Enddo;
   Else;
     Exsr Nogrades;
   Endif;
/End-Free
```

First, this example chains to the Studgrades file, using a *partial* composite key (with fewer key values than in the actual file) to read the first course for the given student in the given semester. If the Chain finds a record, the program sets up a loop that continues until %Eof comes on for Studgrades. Within the loop, the program executes subroutine Printgrade to print grades and then executes a Reade to bring in the next course for the student being processed. The Reade operation within the loop will set %Eof on when no more records are found for that student/semester. If the original Chain fails, control drops to the Else and the program executes subroutine Nogrades to indicate that the student/semester was not in the file.

Note that we could have achieved the same effects by issuing a Setll to position the file and then, provided the operation was successful, using a Reade to read the first record of the set. A successful Chain reads a record and positions the file to the desired location in one operation.

RPG IV lets you access a database file based on a partial key list provided the portion you want to use is the major, or top-level, key field (or fields). That is, given the Studgrades file definition here, the following partial key lists would be valid:

- Studnbr
- (Studnbr:Semester)

But the following would *not* be valid:

- Semester
- Coursenbr
- (Studnbr:Coursenbr)

Thus, we can get a list of all courses for a given student but not a list of all students who have taken a given course; the database file would need to be keyed differently, perhaps using a logical file, to allow this kind of access.

%Kds (Key Data Structure)

The **%Kds (Key data structure) function** lets you use the subfields in a data structure as the search arguments for any file operation that supports a composite key. The %Kds function follows the general form

```
%Kds(data-structure {:number-of-keys} )
```

When you substitute the %Kds function for the list of key values, the program will use the current values of the subfields in the named data structure as the composite key list for the operation. There are no special requirements for defining the data structure, but the base types of the subfields in the data structure must be compatible with the key fields in the file; if the formats or lengths differ, the subfield values will be converted to the proper format and length, using the same rules that Eval uses to assign values. The following code defines a data structure called Studsmster and then uses it as a key to Chain to the Studgrades file:

```
*.. 1 ...+... 2 ...+... 3 ...+... 4 ...+... 5 ...+... 6 ...+... 7 ...+... 8
DName++++++++++ETDsFrom+++To/Len+IDc.Keywords+++++++++++++++++++++++++++++++
D Studsmstr       DS
D   Studnbr                    9 0
D   Semester                   5 0
D   Coursenbr                  7
 /Free
    Chain %Kds(Studsmstr) Studgrades;
 /End-Free
```

If you want to specify a partial key, you can code a second argument to the %Kds function, to tell it how many key fields to use (only Student and Semester in the following example):

```
Chain %Kds(Studsmstr:2) Studgrades;
```

In connection with this support, you could use a variation of the Extname keyword to define a data structure that will automatically extract just the key fields from a record format, eliminating the necessity to key the subfields explicitly. The following code would create an externally described data structure with just the key fields from the Studgrades file:

```
*.. 1 ...+... 2 ...+... 3 ...+... 4 ...+... 5 ...+... 6 ...+... 7 ...+... 8
DName+++++++++++ETDsFrom+++To/Len+IDc.Keywords+++++++++++++++++++++++++++++++
D Studsmstr      E DS                  Extname(Studgrades:*Key)
```

The Likerec keyword also allows you to limit the data structure to key fields only:

```
*.. 1 ...+... 2 ...+... 3 ...+... 4 ...+... 5 ...+... 6 ...+... 7 ...+... 8
FFilename++IPEASFRLen+LKLen+AIDevice+.Keywords+++++++++++++++++++++++++++++++
DName+++++++++++ETDsFrom+++To/Len+IDc.Keywords+++++++++++++++++++++++++++++++
FStudgradesIF   E          K Disk

D Studsmstr        DS                  Likerec(Studrec:*Key)
```

The %Kds function will take the top-level subfields (i.e., those starting at the beginning) from the data structure. The subfields cannot be arrays (although the data structure can be an array data structure if you use an index).

Operations for Output Files

The operations we've looked at so far are appropriate for input files. A few file I/O operations deal with output—that is, writing new records to database files. Until now, the output of your programs has been reports, but you can also designate a database file as program output. The File specification entries in this case are similar to the input files we've used until now, except that output files use an O for output, in position 17, and a blank in position 18:

```
*.. 1 ...+... 2 ...+... 3 ...+... 4 ...+... 5 ...+... 6 ...+... 7 ...+... 8
FFilename++IPEASFRlen+LKLen+AIDevice+.Keywords+++++++++++++++++++++++++++++++
   // File specification for a program that writes records to a new file
FCustmast   O   E          K Disk
```

Once you've defined a File specification as output, two RPG IV operations let you output records to the file:

- Except (Calculation Time Output)
- Write (Write a Record to a File)

Note
The File specification must name a file that will already exist when the program executes. If the file is externally described, it must already exist when the program is compiled. The RPG program itself cannot actually create a new file object; it simply adds new records to an existing file object, which may or may not already contain records. If the file already contains records, new ones are added to the end of the file. To review creating the file object, see Chapter 3.

Except (Calculation Time Output)

You have already used the **Except (Calculation Time Output) operation** to write to printer files; you can also use Except to write new records to a database file. The form of the Except statement used to write to database files is no different than the form used for printer files.

The Except operation optionally can designate a named E line on the output. When the program reaches the Except operation, it writes the named E lines (if the Except includes a line name in Factor 2) or all unnamed E lines (if the Except operation appears alone on the Calculation specification) from the Output specifications.

If the file is an externally described file, in the Output specifications you need to enter the record format name, rather than the file name itself, in positions 7–16. Then list all the fields making up the record. Omitting a field or fields from the list causes default values (usually zeros or blanks) to be written to the record for that field. Rather than listing all the fields, you can simply code *All, which has the same effect as including all the field names. The following code demonstrates how you could write records to a customer file using Except:

```
*.. 1 ...+... 2 ...+... 3 ...+... 4 ...+... 5 ...+... 6 ...+... 7 ...+... 8
FFilename++IPEASFRLen+LKLen+AIDevice+.Keywords+++++++++++++++++++++++++++++++
OFilename++DF..N01N02N03Excnam++++B++A++Sb+Sa+...............................
FCustomers O    E          K Disk
 ...
 /Free
    Except Record;
 /End-Free
 ...
OCustrec   E           Record
O                      *ALL
```

Write (Write a Record to a File)

Rather than using the Except operation and Output specifications, most programmers prefer to use the **Write (Write a Record to a File) operation** to output database records more directly, without Output specifications. The Write operation designates the file name (or the record format, for externally described files) to which the record will be written. The Write operation takes the following general form:

```
Write filename {data-structure};
```

With a Write operation, the current program values for all the fields making up the record definition are written to the file.

For program-described files, you must specify an additional argument for the Write operation to name a data structure to supply the record data (for externally described files, the data structure is optional). When you include a data structure, the Write operation will transfer data directly from the data structure to the record. The following example demonstrates the use of a data structure with the Write operation:

```
*.. 1 ...+... 2 ...+... 3 ...+... 4 ...+... 5 ...+... 6 ...+... 7 ...+... 8
FFilename++IPEASFRLen+LKLen+AIDevice+.Keywords++++++++++++++++++++++++++++++++
DName++++++++++ETDsFrom+++To/Len+IDc.Keywords+++++++++++++++++++++++++++++++++
FCustmast  O    E            Disk

D Customer         DS                    Likerec(Custrec:*Output)

 /Free
    Write Custmast Customer;
 /End-Free
```

If the file is program-described, the data structure can be any data structure with the same length as the file's declared length. If the file is externally described, it must be defined using the Extname or Likerec keyword, specifying *Output fields—Extname(...:*Output) or Likerec(...:*Output)—as this example illustrates.

Update Files and I/O Operations

A common data processing task is file maintenance. File maintenance, or updating, involves adding or deleting records from database files, or changing the information in database records, to keep the information current and correct. Records that do not exist cannot be changed or deleted; if a file has unique keys, a second record with the same key should not be added to the file. Accordingly, file maintenance routines typically require first determining whether the record exists in the file (through a Chain or Setll) and then determining what update option is valid, given the found record's status.

RPG IV includes an update file type, signaled by U (for Update) in position 17 of the File specifications, which lets you read, change, and then rewrite records to the file, as well as add and delete entire records. You can use any database file as an update file simply by coding it as such in the File specifications. If the maintenance procedure involves adding new records, you must signal that fact in the File specifications by entering an A (for Add) in position 20.

```
*.. 1 ...+... 2 ...+... 3 ...+... 4 ...+... 5 ...+... 6 ...+... 7 ...+... 8
FFilename++IPEASFRLen+LKLen+AIDevice+.Keywords+++++++++++++++++++++++++++++++++
FCustomers UF A E           K Disk
```

An update file supports both input and output operations. If you define a file as an update full procedural file, you can use all the input operations we've discussed so far—Chain, Read, Reade, Readp, Readpe, Setll, and Setgt—to access records in the file. If you define the file for add capability (the A on the File specifications), you can use the Write operation to add new records to the file. Two additional I/O operations can be used only for update files:

- Delete (Delete Record)
- Update (Modify Existing Record)

Delete (Delete Record)

The **Delete (Delete Record) operation** deletes a single record from an update file. Delete takes the following general form:

```
Delete {search-argument} filename;
```

With the Delete operation, you must code a file name or, if the file is externally described, a record format name. The first Delete operand is optional; if you leave it blank, the system deletes the record most recently read from that file.

```
Delete Customers;
```

The record must have been previously read by an input operation (e.g., Chain or Read). If you use this form of Delete without first retrieving a record from the file, you will get a system error message. To cover this case, you should use the %Found function to detect instances wherein the record to be deleted is not found in the file.

```
/Free
    // This code deletes the record of customer 100 if the record exists
    // in the file.
    Chain '100' Customers;
    If %Found(Customers);
      Delete Customers;
    Endif;
/End-Free
```

The second form of Delete retrieves a record and then deletes it. If you code a search argument to specify which record is to be deleted, you can enter a variable name, a literal, a constant, or a composite key. If duplicate records exist in the file, the system deletes only the first record that matches the search argument. An error will occur if the record cannot be found (Chapter 14 discusses how to capture the error).

```
/Free
   // This code deletes the record of customer 100 if the record exists
   // in the file. An error occurs if the record does not exist.
   Delete '100' CustMaster;
/End-Free
```

Note
The Delete operation logically deletes records from a file rather than physically removing them. Although as a result of Delete a record is no longer accessible to programs or queries, the record actually remains on disk until the file containing the deleted record is reorganized.

Update (Modify Existing Record)

The **Update (Modify Existing Record) operation** modifies the record most recently read from an update file. The required operand names the file (for program-described files) or the record format (for externally described files) to be updated. Update takes the following general form:

```
Update name {data-structure};
```

Before your program can update a record, it must have successfully that record with a Chain, Read, Reade, Readp, or Readpe operation. If you update a record without first retrieving one, you will get a system error message. To cover this case, you should use the %Found function to detect instances wherein no record has been retrieved.

Update causes the current program values of all the record's fields to be rewritten to the file. The typical procedure involving Update is to retrieve a record, change one or more of its fields' values, and then use Update to rewrite the record with its new values. You cannot issue multiple Updates for a single read operation; each Update must be preceded by a record retrieval.

```
/Free
   Chain Custnbr Custmast;
   If %Found(Custmast);
     Balancedue += Invoiceamt;
     Lastdate = Invoicedate;
     Update Custrec;
   Else;
     Exsr Nocustomer;
   Endif;
/End-Free
```

In this example, the program will retrieve a record from the Custmast file for a given Custnbr. If a record is found for that customer, the Balancedue and Lastdate fields (presumably in the Custmast file) will be adjusted; following that, the record (which uses the Custrec format) in the file will be updated. If no record can be found for that customer, the Nocustomer subroutine will be invoked.

The optional second operand names a result data structure for the Update operation. If you specify a data structure, the record is updated directly from the data structure, instead of field by field. The following example demonstrates the use of a data structure with the Update operation:

```
*.. 1 ...+... 2 ...+... 3 ...+... 4 ...+... 5 ...+... 6 ...+... 7 ...+... 8
FFilename++IPEASFRLen+LKLen+AIDevice+.Keywords+++++++++++++++++++++++++++++++
DName++++++++++++ETDsFrom+++To/Len+IDc.Keywords++++++++++++++++++++++++++++++++
FCustmast  O    E             Disk

D Customer        DS                      Likerec(Custrec:*Input)

 /Free
    Chain Custnbr Custmast;
    If %Found(Custmast);
      Balancedue += Invoiceamt;
      Lastdate = Invoicedate;
      Update Custrec Customer;
    Else;
      Exsr Nocustomer;
    Endif;
 /End-Free
```

If the file is program-described, the data structure can be any data structure with the same length as the file's declared length. If the file is externally described, it must be defined using the Extname or Likerec keyword, specifying *Input fields—Extname(...:*Input) or Likerec(...:*Input)—as this example illustrates.

Using the %Fields (Fields to Update) Function

The Update operation rewrites all of a database record's fields to the file. In the previous example the current values of Balancedue and Lastdate—along with every other field in Custrec—are updated by the Update operation. If your program logic has changed field values that you do not want to be updated, you can use the **%Fields (Fields to update) function** to list just those fields that are to be rewritten:

```
 /Free
    Chain Custnbr Custmast;
    If %Found(Custmast);
      Balancedue += Invoiceamt;
      Lastdate = Invoicedate;
      Update Custrec %Fields(Balancedue:Lastdate);
    Else;
      Exsr Nocustomer;
    Endif;
 /End-Free
```

The %Fields function specifies a list of fields to be updated in the record (Balancedue and Lastdate in this example); the unlisted fields will remain unchanged in the database file.

While most programmers prefer to use the %Fields function for this situation, early releases of RPG IV used the Except operation and Output specifications to designate which fields are to be rewritten:

```
*.. 1 ...+... 2 ...+... 3 ...+... 4 ...+... 5 ...+... 6 ...+... 7 ...+... 8
OFilename++DF..NØ1NØ2NØ3Excnam++++B++A++Sb+Sa+................................

/Free
   Chain Custnbr Custmast;
   If %Found(Custmast);
     Balancedue = Balancedue + Invoiceamt;
     Lastdate = Invoicedate;
     Except Custupdate;
   Else;
     Exsr Nocustomer;
   Endif;
/End-Free

OCustrec     E             Custupdate
O                          Balancedue
O                          Lastdate
```

File and Record Locking

Any multiuser system needs to address the problems related to simultaneous use of the same database file. Otherwise, it is possible that if two users access the same record for update, make changes in the record, and then rewrite it to the file, one of the user's changes might get lost—a condition sometimes called **phantom updates**. Two approaches you can use to deal with this type of problem are **file locking** and **record locking**.

The easiest kind of locking is to limit access to a file to one user at a time—a condition known as file locking. Although i5/OS permits you to lock files at a system level by issuing CL commands, most of the time you want to allow multiple users access to the same files at the same time. RPG IV includes built-in, automatic locking features at a record level.

If your program designates a file as an update file, RPG IV *automatically* places a lock on a record when it is read within your program. Updating that record or reading another record releases the record from its locked state. While the record is locked, other application programs can access the record if they have defined the file as an input file but not if they, too, have defined the file as an update file. Other application programs can access other records in the file, even if they have defined the file as an update file; but two programs cannot access the same record in update mode simultaneously. This solution eliminates the problem of lost updates.

However, record locking can cause waiting and access problems for users if programmers don't structure their code to avoid locks except when absolutely necessary. The nightmare scenario you should keep in mind when designing update programs is that of the user who keys in a request to update a record, pulls up the screen of data preparatory to making changes in the record, and then realizes it's lunch time and disappears for an hour. Meanwhile, the record lock prevents all other users from accessing the record.

One solution to this problem lies with the **(N) operation code extender**, which you can use with Read, Reade, Readp, Readpe, and Chain to specify that the input operation to an update file be done without locking the record. You can use this feature to avoid unnecessary locking. Another, less common, solution is the **Unlock (Unlock a Data Area or Release a Record) operation**. If you've read a record with a lock and want to release the lock, you can use this operation along with a file name to release the most recently locked record in that file:

```
/Free
   // Random read of an update file automatically locks the record.
   Chain CustNbr CustMaster;

   // Random read of an update file with operation extender N
   // keeps the record unlocked.
   Chain(n) Custnbr Custmaster;

   // Release most recently read record in CustMaster.
   Unlock Custmaster;
/End-Free
```

If you start releasing record locks in update procedures, however, be aware that you can easily code yourself right back into the phantom update problem that caused systems to incorporate record locking in the first place. If you aren't including some provision that checks to make sure another user has not updated a record between the time you first accessed the record and the time you are about to rewrite the record with the values from your program, leave all record locking in place. With concise programming practices, you should be able to minimize the processing time that a record is locked; when you are sure that you will not be updating a record in an update file, be sure to retrieve it with the (N) extender to prevent locking the record or Unlock it.

Beyond record locking considerations, generally accepted programming practice dictates that a program should not keep a file open any longer than it needs to access the required data from the file. RPG IV automatically opens your files at the beginning of processing and then closes them all at the end of processing. If your program needs access to a file for only a portion of its total running time, you should take control of the file opening and closing rather than letting RPG IV manage those tasks for you. RPG IV includes two operations to give you this capability:

- Open (Open a File)
- Close (Close Files)

You can open and close files that RPG IV opened automatically. If you want to prevent the file's initial automatic open, you must make an additional entry within the File specification. The **Usropn (User Open) keyword**, coded in the Keywords area of the File specification, prevents the file from being implicitly opened by RPG IV and signals that the opening of the file will be explicitly coded within the program:

```
*.. 1 ...+... 2 ...+... 3 ...+... 4 ...+... 5 ...+... 6 ...+... 7 ...+... 8
FFilename++IPEASFRlen+LKlen+AIDevice+.Keywords+++++++++++++++++++++++++++++++++
FCustMast  UF A E           K Disk    Usropn

/Free
   Open Custmast;
   ...
   Close Custmast;
/End-Free
```

The Close operation can also close all the open files in a single statement:

```
Close *All;
```

You can open a given file more than once within a program, provided the file is closed before each successive open. When you close—and then subsequently reopen—a file, it is repositioned to the beginning of the file (%Eof will be off).

Trying to open a file that's already open causes an error; trying to close a file that's already closed does not produce an error. To avoid opening an already open file, you can use the **%Open (Return open file condition) function** to check a file's open condition:

```
/Free
   If Not %Open(Custmast);
      Open Custmast;
   Endif;
/End-Free
```

Note
File opens and closes have a significant performance impact on the system, and you should avoid repeatedly opening and closing the same file while a program is running. Reserve this capability for those situations where it is truly necessary.

Putting It All Together

Now that you've learned about RPG IV's input and output operations, you might find some sample programs helpful to demonstrate how to apply these operations. Accordingly, read the scenarios that follow and study the program solutions to develop a sense of when to use the various I/O operations.

Example 1

In the first scenario, a company has decided to give all its employees a five percent pay raise. Assume that an externally described master file of employees (Empmaster) exists, that the record format within the database file is Emprecord, and that the pay field is Pay. The file is keyed on employee ID. The following code shows a solution for this problem.

```
*.. 1 ...+... 2 ...+... 3 ...+... 4 ...+... 5 ...+... 6 ...+... 7 ...+... 8
FFilename++IPEASFRLen+LKLen+AIDevice+.Keywords+++++++++++++++++++++++++++++
   // *******************************************************************
   // This program gives each employee in the Empmaster file a 5% raise.
   // *******************************************************************

FEmpmaster UF   E              Disk

 /Free
    Read Empmaster;

    Dow Not %Eof(Empmaster);
      Eval(H) Pay = Pay * 1.05;
      Update Emprecord %Fields(Pay);
      Read Empmaster;
    Enddo;

    *Inlr = *On;
    Return;
 /End-Free
```

In this solution, the file is declared as an update file, but because we are not asked to add new records to the file, the program does not specify that record addition should be enabled. Even though the master file is keyed, we are processing the records sequentially because we want to process all the records in the file and the order of processing is not important for this solution. Because all employees are to receive the raise, the calculations consist of a simple loop that sequentially reads through the file, calculates the new pay for each employee, and then updates the employee's record (just the Pay field).

Example 2

Now let's complicate the problem a little. Instead of giving every employee a raise, the company wants to give only selected employees a five percent raise; a transaction file called Raisetrans contains the IDs of these employees (in field Empid).

The processing requirements of this problem vary from the first scenario because now we need to access only those employees in Empmaster who appear in file Raisetrans. Every record in Raisetrans, however, must be processed. Accordingly, we want to sequentially process Raisetrans and use the information on each record to randomly access an Empmaster record to update.

To provide for the possible error where Raisetrans contains one or more employee IDs not found in the master file, we'll include an externally described printer file, Errprint, with a record format called Notfound; if the program cannot find an employee in the master file, it will use this format to report the error. The sample program is shown on page 270.

Embedding SQL Statements in RPG

In this chapter we've discussed reading and updating files using RPG operations (Read, Chain, Update, Delete, and so on) to access the database directly. Structured Query Language (SQL) also has statements to access and manipulate database files. RPG IV supports embedding SQL statements in an RPG program, allowing you to use industry-standard syntax and provide a measure of platform independence for your applications. Usually, embedded SQL statements are Data Manipulation Language (DML) statements, but they can also be Data Definition Language (DDL) statements. In addition, embedded SQL supports several special statements that are used only in programs.

Embedded SQL is especially suited for "set-at-a-time" file manipulation, wherein you perform operations against a number of records using a single SQL statement. It is also useful when you want to improve the user interface to SQL or control access to SQL statements programmatically. Embedding SQL statements in an RPG IV program gives the program access to SQL functions that may not be available in RPG.

RPG IV stores source code that includes embedded SQL statements in a source file member using SEU type SQLRPGLE. The CRTSQLRPGI (Create SQL ILE RPG Object) command compiles the program.

Each SQL statement must be preceded by a special compiler directive, Exec SQL, and followed by a semicolon:

```
Exec Sql Update Maillist Set Errorcode = 'ST420' Where State = '  ';
```

This statement would update a Maillist file, changing field Errorcode to have a value of "ST420" in each record where the State field is blank. Note that every record that fits the condition in the Where clause would be updated, without requiring the use of a loop to read, evaluate, and update each record individually. The program that includes this statement would also not require the use of a File specification to declare the Maillist file.

To integrate embedded SQL statements with RPG variables, SQL uses "host variables," which are variables defined in the program's RPG syntax but accessible by the SQL syntax. Using host variables, the SQL and RPG portions of the program can pass information to each other:

```
Dltstate = 'TX';
Exec Sql Delete From Maillist Where State = :Dltstate;
```

In this example, the variable Dltstate (defined elsewhere in the program) is assigned a value in an RPG IV expression, using an implied Eval operation. The subsequent SQL statement substitutes the value of Dltstate, preceding it with a colon (:) character. The net effect of the two statements would be to delete all the "TX" records from the Maillist file. Host variables are always preceded by a colon in the SQL statement but appear without a colon in the RPG syntax; both notations refer to the same variable.

To use SQL to read a single record into an RPG program, SQL uses a special variation of its Select statement:

```
Pgmaccount = 'G5X67';
Exec Sql Select Firstname, Lastname, City, State
         Into :Pgmfirstname, :Pgmlastname, :Pgmcity, :Pgmstate
         From Maillist
         Where Account = :Pgmaccount;
```

SQL's Select Into statement will read fields from a record into corresponding host variables in the RPG program. Notice that the SQL statement can span several lines without using any continuation characters; the SQL statement ends with a semicolon.

To read multiple records and process them individually, SQL uses a special construct called a "cursor," which uses a Select statement to define the records to be read. A special SQL statement, Fetch Into, then reads individual records from a cursor in a loop. SQL treats the cursor like a file definition in RPG; like a file, a cursor must be declared (defined), opened, and closed using special SQL statements. In addition to reading records, SQL can use cursors to add, update, and delete records.

```
Exec Sql Declare C1 Cursor
         For Select Address, State, Zipcode
             From Mmaster
         For Update Of Delpoint, Carroute;

Exec Sql Open C1;

Dou Sqlcode <> 0;
  Exec Sql Fetch C1 Into :Address, :State, :Zipcode;
  If Sqlcode = 0;
    // Processing statements go here
    Exec Sql Update Mmaster
             Set Delpoint = :Delpoint, Carroute = :Carroute
             Where Current Of C1;
  Endif;
Enddo;

Exec Sql Close C1;
```

This example declares and opens a cursor named C1, associating it with an SQL Select statement. The subsequent RPG Dou loop fetches records from the cursor, individually processing and updating them. Sqlcode is a reserved variable used by embedded SQL to indicate the success or failure of an SQL statement. Finally, the SQL Close statement closes the cursor.

SQL is a powerful means of extending an RPG program's database capabilities. The topic can be a complex one, complete and separate from simple RPG IV. A complete discussion of embedded SQL goes beyond the scope of this text.

```
*.. 1 ...+... 2 ...+... 3 ...+... 4 ...+... 5 ...+... 6 ...+... 7 ...+... 8
FFilename++IPEASFRlen+LKlen+AIDevice+.Keywords+++++++++++++++++++++++++++++
DName++++++++++ETDsFrom+++To/Len+IDc.Keywords+++++++++++++++++++++++++++++++
   // **************************************************************
   // This program updates employees' pay by 5% based on employee IDs
   // contained in file RaiseTrans.
   // **************************************************************

FRaisetransIF    E               Disk
FEmpmaster  UF   E             K Disk
FErrprint   O    E               Printer Oflind(Endofpage)

D Endofpage        S               N    Inz(*On)

 /Free
    Read RaiseTrans;
    Dow Not %Eof(Raisetrans);
      Exsr Process;
      Read Raisetrans;
    Enddo;

    *Inlr = *On;
    Return;

   // *******************************************************************
   //
   // Subroutine to write Heading lines
   //
    Begsr Overflow;
      If Endofpage;
        Write Errheads;
        Endofpage = *Off;
      Endif;
    Endsr;

   // *******************************************************************
   //
   //  Subroutine to process Empmaster records
   //
    Begsr Process;
      Chain Empid Empmaster;
      If %Found(Empmaster);
        Eval(H) Pay = Pay * 1.05;
        Update Emprecord %Fields(Pay);
      Else;
        Exsr Overflow;
        Write Notfound;
      Endif;
    Endsr;
 /End-Free
```

Example 3

Now let's change the problem again, complicating it further. This time, the employers want to give raises to all the employees in certain departments; the Depttrans file contains the names of the departments to receive the raise.

The best way to solve this problem is to define a logical file over the Empmaster file, keyed on department, and then use the logical file for updating the employees. This approach lets you use Setll to locate the appropriate departments within the file and then use Reade to process all the employees within each department. The following program shows a solution using this approach. Note that we've omitted the error handling to let you focus more easily on the file accessing used in the program.

```
*.. 1 ...+... 2 ...+... 3 ...+... 4 ...+... 5 ...+... 6 ...+... 7 ...+... 8
  // *****************************************************************
  // This program updates employees' pay by 5% based on departments
  // contained in file DeptTrans. EmpMasterL is a logical file of
  // employees, keyed on department.
  // *****************************************************************

FDepttrans IF   E              Disk
FEmpmasterlUF   E            K Disk

 /FREE
    Read Depttrans;
    Dow Not %Eof(Depttrans);              // Loop To Process Each Department.
      Setll Dept Empmasterl;
      If %Equal(Empmasterl);
        Reade Dept Empmasterl;
        Dow Not %Eof(Empmasterl);         // Loop For All Employees In A Dept.
          Eval(H) Pay = Pay * 1.05;
          Update Emprecordl %Fields(Pay);
          Reade Dept Empmasterl;
        Enddo;
      Endif;
      Read Depttrans;
    Enddo;

    *Inlr = *On;
    Return;
 /End-Free
```

As you begin to write programs that require you to access several files, try to decide how to handle access to each file. Ask yourself how many records in each file you will need to process. If you need to access all the records in the file or a subset (or subsets) of the records based on a common value of a field, then sequential access, using Read or Reade (for subsets of sequential records), is appropriate. If you need to select only certain records from the file, random access, using Chain, would be best. And don't forget that i5/OS's facility for defining keyed logical files lets you retrieve records based on any field. Often, defining logical files goes hand in hand with developing programs.

Chapter Summary

In this chapter, you learned many I/O operations appropriate to input, output, and update files. Read, Reade, Readp, and Readpe are input operations used to access records sequentially from a full procedural file whose type is declared as input or update. You can use the Setll and Setgt operations to position the file before a sequential read operation. Chain randomly retrieves a record and also positions the file for subsequent sequential reading, if desired. These operations use the %Eof , %Found, and %Equal functions to return information to the program about the success or failure of the operation.

Many file I/O operations let you position a file or retrieve a record based on a composite key. You can either list the individual values that comprise the composite key or use the %Kds function to associate a data structure with the composite key. By using a partial composite key, you can initiate access to sets of records that share a common value on the first field (or fields) of a composite key.

You can use Write or Except to put records into an output file or an update file. Operations Update and Delete are specific to update files. You cannot Update a record without having first read it; you can, however, Delete a record without first retrieving it if you indicate the key of the record to delete in the operation. The Update operation normally changes all the fields in a record; if you want to change only specific fields, you can use the %Fields function.

i5/OS includes built-in record locking to prevent the problem of phantom updates. Techniques, including use of the (N) operation code extender or the Unlock operation, exist to minimize record locking, but you should not use them if their implementation might cause lost updates to occur.

The following table summarizes the functions and operation codes discussed in this chapter.

Function or operation	Description	Syntax
Chain	Random retrieval from a file	Chain{(ehmnr)} *search-argument file-format-name {data-structure}*
Close	Close files	Close{(e)} *file-name* | *All
Delete	Delete record	Delete{(ehmr)} *{search-argument} file-format-name*
%Eof	End (or beginning) of file	%Eof{(*file-name*)}
%Equal	Exact match for Setll	%Equal{(*file-name*)}
Except	Calculation time output	Except {*name*}
%Fields	Fields to update for Update	%Fields(*name {: name ...}*)
%Found	Record found for Chain, Delete, Setgt, Setll	%Found{(*file-name*)}
%Kds	Key data structure	%Kds(*data-structure-name {: number-keys}*)
%Open	Return open file condition	%Open(*file-name*)
Open	Open file for processing	Open{(e)} *file-name*
Read	Read a record	Read{(en)} *file-format-name {data-structure}*
Reade	Read equal key	Reade{(ehmnr)} *search-argument file-record-name {data-structure}*
Readp	Read prior record	Readp{(en)} *file-record-name {data-structure}*
Readpe	Read prior equal key	Readpe{(ehmnr)} *search-argument file-record-name {data-structure}*
Setgt	Set greater than	Setgt{(ehmr)} *search-argument file-record-name*
Setll	Set lower limit	Setll{(ehmr)} *search-argument file-record-name*
Unlock	Unlock a data area or release a record	Unlock{(e)} *dtaara-record-file*
Update	Modify existing record	Update{(e)} *file-record-name {data-structure}* Update{(e)} *file-record-name* %Fields(*name {: name ...}*)
Write	Create new record	Write{(e)} *file-record-name {data-structure}*

Key Terms

Chain operation
composite key
concatenated key
Delete operation
Except operation
file access
file locking
(N) operation code extender
phantom updates
random access
read operation
Reade operation
Readp operation
Readpe operation
record locking

result data structure
sequential access
Setgt operation
Setll operation
Unlock operation
Update operation
Usropn keyword
Write operation
%Eof function
%Equal function
%Fields function
%Found function
%Kds function
%Open function

Discussion/Review Questions

1. Describe the difference between sequential and random record retrieval.
2. What does "position the file" mean?
3. What are the differences between the Setgt and Setll operations?
4. Because Reade and Readpe imply reading records with matching keys, would you ever use them in programs accessing files with UNIQUE keys? Explain your answer.
5. When is it appropriate to use a Reade as opposed to a Read operation?
6. What does the term "file maintenance" mean? What kinds of files are likely to need maintenance?
7. Is any difference in results possible when you update a file using Except rather than Update?
8. Give an example of when you would use a partial key to access a record.
9. What would be the advantage of using the %Kds function?
10. Why should you use %Found before performing a Delete operation?
11. Because designating a file type as update gives you maximum flexibility in which I/O operations you can use with that file, why don't programmers designate all their files as update files, just in case? That is, why bother with input and output files?
12. What is the difference between a file lock and a record lock? Which technique do you think is easier for an operating system to implement? Why? Which technique is preferable from a user standpoint? Why?
13. What is defensive programming? What defensive programming technique is described in this chapter? Research and list additional ways to be a defensive programmer.
14. When using the %Eof function, why is it good programming practice to include a file name in the statement?
15. When using the Delete operation, what must be done before the record can be deleted?
16. Why is a Read NOT required after a chain operation?

Exercises

1. Assume you had a logical file of customers, CustLZip, keyed on zip code. Write the Calculation specifications that would let you print an exception line, CustLine, for every customer whose zip code matched ZipIn. If no customers have that zip code, print exception line NoCust.
2. Your company sequentially assigns a unique customer number to each new customer. Assume customer file CustMaster is keyed on customer number, field CustNbr. Write the Calculation specifications necessary to determine what number should be assigned to the next new customer.
3. You have a sales file, SalesFile, keyed on a composite key of store, department, and salesperson. (Duplicate keys are present because each record represents one sale.) Write the Calculation specifications needed to total all the sales for a given department within a given store. Field Dept contains the desired department; field Store holds the store. The sales field that you want to accumulate is SalesAmt. Modify your code so that it totals all the sales of the store represented in Store.

4. Write the File specifications and Calculation specifications needed to let you randomly retrieve a customer in file CustMast based on the customer number in CustNbr, subtract Payment from BalanceDue, and rewrite the record. Execute subroutine NoCust if the customer is not found in the file.

5. You have a transaction file, CustTrans, of records to be added, deleted, or changed in the CustMaster master file. The Code field of the transaction record contains an A, D, or C, denoting whether the record is to be added, deleted, or changed, respectively, while the number of the customer to add, delete, or change is contained in transaction field CustNo. Write the File specifications and Calculation specifications that will let you appropriately process each record in the transaction file. Add is a valid option if the customer does not already exist in CustMaster; Change and Delete are valid only if the customer does exist in CustMaster. Execute subroutine AddRecord for valid adds, ChgRecord for valid changes, and DltRecord for valid deletions; for all invalid transactions, execute subroutine TransError. (Don't code the details of these subroutines; stop at the point of coding the Exsr statements.)

Programming Assignments

1. GTC Telephone Company wants a program to update its customer master file (GTCSTP) based on data contained in the payments transaction file (GTPAYP). Data files are described in Appendix F. For each record in the payment file, randomly retrieve the appropriate customer, subtract the payment amount from the amount owed, change the date-of-last-payment field, and rewrite the customer record. Also prepare the audit report shown in the following printer spacing chart. Notice that if a customer in the payment file is not found in the customer file, an error notation should appear on the report.

```
XX/XX/XX        GTC Payments Processed   Page XX0X
                      Audit Report

    Customer          Date Received      Amount

    (XXX)XXX-XXXX       XX/XX/XX        X,XX0.XX
    (XXX)XXX-XXXX       XX/XX/XX        X,XX0.XX  Record Not Found
    (XXX)XXX-XXXX       XX/XX/XX        X,XX0.XX

                          TOTAL      XXX,XX0.XX

    X0X CUSTOMERS Not IN MASTER FILE
```

2. CompuSell wants a program that will generate purchase orders for those items in the inventory file that need reordering—that is, items whose quantity on hand is less than or equal to their reorder point. For any inventory item that meets this criterion and has not already been reordered (i.e., the reorder code field is still blank), include that item on a purchase order and rewrite the record to the inventory file with an R in the reorder code field to signal that the item has been reordered.

Only one purchase order should be completed per supplier—that is, all items to be purchased from the same supplier should appear on the same purchase order. The format of the purchase order is shown below. Note that the item number is the supplier's product number, not CompuSell's. The unit cost is the current cost figure, and the quantity (QTY) is the reorder quantity in the inventory file.

```
                 1         2         3         4         5         6         7         8         9
        1234567890123456789012345678901234567890123456789012345678901234567890123456789012345678901234567890
 1                                                                                      XX/XX/XX
 2                                   Compusell Industries
 3                                     5260 Haworth
 4                                   Kalamazoo  Mi  49008-0010
 5
 6 Purchase Order To:
 7
 8  Supplier: XXXXXXXXXXXXXXXXXXXXXXXXX  Contact: XXXXXXXXXXXXXXXXXXXXXXXXXXXXXXX
 9            XXXXXXXXXXXXXXXXXXXXX               (XXX)XXX-XXXX
10            XXXXXXXXXXXXXX   XX XXXXX-XXXX
11
12  Item Number       Description           Unit Cost     Qty        Extension
13    XXXXXXXX   XXXXXXXXXXXXXXXXXXXXXXXXXXX  X,XXi.XX     X,X0X    XX,XXX,XX0.XX
14    XXXXXXXX   XXXXXXXXXXXXXXXXXXXXXXXXXXX  X,XX0.XX     X,X0X    XX,XXX,XX0.XX
15    XXXXXXXX   XXXXXXXXXXXXXXXXXXXXXXXXXXX  X,XX0.XX     X,X0X    XX,XXX,XX0.XX
16
17                                           Order Total         $XXX,XXX,XX0.XX
18
19                                           Total Parts             XXXXX0X
20
21                      Authorized Signature_____
22
```

You will need to use data from CompuSell's inventory master file (CSINVP) and supplier file (CSSUPP), both described in Appendix F. You also will need to create a logical file so that the inventory records can be processed in supplier number order.

3. CompuSell wants you to write a program to process goods received from suppliers. As the company receives ordered goods from suppliers, the items are added to inventory, and a record of each received item is added to the goods received file (CSRCVP). The contents of this file are then run in batch to update the inventory file, CSINVP. Appendix F describes these files.

Hint: The file CSRCVP doesn't contain the part number, which is required to read the CSINVP file; it does contain the PO number and the line item number. This will allow you to access the part number by reading the Purchase Order detail file (CSPOD) and then reading the CSINVP file.

For each item in CSRCVP, the following changes must be made in the corresponding record of CSINVP:

a) The quantity on hand must be changed to reflect the additional goods.

b) The reorder code should be changed to spaces.

c) If the current charge from the supplier is not identical to the current and average costs stored in the inventory file, two changes must be made—first, the inventory file's current cost must be changed to reflect the new cost, and, second, the average cost must be recalculated and updated.

To calculate new average cost, multiply the old average cost by the old quantity on hand, add this value to the cost of the items that have just come in, and divide by the new total quantity on hand. Thus, if you had 10 units in stock with an average cost of $3 and received 20 more units at a cost of $4, the new average cost would be:

$$(10 * 3 + 20 * 4) / 30 = \$3.67$$

In addition to updating the inventory file, your program should produce the following report to serve as an audit trail of the updating. Note that if there is an error in an item number in CSRCVP, so that a corresponding item does not exist in CSINVP, the report should note that fact by printing two special lines, as shown. The second line contains an

```
              1         2         3         4         5         6         7         8         9
   12345678901234567890123456789012345678901234567890123456789012345678901234567890123456789 0
 1  XX/XX/XX              Compusell Inventory Update Report            PAGE XXØX
 2                          Received Goods Processed
 3
 4 Supplier    Item    Qty    New Qty  Previous          New         Previous      New Avg.
 5   ID         No     Rcvd   On Hand    Cost            Cost        Avg. Cost      Cost
 6
 7 XXXXXXXX  XXXXXX   XXØX     XXØX    X,XXØ.XX       X,XXØ.XX       X,XXØ.XX      X,XXØ.XX
 8 XXXXXXXX  XXXXXX   XXØX     XXØX    X,XXØ.XX       X,XXØ.XX       X,XXØ.XX      X,XXØ.XX
 9 XXXXXXXX   Item Not Found In Inventory File; Recheck Supplier ID
10         XXXXXXXXXXXXXXXXXXXXX  *** Record Not Processed ***
11 XXXXXXXX  XXXXXX   XXØX     XXØX    X,XXØ.XX       X,XXØ.XX       X,XXØ.XX      X,XXØ.XX
12
13 Total Records Processed XØX
14 Total Error Records     XØX
15
```

image of the problem record from CSRCVP. This report requires Total lines for the number of records processed and the total number of records in Error.

4. Wexler University wants you to write a program that will generate a transcript, shown below, of completed courses for each student in the transcript request file, WUTRANSP. The program will also require the use of the student master file (WUSTDP), the course file (WUCRSP), and the earned credits file (WUCRDP). Appendix F describes each of these files.

Courses should be listed in chronological order. Note that under SEMESTER, the school wants WIN to be printed for semester code 1, SUM for semester code 2, and FAL for semester code 3; the XX to the right of this code represents the year the course was taken.

```
         1         2         3         4         5         6         7         8
123456789012345678901234567890123456789012345678901234567890123456789012345678901234567890
1                         Wexler University Official Transcript
2                              Date Issued: XX/XX/XX
3
4 Student:    XXXXXXXXXXXXXXX XXXXXXXXXX    Date Admitted: XX/XX/XX
5             XXX-XX-XXXX                   Major: XXX
6
7             Credits Earned: XØX           Grade Point Average: Ø.XX
8             Graduated:  XX/XX/XX          Degree Granted: XXX
9
10   Course          Title                  Semester    Credits        Grade
11   XXXXXX    XXXXXXXXXXXXXXXXXXXXXXXXXX    XXX XX         X             XX
12   XXXXXX    XXXXXXXXXXXXXXXXXXXXXXXXXX    XXX XX         X             XX
13   XXXXXX    XXXXXXXXXXXXXXXXXXXXXXXXXX    XXX XX         X             XX
14
15
16                                          Total Credits  XØX
```

Note

The line showing graduation date and degree granted should be printed only if the student has, in fact, graduated, as signaled by nonblank values in those fields of the student's master record.

5. Wexler University wants you to write a program that will generate class lists to distribute to all instructors. Because these lists are sent to the individual instructors, begin each instructor's list on a new page. You will need to access data from several files to obtain the output: the current enrollment file (WUENRLP), the student master file (WUSTDP), the current sections file (WUSCTP), the course file (WUCRSP), and the instructor file (WUINSTP). Appendix F describes these data files. Follow your instructor's directions for accessing these files of data. Hint: You will need to use logical files to solve this problem. The class lists should be formatted as follows:

```
          1         2         3         4         5         6         7         8
 12345678901234567890123456789012345678901234567890123456789012345678901234567890
 1              Wexler University Class List 20XX
 2
 3 Instructor: XXXXXXXXXXXXXXX Dept: XXX
 4
 5    Dept   Course  Title                       Credits    Section
 6    XXX    XXX     XXXXXXXXXXXXXXXXXXXXXXXXXX      X       XXXXX
 7
 8           Student                Soc. Sec.    DCode    Major
 9           XXXXXXXXXXXXXXX XXXXXXXXXX   XXX-XX-XXXX    X       XXX
10           XXXXXXXXXXXXXXX XXXXXXXXXX   XXX-XX-XXXX    X       XXX
11           XXXXXXXXXXXXXXX XXXXXXXXXX   XXX-XX-XXXX    X       XXX
12
13              SECTION ENROLLMENT: XØX STUDENTS
14
15
16    Dept   Course  Title                       Credits    Section
17    XXX    XXX     XXXXXXXXXXXXXXXXXXXXXXXXXX      X       XXXXX
18
19           Student                Soc. Sec.    DCode    Major
20           XXXXXXXXXXXXXXX XXXXXXXXXX   XXX-XX-XXXX    X       XXX
21           XXXXXXXXXXXXXXX XXXXXXXXXX   XXX-XX-XXXX    X       XXX
22           XXXXXXXXXXXXXXX XXXXXXXXXX   XXX-XX-XXXX    X       XXX
23           XXXXXXXXXXXXXXX XXXXXXXXXX   XXX-XX-XXXX    X       XXX
24
25              Section Enrollment: XØX Students
```

6. GTC has converted to a new computer system. This system requires that all text fields in the Customer Master file be in proper case. Write a program to convert the following fields in the file GTCSTP. You learned how to manipulate strings in Chapter 6, and this program requires you to update the GTCSTP file.

Field name	Current contents	After conversion
CFNAME	AMY	Amy
CLNAME	GRASHUIS	Grashuis
CSTRET	1212 35TH ST.	1212 35th St.
CCITY	SWAMP HOLLAR	Swamp Hollar

7. CompuSell has a business partner that will require a copy of its Customer Master file. This company has specified the requirements for this file. Examples of these requirements are shown in the table below. Write a program that will read the CSCSTP file and output the following fields to the file CSCSTPA. The date format will change (Chapter 7) and the BALDUE field will be padded with '*' (Chapter 6). It will be necessary to create the CSCSTPA file. Note - the field types of the file CSCSTPA will differ from the CSCSTP.

Field name	Current contents	After conversion
CUSTNO	100001	10-0001
CLNAME	NARIZA	Nariza
CFNAME	ABDUL HALIM	Abdul Halim
CSTREET	5652 N. 46TH ST.	5652 N. 46th St.
CCITY	KALAMAZOO	Kalamazoo
CSTATE	MI	MI
CZIP	490080000	49008-0000
CPHONE	6161254115	616-125-4115
ORDDAT	1211997	19971211
BALDUE	0	******.*

Chapter 11

Writing Interactive Applications

Chapter Overview
In this chapter, you will learn how to define display files and how to use them to develop interactive applications.

Batch and Interactive Programs

So far, the programs you have written were designed to run in batch. In **batch processing**, once a program begins to run, it continues to execute instructions without human intervention or control. Most batch applications in the business environment involve processing one or more transaction files sequentially; the programs end when the transaction files reach end of file.

Interactive applications, in contrast, are user driven. As the program runs, a user at a workstation interacts with the computer—selecting options from menus, entering data, responding to prompts, and so on. The sequence of instructions the program executes is determined in part by the user; the program continues until the user signals that he or she is ready to quit.

This dialogue between the user and the computer is mediated through what i5/OS calls display files. **Display files** define the screens that the program presents as it runs. Display files allow values keyed by the user in response to the screen to be input as data to the program. Thus, display files serve as the mechanism that lets the user and program interact.

Display Files

You define display files externally to the program that uses them. The procedure for creating a display file is similar to the procedure followed to create a physical or logical file. You code display files using Data Description Specifications (DDS), enter the specifications using an editor to create a source member (with type DSPF), and then compile the source code to create an object; the command to compile display file source is CRTDSPF (Create Display File). IBM also provides utilities—**Screen Design Aid (SDA)** and **CODE Designer**—that automatically generate the DDS source code as you design and create display screens in an interactive environment.

Just like database and printer file definitions, display file definitions include entries at one of three levels: file, record, or field-level. File-level entries appear at the very beginning of the definition and apply to all the record formats within the file. Record-level entries are associated with a single record format (usually a single screen). Field-level entries are coded for specific fields or constants within a record format.

Each record format defines what is written to or read from the workstation in a single input/output (I/O) operation. On an output operation, the record may fill an entire screen with prompts and/or values; on an input operation, the record may read several values keyed from the workstation. Unless you make special provisions, only one screen is displayed at a time. When a different record format is written, the first screen is erased before the second one is shown.

As an introduction to DDS coding for display files, consider the following situation. A school identifies each of its semester offerings through a section number. For each section, the school stores information about the course with which this section is associated, the days and time it meets, the assigned room, the section enrollment, and the instructor. This data is stored in file Sections; its physical file definition is shown on the following page.

```
*.. 1 ...+... 2 ...+... 3 ...+... 4 ...+... 5 ...+... 6 ...+... 7 ...+... 8
A..........T.Name++++++RLen++TDcB......Functions++++++++++++++++++++++++++++
 * Physical file SECTIONS definition
A          R SECREC
A            SECTNO         5              TEXT('Section number')
A            DAYS           3              TEXT('Days class meets')
A            BEGTIME        4  Ø           TEXT('Time class starts')
A            ROOM           4  Ø           TEXT('Classroom')
A            ENROLL         3  Ø           TEXT('Current enrollment')
A            INSTR         15              TEXT('Instructor')
A            COURSE         6              TEXT('Course identifier')
A          K SECTNO
```

The school wants a simple online inquiry program that will let a user enter a section number and then display information about that section. The application displays the following input, or entry, screen:

```
                    Section Inquiry
    Type value, then Enter.

        Section number . . _____


    F3=Exit
```

The DDS of the display file record format needed to produce the above screen is shown below.

```
*.. 1 ...+... 2 ...+... 3 ...+... 4 ...+... 5 ...+... 6 ...+... 7 ...+... 8
AANØ1NØ2NØ3T.Name++++++RLen++TDcBLinPosFunctions++++++++++++++++++++++++++++
A          R SECT1
A                                         CAØ3(Ø3 'F3=Exit')
A                                      1 28'Section Inquiry'
A                                      3  2'Type value, then Enter.'
A                                      5  5'Section number . .'
A            SECTION        5A  I  5 24
A                                     23  2'F3=Exit'
```

Notice that each record format begins with an identifier, an R in position 17, followed by a name for that format—in this case, SECT1—beginning in position 19 (*Name++++++*). Below the record format line appear all the fields and literals that are to make up the format. You must indicate the location of each literal and field on this screen by specifying the screen line on which the literal or field is to appear (in positions 39–41, Lin) as well as its starting column position within that line (in positions 42–44, Pos). You code the literals themselves, such as 'Section Inquiry', in the Functions area, positions 45–80 of the DDS line. You must enclose them in apostrophes (').

You enter field names left-adjusted in positions 19–28. Each field needs an assigned usage, which you code in position 38 (*labeled B*). Usage codes include I for input, O for output, or B for both input and output. SECTION, the only field in the sample definition, is an input field because its value is to be entered by the user and read by (input to) the program. Its usage code is therefore I.

You must further define each field by specifying its length in positions 30–34 (*Len++*), data type in position 35 (*T*), and—for numeric fields—number of decimal positions in positions 36–37 (*Dc*).

For display files, column 35 is actually more appropriately called "data type/keyboard shift" because it allows many more possible values than are permitted for field definitions of physical files. These additional values affect the **keyboard shift attribute** of different workstations to limit what characters users can enter. Although a complete description of allowable values is beyond the scope of this text, the following table describes four commonly used values.

Keyboard shift value	Description
A (Alphanumeric shift)	Used for character fields; puts keyboard in lower shift; lets user enter any character
X (Alphabetic only)	Used for character fields; lets user enter only A–Z, commas, periods, dashes, and spaces; sends lowercase letters as upper case
S (Signed numeric)	Used for numeric fields; lets user enter digits 0–9 but no signs; uses Field- key for entering negative values
Y (Numeric only)	Used for numeric fields; lets the user enter digits 0–9, plus or minus signs, periods, commas, and spaces

One very important distinction between keyboard shift values S and Y is that Y lets you associate edit codes and edit words with the field, while S does not.

Because our sample application treats SECTION as a character field, a decimal position entry is not appropriate. The type is A, or character. Because A is the default type for character fields, we could have omitted the A. The default type for numeric fields is S unless you associate an edit code or word with the field; in that case, the system assumes a default type value of Y.

The line below the record format definition, CA03(03 'F3 = Exit'), establishes a connection between function key F3 and the 03 indicator. You haven't used indicators much previously in this text. The need for them is rapidly disappearing from RPG IV, but an indicator is still the primary means by which a DDS display file communicates conditions with an RPG program. When you code interactive applications, indicators communicate between the screen and the program that uses the screen. Control generally returns from the screen to the program when the user presses the Enter key or a function key that has been assigned a special meaning. In this screen, for instance, the user is prompted to press F3 to exit the program. But because you cannot reference the function key directly within an RPG IV program, an indicator must serve as a mediator.

The DDS line CA03(03 'F3 = Exit') accomplishes three things. First, the CA03 portion establishes F3 as a valid command key in this application; only those function keys explicitly referenced within the DDS are valid, or enabled, during program execution. Second, the 03 within the parentheses associates indicator 03 with F3 so that when F3 is pressed, indicator 03 is turned on. Although you can associate any indicator (01–99) with any function key, it makes good programming sense to associate a function key with its corresponding numeric indicator to avoid confusion. Last, by referencing the function key as CA (Command Attention) rather than CF (Command Function), the code is saying to return control to the program without the input data values (if any) that the user has just entered. If the line were coded CF03(03 'F3 = Exit'), control would return to the program with the input data.

The information within apostrophes—'F3 = Exit'—serves only as documentation. You could omit it (e.g., code only CA03(03)) without affecting how the screen functions. Good programming practice, however, suggests including such documentation.

We can now look at the design of the second screen the application needs. It's an information screen, or panel, used to display the requested information. The specific values shown give you a sense of what the screen might look like when the program is running.

```
         Section Information

Section number . . . . . . 12435
Course . . . . . . . . . . BIS350
Instructor . . . . . . . . Johnson
Room . . . . . . . . . . . 1120
Meets on days  . . . . . . MWF
Starting time  . . . . . . 10:30
Enrollment . . . . . . . . 36




Press Enter to continue.

F3=Exit  F12=Cancel
```

This screen will require a second record format within the display file. The DDS for this record format is:

```
*.. 1 ...+... 2 ...+... 3 ...+... 4 ...+... 5 ...+... 6 ...+... 7 ...+... 8
AAN01N02N03T.Name++++++RLen++TDcBLinPosFunctions++++++++++++++++++++++++++++++
A                                         REF(SECTIONS)
A           R SECT2
A                                         CA03(03 'F3=Exit')
A                                         CA12(12 'F12=Cancel')
A                                     1 10'Section Information'
A                                     3  2'Section number . . . . . . .'
A             SECTNO    R        O    3 29
A                                     4  2'Course . . . . . . . . . .'
A             COURSE    R        O    4 29
A                                     5  2'Instructor . . . . . . . .'
A             INSTR     R        O    5 29
A                                     6  2'Room . . . . . . . . . . .'
A             ROOM      R        O    6 29
A                                     7  2'Meets on days  . . . . . .'
A             DAYS      R        O    7 29
A                                     8  2'Starting time  . . . . . .'
A             BEGTIME   R        O    8 29
A                                     9  2'Enrollment . . . . . . . .'
A             ENROLL    R        O    9 29
A                                    21  2'Press Enter to continue.'
A                                    23  2'F3=Exit'
A                                    23 11'F12=Cancel'
```

This code represents a "bare bones" record format to describe the screen. Note that the fields represented in SECT2 are given an O, for Output, usage. That's because their values are going to be sent from the program to the screen. Instead of including length and decimal position entries, these field entries contain an R in position 29. This R (for Reference) signals that the fields are defined elsewhere and that their definitions can be obtained from that source. The source, in this case, is the file SECTIONS, as indicated by the first line of the DDS, which specifies keyword REF followed by the file name in parentheses. REF is a file-level keyword that should appear at the beginning of the DDS, before any record format definitions.

If you define a field through referencing, and if the referenced database field includes an edit code or edit word associated with it in the database file, that editing is automatically incorporated into the display file. (If the referenced field is unedited, or if the field is defined within the display file itself, you can add editing within the display file; we discuss how to do this later in this chapter.)

Notice that record format SECT2 enables function key F12 as well as F3. Generally accepted iSeries screen design standards use F12, Cancel, to signal that the user wants to back up to the previous screen, while F3, Exit, means to exit the entire application.

Putting the two format definitions together completes the DDS for the display file, called SECTINQR. We've added one file-level keyword, INDARA, to the DDS. INDARA organizes all the indicators that the display file uses into relative positions in a 99-byte data structure—indicator 03 in position 3, indicator 12 in position 12, and so on. We'll use this data structure in the RPG IV program to avoid referring to numbered indicators; instead, we'll be able to assign them meaningful names.

```
*.. 1 ...+... 2 ...+... 3 ...+... 4 ...+... 5 ...+... 6 ...+... 7 ...+... 8
AAN01N02N03T.Name+++++RLen++TDcBLinPosFunctions++++++++++++++++++++++++++++
 * Display file SECTINQR, containing two record formats
A                                          REF(SECTIONS)
A                                          INDARA
A           R SECT1
A                                          CA03(03 'F3=Exit')
A                                       1 28'Section Inquiry'
A                                       3  2'Type value, then Enter.'
A                                       5  5'Section number . .'
A             SECTION        5A  I      5 24
A                                      23  2'F3=Exit'
A           R SECT2
A                                          CA03(03 'F3=Exit')
A                                          CA12(12 'F12=Cancel')
A                                       1 10'Section Information'
A                                       3  2'Section number . . . . . . .'
A             SECTNO         R       O  3 29
A                                       4  2'Course . . . . . . . . . .'
A             COURSE         R       O  4 29
A                                       5  2'Instructor . . . . . . . .'
A             INSTR          R       O  5 29
A                                       6  2'Room . . . . . . . . . . .'
A             ROOM           R       O  6 29
A                                       7  2'Meets on days  . . . . . .'
A             DAYS           R       O  7 29
A                                       8  2'Starting time  . . . . . .'
A             BEGTIME        R       O  8 29
A                                       9  2'Enrollment . . . . . . . .'
A             ENROLL         R       O  9 29
A                                      21  2'Press Enter to continue.'
A                                      23  2'F3=Exit'
A                                      23 11'F12=Cancel'
```

Before looking at some of the many additional features available for defining display files, let's develop the section inquiry program to see how display files are used in interactive programs. Recall that the user wants to enter a section number to request section information from the Sections file. The program should display the retrieved information on the screen. The user can then enter another section number or signal that he or she is finished by pressing F3.

In writing the program, you must define display file Sectinqr, like any other kind of file, in the File specifications. Display files are full procedural, externally described files. However, because the concept of "key" is not applicable to this kind of file, you leave position 34 blank. What about type (position 17)? You have worked with input files (I), output files (O), and update files (U). Display files represent a new type: combined, or C. A **combined file** supports both input and output, but as independent operations. You cannot update a combined file.

Next, the device for display files is Workstn. Finally, we'll code the Indds keyword, which instructs RPG to store the indicators passed to and from this display file in the data structure named Indicators; we'll discuss this data structure a little later. The following code shows the complete File specifications for the section inquiry program.

```
*.. 1 ...+... 2 ...+... 3 ...+... 4 ...+... 5 ...+... 6 ...+... 7 ...+... 8
FFilename++IPEASFRLen+LKLen+AIDevice+.Keywords++++++++++++++++++++++++++++++++
FSections  IF   E          K Disk
FSectinqr  CF   E            Workstn Indds(Indicators)
```

Because both files are externally described, the program will have no Input specifications, nor Output specifications for that matter. The only part of the program left to code is the Calculation specifications. Before we jump into this coding, however, it pays first to think through the logic of a solution. Interactive programs are extremely prone to "spaghetti coding," primarily because the flow of control is less straightforward—depending on which function key a user presses, you may need to repeat, back up, or early exit out of different routines.

The present program will need to loop until the user presses F3 in response to either screen 1 or screen 2. If the user presses F12 at screen 2 to back up, that effectively is the same in this program as hitting the Enter key because in both cases the user should next see screen 1 again.

A rough solution written in pseudocode would look like the following:

```
While user wants to continue (no Exit)
    Display first screen
    Obtain user's response to the screen
    If user wants to continue (no Exit)
        Random read section file to get section information
        If record found
            Display second screen
            Obtain user's response
        Endif
    Endif
Endwhile
```

You can easily develop the RPG IV calculations from the pseudocode once you know how to send screens of data to the user and read user input.

Performing Screen I/O

The allowable operations for screen I/O are **Write, Read,** and **Exfmt (Execute Format)**. All three operations require an operand to designate a record format name.

The Write operation displays a screen and returns control to the program without waiting for user input. A subsequent Read operation sends control to the currently displayed screen, waits for the end of user input (signaled by the user's pressing either the Enter key or any other enabled special key), and returns control to the program.

The Exfmt operation combines the features of Write and Read; it first writes a record to the screen and then waits for user input to that screen. When the user has finished inputting, the system reads the data back from the screen and returns control to the program. Because in most screen I/O you want to display some information and then wait for a user response, Exfmt is the operation you will use most frequently in your interactive programs.

The following code shows an RPG IV implementation of the pseudocode solution to the section inquiry problem.

```
/Free
   Dow Not *In03;
     Exfmt Sect1;
     If Not *In03;
        Chain Section Sections;
        If %Found(Sections);
           Exfmt Sect2;
        Endif;
     Endif;
   Enddo;

   *Inlr = *On;
   Return;
/End-Free
```

In this code, indicator 03, which is turned on when the user presses F3, controls the main program loop. Because the user can signal "Exit" at screen SECT1, the calculations need an If operation following the return from the SECT1 screen to check for this possibility. Because the user may have keyed in a wrong section number, which would cause the Chain operation to fail, the program executes the information panel, SECT2, only if the chaining found a record.

Using an Indicator Data Structure

We can eliminate the somewhat obscure reference to *In03 in the above code by including a definition for a special data structure called an **indicator data structure**. You'll recall that the Indara keyword in the DDS for the display file instructed the system to organize all the display file's indicators into a 99-byte data area. In the RPG IV program, the File specification for the display file included the Indds keyword; this keyword moves the indicator area from DDS into the data structure named as the keyword value. Given these two requirements (the INDARA keyword in DDS and the Indds keyword in the File specification), we can then include a Definition specification for the data structure that will contain the indicators. The code for this definition is shown here:

```
*.. 1 ...+... 2 ...+.... 3 ...+... 4 ...+... 5 ...+... 6 ...+... 7 ...+... 8
DName++++++++++ETDsFrom+++To/L+++IDc.Keywords++++++++++++++++++++++++++++++++
   // Indicator data structure
D Indicators      DS                  99
D  Exit                          3      3N
D  Cancel                       12     12N
```

In this definition, position 3 in the data structure corresponds to *In03, and position 12 corresponds to *In12; these positions are assigned to indicator (data type N) variables named Exit and Cancel, respectively. Note that this definition uses From and To positions to specify exact positions of fields within the data structure, instead of field length. In defining this special data structure, this notation serves us well in describing which indicator we are naming and in letting us skip over unused portions of the indicator data structure. Once we've included this definition, we'll refer to Exit instead of *In03 in the RPG IV code, making the program more readable:

```
Dow Not Exit;
  Exfmt Sect1;
  If Not Exit;
    Chain Section Sections;
    If %Found(Sections);
      Exfmt Sect2;
    Endif;
  Endif;
Enddo;

*Inlr = *On;
Return;
```

Caution
If you specify an Indds keyword in a File specification, you can no longer refer to the indicators in that file using the *In notation. You must use the indicator data structure to communicate the indicator state, and you must refer to the indicators by their subfield names in the data structure. If your program refers to *In03, that indicator state will not be communicated with the DDS; you must use the named variable (Exit in the above example) to set indicator 03 in the DDS.

Additional DDS Keywords
Although the DDS definition for the previous example would work, it represents a minimalist approach to screen design—it contains no "bells and whistles." More important, perhaps, as the DDS is presently coded, numeric fields would be displayed without editing, and information about a possible important program event—a section not found in the file—is not conveyed to the user. You can include these and other kinds of special effects by using keywords.

You have already been introduced to three keywords used with display files (CA*nn*, CF*nn*, and REF). DDS includes a long list of permissible keywords for display files to let you change a screen's appearance or the interaction between screen and user. This section discusses some of the major keywords. Refer to IBM's manual *DDS Reference: Display Files* for more detail.

Keywords are always coded in positions 45–80 (the Functions area) of the DDS line. Keywords apply at a file, record, or field-level. Some keywords can be used with two levels, while others are appropriate to just one level. Where you code the keyword determines the level with which the keyword is associated.

File-Level Keywords
File-level keywords must always appear as the first lines in the DDS, before any record format information. If you have several file-level keywords, the order in which you code them does not matter. You have already encountered two file-level keywords: REF, used to indicate a database file that contains definitions of fields used in the screen, and INDARA, used to organize indicators into a 99-byte data structure.

The CA*nn* (Command Attention) and CF*nn* (Command Function) keywords, which we've already discussed, enable the use of function keys and associate the keys with program indicators.

You can use as many function keys as are appropriate to your application by including a CA*nn* or CF*nn* keyword for each one.

If you code these keywords at a file level, they apply to all the record formats within the file. Alternatively, you can associate them with individual record formats, as we did in the section inquiry example; in that case, the keys are valid only during input operations for the screen or screens with which they are associated.

A commonly used file-level keyword is PRINT. This keyword enables the Print key during the interactive application to let the user print the current screen. Without this keyword, the Print key is disabled. You can also use PRINT as a record-level keyword to enable the key for some screens but not others.

Keyword MSGLOC (Message Location) specifies the position of the message line for error and other messages. The keyword's format is

```
MSGLOC(line)
```

Without this keyword, the message line position defaults to the last screen line (line 24 on a standard 24 x 80 screen).

Keyword VLDCMDKEY (Valid Command Key) is a file or record-level keyword used to turn on an indicator when the user presses *any* valid (enabled) command key. Note that command keys include any special key, such as the Roll up key, in addition to function keys. The format for this keyword is

```
VLDCMDKEY(indicator ['text'])
```

The indicator can be any numbered indicator (01–99); the text description is optional and serves only as documentation.

VLDCMDKEY is useful because it lets the program differentiate between control returned as a result of the Enter key and control returned by any other key. You often need to set up separate logic branches based on this distinction.

Record-Level Keywords

Record-level keywords appear on the line on which the record format is named and/or on lines immediately following that line, preceding any field or literal definition. These kinds of keywords apply only to the screen with which they are associated. They do not carry over to or influence other record formats defined within the file.

You can use keywords CA*nn*, CF*nn*, PRINT, and VLDCMDKEY as record-level keywords as well as file-level keywords. Keyword BLINK, on the other hand, is strictly a record-level keyword. BLINK causes the cursor to blink during the display of the record format with which it is associated.

OVERLAY is a record-level keyword that specifies that the record format be displayed without clearing the previous display. OVERLAY works only when the record formats involved do not overlap lines on the screen.

The following DDS demonstrates the use of record-level keywords.

```
*.. 1 ...+... 2 ...+... 3 ...+... 4 ...+... 5 ...+... 6 ...+... 7 ...+... 8
AAN01N02N03T.Name+++++RLen++TDcBLinPosFunctions+++++++++++++++++++++++++++++
 * Sample DDS showing record level keywords
A          R SAMPLE                     PRINT
A                                       CA03(03 'F3=Exit')
A                                       CA12(12 'F12=Cancel')
A                                       VLDCMDKEY(30 'Any valid key')
A                                       OVERLAY
```

Field-Level Keywords

A **field-level keyword** applies only to the specific field with which it is associated. A field can have several keywords. The first keyword appears on the same line as the field definition or on the line immediately following the definition. You can code additional keywords on the same line (provided there is room) or on successive lines. All keywords for a field must be coded before the next field definition line.

Two field-level keywords control the format of numeric output fields on the display: **EDTCDE (Edit Code)** and **EDTWRD (Edit Word)**. Recall that only numerically defined fields can be edited and that the field type specification in column 35 of the DDS must be Y or blank to use editing for a displayed field.

Display file edit codes and edit words match those used within RPG IV itself and have the same meaning as in RPG IV. EDTCDE's format is

```
EDTCDE(editcode [*|$])
```

The parentheses should contain a valid edit code, such as 1, optionally followed by a single asterisk (*) to provide asterisk protection or a single dollar sign ($) to supply a floating dollar sign.

The format for EDTWRD is

```
EDTWRD('editword')
```

To review RPG IV edit words and edit codes, see Chapter 2.

The following DDS sample shows the use of keywords EDTWRD and EDTCDE. Note that because editing is a concept related to output, the use of EDTWRD and EDTCDE is appropriate for fields defined for output usage or fields used for both input and output, but not for fields defined to be used for input only.

```
*.. 1 ...+... 2 ...+... 3 ...+... 4 ...+... 5 ...+... 6 ...+... 7 ...+... 8
AAN01N02N03T.Name+++++RLen++TDcBLinPosFunctions+++++++++++++++++++++++++++++
 * Sample DDS showing the use of editing keywords
A          R SAMPLE
A            SOCSEC      9Y 00  4 10EDTWRD('   -   -    ')
A            NAME        20  0  5 10
A            BILLDATE    6Y 00  6 10EDTCDE(Y)
A            AMOUNTDUE   7Y 20  7 10EDTCDE(1 $)
```

Another field-level keyword, **DSPATR (Display Attribute),** determines the appearance of fields on the screen. You can use DSPATR more than once for a given field, and you can include more than one attribute with the same keyword. The keyword is followed by parentheses containing the codes of the desired attributes. The following attributes can be assigned to all types of fields (input, output, or both):

Attribute	Meaning
BL	Blinking field
CS	Column separator (a vertical bar separating each position within a field)
HI	High intensity
ND	Nondisplay (keyed characters don't appear on screen)
PC	Position cursor (position cursor to the first character of this field)
RI	Reverse image
UL	Underline

The following code illustrates the use of **display attributes**.

```
*.. 1 ...+... 2 ...+... 3 ...+... 4 ...+... 5 ...+... 6 ...+... 7 ...+... 8
AAN01N02N03T.Name++++++RLen++TDcBLinPosFunctions+++++++++++++++++++++++++++++
 * Sample DDS illustrating display attributes
A          R SAMPLE
A            SOCSEC        9Y 00  4 10DSPATR(ND)
A                                    DSPATR(UL)
A            NAME         20  0  5 10DSPATR(BL UL)
A            BILLDATE      6Y 00  6 10EDTCDE(Y)
A                                    DSPATR(RI)
A                                    DSPATR(PC HI BL)
```

Caution

This sample is not intended to set a style standard to be followed. A screen with so many bells and whistles would be distracting to the user. In general, you should use such features sparingly and consistently to draw attention to specific fields on the screen or to problems with which the user must deal.

Another important set of field-level keywords concerns **data validation**. Every programmer should recognize the extreme importance of preventing invalid data from entering the system; corrupt data files can cause abnormal endings or incorrect processing. Although no way exists to completely ensure that values a user enters are correct, by validating data as tightly as possible, you can eliminate some kinds of errors.

The four major keywords used for validating user entry are

- VALUES
- RANGE
- COMP
- CHECK

Each of these keywords lets you place restrictions on what the user can enter. Violating these restrictions causes the system to display an appropriate error message on the message line and to display the field in reverse image to force the user to change the entered value.

The *VALUES* keyword lets you specify the exact valid values allowed for a field. The keyword format is

```
VALUES(value1 value2 . . .)
```

Up to 100 values can be entered. You must enclose character values within apostrophes.

The **RANGE** keyword lets you specify a range within which the user's entry must fall to be considered valid. The format for this keyword is

```
RANGE(lowvalue highvalue)
```

If you use RANGE with character fields, the low and high values must each be enclosed in apostrophes. The valid range includes the low and high values, so the entered value must be greater than or equal to the low value and less than or equal to the high value to be considered valid.

The **COMP** keyword lets you specify a relational comparison to be made with the user's entered value to determine validity. This keyword's format is

```
COMP(relational-operator value)
```

The relational operator can be one of the following:

Operator	Meaning
LT	Less than
LE	Less than or equal to
EQ	Equal to
GE	Greater than or equal to
GT	Greater than
NL	Not less than
NE	Not equal to
NG	Not greater than

The **CHECK** keyword is a field-level keyword that you can use for validity checking. Its format is

CHECK(*code* [. . .])

That is, you can associate one or more validity checking codes with a single CHECK entry. Some of these validity codes are ME (Mandatory Enter), MF (Mandatory Fill), and AB (Allow Blank).

For Mandatory Enter fields, the user must enter at least one character of data (the character could be a blank); the user cannot simply bypass the field. Mandatory Fill specifies that each position in the field have a character in it. (Again, a blank is considered a character.) Allow Blank provides the user with an override option for a field that fails a validity check. For example, if a field has a VALUES keyword associated with it and the user is uncertain which value is appropriate to the record he or she is entering, the user can simply enter blanks and the value will be accepted. The following DDS demonstrates the use of keywords for data validation.

```
*.. 1 ...+... 2 ...+.... 3 ...+... 4 ...+... 5 ...+... 6 ...+... 7 ...+... 8
AAN01N02N03T.Name++++++RLen++TDcBLinPosFunctions++++++++++++++++++++++++++++++
 * Sample DDS illustrating the use of keywords for data validation
A          R SAMPLE
A            DEPT        3   I  4 10VALUES('CIS' 'DPR' 'MGT')
A                                  CHECK(MF AB)
A            MONTH       2Y 0I  6 10RANGE(1 12)
A            REGHOURS    3Y 1I  7 10COMP(LE 40)
```

The CHECK keyword also supports parameter values concerned with functions other than validity checking. CHECK(LC), for example, lets the user enter lowercase (as well as uppercase) letters for character fields. Without this keyword, all user-entered alphabetic characters are returned to the program as upper case. You can use CHECK at a field, record, or file-level, depending on how broadly you want to enable lowercase data entry.

One field-level keyword of major importance is **ERRMSG** (Error Message). When an error message is in effect for a field, the message is displayed on the message line of the screen, and the field with which the message is associated appears on the screen in reverse image. The format for the ERRMSG keyword is

ERRMSG('*message-text*' [*indicator*])

If you specify an indicator, the indicator is turned off as part of the input operation that follows the display of the error message. Error messages are useful for conveying information about program processing problems to the user's screen.

Last, two field-level keywords serve as built in variables to display the date and/or time on the screen. **TIME**, entered as a keyword along with screen line and column position values, causes the system time to be displayed in *hhmmss* format (hours, minutes, and seconds). The time is displayed with the default edit word '0b:bb:bb' unless you specify an alternate display format. You can display the current date by using keyword **DATE** along with line and column entries. DATE appears as a six-position, unedited value unless you associate an edit code or word with it.

```
*.. 1 ...+... 2 ...+... 3 ...+... 4 ...+... 5 ...+... 6 ...+... 7 ...+... 8
AAN01N02N03T.Name++++++RLen++TDcBLinPosFunctions++++++++++++++++++++++++++++
 * Sample DDS illustrating the use of DATE and TIME keywords
A           R SAMPLE
A                                  1  5TIME
A                                  1  60DATE EDTCDE(Y)
```

Conditioning Indicators

So far, we've discussed field-level keywords as though they are always in effect. However, if this were the case, many would be of little value. Why, for instance, would you want an error message to be displayed each time a field appears on the screen? In fact, you can condition most individual field-level keywords on one or more indicators. The status of these indicators when the screen is displayed determines whether the keywords are in effect. In fact, not only can you condition keywords, but you can also associate fields and literals with indicators to control whether the field or literal appears on the screen.

Moreover, you can use multiple indicators, in AND and/or in OR relationships, to condition screen events. You can include up to three indicators on a DDS line; these indicators are in an AND relationship with one another, such that all the indicators on the line need to be on for the event they are conditioning to occur. If you need to use more than three indicators to control an event, you can signal an AND by coding A in position 7 of the DDS line.

If you want an event to occur if one of several indicators is on (i.e., you want to express an OR relationship), code one indicator per line, with an O in position 7 of the second (and successive) lines. The keyword, field, or literal conditioned by these indicators should appear on the last line of the set.

```
*.. 1 ...+... 2 ...+... 3 ...+... 4 ...+... 5 ...+... 6 ...+... 7 ...+... 8
AAN01N02N03T.Name++++++RLen++TDcBLinPosFunctions++++++++++++++++++++++++++++
 * Sample DDS showing the use of indicators
A           R SAMPLE
A 10          FLDA         10   0   4 15
A N10         FLDB         12   0   4 30
A             FLDC          5   0   6  5
A 20 25                              DSPATR(HI)
A 30
AO 40                                DSPATR(UL)
A 10                             15  5'Indicator 10 is on'
```

The above code causes FLDA to be displayed if indicator 10 is on, while FLDB is displayed only if indicator 10 is off (signaled by the N in position 8). FLDC will always appear, but it will be displayed in high intensity only if indicators 20 and 25 are both on; it will be underlined if either indicator 30 or indicator 40 is on. The literal 'Indicator 10 is on' will be displayed only if indicator 10 is, in fact, on.

Because you can turn indicators on or off as part of your program logic, they provide a way for program events to control screen display. For example, in our sample program, if the user entered a section number that didn't exist in the SECTIONS file, it would be nice not only to return the user to the first screen but also to return with the erroneous section number displayed in reverse video, with the message "Section not found" shown at the bottom of the screen and with the cursor positioned on the field. We can easily cause this to happen by making a few changes in the first screen format. First we'll use the ERRMSG keyword to display a message when an unsuccessful Chain occurs; we'll use indicator 90 to condition the ERRMSG keyword, showing it only if *In90 is on.

```
*.. 1 ...+... 2 ...+... 3 ...+... 4 ...+... 5 ...+... 6 ...+... 7 ...+... 8
AAN01N02N03T.Name++++++RLen++TDcBLinPosFunctions+++++++++++++++++++++++++++++++
A* Display file SECTINQR, containing two record formats
A                                         REF(SECTIONS)
A                                         PRINT
A                                         INDARA
A            R SECT1
A                                         BLINK
A                                         CA03(03 'F3=Exit')
A                                    1 28'Section Inquiry'
A                                    3  2'Type value, then Enter.'
A                                    5  5'Section number . .'
A            SECTION        5A  B    5 24
A N90                                      DSPATR(HI UL)
A  90                                      ERRMSG('Section not found' 90)
A                                   23  2'F3=Exit'
A            R SECT2
A                                         CA03(03 'F3=Exit')
A                                         CA12(12 'F12=Cancel')
A                                    1 10'Section Information'
A                                    3  2'Section number . . . . . .'
A            SECTNO        R         0 3 29
A                                    4  2'Course . . . . . . . . . .'
A            COURSE        R         0 4 29
A                                    5  2'Instructor . . . . . . . .'
A            INSTR         R         0 5 29
A                                    6  2'Room . . . . . . . . . .'
A            ROOM          R         0 6 29EDTCDE(Z)
A                                    7  2'Meets on days . . . . . .'
A            DAYS          R         0 7 29
A                                    8  2'Starting time . . . . . .'
A            BEGTIME       R         0 8 29EDTWRD(' 0:  ')
A                                    9  2'Enrollment . . . . . . . .'
A            ENROLL        R         0 9 29EDTCDE(3)
A                                   21  2'Press Enter to continue.'
A                                   23  2'F3=Exit'
A                                   23 11'F12=Cancel'
```

Note that one of the changes includes changing the usage of field SECTION to B (both) so the erroneous section number will be returned to the screen. If indicator 90 is off, the field is underlined and shown in high intensity (bold). If 90 is on, the error message is displayed and the field appears in reverse image.

A few extra keywords give the display file more functionality: PRINT (to enable the Print key) and BLINK (to cause the cursor to blink).

The only additions to record format SECT2 were to add editing to fields ROOM, DAYS, and ENROLL to achieve the format shown in the sample screen given earlier in the chapter (page 284).

A few simple changes to the RPG IV program will enable it to display the error message if the Chain fails. First, we'll define position 90 in the Indicators data structure, to give it a name:

```
*.. 1 ...+... 2 ...+... 3 ...+... 4 ...+... 5 ...+... 6 ...+... 7 ...+... 8
DName+++++++++++ETDsFrom+++To/L+++IDc.Keywords++++++++++++++++++++++++++++++++
    // Indicator data structure
D Indicators      DS             99
D Exit                     3      3N
D Cancel                  12     12N
D Sectnotfnd             90     90N
```

Then, we'll make a simple change to the logic to support the Sectnotfnd field:

```
/Free
   Dow Not Exit;
     Exfmt Sect1;
     If Not Exit;
       Chain Section Sections;
       Sectnotfnd = Not %Found(Sections);
       If %Found(Sections);
         Exfmt Sect2;
       Endif;
     Endif;
   Enddo;
/End-Free
```

Because Sectnotfnd is an indicator, with a value of *On or *Off, we can simply use an assignment expression to move the result of the %Found function (also either *On or *Off) to Sectnotfnd and, consequently, to *In90.

Interactive File Maintenance

A common data processing task is **file maintenance**—that is, adding, deleting, and changing records in a company's database files. Over the past decade, programmers have implemented an increasing amount of such updating through interactive, rather than batch, processing.

In a typical update program, the user specifies the key of a record and signals whether that record is to be added, changed, or deleted. Because businesses typically want key field values to master records to be unique (e.g., they would not want the same customer number to be assigned to two customers), a user request to add a record with a key that matches the key of a record already in the file generally is handled as an error. Similarly, it is impossible to change or delete a record that does not exist in the file.

As a result, the first tasks of an update program are to accept the user's update option request (add, delete, or change) and the key of the record to be maintained and to check the file for the existence of a record with that key before giving the user the chance to actually enter data values.

A critical concern of interactive updates is how to detect invalid data entries to prevent corrupting the business's database files. The system offers three methods of safeguarding against invalid data:

- Using validation keywords within the database definitions themselves, provided those fields are displayed for input and reference back to the database file
- Including validation keywords within the display file
- Validating field values within the program, after they are read from the screen

The operating system handles some validation automatically for you. For example, the system will not let a user enter a nonnumeric value for a numerically defined field. Or, if you have specified type X for a character field, the system will permit alphabetic entries only. The use of validation keywords also automatically limits what the user can enter without the need for further programming on your part. For example, if you specify VALUES('A' 'C' 'D') for field CODE, attempts by the user to enter any value other than 'A', 'C' or 'D' will automatically cause an error message to appear on the bottom line of the screen and field CODE to be displayed in reverse video.

You should always validate your data as tightly as possible, given the nature of the data. For some fields (e.g., name), the best you can do is ensure that the user enters some value rather than skipping over the field; for other fields (e.g., gender code), you will be able to specify permissible values for the entered data. Never overlook validating data at any point where it enters the system.

To illustrate screen and program design for interactive updating, we will develop a program to update the university's SECTIONS file. To refresh your memory, the file definition is reproduced here:

```
*.. 1 ...+... 2 ...+... 3 ...+... 4 ...+... 5 ...+... 6 ...+... 7 ...+... 8
A..........T.Name++++++RLen++TDcB......Functions++++++++++++++++++++++++++++++
 * Physical file SECTIONS definition
A           R SECREC
A             SECTNO        5            TEXT('Section number')
A             DAYS          3            TEXT('Days class meets')
A             BEGTIME       4  Ø         TEXT('Time class starts')
A             ROOM          4  Ø         TEXT('Classroom')
A             ENROLL        3  Ø         TEXT('Current enrollment')
A             INSTR        15            TEXT('Instructor')
A             COURSE        6            TEXT('Course identifier')
A           K SECTNO
```

The first screen of the application is shown below. The user keys in a section number and an action code to specify whether he or she wants to add, change, or delete the section. If the user tries to enter an invalid action code, an error message is displayed. If the user enters a section with an action code inappropriate for that section—that is, tries to add a section already in the file or tries to change or delete a section not in the file—an appropriate error message appears on the screen.

```
                         Section File Maintenance

Type values, then Enter.

     Section number . .  _____
     Action code  . . .  _      A=Add
                                C=Change
                                D=Delete













 F3=Exit
```

If the user's entries are valid and appropriate, screen 2 is displayed, with blank fields if the user is in Add mode or with the field values from the selected record displayed if the mode is Change or Delete. A prompt appropriate to each mode appears at the bottom of the screen. Some data validation takes place as the user enters values. When the user presses Enter, the program performs the appropriate action and then returns the user to the first screen. If the user presses F12 at the second screen, no maintenance is done for that record, and the user is returned to the first screen. Pressing F3 at the second screen causes a program exit without maintenance of the last displayed data. The following screen illustrates the layout of screen 2.

```
                         Section File Maintenance        ADD
     Section number . . . . . . XXXXX
     Course . . . . . . . . . . XXXXXX
     Instructor . . . . . . . . XXXXXXXXXXXXXX
     Room . . . . . . . . . . . XXXX
     Meets on days  . . . . . . XXX
     Starting time  . . . . . . XX:XX
     Enrollment . . . . . . . . XXX










     Press Enter to add

     F3=Exit   F12=Cancel
```

The DDS for the display file, SECTMAIN, is coded as follows:

```
*.. 1 ...+... 2 ...+... 3 ...+... 4 ...+... 5 ...+... 6 ...+... 7 ...+... 8
AAN01N02N03T.Name++++++RLen++TDcBLinPosFunctions++++++++++++++++++++++++++++++
 * Display file SECTMAIN, used for interactively maintaining the
 * SECTIONS file
A                                           REF(SECTIONS)
A                                           PRINT
A                                           INDARA
A                                           CA03(03 'F3=Exit')
A                                           VLDCMDKEY(10)
A              R SCREEN1
A                                        1 28'Section File Maintenance'
A                                        3  2'Type values, then Enter.'
A                                        5  5'Section number . .'
A                SECTION       5    B    5 24
A 30
AO 31
AO 32
AO 91                                       DSPATR(PC)
A 30                                        ERRMSG('Record already exists' 30)
A 31                                        ERRMSG('No record for change' 31)
A 32                                        ERRMSG('No record for delete' 32)
A 91                                        ERRMSG('I/O error' 91)
A                                        6  5'Action code . . . .'
A                ACTION        1    I    6 24VALUES('A' 'C' 'D')
A                                        6 30'A=Add'
A                                        7 30'C=Change'
A                                        8 30'D=Delete'
A                                       24  2'F3=Exit'
A              R SCREEN2                     CA12(12 'F12=Cancel')
A                                        1 28'Section File Maintenance'
A                MODE          6    O    1 60DSPATR(HI)
A                                        3  2'Section number . . . . .'
A                SECTNO      R        O  3 29
A                                        4  2'Course . . . . . . . . . .'
A                COURSE      R        B  4 29
A 40                                        DSPATR(PR)
A                                        5  2'Instructor . . . . . . . . .'
A                INSTR       R        B  5 29
A 40                                        DSPATR(PR)
A                                        6  2'Room . . . . . . . . .'
A                ROOM        R        B  6 29EDTCDE(Z)
A 40                                        DSPATR(PR)
A                                        7  2'Meets on days  . . . . . .'
A                DAYS        R        B  7 29VALUES('MWF' 'TTH')
A 40                                        DSPATR(PR)
A                                        8  2'Starting time  . . . . . .'
A                BEGTIME     R        B  8 29EDTWRD(' 0:  ')
A 40                                        DSPATR(PR)
A                                        9  2'Enrollment . . . . . . . .'
A                ENROLL      R        B  9 29EDTCDE(3)
A 40                                        DSPATR(PR)
A                                       21  2'Press Enter to '
A                MODE2         6    O   21 17DSPATR(HI)
A                                       23  2'F3=Exit'
A                                       23 11'F12=Cancel'
```

This DDS contains one DSPATR entry you have not seen before: DSPATR(PR) protects input-capable fields (i.e., usage I or B) from input keying. Because you can condition display attributes with indicators, you can use this attribute to permit or prevent a user from keying a value into a field, depending on processing needs at that time. The maintenance program shown later in this chapter uses DSPATR(PR) to prevent the user from changing field values within a record when he or she has selected the delete option.

Notice in the above DDS for record format SCREEN2 that SECTNO is Output only to prevent the user from modifying that field. Also, record format SCREEN1 uses indicators to display error messages differentially, depending on processing outcomes within the program. Because SECTION should appear in reverse image with the cursor positioned to that field for any file error, DSPATR(PC) is conditioned by four indicators in an "OR" relation; if any one of the four indicators is on, the display attributes will be in effect. DSPATR(PR), or protected, is enabled for all SCREEN2 input-capable fields during deletion mode to prevent the user from changing these fields.

Before jumping into the RPG IV code required to implement this interactive application, let's work out the logic of what the application should do. Typically this "think before acting" approach to programming leads to more structured code. And remember, when coding for interactive applications, it is hard to resist falling into the GOTO habit. The pseudocode below illustrates the logic needed for this maintenance program. Notice that the pseudocode breaks the program into separate modules based on the function the code performs.

Program Mainline
While user wants to continue
   Display screen 1
   Read screen 1
   Select
      When user signals exit
         Leave
      When action is Add
         Do subroutine Addrecord
      When action is Change
         Do subroutine Chgrecord
      When action is Delete
         Do subroutine Dltrecord
   Endselect
Endwhile
End program

Subroutine Addrecord
Chain to Section file
If record found
   Set on error indicator (Adderror)
Else
   Zero and blank all record fields except section number
   Display screen 2
   Read screen 2
   If not valid command key
      Write record to file
   Endif
Endif
End subroutine

Subroutine Chgrecord
Chain to Section file
If record not found
   Set on error indicator (Chgerror)
Else
   Display screen 2
   Read screen 2
   If not valid command key
     Update record to file
   Endif
Endif
End subroutine

Subroutine Dltrecord
Chain to Section file
If record not found
   Set on error indicator (Dlterror)
Else
   Display screen 2
   Read screen 2
   If not valid command key
     Delete record from file
   Endif
Endif
End subroutine

Once you have the pseudocode worked out, coding the RPG IV is simple. In the following program, notice that indicators turned on within the program to control screen display may need to be turned off. Those indicators associated with error messages in the screen are set off automatically.

```
*.. 1 ...+... 2 ...+... 3 ...+... 4 ...+... 5 ...+... 6 ...+... 7 ...+... 8
  // **********************************************************
  // This program interactively maintains file SECTIONS.      *
  // **********************************************************

FSections  UF A E          K Disk
FSectmain  CF   E            Workstn Indds(Indicators)

  // ------------------------------------------------ Indicator data structure
D Indicators      DS
D  Exit                    3      3N
D  Cmdkeypressed          10     10N
D  Cancel                 12     12N
D  Adderror               30     30N
D  Chgerror               31     31N
D  Dlterror               32     32N
D  Protect                40     40N
```

continued...

continued...

```
/Free
   Dow Not Exit;
     Protect = *Off;
     Cancel = *Off;
     If Not Adderror And Not Chgerror And Not Dlterror;
       Section = *Blanks;
     Endif;

     Exfmt Screen1;

     Select;
       When Exit;
         Leave;
       When Cancel;
         Iter;
       When Action = 'A';
         Exsr Addrecord;
       When Action = 'C';
         Exsr Chgrecord;
       When Action = 'D';
         Exsr Dltrecord;
     Endsl;

   Enddo;

   *Inlr = *On;
   Return;

// ***************************************************************
//   Subroutine Addrecord: Processes an Add action request      *
// ***************************************************************
   Begsr Addrecord;
     Chain Section Sections;
     Adderror = %Found(Sections);   //Set Adderror If Record Already Exists

     If Not %Found(Sections);
       Mode = 'Add';
       Mode2 = 'add';
       Sectno = Section;
       Exsr Initial;
       Exfmt Screen2;

       If Not Cmdkeypressed;
         Write Secrec;
       Endif;

     Endif;

   Endsr;

// ***************************************************************
//   Subroutine Chgrecord: Processes a Change request           *
// ***************************************************************
   Begsr Chgrecord;
     Chain Section Sections;
     Chgerror = Not %Found(Sections);
```

continued...

continued...

```
        If %Found(Sections);
          Mode = 'Change';
          Mode2 = 'change';
          Exfmt Screen2;

          If Not Cmdkeypressed;
            Update Secrec;
          Endif;

        Endif;

      Endsr;

// ***********************************************************
//   Subroutine Dltrecord: Processes a Delete request        *
// ***********************************************************
   Begsr Dltrecord;
     Chain Section Sections;
     Dlterror = Not %Found(Sections);

     If %Found(Sections);
       Mode =  'Delete';
       Mode2 = 'delete';
       Protect = *On;
       Exfmt Screen2;

       If Not Cmdkeypressed;
         Delete Secrec;
       Endif;

     Endif;

   Endsr;

// ***********************************************************
//   Subroutine Initial: Initializes record fields to blanks *
//   and zeros preparatory to an Add.                        *
// ***********************************************************
   Begsr Initial;
     Course = *Blanks;
     Instr = *Blanks;
     Room = *Zeros;
     Days = *Blanks;
     Begtime = *Zeros;
     Enroll = *Zeros;
   Endsr;
/End-Free
```

Many RPG IV programmers feel that the fields used in the display file should not be the same as the database fields, and in some applications, depending on the program design, such separate definition in fact may be necessary to prevent losing values input by the user (or read from the database). To implement this approach, simply define the display file fields independently, giving them new names. Then, in your RPG IV program, add two subroutines—one that assigns the screen field values to the database fields and one that does the reverse (assigns the database fields to the screen fields). Before you add or update a record, execute the subroutine that assigns the screen fields to the database fields. Before you display the data entry screen for a change or delete, execute the subroutine that assigns the database fields to the screen fields.

Screen Design and CUA

The screens illustrated in this chapter are based on a set of design standards called **Common User Access (CUA)**. IBM developed and promotes CUA as a way of standardizing user interfaces across platforms. All the iSeries screens follow these standards.

Screens can be classified into one of four panel types:

- menu
- list
- entry
- information

Under CUA, all panels have the same general layout: a panel title on the first screen line, an optional information area, an instruction area, a panel body area (where either the menu, list, data entry fields, or informational output occurs), and, at the bottom of the screen, a command area, a list of function keys, and a message line. The following screen illustrates the layout for these types of panels.

```
Panel ID                        Panel Title

   Optional information area (on menu, list, or info)
     and/or controlling fields for list panel

   Instruction area (on menu, entry, or list)

   Panel body area
      -    Menu choices on menu panel
      -    List area on list panel
      -    Entry prompts on entry panel
      -    Information prompts on information panel




   Optional command area
   Function key area
   Message area
```

CUA provides specific guidelines for row and column placement of screen items, vertical alignment of screen columns, capitalization and punctuation, function key use, error condition handling, and so on. Although you may think such standards stifle creativity, there are two excellent reasons for standardizing the user interface.

First, a standardized interface makes it easier for users to learn new applications because the interface is consistent with other applications. If F3 is always the Exit key across applications, for instance, and F12 always backs up to the previous screen, users don't have to learn new commands counter to those they've used in other applications.

A second major reason for adopting CUA (or other) standards is that such standards can improve programmer productivity. If you adopt a set of design standards, you can easily develop a set of generic DDS descriptions—one for each panel type—that you can then easily tailor to your specific applications.

Chapter Summary

Display files, defined in DDS, are the mechanism that lets a user and a program interact. Each record screen format of a display file defines a screen. The screen format may include literals to be displayed and fields for output, input, or both. Each data item is positioned on the screen based on line and column DDS entries.

DDS relies on keywords to achieve specific desired effects. You can associate some keywords with the entire file, others with a specific record format, and others yet with specific fields. Keywords enable function keys, determine the appearance and format of displayed items, control what the user can enter as input values, and associate error messages with fields.

You can condition most keywords, as well as fields and literals, by indicators. If the indicator is on at display time, the keyword is in effect (or the field or literal is displayed); if the indicator is off, the effect or data item with which the indicator is associated is suppressed. The indicators are turned on within a program to control screen display. On the display side, you can associate valid command keys with indicators to convey information back to the program. While DDS requires the use of numbered indicators to condition fields, RPG lets you map those indicators to an indicator data structure wherein you can name the indicators.

Today's businesses frequently use interactive applications to display database information or the results of processing data; more and more companies also use interactive applications for file maintenance. In the latter case, you should pay special attention to validating user's entries to maintain data file integrity.

An interactive program uses display files as full procedural, combined (both input and output) files, coded with a Workstn device. To display a screen, the program writes a display record; to retrieve user input, the program will read the display record. The Exfmt operation combines the write and read operations into a single operation.

The following table summarizes the functions and operation codes discussed in this chapter:

Function or operation	Description	Syntax
Exfmt	Write then read screen	Exfmt{(E)} *format-name*
Read	Read a screen	Read{(E)} *format-name* {*data-structure*}
Write	Display a screen	Write{(E)} *format-name* {*data-structure*}

IBM has developed a set of screen design guidelines, called Common User Access (CUA), that can standardize iSeries interactive applications. Such standards of screen design can make it easier for users to learn new applications and for programmers to develop new applications more efficiently.

Key Terms

batch processing
CHECK keyword
CODE Designer
combined file
Common User Access (CUA)
COMP keyword
conditioning indicators
data validation
DATE keyword
display attributes
display files
DSPATR keyword
EDTCDE keyword
EDTWRD keyword

ERRMSG keyword
Exfmt operation
file-level keywords
file maintenance
indicator data structure
interactive applications
keyboard shift attribute
Read operation
RANGE keyword
record-level keywords
Screen Design Aid (SDA)
TIME keyword
VALUES keyword
Write operation

Discussion/Review Questions

1. Contrast batch and interactive applications.
2. What are the permissible I/O operations that can be used with record formats or display files? What are the effects of each?
3. Describe how a combined file differs from an update file.
4. What lets the system determine whether you are using a keyword as a file-, record-, or field-level keyword?
5. What's the difference between referring to a function key as CA (Command Attention) and CF (Command Function)? How does each affect your program?
6. Explain the meaning of the following display attribute codes: BL, CS, ND, HI, UL, RI, PC.
7. Why might you want to know, in general, whether a user pressed an enabled function key or a special key (i.e., use the VLDCMDKEY keyword) when each valid key has its own indicator whose status can be checked within your program?
8. What are the relational codes used with COMP in DDS display files?
9. What's the difference between Mandatory Enter and Mandatory Fill?
10. What happens when an error message (ERRMSG) is in effect for a field? Describe the screen effects.
11. How can program events influence screen display, and how can screen input influence program flow of control?
12. Describe how a record's existence affects the validity of adding, deleting, or changing the record when maintaining a file with unique keys.
13. Discuss the pros and cons of adopting IBM's CUA standards in your screen design.
14. What impact do you think graphical user interfaces (GUIs), as typified by Microsoft's Windows environment and Internet browsers, will have on future iSeries interactive applications?

Exercises

1. Assume that your school has a student file containing name, sex, total credits accumulated, residency code, grade point average, major (or degree program), and student classification. Write the DDS for a record format that prompts the user to enter values for these fields, including as many validation keywords as are appropriate.

2. Write a DDS record format that would prompt the user to enter salesperson number, date of sale, and amount of sale. The cursor should blink, salesperson number should be underlined with column separators, date of sale should be displayed in high intensity, and amount of sale should be in reverse image and blinking.

3. Rewrite the DDS from Exercise 2 so that the salesperson number is underlined if indicators 10 and 12 are on and is displayed with column separators if 10 or 12 is on. Date of sale should be displayed in high intensity only if indicator 10 is on. Amount of sale should be in reverse image and blinking if 10 and 12 are on or if 14 and 16 are on.

4. Write the pseudocode for a program to allow interactive processing of received goods. The program should let a user enter a product number (on Screen1), determine whether that product number exists in the file, and either display an error message (on Screen1) if the product number is incorrect or display a second screen (Screen2) that asks the user to enter the quantity of the product received. The amount entered should be added to the current quantity on hand and the product record then updated. Include provisions for exiting and canceling.

5. Write the RPG IV for the pseudocode of Exercise 4. Don't code the DDS. Make up whatever file and field names you need. Document whatever indicators you use.

Programming Assignments

1. CompuSell wants you to develop an interactive application that will let the company enter its product number for an item and display a screen of information about the supplier of that product. The screen should include all the information in the supplier file CSSUPP. You also must use inventory file CSINVP to obtain the correct supplier number for the item in question. Appendix F describes the data files.

    Develop the DDS and the RPG IV program for this application. Design your application with two screens: one inquiry screen and one informational display. Write your program to loop so that following the display of the requested information, the program prompts the user for a new product number; continue until the user signals that he or she is finished. Display the appropriate error message for invalid entry of the Product Number. Follow your instructor's directions for testing this program.

Screen One:

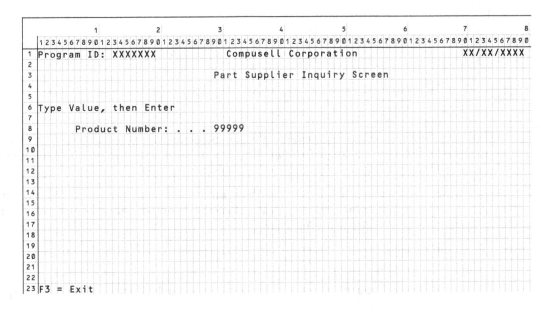

Screen Two:

```
          1         2         3         4         5         6         7         8
 123456789012345678901234567890123456789012345678901234567890123456789012345678 90
1 Program ID: XXXXXXX              Compusell Corporation              XX/XX/XXXX
2
3                             Part Supplier Inquiry Screen
4
5
6      Supplier code . . . . . X0X
7      Name. . . . . . . . . XXXXXXXXXXXXXXXXXXXXXXXXXXX
8      Contact person  . . . . XXXXXXXXXXXXXXXXXXXXXXXXXXXXXXXX
9      Street  . . . . . . . . XXXXXXXXXXXXXXXXXXXXX
10     City  . . . . . . . . . XXXXXXXXXXXXXXX
11     State . . . . . . . . . XX
12     Zip . . . . . . . . . . 99999-9999
13     Phone . . . . . . . . . 999-999-9999
14
15
16
17
18
19
20
21
22
23      Press Enter to continue.
24
25 F3=Exit
```

2. CompuSell wants you to write an interactive file maintenance program for its customer master file, CSCSTP (described in Appendix F). The criteria for this program are listed below. Follow your instructor's directions for testing this program.

   a. When the user adds a new customer, your program must determine the appropriate number to assign the customer (numbers are assigned sequentially) and provide the number automatically for the user.

   b. Automatically use the system date for the date of last order and assign balance due a value of zero.

   c) If a customer number is entered and there is no matching customer number, display an error message.

   d) For a change request, let the user change any field except the customer number.

   e) Do not let the user delete a record if the customer has a balance greater than zero. Display an error message and prompt for another customer number.

Selection Screen: This screen allows the user to select whether they want to add, change, or delete a record.

```
           1         2         3         4         5         6         7         8
  123456789012345678901234567890123456789012345678901234567890123456789012345678901
 1 Program ID: XXXXXXX              Compusell Corporation             XX/XX/XXXX
 2
 3                           Customer File Maintenance
 4
 5
 6   Type choice, then Enter.
 7
 8      Customer Number. . , 999999
 9
10      Action code . . . . X
11         A = Add
12         C = Change
13         D = Delete
14
15
16   Enter Customer. Number . . .
17
18
19
20
21
22
23
24  F3=Exit  F12=Cancel
25
```

Change Record Screen: This screen allows the user to change the information in the file.

```
           1         2         3         4         5         6         7         8
  123456789012345678901234567890123456789012345678901234567890123456789012345678901
 1 Program ID: XXXXXXX              Compusell Corporation             XX/XX/XXXX
 2
 3                           Customer File Maintenance       CHANGE
 4
 5 Customer Number . . . . 999999
 6 First Name  . . . . . . XXXXXXXXXX
 7
 8 Last Name . . . . . . . XXXXXXXXXXXXXX
 9
10 Street Address  . . . . XXXXXXXXXXXXXXXXXXXX
11
12 City  . . . . . . . . . XXXXXXXXXXXXXX
13
14 State . . . . . . . . . XX
15 Zip . . . . . . . . . . 99999-9999
16 Phone . . . . . . . . . 999-999-9999
17 Last order date . . . . 99/99/9999
18 Balance owed  . . . . . 999.99
19
20
21
22 Press Enter to change
23
24
25 F3=Exit  F12=Cancel
```

3. Wexler University wants you to write an interactive file maintenance program for its instructor file, WUINSTP (see Appendix F). Design screens appropriate for the application. Let the users add, delete, or change instructor records. Do not let them change the Social Security number or add a record with a duplicate Social Security number. Include as much data validation as you can, given the nature of the data fields being entered. Follow your instructor's directions for testing this program.

Selection Screen: The user enters the instructor ID and the Action they want to perform. If the instructor ID does not exist, a message is displayed.

```
          1         2         3         4         5         6         7         8
 1234567890123456789012345678901234567890123456789012345678901234567890123456789 0
 1 Program ID: XXXXXXX              Wexler University                 XX/XX/XXXX
 2
 3                          Instructor File Maintenance
 4
 5  Type values, then Enter
 6
 7       Social security number  . . 999999999
 8       Action code . . . . . . . . X
 9            A = add record
10            C = change record
11            D = delete record
12
13
14
15
16
17
18
19
20
21
22
23  F3=Exit   F12=Cancel
24
25
```

Change Record Screen: This screen should perform edits to verify that the correct information is entered.

```
         1         2         3         4         5         6         7         8
1234567890123456789012345678901234567890123456789012345678901234567890123456789 0
1 Program ID: XXXXXXX              Wexler University                  XX/XX/XXXX
2
3                          Instructor File Maintenance
4
5     Social Security Number  . . 999999999
6     First name . . . . . . . . XXXXXXXXXX
7     Last name . . . . . . . . . XXXXXXXXXXXXXX
8     Department . . . . . . . . XXX
9     Salary . . . . . . . . . . $999,999.99
10    Rank . . . . . . . . . . . 9
11    Sex . . . . . . . . . . . X
12    Date of hire . . . . . . . MM/DD/YYYY
13    Marital status . . . . . . X
14    Number of dependents. . . . 99
15    Tenured (Y/N) . . . . . . . X
16    Preferred title . . . . . . 9
17
18
19
20 When finished, press Enter to change
21
22 F3=Exit   F12=Cancel
```

4. CompuSell wants you to write an interactive application to enter customer orders. The application should begin by determining the appropriate starting order number, based on the last order number in orders file CSORDP.

a) The main process loop should then begin by requesting the customer number; only orders for established customers (those in customer master file CSCSTP) can be processed. If the customer exists, the program should set up a loop to let the user enter ordered items until the order is complete.

b) For each item, the user should enter the product number and the quantity desired.

c) If the product is not in the inventory file CSINVP, or if the quantity on hand is less than the quantity desired, inform the user through error messages that the item cannot be ordered; otherwise, update the quantity on hand field of the inventory file to reflect the new, lower quantity on hand and write a record to the order/products file (CSORDPRP) for that item.

d) When the user has finished entering items for a customer, determine whether payment was included in the order, and if so, for how much.

e) A record should be written to the CSORDP file, leaving the amount due zero. (The files CSORDP and CSORDPRP will be used by different programs to generate pick lists and invoices.) See Appendix F for file descriptions.

Screen One: This screen allows the user to input the customer number to retrieve the customer information.

```
                  1         2         3         4         5         6         7         8
     1234567890123456789012345678901234567890123456789012345678901234567890123456789012345678901234567890
 1 |Program ID: XXXXXXX            Compusell Corporation                    XX/XX/XXXX
 2 |
 3 |                            Order Entry System
 4 |
 5 |Type value, then Enter.
 6 |
 7 |   Customer number . . ,  999999
 8 |
 9 |
10 |
11 |
12 |
13 |
14 | F3=Exit   F12=Cancel
15 |
```

Screen Two: This screen prompts for the part number and quantity to order.

```
                  1         2         3         4         5         6         7         8
     1234567890123456789012345678901234567890123456789012345678901234567890123456789012345678901234567890
 1 |Program ID: XXXXXXX            Compusell Corporation                    XX/XX/XXXX
 2 |
 3 |                            Order Entry System
 4 |
 5 | Type values, then Enter.
 6 |
 7 |    Customer number . . ,  999999
 8 |    Customer name . . . . XXXXXXXXXX XXXXXXXXXXXXXXX
 9 |    Order number  . . . . 99999
10 |
11 |
12 |    Product number  . . . 999999
13 |
14 |    Quantity ordered  . . 9999
15 |
16 |
17 |    Press F3 when finished with items.
18 |
19 |
20 |
21 |
22 |
23 | F3=Exit   F12=Cancel
24 |
25 |
```

Screen Three: This screen displays the part number information and gives the users the option to cancel the order.

```
                1              2              3              4              5              6              7              8
   1234567890123456789012345678901234567890123456789012345678901234567890123456789012345678901234567890
 1 Program ID: XXXXXXX              Compusell Corporation                    XX/XX/XXXX
 2
 3                                    Order Entry System
 4
 5 Type values, then Enter.
 6
 7     Customer number . . , 999999
 8     Customer name . . . . XXXXXXXXXX XXXXXXXXXXXXXXX
 9     Order number  . . . . 99999
10
11
12     Product number  . . . 999999
13     Product description . XXXXXXXXXXXXXXXXXXXXXXXXXXX
14     Quantity ordered  . . 9999
15
16        Press Enter to confirm.
17
18
19
20
21 F3=Exit   F12=Cancel
```

5. Wexler University wants you to write a program that will provide an online registration system for its students. The registration system should work as follows:

   a. The student is prompted to enter their Social Security number. If the student is not found in the student master file, the program should not let the student proceed and an Error displayed on the screen.

   b. If the student is in the file, they are allowed to register for courses until signaling that they are finished.

   c. For each desired course, the student will enter the section number. If the section number is invalid, the student should be informed and an Error displayed on the screen.

   d. If the number is valid, the program should display the student name, student ID, course identification, title, and credits on the screen, along with the time and days the section meets and an indication of whether the section is full (a message should be displayed showing the section is full) or not full (current enrollment < cap).

   e. If the section is not full, and if the student indicates that this is, in fact, the course and section into which he or she wants to enroll, the program should confirm the enrollment to the student, update the current enrollment figure in the current section record by adding 1 to the field CURENL, and add a record to the current enrollment file for this student in this section.

   f. When the student has finished enrolling, the program should return to the initial screen to let the next student enroll. This process should continue until the user presses F3 to exit the application completely.

Your program will use files WUSTDP, WUSCTP, WUCRSP, and WUENRLP (Appendix F describes these files). Follow your instructor's directions for testing this program.

Selection Screen: This screen allows the user to input the student ID number. It will display a message if the student number does not exist.

```
          1         2         3         4         5         6         7         8
 12345678901234567890123456789012345678901234567890123456789012345678901234567890
 1 Program ID: XXXXXXX            Wexler University                    XX/XX/XXXX
 2
 3                              Registration System
 4
 5 Type value, then Enter.
 6
 7     Student number  . . 999999999
 8
 9
10
11
12
13
14
15
16
17
18
19
20
21 F3=Exit  F12=Cancel
```

Section Screen: This screen displays the student name and ID. It also prompts for the section number the student wants to register.

```
          1         2         3         4         5         6         7         8
 12345678901234567890123456789012345678901234567890123456789012345678901234567890
 1 Program ID: XXXXXXX            Wexler University                    XX/XX/XXXX
 2
 3                              Registration System
 4
 5
 6    Student Number  . . 999999999
 7
 8    Student Name . . .  XXXXXXXXXX XXXXXXXXXXXXXX
 9
10
11 Type value, then Enter.
12
13    Section number  . . . 99999
14
15
16
17
18
19
20 F3=Exit   F12=Cancel
21
```

Confirmation Screen: This screen allows the user to verify that they want to register for this class. Pressing the F12 key will cause the program to return to the section screen.

```
            1         2         3         4         5         6         7         8
   12345678901234567890123456789012345678901234567890123456789012345678901234567890
 1 Program ID: XXXXXXX            Wexler University                       XX/XX/XXXX
 2
 3                               Registration System
 4
 5
 6    Student Number  . . 999999999
 7
 8    Student Name . . .  XXXXXXXXXX XXXXXXXXXXXXXXX
 9
10
11
12    Section number  . . . 99999
13
14    Dept  Course#  Description
15    ACT    201     XXXXXXXXXXXXXXXXXXXXXXXXX       9 Credits
16
17    Class Meets:
18
19    Day of Week XXX Time 99:99 Room: X999
20
21
22    Press Enter to confirm enrollment.
23
24
25 F3=Exit   F12=Cancel
```

Chapter 12

Calling Programs and Passing Parameters

Chapter Overview

This chapter discusses modular programming and shows you how RPG IV programs can communicate with one another by passing data values as parameter arguments. You'll also learn how to define prototypes and procedure interfaces. Finally, the chapter also introduces calling APIs from within an RPG IV program and sharing data among programs through data areas.

Modular Programming

As concern about program development and maintenance efficiencies has grown, programmers have become increasingly interested in developing small, standalone units of code (rather than monolithic programs thousands of lines long). This approach, which is often called **modular programming**, offers many advantages.

First, if you develop code in small, independent units, you often can reuse these units because it is common for several applications to share identical processing requirements for some parts of their logic. Furthermore, small programs are easier to test than large programs. In addition, code changes are less likely to cause unexpected—and unwanted—side effects when they are made within a small, standalone module rather than in a routine that is embedded within a gigantic program. Finally, because you can separately develop and test such modules, a modular approach to programming makes it easier to divide an application development project among members of a programming team, each with responsibilities for developing different modules.

RPG IV provides the Callp (Call a Prototyped Procedure or Program) operation to let you adopt this modular approach to program development. Before discussing this operation in detail, you need to understand how the call affects flow of control. When program execution reaches a call statement, control passes to the called program (which is itself a *PGM object). The called program executes until it reaches a Return statement; at this point, control returns to the calling program, at the statement immediately following the call.

Figure 12.1 illustrates this flow of control among calling and called programs.

Figure 12.1
Flow of Control with Calls

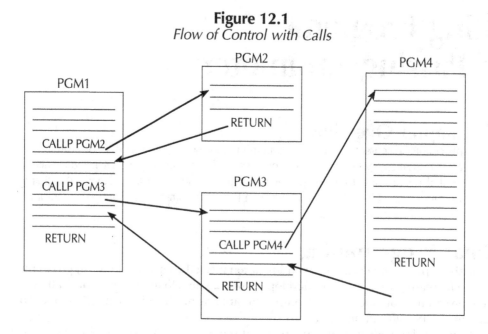

As you can see, the flow of control with a call is like that of an Exsr operation, except that a call invokes an external program (or a subprocedure, discussed in the next chapter) rather than a subroutine internal to the program. A called program can in turn call other programs, but it should not recursively call itself or its calling program.

Prototyping the Call Interface

A call would be of limited value if it did not permit the called and calling programs to share data. While an RPG IV program can normally access the value of any variable from anywhere within the program, this "global" feature of variables does not extend across program boundaries. It is said that the **scope**—that is, the extent of influence—of a variable is limited to the program in which it is defined. That means if you want a called program to process some data and send the results of the processing back to the calling program, you need to make special provisions to let this sharing take place.

The Callp operation passes parameters to communicate values between the calling program and the called program. **Parameters**—sometimes referred to as **arguments**—are values, usually contained in variables, that a program can pass to another program; the called program can then accept the parameters and use those values to control its processing.

Before you can use Callp to call a program, you must define the **call interface** to the called program. The basic program call interface includes the following information:

- The name of the program to call
- The number of parameters to pass, their data attributes, and the order in which they are passed

To define this interface, you define a special structure called a **prototype**. The RPG IV compiler uses the prototype to call the program correctly and to ensure that the caller passes the correct parameters to the called program. A prototype must be in the Definition specifications of the calling program; many programmers prefer to include prototypes at the beginning of the Definition specifications. If the calling program calls more than one program, it must include a prototype for each call interface.

To code a prototype, you define a structure similar to a data structure. The prototype definition has two parts:

- The prototype definition itself (the prototype header)
- The description(s) of parameter(s) to be shared between the programs

The following is an example of a prototype for a program call interface:

```
*.. 1 ...+... 2 ...+... 3 ...+... 4 ...+... 5 ...+... 6 ...+... 7 ...+... 8
DName++++++++++ETDsFrom+++To/L+++IDc.Functions++++++++++++++++++++++++++++++++
D Updcust        PR                  Extpgm('AR003')
D                                5
D                                7 0
```

PR, coded in positions 24–25 (*Ds*) signals the beginning of a prototyped call interface. You must name the prototype in positions 7–21 (*Name+++++++++++*). Code the external name of the program associated with this prototype, using the Extpgm keyword; the program is the object that the caller will execute when you perform the call. The Extpgm entry is usually a literal, but it could be a named constant or a field specifying the name of the program. The Extpgm name must match the actual name of the called program; the name of the prototype need not match the name of the external program, although you may find it convenient to use matching names. The Extpgm entry is case sensitive—which usually means that it must be in all uppercase characters. In the above example, when you perform a call to the Updcust prototype, program AR003 will actually be called.

If there are no parameters to be passed to the called program, the prototype will consist of just the single prototype header line:

```
*.. 1 ...+... 2 ...+... 3 ...+... 4 ...+... 5 ...+... 6 ...+... 7 ...+... 8
DName++++++++++ETDsFrom+++To/L+++IDc.Functions++++++++++++++++++++++++++++++++
D Sleep         PR                  Extpgm('SLEEP')
```

If the call interface involves passing parameters, describe the parameters on subsequent lines, following the PR header. Indicate a parameter's length in positions 33–39 (*To/L+++*); for numeric fields code a decimal positions entry in positions 41–42 (*Dc*). Code the parameter's data type in position 40 (*I*); if the type entry is blank, the prototype will assign default data types: packed decimal for numeric parameters (i.e., those with decimal positions), character for others. In the prototype shown earlier (Updcust), there are two parameters: a five-character field and a seven-digit (packed) numeric field with zero decimals. A prototype can list a maximum of 255 parameters for a called program.

Note that you need not name the parameters. You may find it convenient to document the parameter usage by naming the parameters (in positions 7–21), but the compiler will treat these names as comments:

```
*.. 1 ...+... 2 ...+... 3 ...+... 4 ...+... 5 ...+... 6 ...+... 7 ...+... 8
DName++++++++++ETDsFrom+++To/L+++IDc.Functions++++++++++++++++++++++++++++++++
D Updcust         PR                  Extpgm('AR003')
D   Company                     5
D   Customer                    7 0
```

In the above example, the compiler will not define variables called Company or Customer; these names are merely comments to indicate the purpose for each of the two parameters. If the program needs variables named Company and Customer, you must define them separately.

Callp (Call a Prototyped Procedure or Program)

The **Callp (Call a Prototyped Procedure or Program) operation** takes the form

```
Callp prototype(parm1: parm2: ... parmn)
```

Callp passes control to the program object (type *PGM) associated with the prototype named in the required first argument. List any parameters in parentheses immediately following the prototype name; if there are no parameters, you must code empty parentheses, (), instead.

```
Callp Updcust(Company:Custnbr);
```

The code in the above example, when coupled with the prototype shown earlier, would call program AR003, named in the Updcust prototype, passing fields Company (five characters) and CustNbr (seven digits, packed) as parameters. Note that Company and Custnbr would be defined elsewhere in the program and that their definitions must match those in the prototype definition. If the parameters passed by Callp do not match the number, order, and data types of the parameters in the prototype definition, the program will not compile.

Actually coding the Callp operation is optional in the free-format specification. You may let the compiler infer the Callp operation, instead of explicitly coding it, as the following example illustrates:

```
UpdCust(Company:CustNbr);
```

This code would call program AR003, named in the Updcust prototype, just like the previous example. Most programmers prefer to omit explicitly coding the Callp operation, as this abbreviated syntax matches similar call operations in other computer languages, such as C or Java.

The Procedure Interface

Recall the flow of control illustrated in Figure 12.1. In the calling program (e.g., PGM1), RPG IV uses the prototype definition to describe the list of parameters that it will pass on to the called program (e.g., PGM2). The called RPG IV program also uses a prototype definition to describe the corresponding list of parameters that it will receive from the caller. (Languages other than RPG IV may use mechanisms other than prototypes for this purpose.)

The prototypes in each program must match each other. That is, they must have the same number of parameters, and the corresponding parameters between the two programs must have the same data attributes. RPG IV passes parameter arguments by passing the address of the storage location represented by the parameter, so in fact these corresponding parameters reference the same storage location within the computer. The data names of the parameters used in the caller and the called program need not be the same.

To access those storage locations passed by the calling program, the called program must include a **procedure interface** definition (in addition to a prototype). Like the prototype, the procedure interface describes the parameters that the called program will share with the caller. Unlike the prototype, however, the procedure interface defines variable names to hold the parameter values that the called program will receive, allowing you to refer to and manipulate those parameter values.

Tip

If there are no parameters involved in calling a program, the called program need not have a prototype or a procedure interface. You may still want to code each of them, however, for consistency among your programs, and to promote future enhancements in the application. Regardless of any parameter passing considerations, Callp requires that the calling program always have a prototype.

The procedure interface is coded similarly to the prototype. The program's procedure interface must appear after the primary program prototype, and many programmers prefer to code the procedure interface immediately following the prototype in the Definition specifications. The procedure interface has two parts:

- The procedure interface itself (the header)
- The definition(s) for parameter(s) to be received by the called program

The following is an example of a primary program prototype and a matching procedure interface. These definitions would appear as the first definitions in program AR003 (the called program):

```
*.. 1 ...+... 2 ...+... 3 ...+... 4 ...+... 5 ...+... 6 ...+... 7 ...+... 8
DName+++++++++++ETDsFrom+++To/L+++IDc.Functions++++++++++++++++++++++++++++++
D Main            PR                    Extpgm('AR003')
D                                5
D                                7 0
D Main            PI
D   Company                      5
D   Customer                     7 0
```

PI, coded in positions 24–25 (*Ds*) signals the beginning of a prototyped call interface. You must name the procedure interface in positions 7–21 (*Name+++++++++++*). This name must match the name in the called program's prototype.

Tip
Many programmers standardize on a common name, such as Main, for prototypes and procedure interfaces in called programs. This practice fortifies the role of the prototype and procedure interface to describe the "main procedure" in an RPG IV program.

If the call interface involves passing parameters, define the parameters on subsequent lines, following the PI header. Name the parameter variable in positions 7–21 (*Name+++++++++++*). Indicate its length in positions 33–39 (*To/L+++*); for numeric fields code a decimal positions entry in positions 41–42 (*Dc*). Code the parameter's data type in position 40 (*I*); if the type entry is blank, the default is packed decimal for numeric parameters (variables with decimal positions) and character for parameters with blanks in positions 41–42. The data attributes and length of parameters in the procedure interface must match the corresponding parameter entries in the prototype. In the above procedure interface, there are two parameters: Company, a five-character variable, and Customer, a seven-digit packed decimal variable with zero decimals.

Changing Parameters, the Return Operation, and *Inlr

Because RPG IV passes parameter arguments by passing the address of the storage location represented by the variable (called **passing by reference**), changes in the parameter variables within the called program result in the same changes in the parameter variables of the calling program. In the following example, variable Okay has a value of *Off before the call to another program. As part of its processing, the called program changes the value of Flag (the first parameter). Upon return to the caller, Okay now would have a value of *On because Okay and Flag reference the same storage location.

```
Calling program
*.. 1 ...+... 2 ...+... 3 ...+... 4 ...+... 5 ...+... 6 ...+... 7 ...+... 8
DName++++++++++ETDsFrom+++To/L+++IDc.Functions+++++++++++++++++++++++++++++++
D Nextpgm        PR                     Extpgm('CALLEE')
D                                   N

D Okay           S               N     Inz(*Off)

 /Free
    Nextpgm(Okay);                                     // Okay = *Off before call
                                                       // Okay = *On after call
 /End-Free
```

Called program
```
*.. 1 ...+... 2 ...+... 3 ...+... 4 ...+... 5 ...+... 6 ...+... 7 ...+... 8
DName+++++++++++ETDsFrom+++To/L+++IDc.Functions+++++++++++++++++++++++++++++
D Main            PR                     Extpgm('CALLEE')
D                                   N
D Main            PI
D   Flag                            N

 /Free
    Flag = *On;                                  // Change value of Flag
    *Inlr = *On;
    Return;
 /End-Free
```

The system returns control to the calling program when it encounters a Return statement in the called program. If the LR indicator is also on when the Return is executed, the system resources tied up by the called program are released; a subsequent call to the program causes it to start up again as though for the first time. On the other hand, if LR is not on within the called program upon return, the called program remains activated. As a result, a subsequent call to that program will find all the variables (except parameter variables) and indicators of the called program to have the values they had at the time of the previous Return. Moreover, any files used by the called program will still be open as a result of the previous call. The following examples illustrate this behavior.

Calling program
```
*.. 1 ...+... 2 ...+... 3 ...+... 4 ...+... 5 ...+... 6 ...+... 7 ...+... 8
DName+++++++++++ETDsFrom+++To/L+++IDc.Functions+++++++++++++++++++++++++++++
D Samplepgm       PR                     Extpgm('SAMPLEPGM')

D X               S              3U 0

 /Free
    For X = 1 To 100;
       Samplepgm();
    Enddo;

    *Inlr = *On;
    Return;
 /End-Free
```

Called program *(SAMPLEPGM)*
```
*.. 1 ...+... 2 ...+... 3 ...+... 4 ...+... 5 ...+... 6 ...+... 7 ...+... 8
DName+++++++++++ETDsFrom+++To/L+++IDc.Functions+++++++++++++++++++++++++++++
D   Count         S              5U 0

 /Free
    Count += 1;
    Return;
 /End-Free
```

In this example, SAMPLEPGM executes a Return statement without turning on LR. SAMPLEPGM remains active, and each time the caller calls it, variable Count will be incremented by 1, having retained its latest value from its latest invocation. Notice that setting *Inlr in the calling program will not affect *Inlr in SAMPLEPGM; each program will have its own copy of *Inlr. Indeed, even after the caller has ended, SAMPLEPGM will still be active, because its *Inlr has not been set on.

If we substitute the following version of SAMPLEPGM, where LR is turned on before the Return operation, the program is deactivated, and Count will initially be 0 each time SAMPLEPGM is called:

Called program *(SAMPLEPGM)*
```
*.. 1 ...+... 2 ...+... 3 ...+... 4 ...+... 5 ...+... 6 ...+... 7 ...+... 8
DName+++++++++++ETDsFrom+++To/L+++IDc.Functions++++++++++++++++++++++++++++++
D   Count         S              5U 0

 /Free
    Count += 1;
    *Inlr = *On;
    Return;
 /End-Free
```

Whether or not you should turn on LR before returning from a called program, then, depends on whether you want the called program to start afresh each time the calling program invokes it or you want the called program to pick up where it left off on the previous call (within a given run). Failure to correctly handle the LR indicator can cause undesired effects in the called program.

You should ensure that a program ends with LR on after a process is finished with it. For example, we could use the following SAMPLEPGM to ensure that it would remain active for only 100 calls (matching the For loop in the calling program):

Called program *(SAMPLEPGM)*
```
*.. 1 ...+... 2 ...+... 3 ...+... 4 ...+... 5 ...+... 6 ...+... 7 ...+... 8
DName+++++++++++ETDsFrom+++To/L+++IDc.Functions++++++++++++++++++++++++++++++
D   Count         S              5U 0

 /Free
    Count += 1;
    *Inlr = (Count = 100);
    Return;
 /End-Free
```

In this version of SAMPLEPGM, LR remains off until Count is equal to 100. At that point, the Return operation will close the program completely. If there were any files involved in SAMPLEPGM, they would be closed. A subsequent call to SAMPLEPGM would cause it to be invoked with fresh variable initialization and file opens. This example illustrates one method for ending SAMPLEPGM gracefully; another common technique would be for the caller to pass a parameter to SAMPLEPGM indicating whether or not it should close down. The following example demonstrates this approach.

<u>Calling program</u>

```
*.. 1 ...+... 2 ...+... 3 ...+... 4 ...+... 5 ...+... 6 ...+... 7 ...+... 8
DName++++++++++ETDsFrom+++To/L+++IDc.Functions++++++++++++++++++++++++++++++++
D Samplepgm       PR                    Extpgm('SAMPLEPGM')
D                                    N

D Shutdown        S                  N
D X               S                  3U 0

 /Free
    For X = 1 To 100;
      Shutdown = (X = 100);
      Samplepgm(Shutdown);
    Enddo;

    *Inlr = *On;
    Return;
 /End-Free
```

<u>Called program</u> *(SAMPLEPGM)*

```
*.. 1 ...+... 2 ...+... 3 ...+... 4 ...+... 5 ...+... 6 ...+... 7 ...+... 8
DName++++++++++ETDsFrom+++To/L+++IDc.Functions++++++++++++++++++++++++++++++++
D Main            PR                    Extpgm('SAMPLEPGM')
D                                    N
D Main            PI
D   Closepgm                         N

D   Count         S                  5U 0

 /Free
    Count += 1;
    *Inlr = Closepgm;
    Return;
 /End-Free
```

In this example, the caller controls whether or not SAMPLEPGM will turn on *Inlr, by setting the value of the Shutdown parameter, which it passes to SAMPLEPGM. Notice that the parameter need not have the same name in both programs (although the names could match, if you wish).

Fitting the Pieces

Here is a summary of the requirements for having one RPG IV program call another RPG IV program. The calling program includes

- A prototype definition to describe the parameters to be passed
- The Callp operation to execute the call

The called program includes

- A prototype definition to describe the parameters to be received
- A procedure interface to receive the parameters and define their variables
- The Return operation to return control to the calling program

In the following example "snippets," program AR001 calls AR003, passing it three parameters: Cpyname (with a value of 'CSELL'), Custnbr (10487) and Okay (*Off). Study this example to understand the relationship between the programs, as well as the relationship between the prototype and the procedure interface. (Program AR001 receives no parameters, but the example includes a prototype and a procedure interface for the sake of consistency.)

(Program AR001)

```
*.. 1 ...+... 2 ...+... 3 ...+... 4 ...+... 5 ...+... 6 ...+... 7 ...+... 8
DName++++++++++ETDsFrom+++To/L+++IDc.Functions+++++++++++++++++++++++++++++++
  // ----------------------------------------- Primary prototype/interface
D Main            PR                  Extpgm('AR001')
D Main            PI

  // ----------------------------------------- Prototype(s) for called program(s)
D Updcust         PR                  Extpgm('AR003')
D                               5
D                               7 0
D                               N

D Cpyname         S               5
D Custnbr         S               7 0
D Okay            S               N   Inz(*Off)

 /Free
    Cpyname = 'CSELL';
    Custnbr = 10487;
    Updcust(Cpyname:Custnbr:Okay);

    If Okay;               // If AR003 executed normally, Okay will be *On
      Exsr Process;
    Endif;
 /End-Free
```

(Program AR003)

```
*.. 1 ...+... 2 ...+... 3 ...+... 4 ...+... 5 ...+... 6 ...+... 7 ...+... 8
DName++++++++++ETDsFrom+++To/L+++IDc.Functions+++++++++++++++++++++++++++++++

D Main            PR                  EXTPGM('AR003')
D                               5
D                               7 0
D                               N
D Main            PI
D Company                     5
D Customer                    7 0
D Flag                        N

 /Free
 // Company = 'CSELL'(Value received from first parameter)
 // Customer = 10487 (Value received from second parameter)
 // Flag = *Off (Valued received from third parameter)

    Flag = *On;                              // Change value of Flag
    *Inlr = *On;
    Return;
 /End-Free
```

Because RPG IV passes parameter arguments by passing the address of the storage location represented by the variable (called passing by reference), both programs AR001 and AR003 in this example are, in effect, sharing the same storage address for the three parameters, even though they may refer to those addresses by different names. If program AR003 changes any of the parameter variables, the values of the corresponding parameters in AR001 will also change. For example, in AR001, the value of Okay is *Off. After AR001 calls AR003, the value of Okay (the third parameter) will be *On, because AR003 changed the value of Flag (the name by which it refers to the third parameter).

Passing Parameters by Read-Only Reference

Prototypes provide an effective ways to describe the data items to be passed between programs. Prototypes also offer some flexibility in the method the system will use to pass those parameters.

By default, RPG IV passes parameter arguments by sharing the address of the storage location represented by the variable (passing by reference). If the called program changes the value of the parameter variable, the change will be recognized by the calling program. When a program passes a parameter by reference, the parameter's value must exist within a variable; to pass the parameter, you name the variable in parentheses following the Callp operation.

While passing by reference is the default, prototypes support an alternative method of passing parameters between programs: **read-only reference**. Passing parameters by read-only reference offers several advantages over passing parameters by reference:

- The parameter values need not be represented in a variable.
- The parameter data types need not exactly match the prototype.
- The system offers some protection against the parameter values being changed by the called program.

On occasion, you may want to be able to pass expressions or literals, instead of variables, to dynamically called programs. This capability gives you more flexibility in coding the Callp operation than being limited to representing the parameter value in a variable. When RPG IV passes a parameter by read-only reference, it can first evaluate an expression or a literal and then make a temporary copy of that value before invoking the called program; the calling program will then pass a pointer to the memory occupied by the copy. To specify read-only reference, you code the Const keyword in the prototype:

```
*.. 1 ...+... 2 ...+... 3 ...+... 4 ...+... 5 ...+... 6 ...+... 7 ...+... 8
DName++++++++++ETDsFrom+++To/L+++IDc.Functions++++++++++++++++++++++++++++++
D Updcust         PR                  Extpgm('AR003')
D                             5  0 Const
D                             7  0 Const

 /Free
    Updcust(5:Custnumber);
 /End-Free
```

This example calls a program, passing two parameters; the first parameter is passed as a literal (5), while the second one is passed as a variable (Custnumber). You could also code an expression as the parameter when passing by read-only reference:

```
*.. 1 ...+... 2 ...+... 3 ...+... 4 ...+... 5 ...+... 6 ...+... 7 ...+... 8
DName++++++++++ETDsFrom+++To/L+++IDc.Functions++++++++++++++++++++++++++++++
D Addcust          PR                     Extpgm('AR001')
D                                     5   0 Const
D                                     7   0 Const

 /Free
    Updcust(5 : Lastcustomer + 1);
 /End-Free
```

In the preceding example, the second parameter is an expression. You can mix passing methods in the same prototype, if necessary. If you omit the Const keyword for a parameter, the parameter is passed by reference.

The Const keyword allows you some flexibility in passing parameters of slightly different data formats than the prototype specifies. For example, you might pass an integer when a prototype calls for a packed decimal field. As long as the field's value is appropriate for the data type, the prototype will manage this minor mismatch.

When a program passes a parameter by read-only reference, the called program should avoid changing the value of that parameter. Because the passed parameter may be a copy of the actual information, the calling program may not see any changes that the called program makes to that parameter value. Indeed, if the called program includes a prototype and a procedure interface, the compiler will prevent the program from changing the parameter. In the following example, program AR001, the called program, would not be allowed to change the values of Company or Customer:

Calling program
```
*.. 1 ...+... 2 ...+... 3 ...+... 4 ...+... 5 ...+... 6 ...+... 7 ...+... 8
DName++++++++++ETDsFrom+++To/L+++IDc.Functions++++++++++++++++++++++++++++++
D Addcust          PR                     Extpgm('AR001')
D                                     5   0 Const
D                                     7   0 Const

 /Free
    Updcust(5 : Lastcustomer + 1);
 /End-Free
```

Called program
```
*.. 1 ...+... 2 ...+... 3 ...+... 4 ...+... 5 ...+... 6 ...+... 7 ...+... 8
DName++++++++++ETDsFrom+++To/L+++IDc.Functions++++++++++++++++++++++++++++++
D Main             PR                     Extpgm('AR001')
D                                     5   0 Const
```

```
D                                   7   0 Const
D Main              PI
D   Company                         5   0 Const
D   Customer                        7   0 Const

 /Free
      // (Some processing goes here...cannot change Company or Customer)
     *Inlr = *On;
     Return;
 /End-Free
```

If the called program does not have a PR/PI combination—for example, if the called program is written in another language that does not support prototyping, such as CL—it may be allowed to change the parameter values, but you should avoid doing so, since you cannot be sure whether or not the calling program will recognize the change.

Tip
To improve the flexibility of your coding, and to help protect the integrity of the calling program's data, use read-only reference as the preferred method for passing parameters between programs. If the calling program needs to access any changes made by the called program, pass by reference; or if there is a large number of parameters to be passed, pass by reference to improve the performance of the call.

Using a Modular Approach

You will find a wide variation in the extent to which different companies use RPG IV's calling features. Some companies incorporate calls within menu programs that present application choices to users; the menu programs will then call the selected programs to perform the desired processing. Typically, this kind of program does not require passing data between the calling program and the programs it calls.

Another application of RPG IV's calling features is to access a routine that performs a specific task, without recoding the routine every time you need it. For example, we might write a routine to determine the day of the week for a given date in *ISO format. You could perform this day-of-the-week "calculation" within a called program. The calling program would include two parameters: one to contain the given date and one to store the calculated day of the week. The called program would determine the day of the week of the value represented in the first parameter, store the result in the second parameter, and then return control to the calling program.

Another example of a routine that many programs might call is one that converts a numeric value representing dollars and cents (e.g., 123.43) to its representation in words (e.g., one hundred twenty-three dollars and 43 cents). The logic required for such a conversion is not trivial, and companies do not want to continually reinvent that particular wheel.

Calling an external program offers an additional significant advantage over an Exsr operation: The called program does not have to be created from RPG IV source. You can write a program in any high-level language (HLL) supported by the System i, or in i5/OS's CL, compile it, and then call it from an RPG IV program.

Similarly, you can call an RPG IV program from a CL program or from one written in a different HLL supported by the System i. The RPG IV program's Return statement returns control to whatever program called it.

This flexibility lets you break down a problem into logical units, write each unit in the language best suited for developing the algorithm required by that unit, and then call the units to perform their processing as needed. Although this multilanguage approach to program development has not been not widely used in the System i world previously, its use is growing as cooperative processing and the use of graphical user interfaces (GUIs) demand more sophisticated capabilities than those RPG IV alone can offer. As a result, modular programming is becoming more common in IT departments that use RPG IV. IBM's Integrated Language Environment (ILE) encourages modular programming techniques; as more programmers adopt ILE concepts in their applications, modular programming is a natural companion technology.

APIs

You have learned how an RPG IV program can call another program written in RPG IV (or any other System i language) by using Callp. You can also use Callp to access application programming interfaces, or **APIs**. APIs are programs built into the operating system that let you access lower-level machine functions or system data not otherwise available within an HLL program.

Many different APIs exist; each provides a different, specific capability. For example, API QUSLSPL (List Spooled Files) builds a list of spooled files (i.e., reports) from an output queue; a related API, QUSRSPLA (Retrieve Spooled File Attributes), retrieves this data into a program. You can use APIs to obtain information about a job, a database file, a library, or any other kind of object on the system. Almost all APIs have a required, specific set of parameters used to pass values from your program, return values to your program, or both. Many APIs also require a special kind of storage area, called a **user space**, to receive their output or to supply their input. User spaces are defined, permanent locations in storage; they are similar to data areas, which we describe in detail later in this chapter. How do user spaces originate? An API, QUSCRTUS (Create User Space), creates a user space for use by other APIs. Although a complete discussion of APIs is beyond the scope of this text, we will take a closer look at two often-used APIs to give you a sense of how you might use APIs within your RPG IV programs.

The first API we'll consider is QUSCMDLN (Display Command Line Window). This API presents an i5/OS system command line as a popup window within your program. Say, for example, that you were writing an interactive application in which you wanted to give the user access to the system command line so he or she could check the status of a spooled file, send a message to another user, or whatever. In your display file, you would enable a function key (e.g., F21, mapped via an indicator data structure to field Fkey21) to signal the user's request for a command line, and you would include a prompt at the bottom of the screen to inform the user of this feature (e.g., 'F21=Command Line'). Then, within your RPG IV program upon return from the display, you would check the status of the indicator associated with that function key. If the indicator's value indicates the user has pressed the function key, your program would call API QUSCMDLN to pop up the command line on the current screen:

```
*.. 1 ...+... 2 ...+... 3 ...+... 4 ...+... 5 ...+... 6 ...+... 7 ...+... 8
DName++++++++++ETDsFrom+++To/L+++IDc.Keywords+++++++++++++++++++++++++++++++++
D ShowcmdLine      PR                     Extpgm('QUSCMDLN')

 /Free
   Exfmt Screen1;
   If Fkey21;
     Showcmdline();
   Else;
    . . .
   Endif;
 /End-Free
```

When the user finishes with the command line and exits from it, control returns to your program, which resumes processing from the point of the call. Notice that QUSCMDLN, unlike most APIs, uses no parameters. The second API we'll look at, QCMDEXC (Execute Command), is more typical in its format.

What does QCMDEXC do? Occasionally within an RPG IV program, you would like to communicate directly with the operating system to issue a CL command. You might, for example, want to override one database file with another or send a message reporting on the program's progress to the user. API QCMDEXC lets you execute such a CL command from within an HLL program.

Any program can call QCMDEXC. QCMDEXC normally expects to receive arguments for two parameters: The first parameter should contain the command the system is to execute, and the second should contain the command's length. (The variable representing this length must be defined as a numeric field with 15 positions, five of which are decimal positions.)

The following example illustrates using an expression to build a command, then using the implied Callp to execute it:

```
*.. 1 ...+... 2 ...+... 3 ...+... 4 ...+... 5 ...+... 6 ...+... 7 ...+... 8
DName++++++++++ETDsFrom+++To/L+++IDc.Keywords+++++++++++++++++++++++++++++++++
D Runcmd         PR                     Extpgm('QCMDEXC')
D                           3000         Const OPTIONS(*VARSIZE)
D                           15  5 Const

D Cmd                       3000         Varying
D User                        10         Inz(*User)

 /Free
    Cmd = 'WRKSPLF SELECT(' + User + ')';
    Runcmd(Cmd:%Len(Cmd));
 /END-FREE
```

In this example, the RPG IV program will execute the WRKSPLF (Work with Sppoled Files) CL command for the program's current user. The prototype specifies passing by read-only reference (using the Const keyword); this option allows embedding an expression as a parameter in the call (e.g., %Len(Cmd)). Using the variable-length field Cmd simplifies the string expression used to construct the command, and using Options(*Varsize) in the prototype allows us to pass less data than the prototype specifies.

You can see that APIs provide you with a variety of callable routines to access the resources of the System i in ways not possible with RPG IV alone. If you are interested in learning more details about APIs, see IBM's online API documentation.

Data Areas

Parameters let calling and called programs share data. **Data areas** are system objects that represent storage locations used to share data between programs within a job or between jobs. However, one program does not have to call another to share the data if the data resides in a data area; nor does a calling program have to pass parameters to a called program to share the data. You can use data areas to store information of limited size (up to 2,000 bytes), independent of database files or programs.

The system automatically creates a **local data area (LDA)** for each job in the system. Each LDA is 1,024 positions long, with type character; initially, blanks fill the LDA. When you submit a job with the CL SBMJOB (Submit Job) command, the value of your LDA is copied into the LDA of the submitted job so that the submitted job can access any data values stored in the LDA by your initial job. When a job ends, its LDA ceases to exist.

You also can create more permanent data areas with the CRTDTAARA (Create Data Area) command. A data area created in this way remains an object on the system until it is explicitly removed; any program, regardless of its job, can access such a data area.

Programmers use data areas to store small quantities of data used frequently by several programs or by the same program each time it is run. For example, they might prefer storing within a data area the next order number or customer number to be assigned, to avoid having to retrieve that information from a database file of orders or customers. Programmers sometimes use a data area to store constant values used by several programs, such as tax rates or discounts, or to transfer the processing results of one program to another.

Data Area Data Structures

As a programmer, you should understand how to access data areas from within an RPG IV program. To make a data area accessible to an RPG IV program, define a data structure for the data area. A U in position 23 (T) of a data-structure definition identifies it as a **data area data structure**.

If you do not provide a name for a data area data structure, the data structure automatically represents the LDA. If you want the data structure to contain data from a different data area, you must provide a name for the data structure; usually that name matches the external name of the data area in the system (otherwise, the Dtaara keyword provides the external name of the data area). The following code illustrates three data area data structures.

```
*.. 1 ...+... 2 ...+... 3 ...+... 4 ...+... 5 ...+... 6 ...+... 7 ...+... 8
DName++++++++++ETDsFrom+++To/L+++IDc.Keywords+++++++++++++++++++++++++++++++
   // The data structure below represents the local data area (LDA).
D                 UDS
D Invno                        8  0

   // The data structure below represents data area Receipts.
D Receipts        UDS
D   Store1                     10  2
D   Store2                     10  2
D   Store3                     10  2

// The NextRes data structure represents the ResCounter data area.
D Nextres         UDS               Dtaara(Rescounter)
D   Nextresnbr                  7  0
```

The contents of any data area defined via a data structure, as in the above examples, are read into the program at program initialization. The data area is then locked to prevent other programs from accessing it. When the program ends, the system writes the contents of the data structure from the program back to the data area and removes the lock.

If your program needs to process a data area data structure more explicitly than simply reading and locking it when the program begins and then writing/unlocking it when the program ends, it can use three operation codes related to data area processing:

- In (Retrieve a Data Area)
- Out (Write a Data Area)
- Unlock (Unlock a Data Area)

The **In (Retrieve a Data Area)** and **Out (Write a Data Area) operations** allow you to retrieve and write a data area in a program, as well as to control the locking or unlocking of a data area. When a program locks a data area, other programs can read the data area but cannot update it; this is called an **exclusive lock**. The **Unlock (Unlock a Data Area) operation** unlocks a data area without updating it.

```
*.. 1 ...+... 2 ...+... 3 ...+... 4 ...+... 5 ...+... 6 ...+... 7 ...+... 8
DName++++++++++ETDsFrom+++To/L+++IDc.Keywords+++++++++++++++++++++++++++++++
D Nextres         UDS               Dtaara(RESCOUNTER)
D   Nextresnbr                  7  0

 /Free
    Unlock Nextres;
    ...
    In *Lock Nextres;
    Nextresnbr += 1;
    Out Nextres;
 /End-free
```

In the preceding example, the data area RESCOUNTER is unlocked near the beginning of the program so that other programs can read and update it. When this program is ready to find the value of Nextresnbr, it will use the In operation to retrieve the data area and lock it; it will then promptly update the data area with a new value. If the subsequent Out operation does not specify *Lock, the data area will be automatically unlocked after the update; if the lock is to remain in effect, specify *Lock:

```
Out *Lock Nextres;
```

*Lock cannot be specified for the local data area. The Unlock operation can also unlock all the data areas locked by a program:

```
Unlock *Dtaara;
```

Chapter Summary

Programming experts advocate a modular approach to programming, in which you break complex processing down into separate programs or modules, each focused on accomplishing a single function. Other programs can then call these programs. If a routine is compiled and bound into a separate *PGM object, you use operation Callp to invoke that program. The System i lets you write calling and called programs in any mix of languages available on the system, including CL.

In RPG IV, all variables are global within a program but local to the program. To share data between a calling and a called program, both programs use parameters to define the shared data. These parameters are described by a prototype definition and appear as arguments to a Callp operation. The procedure interface definition lets the called program accept parameter values and assign them to variables.

When you pass parameters by reference, the corresponding parameter variables in the calling and called programs share a common storage location. As a result, changes to a parameter's value in one of the programs affect the corresponding parameter's value in the other program. Using prototype definitions, you can also pass parameters by read-only reference, a method that improves the call's flexibility and avoids problems with parameters being changed by called programs.

The LR indicator controls whether or a not a called program will completely "shut down" when it returns to its caller. If *Inlr is off when a program returns, the program will remain active; if *Inlr is on, the program will start fresh the next time it is called. You should ensure that a program ends with *Inlr on after a process is finished with it.

IBM offers several built-in system programs, called APIs, which you can call from your RPG IV program to accomplish various kinds of lower-level processing. API QUSCMDLN presents a system command line for use within a program. API QCMDEXC lets you execute a CL command from within your program; you simply pass the command as a parameter to QCMDEXC, along with another parameter that specifies the command's length.

The System i also provides data areas (special storage areas defined on the system) for sharing values between programs. The programs do not have to call one another to access the same data area. A temporary local data area (LDA) is automatically available for each job; you also can define permanent data areas that any program can subsequently access. You access the contents of a data area within an RPG IV program by defining a special data structure—a data area data structure. Data contained in data area data structures is automatically retrieved at the start of a program and written back to the data area at the end of the program.

The following table summarizes the operation codes discussed in this chapter:

Function or operation	Description	Syntax
Callp	Call a prototyped procedure or program	{Callp{(emr)}} name({parm1 : parm2 : ...})
In	Write a data area	In{(e)} {*Lock} data-area-name
Out	Write a data area	Out{(e)} {*Lock} data-area-name
Return	Return to caller	Return
Unlock	Unlock a data area	Unlock{(e)} {*Lock} data-area-name

Key Terms

APIs
arguments
call interface
Callp operation
data area data structure
data areas
exclusive lock
In operation
local data area (LDA)
modular programming

Out operation
parameters
passing by reference
procedure interface
prototype
read-only reference
Return operation
scope
Unlock operation
user space

Discussion/Review Questions

1. What does "modular programming" mean?
2. What are the advantages of a modular approach to application development?
3. What effect does LR have on a called program?
4. What is the purpose of the prototype definition?
5. List the parts of a prototype definition.
6. List the rules that must be observed when defining a prototype.
7. What are the default data attributes for numeric and character data types?
8. When passing by reference, why is a change in a parameter variable reflected in the called program?
9. What is the purpose of the procedure interface?
10. Explain the difference between passing by reference and read-only reference. Why would you use one instead of the other?
11. Explain the use of API QUSCMDLN and QCMDEXC.
12. Research the APIs that are available to programmers, and select five, list them, and explain how you might use them.
13. What is an LDA?
14. Why might you use a data area rather than a database file to store values?
15. Describe how to access a data area through a data area data structure.

Exercises

1. Write the RPG IV code to call either ProgA, ProgB, or ProgC, depending on whether the value of field Option is 1, 2, or 3. No parameters are needed with any of the calls.

2. Write the portion of a calling program that passes a date of numeric data type in *yymmdd* format to a called program to convert the date to a date in month-name, day, and four-digit-year format (e.g., January 1, 1993).

3. Write the entire RPG IV program that would be called in Exercise 2 to convert the date to the desired format.

4. Assume a data area named CheckValue contains a six-position number representing the last check number used, a six-position date reflecting the most recent date on which the check-writing program was run, ten positions containing the name of the last user running the check-writing program, and four positions reflecting the number of checks written during the last program run. Code a data area data structure to enable access to this data area.

5. At a certain point in an RPG IV program, you need to delete a database file. The name of the file to be deleted is contained in field FileName, a ten-position character field. The CL command to delete a file is DLT (Delete File), used as follows:

```
DLTF FILE(*CURLIB/xxxxxxxxxx)
```

where *xxxxxxxxxx* represents a file name. Write the code to execute this command.

6. Write the RPG IV code to incorporate the file name from field FileName in the proper location within the DLTF command, and then call API QCMDEXC to carry out the command.

Programming Assignments

1. Develop an interactive menu application that presents the user with a choice for executing one of four programs you have written this semester. (Your instructor may tell you which applications to include; preferably, the programs will be part of the same application system and include at least one interactive application.)

   a. Your program should call the appropriate program based on the user's choice. Upon return from the called program, the user should again see the menu for another selection. This cycle should continue until the user signals Exit at the menu.

   b. Design your menu to be user friendly; display messages if the user inputs incorrect choices.

   c. Include informational messages signaling the results of processing for non-interactive applications, so that the user knows the selected program was executed.

   d. Allow the user access a CL command line from the menu by pressing F21.

2. As part of its billing procedure, GTC needs to perform a number of conversions to data stored in the GTCLSP file when used in several programs. The company decides to perform these conversions through a called program with procedures to perform each conversion. The conversions are listed below. Each conversion will be done in a called procedure in a separate called program, and the converted value will be returned to the calling program.

   a. GTC needs to convert military time to standard time. This procedure will receive a parameter argument in *hhmm* format, where the hours are based on a 24-hour clock (i.e., military time); convert that value to time expressed on a 12-hour clock, with a.m. or p.m.; and return the converted value. For example, if the called program was passed 1530, it should convert that value to 3:30 p.m.

   b. Convert the date stored in the field CALDAT to a native date. The called procedure will accept the CALDAT field and return the converted date.

   c. Format the first name and last name fields so that the name is displayed with the first letter capitalized and the balance of the name in lower case.

   To test your program, create a logical file that uses GTC's Customer Master file GTCSTP and the calls transaction file, GTCLSP (described in Appendix F) as the input files to a calling program that passes the time-of-call value from each record to the called program and generates the following report to reflect the converted time returned by the called program:

```
          1         2         3         4         5         6         7         8
 123456789012345678901234567890123456789012345678901234567890123456789012345678901234567890
 1 XX/XX/XX                                                                    Page XXØX
 2                          GTC Time Conversion Test Report
 3
 4 Phone         First           Last            Call       Military   Converted
 5 Number        Name            Name            Date       Time        Time
 6 999-999-9999  XXXXXXXXXXXX    XXXXXXXXXXXXXXX 99/99/9999  XXXX       ØX:XX AM
 7 999-999-9999  XXXXXXXXXXXX    XXXXXXXXXXXXXXX 99/99/9999  XXXX       ØX:XX AM
 8 999-999-9999  XXXXXXXXXXXX    XXXXXXXXXXXXXXX 99/99/9999  XXXX       ØX:XX AM
 9
10                                              Total Calls Processed XXXØX
11
```

3. GTC needs to convert time from military to standard time and determine the day of the week from a given date, both as part of its billing procedure. The programmers decide to implement each of these conversions as called programs. Write two called programs to accomplish these tasks. Programming Assignment 2, above, describes more details of the time conversion. For the called program that determines the day of the week, use the algorithm shown below.

Algorithm to determine day of week from a date in numeric format:

a. Initialize known date

b. Convert given date to date data type

c. Calculate number-of-days from known date to converted date

d. Calculate day-of-week (remainder from number-of-days / 7)

e. Use the code below to assign the day-of-week Text.

```
IF day-of-week = 0
        name-of-day = "Sunday"
ELSE
        IF day-of-week = 1
                name-of-day = "Monday"
ELSE
        IF day-of-week = 2
                name-of-day = "Tuesday"
ELSE
        . . .
ENDIF
```

Test your two called programs by generating the following report, using the date-of-call and time-of-call fields of GTC's calls transaction file (GTCLSP) for your test data. For the report's Day of the Week column, print the appropriate name of the day (e.g., SUNDAY). Like the previous assignment, this assignment will require a logical file.

```
          1         2         3         4         5         6         7         8         9
 1234567890123456789012345678901234567890123456789012345678901234567890123456789012345678901234567890
 1 XX/XX/XX                                                                      Page XX0X
 2                          GTC Time Conversion Test Report
 3
 4 Phone         First       Last            Call        Day of    Military  Converted
 5 Number        Name        Name            Date        the Week  Time      Time
 6 999-999-9999  XXXXXXXXX   XXXXXXXXXXXXXXX 99/99/9999  XXXXXXXXX XXXX      0X:XX AM
 7 999-999-9999  XXXXXXXXX   XXXXXXXXXXXXXXX 99/99/9999  XXXXXXXXX XXXX      0X:XX AM
 8 999-999-9999  XXXXXXXXX   XXXXXXXXXXXXXXX 99/99/9999  XXXXXXXXX XXXX      0X:XX AM
 9
10                                                       Total Calls Processed XXX0X
```

4. CompuSell wants you to write a label-printing program for its customers in file CSCSTP (Appendix F); the company wants your program to print two-across labels. Each of the labels reading across should represent the same customer. The printer will be loaded with continuous-label stock when this program is run. Each label is five print lines long. The desired format for the labels is shown below.

a. The names, addresses, and city should be printed in lower case (except for the first letter of each word). Rather than writing a conversion routine repeatedly for each of the fields, you decide to write the procedure once as a called program so that it will be available for use in other programs.

b. The label program successively calls the procedure in the called program to convert first name, last name, street address, and city to the desired format for each customer before printing the label.

Note: the information within parentheses is included to let you know what should appear on the label, but this information should not appear in your output.

```
         1         2         3         4         5         6         7         8         9         1
         1234567890123456789012345678901234567890123456789012345678901234567890123456789012345678901234567890
 1        XXXXXXXXX XXXXXXXXXXXXXXX            XXXXXXXXX XXXXXXXXXXXXXXX     (first, last name)
 2        XXXXXXXXXXXXXXXXXXXXX                XXXXXXXXXXXXXXXXXXXXX         (street address)
 3        XXXXXXXXXXXXXXX  XX XXXXX-XXXX        XXXXXXXXXXXXXXX  XX XXXXX-XXXX  (city, state, zip)
 4
 5
 6        XXXXXXXXX XXXXXXXXXXXXXXX            XXXXXXXXX XXXXXXXXXXXXXXX
 7        XXXXXXXXXXXXXXXXXXXXX                XXXXXXXXXXXXXXXXXXXXX
 8        XXXXXXXXXXXXXXX  XX XXXXX-XXXX        XXXXXXXXXXXXXXX  XX XXXXX-XXXX
 9
10        Total Number of Labels   XXXØX
11
```

5. Wexler University wants a Payroll report for the hourly employees. This report will require a logical file built over the WUHRLYP file. All calculations and conversions should be performed in individual procedures in called programs.

    The report requirements are below:

    a. The report should be in employee last name, first name order.

    b. The employee name should be in proper case (first letter capitalized and the balance of the name in lower case).

    c. The hire date should be converted to a native date field.

    d. The employee receives the normal rate of pay (RATE) for the regular hours and 1.5 the rate of pay for overtime (OTHRS). The tax rate is 25 percent.

```
         1         2         3         4         5         6         7         8         9         10
1234567890123456789012345678901234567890123456789012345678901234567890123456789012345678901234567890
1 XX/XX/XX                                                                                 Page XXØX
2                          Wexler University Employee Payroll Report
3
4 Social Sec.   First        Last              Regular    Overtime    Gross                   Net Pay
5 Number        Name         Name              Hours      Hours       Pay        Tax
6 999-99-9999   XXXXXXXXXX   XXXXXXXXXXXXXXX   XXØ        XXØ         X,XXX.ØX   X,XXX.ØX    X,XXX.ØX
7 999-99-9999   XXXXXXXXXX   XXXXXXXXXXXXXXX   XXØ        XXØ         X,XXX.ØX   X,XXX.ØX    X,XXX.ØX
8 999-99-9999   XXXXXXXXXX   XXXXXXXXXXXXXXX   XXØ        XXØ         X,XXX.ØX   X,XXX.ØX    X,XXX.ØX
9                           Report Totals      XXXØ       XXXØ        XØX,XXX.ØX XØX,XXX.ØX  XØX,XXX.ØX
10
11
12 Total Employees Processed XXXØX
13
```

6. In Chapter 11, CompuSell wanted an interactive file maintenance program for its customer master file, CSCSTP (described in Appendix F). The criterion for this program is described in Chapter 11, programming assignment 2. The only change for this assignment is to store the last assigned customer number in a data area.

Note: You will need to read the data area, add 1 to it for the new customer number, and write the new value back to the data area. If you have written this program for a previous assignment, convert it to use a data area. Otherwise, write the program using a data area.

Chapter 13

Building Modular Programs with Procedures

Chapter Overview

This chapter continues coverage of modular programming techniques by discussing procedures. You'll learn how procedures differ from subroutines and called programs and the advantages of using procedures. You'll also learn how to create modular components and bind them to callable program objects. Finally, this chapter will introduce several other application development topics related to the Integrated Language Environment (ILE): service programs, binding directories, and binder language.

Dynamic Program Calls and Static Binding

In the previous chapter, we discussed a modular approach to programming in terms of calling separate executable program (*Pgm) objects. In this environment, the calling programs and the called programs are complete in themselves, having been individually compiled. This technique is called a **dynamic program call**. With this technique, when you run a program that uses the Callp operation to invoke another program, the system goes "looking" for the called program dynamically, during runtime, using an internal process known as **resolution**. The calling program depends upon the existence of the called program not at the time you compile it, but at the time you actually run it. The programs are never physically connected to each other, but they can execute in concert with each other at run time.

If an application is "call intensive" (that is, if one program calls another program hundreds, or even thousands, of times), this dynamic resolution takes time and may degrade system performance—in some instances, severely—compared to performance if the programmer handled the code in the called programs as subroutines internal to the calling program.

When IBM introduced the Integrated Language Environment (ILE) to i5/OS, it included the option of connecting RPG IV modules *before* runtime. This **static binding** alleviates some of the performance degradation found with dynamic program calls. With static binding, the calling component and the called component are bound together into a single called program object. The resolution process take place one time—when the program is first created—and has already been accomplished by the time the program runs.

Here is how static binding works. When you compile source code with the **CRTRPGMOD (Create RPG Module) command**, the compiler creates a *Module object, rather than an executable program (*Pgm) object. A module (sometimes called a **compile unit**) contains compiled, executable code, but you cannot run a module by itself; its purpose is to be a building block for the eventual program object. To form the runnable program, you must carry out a separate binding procedure, invoked through the **CRTPGM (Create Program) command**.

Because the binding step in this process physically copies the compiled code from the module(s) into the program object, this model of static binding is called **bind-by-copy**. When the program runs, the binding has already been completed, so performance is not affected. Figure 13.1 illustrates the two-step compile-then-bind process graphically.

Figure 13.1
Compiling and Binding an ILE Program

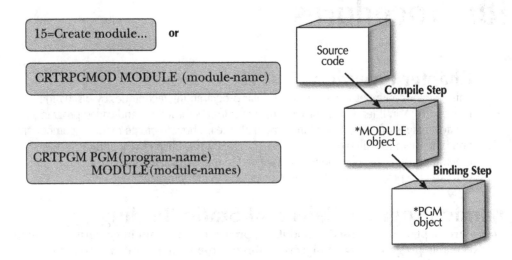

A program can comprise one or more compiled modules. If some modules are to call others, you can link them together during this binding step to form a single executable *Pgm object. The modules need not even be written in the same language; an ILE program might consist of RPG IV modules and CL modules bound to the same program. When you create the program, you must designate one of the modules as the **entry module** for the program; this is the first module that will execute when you invoke the program, and it will serve as the "driver" for the program. The resulting ILE program is called a **single entry point program**, because it always begins execution at the beginning of a single module. Figure 13.2 illustrates the process of creating an ILE program from several modules, using the bind-by-copy process.

Figure 13.2
Creating an ILE Program from Multiple Modules

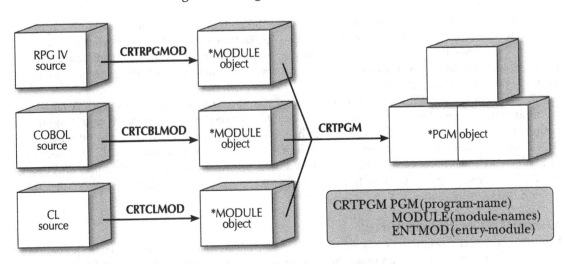

An alternate static binding technique, called **bind-by-reference,** binds *Module objects together to form a **service program** (*Srvpgm) object. Service programs are not standalone executable objects but instead serve as containers for module code that other programs can access. Any of the modules bound into a service program can be an entry point into the service program; it is known as a **multiple entry point program**. A single entry point program can invoke the compiled code in a multiple entry point service program, similarly to the way one program object can dynamically call another. Service programs combine some of the performance advantages of bind-by-copy static binding with the modularity and flexibility advantages of the dynamic program call. We'll reserve a more complete discussion of service programs for later in this chapter.

Procedures and Subprocedures

Procedures are IBM's most recent RPG enhancement for developing modular, reusable code. In the past, RPG programs consisted of single-procedure programs. With the introduction of procedures, a program can now consist of a main procedure and, optionally, one or more **subprocedures**. Moreover, subprocedures can exist either within the same module as a main procedure or in standalone modules, where they can readily be bound to and accessed by several different programs.

A subprocedure is like a subroutine, but with several important differences. First, the subprocedure can be created independently of what we traditionally have called a program but now more accurately call a main procedure. A program's procedures can be coded in separate source members and compiled into separate modules, then bound together when the program is created. A procedure is not a system object, but it is a segment of executable code contained within a compiled module object; a module can contain one or more procedures.

The second important difference between a subprocedure and a subroutine lies in the scope of the variables used in the two kinds of routines. For a program containing subroutines (no subprocedures), all data definition is **global**; that is, all variables are equally accessible by both the main calculations and the subroutines they execute. In contrast, subprocedures introduce the concept of **local variables** to RPG. Local variables are recognized only within the subprocedure in which they are defined. Data values are communicated from main procedures to subprocedures by passing parameters.

A third difference between subprocedures and subroutines is that subprocedures are recursive; a procedure can actually call itself (actually a new copy of itself). Some applications can make good use of the recursive functionality of subprocedures. For example, in a manufacturing application, a complex component might consist of yet other components, each of which might require identical subprocedure processing at its own level.

Another important difference between subprocedures and subroutines is the **return value.** A subprocedure, like a built-in function, may return a value to the calling procedure outside the context of any parameter variable. This capability effectively lets you incorporate user-defined functions into your programs, using your own functions as easily as you can use RPG IV's built-in functions. Once a subprocedure has been created, if it returns a value to the calling procedure, you invoke it the same way you invoke a function. To invoke a subprocedure that does not return values, you use the Callp operation.

Using Local Procedures

Up until now, all the programs we have written have consisted of a main procedure only, coded in a single source member. The main procedure comprises all the normal RPG IV specifications in the order that we have previously discussed:

- H—Control specifications
- F—File specifications
- D—Definition specifications
- I—Input specifications
- C—Calculation specifications
- O—Output specifications

You can include the code for a subprocedure in the same source member as the main procedure for a program. Using this technique, a single source member includes the main procedure and one or more subprocedures in the same compile unit. This type of subprocedure, commonly called a **local procedure,** might be appropriate when the function performed by the procedure is needed by only one program in an application; or it might be useful when a simple subroutine won't do—for example, when you want to take advantage of parameter passing, local variables, or a return value. Local procedures are also useful in a top down approach to program design, because you can encapsulate the complexity of a process within a procedure, in much the same way that you can simplify a program by relegating complex code to a subroutine. The code for a local procedure appears after the last line of code in the main procedure (but before any compile time data).

Tip
Don't be confused or overly concerned about the differences between a procedure and a subprocedure. The term "subprocedure" is simply used by RPG IV to distinguish a program's main procedure from other procedures in the program.

To understand the basic coding requirements for a procedure, let's look at an example. The following program demonstrates how to code a main procedure and a local procedure to convert a Fahrenheit temperature value into its Celsius equivalent. Although the program is complete as shown, it has been abbreviated to concentrate those lines that relate to procedures.

```
*.. 1 ...+... 2 ...+... 3 ...+... 4 ...+... 5 ...+... 6 ...+... 7 ...+... 8
   // ------------------------------------------------- Main procedure PR/PI
D Main             PR                    Extpgm('THISPGM')
D Main             PI

   // -------------------------------------------------------- Prototypes
D Celsius          PR            5  0
D                                5  0

   // ----------------------------------------------------- Global variables
D Metrictemp       S             5  0
D Englishtemp      S             5  0
D Status           S             8

   // ------------------------------------------------------------------
   //
   // Main procedure
   //
   // ------------------------------------------------------------------

/Free
   Englishtemp = 212;
   Metrictemp = Celsius(Englishtemp);

   If Celsius(Englishtemp) > 0;
     Status = 'Thawed';
   Else;
     Status = 'Freezing';
   Endif;

   *Inlr = *On;
   Return;
/End-Free

   // ------------------------------------------------------------------
   //
   // Procedure ... Celsius ... Converts Fahrenheit to Celsius
   //
   // ------------------------------------------------------------------
P Celsius          B

D                  PI            5  0
D Fahrenheit                     5  0

   // ----------------------------------------------------- Local variables
D Temperature      S             5  0
```

continued...

continued...

```
 /Free
    Eval(H) Temperature = (5/9) * (Fahrenheit - 32);
    Return Temperature;
 /End-Free

P Celsius            E
```

Coding the Main Procedure

The first section of code should be familiar to you by now. We've started with a primary PR/PI combination to identify the main procedure interface into the program. If the program required any parameters, the interface would have reflected those parameters. Since this program does not require parameters, we could have omitted this PR/PI combination, but we included it as a matter of good style:

```
DName++++++++++ETDsFrom+++To/L+++IDc.Functions++++++++++++++++++++++++++++
D Main            PR                    Extpgm('THISPGM')
D Main            PI
```

Next in the code come Definition specifications to define the **prototype** for the Celsius subprocedure. This prototype lets the compiler compare the parameter definitions in the calling and the called procedures for inconsistencies that could cause difficult-to-locate bugs when the program is executed. By now, you should be familiar with this structure. Notice the differences in the prototype header for this prototype compared to the prototypes we discussed in the previous chapter. In addition to naming the subprocedure (in this case, Celsius), the first line of the prototype identifies the length (positions 33–39), data type (position 40), and any decimal positions (positions 41–42) of the value the subprocedure will return to the caller. This entry defines the subprocedure's **return value**.

```
DName++++++++++ETDsFrom+++To/L+++IDc.Functions++++++++++++++++++++++++++++
D Celsius         PR              5  0
D                                 5  0
```

A subprocedure can have only a single return value. The return value can be any supported data type; it can also be a data structure (using the Likeds keyword) or an array (using the Dim keyword). Notice that the prototype does not include the Extpgm keyword; the Extpgm keyword specifies a dynamic program call, so it is not appropriate for this static procedure call. (If the name of the prototype does not match the name of the procedure, or if the procedure name is case sensitive, you can use the Extproc keyword to name the procedure.)

The next Definition specification (without any entry in positions 24–25) identifies the attributes of the single parameter to be passed to the subprocedure by the caller. If there were additional parameters, you would code additional Definition specifications.

This program will also need to define a few standalone variables—work fields—to complete its task. The S in position 24 of the definitions separates the prototype from the standalone variables.

```
DName++++++++++ETDsFrom+++To/L+++IDc.Functions+++++++++++++++++++++++++++++
D Metrictemp      S              5 0
D Englishtemp     S              5 0
```

Because these variables are defined within the main procedure portion of the program, they are **global variables**. The values of Metrictemp and Englishtemp will be available throughout the entire compile unit and can be changed from anywhere within the compile unit—both the main procedure and the Celsius subprocedure.

The next block of calculations represents the main procedure's processing steps:

```
Englishtemp = 212;
Metrictemp = Celsius(Englishtemp);
If Celsius(Englishtemp) > 0;
  Status = 'Thawed';
Else;
  Status = 'Freezing';
Endif;

*Inlr = *On;
Return;
```

Because the prototype for the Celsius subprocedure includes a return value, the main procedure can now use Celsius like a function when it needs to convert a Fahrenheit temperature to its Celsius equivalent. In the main procedure (i.e., the calling procedure), you could assign the value of the Celsius subprocedure to another variable or use it in an If statement. The main procedure doesn't need to know what process Celsius will use to perform the conversion; the main procedure needs only to pass the Englishtemp variable as a parameter, in parentheses, to Celsius and then process the return value from Celsius.

You can also call subprocedures using the Callp operation, using the form

```
{Callp} prototype({parm1: parm2: ... parmn});
```

You should use this method for calling procedures only when the subprocedure does not return a value. Otherwise, invoke the subprocedure like a function.

Tip
It is often useful—as well as documentary—to give the subprocedure a meaningful name that describes the return value.

The main procedure ends with a couple of familiar lines, to turn on *Inlr—that is, close down the program—and return to its caller. If the program included File specifications, Input specifications, or Output specifications, they would appear in their normal sequence in the main procedure, *before* any subprocedures.

Coding the Local Subprocedure

After coding the main procedure, the program includes the local subprocedure. Every subprocedure begins and ends with **Procedure Boundary specifications.** The P-spec is a new type of specification that forms the beginning and ending boundaries of the procedure. It includes a P in position 6, the name of the subprocedure in positions 7–21 (*Name*++++++++++), and in position 24 either a B to indicate the beginning of the subprocedure, or an E to mark its end:

```
PName++++++++++..T.................Functions++++++++++++++++++++++++++++++
P Celsius             B
 ...
P Celsius             E
```

Between the boundaries of the two P-specs you may code definitions (D-specs) and calculations (C-specs); no other specifications may appear within a subprocedure.

The first Definition specification (with PI in positions 24–25) inside the subprocedure defines the **procedure interface** of the subprocedure. Remember that the procedure interface accepts the parameters and assigns their values to variables in the procedure. Like the prototype, now the procedure interface includes the length and type of the subprocedure's return value. The following Definition specification defines the variable (Fahrenheit) that is to receive the value of the parameter passed to the subprocedure. As with the prototype, had there been more parameters, we would have coded more Definition specifications.

```
DName++++++++++ETDsFrom+++To/L+++IDc.Functions+++++++++++++++++++++++++++++
D                  PI             5 0
D Fahrenheit                      5 0
```

The procedure interface must match exactly the prototype for the procedure. The data attributes of the return value and the parameters must be the same in both definitions. If there are any keywords, they must match as well. If there is a mismatch, the compile will fail. For a static procedure call, the procedure interface need not be named; an RPG IV subprocedure can have only one interface.

The final Definition specification defines Temperature, a standalone variable (with an S in position 24). In addition to standalone variables, you can code local data structures, arrays, tables, and named constants within a subprocedure.

```
DName++++++++++ETDsFrom+++To/L+++IDc.Functions+++++++++++++++++++++++++++++
D Temperature     S             5 0
```

The definitions described within the subprocedure have a **local scope.** In this example, variables Fahrenheit and Temperature are local—they are restricted to the subprocedure in which they are defined. No other procedure will recognize that these variables exist; they cannot be referenced or changed outside the boundaries of the Celsius subprocedure. In fact, if the program were to contain several subprocedures, each one could have local variables with identical names, even if they had different data attributes.

If we had needed to do so, the Celsius subprocedure could also have processed the Metrictemp and Englishtemp variables. Those variables, which are defined in the main procedure, have a **global**

scope; they can be accessed from anywhere in the compile unit. The main procedure cannot define local variables. The main procedure cannot access a subprocedure's local variables.

Tip

As a general rule, you should define variables with the narrowest scope that will accomplish your program's goal. Instead of accessing global variables in a subprocedure, you should pass parameters to share information between the main procedure and any subprocedures. In a large program, consisting of many modules, this practice will help avoid confusion and errors and make your programs easier to maintain.

The Calculation specifications inside the subprocedure do the actual work of the subprocedure. In this case, the subprocedure accepts the sole parameter into local variable Fahrenheit and then converts it to the appropriate value in local variable Temperature. Following that assignment, the Return operation immediately returns control back to the main procedure; but this operation is not the simple Return that we have used before. Note that the name of the variable containing the calculated value (Temperature) is included with the Return operation to allow the subprocedure to return this value to the calling procedure.

```
Eval(H) Temperature = (5/9) * (Fahrenheit - 32);
Return Temperature;
```

It's important to understand that the subprocedure is *not* returning the Temperature variable itself, but only the value of that variable. It is the responsibility of the main procedure to use that value in its proper context—for example, assigning it to another variable or using it in an If statement.

As an alternative to coding the Return statement with a variable, you can code an expression or a literal; the subprocedure will return the value of the expression or literal. The following Return statement would accomplish the same end as the previous example (without the need for the Temperature variable):

```
Return(H) (5/9) * (Fahrenheit - 32);
```

Any local variables defined inside a subprocedure are allocated by default in **automatic storage**, which is allocated only while the subprocedure is active. Each time the subprocedure is called during the execution of a program, those variables are automatically reinitialized; they do not retain their values from previous iterations of the subprocedure. On the rare occasion that a local variable must preserve its value between subprocedure calls, you can define it with the Static keyword to allocate it in **static storage,** which remains active until the program's main procedure ends with *Inlr on.

Creating the Single-Module Program

To create a single-module program that uses a local procedure, such as the one we've been discussing, you must first compile it to a *Module object with the CRTRPGMOD command. Once the module has successfully compiled, you must bind it using the CRTPGM command. Figure 13.1 illustrated this process.

As an alternative, the **CRTBNDRPG (Create Bound RPG Program) command** will let you create a single-module program, combining the compile and binding steps into a single command. But the default options for the CRTBNDRPG command will cause the compile to fail if you try to use it to create a program with subprocedures. You can, however, make a change when you execute the CRTBNDRPG command to allow subprocedures. If you execute the command with the DFTACTGRP(*NO) option, it will allow the use of local subprocedures. This option specifies that the program should not be forced to run in the job's default activation group. An **activation group** is a subdivision of a job that ILE enlists to keep track of the resources a job uses; one job can have several activation groups in use simultaneously. Programs that are forced to run in the default activation group do not strictly conform to ILE concepts and do not support procedures. If it is free to create the program to run in other activation groups, the CRTBNDRPG command will support subprocedures. A complete discussion of activation groups goes beyond the scope of this text.

Creating Nomain Modular Procedures

Now that you understand how to code a procedure, how to call it, and how to create a program that uses it, let's take this modular programming tool one step further. Until now, the programs that we've been coding have all been complete programs in a single source member. ILE programs, however, can comprise more than one compile unit. An ILE program can be made up of several compiled modules, each of which represents only a portion of the entire program. The program's individual modules are coded and compiled independently from each other and then bound together when you create the program with the CRTPGM command. This concept lets you work with small pieces of code, which preferably perform single functions, and then use those pieces just like building blocks to create an entire program. A given module might be reusable in many different programs, even though you would have to code, maintain and compile only a single instance of it. Even though it's not a complete program by itself, the module would offer a service (i.e., a procedure) or a group of services that other programs might use.

Figure 13.2 illustrated the process of creating a multiple-module program. First, the compile step compiles each source member, creating a module (*Module) object. Then, the binding step gathers all the modules necessary for the program and binds them into the eventual program (*Pgm) object. During the binding step, one of those modules is designated the entry module for the program. The entry module is the first user-written code that executes when the program is loaded; this module includes the program's main procedure. The other modules in the program do not have a main procedure and cannot be the entry module; their subprocedures must be called from another procedure in the program, either the main procedure or another subprocedure.

Coding the Main Procedure

To understand the concept of a multiple-module program, let's revisit the program to convert a Fahrenheit temperature value into its Celsius equivalent. This time, though, we'll separate the program's main procedure from the Celsius procedure, putting each into a separate source member.

Source member THISPGM:

```
*.. 1 ...+... 2 ...+... 3 ...+... 4 ...+... 5 ...+... 6 ...+... 7 ...+... 8
   // ------------------------------------------------- Main procedure PR/PI
D Main            PR                       Extpgm('THISPGM')
D Main            PI

   // --------------------------------------------------------- Prototypes
D Celsius         PR              5 0
D                                 5 0

   // ------------------------------------------------- Global variables
D Metrictemp      S               5 0
D Englishtemp     S               5 0
D Status          S               8

   // ---------------------------------------------------------------------
   //
   // Main procedure
   //
   // ---------------------------------------------------------------------

 /Free
    Englishtemp = 212;
    Metrictemp = Celsius(Englishtemp);

    If Celsius(Englishtemp) > 0;
      Status = 'Thawed';
    Else;
      Status = 'Freezing';
    Endif;

    *Inlr = *On;
    Return;
 /End-Free
```

The first source member, THISPGM, contains the code for only the main procedure of the program. Everything in this source member should be familiar to you by now; after stripping out the subprocedure code, we made no changes to this source member. Notice that the program calls the Celsius subprocedure twice—in the assignment expression and in the If statement—but the actual code for the Celsius subprocedure is not in this source member.

This source member still requires a prototype for the Celsius subprocedure. The compiler will use that prototype to check the validity of the subprocedure calls, ensuring that they pass the correct number and type of parameters and that the return value will be compatible with the context of the call.

Coding the Nomain Procedure(s)

The CELSIUS source member contains the code only for the Celsius subprocedure. A few minor changes were necessary to make this source work as an independent modular procedure.

<u>Source member CELSIUS:</u>

```
*.. 1 ...+... 2 ...+... 3 ...+... 4 ...+... 5 ...+... 6 ...+... 7 ...+... 8
  // ---------------------------------------------------------------------
  //
  // Procedure Celsius Converts Fahrenheit to Celsius
  //
  // ---------------------------------------------------------------------
H Nomain

  // -------------------------------------------------------- Prototypes
D Celsius         PR              5 0
D                                 5 0

  // ----------------------------------------------------- Begin procedure
P Celsius         B                      Export

D                 PI              5 0
D Fahrenheit                      5 0

  // ----------------------------------------------------- Local variables
D Temperature     S               5 0

 /Free
    Eval(H) Temperature = (5/9) * (Fahrenheit - 32);
    Return Temperature;
 /End-Free

P Celsius         E
```

Note, first, the Control (Header) specification. This specification, with its Nomain keyword, is required when a module contains no main procedure but only a subprocedure (or subprocedures). The Nomain keyword prevents the code in this compile unit from being an entry module for a program; instead this compile unit will consist solely of one or more subprocedures, which will ultimately be bound to other modules (in this case, THISPGM) to construct a complete program.

Next in the code come Definition specifications to define the procedure prototype. By now, you should be familiar with this structure. In this source member, the prototype serves to check the validity of the procedure interface, which is coded later. This procedure prototype must appear in every module that calls this subprocedure, as well as in the subprocedure itself. This prototype should match the prototype in the source for the main procedure, or else the eventual binding step will fail.

The prototype appears near the top of the source member, in the global definitions. If there are other global variables, data structures, or constants, they can also appear in this area, before any subprocedures. Without special coding, global definitions in the individual source members are limited in scope to the source member in which they are coded and to the module into which they are compiled. Even after the modules are bound to a program, their global definitions will not normally cross modular boundaries.

Storing Prototypes in /Copy Members

A prototype definition for a program/procedure must appear in every module that refers to that program/procedure. Further, the prototype must be identical in each module. To alleviate the need for redundant, possibly erroneous, coding, RPG IV supports a /Copy function that allows you to store source records in a secondary source member— sometimes called a **copybook**—and then copy that source member into the primary source member at compile time. With this capability you can reuse a single copy of one or more prototypes without having to retype the code in every module.

To use a copybook for prototypes, use an editor to store just the prototype definition in a source member (PROTOTYPES in this example):

```
DName++++++++++ETDsFrom+++To/L+++IDc.Functions+++++++++++++++++++++++++++++++
 // ---------------------------------------- Prototype for CELSIUS procedure
D Celsius           PR             5 0
D   Fahrenheit                     5 0
```

The copybook could contain prototypes for other procedures, especially if those procedures are loosely related to each other and tend to be used together. If the compiler encounters a prototype for a procedure that it doesn't eventually call, it will overlook the unused prototype.

In each source member that refers to the procedure (the procedure source member and each member that calls it), at the point where the prototype would normally appear, instead of coding the prototype, you will code the following **compiler directive**:

```
*.. 1 ...+... 2 ...+... 3 ...+... 4 ...+... 5 ...+... 6 ...+... 7 ...+... 8
 /Copy Mylib/Mysource,Prototypes
```

A compiler directive gives an instruction to the compiler to perform an action or switch processing modes. You've already used the /Free and /End-free compiler directives to switch into and out of free-format processing. The **/Copy** directive causes records from a secondary source member to be copied into the primary source member at the point where the directive occurs. In this example, the copybook member Prototypes is in source file Mysource within library Mylib.

Because the prototype is coded within fixed-format code, the /Copy directive should begin in position 7 and must be followed by exactly one space and the path to the copybook. You must specify a member name. If you do not specify a library (e.g., Mylib), the /Copy function will search the library list for the copybook:

```
*.. 1 ...+... 2 ...+... 3 ...+... 4 ...+... 5 ...+... 6 ...+... 7 ...+... 8
 /Copy Mysource,Prototypes
```

If you do not specify a source file name (e.g., Mysource), the system will use the name QRPGLESRC:

```
*.. 1 ...+... 2 ...+... 3 ...+... 4 ...+... 5 ...+... 6 ...+... 7 ...+... 8
 /Copy Prototypes
```

In addition to using /Copy to reuse prototype source, you can use copybooks to reuse other source as well. The /Copy directive can appear anywhere in the source. It will cause the compiler to include records from the copybook at the point where the /Copy directive occurs. The copybook records must fit the context of the file being compiled;

continued...

continued...

you cannot, for example, include F-spec records from a copybook inside the C-specs. The compiler listing will show all the merged source code.

Copybook members are considered to be fixed-format records, even if the /Copy directive is included within free-format specifications. If the copybook contains free-format specifications, be sure the copybook itself includes the appropriate /Free and /End-free directives. In a block of free-format specifications, you can indent the /Copy directive.

The copybook can also include /Copy directives, if necessary, to merge nested copybook records as well as the original copybook. You should avoid nesting so deeply that the architecture becomes difficult to understand; you must also take care not to have copybooks copy each other infinitely. You can use the Copynest keyword on the H-specification to control how many nesting levels can occur (the default is 32 levels).

Another compiler directive, /Include, performs the same function as /Copy:

```
*.. 1 ...+... 2 ...+... 3 ...+... 4 ...+... 5 ...+... 6 ...+... 7 ...+... 8
/Include Mylib/Mysource,Prototypes
```

As long as your program does not include embedded Structure Query Language (SQL) statements, you can use either /Copy or **/Include**. A detailed discussion of embedded SQL goes beyond the scope of this text.

Next comes the Procedure Boundary specification to indicate the beginning of the Celsius subprocedure itself. To make this procedure available to other modules with which it will be eventually bound, we've added the **Export** keyword to the beginning P-spec. Without the Export keyword, other modules in the bound program would not be able to call the Celsius subprocedure. The Export keyword lets other modules "see" the Celsius subprocedure (but not its local data).

This subprocedure can now be used like a function in any procedure that needs to convert a Fahrenheit temperature to its Celsius equivalent. Because the Celsius procedure exists as a separate entity, you can compile it once and then bind it to any program that will require the function. Any source member that needs the Celsius function must include a prototype for it, but the actual subprocedure code will reside in only one place.

Creating a Multiple-Module Program

To create an ILE program that uses multiple modules, such as the one we've been discussing, you must first compile each source member to a *Module object with the CRTRPGMOD command:

```
CRTRPGMOD MODULE(THISPGM)
CRTRPGMOD MODULE(CELSIUS)
```

Once the modules have successfully compiled, you must bind them using the CRTPGM command:

```
CRTPGM PGM(THISPGM) MODULE(THISPGM CELSIUS) ENTMOD(THISPGM)
```

The PGM (Program) parameter names the program to be created; this will typically be the same name as the main procedure's module. The MODULE parameter lists up to 300 modules which will be bound to the program. The ENTMOD (Entry Module) parameter names the entry module—that is, the main procedure module—for the program. Figure 13.2 illustrated the process graphically.

After you have created the program object, you can run it using the CALL command. The modules that were used to construct the program are not used to run the program; the bound program object contains all the code necessary to run the program. If a module might be used in several programs, you should retain the compiled module so that it will not be necessary to recompile the source when you want to reuse the code.

Passing Parameters by Value

Recall from the previous chapter that programs can pass parameters by reference (when you want two programs to share the same memory space) or by read-only reference (when you want to avoid sharing the same memory space). Procedures can also pass parameters by reference or by read-only reference. In addition, procedure calls (but not program calls) can use a third method for passing parameters: **pass by value**.

When you include the Value keyword for a parameter within a prototype, you can pass the parameter's actual value instead of sharing the address of the parameter. The called procedure must allocate its own memory for the parameter instead of sharing the same memory address that the caller is using. If the called procedure changes the value of the parameter, the calling procedure will not recognize the change; its data is thus protected from being changed by the called procedure. Passing by value applies only to statically bound procedure calls.

```
DName++++++++++ETDsFrom+++To/L+++IDc.Functions++++++++++++++++++++++++++++++
D Celsius          PR             5 0
D                                 5 0 Value
```

In this example, we've changed the Celsius prototype to pass the parameter by value instead of reference. Any procedure that uses Celsius can be assured that the variable that the caller uses for the parameter will be protected from any changes that Celsius might make to the parameter value. In the Celsius procedure, the procedure interface definition must also specify the Value keyword to match the prototype:

```
DName++++++++++ETDsFrom+++To/L+++IDc.Functions++++++++++++++++++++++++++++++
D                  PI             5 0
D Fahrenheit                      5 0 Value
```

You can mix passing methods if necessary. If you omit the Value keyword for a parameter, the parameter is passed by reference; if you specify the Const keyword for a parameter, the parameter is passed by read-only reference. When you pass parameters by value or by read-only reference, you can pass literals and expressions as well as variables:

```
Zero = Celsius(32);
If Celsius(Englishtemp + 40) > 25;
  Status = 'Too hot';
Endif;
```

Because the parameter is passed by value, the example can pass a literal (32) or an expression (Englishtemp + 40) as well as a numeric variable.

Tip
To improve the flexibility of your coding, and to protect the integrity of a procedure's data, always pass parameters by value, unless the calling procedure needs to access any changes made by the called procedure (in that case, pass by reference). There is one exception to this general rule: If you must pass a large number of parameters, passing by reference might perform faster than passing by value.

Using Export and Import

As we mentioned earlier, the Export keyword can be used to make a subprocedure available outside the module in which it is coded. In a modular programming environment you can also use Export to define a variable whose value is available across modules. You must define the variable in the Definition specifications within each relevant procedure. In the module that will actually allocate the storage for the variable, specify the Export keyword for the variable's definition. In the other modules that will reference the variable, specify the **Import** keyword. Data items coded with Export and Import should not be used as parameters. The procedure exporting the data item is responsible for any initialization of that variable.

Module PRIMARY:
```
*.. 1 ...+... 2 ...+... 3 ...+... 4 ...+... 5 ...+... 6 ...+... 7 ...+... 8
DName++++++++++ETDsFrom+++To/L+++IDc.Keywords+++++++++++++++++++++++++++++++
D Proca           PR

  // Superglobal field
D Vara             S              9  2 Export Inz(200)

 /Free
    Proca();
 /End-Free
```

Module PROCA:
```
*.. 1 ...+... 2 ...+... 3 ...+... 4 ...+... 5 ...+... 6 ...+... 7 ...+... 8
DName++++++++++ETDsFrom+++To/L+++IDc.Keywords+++++++++++++++++++++++++++++++
D Proca           PR

  // Vara gets its value from module PRIMARY
D Vara             S              9  2 Import

P Proca           B
P Proca           E
```

If these two modules were compiled and bound to a program, the primary module would allocate the storage for Vara; both modules would use the same storage for Vara, which would be a "superglobal" definition. Usually you will find it more convenient and flexible to pass parameters between procedures, rather than using Export and Import to define such intermodular variables.

Using a Binding Directory

When it is constructing a program, the binding step copies into the resulting program object the compiled code from all the programs you list in the MODULE parameter of the CRTPGM command. You can list up to 300 individual modules in this parameter. If the program includes more than just a few modules, however, it would be tedious and error-prone to individually list the modules. To alleviate the need to list all the modules, ILE uses a special system object called a **binding directory** (type *BNDDIR).

A binding directory is simply a list of modules that might be reused when binding programs. Instead of requiring you to list each and every module that you want bound to a program, the CRTPGM command allows you to refer to one or more binding directories to find necessary modules that you may not have listed. The command's BNDDIR parameter allows you to list up to 300 binding directories:

```
CRTPGM  PGM(pgm-name)         +
        MODULE(module-names) +
        ENTMOD(entry-module) +
        BNDDIR(binding-directories)
```

You can use a binding directory to store the names of modules that you intend to reuse among many different programs. The **CRTBNDDIR (Create Binding Directory) command** will create the binding directory object; the **WRKBNDDIRE (Work with Binding Directory Entries) command** provides a convenient means of adding and removing module names in the binding directory. The binding directory does *not* contain any code; it contains only the module names, with the compiled code remaining in the module objects themselves.

When you include a binding directory value in the CRTPGM command, the binder will bind all the modules that you explicitly list in the MODULE parameter. If any of those modules call a procedure that cannot be found in the explicitly listed modules, the binder will search the binding directory (directories) in order until it finds a module that includes the procedure it needs. It will then bind that module to the program just as if you had explicitly listed it. If the binder does not need any of the procedures in a module, it will ignore that module and will not bind it.

After the binder has processed all the listed modules and all the binding directories, if it has been able to resolve all the procedure references, the program will be created. If the binder is unable to find all the necessary procedures, the binding step will fail and the program will not be created.

Updating ILE Programs

When the binder creates a program, it copies the compiled code from all the listed modules, along with the code from those modules it needs from any binding directories. The source code has gone through two steps on its way to being part of a program:

1. The compile step, which converted the source code to executable instructions stored in a module

2. The binding step, which copies the compiled code from the module to the program

If you should need to modify the code, you'll need to go through those same two steps to ensure that the program you are running is using the latest version of the instructions. Once you have modified the source code, you'll recompile it with the CRTRPGMOD command.

Instead of recreating the entire program anew, though, you can use the **UPDPGM (Update Program) command** to accomplish an abbreviated binding step. The UPDPGM command lets you list just the module (or modules) that you want to remove from the original program, replacing its code with the new version that now resides in the newly recompiled module:

```
UPDPGM PGM(program-name) MODULE(module-names)
```

The UPDPGM command performs the same functions as the CRTPGM command, except that it replaces only the changed modules (i.e., those you list) in an existing program. The unchanged modules are not affected.

To see the modules that make up an ILE program, use the **DSPPGM (Display Program) command**, which shows information about a program object:

```
DSPPGM PGM(pgm-name) DETAIL(*MODULE)
```

Creating Service Programs

Earlier in this chapter, we referred to an alternative to the bind-by-copy model for binding modules to programs. This technique, called bind-by-reference, uses a different kind of program called a service program (type *SRVPGM). Service programs are not standalone executable objects but instead serve as containers for procedures that other programs can access. A service program is a means of reusing procedures without physically copying them into each program that needs them.

A service program is a multiple entry point program; it does not have a main procedure. Instead, any of the modules bound into a service program can be an entry point into the service program. A single entry point program can invoke any procedure in a multiple entry point service program, similarly to the way one program object can dynamically call another. Service programs combine some of the performance advantages of bind-by-copy static binding with the modularity and flexibility advantages of the dynamic program call.

There are no unique coding requirements for procedures that will reside in a service program. The procedures in a service program are coded in Nomain modules; they will typically use the Export keyword to be sure that they will be available to single entry point programs that use the service program. The code uses the same syntax that we already discussed: prototypes, procedure interfaces, P-specs, Return, and so on. After entering the source code for the module, you will compile the module normally, using the CRTRPGMOD command.

Tip
If you want to "hide" a procedure in a service program, so that it may be invoked only by other procedures in the same module object, omit the Export keyword.

As you might expect, you must next bind the appropriate module objects to make use of them. Just as with single entry point programs, service programs can be bound from a single module or from multiple modules and may include modules written in different languages. You'll recall that the CRTPGM command performs the binding step for a single entry point program. The **CRTSRVPGM (Create Service Program) command** performs the same function for a multiple entry point service program:

```
CRTSRVPGM SRVPGM(srvpgm-name)  +
          MODULE(module-names) +
          BNDDIR(binding-directories)
```

The CRTSRVPGM command looks very much like the CRTPGM command and serves very much the same purpose. Notice, though, that there is no parameter to designate an entry module; because a service program is a multiple entry point program, there is no single entry module. Also notice that the CRTSRVPGM command supports the using of a binding directory; if a procedure in the service program invokes a procedure that is not in the explicit module list, it will search the binding directories in order until it finds a module that includes the procedure it needs. If the binder finds all the procedures it needs, the end result of a successful binding step will be a *Srvpgm object.

Using Service Programs

A single entry point program—or another service program—can invoke any of the procedures in a service program. But the calling program does not call the service program itself; because a service program does not have a main procedure, you cannot call it. Instead, the caller invokes an individual procedure in a service program, using the same syntax that it would use if the procedure were bound to it by copy:

```
Metrictemp = Celsius(Englishtemp);
If Celsius(Englishtemp) > 0;
   Status = 'Thawed';
Else;
   Status = 'Freezing';
Endif;
```

If there are no differences between the way you invoke a procedure in a module and the way you invoke it in a service program, how will your program know which technique to use? The answer to that question lies in the way that you bind the procedure to the calling program.

Recall that when you bind a module to a program, the binder physically copies the executable code from the module into the program—hence the term "bind-by-copy." When you bind a service program to a single entry point program, the binder does *not* physically copy the code. Instead, the binder makes a reference associating the single entry point program with the service program and each of the procedures in it—"bind-by-reference." You can think of the program as jotting a note to itself—a reminder that when it comes time to load itself at runtime it must also load any service programs that have been bound to it by reference. Once the program and any of its associated service programs have been loaded, all the procedures work together as a unit, regardless of whether they were bound by copy or by reference.

Regardless of how many programs use the procedures in a service program, there is only one copy of the executable code, in the service program. If many programs use a procedure, bind-by-reference avoids the redundancy of bind-by-copy and may avoid the need to update many programs when a procedure needs to be corrected or enhanced.

When you use the CRTPGM command to bind a single entry point program, you make the choice between bind-by-copy or bind-by-reference:

```
CRTPGM  PGM(pgm-name)           +
        MODULE(module-names)    +
        ENTMOD(entry-module)    +
        BNDSRVPGM(srvpgm-names) +
        BNDDIR(binding-directories)
```

Any modules that you list in the MODULE parameter will be bound to the program by copy. Any service programs that you list in the BNDSRVPGM (Bind service program) parameter will be bound to the program by reference. All the exported procedures in that service program will be available to the bound program, whether or not the bound program uses all of them.

Caution

You should organize service programs efficiently to avoid unnecessarily activating a large number of procedures that will not be used by the bound program. The procedures in a single service program should be closely related to each other—a concept know as cohesion. As a general rule, most of the time that you activate a service program, most of the procedures in it should be used.

When you create a service program, its procedures might refer to other procedures that reside in other service programs. In that case, the CRTSRVPGM binding step can bind additional service programs by referring to them in the BNDSRVPGM parameter:

```
CRTSRVPGM  SRVPGM(srvpgm-name)    +
           MODULE(module-names)   +
           BNDSRVPGM(srvpgm-names) +
           BNDDIR(binding-directories)
```

Recall that a binding directory—a list of reusable modules—allows the binder to find necessary modules that you may not have explicitly listed with the binder command. In addition to module entries, a binding directory can store the names of service programs that you intend to reuse among many different programs. If the binder finds the procedure it needs in a module entry, it will bind the module by copy; if it finds the procedure it needs in a service program entry, it will bind the service program (and all its procedures) by reference.

Maintaining Service Programs

If you should need to modify the code in a service program procedure, you'll need to go through the compile-then-bind process to apply those changes to the service program. Instead of recreating the entire service program, though, you can use the **UPDSRVPGM (Update Service Program) command** to complete an abbreviated binding step. The UPDSRVPGM command lets you list just the module (or modules) that you want to remove from the original service program, replacing its code with the new version that now resides in the newly recompiled module:

```
UPDSRVPGM PGM(srvpgm-name) MODULE(module-names)
```

The UPDSRVPGM command performs the same functions as the CRTSRVPGM command, except that it replaces only the changed modules (i.e., those you list) in an existing service program. The unchanged modules are not affected.

To see the modules that make up a service program, use the **DSPSRVPGM (Display Service Program) command**, which shows information about a *Srvpgm object:

```
DSPSRVPGM SRVPGM(srvpgm-name) DETAIL(*MODULE)
```

Understanding the Service Program Signature

If you make a change to a service program that does not affect its external interface (e.g., the parameters or return value of exported procedures), the programs that use that service program will not require any action on your part to reflect the change. Whether or not you will need to rebind those programs depends upon the **service program signature**. The signature is an attribute of a service program that identifies its external interface—the exported procedures (and data items) it contains.

When you bind a service program to a calling program or service program, the caller makes a note of the service program's signature. At runtime when the caller is loading itself and any associated service programs, it checks each service program to ensure that it still supports the signature the caller is expecting. If the signatures in the caller and the service program match, the caller can use the service program; if there is a mismatch the program load will fail.

Using Binder Language

You can explicitly control the service program signature using a special syntax called **binder language**. Binder language consists of three commands that define the external interface of a service program. Using an editor, you enter these commands into a source member (source type BND), and then refer to that source member when you create the service program. The three binder language commands are

- STRPGMEXP (Start Program Export List)
- EXPORT (Export a Program Symbol)
- ENDPGMEXP (End Program Export List)

To understand how binder language relates to the service program signature, consider two hypothetical procedures, DAYOFWEEK and DAYNAME. These procedures have been coded in two Nomain modules that you have compiled and want to bind to create a new service program, DATESRVPGM. Before running the binder, you should create a new source member to store the binder language that will define the signature. Usually, the source member will be named the same as the service program, DATESRVPGM in this example:

```
STRPGMEXP PGMLVL(*CURRENT)
EXPORT SYMBOL('DAYOFWEEK')
EXPORT SYMBOL('DAYNAME')
ENDPGMEXP
```

The **STRPGMEXP binder language statement** forms the beginning of the binder language to define a service program signature. Specifying *CURRENT indicates that the signature will be the current signature; this is the default value. The **ENDPGMEXP statement** indicates the end of the signature.

Between the beginning and the ending statements, **EXPORT statements** list the procedures that will be included in the signature (DAYOFWEEK and DAYNAME). The order of the procedures in the binder language affects the signature, and you should not change the order after the service program has been created. The procedures must have been created with the Export keyword in the RPG IV source. In the rare case that the procedure names are case sensitive, the names must be enclosed between apostrophes ('). In addition to procedures, you could also list data items defined with the Export keyword.

You cannot compile the binder language source member. Instead, you refer to it when you create the service program:

```
CRTSRVPGM SRVPGM(DATESRVPGM)         +
          MODULE(DAYOFWEEK DAYNAME)  +
          EXPORT(*SRCFILE)           +
          SRCFILE(QSRVSRC)           +
          SRCMBR(DATESRVPGM)
```

When the binder is constructing the service program's signature it will use the binder language in source member DATESRVPGM (in source file QSRVSRC) as the basis for generating the signature.

After the service program is created, you can view the resulting signature using the DSPSRVPGM command:

```
DSPSRVPGM SRVPGM(DATESRVPGM) DETAIL(*SIGNATURE)
```

The signature is a system-generated 16-byte string. If this service program is bound a caller, the caller will also store the current signature from the service program. When the caller and the service program are loaded at runtime, their signatures must match. To view the service programs used by the caller, along with their expected signatures, you can use the DSPPGM or DSPSRVPGM command, depending upon the caller's object type:

```
DSPPGM PGM(pgm-name) DETAIL(*SRVPGM)
DSPSRVPGM SRVPGM(srvpgm-name) DETAIL(*SRVPGM)
```

Maintaining Multiple Signatures

The use of binder language goes well beyond using it to create a single signature for a service program. A service program can simultaneously accommodate many different signatures, representing many different public interfaces. The service program has only one current signature, but it can retain any number of previous signatures. When you bind a service program to a caller, the binder associates the two objects using the current signature. But if there exist any callers that know the service program by a previous signature, those callers can continue to use the service program without recompiling or rebinding. The binder uses binder language to manage each of those signatures.

To understand why you might want a service program to have multiple signatures, consider the previous example, DATESRVPGM. For the sake of discussion, let's suppose that the binder language for this service program generated a signature of "ABC" (the actual signature would be a system-generated string). If this service program were in use for some time, it's probable that there would be many programs using it, tied to its "ABC" signature. Those programs could call its DAYOFWEEK and DAYNAME procedures.

After some time using the service program, it might be desirable to create a new procedure and package it within the service program. For example, we might want an ENDOFMONTH procedure to return the date of the end of the month. We could code this procedure in yet a third Nomain module and then bind it to the DATESRVPGM. But to avoid having to rebind all the existing programs that use DATESRVPGM—but which do not use the new ENDOFMONTH procedure—we should first modify the binder language source as follows:

```
STRPGMEXP PGMLVL(*CURRENT)
EXPORT SYMBOL('DAYOFWEEK')
EXPORT SYMBOL('DAYNAME')
EXPORT SYMBOL('ENDOFMONTH')
ENDPGMEXP

STRPGMEXP PGMLVL(*PRV)
EXPORT SYMBOL('DAYOFWEEK')
EXPORT SYMBOL('DAYNAME')
ENDPGMEXP
```

This binder language changes the existing signature to be the *PRV (previous) signature and adds a new *CURRENT signature that includes all three procedures (DAYOFWEEK, DAYNAME, and ENDOFMONTH) now in the service program.

After updating and saving the source member, we can rebind the service program:

```
CRTSRVPGM SRVPGM(DATESRVPGM)                          +
          MODULE(DAYOFWEEK DAYNAME ENDOFMONTH) +
          EXPORT(*SRCFILE)                            +
          SRCFILE(QSRVSRC)                            +
          SRCMBR(DATESRVPGM)
```

The command's EXPORT, SRCFILE, and SRCMBR parameters would default to the values shown above (with SRCMBR being the same name as the service program), so we could simply enter the following command:

```
CRTSRVPGM SRVPGM(DATESRVPGM)                        +
          MODULE(DAYOFWEEK DAYNAME ENDOFMONTH)
```

Because we are adding a new module to the service program, we cannot use the UPDPGM abbreviated binder. The binder will recreate the service program, but with two signatures now (the original "ABC" and the new current one—let's call it "DEF.")

If any existing callers associate the "ABC" signature with this service program, they will continue to run without any changes. They will be able to call the DAYOFWEEK and DAYNAME procedures—but not the new ENDOFMONTH procedure. Any new programs that are bound using this service program will associate with the current signature, "DEF," and will be able to call any of the three procedures. Any existing programs that are rebound will be bound to the new current signature.

We could continue to enhance this service program, adding new procedures and updating the binder language each time:

```
STRPGMEXP PGMLVL(*CURRENT)
EXPORT SYMBOL('DAYOFWEEK')
EXPORT SYMBOL('DAYNAME')
EXPORT SYMBOL('ENDOFMONTH')
EXPORT SYMBOL('ENDOFWEEK')
EXPORT SYMBOL('NEXTMONDAY')
ENDPGMEXP

STRPGMEXP PGMLVL(*PRV)
EXPORT SYMBOL('DAYOFWEEK')
EXPORT SYMBOL('DAYNAME')
EXPORT SYMBOL('ENDOFMONTH')
ENDPGMEXP

STRPGMEXP PGMLVL(*PRV)
EXPORT SYMBOL('DAYOFWEEK')
EXPORT SYMBOL('DAYNAME')
ENDPGMEXP
```

Each time, the old "current" signature becomes a previous signature, and a new current signature is added. Service programs, signatures, and binder language allow you a great deal of flexibility in packaging your procedures efficiently, reusing them throughout your applications, and enhancing them with a minimum impact on those programs that use them.

Chapter Summary

The Integrated Language Environment (ILE) enhances traditional module programming techniques by supporting static procedure binding as well as dynamic program calls. Static binding involves a two-step compile-then-bind process to connect RPG IV modules before runtime, saving the runtime overhead of object resolution and improving performance. ILE compilers create *Module objects—not programs—and then bind those modules to form runnable program (*Pgm) objects. A single entry point ILE program can comprise one or more compiled modules; one of the modules serves as the entry module and contains the main procedure. This binding model is called bind-by-copy.

A procedure is a segment of code, like a subroutine, but with many additional capabilities. Procedures support parameters and can use several parameter passing methods: value, reference, or read-only reference. When it passes parameters by value, a caller can protect its data from being inadvertently changed by the called procedure. Procedures can define their own local variables or can use global variables. Because they support a return value, you can incorporate procedures into your RPG IV code just like functions; if a procedure does not return a value, you can call it with the Callp operation.

You can code local procedures, which appear in the same source member as the main procedure; or you can code procedures as independent Nomain modules and then bind the modules together when it comes time to create the callable program. The coding requirements are similar for either programming model.

Procedures require a prototype and a procedure interface to describe the return value and any parameters to be passed. The procedure's local definitions, as well as the code to perform the procedure's work, appear between two Procedure Boundary specifications.

A binding directory is a list of reusable modules; you can refer to the binding directory instead of listing all the modules when you use the CRTPGM command to bind a program.

A service program acts as a procedure container to serve other programs with the procedures they need. The compiled code, however, resides in the service program. The *Srvpgm object is a multiple entry point program, with each of its procedures as an entry point. The binding model that uses service programs is call bind-by-reference. When a program uses bind-by-reference, it loads any necessary service programs at the same time that it activates itself; it can then easily use the procedures in the service program.

Through the use of binder language, a service program can incorporate multiple signatures. The capability allows you to make changes to the service program without having to change all the programs that are associated with the service program.

This chapter discusses the following CL commands, which are used to compile, bind, rebind, or display ILE programs:

- CRTRPGMOD (Create RPG Module)
- CRTPGM (Create Program)
- CRTSRVPGM (Create Service Program)
- UPDPGM (Update Program)
- UPDSRVPGM (Update Service Program)
- CRTBNDRPG (Create Bound RPG Program)
- DSPPGM (Display Program)
- DSPSRVPGM (Display Service Program)

The following table summarizes the operation codes and functions discussed in this chapter:

Function or operation	Description	Syntax
Callp	Call a prototyped procedure or program	{Callp{(emr)}} *name*({*parm1* : *parm2* : ...})
Return	Return to caller	Return{(hmr)} *expression*

Key Terms

activation group
automatic storage
bind-by-copy
bind-by-reference
binder language
binding directory
compile unit
compiler directive
/Copy
copybook
CRTBNDDIR command
CRTBNDRPG command
CRTPGM command
CRTRPGMOD command
CRTSRVPGM command
DSPPGM command
DSPSRVPGM command
dynamic program call
ENDPGMEXP statement
entry module
Export keyword
EXPORT statements
global scope
global variables

Import keyword
/Include
local procedure
local scope
local variables
multiple entry point program
pass by value
Procedure Boundary specifications
procedure interface
procedures
prototype
resolution
return value
service program
service program signature
single entry point program
static binding
static storage
STRPGMEXP statement
subprocedures
UPDPGM
UPDSRVPGM
WRKBNDDIRE

Discussion/Review Questions

1. Explain the similarities of subprocedures and subroutines.
2. What advantages do subprocedures have over subroutines?
3. What are the advantages of service programs over using a called program (example using CallP)?
4. Although static binding leads to improved system performance, when might you still want to use dynamic binding to call a program?
5. How do subprocedures improve the reusability and reliability of an application?
6. Describe the distinction between a parameter and a return value.
7. What is required to allow a local variable to retain its value between calls to a subprocedure?
8. What are the benefits of multiple-module programs?
9. List the benefits of static binding vs. dynamic program calls.
10. What is the Static keyword used for when coding modules?
11. Why is the use of binder language important to the maintenance of service programs?
12. What is the significance of signatures when coding service programs?
13. What is the importance of using binding directories?
14. Why would a parameter be passed by value?
15. Why would a Prototype be stored in a copybook?

Exercises

1. Write the RPG IV code to define two procedures. The first procedure (DATEDIFF) will accept two parameters, StartDate and EndDate. It should return the number of days between the two dates. The second procedure (FUTDATE) will accept two parameters, a date (InDate) and number of days (NbrOfDays), and return the date in the future.
2. List the steps needed to create a service program. Give an example of a service program with three modules.
3. Write the RPG IV code for two modules; one module will export a variable and the other will import the same variable.
4. Research Web Services on the Internet; how can RPG IV be used in this technology? Write a report on what you have discovered.

Programming Assignments

1. CompuSell has been expanding its overseas sales. As a result, they need a service program that will convert currencies. This service program should accept two parameters, the amount and the currency to be converted. The service program will return the converted amount.

   Although a number of applications will use this service program, the sales department needs an interactive screen to assist its sales staff. This application will allow the user to enter an amount and the currency abbreviation. The generally accepted abbreviations can be found on the Internet (for example, United States Dollar—USD, Canada Dollar—CAD). The user has the ability to continue running this application until pressing F3. An example of the screens is shown below.

   Screen 01: Enter Data

```
         1         2         3         4         5         6         7         8
1234567890123456789012345678901234567890123456789012345678901234567890123456789 0
 1 xx/xx/xx                    Compusell International                    hh:mm:
 2 ss
 3                        Currency Conversion Screen
 4
 5
 6
 7 Type values, then Enter.
 8
 9        Amount to be converted:        999999.99
10
11        Currency to be converted to:  XXXX
12
13
14
15
16
17
18
19
20
21
22
23
24 F3=Exit   F12=Cancel
25
```

Screen 02: Display Data

```
                1              2              3              4              5              6              7              8
     1234567890123456789012345678901234567890123456789012345678901234567890123456789012345678901234567890
  1  xx/xx/xx                      Compusell International                                        hh:mm:ss
  2                              Currency Conversion Screen
  3
  4
  5
  6  .
  7
  8          US Amount to be converted:        999999.99
  9
 10          Currency converted to:            XXXX
 11
 12          Amount converted:                 999999.99
 13
 14
 15  Press Enter for to enter next amount
 16
 17
 18
 19
 20
 21
 22
 23
 24  F3=Exit    F12=Cancel
 25
```

2. Wexler University needs a service program to return the day of the week for any date. The service program should accept a date and return the day of the week. A number of applications will eventually use this service program; however, the scheduling department would like an interactive screen to accomplish this. The user has the ability to continue running this application until pressing F3. An example of the screens is shown below.

Screen 01: Enter Date

```
          1         2         3         4         5         6         7         8
 1234567890123456789012345678901234567890123456789012345678901234567890123456789 0
 1 xx/xx/xx                    Wexler University                      hh:mm:ss
 2                            Day of the Week Screen
 3
 4
 5
 6 Type values, then Enter.
 7
 8                        Inquire Date: XX/XX/XXXX
 9
10
11
12
13
14
15
16
17
18 F3=Exit   F12=Cancel
19
```

Screen 02: Display Day of the Week

```
          1         2         3         4         5         6         7         8
 1234567890123456789012345678901234567890123456789012345678901234567890123456789
 1 xx/xx/xx                    Wexler University                      hh:mm:ss
 2                            Day of the Week Screen
 3
 4
 5
 6
 7
 8                        Inquire Date:      66/66/9999
 9
10                        Day of the Week; XXXXXXXXX
11
12
13
14
15
16 Press Enter to enter next Date
17
18
19
20
21
22
23 F3=Exit   F12=Cancel
24
25
```

3. A German company has approached CompuSell with an opportunity for a merger. As part of the merger negotiations, the board of directors has been asked for a report listing the value of CompuSell's inventory in the following currencies: Deutsche (Germany) Marks—DEM and Euro—EUR. The report details are below.

   a. This will require a NOMAIN module with two procedures. One procedure will be called to convert Deutsche (Germany) Marks and the other to convert Euro—EUR each time a record is processed.

   b. The report will be in part number order and will require a logical file built over file CSINVP.

   c. Totals will be printed on a separate page at the end of the report.

Note: The grid has been split to allow the report to be formattted for the textbook.

```
                1         2         3         4         5         6         7
       1234567890123456789012345678901234567890123456789012345678901234567890
    1  XX/XX/XXXX                            Compusell Inventory Cost Report
    2
    3                                              ----- Current Cost -------
    4  Product Product                       On Hand US        Deutsche   Euro
    5  Number  Description                      Qty  Dollars   Marks
    6  999999  XXXXXXXXXXXXXXXXXXXXXXXXXX     9,999  99999.99  99999.99  99999.99
    7  999999  XXXXXXXXXXXXXXXXXXXXXXXXXX     9,999  99999.99  99999.99  99999.99
    8  999999  XXXXXXXXXXXXXXXXXXXXXXXXXX     9,999  99999.99  99999.99  99999.99
    9
   10  Report
   11  Totals          Current Cost       Average Cost        Selling Price
   12  US Dollars:   $999,999,999.00     $999,999,999.00     $999,999,999.00
   13  Deutsche:     $999,999,999.00     $999,999,999.00     $999,999,999.00
   14  Euro:         $999,999,999.00     $999,999,999.00     $999,999,999.00
   15
```

```
                            1         1         1         1
                8         9 0         1         2         3
       123456789012345678901234567890123456789012345678901234567890012
       - Currency Conversion                            Page XXX0

         ----- Average Cost -------   ----- Selling Price -------
       US        Deutsche   Euro     US        Deutsche   Euro
       Dollars   Marks               Dollars   Marks
       99999.99  99999.99   99999.99  99999.99  99999.99  99999.99
       99999.99  99999.99   99999.99  99999.99  99999.99  99999.99
       99999.99  99999.99   99999.99  99999.99  99999.99  99999.99

       Report
       Totals        Current Cost       Average Cost       Selling Price
       US Dollars:  $999,999,999.00    $999,999,999.00    $999,999,999.00
       Deutsche:    $999,999,999.00    $999,999,999.00    $999,999,999.00
       Euro:        $999,999,999.00    $999,999,999.00    $999,999,999.00
```

4. Wexler University Human Resources Department wants a report showing an instructor's employment anniversary; recognition is given for 5, 10, 15, and 20 years of service. Your instructor will tell you whether your solution should use bind-by-reference (i.e., a service program) or bind-by-copy.

   a. This report is run on the first of each month and will only print instructors with anniversary dates in the current month. Example: If the instructor was hired in July, his or her name will only appear on the report in July on the 5-, 10-, 15-, and 20-year anniversaries.

   b. The report should be sorted by the instructor last name, then first name. The report is based on the WUINSTP file.

   c. The number of years of service is printed on the right of the report line.

```
         1         2         3         4         5         6         7         8         9
1234567890123456789012345678901234567890123456789012345678901234567890123456789012345678901234567890
XX/XX/XX                                                                        Page XXØX
                Wexler University Instructor Anniversary Report

Instructor      First         Last             Hire         Anniversary
Number          Name          Name             Date         Certificate
999-999-9999    XXXXXXXXXX    XXXXXXXXXXXXXXXX 99/99/9999    99 Years
999-999-9999    XXXXXXXXXX    XXXXXXXXXXXXXXXX 99/99/9999    99 Years
999-999-9999    XXXXXXXXXX    XXXXXXXXXXXXXXXX 99/99/9999    99 Years

                                                 Total Call Processed XXXØX
```

5. You were asked to produce a report in Chapter 12 (Programming Assignment 3) using separately called programs. To simplify this process and allow other applications access to these procedures, you have been asked to create a service program with separate procedures to accomplish this task. Refer to Chapter 12, Programming Assignment 3 for the details of this assignment.

Chapter 14

Handling Errors

 ## Chapter Overview

This chapter covers a variety of error handling techniques that you can use to make your programs more reliable.

Capturing Operation Code Errors

Without explicit error handling within your program, any runtime error will cause the system to suspend the program and send a message to the interactive user or the system operator (when the program is running in batch). You can anticipate some errors that might occur during the execution of a program. For those cases, most programmers prefer to practice defensive programming; that is, to handle errors internally within the program rather than letting them cause a program **abend** (abnormal ending). You could use one of several alternative methods to handle errors. RPG IV supports facilities to process errors at any of three scopes:

- Errors that occur on a specific operation code
- Errors that occur in a block of code
- Errors that occur anywhere in the program

Using the (E) Extender

Many operation codes allow you to code an **(E) operation code extender**, in parentheses immediately following the operation code. The purpose of the (E) extender is to allow the program to continue when an error occurs on that operation code. Of the operation codes we have discussed thus far in this text, the following ones support an (E) extender:

• Callp	• Exfmt	• Readp	• Unlock
• Chain	• Open	• Readpe	• Update
• Close	• Read	• Setgt	• Write
• Delete	• Reade	• Setll	

When an error occurs on an operation that uses the (E) extender, the program will not be suspended; it will instead continue as if no error had occurred. It is then left up to the program to perform processing appropriate to the error. Common errors that might occur include:

- Attempting to divide by zero
- Using an invalid date/time/timestamp value
- Insufficient authority to use a data area
- Invalid array index
- Variable too small to hold result
- Decimal data error

All the file I/O operation codes support the use of the (E) extender. Some errors that could occur for a file operation include:

- Attempting to retrieve a locked record
- Attempting to retrieve a record from a closed file
- Attempting to open an already open file

Note that if a file I/O operation cannot find a record or reaches end of file, an error condition is *not* signaled. You should already be familiar with the %Found and %Eof functions, which are used to capture those conditions.

If an error occurs during an operation that includes the (E), the program simply continues to the next sequential instruction:

```
Read(E) Sample;
Dow Not %Eof(Sample);
  Chain(E) Samp Otherfile;
  Exsr Calcs;
  Read(E) Sample;
Enddo;
```

Although this method prevents an abend of your program, it simply ignores the error—a potentially dangerous practice. A better method would be to include an error routine that the program executes immediately upon encountering an error. You can easily use two functions to capture an error:

- %Error (Return Error Condition)
- %Status (Return File or Program Status)

%Error (Return Error Condition) Function

If an error occurs during an operation that includes the (E), the **%Error function** is turned on and the program continues. By checking the status of the %Error function after each operation that uses the (E) extender, your program could appropriately execute a special routine should any error occur.

```
Read(E) Sample;
  If %Error;
    Exsr Error;
  Endif;
Dow Not %Eof(Sample);
  Chain(E) Samp Otherfile;
    If %Error;
      Exsr Error;
    Endif;
  Exsr Calcs;
  Read(E) Sample;
    If %Error;
      Exsr Error;
    Endif;
Enddo;
```

Remember that the %Error function is tied to the (E) extender. Its value always pertains to the most recently executed operation code with the (E) extender—even if the appearance of %Error does not immediately follow that operation code. If an error occurs on an operation code without the (E) extender, the value of the %Error function remains unchanged.

%Status (Return File or Program Status) Function

The %Error function provides a generic on/off indicator if its related operation ends in error; but it gives you no indication of the specific nature of the error. RPG IV can provide more specific **status codes** that will identify an error when it occurs. The **%STATUS (Return file or program status) function** provides the most recent status code to your program. RPG categorizes errors into two classes:

- Program errors
- File errors

The %Status function value is set whenever the program status or file status changes, usually when an error occurs. %Status is a numeric value; it is set to 0 before any operation with an (E) extender begins. Operation codes without the (E) extender may also set the value of %Status (but not the value of %Error).

The following table lists a few common status codes. Status code values below 100 are not considered errors. Status codes between 100 and 999 are program errors; status codes between 1000 and 9999 are file errors. Appendix A includes a complete list of status codes.

Status Code	Description
00000	No error occurred
00102	Divide by zero
00103	Variable too small to hold result
00112	Invalid date/time/timestamp value
00121	Invalid array index
00414	Insufficient authority to use a data area
00907	Decimal data error
01211	File I/O to a closed file
01215	Attempt to open an already open file
01218	Record locked

Usually, you'll use %Status in conjunction with the (E) extender and the %Error function, as the following example shows. If you code a file name in parentheses immediately following the %Status function, the value will be the most recent value for that file; if you omit the file name, %Status will refer to the most recent change to the program or file status code.

```
Read(E) Salesfile;
Select;
  When %Error And %Status(Salesfile) = 01218;
    Exsr Lockedrec;
  When %Error;
    Exsr Fileerr;
  When %Eof(Salesfile);
    *Inlr = *On;
    Return;
  Other;
    Exsr Process;
Endsl;
```

Including all these checks, however, greatly increases the length of your program and still doesn't solve the problem of errors generated by operations (such as Eval) that do not permit the use of the (E) extender.

Fortunately, two alternate methods of error trapping exist. The Monitor (Begin a Monitor Group) and On-error (On Error) operations allow you to check for errors that occur within a block of code in an RPG IV program. The INFSR and *PSSR subroutines allow you to check for errors anywhere in the program that are not otherwise handled.

Monitor and On-error Operations

Using the (E) extender with the %Error function and the %Status function greatly improves the ability of your program to prevent runtime errors in a specific operation from ending your program abnormally. But not all operation codes support an (E) extender; for example, the commonly used Eval operation does not support the (E) extender, although it can still generate errors. For such operation codes, RPG IV supports an alternate means of trapping errors: the **Monitor (Begin a Monitor Group)** and **On-error (On Error)** operations.

These operations are intended to provide error trapping within a block of multiple code lines in a program, but they can also provide error trapping for a single line of code. The concept behind Monitor and On-error is that you can isolate a block (or a line) of code to execute; if an error occurs in that block, you can provide error handling code specifically for that block. In some computer languages, this concept is called "try and catch" because the program tries to execute a block of code and catches any errors that occur in the block.

The Monitor and **Endmon (End a Monitor Group)** operations form **monitor groups**—code for which you will provide error handling routines. A monitor group consists of a monitor block, followed by one or more On-error blocks, and finally an Endmon operation. The monitor block contains the code you think could generate an error; the On-error blocks contain the code to process any errors that occur in the monitor block.

If an error occurs while processing any line (without an (E) extender) in a monitor group, control immediately passes to the first On-error block within the monitor group. Each On-error operation lists one or more errors for which it is responsible; these errors correspond to the status codes from 00100 to 09999; or you can specify *File for file errors, *Program for program errors, or *All for any errors. The code following an On-error operation forms an On-error block and will be executed if the error that occurred matches the On-error statement. Only the first matching On-error statement will be processed; if there are no matching On-Error statements, none will be processed. Once an On-error block has been processed, or if the monitor block executed without error, control will pass to the Endmon statement that ends the group; it cannot return directly to the monitor block.

The following example shows a typical use of Monitor and On-error:

```
Monitor;
  Read Sample;
  Dow Not %Eof(Sample);
    Chain Samp Otherfile;
    Exsr Calcs;
    Read Sample;
  Enddo;
On-error 01218;
  Exsr Lockedrec;
On-error 01211:01215;
  Exsr Opensample;
On-error *File;
  Exsr Fileerr;
On-error *All;
  Exsr Generr;
  *Inlr = On;
  Return;
Endmon;
```

In this example, if the code in the Monitor block finishes without error, the program will skip the On-error blocks and pass control to the line following the Endmon operation. If an error occurs, however, control will pass to the first On-error block whose status code matches the status code generated by the error. Once the code in the appropriate On-error block has executed, control will pass to the line following the Endmon operation.

A monitor group can appear anywhere in an RPG IV program, and you can nest monitor groups (innermost groups are considered first). Notice that the program no longer needs to use the (E) extender to monitor for errors. If any of the operations (e.g., Read or Chain) generates an error, the On-error blocks will automatically take control; in fact if the Calcs subroutine in the above example generates an error, the On-error groups will handle the error (unless Calcs also is coded with its own monitor blocks). It's a good idea to finish up the block with a "catch-all" On-error *All statement to handle generic errors.

Note
If the line of code that generated the error in a monitor block does include the (E) extender, then %Error and %Status will be set, but the On-error blocks will not get control.

The following example illustrates how you might use Monitor and On-error to handle errors that occur for an Eval operation:

```
Monitor;
  Eval(H) Foreign = Local / Buyrate;
On-error 00102;                     // Divide by zero
  Foreign = 0;
On-error 00103;                     // Result too small
  Foreign = 9999999.99;
Endmon;
```

In this example, which might be used in a currency conversion program, if the expression encounters a divide-by-zero error, Foreign will be 0; if the Buyrate variable value is so small that the expression result could not fit into Foreign, the program will assign a value of 9999999.99 to Foreign. Notice in the above example the use of comments to document the conditions.

Tip

To make your program more documentary, you could assign named constants to status codes, as the following example shows:

```
*.. 1 ...+... 2 ...+... 3 ...+... 4 ...+... 5 ...+... 6 ...+...
DName++++++++++ETDsFrom+++To/Len+IDc.Keywords++++++++++++++++++

D Dividebyzero    C                    00102
D Resultoverflow  C                    00103
D Recordlocked    C                    01218

 /Free
    Monitor;
      Eval(H) Foreign = Local / Buyrate;
    On-error Dividebyzero;
      Foreign = 0;
    On-error Resultoverflow;
      Foreign = 9999999.99;
    Endmon;

    Read(E) Salesfile;
    If %Status(Salesfile) = Recordlocked;
      Exsr Wait;
    Endif;
 /End-Free
```

You should consider using a copybook (discussed in Chapter 13) to store the constants that represent status codes and then including that copybook (with the /Copy function) in any programs that will use status codes.

Finding Data Errors

Some of the most frequent processing errors occur as a result of invalid or unexpected data values. For example, a date variable might contain a nonexistent date; or a numeric variable might contain a nonnumeric value; or a conversion function might encounter problems when converting a character value to a numeric value. RPG IV offers several approaches to dealing with invalid data. We've already discussed how to capture these types of errors when they occur, through the use of the %Error and %Status functions and the Monitor and On-error operations. RPG IV features several options to capture these errors before they occur.

Decimal Data Errors

One of the most common errors is the **decimal data error**—the error that occurs when a program tries to process a numeric variable that contains nonnumeric information. This situation may occur, for example, if you are processing data that comes from another system or application. The decimal data error generates a status code of 00907, which you can capture in the program. Perhaps the easiest way to catch a decimal data error is to attempt a numeric expression:

```
*.. 1 ...+... 2 ...+... 3 ...+... 4 ...+... 5 ...+... 6 ...+... 7 ...+... 8
DName++++++++++ETDsFrom+++To/Len+IDc.Keywords+++++++++++++++++++++++++++++++

D Decimalerror    C                      00907

 /Free
    Monitor;
      Transamt += 0;
    On-error Decimalerror;
      Transamt = 0;
    Endmon;
 /End-Free
```

In this example, the program attempts to add zero to the Transamt variable. If the Transamt variable is numeric, it will remain unchanged and can be processed. If Transamt contains invalid numeric characters, the expression will cause a 00907 status code, and its value will be set to zero. Instead of changing the value to zero, you could code alternative processing.

In case you want the system to detect and fix decimal data errors *before* processing any input data, the compile commands (CRTRPGMOD or CRTBNDRPG) have a FIXNBR parameter that will fix invalid numeric data. Any of the following compile command parameter combinations are valid—FIXNBR(*NONE) is the default:

- FIXNBR(*NONE)
- FIXNBR(*ZONED)
- FIXNBR(*INPUTPACKED)
- FIXNBR(*ZONED *INPUTPACKED)

If you compile the module with the FIXNBR(*ZONED *INPUTPACKED) option, the program will fix decimal data errors that occur in any zoned or packed numeric variables that the program uses. For zoned variables, invalid data (blanks, invalid digits) will be treated as zeros; invalid signs will be generally treated as positive. For packed variables, the entire variable is set to zero.

The compiler options to fix decimal data errors are not very flexible and may cause your programs to get incorrect results. Most programmers prefer to individually check "problem" input field rather than let the program fix them en masse.

Numeric Conversion Errors

Previously, we have discussed several functions that will convert a character value to a numeric value:

- %Dec (and %Dech) to convert to packed decimal
- %Int (and %Inth) to convert to integer
- %Uns (and %Unsh) to convert to unsigned integer

If you use these functions to convert a character value, the following rules apply to the character value:

- An optional sign (+ or -) can precede or follow the data value.
- A decimal point (. or ,) is optional.
- Blanks can appear anywhere in the data.
- The remaining data must include only digits (0–9).
- Floating point data is not allowed.

If one of these functions encounters invalid numeric data, it will generate a status code of 00105. Perhaps the easiest way to catch a **conversion error** is to attempt the conversion:

```
*.. 1 ...+... 2 ...+... 3 ...+... 4 ...+... 5 ...+... 6 ...+... 7 ...+... 8
DName+++++++++++ETDsFrom+++To/Len+IDc.Keywords++++++++++++++++++++++++++++++

D Numbererror     C                     00105

/Free
   Monitor;
     Numfield = %Dec(Charfield:13:2);
   On-error Numbererror;
     Numfield = 0;
   Endmon;
/End-Free
```

In this example, the program converts the Charfield variable (data type A) to packed decimal format (13 digits, two decimal places) and places the value in the Numfield variable (data type P). If the program cannot successfully convert the value, it will return status code 00105, and the Numfield variable will be set to zero.

If you want to check the data value *before* attempting the conversion, you can use the %Check function to see if any invalid characters appear in Charfield:

```
If %Check(' +-.,0123456789':Charfield) = 0;
  Numfield = %Dec(Charfield:13:2);
Endif;
```

The %Check function will ensure that Charfield contains only the characters that can be converted. It does not, however, ensure that they will be in the proper places. Depending upon the specific circumstances, you could use other functions (e.g., %Scan, %Subst) to validate the position of various characters.

Date and Time Errors

If you try to process a date, time, or timestamp variable that contains an invalid value, the program will generate error RNQ0112. The status code will be 00112, which you can, of course, capture:

```
*.. 1 ...+... 2 ...+... 3 ...+... 4 ...+... 5 ...+... 6 ...+... 7 ...+... 8
DName++++++++++ETDsFrom+++To/Len+IDc.Keywords+++++++++++++++++++++++++++++
D Dateerror      C                00112

 /Free
    Monitor;
      Duedate = Invoicedate + %Days(30);
    On-error Dateerror;
      Duedate = %Date() + %Days(30;
    Endmon;
 /End-Free
```

In this example, Duedate (type D) is calculated to be 30 days after Invoicedate (type D). If Invoicedate contains an invalid value, or if the expression causes Duedate to have an invalid value, Duedate will be set to 30 days from the current system date.

Caution
Remember from Chapter 7 that the format you use for a date field may affect its range of valid values.

The **Test (Test Date/Time/Timestamp) operation** can check the validity of date, time, or timestamp variables *before* you try to process them. To check variables with data types D, T, or Z, the operation takes the following form:

```
Test(e) date-field;
```

The %Error function is turned on if the variable contains an invalid date/time value. The following example demonstrates this use of the Test operation.

```
Test(e) Todaysdate;
If %Error;
  Todaysdate = %Date();
Endif;
```

In this example, Todaysdate is a date (type D) variable. If it doesn't contain a valid date value, the Test operation will turn on the %Error function; subsequent lines will assign the current system date to Todaysdate. When you use Test to check data type D, T, or Z variables, they can be in any valid format without any special coding.

You can also use the Test operation to check character or numeric variables *before* using them as dates, times, or timestamps. When you use it with these data types, the Test operation takes one of the following forms, depending upon data type:

```
Test(de) format field-name;
Test(te) format field-name;
Test(ze) format field-name;
```

To use Test to check character and numeric fields for valid date/time data, you must include an operation extender—(D) for date, (T) for time, (Z) for timestamp—to identify which test you want to perform. Be sure to also include the (E) extender to support the %Error function. Before coding the name of the variable to test, you must also code the date/time display format (e.g., *Iso, *Mdy, *Usa) you want to compare to your data. Consider the following examples, in which Userdate and Usertime are numeric fields.

```
Test(de) *Iso Userdate;
Test(te) *Hms Usertime;
```

When testing the date/time validity of character variables, RPG IV also checks to see that valid separator characters are included in the value. If the character value does not include separators, you can override the separator with a 0. Assume in the following examples that Userdate and Usertime are character fields without separators:

```
Test(de) *Iso0 Userdate;
Test(te) *Hms0 Usertime;
```

The INFSR Subroutine

You can designate a subroutine to automatically execute when the main procedure encounters a file error; this file error subroutine is commonly called the **INFSR subroutine**. This subroutine will take control if a file I/O operation encounters an error that is not handled by one of the other error handling mechanisms (e.g., an (E) extender or a Monitor group). You can also explicitly execute an INFSR subroutine with the Exsr operation. One subroutine can handle errors for several files, or you can code multiple INFSR subroutines in a single program.

To add an INFSR subroutine to your program, you must include the Infsr keyword on the file specification for the file you want to associate with the subroutine. With this keyword, you name the subroutine that you want to handle that file's errors. This name can be any subroutine (including the *PSSR subroutine, discussed later in this chapter).

There are no unique requirements for an INFSR subroutine. You can use any RPG IV operations, but you should avoid using the INFSR to perform file I/O operations to the same file that caused the error. The following example shows how you might use an INFSR subroutine:

```
*.. 1 ...+... 2 ...+... 3 ...+... 4 ...+... 5 ...+... 6 ...+... 7 ...+... 8
FFilename++IPEASFRLen+LKLen+AIDevice+.Keywords++++++++++++++++++++++++++++++
FCustomers UF   E           K Disk    Infsr(Custinfsr)
FBacklog   O    E           K Disk
...
 /Free
    Chain (Company:Customer) Custrec;
    If %Found(Customers);
      Lasdat = %Date();
      Update Custrec %Fields(Lasdat);
    Endif;
...
    Begsr Custinfsr;
      Write Backrec;
      *Inlr = *On;
    Endsr '*CANCL';
 /End-Free
```

In this example, the Custinfsr subroutine is designated as the file error subroutine by the Infsr keyword on the File specification for Customers. If an error occurs for the Chain or Update operations associated with the Customers file, this subroutine will take control. The Custinfsr subroutine writes a Backrec record to the Backlog, turns on *Inlr, and then ends.

Notice the Endsr operation, which has an extra entry that we have not seen before. This optional entry indicates the **return point** for the subroutine; it is valid only with error handling subroutines. This entry indicates what the program should do when it is finished executing the subroutine. It will usually be one of the following entries:

- '*DETC' to continue the program at the top of the calculations
- '*CANCL' to cancel the program

The entry can be a literal, constant or variable (six characters) with the desired value. If you do not code a return point, one of two things happens: (1) if the subroutine has been executed as the result of a file error, the program will generate an error; (2) if the subroutine has been executed as the result of an Exsr operation, control will return to the next sequential instruction (just like a normal subroutine).

Several limitations on the INFSR subroutine cause most programmers to prefer other error handling mechanisms instead. First, the INFSR subroutine handles file errors that occur in the main procedure, not in subprocedures; the INFSR must appear in the main procedure. Next, if an error occurs when the program is initially opening a file, the INFSR will not get control; only those errors that occur once the program is running will cause the INFSR to take over. Finally, the INFSR cannot easily return to the point of the error after executing. For these reasons, most programmers will use Monitor groups or the %Error and %Status functions—or the *PSSR subroutine, discussed later in this chapter—instead of, or in conjunction with, an INFSR subroutine.

The File Information Data Structure

For each file in an RPG IV program, you can define a **file information data structure** to provide feedback to your program about the current status of a file, along with details about any file errors that may have occurred. You can use the file information data structure in combination with a INFSR subroutine, if you wish, or you can use either construct independently. To name a file information data structure, use the Infds keyword in the File specification:

```
*.. 1 ...+... 2 ...+... 3 ...+... 4 ...+... 5 ...+... 6 ...+... 7 ...+... 8
FFilename++IPEASFRLen+LKLen+AIDevice+.Keywords++++++++++++++++++++++++++++++++
FCustomers UF    E           K Disk    Infds(Custinfds)
```

You must, of course, then define the data structure in the Definition specifications; it may be externally described, if you wish. The file information data structure appears in the main procedure; the same data structure will be used by any procedure using the file.

The subfields in the file information data structure are in predetermined locations, documented in IBM's *ILE RPG Language Reference*. Some of the information available in the file information data structure includes:

- The name of the file
- The record being processed when the error occurred
- The last operation being processed when the error occurred
- The RPG IV routine in which the error occurred
- The status code

Some of the information and its location in the file information data structure is specific to the device coded in positions 36–42 on the File specification. For example, if the device is a printer file, the information includes the current line number and the current page count; if the device is a workstation file, the information includes a variable identifying which key has been pressed; for a database (disk) file, the information includes the current record count.

Here is an example of a file information data structure:

```
*.. 1 ...+... 2 ...+... 3 ...+... 4 ...+... 5 ...+... 6 ...+... 7 ...+... 8
FFilename++IPEASFRLen+LKLen+AIDevice+.Keywords++++++++++++++++++++++++++++++++
DName++++++++++ETDsFrom+++To/Len+IDc.Keywords++++++++++++++++++++++++++++++++
FCustomers UF    E           K Disk    Infds(Custinfds)

D Custinfds       DS                        Qualified
D   Filename                  1      8
D   Fileopen                  9      9N
D   Endoffile                10     10N
D   Opcode                   16     21
D   Routine                  22     29
```

To find the correct location for other subfields, refer to IBM's documentation. A complete discussion of the file information data structure goes beyond the scope of this text.

The *PSSR Subroutine

If you include a subroutine named *PSSR within your program, that subroutine will automatically receive control when an unhandled program error occurs anywhere in the code. The ***PSSR subroutine** provides a "last defense" against errors—to handle those errors that you have not processed with the (E) extender, the %Error function, the %Status function, or Monitor groups.

The following example shows a basic *PSSR subroutine:

```
Begsr *PSSR;
   Dump(A);
   *Inlr = *On;
Endsr '*CANCL';
```

This *PSSR subroutine will cause the program to issue a formatted RPG **program dump**. A dump is a report that will show the details of the error, the current state of all files, and the current values of all the variables in the program. It is useful when you need to **debug** a problem with a running program. The **Dump (Program Dump) operation** issues the program dump and then continues with the next line in the program. The **(A) extender** on the Dump operation ensures that the dump will always be issued, regardless of other debugging or optimization entries coded in your program.

Like the INFSR subroutine, the *PSSR subroutine can include a return point on its Endsr operation. If you do not code a return point, one of two things happens: (1) if the subroutine has been executed as the result of a program error, the program will generate an error; (2) if the subroutine has been executed as the result of an Exsr operation, control will return to the next sequential instruction (just like a normal subroutine).

If the *PSSR subroutine is more complex than the one shown above, you'll want to be careful to avoid errors that might occur within the *PSSR subroutine itself. If an unhandled error occurs in the *PSSR subroutine, that error can cause endless reiteration of the *PSSR subroutine. You can avoid this endless recursion by defining a variable to "remember" whether or not the *PSSR subroutine has already executed:

```
*.. 1 ...+... 2 ...+... 3 ...+... 4 ...+... 5 ...+... 6 ...+... 7 ...+... 8
DName+++++++++++ETDsFrom+++To/Len+IDc.Keywords++++++++++++++++++++++++++++++++
D Pssrdone        S              N   Inz(*Off)

 /Free
    Begsr *PSSR;
      If Pssrdone;
        *Inlr = *On;
        Return;
      Endif;

      Pssrdone = *On;

      Dump(A);
      // Additional error processing goes here

    Endsr;
 /End-Free
```

The *PSSR subroutine handles program errors that occur. To have this subroutine control file errors as well, you must explicitly designate *PSSR as the error handler for the files. This assignment is quite straightforward; simply use the Infsr keyword as part of the file definition and include *PSSR in parentheses after the keyword.

```
*.. 1 ...+... 2 ...+... 3 ...+... 4 ...+... 5 ...+... 6 ...+... 7 ...+... 8
FFilename++IPEASFRLen+LKlen+AIDevice+.Keywords+++++++++++++++++++++++++++++
FCustomers UF    E          K Disk     Infsr(*PSSR)
```

Although any subroutine could be used for file error handling, most programmers prefer to combine program error handling and file error handling within a *PSSR subroutine.

The Program Status Data Structure

Within an RPG program you can define a **program status data structure** (PSDS) to make program error information available to the program. These program errors include such things as attempts to divide by zero, attempt to use an invalid array index, or errors on a Callp operation. In addition to error information, the PSDS includes other information, such as the user identifier of the current user and the job name/number. The program status data structure is coded with an S in position 23 of the data structure definition:

```
*.. 1 ...+... 2 ...+... 3 ...+... 4 ...+... 5 ...+... 6 ...+... 7 ...+... 8
DName++++++++++ETDsFrom+++To/Len+IDc.Keywords+++++++++++++++++++++++++++++++
D                 SDS
D  Jobname              244    253
D  Jobuser              254    263
D  Jobnumber            264    269  0
D  Currentuser          358    367
```

The subfields in the program status data structure are in predetermined locations, documented in IBM's *ILE RPG Language Reference*. The PSDS can be externally described, if you wish.

You can handle most errors in a program with a combination of the (E) extender, the %Error and %Status functions, and the use of Monitor groups. The INFSR and *PSSR subroutines, along with the file information and program status data structures, provide more detailed error handling. It is left to you, the programmer, to determine the best response to the error—perhaps ignoring the error and continuing; perhaps writing a line to an error report and continuing; or perhaps noting the error and bringing the program to a normal ending. While the optimal design of error handling logic can be very complex, as you gain more experience with the language, you will no doubt begin to incorporate these tools in your programs.

Chapter Summary

RPG IV supports facilities to process errors at a specific error code, with a block of code, or anywhere in the program.

The (E) extender on an operation code allows a program to continue processing if the operation generates an error. Without the (E) extender, the program will be suspended while it waits for a response to an error message.

The %Error function returns a simple on/off indicator to let the program know if an error has occurred; it is always associated with the last operation code that used an (E) extender. The %Status function returns a numeric value that identifies a specific error condition. Status codes from 00100 to 00999 are used to describe program errors; status codes from 01000 to 09999 describe file I/O errors.

The Monitor and On-error operations allow you to check for errors that occur within a block of code by creating Monitor groups that include the code to process and its error handling instructions in a single block.

Some of the most frequent processing errors occur as a result of invalid or unexpected data values. These errors include decimal data errors, numeric conversion errors, and invalid date values. Wherever possible, you should check for these types of errors before processing the data. The Test operation will check date/time variables for valid values and can also be used to validate numeric and character fields that are used to store date values.

If you use INFSR and *PSSR subroutines, they will automatically execute when a file error or a program error occurs that is not otherwise handled by another mechanism. The file information and program status data structures can also be used to gain more information about any errors that occur.

The following table summarizes the operation codes and functions discussed in this chapter:

Function or operation	Description	Syntax
Dump	Program dump	Dump{(a)} {identifier}
Endmon	End a Monitor group	Endmon
%Error	Error	%Error
Monitor	Begin a Monitor group	Monitor
On-Error	On error	On-error {exception-id1:exception-id2...}
%Status	File or program status code	%Status{(file-name)}
Test	Test date/time/timestamp	Test{(detz)} {format} tested-field

Key Terms

(A) extender
abend
conversion error
debug
decimal data error
Dump operation
(E) operation code extender
Endmon operation
%Error function
file information data structure
INFSR subroutine

monitor groups
Monitor operation
On-error operation
program dump
program status data structure
*PSSR subroutine
return point
status codes
%Status function
Test operation

Discussion/Review Questions

1. Discuss different options for trapping errors (or not trapping errors) within a program, giving the pros and cons of each method.
2. Why might a programmer want to convert one data type to another in an RPG program? For example, why might you want to convert a packed decimal number to a character field? Which built-in functions would you use to perform the conversion?
3. What is the INSFR subroutine? Give an example of how (and why) this is used.
4. What is the *PSSR subroutine and why is it used? Give an example.
5. Investigate the problems that can be caused by writing a program that is not prepared to handle errors. Programming professionals and your instructor are good resources for information. Write a report.
6. Summarize the rules that are applied to numeric data if the FIXNBR compile command is used when compiling a program.
7. Investigate IBM's online documentation to find the list of subfields that are available for the file information data structure. Compile a list of subfields you think might be beneficial in your programming efforts.

Exercises

1. Write the RPG IV code to read a record from CSCSTP. Check for the errors you think might occur.
2. Write the RPG IV code to check for a divide-by-zero error.
3. Write the RPG IV code to check for a result of a math operation being too large for the result field.
4. Write the RPG IV code to monitor the conversion of character data to a packed decimal, integer, and unsigned integer.
5. After completing Review Question 7 above, write a file information data structure using the CSCSTP file. Using RPG IV code, give an example of the use of each subfield.
6. Write the F-specs and the other required code to use the *PSSR subroutine. Write a sample of how it would be used.

Programming Assignments

1. GTC Telephone Company wants a program to prepare customer bills. This program will update two fields in the customer master file: current billed amount (CURBIL) and balanced owed (AMTOWE). This program needs to run during regular business hours so it needs to include the following programming features:
   a. INFSR to check for file I/O problems.
   b. *PSSR subroutine to handle unrecoverable errors.
   c. All supported functions should have an (E) extender.
   d. A Monitor group should be included with the appropriate errors checked and handled appropriately.
   e. Use the functions %Error and/or %Status when needed.

Requirements for this program: The report will be in customer name order. You will need to create a logical over the GTCSTP file and access the GTCLSP file for the call data.
   a. Each new customer will start on a new page.
   b. The call day of the week should be displayed on the report.
   c. The time needs to be converted from military time.
   d. The billing demographics should be in proper case.
   e. The federal tax, state tax, and past due charge percentages should be a runtime table. Be sure to check for this file's existence before processing starts.

Note: Programs developed in the previous two chapters can be used to satisfy a number of the requirements for this program.

```
          1         2         3         4         5         6         7         8
 1234567890123456789012345678901234567890123456789012345678901234567890123456789012345678
 1 xx/xx/xx                    GTC Incorporated                    ProgID XXXXXXXX
 2
 3                               P.O Box 123
 4                            Lawrence MI, 49067
 5
 6 Bill For: XXXXXXXXXXXXXXX XXXXXXXXXXXXXXXXXXXX
 7           XXXXXXXXXXXXXXXXXXXXXX
 8           XXXXXXXXXXXXXXX XX, XXXXX-XXXX
 9           (XXX) XXX-XXXX
10
11                                       Billing Date: XX/XX/XXXX
12 GTC Current Charges
13      Local Service                          18.95
14      Intrastate Access                      12.00
15
16 Call       Day Of    Number      *******    Call    *******
17 Date       The Week  Called       Time      Minutes   Cost
18 XX/XX/XXXX XXXXXXXXX XXX-XXX-XXXX XX:XX A.M    XX0    XX0,X0
19 XX/XX/XXXX XXXXXXXXX XXX-XXX-XXXX XX:XX P.M    XX0    XX0,X0
20 XX/XX/XXXX XXXXXXXXX XXX-XXX-XXXX XX:XX A.M    XX0    XX0,X0
21 XX/XX/XXXX XXXXXXXXX XXX-XXX-XXXX XX:XX P.M    XX0    XX0,X0
22 Number of Calls X0X              Calls Total Cost: XX,XX0.XX
23
24              3% Federal Excise Tax on X,XX0.XX     XX0.XX
25              4% State Tax on X,XX0.XX              XX0.XX
26                                                ==========
27 Charges This Billing Period                     XX,XX0.XX
28      Balance Past Due                           XX,XX0.XX
29 5% Past Due Charge                                XX0.XX
30                            Total Due:            XX,XX0.XX
```

2. GTC Telephone Company had you write a program in Chapter 10, Programming Assignment 1, to process a transaction file and create a report. This program has caused problems because a previous program in the nightly processing had deleted the transaction file. You have been asked to modify this program to include the INFSR subroutine. If there is a file I/O problem on any file, a report should be produced and the program should be canceled. Refer to Chapter 10 for details on this program.

3. CompuSell had you write a program in Chapter 10, Programming Assignment 3, that processes a Goods Received file. This program runs in a nightly batch job stream and has caused a number of problems. You have been asked to modify this program to include an INFSR, *PSSR subroutine, and %Status to check the calculations. Refer to Chapter 10 for details on this program.

4. You developed a program in Chapter 13, Programming Assignment 3, to convert currencies for a cost report. You have been asked to have this program use a runtime table to get the exchange rates at the time the program is run. As part of this modification, you should incorporate more robust error checking. This will include a file information data structure and status checking on all math functions in this program. Refer to Chapter 13 for details on this program.

5. CompuSell wants you to write an interactive program that its shipping department can use to calculate shipping charges based on destination and weight of package. Include the following programming features:

   a. INFSR to check for file I/O problems.

   b. *PSSR to subroutine to handle unrecoverable errors.

   c. All supported functions should have an (E) extender.

   d. A Monitor group should be included with the appropriate errors checked and handled appropriately.

   e. Use the functions %Error and/or %Status when needed.

   Requirements for this program: Skills learned in chapter 9 will be needed to code this program.

   a. Two files of table information related to shipping exist: the zip/zone table file (CSZPZNP) and the charges table file (CSCHGP). (Appendix F describes these files.)

   b. The files will be loaded into runtime tables.

   c. Your program should let a user enter the first three digits of the zip code of a package's destination and the pounds and ounces of the package weight and, based on the entered information, calculate the appropriate shipping charge and display the charge to the user.

d. Note that any package with ounces greater than zero should get charged the rate appropriate for the next pound. That is, a package weighing seven pounds and three ounces should get charged at the eight-pound rate.

Screen One: This input screen allows the user to input the zip code (first three digits) and the weight of the package.

```
         1         2         3         4         5         6         7         8
 1234567890123456789012345678901234567890123456789012345678901234567890
 1 XX/XX/XX                                           Program ID XXXXXXX
 2
 3                  CompuSell Shipping Charge Calculator
 4
 5
 6
 7
 8     Type values, then Enter
 9
10        Zip code . . 999     (first 3 digits)
11
12
13        Shipping Weight
14           Pounds . . 999
15           Ounces . . 99
16
17
18
19
20
21
22 F3=Exit   F12=Cancel
23
24
25
```

Screen Two: This screen shows the results of the inquiry. Pressing Enter will return the user to the first screen.

```
                1         2         3         4         5         6         7         8
       1234567890123456789012345678901234567890123456789012345678901234567890123456789 0
    1  XX/XX/XX                                                    Program ID XXXXXXX
    2
    3                      CompuSell Shipping Charge Calculator
    4
    5
    6
    7  Type values, then Enter
    8
    9        Zip code . . . . . . . .  666
   10
   11        Shipping Weight
   12          Pounds . . . . . . . .  666
   13          Ounces . . . . . . . .  6
   14
   15
   16        Shipping Charges . . . .    6.66
   17
   18        Press Enter to continue.
   19
   20
   21
   22
   23
   24  F3=Exit   F12=Cancel
   25
```

Chapter 15

Programming with Subfiles

Chapter Overview

This chapter extends your ability to write interactive applications by introducing you to the concept of subfiles.

Subfiles

In Chapter 11, you were introduced to interactive programs. You learned how to write inquiry and maintenance programs whose logic required the display of information one record at a time. Some kinds of applications require the use of **list panels**, in which data from many records is displayed on a screen for review, selection, or update. RPG IV has a special feature called subfiles to handle this kind of program requirement.

A **subfile** is a collection of records that is handled as a unit for screen input/output (I/O). Although subfile processing can get quite complicated, you can learn basic subfile processing techniques without great difficulty. As a prelude to discussing coding requirements for subfiles, consider the following problem description.

In Chapter 11, we worked with a file of course-section information and developed an interactive application to display detailed section information based on a section number entered by the user. The record layout of that file, SECTIONS, is repeated below.

```
*.. 1 ...+... 2 ...+... 3 ...+... 4 ...+... 5 ...+... 6 ...+... 7 ...+... 8
A..........T.Name++++++RLen++TDpB......Functions++++++++++++++++++++++++++++++
 * Physical file SECTIONS definition
A           R SECREC
A             SECTNO         5              TEXT('Section number')
A             DAYS           3              TEXT('Days class meets')
A             BEGTIME        4   0          TEXT('Time class starts')
A             ROOM           4   0          TEXT('Classroom')
A             ENROLL         3   0          TEXT('Current enrollment')
A             INSTR         15              TEXT('Instructor')
A             COURSE         6              TEXT('Course identifier')
A           K SECTNO
```

Now, assume that the same school wants an application in which the user can enter a course name to see a list of all the sections offered for that course. The desired screen layouts are shown on the following page.

```
                          Course Inquiry

        Type value, then Enter.

           Course number . .  ____




        F3=Exit
```

```
                     XXXXXX Course Information

              Section    Instructor       Room   Days   Time    Enroll.
              XXXXX   XXXXXXXXXXXXXX   XXXX   XXX   XX:XX    XØX
              XXXXX   XXXXXXXXXXXXXX   XXXX   XXX   XX:XX    XØX
              XXXXX   XXXXXXXXXXXXXX   XXXX   XXX   XX:XX    XØX




        Press Enter to continue.

        F3=Exit  F12=Cancel
```

Notice that the second screen contains information from many section records rather than just one. This fact means that you will need to use subfiles to implement the solution.

Your first step, before beginning the screen definition, is to create a logical file over file SECTIONS to access the records in order by course and, within course, by section. The following DDS provides the definition for that logical file, SECTIONL:

```
*.. 1 ...+... 2 ...+... 3 ...+... 4 ...+... 5 ...+... 6 ...+... 7 ...+... 8
A..........T.Name++++++.Len++TDpB......Functions++++++++++++++++++++++++++++++
 * Definition of SECTIONL, a logical file over physical file SECTIONS
A          R SECREC                      PFILE(SECTIONS)
A          K COURSE
A          K SECTNO
```

Now consider the display file, SECTINQ. The first screen definition is identical to the layout of the screen in Chapter 11; only the literals need to be changed. Note, though, that we've moved CA03 to make it a file-level keyword. The following DDS defines this screen.

```
*.. 1 ...+... 2 ...+... 3 ...+... 4 ...+... 5 ...+... 6 ...+... 7 ...+... 8
AAN01N02N03T.Name++++++RLen++TDpBLinPosFunctions+++++++++++++++++++++++++++++
A                                        INDARA
A                                        CA03(03 'F3=Exit')
A          R CRSEINQ
A                                        BLINK
A                                      1 28'Course Inquiry'
A                                      3  2'Type value, then Enter.'
A                                      5  5'Course number . .'
A            COURSENO      6A   B   5 24
A N90                                     DSPATR(UL)
A N90                                     DSPATR(HI)
A  90                                     ERRMSG('Course not found' 90)
A                                     23  2'F3=Exit'
```

The second screen will require subfile definition. Using a subfile to display multiple records on a screen requires two record formats: one to define a subfile record and one to control the subfile and its display.

Subfile Record Formats

The **subfile record format** describes the fields that are to appear on the screen. Because in this example the screen and database fields are the same, the database file containing the field definitions is noted with record-level keyword REF.

A new record-level keyword, **SFL** (Subfile), is also required; this keyword identifies the record format as a subfile. The remaining information in the subfile record format describes the fields to appear, their locations on the screen, and any editing or other special keywords desired. The line number associated with each field represents the line on which the first record of the subfile is to appear.

The following DDS illustrates the subfile record format of our application.

```
*.. 1 ...+... 2 ...+... 3 ...+... 4 ...+... 5 ...+... 6 ...+... 7 ...+... 8
AAN01N02N03T.Name++++++RLen++TDpBLinPosFunctions+++++++++++++++++++++++++++++
A                                        REF(SECTIONS)
A          R SFLSECT                     SFL
A            SECTNO    R        0   4 14
A            INSTR     R        0   4 23
A            ROOM      R        0   4 41
A            DAYS      R        0   4 49
A            BEGTIME   R      Y 0   4 57EDTWRD('0 :  ')
A            ENROLL    R      Y 0   4 66EDTCDE(3)
```

Subfile Control Record Formats

The **subfile control record format** must immediately follow the subfile record format. This record format controls the display of the subfile records through the use of special record-level keywords. In addition, programmers often include the column headings for the subfile display as part of this record format.

The subfile control record format requires several record-level keywords. The required keywords and their functions are as follows:

- **SFLCTL** *(Subfile Control)* identifies a record as the subfile control record for the subfile named within the parentheses after the keyword.

- **SFLDSP** *(Subfile Display)* displays the subfile itself if SFLDSP is active when an output operation is performed on the subfile control record. This keyword generally is conditioned by an indicator to control whether the subfile is displayed on a given output operation.

- **SFLPAG** *(Subfile Page)* defines how many subfile records are to be displayed at one time on the screen. The number follows the keyword and is enclosed in parentheses. You typically determine this number by calculating the number of available screen lines, after taking into account all other lines to be displayed along with the subfile.

- **SFLSIZ** *(Subfile Size)* indicates the number of records in the entire subfile. The value, enclosed in parentheses immediately after the SFLSIZ keyword, should be either equal to or greater than the SFLPAG value. If the value is greater, you can make it large enough to accommodate the maximum number of records you would normally have in the subfile. (If you underestimate, however, the system will automatically extend the subfile to make room for the additional records.) A subfile cannot contain more than 9,999 records. If SFLSIZ is greater than SFLPAG, i5/OS automatically handles paging through the subfile when the user presses the page (or roll) keys and displays a plus sign (+) or a "More..." indicator at the bottom of the screen to indicate there are subfile records not yet displayed.

Subfile control record-level keywords that are optional but usually used include the following:

- **SFLDSPCTL** *(Subfile Display Control)* enables the display of any output fields or constants described within the control record format. The keyword generally is conditioned with the same indicator used for the SFLDSP keyword.

- **SFLCLR** *(Subfile Clear)* clears the subfile of any records if it is active when an output operation is performed on the subfile control record. An option indicator is required for this keyword, or the system would clear the subfile on every output operation to the control record. The indicator often is the reverse of the indicator used for keywords SFLDSP and SFLDSPCTL, so that you clear the subfile in one output operation and display the subfile and the control-record information in a second output operation.

The following DDS illustrates a subfile control record format. Notice that when indicator 50 is on, the system will clear the subfile; when 51 is on, the system will display both the subfile record format and the subfile control record format. Also note that the control record format includes screen column headings for the subfile.

```
*.. 1 ...+... 2 ...+... 3 ...+... 4 ...+... 5 ...+... 6 ...+... 7 ...+... 8
AAN01N02N03T.Name++++++RLen++TDpBLinPosFunctions++++++++++++++++++++++++++++
A* Subfile control record format for course inquiry application
A            R CTLSECT                       SFLCTL(SFLSECT)
A                                            SFLPAG(15)
A                                            SFLSIZ(80)
A    50                                      SFLCLR
A    51                                      SFLDSPCTL
A    51                                      SFLDSP
A              COURSENO      6A  O  1 28
A                                   1 35'Course Information'
A                                   3 12'Section'
A                                   3 24'Instructor'
A                                   3 41'Room'
A                                   3 49'Days'
A                                   3 57'Time'
A                                   3 64'Enroll.'
```

Loading the Subfile

As we indicated above, the relationship between subfile size and subfile page can vary. Programmers use several different approaches to defining this interrelationship and to loading data into the subfile. The method used depends in part on a program's anticipated processing requirements. We will develop our sample program using three different techniques to give you a sense of the variation and the rationale for each method.

Loading the Entire Subfile

The first approach to defining and loading a subfile involves defining the subfile size large enough to hold the maximum expected number of records and then loading all the appropriate data into the subfile before any record display. This method is the easiest to code but results in the slowest initial response time. Once display begins, however, paging through the subfile is fast. This method is least appropriate when there are a large number of records to be loaded and the user is unlikely to want to see most of them.

The following code shows the complete DDS for this application method. SFLSIZ is defined with a value of 80, and SFLPAG's value is 15.

```
*.. 1 ...+... 2 ...+... 3 ...+... 4 ...+... 5 ...+... 6 ...+... 7 ...+... 8
AAN01N02N03T.Name++++++RLen++TDpBLinPosFunctions+++++++++++++++++++++++++++++
 * Display file SECTINQ, coded for loading the entire subfile at once
A                                         INDARA
A                                         CA03(03 'F3=Exit')
A                                         CA12(12 'F12=Cancel')
A                                         REF(SECTIONS)
 * Record format of initial inquiry screen
A             R CRSEINQ
A                                         BLINK
A                                      1 28'Course Inquiry'
A                                      3  2'Type value, then Enter.'
A                                      5  5'Course number . .'
A               COURSENO      6A  B   5 24
A N90                                     DSPATR(UL)
A N90                                     DSPATR(HI)
A  90                                     ERRMSG('Course not found' 90)
A                                     23  2'F3=Exit  F12=Cancel'
 * Record format for subfile
A             R SFLSECT                    SFL
A               SECTNO      R       0  4 14
A               INSTR       R       0  4 23
A               ROOM        R       0  4 41
A               DAYS        R       0  4 49
A               BEGTIME     R    Y  0  4 57EDTWRD('0 : ')
A               ENROLL      R    Y  0  4 66EDTCDE(3)
 * Record format for subfile control
A             R CTLSECT                    SFLCTL(SFLSECT)
A                                          SFLPAG(15)
A                                          SFLSIZ(80)
A  50                                      SFLCLR
A  51                                      SFLDSPCTL
A  51                                      SFLDSP
A                                          OVERLAY
A               COURSENO     6A  O   1 28
A                                      1 35'Course Information'
A                                      3 12'Section'
A                                      3 24'Instructor'
A                                      3 41'Room'
A                                      3 49'Days'
A                                      3 57'Time'
A                                      3 64'Enroll.'
 * Footer record format
A             R FOOTER
A                                     21  2'Press Enter to continue.'
A                                     23  2'F3=Exit  F12=Cancel'
```

Notice the inclusion of a footer record definition, which contains prompts about active function keys. This record format is needed because the control record format cannot reference screen lines that would fall both above the subfile display (i.e., the column headings) and below the subfile (the function key prompts). The control record format includes the record-level keyword **OVERLAY** so that the footer record format will not be erased when the subfile is displayed.

With the display file definition complete, we can turn to the requirements for the program that will use it.

First, for all subfile applications, RPG IV requires you to identify a subfile within the File specification of the display file with which you want to associate the subfile. In addition, as part of the display file's definition, you need to identify a field that your program will use to represent a subfile record's relative record number. **Relative record number** simply means the position of the record within the subfile (e.g., first subfile record, second subfile record). This field is needed because RPG IV writes records to a subfile (and retrieves records from a subfile) based on the value of the relative record number.

You associate the subfile and relative record number field with a workstation file by using keyword Sfile in the Keywords area of the File specification (positions 44–80). The subfile record format name (e.g., Sflsect), a colon (:), and the field to be used to store the relative record number (e.g., Rrn) appear within parentheses following the keyword:

```
*.. 1 ...+... 2 ...+... 3 ...+... 4 ...+... 5 ...+... 6 ...+... 7 ...+... 8
FFilename++IPEASFRLen+LKLen+AIDevice+.Keywords+++++++++++++++++++++++++++++++
FSectionl   If   E          K Disk
FSectinq    Cf   E              Workstn Sfile(Sflsect:Rrn)
F                                       Indds(Indicators)
```

Next, you need to design the calculations. In our application, once the user has entered the desired course, the program needs to use that value to access the appropriate records in logical file SECTIONL and write them to the subfile; loading the subfile continues until no additional appropriate records (i.e., no more sections for that course) exist. Then the subfile can be displayed by executing the subfile control record format. Because SLFPAG is less than SLFSIZ, the system will handle any user request to page up or page down. Upon return, the program should either end or request another course, depending on whether the user pressed F3 or Enter. The following pseudocode illustrates the logic needed for this application.

```
While user wants to continue;
   Display inquiry screen;
   If user doesn't want to exit;
      Access start of appropriate sections;
      If section not found;
         Turn on error indicator;
      Else;
         Clear subfile;
         Load subfile;
         Display subfile;
      Endif;
   Endif;
Endwhile;
```

The pseudocode for loading the subfile using this method of handling subfiles is as follows:

Read a matching section record;
While there are more appropriate section records;
  Increment relative record number;
  Write a record to the subfile;
  Read a matching section record;
Endwhile;

The following code illustrates the RPG IV implementation of the design we've depicted in pseudocode.

```
*.. 1 ...+... 2 ...+... 3 ...+... 4 ...+... 5 ...+... 6 ...+... 7 ...+... 8
DName++++++++++ETDsFrom+++To/L+++IDc.Keywords++++++++++++++++++++++++++++++++
     // Indicator data structure
D Indicators      DS
D  Exit                          3      3N
D  Cancel                       12     12N
D  Sflclr                       50     50N
D  Slfdsp                       51     51N
D  Crsnotfnd                    90     90N

     . . .
    /Free
     // Calculations for subfile application when entire subfile is loaded
     // before any display takes place
       Dow Not Exit;                       // Process loop until user wants to exit
         Exfmt Crseinq;
         If Not Exit;
           Setll Courseno Sectionl;
           If Not %Equal(Sectionl);   // No matching section in file
             Crsnotfnd = *On;         // Turn on error indicator
           Else;
             Exsr Clearsfl;           // Otherwise, clear and then load subfile
             Exsr Loadsfl;
             Write Footer;            // Write footer to screen
             Exfmt Ctlsect;           // Show subfile via control record format
           Endif;
         Endif;
       Enddo;

       *Inlr = *On;
       Return;
```

continued...

continued...

```
 // ********************************************************************
 //
 // Subroutine to clear the subfile and reset RRN to 0
 //
   Begsr Clearsfl;
     Sflclr = *On;
     Sfldsp = *Off;
     Write Ctlsect;
     Sflclr = *Off;
     Rrn = 0;
   Endsr;

 // ********************************************************************
 //
 // Subroutine to load the subfile until no more section records
 //
   Begsr Loadsfl;
     Reade Courseno Sectionl;
     Dow Not %Eof(Sectionl);
       Rrn += 1;
       Write Sflsect;
       Reade Courseno Sectionl;
     Enddo;
     Sfldsp = (Rrn > 0);
   Endsr;
 /End-Free
```

Note in these calculations that the subfile is loaded by writing records to the subfile record format based on the relative record number field, which is incremented before each successive write operation. The program displays the subfile by executing the subfile control record format. A **Write operation** to the control format—with the Sflclr indicator on—clears the subfile; the program also uses Write, rather than Exfmt, to display the Footer format because a user response to that display is not required.

In this implementation of the subfile application, subfile size is greater than subfile page, and the size is large enough to handle the maximum number of records that the subfile normally would be expected to hold. The program stores all relevant database records in the subfile before any display. With this approach, i5/OS automatically enables the page keys and signals, through a plus sign in the lower-right screen corner, that more subfile records are available for viewing. From a programmer's viewpoint, this technique is the simplest to code. Unfortunately, this method may result in poor response time when the application is used.

The cause of the slow system response is that this technique requires the system to access all the records that meet the selection criterion and store them in the subfile before displaying the first page of the subfile. If the subfile size is small, performance will be satisfactory, but as the subfile size increases—to, say, hundreds of records—response time will degrade noticeably. In that case, especially if the user typically does not scroll much throughout the subfile, it may make sense to build the subfile a page at a time as the user requests additional pages.

Loading the Subfile a Page at a Time

The other methods of subfile building load the subfile a page at a time. Two variations exist for this technique.

Variation 1: Subfile Size Greater Than Page

This method of subfile handling relies on the fact that the system will automatically expand a subfile, regardless of its stated size, as your program adds more records to it. Because this additionally allocated room is not contiguous on disk, performance degrades as the number of pages in the subfile increases, but the technique works well when the number of records usually required within the subfile is small.

This method entails loading the subfile one page at a time based on the user's request for additional pages. Paging within the subfile records already loaded is handled automatically by the operating system. When the user attempts to scroll past the last page in the subfile, however, control returns to the program, which must load an additional page (if additional appropriate records exist).

To use this method, you must add three keywords to the subfile control record format. First, the PAGEDOWN keyword (or its equivalent, ROLLUP) must be associated with an indicator to let the system send control back to the program when a page down request exceeds the current limits of the subfile. You must also add the **SFLEND** (Subfile End) keyword, conditioned by an indicator.

Keyword SFLEND, its associated indicator, and the Page down key work together to determine what happens when the user tries to scroll past the current limits of the subfile. If indicator SFLEND is off, the system displays a plus sign and returns control to the program to load the next page; if SFLEND is on, the plus sign is not displayed, and control is not returned to the program for additional loading. Thus, the program should turn on SFLEND when no additional records remain to be put into the subfile. The system will then prohibit user attempts to scroll past the last page of records in the subfile.

The third keyword needed is **SFLRCDNBR** (Subfile Record Number), coded within the subfile control record format opposite a hidden field. The value of the hidden field determines which page of the subfile is displayed when the subfile control format is written. Without this keyword and its associated field, when the program writes the control record after loading a new page into the subfile, it will by default display the first page of the subfile rather than the newly loaded page. Using parameter value **CURSOR** with keyword SFLRCDNBR causes the cursor to be positioned on that record upon display.

Note that you signify a hidden field by entering an H in position 38 (Usage) of the DDS specifications. Hidden fields do not include a screen location specification because, although they are part of the screen, they are not displayed. Your program can write a value to a hidden field and read the field's value, but the user cannot see or change the value of the field.

The following DDS shows the changes this method requires in the subfile control record format. Note that because the initial inquiry screen, the portion of the control record format defining the column headings, and the footer record format are unchanged from our first example, this DDS does not repeat those lines.

```
*.. 1 ...+... 2 ...+... 3 ...+... 4 ...+... 5 ...+... 6 ...+... 7 ...+... 8
AANØ1NØ2NØ3T.Name++++++RLen++TDpBLinPosFunctions++++++++++++++++++++++++++++++++
 * Display file SECTINQ, coded for loading the subfile one page at a time,
 * with subfile size one greater than page
A                                        INDARA
A                                        CAØ3(Ø3 'F3=Exit')
A                                        CA12(12 'F12=Cancel')
A                                        REF(SECTIONS)
            . . .
 * Record format for subfile
A           R SFLSECT                    SFL
A             SECTNO    R         0  4 14
A             INSTR     R         0  4 23
A             ROOM      R         0  4 41
A             DAYS      R         0  4 49
A             BEGTIME   R      Y  0  4 57EDTWRD('Ø :  ')
A             ENROLL    R      Y  0  4 66EDTCDE(3)
 * Record format for subfile control
A           R CTLSECT                    SFLCTL(SFLSECT)
A                                        SFLPAG(15)
A                                        SFLSIZ(16)
A 50                                      SFLCLR
A 51                                      SFLDSPCTL
A 51                                      SFLDSP
A                                        OVERLAY
A                                        PAGEDOWN(52 'Page Down')
A 55                                      SFLEND
A             SFLRCD        4S ØH         SFLRCDNBR(CURSOR)
A             COURSENO      6A  0  1 28
A             . . .
```

The major logic changes in the RPG program center on loading the subfile a page at a time. Each time control returns to the program from the screen, if the page key triggered the return, the program must load the next page of the subfile and return control to the screen.

When there are no more records left to load, the program should turn on the SFLEND indicator to disable scrolling past the last subfile page. To determine whether additional pages can be built, the program needs to read one additional record after loading an entire subfile page before displaying the new page. The following code illustrates this technique.

```
*.. 1 ...+... 2 ...+... 3 ...+... 4 ...+... 5 ...+... 6 ...+... 7 ...+... 8
DName+++++++++++ETDsFrom+++To/L+++IDc.Keywords++++++++++++++++++++++++++++++
  // Indicator data structure
D Indicators      DS                  99
D  Exit                          3      3N
D  Cancel                       12     12N
D  Sflclr                       50     50N
D  Sfldsp                       51     51N
D  Pagdwn                       52     52N
D  Sflend                       55     55N
D  Crsnotfnd                    90     90N
  // Work field
D Loop            S              10U 0
 . . .
 /Free
  // Calculations for subfile application when subfile is built
  // one page at a time

    Dow Not Exit;                       // Process loop until user wants to exit
      Exfmt Crseinq;
      If Not Exit;
        Chain Courseno Sectionl;
        If Not %Found(Sectionl);  // No matching section in file
          Crsnotfnd = *On;        // Turn on error indicator
        Else;                     // Clear and then load subfile
          Exsr Clearsfl;
          Exsr Loadsfl;
          Sflend = *Off;          // Initialize SFLEND indicator to off
          Write Footer;           // Write footer to screen
          Exfmt Ctlsect;          // Show subfile via control record format
          Dow Pagdwn;             // Load/display page when pag key pressed
            Exsr Loadsfl;
            Exfmt Ctlsect;
          Enddo;
        Endif;
      Endif;
    Enddo;

    *Inlr = *On;
    Return;

  // *********************************************************************
  //
  // Subroutine to clear the subfile and reset RRN to 0
  //
    Begsr Clearsfl;
      Sflclr = *On;
      Sfldsp = *Off;
      Write Ctlsect;
      Sflclr = *Off;
      Rrn = 0;
    Endsr;
```

continued...

continued...

```
// ********************************************************************
//
// Subroutine to load one page of subfile or until no more records exist
//
  Begsr Loadsfl;
    Sflrcd = Rrn + 1;

    For Loop = 1 To 15;              // Loop 15 times to load the page
      Rrn += 1;
      Write Sflsect;
      Reade Courseno Sectionl;
      Sflend = Not %Found(Sectionl);
      If Sflend;                     // Early exit if no more matching records
        Leave;
      Endif;
    Endfor;
    Sfldsp = (Rrn > 0);
  Endsr;
/End-Free
```

Notice in this code that, in contrast to the code of the first method, subroutine Loadsfl reads and writes only 15 records to the subfile—that is, one page. If no additional appropriate sections remain before the page is full, the looping ends. In the mainline, a loop of load-and-display continues until the user presses some key other than the Page down key.

Variation 2: Subfile Size Equals Page

Setting subfile size equal to page is most appropriate when the user is likely to want to scroll through a large number of records—for example, to do generic searches. Response time is medium and consistent regardless of the number of records viewed.

With this method, the subfile stores only one page of records. Scrolling forward requires replacing the existing page with the next page through loading; scrolling backward requires replacing the existing page with records already read. The program logic required by this technique is therefore more complicated than that of the other methods. Moreover, the method of backward scrolling used will depend on whether you are accessing records by unique keys, non-unique keys, partial keys, or relative record numbers. As an alternative to enabling **PAGEUP** (or **ROLLDOWN**), programmers often require users to restart the subfile at the beginning to review records already displayed. This is the method illustrated here.

The DDS for this implementation is similar to that used when subfile size is one greater than subfile page, except that subfile size equals subfile page and keyword SFLRCDNBR is not used. (Because the subfile is only one page long, positioning the subfile upon redisplay is not a problem with this technique.) Note that the control record format includes keywords PAGEDOWN and SFLEND, and function key F5 is enabled to signal restarting the course display. Also note that the illustration omits the initial inquiry screen and the screen column headings from the subfile control record format; these remain identical to those of the previous methods. The footer prompt line now indicates that F5 restarts the subfile.

```
*.. 1 ...+... 2 ...+... 3 ...+... 4 ...+... 5 ...+... 6 ...+... 7 ...+... 8
AANØ1NØ2NØ3T.Name++++++RLen++TDpBLinPosFunctions++++++++++++++++++++++++++++++
 * Display file SECTINQ, where subfile size equals subfile page
A                                       INDARA
A                                       CAØ3(Ø3 'F3=Exit')
A                                       CA12(12 'F12=Cancel')
A                                       REF(SECTIONS)
         . . .
 * Record format for subfile
A           R SFLSECT                    SFL
A             SECTNO     R        0  4 14
A             INSTR      R        0  4 23
A             ROOM       R        0  4 41
A             DAYS       R        0  4 49
A             BEGTIME    R     Y  0  4 57EDTWRD('Ø :   ')
A             ENROLL     R     Y  0  4 66EDTCDE(3)
 * Record format for subfile control
A           R CTLSECT                    SFLCTL(SFLSECT)
A                                        SFLPAG(15)
A                                        SFLSIZ(15)
A 50                                     SFLCLR
A 51                                     SFLDSPCTL
A 51                                     SFLDSP
A                                        OVERLAY
A                                        PAGEDOWN (52 'Page Down')
A 55                                     SFLEND
A                                        CAØ5(Ø5 'Restart course')
A                                        VLDCMDKEY(Ø6)
A             COURSENO    6A   0  1 28
         . . .
 * Footer record format
A           R FOOTER
A                                    21  2'Press Enter to continue.'
A                                    23  2'F3=Exit  F5=Restart Sections'
A                                    23 32'F12=Cancel'
```

Although the needed DDS changes are minimal, this method requires some major changes to the RPG IV program. First, before each loading of the subfile, the program must clear the subfile because the new records should completely replace those previously displayed. Second, the program must check the page key indicator and indicator 05 upon return from the screen to determine whether to put the next set of section records into the subfile or to chain to the first section record again and load the first set of records back into the subfile.

```
*.. 1 ...+... 2 ...+... 3 ...+... 4 ...+... 5 ...+... 6 ...+... 7 ...+... 8
DName++++++++++ETDsFrom+++To/L+++IDc.Keywords+++++++++++++++++++++++++++++++++
  // Indicator data structure
D Indicators      DS             99
D  Exit                     3    3N
D  Refresh                  5    5N
D  Cancel                  12   12N
D  Sflclr                  50   50N
D  Pagdwn                  52   52N
D  Sflend                  55   55N
D  Crsnotfnd               90   90N
  // Work field
D Loop           S              10U 0
  . . .
 /Free
  // Calculations for subfile application when subfile size equals page

     Dow Not Exit;                          // Process loop until user exits
       Exfmt Crseinq;
       If Not Exit;
         Chain Courseno Sectionl;
         If Not %Found(Sectionl);           // No match section in file
           Crsnotfnd = *ON;                 // Turn on error indicator
         Else;
           Dou Not Refresh And Not Pagdwn;  // Loop until no action
             If Refresh;
               Chain Courseno Sectionl;
             Endif;
             Exsr Clearsfl;                 // Clear and load subfile
             Exsr Loadsfl;
             Write Footer;                  // Display footer and subfile
             Exfmt Ctlsect;
           Enddo;
         Endif;
       Endif;
     Enddo;

     *Inlr = *On;
     Return;

  // ********************************************************************
  //
  // Subroutine to clear the subfile and reset RRN to 0
  //
     Begsr Clearsfl;
       Sflclr = *On;
       Sfldsp = *Off;
       Write Ctlsect;
       Eval Sflclr = *Off;
       Rrn = 0;
     Endsr;
```

continued...

continued...

```
// ********************************************************************
   // Subroutine to load one page of subfile or until no more records. First
   // record of page already read by CHAIN or previous READE.
      Begsr Loadsfl;
         For Loop = 1 To 15;              // Loop 15 times to load the page
            Rrn += 1;
            Write Sflsect;
            Reade Courseno Sectionl;
            Sflend = Not %Found(Sectionl);
            If Sflend;                     // Early exit if no more matching records
               Leave;
            Endif;
         Endfor;
         Sfldsp = (Rrn > 0);
      Endsr;
 /End-Free
```

Subfiles and Change

Assume you wanted to list sections of a course not just to inspect the data but also to make changes in the data—perhaps you need to assign different instructors to sections or reschedule some sections to different rooms. The **Readc (Read Next Changed Record) operation**, used only with subfiles, lets you develop such an application. The Readc operation takes the form

```
Readc{(e)} record-name {data-structure};
```

Generally used within a loop, the Readc operation reads only those subfile records that were changed during a prior Exfmt operation; when no changed subfile records remain to be read, %Eof is turned on. Because of the Readc operation, a user can make as many changes as necessary to various records in the subfile in a single display; all these changes can then be processed when control is returned to the program. If you specify a result data structure the Read operation will transfer data directly from the record to the data structure.

You can use Readc regardless of the technique used to load and display the subfile. For simplicity's sake, we'll modify the first version of the program, in which all the relevant records are loaded into the subfile at one time, to demonstrate how to use this operation.

We need to make a few changes in the display file. First, the subfile fields need to be different from the database fields. Without this change, rereading a database record preparatory to updating it would obliterate any changes to subfile field values. Also, the usage of most of the subfile fields needs to be B (both input and output) to let users change the fields' values; section number remains output only, to prevent changes to the key. Last, some of the screen captions and prompts require changes to better suit the new application. The following DDS reflects all these modifications.

```
*.. 1 ...+... 2 ...+... 3 ...+... 4 ...+... 5 ...+... 6 ...+... 7 ...+... 8
AAN01N02N03T.Name++++++RLen++TDpBLinPosFunctions+++++++++++++++++++++++++++++++
 * Display file SECTUPDT, coded for loading the entire subfile at once
A                                      INDARA
A                                      CA03(03 'F3=Exit')
A                                      CA12(12 'F12=Cancel')
A                                      REF(SECTIONS)
 * Record format of initial inquiry screen
A          R CRSEINQ
A                                      BLINK
A                                    1 28'Course Section Update'
A                                    3  2'Type value, then Enter'
A                                    5  5'Course number . .'
A            COURSENO      6A  B  5 24
A N90                                  DSPATR(UL)
A N90                                  DSPATR(HI)
A  90                                  ERRMSG('Course not found' 90)
A                                   23  2'F3=Exit   F12=Cancel'
 * Record format for subfile
A          R SFLSECT                 SFL
A            SECTNO     R        O  4 14
A            SINSTR        15    B  4 23
A            SROOM          4   0B  4 41
A            SDAYS          3    B  4 49
A            SBEGTIME      4Y   0B  4 57EDTWRD('0 : ')
A            SENROLL       3Y   0B  4 66EDTCDE(3)

 * Record format for subfile control
A          R CTLSECT                 SFLCTL(SFLSECT)
A                                    SFLPAG(15)
A                                    SFLSIZ(80)
A  50                                SFLCLR
A  51                                SFLDSPCTL
A  51                                SFLDSP
A                                    OVERLAY
A            COURSENO      6A  O  1 28
A                                    1 35'Course Information'
A                                    3 12'Section'
A                                    3 24'Instructor'
A                                    3 41'Room'
A                                    3 49'Days'
A                                    3 57'Time'
A                                    3 64'Enroll.'
 * Footer record format
A          R FOOTER
A                                   21  2'Change values as desired;-
A                                       ' press Enter to continue.'
A                                   23  2'F3=Exit   F12=Cancel'
```

The RPG program requires a few changes to enable the updating to take place. First, remember that the database file will be an update type so that records can be read and then rewritten to the file with any changes.

The program logic remains basically the same. The major difference occurs when control is returned to the program following the subfile display. At that point, provided the user did not press F3 or F12, the program needs to loop, using Readc to read any changed subfile record and using that data to update the data file. The loop should continue until no more changed records exist.

The program uses partial keys (to access a group of records) with the Setll and Reade operation; it uses a complete key (to access a specific record for update) with the Chain operation. Finally, because the subfile and database fields are different, the program needs to move values back and forth between corresponding fields at appropriate times. The modified program is shown below.

```
*.. 1 ...+... 2 ...+... 3 ...+... 4 ...+... 5 ...+... 6 ...+... 7 ...+... 8
 // **********************************************************************
 // This interactive program displays sections of a course entered by the
 // user and lets the user update the section information.
 // **********************************************************************
FSectionl  UF   E    K       Disk
FSectupdt  CF   E            Workstn Sfile(Sflsect:Rrn)
F                                    Indds(Indicators)

D Rrn             S            2 0

   // Indicator data structure
D Indicators     DS           99
D  Exit                   3     3N
D  Cancel                12    12N
D  SflClr                50    50N
D  Sfldsp                51    51N
D  CrsNotFnd             90    90N

 /Free
    Dow Not Exit;                             // Process loop until user exits
      Exfmt Crseinq;
      If Not Exit;
        Setll Courseno Sectionl;
        If Not %Equal(Sectionl);              // No matching section in file
          Crsnotfnd = *On;                    // Turn on error indicator
        Else;                                 // Otherwise clear/load subfile
          Exsr Clearsfl;                      // Clear/load subfile
          Exsr Loadsfl;
          Write Footer;                       //Display footer/subfile
          Exfmt Ctlsect;
          If Not Exit And Not Cancel;         // Update database records
            Exsr Updatesr;
          Endif;
        Endif;
      Endif;
    Enddo;
```

continued...

continued...

```
   *Inlr = *On;
   Return;

// ********************************************************************
//
// Subroutine to clear the subfile and reset RRN to 0
//
  Begsr Clearsfl;
    Sflclr = *On;
    Sfldsp = *Off;
    Write Ctlsect;
    Sflclr = *Off;
    Rrn = 0;
  Endsr;

// ********************************************************************
//
// Subroutine to load the subfile until no more section records exist
//
  Begsr Loadsfl;
    Reade Courseno Sectionl;
    Dow Not %Eof(Sectionl);
      Rrn = Rrn + 1;
      Exsr Movedb;
      Write Sflsect;
      Reade Courseno Sectionl;
    Enddo;
    Sfldsp = (Rrn > 0);
  Endsr;

// ********************************************************************
//
// Subroutine to read changed records in the subfile and update the
// database records
//
  Begsr Updatesr;
    Readc Sflsect;
    Dow Not %Eof;
      Chain (Courseno:Sectno) Sectionl;
      If %Found(Sectionl);
        Exsr Movesfl;
        Update Secrec;
      Endif;
      Readc Sflsect;
    Enddo;
  Endsr;
```

continued...

continued...

```
// ********************************************************************
//
// Subroutine to transfer values from database fields to subfile fields
//
   Begsr Movedb;
     Sdays = Days;
     Sbegtime = Begtime;
     Sroom = Room;
     Senroll = Enroll;
     Sinstr = Instr;
   Endsr;

// ********************************************************************
//
// Subroutine to transfer values from subfile fields to database fields
//
   Begsr Movesfl;
     Days = Sdays;
     Begtime = Sbegtime;
     Room = Sroom;
     Enroll = Senroll;
     Instr = Sinstr;
   Endsr;
/End-Free
```

Uses of Subfiles

You can use subfiles in a variety of ways. Subfiles can simply display data, when the user needs only to review information. You can use them for display with selection, so the user can select an entry to obtain more detailed information about the selected record; the user can then update the selected record if desired.

You can use subfiles for data entry of new records to database files, with or without validity checking. You can associate multiple subfiles with a given workstation file. You can display two subfiles simultaneously on the screen. You can transfer data between a program and a subfile by using Chain, Update, and Write operations, as well as Readc; such processing is always based on the relative record numbers of the subfile records. Last, you can display system messages through special message subfiles.

It should be obvious from the above discussion that subfile processing can become complex and that mastery of programming with subfiles, like any kind of programming, comes with practice and experience.

Chapter Summary

Subfiles let users work with more than one database record at a time in an interactive application. Records stored in a subfile are displayed in a single output operation to the workstation file; changes made to subfile records are returned to the program in a single input operation.

Defining subfiles within DDS requires two kinds of record formats: one that defines the fields within the subfile and describes the field locations within a screen line, and a second format, called a subfile control record format, that actually manages the displaying of the subfile information.

You use several required DDS keywords with subfiles. Record-level keyword SFL identifies a record format as a subfile record, while record-level keyword SFLCTL identifies a format as a subfile control record format. Additional required keywords determine how many records appear on the screen at the same time, how much total storage the system allocates to the subfile, and when the subfile and its control record are displayed.

Several different techniques exist for loading and displaying subfiles. These methods differ in the relationship they establish between subfile page and subfile size and in when they write records to the subfile relative to when the subfile display begins. Regardless of the technique you use, all applications involving subfiles require additional entries on the File specifications for the workstation files using the subfiles. You perform all input to and output from a subfile through relative record numbers. The Readc operation lets your application program process just those subfile records that the user has changed.

The following table summarizes the operation codes discussed in this chapter:

Function or operation	Description	Syntax
Readc	Read next changed record	Readc{(e)} *record-name* {*data-structure*}
Write	Displays a subfile	Write {(e)} *record-name*

Key Terms

CURSOR

list panels

OVERLAY

PAGEUP

Readc operation

relative record number

ROLLDOWN

SFL

SFLCLR

SFLCTL

SFLDSP

SFLDSPCTL

SFLEND

SFLPAG

SFLRCDNBR

SFLSIZ

subfile

subfile control record format

subfile record format

Write operation

Discussion/Review Questions

1. What is a subfile?
2. What are the functions of a subfile record format and a subfile control record format in a display file?
3. Describe the meanings of the following display file keywords and which record format each is used with: SFL, SFLCTL, SFLPAG, SFLSIZ, SFLDSP, SFLCLR, SFLDSPCTL.
4. In subfile processing, how are column headings for the subfile and screen footings (i.e., information to be displayed below the subfile) generally handled?
5. What is a File specification continuation line? What information is required on a continuation line when you develop an application using subfiles?
6. What is a hidden field?
7. When do you need to use the keyword SFLRCDNBR?
8. Discuss the relative merits of different approaches to subfile definition and loading.
9. Discuss page-key control and action with the different approaches to subfile definition and loading.
10. How does the READC operation differ from the other read operations of RPG IV?
11. In using subfiles for updating, why do you need to use fields for the subfile that are different from the fields of the database file you are updating?
12. Explain the differences between the different ways to load subfiles. What are the benefits of one over the other?

Exercises

1. Design the screens and write the DDS for an interactive application that lets a user enter a zip code to list the names of all the company's customers residing within that zip code. Create whatever fields you may need, and make the subfile size much greater than page.
2. Write the RPG IV code for Exercise 1. Make up whatever file and field names you need, but be consistent with the definitions used in Exercise 1. Use the technique of loading the entire subfile prior to display.
3. Revise the DDS from Exercise 1 to make subfile size and page equal. Modify the RPG IV code from Exercise 2 to suit this change.
4. Write the pseudocode for an interactive application that displays a list of all a company's product numbers and their descriptions and lets the user place an X in front of those products for which he or she wants more information. The program should then display a screen of detailed product information – quantity on hand, cost, selling price, reorder point, and reorder quantity – for each product selected by the user.
5. Write the generic pseudocode needed to use subfiles for data entry (i.e., for adding large numbers of records to a file).
6. Write the pseudocode for Programming Assignment 5 in this chapter.

Programming Assignments

1. Write an interactive application for Wexler University that will let a user enter a department number to display all the instructors working within that department. Use a logical file built over file WUINSTP (described in Appendix F).

Screen One: The user enters a valid department code and presses Enter. F3 exits the program.

```
              1         2         3         4         5         6         7         8
     1234567890123456789012345678901234567890123456789012345678901234567890
  1  XX/XX/XX                                              Program ID XXXXXXX
  2
  3                         Wexler University
  4                   Instructor Department Inquiry Screen
  5
  6
  7  Type value, then Enter.
  8
  9      Department code . . XXX
 10
 11
 12
 13
 14
 15
 16
 17
 18
 19
 20
 21
 22
 23
 24
 25  F3=Exit
```

Screen Two: This screen lists all of the instructors for a specific department. Pressing F3 exits the program and F12 returns to the previous screen.

```
        1         2         3         4         5         6         7         8
1234567890123456789012345678901234567890123456789012345678901234567890123456789 0
 1 XX/XX/XX                                              Program ID XXXXXXX
 2
 3                          Wexler University
 4                    Instructors for Department 000
 5
 6  Soc. Sec.      Name                   Salary   R  S    Hired     M  D T  T
 7  666-66-6666 0000000000 000000000000000 666,666.66  0  0  6666/66/66  66 0  0
 8  666-66-6666 0000000000 000000000000000 666,666.66  0  0  6666/66/66  66 0  0
 9  666-66-6666 0000000000 000000000000000 666,666.66  0  0  6666/66/66  66 0  0
10  666-66-6666 0000000000 000000000000000 666,666.66  0  0  6666/66/66  66 0  0
11  666-66-6666 0000000000 000000000000000 666,666.66  0  0  6666/66/66  66 0  0
12  666-66-6666 0000000000 000000000000000 666,666.66  0  0  6666/66/66  66 0  0
13  666-66-6666 0000000000 000000000000000 666,666.66  0  0  6666/66/66  66 0  0
14  666-66-6666 0000000000 000000000000000 666,666.66  0  0  6666/66/66  66 0  0
15  666-66-6666 0000000000 000000000000000 666,666.66  0  0  6666/66/66  66 0  0
16  666-66-6666 0000000000 000000000000000 666,666.66  0  0  6666/66/66  66 0  0
17  666-66-6666 0000000000 000000000000000 666,666.66  0  0  6666/66/66  66 0  0
18  666-66-6666 0000000000 000000000000000 666,666.66  0  0  6666/66/66  66 0  0
19  666-66-6666 0000000000 000000000000000 666,666.66  0  0  6666/66/66  66 0  0
20  666-66-6666 0000000000 000000000000000 666,666.66  0  0  6666/66/66  66 0  0
21  666-66-6666 0000000000 000000000000000 666,666.66  0  0  6666/66/66  66 0  0
22
23  F3=Exit   F12=Cancel
24
25
```

2. Write an interactive application for CompuSell that will let a user locate a customer based on a generic name search. That is, the user can enter one or more starting letters of the last name and the program will display the customers by last name, starting with the first customer whose name meets the generic specification and ending when a customer's name no longer matches that specification.

The subfile of customers displayed should include just the last name, first name, and identification of the customers, plus a selection field. If the user chooses (selects) one or more of the records by placing an X, the program then should display all the detailed information about that customer (all the data fields of the customer master file). You will need to use file CSCSTP and a logical file keyed on last name built over this file (see Appendix F for a description of file CSCSTP). Include a generic help screen in your application.

Screen One: A user can enter part of a customer's name and press Enter.

```
                 1         2         3         4         5         6         7         8
       1234567890123456789012345678901234567890123456789012345678901234567890123456789012345678901234567890
    1  XX/XX/XX                                                              Program ID XXXXXXX
    2
    3                    CompuSell Customer Generic Inquiry Screen
    4
    5
    6
    7  Enter name or generic name.
    8
    9     Name . . . . . . .  IIIIIIIIIIIIIIII
   10
   11
   12
   13
   14
   15
   16
   17
   18
   19
   20
   21
   22
   23  F3=Exit   F12=Cancel
   24
   25
```

Screen Two: The user can select a record by placing an X in the selection field. The user is allowed to select a number of customers.

```
                 1         2         3         4         5         6         7         8
       1234567890123456789012345678901234567890123456789012345678901234567890123456789012345678901234567890
    1  XX/XX/XX                                                              Program ID XXXXXXX
    2                 CompuSell Customers Matching Specification
    3
    4      Enter X in selection(s) to see customer details.
    5
    6  Selection     Last Name        First Name    Number
    7      B        0000000000000000   0000000000   666666
    8      B        0000000000000000   0000000000   666666
    9      B        0000000000000000   0000000000   666666
   10      B        0000000000000000   0000000000   666666
   11      B        0000000000000000   0000000000   666666
   12      B        0000000000000000   0000000000   666666
   13      B        0000000000000000   0000000000   666666
   14      B        0000000000000000   0000000000   666666
   15      B        0000000000000000   0000000000   666666
   16      B        0000000000000000   0000000000   666666
   17      B        0000000000000000   0000000000   666666
   18      B        0000000000000000   0000000000   666666
   19      B        0000000000000000   0000000000   666666
   20      B        0000000000000000   0000000000   666666
   21      B        0000000000000000   0000000000   666666
   22
   23  F3=Exit   F12=Cancel
   24
   25
```

Screen Three: This screen displays the customer's information. Pressing Enter will display the next customer selected. If there are no additional customers selected, the program will return the user to the first screen.

```
         1         2         3         4         5         6         7         8
1234567890123456789012345678901234567890123456789012345678901234567890123456789 0
1 XX/XX/XX                                                    Program ID XXXXXXX
2                     CompuSell Customer Information
3
4            Press Enter to see next selected customer.
5
6      Number . . . . 666666
7      Name . . . . . 0000000000 000000000000000
8      Address  . . . 000000000000000000000
9                     000000000000000   00   66666-6666
10     Phone  . . . . 666-666-6666
11     Last order . . 66/66/6666
12     Balance due  . 6,666.66
13
14
15
16
17
18
19
20
21
22
23 F3=Exit   F12=Cancel
24
25
```

3. Write an application for Wexler University that will let a user interactively add or change (but not delete) a course and/or its description in files WUCRSP and WUCRSDSP (see Appendix F). Do not let the user change the course identification or add a duplicate identification. All other fields of either file may be changed. Do not display the line numbers of the description on the screen.

Screen One: This allows the user to enter the department, the course number, and the action code.

```
           1         2         3         4         5         6         7         8
  1234567890123456789012345678901234567890123456789012345678901234567890123456789 0
1 XX/XX/XX                                                      Program ID XXXXXXX
2                          Wexler University
3
4                       Course File Maintenance
5
6
7
8  Type values, then Enter
9
10      Department  . . . . . . . .  BBB
11      Course number . . . . . . .  999
12      Action code . . . . . . . .  I
13         A = add record
14         C = change record
15
16
17
18
19
20
21
22
23 F3=Exit   F12=Cancel
24
25
```

Screen Two: The user can add/change the Title of the course and the number of credits. Pressing Enter will take the user to the next screen. Pressing F12 will return to the previous screen, and F3 will exit the program with no updates.

```
         1         2         3         4         5         6         7         8
1234567890123456789012345678901234567890123456789012345678901234567890123456789 0
1 XX/XX/XX                                                    Program ID XXXXXXX
2                              Wexler University
3
4                            Course File Maintenance
5
6
7 Type values, then Enter
8
9    Course  . . . . . . . . . 000 666
10   Title . . . . . . . . . . BBBBBBBBBBBBBBBBBBBBBBBBBB
11   Credits   . . . . . . . . 9
12
13
14
15
16
17
18
19
20
21
22
23  F3=Exit   F12=Cancel
24
25
```

Screen Three: The user can add/change the Title, Credits, or Course Description. Pressing F3 will exit the program with no updates. Pressing F12 will return to the previous screen, and pressing Enter will update the files and return to the first screen.

```
         1         2         3         4         5         6         7         8
1234567890123456789012345678901234567890123456789012345678901234567890123456789 0
1 XX/XX/XX                                                    Program ID XXXXXXX
2                              Wexler University
3
4                            Course File Maintenance
5
6
7    Course  . . . . . . . . . 000 666
8    Title . . . . . . . . . . BBBBBBBBBBBBBBBBBBBBBBBBBB
9    Credits   . . . . . . . . 9
10
11   Course description:
12 BBBBBBBBBBBBBBBBBBBBBBBBBBBBBBBBBBBBBBBBBBBBBBBBBBBBBBBB
13 BBBBBBBBBBBBBBBBBBBBBBBBBBBBBBBBBBBBBBBBBBBBBBBBBBBBBBBBBB
14 BBBBBBBBBBBBBBBBBBBBBBBBBBBBBBBBBBBBBBBBBBBBBBBBBBBBBBBBBB
15 BBBBBBBBBBBBBBBBBBBBBBBBBBBBBBBBBBBBBBBBBBBBBBBBBBBBBBBBBB
16 BBBBBBBBBBBBBBBBBBBBBBBBBBBBBBBBBBBBBBBBBBBBBBBBBBBBBBBBBB
17 BBBBBBBBBBBBBBBBBBBBBBBBBBBBBBBBBBBBBBBBBBBBBBBBBBBBBBBBBB
18 RRRRRBBBBBBBBBBBBBBBBBBBBBBBBBBBBBBBBBBBBDDDDDDDDDDDDBBBB
19 BBBBBBBBBBBBBBBBBBBBBBBBBBBBBBBBBBBBBBBBBBBBBBBBBBBBBBBBBB
20 BBBBBBBBBBBBBBBBBBBBBBBBBBBBBBBBBBBBBBBBBBBBBBBBBBBBBBBBBB
21 BBBBBBBBBBBBBBBBBBBBBBBBBBBBBBBBBBBBBBBBBBBBBBBBBBBBBBBBBB
22
23  F3=Exit   F12=Cancel
24
25
```

4. GTC Telephone Company wants you to develop an interactive application to process payments from customers. The program should let a user enter a screen full of payments at one time by entering for each payer the payer's phone number and amount paid. This information should be used for two purposes: to update the amount-owed and date-of-last-payment fields in the customer master file (GTCSTP) and to write a record to the payments archive file (GTPAYP). Use the system date for date fields. See Appendix F for file layouts.

Screen One: This screen allows the user to enter customer payments a screen at a time. When the user presses Enter the program validates each customer and updates their payment record.

```
         1         2         3         4         5         6         7         8
1234567890123456789012345678901234567890123456789012345678901234567890123456789012345678901234567890
1  XX/XX/XX                                                    Program ID XXXXXXX
2                         GTC Payment Processing System
3
4     Key in all payments, then Enter.
5
6     Cust. Phone     Payment
7      9999999999     9999.99
8      9999999999     9999.99
9      9999999999     9999.99
10     9999999999     9999.99
11     9999999999     9999.99
12     9999999999     9999.99
13     9999999999     9999.99
14     9999999999     9999.99
15     9999999999     9999.99
16     9999999999     9999.99
17     9999999999     9999.99
18     9999999999     9999.99
19     9999999999     9999.99
20     9999999999     9999.99
21     9999999999     9999.99
22
23  F3=Exit   F12=Cancel
24
25
```

Screen Two: If a phone number is incorrect, this screen is displayed telling the user that the payment has not been processed. At the same time, this information is printed on a report. This report will show the phone number entered and the payment amount.

```
         1         2         3         4         5         6         7         8
 1234567890123456789012345678901234567890123456789012345678901234567890123456789012345678901234567890
 1 XX/XX/XX                                                           Program ID XXXXXXX
 2                          GTC Payment Processing System
 3
 4
 5
 6                      Customer 6666666666 Not Found!
 7
 8                         Payment Not Processed.
 9
10
11
12
13
14
15
16
17
18 Press Enter to continue.
19
20
21
22
23
24
25
```

5. CompuSell wants an Order Entry screen to add and maintain customer orders. This program should include all the error checking described in previous chapters. You will need to use the Customer Master (CSCSTP), Orders (CSORDP), Orders/Products (CSORDPRP) and Inventory Master (CSINVP) described in Appendix F.

   a. This application will prompt for a Customer number. If the customer number is valid, the application will present a screen that will allow the user to change an order or enter a new one.

   b. If the action code is C (for change), a subfile is displayed showing all the orders for the customer. If A (for Add), the user is shown the Add order screen and the order number will be automatically generated using a data area (data areas were covered in Chapter 12).

   c. The user can then maintain the order by adding line items to the order.

   d. On the line item screen, the user can add/change the part number details.

   e. F12 will move the user back a screen and F3 will exit the program with no updates.

Screen One: The user enters a Customer number. If the number is valid, Screen Two is displayed.

```
          1         2         3         4         5         6         7         8
 1234567890123456789012345678901234567890123456789012345678901234567890123456789 0
 1
 2  DD/DD/DD              CompuSell Order Entry Screen          ProgramID XXXXXXX
 3
 4
 5
 6
 7     Enter Customer Number, Then Enter    333333-
 8
 9
10
11
12
13
14
15
16
17
18
19
20
21
22
23
24    F12 = Cancel F3 = Exit
25
```

Screen Two: This screen allows the user to change or add a record. F12 will return to the previous screen, and F3 will exit the program.

```
            1         2         3         4         5         6         7         8
   1234567890123456789012345678901234567890123456789012345678901234567890123456789 0
 1
 2  DD/DD/DD            CompuSell Order Entry Screen            ProgramID XXXXXXX
 3
 4
 5  Customer Information
 6  Cust#  666666
 7
 8  0000000000  000000000000000  6666666666
 9
10  00000000000000000000000  000000000000000 00  666666666
11
12  Enter Action Code: B A = Add C = Change
13
14  Enter Order Number
15
16   If you are adding a new Order you do not need to Enter an Order Number
17
18
19
20
21
22
23   F12 = Cancel F3 = Exit
24
25
```

Screen Three: If the user selected to change an order, this screen is displayed. The user can select the order assigned to this customer to change.

```
            1         2         3         4         5         6         7         8
   1234567890123456789012345678901234567890123456789012345678901234567890123456789 0
 1
 2  DD/DD/DD            CompuSell Order Entry Screen            ProgramID XXXXXXX
 3
 4
 5  Customer Information
 6  Cust#  666666
 7
 8  0000000000  000000000000000  6666666666
 9
10  00000000000000000000000  000000000000000 00  666666666
11
12 Enter an X in the Select Field for the item you want to maintain
13
14            Order                     Amount    Order
15        Select Number Date     Cust#   Paid     Total
16          I    66666  66666666  666666  66,666.66 66,666.66
17          I    66666  66666666  666666  66,666.66 66,666.66
18          I    66666  66666666  666666  66,666.66 66,666.66
19          I    66666  66666666  666666  66,666.66 66,666.66
20          I    66666  66666666  666666  66,666.66 66,666.66
21          I    66666  66666666  666666  66,666.66 66,666.66
22
23   F12 = Cancel F3 = Exit
24
25
```

Screen Four: The user can change the order date or payment information or select an order line item to change.

```
                1         2         3         4         5         6         7         8
       1234567890123456789012345678901234567890123456789012345678901234567890123456789 0
 1
 2      DD/DD/DD              CompuSell Order Entry Screen            ProgramID XXXXXXX
 3
 4
 5      Order#    66666  Customer#   666666 Order Total 6666666-
 6
 7      Payment   9999999- Order Date 99/99/9999
 8
 9
10                 Product                              Ship  Order
11       Select    Number  Description                 Wght  Qty
12          B      999999- BBBBBBBBBBBBBBBBBBBBBBBBB    9999- 9999-
13          B      999999- BBBBBBBBBBBBBBBBBBBBBBBBB    9999- 9999-
14          B      999999- BBBBBBBBBBBBBBBBBBBBBBBBB    9999- 9999-
15          B      999999- BBBBBBBBBBBBBBBBBBBBBBBBB    9999- 9999-
16          B      999999- BBBBBBBBBBBBBBBBBBBBBBBBB    9999- 9999-
17          B      999999- BBBBBBBBBBBBBBBBBBBBBBBBB    9999- 9999-
18
19
20
21
22      Enter C to change a line or A to add an item Press Enter
23
24
25      F12 = Cancel F3 = Exit
```

Screen Five: This screen allows a user to change or add a line item on an order. This screen also allows the user to Press F6 to open a window that allows them to retrieve a list of part numbers from the inventory master. This feature is described in the Appendix F.

```
               1         2         3         4         5         6         7         8
     1234567890123456789012345678901234567890123456789012345678901234567890123456789012345678901234567890
 1
 2    DD/DD/DD              CompuSell Order Entry Screen              ProgramID XXXXXXX
 3
 4
 5
 6       Order Number 66666
 7
 8       Part Number  999999- BBBBBBBBBBBBBBBBBBBBBBBBBBBB
 9
10       Order Qty... 9999-
11
12
13
14
15  Press F6 to List available Parts.
16
17
18 Press Enter to confirm your Change
19
20
21
22
23 F12 = Cancel F3 = Exit
24
25
```

Appendix A

RPG IV Summary

This appendix summarizes RPG IV specifications, keywords, operation codes, functions, and other RPG IV syntax components. The information is current for Version 5 Release 4 (V5R4) of the ILE RPG/400 compilers; earlier releases may not support some of the entries in this appendix.

Usage Conventions

In some syntax illustrations, the following characters have special meaning:

Arguments separated by vertical bars (|) indicate that only one of the shown values may be entered for the argument. For example, in the following syntax illustration,

```
DFTACTGRP(*NO | *YES)
```

either of the following entries would be valid:

```
DFTACTGRP(*NO)
DFTACTGRP(*YES)
```

Arguments enclosed in curly braces ({ }) are optional arguments. For example, in the following syntax illustration,

```
%KDS(data-structure-name {: num-keys})
```

either of the following entries would be valid:

```
%KDS(MYDS)
%KDS(MYDS : 2)
```

Control (H) Specification

```
*.. 1 ...+... 2 ...+... 3 ...+... 4 ...+... 5 ...+... 6 ...+... 7 ...+... 8
HKeywords++++++++++++++++++++++++++++++++++++++++++++++++++++++++++++++++++++++
```

Columns	Description
1–5	Sequence number
6	H
7–80	Control keywords
81–100	Comments

Control Keywords

ACTGRP(*CALLER | *NEW | 'name')	Specifies ILE activation group (valid only with the CRTBNDRPG compile command).
ALTSEQ{(*EXT | *NONE | *SRC)}	Specifies an alternate collating sequence.
ALWNULL(*INPUTONLY | *NO | *USRCTL)	Specifies processing for null-capable fields.
AUT(*ALL | *CHANGE | *EXCLUDE | *LIBCRTAUT | *USE | 'auth-list')	Specifies authority for users without specific authority to compiled object.
BNDDIR('{libr/}name' {. . .})	Specifies binding directory (or directories) to use when binding object.
CCSID(*CHAR:*JOBRUN | *GRAPH:parm | *UCS2:number)	Specifies default graphic character set identifier.
COPYNEST(number)	Specifies maximum nesting level for /COPY members (1-2048).
COPYRIGHT('string')	Provides copyright information to include in module.
CURSYM('symbol')	Specifies character to use as currency symbol, enclosed in apostrophes (').
CVTOPT(*{NO}DATETIME *{NO}GRAPHIC *{NO}VARCHAR *{NO}VARGRAPHIC)	Specifies compiler conversion options for date, time, timestamp, and graphic data types, as well as variable-length data.
DATEDIT(format{separator})	Specifies numeric field format for the Y edit code: *MDY, *YMD, or *DM. Optional separator character defaults to a slash (/); an ampersand (&) indicates a blank separator.
DATFMT(format{separator})	Specifies format for date literals and default format for date fields. Defaults to *ISO.
DEBUG{(*DUMP} {*INPUT} {*XMLSAX} | *NO | *YES)}	Controls which debug aids are generated into compiled module.
DECEDIT(*JOBRUN | 'value')	Specifies character used for decimal point for edited numbers, enclosed in apostrophes ('). Also indicates whether to print leading zeros. Valid values are '.', ',', '0.' and '0,'.
DECPREC(30 | 31 | 63)	Specifies maximum decimal precision of decimal (packed, zoned, binary) intermediate values in expressions.
DFTACTGRP(*NO | *YES)	Specifies whether to force a program to run in the default activation group (valid only with the CRTBNDRPG compile command).

`DFTNAME(name)`	Specifies default name for RPG program or module.
`ENBPFRCOL(*ENTRYEXIT | *FULL | *PEP)`	Specifies whether performance collection is enabled.
`EXPROPTS(*MAXDIGITS | *RESDECPOS)`	Specifies precision rules to be used when evaluating expressions.
`EXTBININT{(*NO | *YES)}`	Specifies whether to process externally described files with binary (no decimal place) fields as if the fields were integers.
`FIXNBR(*{NO}INPUTPACKED *{NO}ZONED)`	Specifies compiler options to fix invalid decimal data.
`FLTDIV{(*NO | *YES)}`	Specifies whether to use floating-point representation for division.
`FORMSALIGN{(*NO | *YES)}`	Specifies whether to prompt for first page (1P) forms alignment on printed forms.
`FTRANS{(*NONE | *SRC)}`	Specifies whether file translation is to be performed, using a translation table in the source.
`GENLVL(number)`	Specifies maximum error level to allow when compiling object (0-20).
`INDENT(*NONE | 'chars')`	Specifies indentation characters (1 or 2) for source listing.
`INTPREC(10 | 20)`	Specifies integer precision.
`LANGID(*JOB | *JOBRUN | 'lang-id')`	Specifies language identifier for some SRTSEQ options.
`NOMAIN`	Indicates that there is no main procedure in this module.
`OPENOPT(*{NO}INZOFL)`	Specifies open printer file option.
`OPTIMIZE(*BASIC | *FULL | *NONE)`	Specifies optimization level for compiled object.

`OPTION(*{NO}DEBUGIO *{NO}EXPDDS`
  `*{NO}EXT *{NO}GEN *{NO}SECLVL`
  `*{NO}SHOWCPY *{NO}SHOWSKP`
  `*{NO}SRCSTMT *{NO}XREF)`
	Specifies compiler options to use for this object.

`PRFDTA(*{NO}COL)`	Enables collection of profiling data.
`SRTSEQ(*HEX | *JOB | *JOBRUN |` `*LANGIDUNQ | *LANGIDSHR | 'name')`	Specifies sort sequence table to use when compiling object.
`TEXT(*BLANK | *SRCMBRTXT |` `'description')`	Specifies text for compiled object.
`THREAD(*SERIALIZE)`	Specifies multithread environment.
`TIMFMT(format{separator})`	Specifies format for time literals and default format for time fields. Defaults to *ISO.
`TRUNCNBR(*YES | *NO)`	Specifies whether to ignore numeric overflow (not valid for expressions).
`USRPRF(*OWNER | *USER)`	Specifies the user profile under which to run the compiled object (valid only with the CRTBNDRPG compiler command).

Date Formats

Option	Description	Format	Valid separators	Edited field length	Example
*ISO	International Standards Organization	yyyy-mm-dd	-	10	2007-12-31
*USA	IBM US Standard	mm/dd/yyyy	/	10	12/31/2007
*EUR	IBM European Standard	dd.mm.yyyy	.	10	31.12.2007
*JIS	Japanese Industrial Standard	yyyy-mm-dd	-	10	2007-12-31
*YMD	Year/month/day	yy/mm/dd	/ - , . &(blank)	8	07/12/31
*MDY	Month/day/year	mm/dd/yy	/ - , . &(blank)	8	12/31/07
*DMY	Day/month/year	dd/mm/yy	/ - , . &(blank)	8	31/12/07
*JUL	Julian	yy/ddd	/ - , . &(blank)	6	07/365

The following formats are valid only with the TEST operation code, for use with legacy date formats.

Option	Description	Format	Valid separators	Edited field length	Example
*CYMD	Century-year/month/day	cyy/mm/dd	/ - , . &(blank)	9	107/12/31
*CMDY	Century-month/day/year	cmm/dd/yy	/ - , . &(blank)	9	112/31/07
*CDMY	Century-day/month/year	cdd/mm/yy	/ - , . &(blank)	9	131/12/07
*LONGJUL	Long Julian	yyyy/ddd	/ - , . &(blank)	8	2007/365
*JOBRUN	Format determined by job description				

Time Formats

Option	Description	Format	Valid separators	Example
*ISO	International Standards Organization	hh.mm.ss	.	19.30.00
*USA	IBM US Standard	hh:mm xM	:	07:30 PM
*EUR	IBM European Standard	hh.mm.ss	.	19.30.00
*JIS	Japanese Industrial Standard	hh:mm:ss	:	19:30:00
*HMS	Hours:minutes:seconds	hh:mm:ss	: , . &(blank)	19:30:00

File (F) Specification

```
*.. 1 ...+... 2 ...+... 3 ...+... 4 ...+... 5 ...+... 6 ...+... 7 ...+... 8
FFilename++IPEASFRLen+LKLen+AIDevice+.Keywords+++++++++++++++++++++++++++++++
```

Columns	Description	
1–5	Sequence number	
6	F	
7–16	File name	
17	File type:	
	C	Combined (input/output)
	I	Input
	O	Output
	U	Update
18	File designation:	
	(Blank)	Output
	F	Full procedural
	P	Primary
	R	Record address
	S	Secondary
	T	Array or table
19	End of file:	
	(Blank)	Allow LR before all records are processed
	E	All records must be processed before LR
20	File addition (for input or update file):	
	(Blank)	Do not add records
	A	Allow record adds
21	Match field sequence:	
	(Blank)	Ascending
	A	Ascending
	D	Descending
22	File format:	
	E	Externally described
	F	Program-described
23-27	Record length (1–32766, blank)	
28	Limits processing:	
	(Blank)	Sequential or random processing
	L	Limits processing
29-33	Length of key or record address (1–2000, blank)	
34	Record address type:	
	(Blank)	Non-keyed processing
	A	Character keys
	D	Date keys
	F	Float keys
	G	Graphic keys
	K	Externally described key
	P	Packed keys
	T	Time keys
	Z	Timestamp keys

35	File organization (for program-described file):	
	(Blank)	Non-keyed
	I	Indexed
	T	Record address
36-42	Device:	
	DISK	Disk file
	PRINTER	Printer file
	SEQ	Sequentially organized
	SPECIAL	Special device
	WORKSTN	Workstation file
43	(Reserved)	
44–80	File keywords	
81–100	Comments	

File Keywords

BLOCK(*NO | *YES)	Allows user control over file record blocking.
COMMIT{(name)}	Commitment control. Optional name is an indicator to control commitment control at runtime.
DATFMT(format{separator})	Default date format and separator for program-described files.
DEVID(field-name)	Field to contain name of device that provided record.
EXTFILE(file-name)	Name of file to open.
EXTIND(*INUx)	File open conditioned by external indicator.
EXTMBR(member-name)	Name of file member to open.
FORMLEN(number)	Form length of PRINTER file.
FORMOFL(number)	Overflow line number of PRINTER file.
IGNORE(recformat{:recformat...})	One or more externally described record formats to ignore. Mutually exclusive with INCLUDE.
INCLUDE(recformat{:recformat...})	One or more externally described record formats to include. Mutually exclusive with IGNORE.
INDDS(data-struct-name)	Data structure to contain INDARA indicators from workstation or printer file.
INFDS(data-struct-name)	Data structure to contain file feedback information.
INFSR(subr-name)	File exception/error subroutine.
KEYLOC(number)	Beginning position of key for program-described indexed files (1-32766).
MAXDEV(*FILE | *ONLY)	Maximum number of WORKSTN file devices.
OFLIND(indicator)	Overflow indicator for PRINTER files. May be indicator variable, *INOA-*INOG, *INOV, or *IN01-*IN99.
PASS(*NOIND)	Do not pass indicators to data management on output, and do not receive them on input.
PGMNAME(program-name)	Program to handle support for SPECIAL file.
PLIST(plist-name)	Parameter list to pass to PGMNAME for SPECIAL file.

`PREFIX(prefix-string{:number})`	Prefix for field names in file. If second argument is used, prefix replaces that number of characters (0-9) in field names.
`PRTCTL(data-struct{:*COMPAT})`	Data structure for dynamic printer forms control information and line count. *COMPAT for RPG III-compatible layout.
`RAFDATA(file-name)`	File containing records for record address file.
`RECNO(field-name)`	Relative record number.
`RENAME(ext-format:int-format)`	Rename record format from external format name to internal format name.
`SAVEDS(data-struct-name)`	Data structure saved and restored for each device.
`SAVEIND(number)`	Indicators up to specified number are saved and restored for each device.
`SFILE(recformat:rrnfield)`	Subfile record format and relative record number field.
`SLN(number)`	Display file starting line number.
`TIMFMT(format{separator})`	Default time format and separator for program-described files.
`USROPN`	Explicit open of file, using OPEN opcode.

Definition (D) Specification

```
*.. 1 ...+... 2 ...+... 3 ...+... 4 ...+... 5 ...+... 6 ...+... 7 ...+... 8
DName++++++++++ETDsFrom+++To/L+++IDc.Keywords+++++++++++++++++++++++++++++++
```

Columns	Description		
1–5	Sequence number		
6	D		
7-21	Data item name. May be blank for filler fields or unnamed data structure.		
22	Externally described:		
	(Blank)		Program-described
	E		Externally described
23	Data structure type:		
	(Blank)		Miscellaneous definition
	S		Program status data structure
	U		Data area data structure
24-25	Type of definition:		
	(Blank)		Data structure subfield
	C		Constant
	DS		Data structure
	PI		Procedure interface
	PR		Prototype
	S		Standalone field, array, or table
26-32	From position or reserved word		
33-39	To position or length		
40	Internal data type:		
	(Blank)		Character if blank decimal positions entry; otherwise, packed numeric for standalone field or zoned numeric for subfield
	A		Character

B	Binary numeric
C	Unicode
D	Date
F	Float numeric
G	Graphic
I	Signed integer numeric
N	Indicator
O	Object
P	Packed-decimal numeric
S	Zoned numeric
T	Time
U	Unsigned integer numeric
Z	Timestamp
*	Basing pointer or procedure pointer

41-42	Decimal positions (0–30, blank)
43	(Reserved)
44–80	Definition keywords
81–100	Comments

Definition Keywords

ALIGN	Aligns data structure subfields of integer or float data type on word boundaries.
ALT(array-name)	Names a main array for use with this alternating array.
ALTSEQ(*NONE)	Definition ignores alternate collating sequence, if any.
ASCEND	Specifies that array or table entries are in ascending order.
BASED(pointer-name)	Names a pointer to the address of the data item.
CCSID(*DFT | number)	Specifies a character code set identifier.
CLASS(*JAVA:class-name)	Names a class for an object definition.
CONST{(constant)}	(1) Specifies the value of a named constant (optional). (2) Indicates that a parameter is passed by read-only reference.
CTDATA	Specifies a compile-time table or array.
DATFMT(format{separator})	Specifies a date format and separator.
DESCEND	Specifies that array or table entries are in descending order.
DIM(numeric-constant)	Defines the number of elements in an array or table.
DTAARA{({*VAR:}data-area-name | *LDA | *PDA)}	Associates the data item with an external data area. May be variable, if *VAR is specified.
EXPORT{(external-name)}	(1) Allows the data item to be accessed by another ILE module, using the IMPORT keyword. This ILE module allocates the storage. (2) Allows a procedure to be accessed by another ILE module.
EXTFLD(field-name)	Renames a subfield in an externally described data structure.

`EXTFMT(code)`	Specifies an external data type for compile-time and pre-runtime numeric arrays and tables: B Binary C Unicode F Float I Signed integer L Left sign P Packed decimal R Right sign S Zoned decimal U Unsigned integer
`EXTNAME(file-name{:format-name}{:ALL` `| *INPUT | *KEY | *OUTPUT})`	Names a file (and optional record format) containing field descriptions used for subfields in data structure. Optionally, may specify fields to use.
`EXTPGM(program-name)`	Names an external program whose prototype is being defined.
`EXTPROC({proc-type` `{:class} :}proc-name)`	Names an external procedure whose prototype is being defined. Normally takes the format EXTPROC(proc-name), but can be any of the following: EXTPROC(*CL:proc-name) for ILE CL procedures that require special data type handling, EXTPROC(*CWIDEN | *CNOWIDEN:proc-name) for ILE procedures that require special data type handling, EXTPROC(*JAVA:class-name:proc-name | *CONSTRUCTOR) for Java methods or for RPG procedures that will be called by Java.
`FROMFILE(file-name)`	Names a file with input data for a pre-runtime array or table.
`IMPORT{(external-name)}`	Indicates that storage for the data item is allocated in another ILE module with the EXPORT keyword. This module can use the same storage.
`INZ(constant)	*EXTDFT	*JOB |` `*LIKEDS	*NULL	*SYS |*USER)`	Initializes the data item.
`LIKE(name)`	(1) Specifies that the data item's attributes (length, type) are based on another variable. (2) Specifies that an object's class is the same as another object.
`LIKEDS(data-struct-name)`	Specifies that a data structure, data structure subfield, return value, or parameter has the same subfields as another data structure.
`LIKEREC(format-name{:*ALL | *INPUT |` `*KEY | *OUTPUT})`	Specifies that a data structure, data structure subfield, return value, or parameter has the same subfields as a record format. Optionally, may specify fields to use.
`NOOPT`	Specifies that no optimization be performed for this data item.
`OCCURS(numeric-const)`	Specifies the number of occurrences of a multiple-occurrence data structure.
`OPDESC`	Passes operational descriptors with parameters defined within a prototype.

OPTIONS({*NOPASS} {*NULLIND} {*OMIT} {*RIGHTADJ} {*STRING} {*TRIM} {*VARSIZE})	Specifies one or more parameter-passing options: *NOPASS Parameter need not be passed. *NULLIND Null byte map will be passed with parameter. *OMIT *OMIT is allowed for parameter. *RIGHTADJ Character, graphic, or UCS-2 parameter is right adjusted. *STRING Parameter may be a pointer or a character expression. *TRIM Parameter will be trimmed of blanks before being passed. *VARSIZE Parameter may be shorter than defined length.
OVERLAY(name{:pos | *NEXT})	Specifies that a data structure subfield overlays the storage of another subfield.
PACKEVEN	Zeroes out the high-order digit when a packed field has an even number of digits.
PERRCD(numeric-const)	Specifies the number of elements per record for an array or table.
PREFIX(prefix-string{:number})	Specifies a string to be prefixed (added or replaced) to subfield names of an externally described data structure.
PROCPTR	Defines an item as a procedure pointer.
QUALIFIED	Specifies that the subfields in a named date structure must be qualified by the data structure name, i.e., they must be referred to in the format *structure.field*.
STATIC	(1) Defines a local variable within static storage, holding its value across procedure calls. (2) Specifies a Java method as a static method. If not specified, the method is assumed to be an instance method.
TIMFMT(format{separator})	Specifies a time format and separator.
TOFILE(file-name)	Specifies a file to which an array or table is to be written.
VALUE	Specifies that a parameter will be passed by value instead of by reference.
VARYING	Indicates a varying-length character or graphic field.

Input (I) Specification

Input Specification: Externally Described Files

```
*.. 1 ...+... 2 ...+... 3 ...+... 4 ...+... 5 ...+... 6 ...+... 7 ...+... 8
IRcdname+++....Ri.................................................
I.............Ext-field+................Field+++++++++L1M1..PlMnZr......
```

Record Identifier Entry

Columns	Description
1–5	Sequence number
6	I
7-16	Record name
17-20	(Blank)
21-22	Record identifying indicator: Blank, 01–99, L1–L9, LR, H1–H9, U1–U8, RT
23-80	(Blank)
81–100	Comments

Field Description Entry

Columns	Description
1–5	Sequence number
6	I
7-20	(Blank)
21-30	External field name to be renamed
31-48	(Blank)
49-62	Internal field name in program
63-64	Control level: Blank, L1–L9
65-66	Matching fields: Blank, M1–M9
67-68	(Blank)
69-74	Field indicators (plus/minus/zero): Blank, 01–99, H1–H9, U1–U8, RT
75-80	(Blank)
81–100	Comments

Input Specification: Program-Described Files

```
*.. 1 ...+... 2 ...+... 3 ...+... 4 ...+... 5 ...+... 6 ...+... 7 ...+... 8
IFilename++SqNORiPos1+NCCPos2+NCCPos3+NCC.....................................
I.........And..RiPos1+NCCPos2+NCCPos3+NCC.....................................
I.......................Fmt+SPFrom+To+++DcField+++++++++L1M1FrPLMnZr......
```

Record Identifier Entry

Columns	Description
1–5	Sequence number
6	I
7-16	File name
16-18	Logical relationship: AND, OR (used only for multiline record identifier specifications)
17-20	Sequence checking options
21-22	Record identifying indicator: Blank, 01–99, L1–L9, LR, H1–H9, U1–U8, RT, **
23-46	Record identification codes
47-80	(Blank)
81–100	Comments

Field Description Entry

Columns	Description
1–5	Sequence number
6	I
7–30	(Blank)
31–34	External format for a date or time field, *VAR for variable-length fields
35	Separator character for a date or time field
36	Data type:
	Blank Zoned decimal or character
	A Character
	B Binary
	C Unicode
	D Date
	F Float numeric
	G Graphic
	I Signed integer
	L Zoned decimal with preceding (left) sign
	N Indicator
	P Packed decimal
	R Zoned decimal with following (right) sign
	S Zoned decimal
	T Time
	U Unsigned integer
	Z Timestamp
37–41	Field location: from position (1–32766)
42–46	Field location: to position (1–32766)
47–48	Decimal positions: Blank, 0–30
49–62	Internal field name in program
63–64	Control level: Blank, L1–L9
65–66	Matching fields: Blank, M1–M9
67–68	Field record relation: Blank, 01–99, L1–L9, MR, U1–U8, H1–H9, RT
69–74	Field indicators (plus/minus/zero): Blank, 01–99, H1–H9, U1–U8, RT
75–80	(Blank)
81–100	Comments

Calculation (C) Specification

Calculation Specification: Free-Format

```
*.. 1 ...+... 2 ...+... 3 ...+... 4 ...+... 5 ...+... 6 ...+... 7 ...+... 8
..Opcode(E)-or-expression;+++++++++++++++++++++++++++++++++++++++++++++++++
```

Columns	Description
1–5	Sequence number
6-7	(Blank)
8-80	Calculation entry (Operation code or expression), followed by a semicolon (;))
81–100	Comments

Operation Codes and Built-in Functions

Opcode or function	Description	Syntax
%ABS	Absolute value	`%ABS(numeric-expression)`
ACQ	Acquire a program device for a WORKSTN file	`ACQ{(E)}  device-name workstn-file`
%ADDR	Get address pointer	`%ADDR(variable{(index-expression)})`
%ALLOC	Allocate storage	`%ALLOC(length)`
BEGSR	Begin a subroutine	`BEGSR subroutine-name`
%BITAND	Bitwise ANDing of the bits of all arguments	`%BITAND(expression : expression {:expression...})`
%BITNOT	Bitwise inverse of the bits of the argument	`%BITNOT(expression)`
%BITOR	Bitwise ORing of the bits of all arguments	`%BITOR(expression : expression {:expression...})`
%BITXOR	Bitwise exclusive ORing of the bits of two arguments	`%BITXOR(expression : expression)`
CALLP	Call a prototyped procedure or program	`{CALLP{(EMR)}} name({parm1 : parm2 : ...})`
CHAIN	Random retrieval from a file	`CHAIN{(EHMNR)} search-argument file-format-name {data-structure}`
%CHAR	Convert to character data	`%CHAR(expression {: format})`
%CHECK	Check characters	`%CHECK(compare-string : base-string {: start})`
%CHECKR	Check characters (reversed)	`%CHECKR(compare-string : base-string {: start})`
CLEAR	Clear data structure, variable, or record format	`CLEAR {*NOKEY} {*ALL} structure-variable`
CLOSE	Close files	`CLOSE{(E)} file-name	*ALL`
COMMIT	Commit group	`COMMIT{(E)} {boundary}`

%DATE	Convert to date	`%DATE({expression {: format}})`
%DAYS	Number of days	`%DAYS(number)`
DEALLOC	Free storage	`DEALLOC{(EN)} pointer`

%DEC
%DECH
	Convert to packed decimal
	(with optional half adjust)
		`%DEC(expression {: precision : decimals})`
		`%DEC(date-expression {: format})`
		`%DECH(expression : precision : decimals)`

%DECPOS	Get number of decimal positions	`%DECPOS(numeric-expression)`
DELETE	Delete record	`DELETE{(EHMR)} {search-argument}` `    file-format-name`
%DIFF	Difference between two dates/times/timestamps	`%DIFF(date1 : date2 : duration-code)`
%DIV	Integer division	`%DIV(dividend : divisor)`
DOU	Do until	`DOU{(MR)} logical-expression`
DOW	Do while	`DOW{(MR)} logical-expression`
DSPLY	Display function	`DSPLY{(E)} {message` `    {message-queue {response}}}`
DUMP	Program dump	`DUMP{(A)} {identifier}`
%EDITC	Apply an edit code	`%EDITC(numeric-expression : edit-code` `    {: fill})`
%EDITFLT	Convert to floating point	`%EDITFLT(numeric-expression)`
%EDITW	Apply an edit word	`%EDITW(numeric-expression : edit-word)`
%ELEM	Number of elements in an array, table, or multiple occurrence data structure	`%ELEM(data-item)`
ELSE	Else	`ELSE`
ELSEIF	Else If	`ELSEIF{(MR)} logical-expression`

ENDDO
ENDFOR
ENDIF
ENDMON
ENDSL
	End a structured group	`ENDxx increment-value`

ENDSR	End of subroutine	`ENDSR {return-point}`
%EOF	End (or beginning) of file	`%EOF{(file-name)}`
%EQUAL	Exact match for SETLL	`%EQUAL{(file-name)}`
%ERROR	Error	`%ERROR`
EVAL	Evaluate expression	`{EVAL{(HMR)}} assignment-statement`
EVALR	Evaluate expression, right-adjust	`EVALR{(MR)} assignment-statement`
EVAL-CORR	Assign corresponding subfields from one data structure to another	`EVAL-CORR{(HMR)} target = source`
EXCEPT	Calculation time output	`EXCEPT {name}`
EXFMT	Write then read format	`EXFMT{(E)} format-name`
EXSR	Invoke subroutine	`EXSR subroutine-name`

FEOD	Force end of data	`FEOD{(EN)} file-name`
%FIELDS	Fields to update for UPDATE	`%FIELDS(name {: name ...})`
%FLOAT	Convert to floating point	`%FLOAT(expression)`
FOR	For	`FOR{(MR)} index {= start} {BY increment}` `    {TO | DOWNTO limit}`
FORCE	Force a file to be read next cycle	`FORCE file-name`
%FOUND	Record found for CHAIN, DELETE, SETGT, SETLL	`%FOUND{(file-name)}`
%GRAPH	Convert to graphic	`%GRAPH(expression {: ccsid})`
%HANDLER	Event handler procedure for XML-SAX or XML-INTO	`%HANDLER(proc-name : comm-area)`
%HOURS	Number of hours	`%HOURS(number)`
IF	IF	`IF{(MR)} logical-expression`
IN	Retrieve a data area	`IN{(E)} {*LOCK} data-area-name`
%INT %INTH	Convert to integer format (with optional half adjust)	`%INTx(expression)`
ITER	Iterate	`ITER`
%KDS	Key data structure	`%KDS(data-structure-name {: num-keys})`
LEAVE	Leave a DO group	`LEAVE`
LEAVESR	Leave a subroutine	`LEAVESR`
%LEN	Get or set length	`%LEN(expression)`
%LOOKUP %LOOKUPLT %LOOKUPLE %LOOKUPGE %LOOKUPGT	Look up element in an array	`%LOOKUPxx(search-argument : array` `    {: start {: num-elems}})`
%MINUTES	Number of minutes	`%MINUTES(number)`
MONITOR	Begin a monitor group	`MONITOR`
%MONTHS	Number of months	`%MONTHS(number)`
%MSECONDS	Number of microseconds	`%MSECONDS(number)`
NEXT	Specify next input for multiple-device file	`NEXT{(E)} program-device file-name`
%NULLIND	Get or set null indicator	`%NULLIND(field)`
%OCCUR	Get or set occurrence of a data structure	`%OCCUR(data-structure)`
ON-ERROR	ON-ERROR	`ON-ERROR {exception-id1:exception-id2...}`
%OPEN	Return open file condition	`%OPEN(file-name)`
OPEN	Open file for processing	`OPEN{(E)} file-name`
OTHER	Otherwise select	`OTHER`
OUT	Write a data area	`OUT{(E)} {*LOCK} data-area-name`
%PADDR	Get procedure address	`%PADDR(proc-name)`
%PARMS	Number of parameters	`%PARMS`

POST	Put information into a file information data structure	`POST{(E)} {program-device} file-name`
READ	Read a record	`READ{(EN)} file-format-name {data-structure}`
READC	Read next changed record	`READC{(E)} record-name {data-structure}`
READE	Read equal key	`READE{(EHMNR)} search-argument` `    file-record-name {data-structure}`
READP	Read prior record	`READP{(EN)} file-record-name` `    {data-structure}`
READPE	Read prior equal key	`READPE{(EHMNR)} search-argument` `    file-record-name {data-structure}`
%REALLOC	Reallocate storage with new length	`%REALLOC(pointer : length)`
REL	Release program device	`REL{(E)} program-device file-name`
%REM	Integer remainder	`%REM(dividend : divisor)`
%REPLACE	Replace character string	`%REPLACE(replacement : source {:start` `    {: length}})`
RESET	Set variable to initial value	`RESET{(E)} {*NOKEY} {*ALL}` `    structure-variable`
RETURN	Return to caller	`RETURN{(HMR)} expression`
ROLBK	Roll back	`ROLBK{(E)}`
%SCAN	Scan character string	`%SCAN(search-arg : source {: start})`
%SECONDS	Number of seconds	`%SECONDS(number)`
SELECT	Begin a select group	`SELECT`
SETGT	Set greater than	`SETGT{(EHMR)} search-argument` `    file-record-name`
SETLL	Set lower limit	`SETLL{(EHMR)} search-argument` `    file-record-name`
%SHTDN	Shut down requested	`%SHTDN`
%SIZE	Size	`%SIZE(data-item {: *ALL})`

SORTA	Sort array	`SORTA array-name`
		`SORTA %SUBARR(array-name : start`
		`    {:num-elements})`

%SQRT	Square root	`%SQRT(numeric-expression)`
%STATUS	File or program status code	`%STATUS{(file-name)}`
%STR	Get or set null-terminated string	`%STR(pointer : length)`
%SUBARR	Get or set portion of an array	`%SUBARR(array-name : start {:num-elements})`
%SUBDT	Subset of a date, time, or timestamp	`%SUBDT(date : duration-code)`
%SUBST	Get or set substring	`%SUBST(string : start : length)`
TEST	Test date/time/timestamp	`TEST{(DETZ)} {format} tested-field`
%THIS	Class instance for native method	`%THIS`
%TIME	Convert to time	`%TIME({expression {: format}})`
%TIMESTAMP	Convert to timestamp	`%TIMESTAMP({expression {:*ISO | *ISO0}})`

%TLOOKUP %TLOOKUPLT %TLOOKUPLE %TLOOKUPGE %TLOOKUPGT	Look up element in a table	`%TLOOKUPxx(search-argument : table` `{: alternate-table})`
%TRIM %TRIML %TRIMR	Trim characters from a string	`%TRIMx(string {: characters})`
%UCS2	Convert to UCS-2	`%UCS2(expression {: ccsid})`
UNLOCK	Unlock a data area or release a record	`UNLOCK{(E)} dtaara-record-file`
%UNS %UNSH	Convert to unsigned integer format, with optional half adjust	`%UNSx(expression)`

UPDATE	Modify existing record	`UPDATE{(E)} file-record-name`
		`    {data-structure}`
		`UPDATE{(E)} file-record-name %FIELDS(name`
		`    {: name ...})`

WHEN	When true then select	`WHEN{(MR)} logical-expression`
WRITE	Create new record	`WRITE{(E)} file-record-name {data-structure}`
%XFOOT	Sum array expression elements	`%XFOOT(array-expression)`
%XLATE	Translate	`%XLATE(from : to : string {: start})`
%XML	Specifies XML document for XML-SAX and XML-INTO	`%XML(document {: option-string})`

XML-INTO	Parse XML document into
	a variable
		`XML-INTO{(EH)} receiver %XML(document`
		`    {: option-string})`
		`XML-INTO{(EH)} %HANDLER(proc-name :`
		`    comm-area)  %XML(document`
		`    {: option-string})`

XML-SAX	Initiate SAX parse for XML
	document
		`XML-SAX{(E)} %HANDLER(proc-name`
		`    : comm-area)  %XML(document`
		`    {: option-string})`

%YEARS	Number of years	`%YEARS(number)`

Operation Code Extenders

Extender	Description
(A)	Always perform a dump, even if DEBUG(*NO) is specified
(D)	1. When used with CALLP, passes operational descriptors for parameters 2. When used with TEST, indicates test for valid date value
(E)	Turns on %Error if operation code does not complete successfully
(H)	Half-adjusts (rounds) numeric expression result
(M)	Expression is calculated using *MAXDIGITS default precision rules
(N)	1. When used with file I/O operation, will not lock record 2. When used with DEALLOC, sets pointer to *NULL 3. When used with FEOD, does not force data to non-volatile storage
(P)	Pads result with blanks or zeros
(R)	Expression is calculated using *RESDECPOS precision rules
(T)	Used with TEST, indicates test for valid time value
(Z)	Used with TEST, indicates test for valid timestamp value

Edit Codes

OPTIONS		EDIT CODES			
Commas	**Print zero balances**	**No sign**	**CR**	**Right -**	**Floating -**
Yes	Yes	1	A	J	N
Yes	No	2	B	K	O
No	Yes	3	C	L	P
No	No	4	D	M	Q

X edit code ensures a hexadecimal F sign for positive values.

Y edit code inserts slash (/) separators and suppresses leftmost zeros for numeric values used as dates.

Z edit code suppresses leading zeros and removes sign for numeric values

Edit codes 5-9 are user-defined.

Status Codes

%Error	On-Error	%Status	Description
*Off	n/a	00000	No exception/error
*Off	n/a	00001	Call program ended with *Inlr = *On
*Off	n/a	00002	Function key pressed
*Off	n/a	00011	End of file (%Eof = *On)
*Off	n/a	00012	Record not found (%Found = *Off)
*Off	n/a	00013	Write to full subfile
*Off	n/a	00050	Conversion resulted in substitution
*On	*Program	00100	String operation, value out of range
*On	*Program	00101	Negative square root
*On	*Program	00102	Divide by zero
*On	*Program	00103	Intermediate result too small to contain result
*On	*Program	00104	Float underflow; intermediate value too small
*On	*Program	00105	Numeric conversion error
*On	*Program	00112	Invalid date/time/timestamp value
*On	*Program	00113	Date overflow or underflow
*On	*Program	00114	Date mapping error
*On	*Program	00115	Invalid length for variable-length field
*On	*Program	00120	Table/array out of sequence
*On	*Program	00121	Invalid array index
*On	*Program	00122	Occur value out of range
*On	*Program	00123	Reset attempt during initialization
*On	*Program	00202	Call to program or procedure ended in error
*On	*Program	00211	Error occurred while calling program or procedure
*On	*Program	00221	Called program tried to use unpassed parameter
*On	*Program	00222	Pointer or parameter error
*On	*Program	00231	Called program returned with Halt indicator on
*On	*Program	00232	Halt indicator is on
*On	*Program	00233	Return ran with Halt indicator on
*On	*Program	00299	RPG dump failed
*On	*Program	00301	Error in method call
*On	*Program	00302	Error converting Java array to RPG parameter, entering Java method
*On	*Program	00303	Error converting RPG parameter to Java array, exiting RPG native method
*On	*Program	00304	Error converting RPG parameter to Java array, preparing Java call
*On	*Program	00305	Error converting Java array to RPG parameter/return value, exiting Java method
*On	*Program	00306	Error converting RPG return value to Java array

*On	*Program	00333	Error on Dsply operation
*On	*Program	00351	Error parsing XML document
*On	*Program	00352	Invalid option for %Xml
*On	*Program	00353	XML document does not match RPG variable
*On	*Program	00354	Error preparing for XML parsing
*On	*Program	00401	Data area not found
*On	*Program	00402	*Pda not valid for non-prestart job
*On	*Program	00411	Data area types/lengths do not match
*On	*Program	00412	Data area not allocated for output
*On	*Program	00413	I/O error while processing data area
*On	*Program	00414	Not authorized to use data area
*On	*Program	00415	Not authorized to change data area
*On	*Program	00421	Error while unlocking data area
*On	*Program	00425	Requested storage allocation length out of range
*On	*Program	00426	Error during storage management operation
*On	*Program	00431	Data area allocated to another process
*On	*Program	00432	Data area *Lock not granted
*On	*Program	00450	Character field not enclosed by SO/SI
*On	*Program	00451	Cannot convert CCSIDs
*On	*Program	00501	Sort sequence not retrieved
*On	*Program	00502	Sort sequence not converted
*On	*Program	00802	Commitment control not active
*On	*Program	00803	Rollback failed
*On	*Program	00804	Commit error
*On	*Program	00805	Rolbk error
*On	*Program	00907	Decimal data error
*On	*Program	00970	Compiler/runtime level check
*On	*File	01011	Undefined record type
*On	*File	01021	Record already exists
*On	*File	01022	Referential constraint error
*On	*File	01023	Trigger program error before operation
*On	*File	01024	Trigger program error after operation
*On	*File	01031	Match field sequence error
*On	*File	01041	Array/table load sequence error
*On	*File	01042	Array/table load sequence error (alternate collating sequence used)
*On	*File	01051	Excess entries in array/table file
*On	*File	01071	Record out of sequence
*On	*File	01121	No Print key DDS keyword indicator
*On	*File	01122	No Page Down DDS keyword indicator
*On	*File	01123	No Page Up DDS keyword indicator

*On	*File	01124	No Clear key DDS keyword indicator
*On	*File	01125	No Help key DDS keyword indicator
*On	*File	01126	No Home key DDS keyword indicator
*On	*File	01201	Record mismatch detected on input
*On	*File	01211	I/O operation to closed file
*On	*File	01215	Open issued to already open file
*On	*File	01216	Error on implicit open/close
*On	*File	01217	Error on explicit open/close
*On	*File	01218	Record locked
*On	*File	01221	Update/delete operation without prior read
*On	*File	01222	Referential constraint error
*On	*File	01231	Error on Special file
*On	*File	01235	Error in Prtctl space/skip entries
*On	*File	01241	Record number not found
*On	*File	01251	Permanent I/O error
*On	*File	01255	Session/device error
*On	*File	01261	Attempt to exceed maximum number of devices
*On	*File	01271	Attempt to acquire unavailable device
*On	*File	01281	Operation to unacquired device
*On	*File	01282	Job ending with controlled option
*On	*File	01284	Unable to acquire second device
*On	*File	01285	Attempt to acquire allocated device
*On	*File	01286	Attempt to open shared file with Savds/Savind
*On	*File	01287	Response indicators overlap Savind indicators
*On	*File	01299	I/O error detected
*On	*File	01331	Wait time exceeded for Workstn file
*On	*File	09998	Internal failure in RPG compiler or runtime routines
*On	*File	09999	Program exception in system routine

Calculation Specification: Fixed-Format

```
*.. 1 ...+... 2 ...+... 3 ...+... 4 ...+... 5 ...+... 6 ...+... 7 ...+... 8
CLØN01Factor1+++++++Opcode(E)+Factor2+++++++Result+++++++Len++D+HiLoEq....
CLØN01Factor1+++++++Opcode(E)+Extended-factor2++++++++++++++++++++++++++++
C..........................Extended-factor2-continuation+++++++++++++++++++
```

Columns	Description
1–5	Sequence number
6	C
7-8	Control level: Blank, L0, L1–L9, LR, SR, AN, OR
9-11	Conditioning indicators: Blank, 01–99, KA–KN, KP–KY, L1–L9, LR, MR, H1–H9, RT, U1–U8, OA–OG, OV
12-25	Factor 1
26-35	Operation code, with optional extender(s)
36-49 or 36-80	Factor 2, or extended Factor 2
50-53	Result field
64-68	Result field length
69-70	Result field decimal positions
71-76	Resulting indicators (high/low/equal): Blank, 01–99, KA–KN, KP–KY, H1–H9, L1–L9, LR, RT, U1–U8, OA–OG, OV
77-80	(Blank)
81–100	Comments

Fixed-Format (Only) Operation Codes

Opcode	Description	Free-Format Alternative
ADD	Add two values together	Expression with + or +=
ADDDUR	Add duration	Expression with + or += and duration functions
ALLOC	Allocate storage	%ALLOC
ANDxx	And operation	AND
BITOFF	Set bits off	%BITAND, %BITNOT
BITON	Set bits on	%BITOR
CABxx	Compare and branch	LEAVE, LEAVESR, ITER, RETURN
CALL	Call a program	CALLP
CALLB	Call a bound procedure	CALLP
CASxx	Conditionally invoke subroutine	EXSR
CAT	Concatenate two character strings	Expression with +
CHECK	Check characters	%CHECK
CHECKR	Check characters (reversed)	%CHECKR
COMP	Compare two values	Expression with =, <, >, <=, >=, or <>
DEFINE	Field definition	LIKE, DTAARA (Definition specification)
DIV	Divide operation	Expression with /, /=, or %DIV
DO	Begin a DO group	FOR

DOUxx	Do until xx	DOU
DOWxx	Do while xx	DOW
EXTRCT	Extract date/time/timestamp	%SUBDT
GOTO	Go to label	LEAVE, LEAVESR, ITER, RETURN
IFxx	If xx	IF
KFLD	Define parts of a key	Data structure (Definition specification), with %KDS
KLIST	Define a composite key	Data structure (Definition specification), with %KDS
LOOKUP	Look up element in an array or table	%LOOKUP, %TLOOKUP
MHHZO	Move high to high zone	%BITAND, %BITOR
MHLZO	Move high to low zone	%BITAND, %BITOR
MLHZO	Move low to high zone	%BITAND, %BITOR
MLLZO	Move low to low zone	%BITAND, %BITOR
MOVE	Move characters from source field to target field	EVAL, EVALR
MOVEA	Move array	%SUBARR
MOVEL	Move left	EVAL
MULT	Multiply	Expression with * or *=
MVR	Move remainder	%REM
OCCUR	Get or set occurrence of a data structure	%OCCUR
ORxx	Or condition xx	OR
PARM	Identify parameters	Prototype (Definition specification)
PLIST	Identify a parameter list	Prototype (Definition specification)
REALLOC	Reallocate storage with new length	%REALLOC
SCAN	Scan character string	%SCAN
SETOFF	Set indicator off	Expression
SETON	Set indicator on	Expression
SHTDN	Shut down	%SHTDN
SQRT	Square root	%SQRT
SUB	Subtract	Expression with – or –=
SUBDUR	Subtract duration	Expression with + or += and duration functions, or %DIFF
SUBST	Substring	%SUBST
TAG	Tag	LEAVE, LEAVESR, ITER, RETURN
TESTB	Test value of bit field	%BITAND
TESTN	Test numeric	MONITOR, ON-ERROR
TESTZ	Test zone	%BITAND
TIME	Time of day	%DATE, %TIME, %TIMESTAMP
WHENxx	When true then select	WHEN
XFOOT	Sum the elements of an array	%XFOOT
XLATE	Translate	%XLATE
Z-ADD	Zero and add	Expression
Z-SUB	Zero and subtract	Expression

Output (O) Specification

Output Specification: Externally Described Files

```
*.. 1 ...+... 2 ...+... 3 ...+... 4 ...+... 5 ...+... 6 ...+... 7 ...+... 8
ORcdname+++D...N01N02N03Excnam++++.................................................
ORcdname+++DAddN01N02N03Excnam++++.................................................
O.........And..N01N02N03Excnam++++.................................................
O..............N01N02N03Field+++++++++.B...........................................
```

Record Identifier Entry

Columns	Description
1–5	Sequence number
6	O
7-16	Record name
16-18	Logical relationship: AND, OR
17	Type of record to write: D Detail E Exception (EXCEPT) H Detail (header) T Total
18	Release record after output: R, blank
18-20	Record addition/deletion: ADD, DEL
21-29	Output conditioning indicators: Blank, 01–99, H1–H9, KA–KN, KP–KY, L1–L9, U1–U8, LR, MR, RT, 1P
30-39	EXCEPT name
40-80	(Blank)
81–100	Comments

Field Description Entry

Columns	Description
1–5	Sequence number
6	O
7-20	(Blank)
21-29	Output conditioning indicators: Blank, 01–99, H1–H9, KA–KN, KP–KY, L1–L9, U1–U8, LR, MR, RT, 1P
30-43	Field name or *ALL
44	(Blank)
45	Reset field contents after writing record: Blank, B
46-80	(Blank)
81–100	Comments

Output Specification: Program-Described Files

```
*.. 1 ...+... 2 ...+... 3 ...+... 4 ...+... 5 ..+... 6 ...+... 7 ...+... 8
OFilename++DF..N01N02N03Excnam++++B++A++Sb+Sa+................................
OFilename++DAddN01N02N03Excnam++++................................
O.........And..N01N02N03Excnam++++................................
O.............N01N02N03Field+++++++++YB.End++PConstant/editword/DTformat++
O.........................................Constant/editword-continues+
```

Record Identifier Entry

Columns	Description
1–5	Sequence number
6	O
7-16	File name
16-18	Logical relationship: AND, OR
17	Type of record to write: D Detail E Exception (EXCEPT) H Detail (header) T Total
18	Fetch overflow/release for printer files: Blank Do not fetch overflow F Fetch overflow R Release device after write
18-20	Record addition/deletion: ADD, DEL
21-29	Output conditioning indicators: Blank, 01–99, H1–H9, KA–KN, KP–KY, L1–L9, U1–U8, LR, MR, RT, 1P
30-39	EXCEPT name
40-42	Space before: Blank, 0–255 lines
43-45	Space after: Blank, 0–255 lines
46-48	Skip before: Blank, 1–255 lines
49-51	Skip after: Blank, 1–255 lines
52-80	(Blank)
81–100	Comments

Field Description Entry

Columns	Description
1–5	Sequence number
6	O
7-20	(Blank)
21-29	Output conditioning indicators: Blank, 01–99, H1–H9, KA–KN, KP–KY, L1–L9, U1–U8, LR, MR, RT, 1P
30-43	Field to write: Blank, field name, table, array, element, named constant, data structure, PAGE, PAGE1–PAGE7, *PLACE, UDATE, *DATE, UDAY, *DAY, UMONTH, *MONTH, UYEAR, *YEAR, *IN, *INxx, *IN(xx)
44	Edit code: Blank, 1–9, A–D, J–Q, X, Y, Z
45	Reset field contents after writing record: Blank, B
46	(Blank)
47-51	End: position, +nnnn, –nnnn, K1–K8
52	External data format:
	Blank Use default format
	A Character
	B Binary
	C Unicode
	D Date
	F Float
	G Graphic
	I Signed integer
	L Preceding (left) minus sign
	N Indicator
	P Packed decimal
	R Following (right) minus sign
	S Zoned decimal
	T Time
	U Unsigned integer
	Z Timestamp
53-80	Constant, edit word, format name, date/time format
81–100	Comments

Procedure (P) Specification

```
*.. 1 ...+... 2 ...+... 3 ...+... 4 ...+... 5 ...+... 6 ...+... 7 ...+... 8
PName+++++++++++..T.................Functions+++++++++++++++++++++++++++++
```

Columns	Description
1–5	Sequence number
6	P
7–21	Procedure name (optional if column 24 contains an E)
22–23	(Reserved)
24	Begin/end procedure: B, E
25–43	(Reserved)
44–80	Procedure keywords
81–100	Comments

Procedure Keywords

EXPORT   Makes a procedure available to be called by another procedure in another module.

Compiler Directives

Directives Used with Free-Format Calculations

/FREE /END-FREE	Begin/end free-format calculation block.

Directives to Copy Code at Compile Time

/COPY {{library/}file,}member /COPY {path/}file	Copies code from another source file or IFS file into compile process.
/INCLUDE {{library/}file,}member /INCLUDE {path/}file	Copies code from another source file or IFS file into compile process. For embedded SQL, /INCLUDE will not be effective unless you compile with CRTSQLRPGI … RPGPPOPT(*LVL2).

Conditional Compilation Directives

/DEFINE condition-name	Defines a condition, and adds it to the list of currently defined conditions.
/EOF	End of file. Compiler ignores the subsequent lines.
/ELSE	If the previous /IF or /ELSEIF was not true, the compiler reads the subsequent lines until /ENDIF.

/ELSEIF {NOT} DEFINED
  (condition-name | *CRTBNDRPG
  | *CRTRPGMOD | *VxRxMx
  | *ILERPG)
	If the previous /IF or /ELSEIF was not true, but the current condition is true, the compiler reads the subsequent lines until /ELSE, /ELSEIF, or /ENDIF.

/IF {NOT} DEFINED *CRTBNDRPG
  | *CRTRPGMOD | *VxRxMx
  | *ILERPG)
	If the condition is true, the compiler reads the subsequent lines until /ELSE, /ELSEIF, or /ENDIF.

/UNDEFINE condition-name	Removes a condition from the list of currently defined conditions.

Directives Used with Embedded SQL

/EXEC SQL /END-EXEC	Begin/end SQL statement in fixed-format calculations.
EXEC SQL	Begins SQL statement in free-format calculations. SQL statement ends with semicolon (;).

Directives Affecting Compiler Listing

/EJECT	Listing skips to next page.
/SPACE number	Listing spaces 1-112 lines.
/TITLE title-information	Specifies title information for each page of compiler listing.

Appendix B

RPG IV Style Guide

Overview

This appendix presents some suggestions for how to write RPG IV programs that are easy to read, understand, and maintain. Professional programmers appreciate the importance of standards in developing programs. The issue of program style goes beyond any one language, but the RPG IV syntax has some unique features that promote specific style guidelines. Here are some simple rules of thumb that you can use to ensure that bad code doesn't happen to otherwise good RPG IV software construction.

These guidelines are based on those originally set forth by Bryan Meyers in "The Essential RPG IV Style Guide" (*NEWS/400*, June 1998), "RPG IV Style Revisited" (*iSeries NEWS*, February 2002), and "RPG IV Style, Standards, and Best Practices" (*iSeries NEWS*, March 2005).

Defining Data

Use the Definition specification to organize all your declarations in one place. Within the D-specs, organize your definitions in a predictable order, by definition type:

- Prototype for main procedure
- Procedure interface for main procedure
- Other prototype definitions
- Named constants
- Data structures
- Standalone variables

Within each definition type, alphabetize the declarations.

Expand Naming Conventions

Perhaps the most important aspect of programming style deals with the names you give to data items (e.g., variables, named constants) and routines. Establish naming conventions that go beyond the traditional six characters, to fully identify variables and other identifiers. Those extra characters can make the difference between program "code" and a program "description."

When naming an item, be sure the name fully and accurately describes the item. The name should be unambiguous, easy to read, and obvious. Although you should exploit RPG IV's allowance for long names, don't make your names too long to be useful. Name lengths of 10 to 14 characters are usually sufficient, and longer names may not be practical in many specifications.

When naming a data item, describe the item. When naming a procedure with a return value, name the procedure after the return value; or use a "get/set" naming convention if the procedure retrieves or assigns a data value.

For subroutines or procedures without a return value, use a verb/object syntax (similar to a CL command) to describe the process. Maintain a dictionary of names, verbs, and objects, and use the dictionary to standardize your naming conventions.

Avoid using special characters (e.g., @, #, $) when naming items. Some of these characters may cause compile errors in some character sets. Although RPG IV allows an underscore (_) within a name, you can easily avoid using this "noise" character if you use mixed case intelligently.

Declare Named Constants Instead of Using Literals

This practice helps document your code and makes it easier to maintain. One obvious exception to this rule is the allowable use of 0 and 1 when they make perfect sense in the context of a statement. For example, if you're going to initialize an accumulator field or increment a counter, it's fine to use a hard coded 0 or 1 in the source.

Indent Data Item Names

Use indentation to improve readability and document data structures. Unlike many other RPG entries, the name of a defined item need not be left justified in the D-specs. Take advantage of this feature to help document your code:

```
DName+++++++++++ETDsFrom+++To/L+++IDc.Functions+++++++++++++++++++++++++++++
D Errmsgds       Ds
D   Errprefix              3
D   Errmsgid               4
D     Errmajor             2      Overlay(Errmsgid:1)
D     Errminor             2      Overlay(Errmsgid:3)
```

To improve readability, always leave position 7 blank. (The same rule applies to H-specifications—leave position 7 blank.)

Use Length Notation for Data Structure Subfields

Use length notation instead of positional notation in data structure declarations. D-specs let you code fields either with specific from and to positions or simply with the length of the field. To avoid confusion and to better document the field, use length notation consistently. For example, code

```
DName+++++++++++ETDsFrom+++To/L+++IDc.Functions+++++++++++++++++++++++++++++
D Rtncode        DS
D   Packednbr                15P 5
```

instead of

```
D Rtncode        DS
D   Packednbr            1    8P 5
```

Use positional notation only when the actual position in a data structure is important. For example, when coding the program status data structure, the file information data structure, or the return data structure from an API, you'd use positional notation if your program ignored certain positions leading up to a field or between fields. Using positional notation is usually preferable to using unnecessary "filler" variables with length notation. Even with positional notation, though, consider overlaying the positionally declared variable with another variable that is declared with length notation to better document the variable:

```
DName++++++++++ETDsFrom+++To/L+++IDc.Functions++++++++++++++++++++++++++++
D Apirtn          DS
D   Pos145                  145    152
D    Packnbr                       15P 5 Overlay(Pos145)
```

When defining overlapping fields, use the Overlay keyword instead of positional notation. The Overlay explicitly ties the declaration of a "child" variable to that of its "parent." Not only does Overlay document this relationship, but if the parent moves elsewhere within the program code, the child will follow.

Avoid Compile Time Arrays

As you decompose a program into its individual procedures, it helps to have all related pieces of code physically and logically self-contained. The traditional compile time array coding separates the array definition from the array data by perhaps thousands of code lines in the program. A better solution would be to code the array (Days in the following example) inside a data structure (Daysctdata):

```
DName++++++++++ETDsFrom+++To/L+++IDc.Functions++++++++++++++++++++++++++++
D Daysctdata      DS
D                            9     Inz('Sunday')
D                            9     Inz('Monday')
D                            9     Inz('Tuesday')
D                            9     Inz('Wednesday')
D                            9     Inz('Thursday')
D                            9     Inz('Friday')
D                            9     Inz('Saturday')
D    Days                    9     Dim(7)
D                                  Overlay(Daysctdata)
```

Avoid Multiple Occurrence Data Structures

The array data structure is a better construct because it uses standard array notation in your program; it doesn't limit you to processing a single occurrence in the same line; and it allows you to deal with those instances where nested (multiple dimension) arrays are useful.

```
DName++++++++++ETDsFrom+++To/L+++IDc.Functions++++++++++++++++++++++++++++
D Customers       DS                Dim(100)
D                                   Qualified
D    Name                    35
D    Address                 35     Dim(2)
D    City                    21
D    State                    2
D    Postalcode              10
```

Use Qualified Data Structures

Qualified data structures force you to qualify their subfield names with the name of the data structure (e.g., Customer.Name, Customer.Address). This feature not only provides good documentation for the data item, telling you where a data item originates, but it also allows you to have identically named subfields in different data structures (e.g., Before.Name, After.Name). To define a qualified data structure, use the Qualified keyword in its definition.

The Likeds and Likerec keywords are also useful when a data structure "inherits" its subfields from another data structure or a record format. You can control the subfields that will appear in a Likerec data structure or an externally described data structure, specifying *All, *Input, *Ouput, or *Key fields.

Observe a One-Keyword-Per-Line Limit

Instead of spreading multiple keywords and values across the entire specification, your program will be easier to read and let you more easily add or delete specifications if you limit each line to one keyword, or at least to closely related keywords (e.g., Datfmt and Timfmt). This rule applies to all specifications that support keywords.

Free-Format Syntax

At current releases, RPG IV is primarily a free-format language, especially in the area of calculation processing. While it's not perfect, the free-format specification effectively renders the traditional fixed-format Calculation specification obsolete. IBM is introducing many new RPG IV features exclusively in free format.

The advantages of free format are well proven. It's easier to read, document, and maintain than fixed-format code, and its syntax is consistent with other modern computer languages. You should use it exclusively, especially when writing new programs or performing extensive maintenance on existing programs. In many cases, if you use the free-format specification, good standards will result automatically, because the free-format specification doesn't allow much of the obsolete baggage and poor practices that fixed-format C-specs allowed.

Avoid mixing fixed-form style and free-form style in your programs. The result is inconsistent and difficult to read. Take full advantage of the more natural order and expanded space afforded by the free-form specification.

Indent Code in Loops and Groups

When you're coding loops and groups, indent the code within a group by a couple of spaces to highlight the structure of the code group, as the following examples illustrate:

```
If %Found;
  Eval(h) Totalpay = Regpay + Ovtpay;
Endif;

Select;
  When Hours <=40;
    Totalpay = Hours * Rate;
  When Dblhours = 0;
    Totalpay = (Hours * Rate) + ((Hours - 40) * Rate * 1.5);
  Other;
    Totalpay = (Hours * Rate) + ((Hours - 40) * Rate * 1.5) +
               (Dblhours * Rate * 2);
Endsl;
```

continued...

continued...

```
Dou %Eof(Master);
  Read(e) Master;
  Select;
    When %Eof(Master);
      Leave;
    When %Error;
      Exsr Errsubr;
    Other;
      Exsr Process;
  Endsl;
Enddo;
```

But don't completely abandon columnar alignment as a tool to aid readability in expressions. Especially when an expression must continue onto subsequent lines, align the expression to make it easier to understand:

```
Totalpay = (Reghours * Rate)       +
           (Ovthours * Rate * 1.5) +
           (Dblhours * Rate * 2);
```

If your program includes embedded SQL statements, integrate the SQL completely by using the same indenting standards for the SQL statements that you use for the rest of the program:

```
If Instate = 'TX';
  Pgmaccount = 'G5X67';
  Exec SQL Select Firstname, Lastname, City, State
           Into :Infirstname, :Inlastname, :Incity, :Instate
           From Master
           Where Account = :Pgmaccount;
  Exsr Process;
Endif;
```

If the SQL statement is a long one, as in the above example, consider coding the individual SQL predicates on separate lines and aligning them as you would multiline expressions.

Use Mixed-Case Source

Closely related to using free-format syntax is the standard to use mixed uppercase and lowercase characters in the source code. Take advantage of this capability to make your program source easy to read. When coding a symbolic name, use mixed case to clarify the named item's meaning and use. Do not code in ALL UPPERCASE or all lowercase characters. Instead, use a logical combination of uppercase and lowercase, perhaps capitalizing each word in the code line:

```
Chain Postalcode Citymaster;
```

Another possibility is to use a notation commonly called "CamelCase," which joins compound words without spaces, capitalizing each section of the compound:

```
Chain PostalCode CityMaster;
```

If—but only if—your installation integrates Java programs into its applications, you might consider Java's traditional "Hungarian" notation, a variation of CamelCase in which the name of the variable indicates its type; the name begins with lowercase characters. Using Hungarian notation, the name "unsCounter" might indicate an unsigned integer, while "decAmount" might indicate a packed decimal number.

For RPG-reserved words and operations, as well as named constants, consider using ALL UPPERCASE characters. No matter which standard you use, be consistent.

Modular Applications

The RPG IV syntax, along with the Integrated Language Environment (ILE), encourages a modular approach to application programming. Modularity offers a way to organize an application, facilitate program maintenance, hide complex logic, and efficiently reuse code wherever it applies.

Write Modular Programs with Procedures

Isolate reusable code in a procedure. Instead of monolithic, all-purpose monsters, write smaller, single-function compile units and bind them to the programs that need them. Eliminate duplicate code, even little bits of it; your coding mantra should be, "Once and only once."

Relegate mysterious code to a well documented, well named procedure. Despite your best efforts, on extremely rare occasions you simply will not be able to make the meaning of a chunk of code clear without extensive comments. By separating such heavily documented, well tested code into a procedure, you'll save future maintenance programmers the trouble of deciphering and dealing with the code unnecessarily.

Procedures and subroutines share many of the same advantages in building modular programs. But procedures have many features that subroutines do not support—parameter passing, local variables, Nomain modules, and service programs, for example. Your standards should favor using procedures over subroutines as a modular programming mechanism.

Use Return Values

As a general rule, a procedure should always return a value to its caller—even if that value is nothing more than an indicator of whether or not the procedure executed successfully. This syntax allows you to embed a procedure call inside an expression, and it makes the program easy to read:

```
Metrictemp = Celsius(Englishtemp);

If Isweekday(Shipdate);
  ...
Endif;

If GetCustomer(Custnbr);
  ...
Endif;
```

Use Binding Directories Consistently

A binding directory is an object that can help organize the "pieces" required to create a program. Using a binding directory to list often reused modules or service programs will prevent tedium and errors by allowing you to refer to the binding directory or directories instead of explicitly listing the required components when you bind a program. To use binding directories effectively, you need a consistent strategy for them. Perhaps the most useful strategy would be to have a generic binding directory that refers to reusable code that crosses applications, along with an application specific binding directory for that code that relates only to one application.

Package Often Reused Procedures in Service Programs
The service program is an elegant means of reusing procedures without physically copying them into each program that needs them. As a general rule of thumb, if a procedure will appear in more than just one or two programs, you should package that procedure in a service program.

Use Binder Language to Control a Service Program Signature
Binder language source will let you explicitly control the signature of a service program, and more importantly, will allow the service program to maintain multiple signatures. This feature means that you can make dramatic changes to a service program—adding, changing, and removing procedures—without ever touching the programs that use the service program.

Parameters and Shared Data
Prototypes (PR definitions) and procedure interfaces (PI definitions) offer many advantages when you're passing data between modules and programs. For example, they avoid runtime errors by giving the compiler the ability to check the data type and number of parameters. Prototypes also let you code literals and expressions as parameters, declare parameter lists, and pass parameters by value and by read-only reference, as well as by reference.

Protect Parameters from Unintended Changes
In a modular programming environment, you might not always know what a called program or procedure is going to do to a parameter's value. To prevent unintentional changes to a parameter, you should generally pass parameters by value when calling a procedure, or by read-only reference (Const) when calling a program:

```
DName++++++++++ETDsFrom+++To/L+++IDc.Functions++++++++++++++++++++++++++++++
D Celsius         PR            5  0
D                               5  0 Value

D Updcust         PR              Extpgm('AR003')
D                               5  0 Const
D                               7  0 Const
```

Only in those cases where the caller truly needs to see any changes to a parameter—such as in the case of an error message—should you pass a parameter by reference.

Not only do these parameter passing methods—value or read-only reference—avoid accidental changes to parameter values, but they also allow the caller to pass literals or expressions as parameters, making the RPG IV code more flexible:

```
Metrictemp = Celsius(Englishtemp);
Metrictemp = Celsius(212);
Metrictemp = Celsius(Englishtemp + 50);
```

Store Prototypes in /COPY Members

For each module, code a /Copy member containing the procedure prototype for each exported procedure in that module. Then include a reference to that /Copy module in each module that refers to the procedures in the called module. This practice saves you from typing the prototypes each time you need them and reduces errors. As an alternative to having many small /Copy members, consider having a master /Copy member that contains prototypes for all or most of your reusable procedures.

You might also explore RPG's conditional compilation directives that will let you use the prototype from the actual procedure source instead of using a universal /Copy member. This technique would avoid introducing unused prototypes into the compile process (although there's no runtime penalty for having unused prototypes during the compile).

Include constant declarations for a module in the same /Copy member as the prototypes for that module. If you then reference the /Copy member in any module that refers to the called module, you've effectively "globalized" the declaration of those constants.

Use IMPORT and EXPORT Only for Global Data Items

The Import and Export keywords let you share data among the procedures in a program without explicitly passing the data as parameters. In other words, they provide a "hidden interface" between procedures. Limit use of these keywords to data items that are truly global in the program—usually values that are set once and then never changed. If you need to share data between modules, you should usually pass parameters instead of using Import and Export to share the data.

Indicators

Historically, indicators have been an identifying characteristic of the RPG syntax, but with RPG IV they are fast becoming relics of an earlier era. Reducing a program's use of indicators may well be the single most important thing you can do to improve the program's readability.

Eliminate Numbered Indicators

RPG IV completely eliminates the need for conditioning indicators and resulting indicators and does not support them in free-form specifications. The indicator data structure (Indds keyword) and a number of functions render obsolete the predefined numbered indicators. Use the file I/O functions (e.g., %Eof, %Found, %Error) and the (E) operation code extender to indicate file exception conditions.

If you must use indicators, name them. RPG IV supports a Boolean data type (N) that serves the same purpose as an indicator. You can use the Indds keyword with a display file specification to associate a data structure with the indicators for a display or printer file; you can then assign meaningful names to the indicators.

Include a description of any indicators you use. Even after you eliminate numbered indicators, a handful of predefined indicators may remain (e.g., the L0–L9 level break indicators or the U1–U8 external indicators). It's especially important to document these indicators, because their purpose isn't usually obvious by reading the program. The preface is a good place to list them.

Always Qualify File I/O Functions

The %Found, %Eof, %Equal, and %Status functions allow you to specify a file name with which to associate the functions' return value. To avoid ambiguous file exception reporting, you should always include the file name with these functions:

```
%Eof(Customers)
```

instead of

```
%Eof
```

The %Error function does not provide for a file name qualifier. Check the %Error function immediately after executing an operation with the (E) extender, or use the %Status function instead.

Structured Programming Techniques

Give those who follow you a fighting chance to understand how your program works by implementing structured programming techniques at all times. Use the structured operation codes—If, Dou, Dow, For, and Select/When/Other—instead of their older fixed-format ancestors. Do not use conditioning indicators to execute loops or groups of code. Don't use Goto, Cab*xx*, or Comp. Employ Iter to repeat a loop iteration, and use Leave or Leavesr for premature exits from loops or subroutines, respectively.

Perform Multipath Comparisons with Select/When/Other Groups

Deeply nested If/Else code blocks are hard to read and result in an unwieldy accumulation of Endifs at the end of the group. Elseif improves the situation somewhat, but Select/When/Other is usually a better and more versatile construct. The same advice goes for the obsolete Cas*xx* opcode; use Select/When/Other instead.

Character String Processing

IBM has greatly enhanced RPG IV's ability to easily manipulate character strings. Many of the tricks you had to use with earlier versions of RPG are now obsolete. Modernize your source by exploiting these new features.

Use a Named Constant to Declare a String

Instead of storing a string constant in an array or table, declare it in a named constant. Declaring a string (such as a CL command string) as a named constant lets you refer to it directly instead of forcing you to refer to the string through its array name and index. Use a named constant to declare any value that you don't expect to change during program execution.

Avoid using arrays and data structures to manipulate character strings and text. Use expressions and functions (e.g., %Subst, %Replace, %Editc) instead.

Use Variable-Length Fields to Simplify String Handling

You can process variable-length fields using simple expressions. Not only does the code look better (eliminating the %Trim function, for example), but it's also faster than using fixed-length fields. For example, use this code:

```
DName++++++++++ETDsFrom+++To/L+++IDc.Functions+++++++++++++++++++++++++++++
D Qualname        S             33     Varying
D Library         S             10     Varying
D File            S             10     Varying
D Member          S             10     Varying

 /Free
    Qualname = Library + '/' + File + '(' + Member + ')';
 /End-Free
```

instead of

```
DName++++++++++ETDsFrom+++To/L+++IDc.Functions+++++++++++++++++++++++++++++
D Qualname        S             33
D Library         S             10
D File            S             10
D Member          S             10

 /Free
    Qualname = %Trim(Library) + '/' + %Trim(File)
             + '(' + %Trim(Member) + ')';
 /End-Free
```

Use variable-length fields as parameters to every string-handling subprocedure (passing by value or read-only reference), as well as for work fields.

Comments

Good programming style can serve a documentary purpose in helping others understand your source code. But use comments judiciously. If you practice good code construction techniques, you'll find that "less is more" when it comes to commenting the source. Too many comments are as bad as too few. Here are some specific commenting guidelines.

Use // Comments Exclusively

RPG IV now uses comments that begin with double slash characters (//) instead of the traditional asterisk (*) in position 7. In free-format code, which does not allow the asterisk format, the comment can begin anywhere in columns 8–80 and can even be on the same line with existing executable statements. The new comment form can also replace asterisk comments in fixed-format specifications, but the comment must be on a line all by itself. For the sake of consistency, use the new form exclusively, even in fixed-format specifications:

```
DName+++++++++++ETDsFrom+++To/L+++IDc.Functions+++++++++++++++++++++++++++++++
 // ---------------------------------------------------------------- Prototypes
D DayofWeek       PR            1 0
D  VarDate                      D

 // ---------------------------------------------------- Standalone variables
D DayNbr          S             5 0

 // ----------------------------------------------------------------------
 // Main processing routine
 // ----------------------------------------------------------------------
 /Free
 // Calculate total pay for employee
 Chain(ne) EmployeeID Employees;
 If %Found(Employees);           // If employee active, calculate total pay
    Eval(h) TotalPay = (RegHours * Rate) + (OvtHours * Rate * 1.5);
 Endif;
 /End-free
```

Use Comments to Clarify–Not Echo–Your Code

Comments that merely repeat the code add to a program's bulk but not to its value. In general, you should use comments for just three purposes:

- To provide a brief program or procedure summary
- To give a title to a subroutine, procedure, or other section of code
- To explain a technique that isn't readily apparent by reading the source

Always include a brief summary at the beginning of a program or procedure. This prologue should include the following information:

- The program or procedure title
- A brief description of the program's or procedure's purpose
- A chronology of changes that includes the date, programmer name, and purpose of each change
- A summary of indicator usage
- A description of the procedure interface (the return value and parameters)
- An example of how to call the procedure

Use "Marker Line" Comments to Organize Code

You can employ "marker line" comments to divide the major sections of your program. For example, you should definitely section off with lines of dashes (-) the declarations, the main procedure, each subroutine, and any subprocedures. Identify each section for easy reference:

```
DName++++++++++ETDsFrom+++To/L+++IDc.Functions++++++++++++++++++++++++++++++
  // ------------------------------------------------------------- Prototypes
D DayofWeek       PR            1 0
D  VarDate                      D

  // --------------------------------------------------- Standalone variables
D DayNbr          S             5 0

  // ------------------------------------------------------------------------
  // Main processing routine
  // ------------------------------------------------------------------------
 /Free
  // Calculate total pay for employee
  Chain(ne) EmployeeID Employees;
  If %Found(Employees);              // If employee active, calculate total pay
      Eval(h) TotalPay = (RegHours * Rate) + (OvtHours * Rate * 1.5);
  Endif;
 /End-free
```

Use blank lines to group related source lines and make them stand out. In general, you should use completely blank lines instead of blank comment lines to group lines of code, unless you're building a block of comments. Use only one blank line, though; multiple consecutive blank lines make your program hard to read.

Avoid Right-Hand Comments

Right-hand "end line" comments in positions 81–100 tend simply to echo the code, can be lost during program maintenance, and can easily become "out of synch" with the line they comment. Especially now that comments can be inline with code, don't use right-hand comments.

Don't Use Positions 1–5

The original RPG IV syntax, which was oriented to using punched paper cards, used positions 1–5 to sequence program line numbers. In RPG IV, these columns are commentary only. You may use them to identify changed lines in a program or structured indentation levels, but be aware that these columns may be subject to the same hazards as right-hand comments.

Avoid Obsolescence

RPG is an old language. After nearly 40 years, many of its original, obsolete features are still available. Don't use them.

Eliminate Obsolete Operation Codes

How do you identify an obsolete operation? Simple answer: If the free-form specification doesn't support it, the operation code is obsolete. In introducing the free-form specification, IBM took advantage of the opportunity to simplify RPG by paring the number of supported operation codes in half to about 60. Appendix A summarizes the preferred substitutions for those operations that you shouldn't use any more.

Choose Functions Over Operation Codes

If a function offers the same function as an operation, use the function instead of the operation. With some operations, you can substitute a function for the operation and use the function within an expression. The functions are preferable if they offer the same capability as the operation codes.

Avoid Program Described Files

Instead, use externally defined files whenever possible.

Use Native Date Data Types to Process Dates

Get rid of the clever date and time routines that you have gathered and jealously guarded over the years. The RPG IV date functions (e.g., %Date, %Diff, %Subdt, %Days) are more efficient, more clear, and more modern. Even if your database includes dates in "legacy" formats, you can use the date functions to manipulate them.

Avoid Programming Tricks

Such maneuvers aren't so clever to someone who doesn't know the trick. If you think you must add comments to explain how a block of code works, consider rewriting the code to clarify its purpose or hiding the complexity of the code in a procedure. Use of the obscure "bit-twiddling" functions (%Bitand, %Bitnot, %Bitor, %Bitxor) may be a sign that your source needs simpifying.

Final Advice

Sometimes good style and efficient runtime performance don't mix. Wherever you face a conflict between the two, choose good style. Hard-to-read programs are hard to debug, hard to maintain, and hard to get right. Program correctness must always win out over speed. Keep in mind these admonitions from Brian Kernighan and P.J. Plauger's *The Elements of Programming Style* (McGraw-Hill; 2nd edition, 1978):

- Make it right before you make it faster.
- Keep it right when you make it faster.
- Make it clear before you make it faster.
- Don't sacrifice clarity for small gains in efficiency.

Appendix C

Program Development Tools

Chapter 1 discussed the program development cycle, including editing the program source, compiling it, binding the resulting module, and finally running the program. This appendix will introduce those features of the System i you need to know to complete these tasks. There are two primary toolsets available for program development:

- Programming Development Manager (PDM)
- WebSphere Development Studio Client for iSeries (WDSc)

PDM consists of application development tools for use in a "green screen" workstation environment, while WDSc is a Windows-based client program.

Before looking at these tools, let's review the System i's object-based architecture. System i libraries are used to organize stored information in objects. A library is analogous to a PC directory (and is itself an object). The System i stores many kinds of objects—data files, job descriptions, commands, output queues, programs, and so on. The type associated with an object determines the kinds of actions you can perform on the object. All object types begin with an asterisk (*).

During the program development cycle, you will be working with three primary kinds of objects: *MODULE, *PGM, and *FILE. Recall that *MODULE objects result from successfully compiling a source member and contain the machine-language version of your source code. A program object (type *PGM) comprises one or more *MODULE objects, bound together. When you call a *PGM object, you are telling the computer to carry out the instructions contained in the object.

Objects with type *FILE are files. Files are further differentiated by attributes, which categorize the nature of the file. The attribute PF-SRC indicates that a file is a source physical file that contains source code. Attribute PF-DTA indicates that an object is a physical database file; attribute LF indicates that an object is a logical database file.

The contents of all database files, regardless of attribute, can be organized into members. A member is a subdivision of a file. A file must exist before you can add members to it. Each program that you edit will be stored as a member within a source physical file; when you compile that source member, you will create a *MODULE object, usually with the same name as the member.

Most installations use a source file named QRPGLESRC to store RPG IV source code. While most installations will store the source code and the object (executable) code in the same library, it is not unusual to store source code in libraries separate from their object (executable) code. Your installation's standards and practices will dictate the name of the source file and the library name within which you will be working.

System i Development Tools

Traditionally, System i developers have used a toolset called Program Development Manager (PDM). PDM consists of server based tools like Programming Development Manager (PDM) for organizing objects, Source Entry Utility (SEU) for editing source code, and Screen Design Aid (SDA) for designing screens. The PDM tools are primarily designed for use with traditional "green screen" workstations.

Recently, IBM has released a development environment called WebSphere Development Studio Client for iSeries (WDSc). This tool is based on an industry standard platform called Eclipse (www.eclipse.org). WDSc is a Windows-based program and includes such tools as Remote Systems

Explorer (RSE) for organizing System i objects, a Live Parsing Extensible Editor (LPEX) for editing source code, and a Screen Designer tool for designing screens. Currently, developers are moving away from the traditional server-based development toolset, in favor of WDSc. The PDM tools are still supported but there are no plans to enhance this toolset in the future.

The utilities in WDSc perform many of the same functions as the traditional tools, but in a graphical Windows environment, offloading the bulk of application development work from the server and onto Windows clients. Instead of PDM's "Work with" screens, WDSc uses Explorer-like windows to help you organize libraries, objects, and members. Instead of SEU, WDSc uses its own more robust graphical LPEX editor. Instead of SDA, WDSc offers a number of screen and report design tools.

WebSphere Development Studio Client also packages a full set of System i language compilers—e.g., ILE RPG/400 (RPG IV), Control Language (CL), COBOL, Java, and C. You can also install the product with Web development tools for creating Internet Web applications. The platform is designed so that a developer will need to learn only one development environment. If the developer needs to write in a different language or for a different platform, WDSc supports the installation of plug-ins to allow development for that language or platform. These tools and more combine to make WebSphere Development Studio Client for System i a feature-filled application toolkit for the System i.

This appendix will discuss both WDSc and PDM, so that you'll be comfortable with either tool, depending upon your installation's practices.

WebSphere Development Studio Client for iSeries (WDSc)

Figure C.1 shows the first screen shown when you start WDSc (Version 7) for the first time. This screen shows a window titled "iSeries RSE Getting Started". This window will guide you through all of the steps required to connect to your System i, edit and compile a member, then run your first program. You can bring this window up at anytime by selecting "Help/iSeries RSE Getting Started" on the top menu.

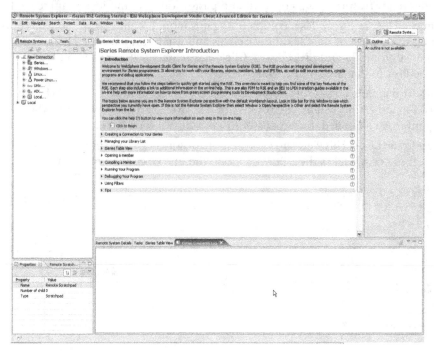

Figure C.1
Remote System Explorer Introduction

There is a learning curve to using WDSc but you'll find that once you spend a little time with it, you'll rarely use the traditional tools once you've mastered WDSc. This appendix will get you started with these important steps in the program development cycle:

- Opening a source member
- Editing a source member
- Compiling a source member
- Running a program

Figure C.2 highlights five views WDSc uses for organizing, editing, and compiling RPG programs:

1. **Remote Systems**—This view lets you navigate the system that you are logged onto. When you use this view you should make comparisons to using Windows Explorer. You can copy, cut, paste, and delete objects. Double clicking a member will open it in the LPEX editor.

2. **LPEX Editor**—This view is where you will edit the source member. The LPEX editor includes many traditional editor features and has some features in common with SEU. It additionally includes many features (e.g., copy, cut and paste) found in modern graphical editors.

3. **Outline**—This view provides a complete organizational outline of the source code you are editing. It shows all of the files and variables and where they are used in the program. It also outlines subroutines and procedures. Clicking on any portion of the outline will move the LPEX editor to that area of the source code.

4. **iSeries Commands Log**—This view is similar to displaying your job log. When you submit any command to the system, the results are displayed here. For example, when you submit a program to be compiled, the results of submission show up here.

5. **iSeries Error List**—This view shows any errors or warnings the compiler found. Clicking on one of these errors takes the LPEX editor to the line of code in question.

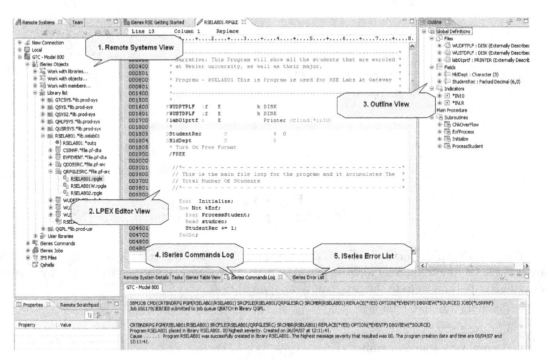

Figure C.2
WDSc Views

Opening a Source Member

Figure C.3 shows a portion of the Remote Systems Explorer (RSE). The RSE shows a graphic representation of the system that you are connected to. Clicking the (+) sign by the Library List icon will display the libraries in your library list as if you had used the DSPLIBL (Display Library List) command on the i5/OS command line. If you aren't logged on to the system you will be presented with a login window; enter your System i user ID and password, and then click OK as shown.

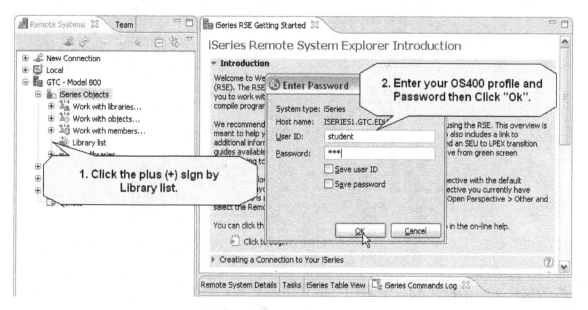

Figure C.3
Logging On and Expanding the Library List

After you have successfully logged onto the server, you need to expand (Click the (+) sign) the Library List icon. You will then see all of the libraries in your library list. The next step is to expand the library that contains the source file you want to edit. Finally, right click the member and select Open with Remote Systems LPEX Editor. Figure C.4 illustrates the process.

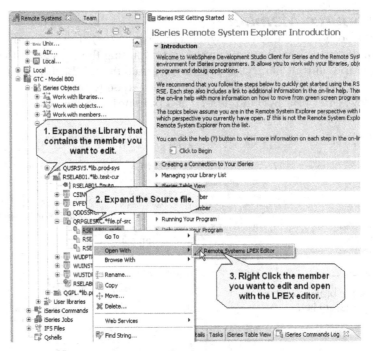

Figure C.4
Opening a Source Member

Editing a Source Member

The source member is now open in the LPEX Editor (Figure C.5) and then you can edit the source member much like a typical document. You can easily copy within the member or between members as you would copy within a document. When using WDSc, the programmer can verify a program before compiling it.

Perhaps one of the most useful features for new programmers is Content Assist. You can type the keyword (or a portion of it) and press Ctrl+Space; WDSc will then propose, display, and insert code completions at the cursor position.

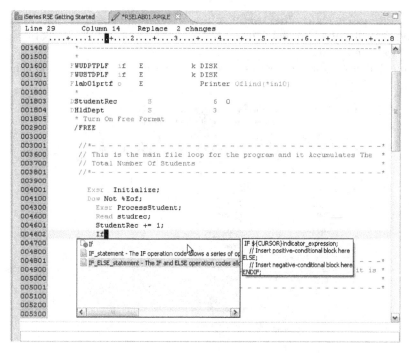

Figure C.5
LPEX Editor with Content Assist

The LPEX editor can provide you with prompts to facilitate code entry. If you are editing a source line and press F4, WDSc will open a separate view that will prompt you for each component of the line. Context-sensitive help is also available from the prompter by pressing F1.

You can access some LPEX functions by typing sequence commands over the sequence number for the appropriate source line(s) and then pressing the Enter key. Here are some common sequence commands:

- *I* to insert a new line below the current line
- *D* to delete the current line
- *DD* to delete a block of lines (type *DD* over the sequence numbers of the first and last lines in the block)
- *C* to copy the current line (to indicate the desired location, type either *A* (after) or *B* (before) over the sequence number of the target line)
- *CC* to copy a block of lines (type *CC* on the first and last lines of the block, then *A* or *B* at the desired target location
- *M* to move the current line (to indicate the desired location, type either *A* or *B* over the sequence number of the target line)
- *MM* to move a block of lines (type *MM* on the first and last lines of the block, then *A* or *B* at the desired target location
- *RP* to repeat the current line on the next line
- *RPP* to repeat a block of lines (type *RPP* on the first and last lines of the block)

The LPEX editor offers many other useful editing features, including search/replace and source line filters. The list of additional features is beyond the scope of this book but is covered in the WDSc Help documentation.

After making changes to the member, you can the save the member by clicking the save button as shown or press the Crtl+S keys (Figure C.6).

Figure C.6
Saving a Source Member

Compiling a Source Member

After saving the source member, the next step is to compile it into a module or a program object. Right-click the source member and then navigate to the Compile option (Figure C.7). At this point, you have a choice of using the CRTBNDRPG command or the CRTRPGMOD command to compile the source member. When you select a compile command, the source member is compiled in batch on the server.

Figure C.7
Compiling a Source Member

You can use either of the following windows to show the results of the compile job:

- *iSeries Commands Log* (Figure C.8) shows executed commands and the results of batch submissions.
- *iSeries Error List* (Figure C.9) shows any errors or warnings. The severity of the error is indicated by a number 00–99. Typically, an error severity of 30 or higher will prevent a successful compile. Clicking on any of these errors will move the LPEX editor to the line that caused the error.

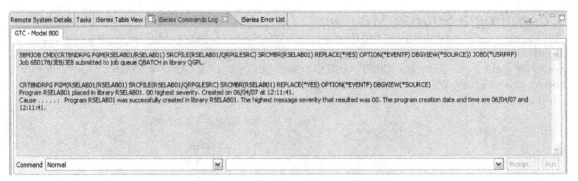

Figure C.8
iSeries Commands Log Showing Successful Compile

	ID	Message	Severity	Line	Location	Connection	
i	RNF7031	The name or indicator ADMDAT is not referenced.	00	13	RSELAB01/QRPGLESRC(RSELAB01)	GTC - Model 800	
i	RNF7031	The name or indicator CHAIR is not referenced.	00	4	RSELAB01/QRPGLESRC(RSELAB01)	GTC - Model 800	
i	RNF7031	The name or indicator CITY is not referenced.	00	7	RSELAB01/QRPGLESRC(RSELAB01)	GTC - Model 800	
i	RNF7031	The name or indicator CLASS is not referenced.	00	14	RSELAB01/QRPGLESRC(RSELAB01)	GTC - Model 800	
i	RNF7031	The name or indicator DCODE is not referenced.	00	12	RSELAB01/QRPGLESRC(RSELAB01)	GTC - Model 800	
i	RNF7031	The name or indicator DEGREE is not referenced.	00	18	RSELAB01/QRPGLESRC(RSELAB01)	GTC - Model 800	
i	RNF7031	The name or indicator DEPT is not referenced.	00	2	RSELAB01/QRPGLESRC(RSELAB01)	GTC - Model 800	
i	RNF7031	The name or indicator DOFFIC is not referenced.	00	5	RSELAB01/QRPGLESRC(RSELAB01)	GTC - Model 800	
i	RNF7031	The name or indicator DPHONE is not referenced.	00	6	RSELAB01/QRPGLESRC(RSELAB01)	GTC - Model 800	
i	RNF7031	The name or indicator GRDDAT is not referenced.	00	15	RSELAB01/QRPGLESRC(RSELAB01)	GTC - Model 800	
i	RNF7031	The name or indicator SMNAME is not referenced.	00	5	RSELAB01/QRPGLESRC(RSELAB01)	GTC - Model 800	
i	RNF7031	The name or indicator STATE is not referenced.	00	8	RSELAB01/QRPGLESRC(RSELAB01)	GTC - Model 800	

Figure C.9
iSeries Error List

Running a Program

After you have compiled the source member—and bound the module to a program, if necessary—
the next step is to run the program object. Use the RSE to navigate to the newly compiled program
object (Figure C.10). Usually, you will select the option to run the program in batch, unless the
program is an interactive program, in which case you'll want to run the program from a workstation
emulation program; WDSc does not offer a server-side workstation display feature.

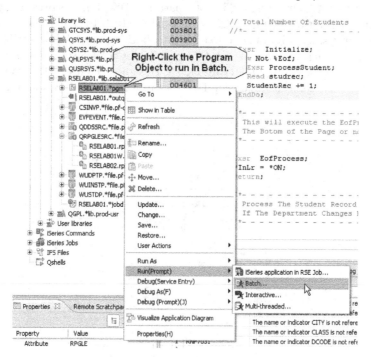

Figure C.10
Running a Program in Batch

Caution
To run a program, you must navigate to the compiled program object itself—not the source
member. You may need to refresh the RSE view by highlighting it and pressing F5.

CODE Designer

You can use WDSc and the LPEX editor to edit source code for DDS source members (e.g., to edit the source for display files and printer files). But it might be more convenient to use a WYSIWYG ("What you see is what you get") graphical tool to design and create these objects. Depending upon which version of WDSc your installation uses, you may be able to use a Screen Designer tool for this purpose.

Another similar tool, CODE Designer, is not a part of WDSc, but it is provided with all WDSc versions as part of an earlier program, CODE and VisualAge RPG for iSeries. This appendix will discuss CODE Designer, since it is available to everyone; both tools work in a similar fashion.

CODE Designer is integrated into WDSc; by right clicking a DDS source member (Display Screen or a Print file) and selecting Open with CODE Designer (Figure C.11), you'll be able to modify the DDS source member using CODE Designer instead of the LPEX editor.

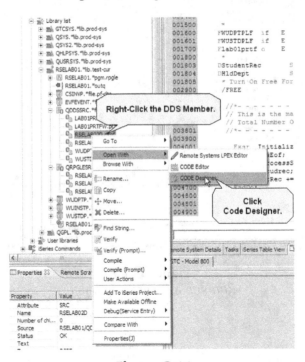

Figure C.11
Opening a Source Member with CODE Designer

CODE Designer allows you to create and maintain both display file (DSPF) source and printer file (PRTF) source; there are no significant differences in the way it works with either type of source member. You place fields on the design window, moving them into their desired positions. Double clicking a field will bring up a window to maintain the properties of the field. Refer to the product's Help for additional information. You are able to easily move fields around, switch between different records, and display the generated DDS source code. Figure C.12 illustrates using CODE Designer with a display file, while Figure C.13 shows it being used with a printer file.

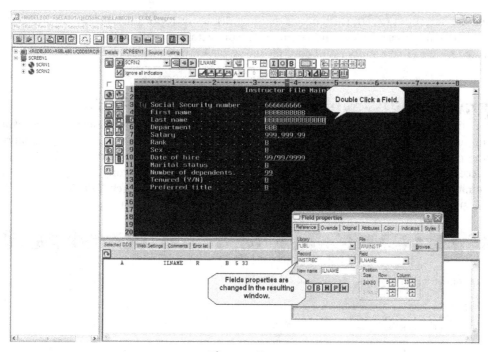

Figure C.12
Designing a Display File with CODE Designer

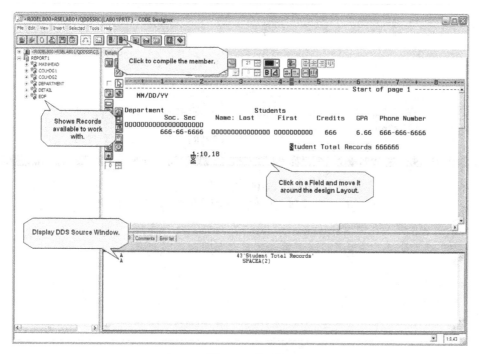

Figure C.13
Designing a Printer File with CODE Designer

After you have used CODE Designer to design a display or report, it will store the generated DDS in a source member. You can then compile it from within CODE Designer, or use RSE to navigate to the source member and compile it, similar to the way you compile RPG source members.

Programming Development Manager (PDM)

Programming Development Manager (PDM) is the primary character-based means for accessing and manipulating libraries, objects, and members. If you are using a "green-screen" workstation or emulation program for your application development, you will use PDM instead of WDSc.

To access PDM from the Main menu, first select option 5, Programming; then, at the resulting Programming panel, select option 2, Programming Development Manager. You will see the PDM menu, illustrated in Figure C.14.

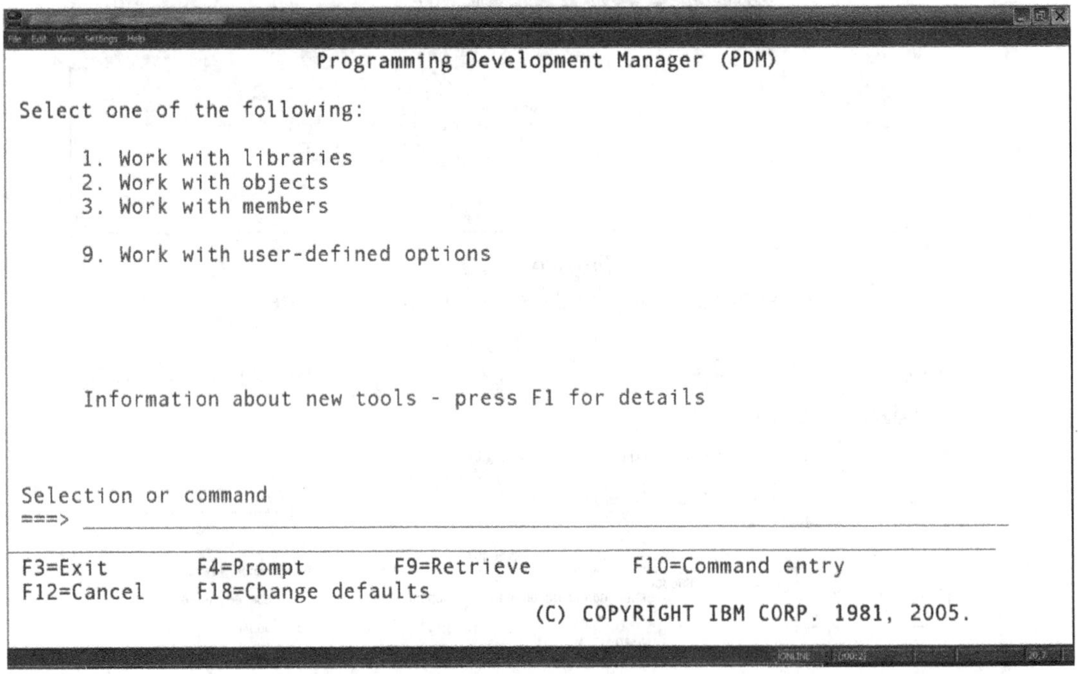

```
                    Programming Development Manager (PDM)

Select one of the following:

       1. Work with libraries
       2. Work with objects
       3. Work with members

       9. Work with user-defined options




       Information about new tools - press F1 for details



Selection or command
===>  _____

F3=Exit      F4=Prompt      F9=Retrieve       F10=Command entry
F12=Cancel   F18=Change defaults
                              (C) COPYRIGHT IBM CORP. 1981, 2005.
```

Figure C.14
Programming Development Manager Menu

Enter/Edit a Source Member

To open a source member for editing, select option 3, Work with members, from the PDM menu, or prompt the WRKMBRPDM (Work with Members Using PDM) command. You will see the prompt shown in Figure C.15, which you will use to select the source file containing the member(s) you want to edit. You may either enter the desired source file or position your cursor on the file prompt and press F4 to see a list of the possible files.

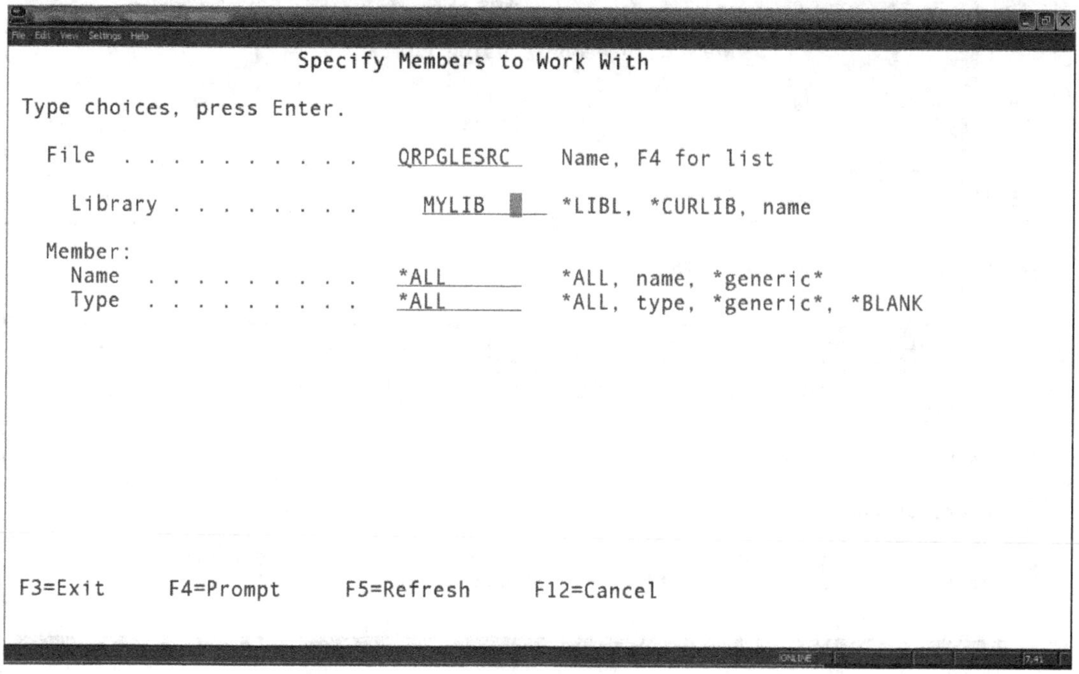

```
                          Specify Members to Work With

 Type choices, press Enter.

   File  . . . . . . . . . .   QRPGLESRC    Name, F4 for list

     Library . . . . . . . .     MYLIB      *LIBL, *CURLIB, name

   Member:
     Name  . . . . . . . . .    *ALL         *ALL, name, *generic*
     Type  . . . . . . . . .    *ALL         *ALL, type, *generic*, *BLANK
```

```
 F3=Exit      F4=Prompt     F5=Refresh     F12=Cancel
```

Figure C.15
Selecting a Source File to Edit

Once you have entered or selected the desired file, the system will display all the members of that file, as shown in Figure C.16. From this screen you can select a source member to edit, print, or compile by keying a 2, 6, or 14, respectively, next to the member with which you want to work. Note that option 14 may not appear on the initial screen; pressing F23 (More options) reveals this and additional options for working with members. However, an option does not have to appear on the screen to be used—provided it is a valid option.

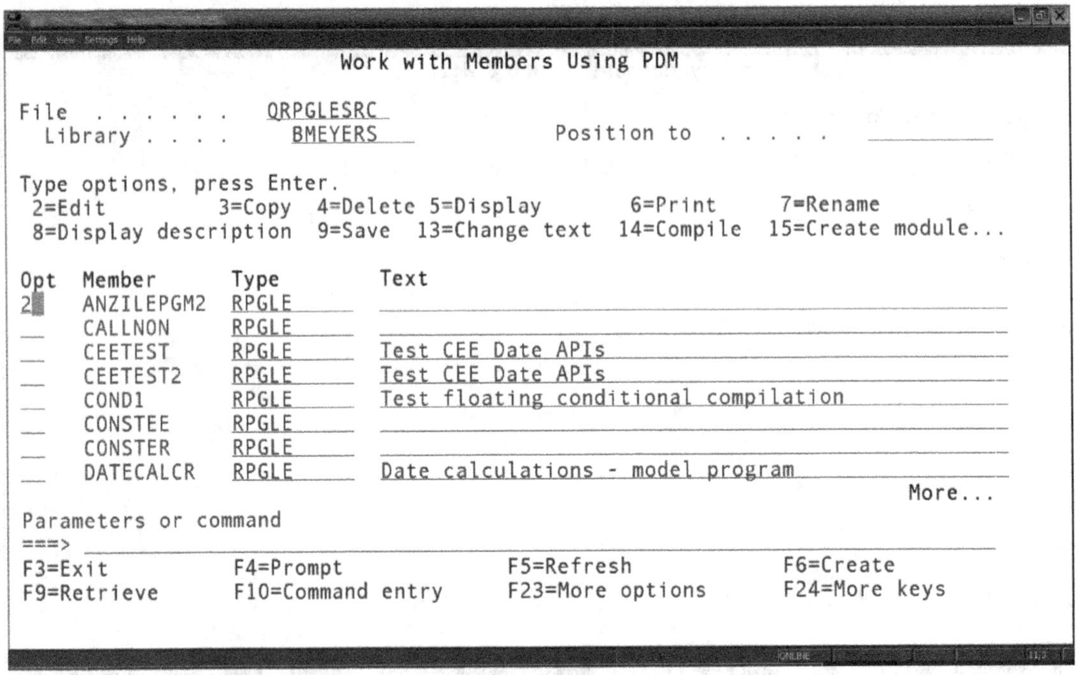

```
                          Work with Members Using PDM

 File  . . . . . .    QRPGLESRC
   Library . . . .      BMEYERS             Position to  . . . . .  _____

 Type options, press Enter.
   2=Edit          3=Copy  4=Delete 5=Display      6=Print     7=Rename
   8=Display description  9=Save  13=Change text  14=Compile  15=Create module...

 Opt  Member      Type      Text
 2    ANZILEPGM2  RPGLE
  _   CALLNON     RPGLE     _____
  _   CEETEST     RPGLE     Test CEE Date APIs
  _   CEETEST2    RPGLE     Test CEE Date APIs
  _   COND1       RPGLE     Test floating conditional compilation
  _   CONSTEE     RPGLE     _____
  _   CONSTER     RPGLE     _____
  _   DATECALCR   RPGLE     Date calculations - model program
                                                                   More...
 Parameters or command
 ===> _____
 F3=Exit         F4=Prompt           F5=Refresh         F6=Create
 F9=Retrieve     F10=Command entry   F23=More options   F24=More keys
```

Figure C.16
Work with Members Using PDM Display

To edit an existing member, enter a 2 to the left of the member name to bring that member into Source Entry Utility (SEU) and continue work on it. If you are creating a new member, press F6=Create to go to the Start SEU screen. You will need to enter the source file name, the member name, and the type.

Figure C.17 illustrates the SEU editor. The editor options in SEU are not as robust as those in WDSc, but the two editors share many of the same functions. For example, the sequence commands, discussed earlier are supported by SEU.

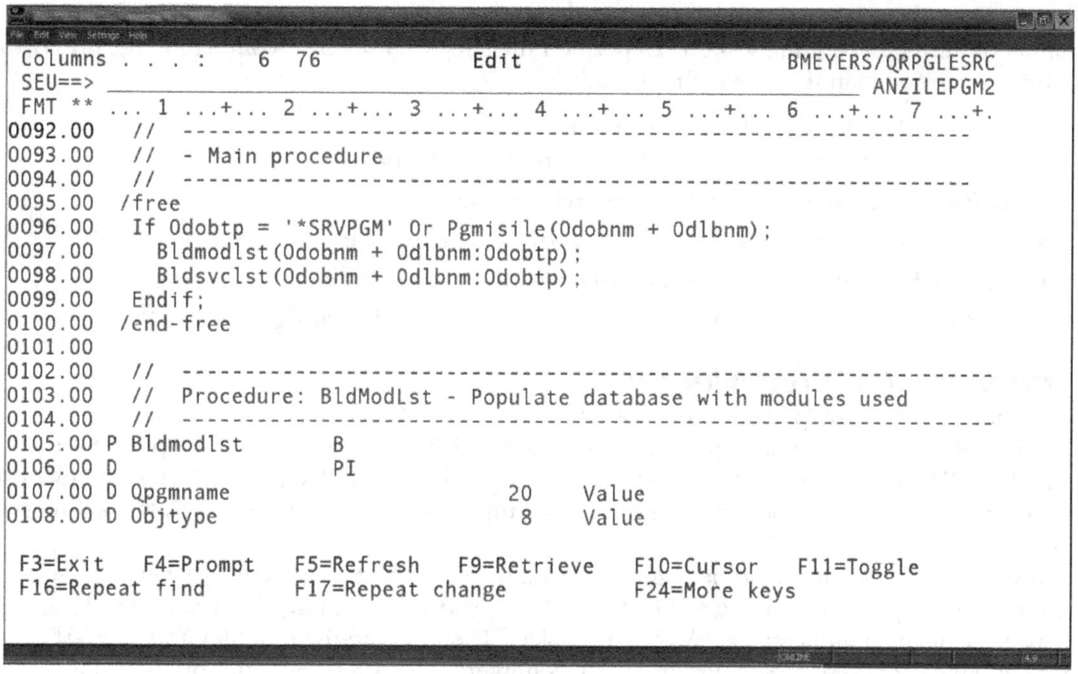

```
 Columns . . . :    6  76            Edit                     BMEYERS/QRPGLESRC
 SEU==> ____________________________________________________________ ANZILEPGM2
 FMT ** ... 1 ...+... 2 ...+... 3 ...+... 4 ...+... 5 ...+... 6 ...+... 7 ...+.
0092.00   //  -------------------------------------------------------------
0093.00   //  - Main procedure
0094.00   //  -------------------------------------------------------------
0095.00  /free
0096.00   If Odobtp = '*SRVPGM' Or Pgmisile(Odobnm + Odlbnm);
0097.00     Bldmodlst(Odobnm + Odlbnm:Odobtp);
0098.00     Bldsvclst(Odobnm + Odlbnm:Odobtp);
0099.00   Endif;
0100.00  /end-free
0101.00
0102.00   //  ---------------------------------------------------------------
0103.00   //  Procedure: BldModLst - Populate database with modules used
0104.00   //  ---------------------------------------------------------------
0105.00 P Bldmodlst       B
0106.00 D                 PI
0107.00 D Qpgmname                      20    Value
0108.00 D Objtype                        8    Value

 F3=Exit   F4=Prompt    F5=Refresh   F9=Retrieve    F10=Cursor   F11=Toggle
 F16=Repeat find        F17=Repeat change           F24=More keys
```

Figure C.17
Source Entry Utility

In addition, you may find the following function keys useful when editing a source member:

- F3 to exit SEU
- F4 to invoke a prompt function (similar to WDSc's prompter) for the current line
- F5 to refresh the display (if you haven't yet pressed Enter)
- F13 (Shift+F1) to change the SEU defaults for the current session (e.g., to enable or disable lowercase alphabetic entry
- F14 (Shift+F2) to search/replace characters in the source member
- F15 (Shift+F3) to browse a second member or a compile output while working in your source code; also lets you copy code from one member into another
- F16 (Shift+F4) to search for the next instance of a character string
- F17 (Shift+F5) to replace the next instance of a character string
- F23 (Shift+F11) to display all possible prompt formats and select the one you want to activate

SEU also supports a command line at the top of the display. You can use this line to enter SEU commands during the editing session. To position the cursor on the SEU command line, press F10. Here are some commands you may find useful:

- *SAVE* to save the member without exiting SEU
- *CANCEL* to leave SEU without saving and return to the previous menu
- *TOP* or *T* to move to the top of the source member
- *BOTTOM* or *B* to move to the bottom of your source member
- *FIND* or *F* to search for a string of characters in the source member
- *CHANGE* or *C* to change a string of characters to some other string

Compiling a Source Member

After editing, enter a compile option to the left of the name of the member you want to compile and bind. The compile option for the CRTBNDRPG command is 14; the option for the CRTRPGMOD command is 15. If the compiled object (either a *MODULE or *PGM) already exists, a Confirm Compile of Member screen appears; you must respond Y (Yes) to the "Delete existing object" option.

If your member is eligible to be compiled using the CRTBNDRPG command, you may use option 14 to compile it and create a *PGM object. Otherwise, you will need to use option 15 to compile the member and create a *MODULE object. Then to bind the module(s) to a *PGM object, use the CRTPGM (Create Program) CL command, which you can enter on the PDM command line.

Your program will not be ready to run until the system returns a message that the processing was completed successfully. To display messages, type DSPMSG (Display Messages) on the command line and press Enter; or in most installations you may type a "dm" shortcut option in any option column of your current screen. If the message says that the processing ended abnormally, you must correct program errors and then reselect option 14.

To correct errors, you may need to refer to the compiler listing for the source member. On many systems you may type "sp" in any option column on any of PDM's screens to obtain a list of your spooled files; alternatively, you can also use the WRKSPLF (Work with Spooled Files) on any command line. From there, you can either print or view the compiler listing. You can also find the compiler listing and view it by using the F15 function key within SEU.

Running a Program

After you have compiled and bound a program, you can run it from within PDM. Select option 2, Work with Objects, from the PDM menu, or prompt the WRKOBJPDM (Work with Objects Using PDM) command. Option 16 (Run) on the resulting display (Figure C.18) will run the program; enter 16 in the left column next to the program object you want to run. Note that although 16 does not appear as an initial option, pressing F23 would reveal it (and other options, as well). Alternately, you can enter the CALL command on any command line:

```
CALL program-name
```

If the program requires input parameters, press F4 to prompt option 16 or the CALL command; you may then enter the necessary parameter values.

```
┌────────────────────────────────────────────────────────────────────────┐
│ File  Edit  View  Settings  Help                                         │
│                     Work with Objects Using PDM                          │
│                                                                          │
│  Library . . . . .   BMEYERS        Position to . . . . . . . .  _____ │
│                                     Position to type  . . . . .  _____ │
│                                                                          │
│  Type options, press Enter.                                              │
│    2=Change        3=Copy        4=Delete      5=Display     7=Rename    │
│    8=Display description          9=Save       10=Restore    11=Move ... │
│                                                                          │
│  Opt   Object      Type        Attribute   Text                         │
│  █_    ANZILEPGM   *PGM        CLLE                                      │
│  __    CALLNON     *PGM        RPGLE                                     │
│  __    CEETEST     *PGM        RPGLE       Test CEE Date APIs            │
│  __    CEETEST2    *PGM        RPGLE       Test CEE Date APIs            │
│  __    COND1       *PGM        RPGLE       Test floating conditional compilation │
│  __    CONSTEE     *PGM        RPGLE                                     │
│  __    CONSTER     *PGM        RPGLE                                     │
│  __    CPYVMASTER  *PGM        RPGLE       Copy VMASTER sample to MMASTER│
│                                                                More...   │
│  Parameters or command                                                   │
│  ===> _____      │
│  F3=Exit          F4=Prompt           F5=Refresh         F6=Create       │
│  F9=Retrieve      F10=Command entry   F23=More options   F24=More keys   │
│  You have reached the top of the list.                                   │
└────────────────────────────────────────────────────────────────────────┘
```

Figure C.18
Work with Objects Using PDM display

Appendix D

Program Testing and Debugging

A major part of a programmer's time is spent ensuring that the programs he or she has written are, in fact, accurately producing the desired results. This procedure involves carefully checking each program's correctness and fixing any errors this checking uncovers—a process often referred to as **debugging**. Program errors fall into one of two broad categories: syntax errors and logic errors.

Syntax Errors

Syntax errors are errors in your use of the programming language. Because the system points out these kinds of errors for you, they are simple to detect and easy to correct, once you have mastered the rules of the language in which you are programming.

The source editor you use (e.g., SEU or LPEX) detects some kinds of syntax errors as you enter program statements. For example, failing to make a required entry within a specification line, forgetting to right adjust a numeric entry within its allocated positions, or including an invalid value in a column (e.g., an F instead of an I, O, U, or C for file type on the File Specifications) causes the editor to highlight the erroneous entry with an accompanying error message. You may need to press the Reset key before the system lets you proceed. Typically, until you correct the error, the error message will remain as a reminder of a problem.

Once you have completely entered your program and have eliminated all syntax errors detected by the editor, your next step is to compile and bind the program. Compiling is the process that translates the statements in your source member into machine code instructions and stores them in a module object. The binding step copies one or more modules into a program object that the computer can then execute.

In attempting to complete the translation process, the ILE RPG/400 compiler often detects additional syntax errors unnoticed by the editor. If your program contains compile errors, the system sends you a message that your job ended abnormally. You can find the cause (or causes) of the difficulties by printing or displaying the *compile listing*, a report of the compilation generated by the compiler. A compile listing includes a listing of your program. The compiler numbers the program statements sequentially in increments of 100 and indicates the date on which each statement was entered (or modified).

Within the program listing, the compiler also indicates how it is interpreting any nesting of structured operators by inserting a B at the beginning of the structure, an E at the end of the structure, and an X for any ELSE it encounters within the structure. The compiler also prints a digit with each of these codes, representing the level of nesting the structure establishes. By cross-checking these digits, you can make sure that the computer has matched the beginnings and ends of the structures as you had intended. Indenting your source code will also help you more easily see your logic structures.

The compiler also provides a cross reference listing to help you diagnose problems. A cross reference listing is a list of all fields and indicators used in your program; it logs every program statement within which each of the fields or indicators occurs. The statement defining the field is annotated with a D (for define), while any statement within which the field's or indicator's value is changed is annotated with an M (for modify). You can use this listing to quickly locate field and/or indicator use within your program listing.

If your program contains syntax errors, the compiler notes the errors by inserting an asterisk (*) and a numeric error code either under the line in error or within the cross reference listing. The error message may also include an alphabetic marker (e.g., "aaa," "bbb," etc.) to help you correlate the error message with the location of the error on the specification line; this feature is especially useful when there are several errors on a single line. At the end of the compile listing, a message summary lists these error codes and provides a message detailing the cause of the problem. Problems vary in severity. A message with a severity of 00 is an informational message noting a condition that will not prevent the program from being compiled; errors with severity of 10 or higher need to be corrected before the program can be compiled normally.

Once you have obtained a "clean compile"—that is, once the system has successfully translated your program into machine language and bound the resulting *MODULE object into a *PGM object—you can begin to check for logic errors that your program may contain.

As a beginning programmer, you may feel frustrated at times by your inability to locate the cause of program errors. With practice, however, you'll find yourself beginning to recognize what kinds of logic errors cause certain output errors, and, as a result, you'll be able to correct your programs with increasing ease. The sign of an excellent programmer is the ability to detect such problems as they occur. But remember, even seasoned programmers make logic mistakes.

Logic Errors

Logic errors are caused by faulty program design. You detect these kinds of errors by having the computer execute your program and then carefully checking the results of the execution. There are two broad classes of logic errors, sometimes called runtime errors and output errors.

Runtime Errors

Runtime errors are errors that prevent your program from reaching a normal end. Runtime errors are easy to detect: Either the program abruptly stops in the middle (an **abend**, or abnormal ending), or the program runs and runs and runs, until finally you or the operator intervenes. (The latter problem signals an infinite loop.) Although detecting the presence of a runtime error is not a problem, discovering the cause of the error can sometimes be difficult. Moreover, the kinds of logic problems that cause abends are different from those that cause infinite loops.

Diagnosing Abends

When your program ends abnormally, the system sends you an error message to inform you of the cause of the problem and where the problem occurred within your program. Sometimes these error messages are not completely clear. By putting your cursor on the message and pressing the Help key you can obtain additional information about the problem. Typical causes of such runtime problems include trying to divide by zero, attempting to carry out a numeric operation on a field that contains non-numeric data, trying to reference an array element beyond the defined limits (or size) of the array, attempting to read past end of file, and trying to update a record before you have read a record.

Once you have located the problem statement and determined the nature of the problem, you often have to trace through your program logic to determine how your program allowed that problem to occur. For example, if the program statement

```
C = A/B;
```

causes an abnormal ending because of an attempt to divide by zero, you need to determine why field B has a value of 0 at the time the system is attempting the division operation. Is B an input field? If so, have you forgotten to read a record before the division? If B is a work field, have you neglected to assign it a nonzero value before the division? Or have you inadvertently assigned 0 to B at the wrong time in your program?

If the problem is one that you could anticipate before the program runs, and if there is a desired process that the program could execute when it encounters the error, you could use some of the error handling techniques discussed in Chapter 14. If you cannot locate the cause of the problem, you may find it useful to run the program in debug mode, a topic discussed later in this appendix.

Diagnosing Infinite Loops

If you have to cancel your job to prevent it from running forever, you know that you have an infinite loop within your program. An infinite loop is a faulty logic structure that causes the computer to repeat the same set of instructions over and over again. The following code shows two obvious infinite loops.

```
Read Customers;
Dou %Eof(Customers);
  Count += 1;
Enddo;

Dou Flag <> Flag;
  Count += 1;
Enddo;
```

In these examples, the causes of the infinite loops are simple to detect. In the first case, no statement exists within the loop to set the value of the %Eof function to *On—the condition needed to end the loop. In the second example, the value of Flag will always be equal to itself, so the loop will never end. (Actually, in these examples, at some point during the execution of the program, the size of Count will be too small to hold its value, causing the program to eventually abend.)

In general, the cause of an infinite loop within a real program is less obvious than it is in these examples. The first thing to realize in trying to diagnose your problem is that you can narrow your focus to the iterative operations in your program: Do, Dou, Dow, and For. The second thing to realize is that somehow the condition that specifies when the looping should stop is not occurring. For example, forgetting to include a Read operation within a loop that continues until end of file is reached will potentially result in an infinite loop. Forgetting to increment a counter in a count-controlled loop (i.e., a For loop) will likewise prevent the loop from ending.

A common cause of infinite loops that you can easily overlook when modifying older, fixed-format programs is a counter defined too small. Study the following example to see whether you can detect the cause of the infinite loop that would result if the program were run.

```
*.. 1 ...+... 2 ...+... 3 ...+... 4 ...+... 5 ...+... 6 ...+... 7 ...+... 8
DName++++++++++ETDsFrom+++To/Len+IDc.Keywords++++++++++++++++++++++++++++++++
CLØNØ1Factor1+++++++Opcode(E)+Factor2+++++++Result++++++++Len++D+HiLoEq....
D Count           S             2 Ø Inz(Ø)

C        Count           Doueq     100
C                        Add       1               Count
C                        Enddo
```

This example results in an infinite loop because Count never attains the value 100. Count is defined as two positions (with zero decimals), so the largest value it can store is 99. Adding 1 to 99 causes the resulting value, 100, to be truncated to 00. You can easily avoid such a potential problem by using the Eval operation or a free-format expression. The Eval operation does not allow high-order truncation; it issues a runtime error to alert you to the problem.

Output Errors

The most insidious kinds of logic errors are not those that cause abnormal program endings or infinite loops, but those that simply result in incorrect output. Some of these errors are very obvious—neglecting to print heading lines on reports, for instance, or omitting an output entry that causes an entire column of information to be missing from a report. Other output errors are less easily detected and require careful checking by hand to discover. You are unlikely to notice errors in complex calculations, for example, if you simply scan the output visually.

Detecting Output Errors

Carefully checking output generated by the computer against the results of your hand calculations is called **desk checking**. How much desk checking is required depends on the complexity of the logic that the program expresses. In general, you should check out enough sets of data to test each logic branch within your program at least once. If, for example, you have written a payroll program that processes workers with overtime hours differently from workers without overtime, you should desk check the output for at least one worker with overtime hours and one without. The more conditional the logic within your program, the more desk checking required to ensure that your program is processing each case correctly.

Don't forget to check the accuracy of subtotals and grand totals. If you have many columns with totals, you generally do not have to manually calculate the total for all columns. If you are doing all your accumulation in the same place within your program and the calculations are all set up in the same way, then if one column's total is correct, the rest should be correct as well—provided you are using the correct fields in the calculations and referencing the correct accumulators in your output.

The final step in checking output is to rigorously compare the computer-generated output with design documents, such as printer spacing charts, to ensure that your output exactly matches the requested format. Are the column headings appropriately centered over the columns? Are the literals spelled correctly (e.g., "Quantity," not "Quanity")? Does the report's vertical alignment match that of the printer spacing chart? Did you edit the output correctly? The programmer's job is to give the designer exactly what he or she requested. Although concern with such formatting details may seem "picky," careful attention to detail is one facet of the preciseness expected of first-rate programmers.

Correcting Output Errors

Once you've discovered an output error, your next job is to discover the cause of the error so you can correct it. A good programmer never makes changes within a program without having a specific reason for doing so. You should locate the precise cause of a problem and fix it; do not, in other words, base your changes on hunches or trial and error.

To find the cause of an error, work backwards: Focus your attention initially on those calculations specifically involved in generating the incorrect output. If after carefully checking these program statements you still have not found a statement that is incorrect, broaden your search to those portions of the program that may be influencing the output more remotely.

It is impossible to be aware of every possible cause of erroneous output, but you should be alert to a number of common errors, many of which are described below, when you are working to debug a program.

Field Problems

Incorrectly defined variables cause overflow (or sometimes truncation), a problem most likely to occur with fields used as accumulators or fields that are the result of complex calculations. Another common field-related problem is a failure to appropriately initialize or reinitialize fields. Forgetting to reset an indicator, counter, or flag variable during repetitive processing is a common cause of erroneous output.

Loops

"Off by one" errors, resulting in a count-controlled loop repeating one too few or one too many times, occur frequently in programs. This kind of error results when you establish the conditional test to end the looping process incorrectly. It often is related to an incorrect initialization of the counter field used to control the looping.

For example, both of the following examples, designed to add all the numbers between 1 and 100, are erroneous. The first example would sum the numbers 1 through 101, while the second would add the values 1 through 99.

```
I = 0;
Sum = 0;
Dow I < 101;
  I += 1;
  Sum += I;
Enddo;

I = 1;
Sum = 0;
Dow I < 100;
  I += 1;
  Sum += I;
Enddo;
```

Another common loop problem is a failure to enter the loop. When you use a looping operator that tests the condition before executing the steps within the loop—when, for example, you want the system to read a file sequentially until it locates a desired code value within a record, process that record, and then resume reading until it finds the next record with that same code value—your program may fail to enter the loop. The following code will correctly find the first record containing the desired code but will continue to process the first record infinitely.

```
Dow Not %Eof(File);
  Dow Code <> Value and Not %Eof(File);
    Read File;
  Enddo;
  Exsr Process;
Enddo;
```

Once the first appropriate record is located, the code field contains the desired value. As a result, the test of the inner loop will always be false and the inner loop will not be executed; no additional records will be read.

IF Logic

Programmers often incorrectly specify the relational comparison used within an If group that is testing for a range of values. For example, if specifications state that pay rate should be less than $45.00, the following pseudocode would be incorrect.

```
If Rate > 45;
     Exsr Error;
Endif;
```

Sometimes output errors are caused by incorrectly nested If operations. Know how the system matches If, Else, and Endif operations, and check the notation of the compiler listing to make sure the system is interpreting your nested If statements the way you intended.

Another common If problem is incorrectly used Ands, Ors, or Nots in compound If tests. Nots, in particular, are prone to errors. For example, if you want to validate a code field that should have a value of S, H, or R, the following code would falsely signal valid values as errors.

```
If Code Not = 'S' Or Code Not = 'H' Or Code Not = 'R';
     Exsr Error;
Endif;
```

Calculations

Sometimes steps in complex calculations are not executed in the correct order. Also, programmers occasionally overlook the possibility that a calculation can result in a negative value. This can be a difficult problem to locate because RPG IV prints or displays all values as absolute (unsigned) values unless field editing includes a provision for a negative sign (however, negative values are handled as negative values during calculation).

For example, when figuring income tax withholding, you often need to subtract a dependent allowance from gross earnings before applying the withholding tax percentage. The relationship between gross earnings and the number of dependents may be such that this subtraction returns a negative value. If you did not anticipate this scenario, the tax will be added to gross earnings (subtracting a negative number), and the same negative tax liability will appear as a positive value on the payroll register report unless the tax field is edited with a code specifying that negative signs should be printed.

Debugging a Program

On occasion, a visual examination of your program will not reveal the source of an output error. Rather than resorting to trial and error, you should use the system's debugging facility. A "debugger" lets you trace a program as it executes, stepping through the program one statement at a time or stopping it at "breakpoints" that you designate so you can examine the values of fields at particular points in execution. Modern debuggers let you view your code as it is executed so that you can examine variable values while stepping through the code on the screen. This procedure can help you locate program errors that might otherwise elude you.

There are several options and methods for using the debugger, including the STRDBG (Start Debug) command and the WebSphere Development Studio Client's Debug Perspective. You will likely use the debugger option that matches your application development environment—STRDBG if you use SEU and PDM, or WDSC if you use that environment. Each of these options has its own advantages and features, but they both have several important debugging facilities in common:

- Debug view
- Breakpoints
- Step mode

Specifying a Debug View

Before you can use a debugger with a program, you must provide one or more debug views for the modules that make up the program. The **debug view** specifies the type of debug data you want stored with the module when you compile it. The debug views are

- compile listing view (*LIST)
- root source view (*SOURCE)
- copy source view (*COPY)
- statement view (*STMT)

Each view offers a different level of source detail.

You choose the debug view when you compile the module (e.g., with the CRTRPGMOD command). Specify the debug view in the compile command's DBGVIEW parameter. For example, you can build a compile listing view by specifying

```
CRTRPGMOD ... DBGVIEW(*SOURCE)
```

The DBGVIEW parameter values also include *ALL, to build all debug views, and *NONE, to omit debugging information from the compiled module.

The compile listing view (*LIST) stores within the module a representation of the actual compile listing, which includes /COPY member text and descriptions for externally described files. Of all the debug view options, the compile listing view offers the most detail and is the most reliable view if the source changes after the module is compiled. The *SOURCE and *COPY views store references to the source at compile time and are not as dependable as the *LIST view. Unlike the *SOURCE and *COPY views, the *LIST view is not tied to the original source member, so you can change, move, or rename the source member without affecting this debug view.

The statement (*STMT) view stores debug information by statement number but does not save a representation of the source. Consequently, you can't display the source when debugging a program with the statement view. This view is most useful when you want to distribute debuggable program code but don't want others to be able to see your source. To completely prevent the ability to debug a module, you can specify DBGVIEW(*NONE).

Breakpoints

One important debugger feature is the ability to set a **breakpoint** at any executable source statement. When a breakpoint is reached, the program stops and lets you analyze the condition of the program at that line of code, just before the program executes it. On the debug screen, you specify breakpoints in either of two ways. Beyond seeing which statement the program will execute next, you can also examine the current value of any variables in the program. Another useful feature is that you can actually change the value of a variable or variables to determine how your program executes when processing that value.

Conditional breakpoints are breakpoints defined to stop your program only when a specific condition is met. Conditional breakpoints are useful when you know your program needs to stop after a specific event. For example, if your program starts to print invalid information when the value of the company field, Cpynbr, changes from '01' to '02', you can set your breakpoint to stop when that happens. Conditional breakpoints can help you find the condition you want to evaluate quickly, without stopping the program several times in search of that condition.

Step Mode

Another way to use debug is to trace the flow of statement execution, using a debugger feature called **stepping**, wherein the system executes all or part of your program one line at a time, stopping after each operation so you can examine the logic flow and program variables.

The debuggers support two varieties of step mode: **step over** and **step into**. In many cases, the difference between the two may be negligible. But if the program you are debugging calls another program or a procedure, these variations will differ. In step over mode, the debugger will treat the call as a single line of code—executing the entire program or procedure before stopping. In step into mode (if you are also debugging the called program) the debugger will treat each line in the called program or procedure as a separate line, stopping at each one.

Debugging with STRDBG

Before you can debug a program, you must place the program into debug mode. The STRDBG (Start Debug) command will name the program (or programs) you want to debug, using the following syntax:

```
STRDBG PGM(program-name program-name ... )
```

A display similar to the one in Figure D.1 will appear, showing the source for the entry module of the program you are debugging. The program(s) will remain in debug mode until you issue the ENDDBG (End Debug) command.

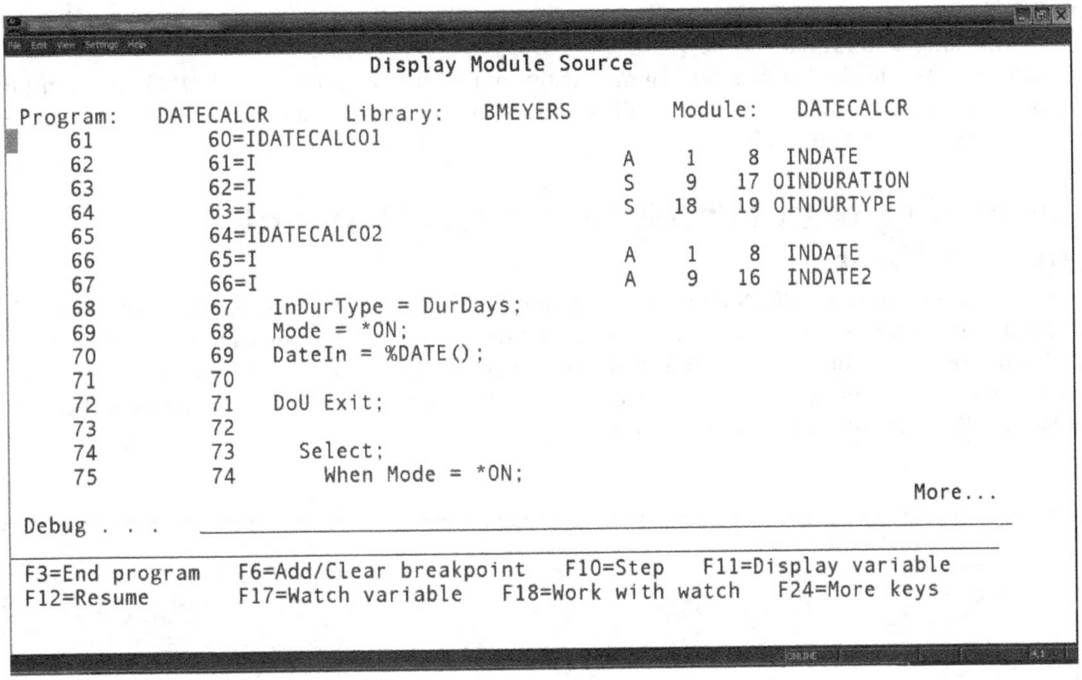

Figure D.1
Debugging with STRDBG

Once in debug mode, you can specify at least one breakpoint, by positioning the cursor on the desired line and pressing F6. Pressing F12 will resume operation, running the program until it encounters the first breakpoint. The debug display will reappear, positioned to the breakpoint.

Using the debug display, you can set other breakpoints—using F6—and execute the program in step mode—using F10 to step over or F22 to step into. To show the current value of a variable, position the cursor on the variable and press F11. The information is displayed on the message line at the bottom of the display; if the information to be displayed exceeds a single line, a separate display is shown so you can view the entire variable information. Another useful feature of debug is that you can actually change the value of a variable or variables to determine how your program executes when processing that value. To modify a variable, use the Eval debugging command, as described below.

In addition to using the function keys to debug a program, you can also type debugging commands on the command line at the bottom of the display. Some of these commands mimic the function of the function keys; other commands expand on the function keys. Here are some common debugging commands:

- Break—to set a breakpoint
- Clear—to clear a breakpoint
- Eval—to show or modify the value of a variable
- Watch—to stop the program whenever and wherever a variable changes
- Step—to execute a program in step mode

Use the Help function—the F1 key—to learn how to use these debugging commands, as well as other commands and function keys.

Once you are finished with a debugging session, remember to issue the ENDDBG command to end the session; this command automatically removes all breakpoints. Before you edit and recompile the program, you must end debug mode.

Debugging with WebSphere Development Studio Client

To debug a program using WebSphere Development Studio Client (WDSc), you must first place the program into debug mode. The easiest way to start a debug session is to set a **service entry point** (SEP) for a program object. To set an SEP, find the program using Remote Systems Explorer (under iSeries Objects). Once you have found the program, right-click it, select Debug (Service Entry) and Set Service Entry Point, as shown in Figure D.2.

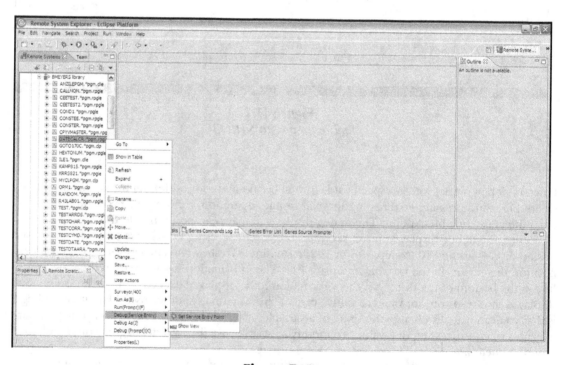

Figure D.2
Setting a Service Entry Point for Debugging

Service entry points appear in the iSeries Service Entry Points view; from here you can change or remove them. When you first set a service entry point, it is associated with your user profile, but you can easily use the Service Entry Points view to modify the SEP to use another user profile. If you recompile the program, you must remove and reset its SEP.

Once you have set the service entry point, the debug session will start automatically within the WDSc Debug perspective (Figure D.3) as soon as the program starts on the iSeries. In the Debug perspective, you can set breakpoints and execute the program in step mode. The Debug perspective displays the source code using the LPEX editor.

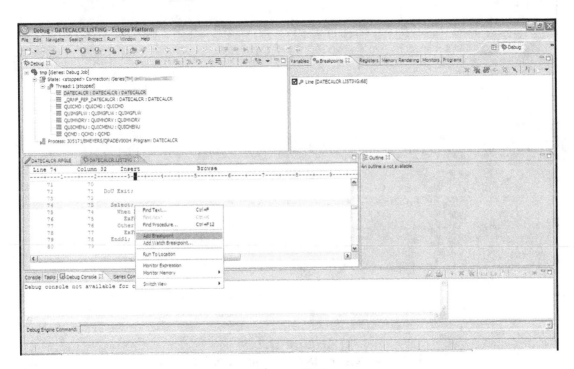

Figure D.3
WDSc Debug Perspective with Breakpoints View

To set a breakpoint, right-click the desired line number and select "Add breakpoint." The breakpoint will be listed in the Breakpoints view, where you can edit or remove it. To run in step mode, select the "Run/Step Into," "Run/Step Over," or "Run/Run to Line" menu option.

To show the current value of a variable, position the mouse over the variable in the LPEX listing. You can also view (and modify) the values of all the program's variables as they change using the Variables view (Figure D.4).

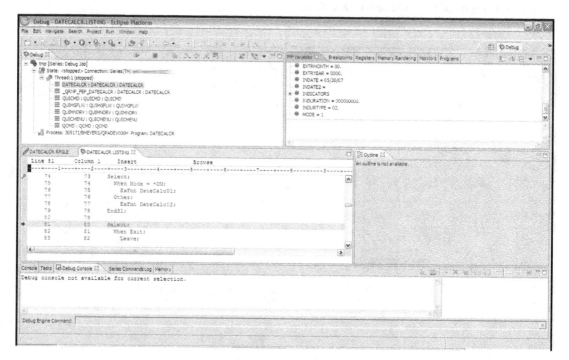

Figure D.4
WDSc Debug Perspective with Variables View

To end the debug session, select the "Run/Terminate" menu option and then—in the Remote Systems Explorer—remove the SEP from the Service Entry Points view.

Appendix E

Maintaining the Past

This appendix discusses the migration of older RPG programs to RPG IV. It also introduces you to features and operations used extensively in earlier versions of the language but now obsolete (although still supported) in RPG IV. The appendix also familiarizes you with RPG's fixed logic cycle, as well as the use of conditioning, resulting, and level indicators.

Evolution and Compatibility

As RPG evolved, IBM's language developers tried to keep the language backward-compatible, so that old program source code could successfully be compiled and then executed with each new version of RPG. Typically, changes to RPG consisted of "add-ons" rather than replacements to older features, so that although the new version of the language might offer a better way to accomplish some programming task, the older method of accomplishing the task would still work. Thus, for example, RPG II programs could be compiled under RPG III with only slight, if any, modification to the source code.

RPG IV, however, introduced fundamental changes to the language. For example, source code lines were lengthened to 100 characters, while previous versions of the language used 80-column specifications. Moreover, RPG IV increased the permitted field name length from six to 4,096 characters, allowed mixed-case entry and blank lines, changed the maximum length of operation names from five to six characters, shifted the location of some fixed-position entries, and changed some code requirements from fixed-position entries to more free-form keywords. All the specification types changed; some were eliminated, and a couple of new ones—the Definition specification and the Procedure Boundary specification—were introduced. As a result, the source code of programs written before RPG IV requires a "facelift" to be compatible with the RPG IV compiler.

Recent releases of RPG IV, especially beginning with Version 5, show noticeable improvements over older releases. As a consequence, the code you maintain may not look much like the code you would write from scratch in RPG IV. Even if all the programs you maintain are written using the RPG IV syntax, it's likely that you will encounter older versions of those programs that could benefit from updates. When you begin working as an RPG IV programmer, you need to understand the programming conventions and styles appropriate to earlier versions of the language to thoroughly understand the programs you encounter.

Fixed-Format Calculations

In this text, we have focused primarily upon RPG IV's free-format syntax for all the operations and processing. This format was introduced to the language at Version 5; it's likely that many of the programs you will maintain were written before Version 5 and will not support free-format operations. Those programs will use a fixed-format Calculation specification instead. The following shows the general format of Calculation specifications:

```
*.. 1 ...+... 2 ...+... 3 ...+... 4 ...+... 5 ...+... 6 ...+... 7 ...+... 8
CLØNØ1Factor1++++++Opcode(E)+Factor2++++++Result++++++++Len++D+HiLoEq....
CLØNØ1Factor1++++++Opcode(E)+Extended-Factor2++++++++++++++++++++++++++++
```

The Calculation specification is identified by a C in position 6. An operation code and any extender must be in positions 26–35 (*Opcode(E)*+). Positions 12–25 (*Factor1+++++++*) and positions 36–49 (*Factor2+++++++*) contain the operands—RPG calls them "factors"—that the operation code will use for its processing. If an operation code returns a result value, the variable that will contain the result is coded in positions 50–63 (*Result+++++++*). All the data must be left aligned within its area; indenting is not allowed. To get an idea of the fixed-format Calculation specification's appearance, consider the following examples:

```
*.. 1 ...+... 2 ...+... 3 ...+... 4 ...+... 5 ...+... 6 ...+... 7 ...+... 8
CLØN01Factor1+++++++Opcode(E)+Factor2+++++++Result++++++++Len++D+HiLoEq....
C         Custnbr      Chain(e)   Customers
C                      If         %Error
C                      Exsr       Custerror
C                      Endif
C         Taxable      Mult(h)    Taxrate        Taxamt
C                      Add        Taxamt         Grossamt
```

The following code would be the free-format equivalent:

```
/Free
  Chain(e) Custnbr Customers;
  If %Error;
    Exsr Custerror;
  Endif;
  Eval(h) Taxamt = Taxable * Taxrate;
  Grossamt += Taxamt;
/End-free
```

Notice that fixed-format Calculation specifications do not require a semicolon (;) delimiter at the end of each line; the fixed-format nature of the specification makes the delimiter unnecessary. The order of the individual parts of the fixed-format specification (Factor 1, Operation Code, Factor 2, Result) may seem unnatural when compared with the free-format code, which begins with an operation code, followed by the factor(s).

Some of the operation codes in the fixed-format example may look unfamiliar to you. Free-format code requires about half the number of operation codes used by the fixed-format C-specs. The Mult (Multiply) operation multiplies Factor 1 by Factor 2 and places the resulting value in the Result field. The Add operation in the above example adds Factor 2 to the Result field, placing the new value in the Result field. Of course, free-format code can utilize arithmetic expressions to accomplish the same purpose; the free-format specification does not support the Mult or Add operations. Appendix A includes a list of those obsolete operation codes not supported in free-format, along with suggested replacements for each.

Using Extended Factor 2

A number of operation codes allow Factor 2 to "spill" beyond its 14-character space, into an
extended Factor 2 area from positions 36–80, including:

- Dou, Dow, For
- Eval, Evalr, Eval-corr
- If, Elseif
- When
- Callp, Return
- On-error

These operations support free-format expressions in the extended Factor 2, even though the
specification is still primarily a fixed-format C-spec. The following example illustrates this use of the
extended Factor 2:

```
*.. 1 ...+... 2 ...+... 3 ...+... 4 ...+... 5 ...+... 6 ...+... 7 ...+... 8
CLØNØ1Factor1+++++++Opcode(E)+Extended-Factor2++++++++++++++++++++++++++++++
C                    Read      Newitems
C                    Dow       Not %Eof
C                    Eval(H)   Unitprofit = Itemcost * .6
C                    Eval      Sellprice = Itemcost + Unitprofit
C                    Eval      Grssprofit = Unitprofit * Qtyrcvd
C                    Eval      Totprofit = Grssprofit + Totprofit
C                    Enddo
```

In fixed-format code, when you extend an expression to multiple lines, you must remember to
include the C in position 6 of subsequent lines:

```
*.. 1 ...+... 2 ...+... 3 ...+... 4 ...+... 5 ...+... 6 ...+... 7 ...+... 8
CLØNØ1Factor1+++++++Opcode(E)+Extended-Factor2++++++++++++++++++++++++++++++
C                    Eval      Grosspay = (Reghours * Rate) +
C                                          (Ovthrs * Rate * 1.5) +
C                                          (Dblhours * Rate * 2)
```

Expressions can be indented within the extended Factor 2. While free-format code allows you to use
an implied Eval or Callp operation under some circumstances, fixed-format code requires you to
explicitly code them.

Defining Work Fields

Fixed-format Calculation specifications allow you to define work variables in the Result field
area without using Definition specifications. With this method, the length of the Result field is
right adjusted in positions 64–68 (Len++). If the field is numeric—for example, as the result of
an arithmetic operation—code the appropriate number of decimal positions, right adjusted, in
positions 69–70 (D+). The following example divides Days by 7, resulting in Weeks; in the same line,
it defines Weeks as a nine-digit packed decimal number with zero decimal positions.

```
*.. 1 ...+... 2 ...+... 3 ...+... 4 ...+... 5 ...+... 6 ...+... 7 ...+... 8
CLØNØ1Factor1+++++++Opcode(E)+Factor2+++++++Result++++++++Len++D+HiLoEq....
C     Days           Div(H)    7             Weeks          9 0
```

This technique for defining work variables is a holdover from RPG III and, before that, RPG II. Good RPG IV style demands that a program instead define all work variables in Definition specifications.

Resulting Indicators

Fixed-format Calculation specifications may utilize positions 71–76 (*HiLoEq*) to set resulting indicators. Resulting indicators are used to reflect the nature of an operation code's result value. For example, an arithmetic operation may set one or more resulting indicators, depending upon whether the result is a positive number, a negative number or zero:

```
CLØNØ1Factor1+++++++Opcode(E)+Factor2+++++++Result++++++++Len++D+HiLoEq
C                   Add       Grssprofit    Totprofit       11 298  98
C                   If        *In98
C                   Exsr      Earnings
C                   Else
C                   Exsr      Losses
C                   Endif
```

For an arithmetic operation, the "Hi" position sets an indicator on if the result is positive; the "Lo" position sets an indicator on if the result is negative; the "Eq" position sets on an indicator if the result is zero. In this example, Grssprofit is added to Totprofit. If the resulting value of Totprofit is positive or zero, indicator 98 will be set on; if Totprofit is negative, indicator 98 would be set off. The program could then test indicator 98. (This example also defines Totprofit as an 11-digit number with two decimals.)

Resulting indicators can also be used to indicate the result of a file I/O operation. Older RPG programs might use this feature instead of using file I/O functions:

```
CLØNØ1Factor1+++++++Opcode(E)+Factor2+++++++Result++++++++Len++D+HiLoEq
C                   Read      Newitems                               99
C                   Dow       Not *In99
C                   Add       Grssprofit    Totprofit       11 298  98
C                   If        *In98
C                   Exsr      Earnings
C                   Else
C                   Exsr      Losses
C                   Endif
C                   Read      Newitems                               99
C                   End
C         Custnbr   Chain     Customers                      97
C                   If        *In97
C                   Exsr      Nocust
C                   Endsr
```

For file I/O operations, a resulting indicator in the "Eq" position typically corresponds to the %Eof function; a resulting indicator in the "Hi" position corresponds to a "Not %Found" condition. The following code could be used in place of the above example:

```
CLØN01Factor1+++++++Opcode(E)+Factor2+++++++Result++++++++Len++D+HiLoEq
C                   Read      Newitems
C                   Dow       Not %Eof(Newitems)
C                   Add       Grssprofit    Totprofit        11 2
C                   If        Totalprofit >= 0
C                   Exsr      Earnings
C                   Else
C                   Exsr      Losses
C                   Endif
C                   Read      Newitems
C                   End
C         Custnbr   Chain     Customers
C                   If        Not %Found(Customers)
C                   Exsr      Nocust
C                   Endsr
```

Good RPG IV style would dictate the elimination of indicators wherever possible to make the code easier to understand, and to reduce the possibility of errors due to redundant and conflicting indicators. Free-format code does not support resulting indicators.

Conditioning Indicators

You can code a conditioning indicator in positions 9–11 (*N01*) of the fixed-format C-spec to control the conditions under which a specification line will be processed. The line will be executed only if the indicator is on when the program encounters the line:

```
CLØN01Factor1+++++++Opcode(E)+Factor2+++++++Result++++++++Len++D+HiLoEq
C       Custnbr     Chain     Customers                               97
C    97             Exsr      Nocust
C    N97            Exsr      Process
```

This example would execute the Nocust subroutine only if indicator 97 is on—that is, only if the preceding Chain operation did not find a record. If the Chain was successful, indicator 97 would be off—which the program would read as "Not 97"—and the Process subroutine would be executed.

Of course a better solution to the above example would be to use an If operation:

```
CLØN01Factor1+++++++Opcode(E)+Factor2+++++++Result++++++++Len++D+HiLoEq
C       Custnbr     Chain     Customers                               97
C                   If        *In97
C                   Exsr      Nocust
C                   Else
C                   Exsr      Process
C                   Endif
```

Or, even better:

```
C           Custnbr        Chain       Customers
C                          If          %Found(Customers)
C                          Exsr        Process
C                          Else
C                          Exsr        Nocust
C                          Endif
```

Or, best:

```
/Free
  Chain Custnbr Customers;
  If %Found(Customers);
    Exsr Process;
  Else;
    Exsr Nocust;
  Endif;
/End-free
```

Though conditioning indicators result in more compact code than the selection and structured operations, the more modern syntax is easier to read and less prone to error.

Moving Data

Fixed-format RPG code usually makes extensive use of three operation codes to accomplish data assignment—transferring a value to a variable. These three operations are Move, Movel (Move Left) and Movea (Move Array). Free-format RPG usually uses a combination of Eval, expressions, and functions to perform assignment operations; free-format code does not support the Move or its related operations.

The Move operation copies the value specified in Factor 2 to the Result field. For example, you could use Move instead of Eval for character assignment operations. Unlike Eval, Move transfers characters from the value (literal or variable) in Factor 2 to the Result field character by character from *right to left*; in this regard, Move is similar to Evalr. But, if the Result field is longer than Factor 2, Move does *not* pad the Result field with blanks; instead, it leaves the additional characters to the left untouched. If padding is required, use a (P) extender. If the result variable is too small to store the Factor 2 value, Move truncates the extra leftmost characters, without warning or error. Movel works the same as Move, except that it moves characters from *left* to *right*. The same rules for padding and field length apply to both Move and Movel.

```
*.. 1 ...+... 2 ...+... 3 ...+... 4 ...+... 5 ...+... 6 ...+... 7 ...+... 8
DName++++++++++ETDsFrom+++To/Len+IDc.Keywords++++++++++++++++++++++++++++++++
D Coursename      S              5    Inz('CS365')
D Padcourse       S             10    Inz('ABCDEFGHIJ')
D Prefix          S              2
```

continued...

continued...

```
CLØNØ1Factor1++++++Opcode(E)+Factor2++++++Result+++++++Len++D+HiLoEq
C                   Move      Coursename    Padcourse
C                             // Padcourse now contains 'ABCDECS365'
C                   Move(p)   Coursename    Padcourse
C                             // Padcourse now contains '      CS365'
C                   Move      Coursename    Prefix
C                             // Prefix now contains '65'
C                   Reset     Padcourse
C                             // Padcourse now contains 'ABCDEFGHIJ'
C                   Reset     Prefix
C                             // Prefix now is blank
C                   Movel     Coursename    Padcourse
C                             // Padcourse now contains 'CS365FGHIJ'
C                   Movel(p)  Coursename    Padcourse
C                             // Padcourse now contains 'CS365     '
C                   Movel     Coursename    Prefix
C                             // Prefix now contains 'CS'
```

Fixed-format RPG might also use these two operations to split fields into smaller units or to rearrange subfields within fields. The following example typifies this use of Move and Movel. The RPG code below switches a "legacy" date (i.e., a date stored as a number or as a character string rather than as a native date value) stored in *yymmdd* format to *mmddyy* format.

```
*.. 1 ...+... 2 ...+... 3 ...+... 4 ...+... 5 ...+... 6 ...+... 7 ...+... 8
CLØNØ1Factor1++++++Opcode(E)+Factor2++++++Result+++++++Len++D+HiLoEq....
                   // Assume YRMODY is a date -- '950329' -- in yymmdd format
C                   Move      Yrmody        Mody          4
                   // Mody now contains '0329'
C                   Movel     Yrmody        Yr            2
                   // Yr now contains '95'
C                   Movel(P)  Mody          Modyyr        6
                   // Modyyr now contains '0329  '
C                   Move      Yr            Modyyr
                   // Modyyr now contains '032995'
```

The Move operation can also be used to change data types, a programming concept known as "casting." Free-format RPG IV uses functions to accomplish casting. Move disregards the decimal positions of numeric fields, and it does not automatically pad a character field with blanks. (You would need to designate the operation extender (P) for this to occur.) The following examples show how to use Move to change data types.

```
*.. 1 ...+... 2 ...+... 3 ...+... 4 ...+... 5 ...+... 6 ...+... 7 ...+... 8
CLØNØ1Factor1++++++Opcode(E)+Factor2++++++Result+++++++Len++D+HiLoEq....
C                   Move      1234          Alpha         4
           // Alpha now contains '1234'
           // Execute desired character operations on Alpha
           //   ...
           // Then move the value to a numeric field so that it can be used with
           // arithmetic operations or edited for output
C                   Move      Alpha         Numeric       4 Ø
```

When you change data types with the Move operation, it is good programming practice to match the size of the result field with the size of the Factor 2 value to avoid errors in data transfer. Matching sizes eliminates inadvertent changes to numeric values; it avoids the truncation of characters or the inclusion of carryover characters from the result field, which can occur if Factor 2 is shorter than the result. The following examples demonstrate how errors in data transfer can happen when using MOVE.

```
*.. 1 ...+... 2 ...+... 3 ...+... 4 ...+... 5 ...+... 6 ...+... 7 ...+... 8
CLØN01Factor1+++++++Opcode(E)+Factor2+++++++Result++++++++Len++D+HiLoEq....
C                   Move      '0000'        Alpha           4
C                   Z-add     0000.0        Numeric         5 1
C                   Move      1.23          Alpha
                                            // Alpha now contains '0123'
C                   Move      Alpha         Numeric
                                            // Numeric now contains 0012.3
C                   Move      32767         Alpha
                                            // Alpha now contains '2767'
C                   Move      59            Alpha
                                            // Alpha now contains '2759'
```

Movea (Move Array) Operation

The Movea (Move Array) operation transfers values from Factor 2 to the Result field of the operation; at least one of the entries—Factor 2 or the Result field—must contain an array name. What makes Movea unusual is that the operation ignores the element boundaries of the array and moves the values, character by character, from the source to the target field or array until either there is nothing left to send or there is no more room in the receiver.

Programmers generally used Movea with character data. It can, however, work with numeric values if the entries in Factor 2 and the Result field have the same numeric length (although not necessarily the same number of decimal positions).

Before the introduction of string operations and functions in RPG IV, programmers used arrays and the Movea operation to inspect and manipulate characters within string fields. This approach involved using Movea to move field values into an array of one-character-long elements. By looping through the elements of the array, you could check each of the characters in the array while the array index served as a positional locator of the character. In this way, you could count, change, or rearrange characters within a string.

To illustrate this concept, assume that a customer file contains records with the field Fname (first name), 12 positions long, and the field Lname (last name), 15 positions long. You want to use the file to generate letters to customers, but you want the letter salutation to read

```
Dear Mary Jones:
```

not

```
Dear Mary       Jones       :
```

The following code uses Movea and arrays to trim trailing blanks from the names and concatenate the desired string. Read the comment lines carefully to understand how the program uses the array to build the salutation.

```
*.. 1 ...+... 2 ...+... 3 ...+... 4 ...+... 5 ...+... 6 ...+... 7 ...+... 8
DName++++++++++ETDsFrom+++To/Len+IDc.Keywords+++++++++++++++++++++++++++++++
CL0N01Factor1+++++++Opcode(E)+Factor2++++++Result++++++++Len++D+HiLoEq....
D Ary             S              1    Dim(35)
D I               S              2 0

C                     Movea(P)  'Dear'        Ary                    '
  // Ary now contains 'Dear

  // Now move Fname into Ary, leaving a blank before the name
C                     Movea     Fname         Ary(6)
  // Ary now contains 'Dear Mary                 '

  // Now loop to inspect the characters of Ary, moving backwards from the
  // last possible position for the last character of Fname, until a
  // nonblank character is found
C                     Eval      I = 17
C                     Dow       Ary(I) = ' '
C                     Eval      I = I - 1
C                     Enddo
  // Given the example, I now has a value of 9

  // Add 2 to I so it points to where Lname should begin
C                     Eval      I = I + 2

  // Move Lname to array, beginning at that position
C                     Movea     Lname         Ary(I)
  // ARY now contains 'Dear Mary Jones          '

  // Now loop to move backwards from the end of the array, looking for
  // the last nonblank character
C                     Eval      I = 35
C                     Dow       Ary(I) = ' '
C                     Eval      I = I - 1
C                     End
  // Given the example, I now has a value of 15

  // Add 1 to I for the colon position
C                     Eval      I = I + 1
C                     Movea     ':'           Ary(I)
  // Ary now contains 'Dear Mary Jones:         '
```

Of course, modern RPG programs would simply use a string expression to accomplish this goal (without arrays or counters):

```
String = 'Dear ' + %Trim(Fname) + ' ' + %Trim(Lname) + ':';
```

Fixed-Format Date Processing

Prior to Version 5, RPG IV used three specific operation codes to perform date processing operations: Adddur (Add Duration), Subdur (Subtract Duration), and Extrct (Extract from Date/Time/Timestamp). These operation codes are not as flexible as the date-related functions and are restricted to the fixed-format Calculation specifications. To help you maintain programs that may use these operations, they are detailed here.

The Adddur operation lets you add a duration coded in Factor 2 to the date specified in Factor 1, storing the answer in the date, time, or timestamp field specified as the Result field. If Factor 1 is blank, the Factor 2 duration is simply added to the Result field. If Factor 1 is present, it may contain any data item representing one of the three date data types, but its type must match that of the Result field.

Factor 2 must contain an integer field (or literal), which represents the number to add, and one of the seven duration codes (listed in Chapter 7), which indicates the kind of duration the number represents. You separate these two portions of Factor 2 with a colon. If the numeric portion of Factor 2 represents a negative value, the duration is subtracted rather than added.

The following examples illustrate the use of Adddur. Assume that fields Billdate, Startdate, and Enddate were defined as type D (date) and fields Starttime and Endtime were defined as type T (time).

```
*.. 1 ...+... 2 ...+... 3 ...+... 4 ...+... 5 ...+... 6 ...+... 7 ...+... 8
CLØN01Factor1++++++Opcode(E)+Factor2++++++Result+++++++Len++D+HiLoEq....
                       // Add 30 days to Billdate to determine Duedate
C         Billdate     Adddur    30:*Days        Duedate

                       // Add field Min, containing a number of minutes,
                       // to Starttime to determine Endtime
C         Starttime    Adddur    Min:*Mn         Endtime

                       // Add 5 years to Duedate
C                      Adddur    5:*Years        Duedate

                       // Subtract 5 months from Enddate to get Startdate
C         Enddate      Adddur    -5:*Months      Startdate
```

The Subdur operation has two uses: One is to subtract a date/time duration from a date/time value (similar to Adddur with a negative duration); the second is to calculate the duration between two date/time units (equivalent to the %Diff function). To subtract a Factor 2 duration from a date/time data item in Factor 1 and store the answer in the Result field, you code the operation the same as you would Adddur. To calculate the duration between two date/time units, place data items of compatible types in both Factor 1 and Factor 2, and place an integer receiving field followed by a duration code that denotes the unit of time involved in the operation in the Result field. Again, a colon separates the two subfactors. The following examples show both uses of Subdur.

```
*.. 1 ...+... 2 ...+... 3 ...+... 4 ...+... 5 ...+... 6 ...+... 7 ...+... 8
CLØNØ1Factor1+++++++Opcode(E)+Factor2+++++++Result+++++++Len++D+HiLoEq....
                        // Subtract 30 days from Duedate to determine Billdate
C       Duedate         Subdur    30:*Days       Billdate

                        // Subtract 5 years from DueDate
C                       Subdur    5:*Y           Duedate

                        // Subtract Birthdate from Today to get Age in years
C       Todaydate       Subdur    Birthdate      Age:*Years

                        // Determine the number of days left to study for a test
C       Examdate        Subdur    Todaydate      Cramtime:*D
```

The third operation for manipulating dates and times, Extrct, extracts a portion of a date, time, or timestamp data item and stores it in the Result field, which can be any numeric or character receiving variable. The Factor 2 date/time data item must be coupled with a duration code to signal which portion of the date/time unit is to be extracted. Factor 1 is always blank for Extrct operations. At Version 5, the %Subdt function performs this task.

```
*.. 1 ...+... 2 ...+... 3 ...+... 4 ...+... 5 ...+... 6 ...+... 7 ...+... 8
CLØNØ1Factor1+++++++Opcode(E)+Factor2+++++++Result+++++++Len++D+HiLoEq....
                        // Determine the birth year of a birth date
C               Extrct    Birthdate:*Y  Birthyear

                        // Extract the month of a loan
C               Extrct    Loandate:*M   Loanmonth
```

Comments
Throughout this text, we have use "double slashes" (//) to indicate the beginning of a program comment. When maintaining older programs, you may encounter comment lines that have an asterisk (*) in position 7 of the specification. This older form of commenting RPG code is valid only for fixed-format specifications. Lines that include asterisk comments cannot contain any executable code; when the RPG compiler encounters an asterisk in position 7, it will ignore the entire line.

Holdovers from RPG III
Some of the programs that you maintain may be RPG III programs. Even some of the RPG IV programs that you encounter may be based on older RPG III programs and may exhibit RPG III characteristics.

In these programs, don't be surprised to see variable names that are very short and written in all uppercase letters. Versions of RPG before RPG IV did not permit mixed-case entry, and they imposed a maximum length of six characters on field names. All specifications in RPG III used fixed-form specifications, without any keywords or free-format.

RPG III Calculations

All Calculation specifications in pre-RPG IV versions of the language use a fixed-format Calculation specification and do not allow an extended Factor 2 form or a free-format specification. The RPG III C-spec is slightly shifted from its RPG IV successor, although its look should be familiar to you:

```
*.. 1 ...+... 2 ...+... 3 ...+... 4 ...+... 5 ...+... 6 ...+... 7 ...
CLØN01N02N03Factor1+++OpcodFactor2+++ResultLenDHHiLoEqComment........
C           DAYS      DIV 7         WEEKS   90H
```

The RPG III specification includes three conditioning indicators in positions 9–17 (*N01N02N03*), all of which must be satisfied before the line can execute. The positions for Factors 1 and 2 are limited to ten characters, and the operation code is limited to five characters (with no operation code extender allowed). Some RPG III operation codes were drastically abbreviated to fit the specification (e.g., REDPE instead of READPE, and LOKUP instead of LOOKUP). The Result field is limited to six characters and the length and decimal positions are also shorter than in RPG IV. Position 53 (*H*) serves as an operation code extender; the above example half adjusts the result.

The EVAL operation was also not available before RPG IV. As a result, programmers used various fixed-format operations to express assignment and arithmetic logic. RPG III did not support expressions or built-in functions. Appendix A includes a list of fixed-format operations, most of which were also available in RPG III.

Looping and Selecting

One set of obsolete operators you may encounter in maintenance programming are DOW*xx*, DOU*xx*, IF*xx*, and WHEN*xx*. These fixed-format structured operators function identically to their modern counterparts DOW, DOU, IF, and WHEN. The major difference is that the older operations do not use conditional expressions. Instead, each operation requires an entry in Factor 1, an entry in Factor 2, and a relational code (replacing the *xx* in the operation) to specify the way in which the two factor entries are to be compared. The following table lists these relational codes and their meanings.

Symbol	Code	Meaning
<	LT	Less than
<=	LE	Less than or equal
=	EQ	Equal
>=	GE	Greater than or equal
>	GT	Greater than
<>	NE	Not equal

Because these older structured operations do not allow expressions, to express a compound condition to check two (or more) relationships, you couple the comparisons with AND*xx* and/or OR*xx* operations to build complex conditional tests.

Carefully examine the following examples to understand how these RPG III structured operations work.

```
*.. 1 ...+... 2 ...+... 3 ...+... 4 ...+... 5 ...+... 6 ...+... 7 ...
CLØN01N02N03Factor1+++OpcodFactor2+++ResultLenDHHiLoEqComment........
 * IF MILES <= 50000:
C           MILES       IFLE 50000
C                       EXSR WRRNTY
C                       ELSE
C                       EXSR YOUPAY
C                       END
 * IF MILES <= 50000 AND MONTHS < 36:
C           MILES       IFLE 50000
C           MONTHS      ANDLT36
C                       EXSR WRRNTY
C                       ELSE
C                       EXSR YOUPAY
C                       END
 * DOW *IN90 = *OFF AND *IN99 = *OFF
C           *IN90       DOWEQ*OFF
C           *IN99       ANDEQ*OFF
 *                      ...
C                       END
```

Defining Data

In RPG III, Definition specifications did not exist. As a result, it used other methods for defining the data items a program would need. Programs written during the RPG III era (and before it) defined each work field within the Calculation specifications, as discussed earlier.

```
*.. 1 ...+... 2 ...+... 3 ...+... 4 ...+... 5 ...+... 6 ...+... 7 ...
CLØN01N02N03Factor1+++OpcodFactor2+++ResultLenDHHiLoEqComment........
C           DAYS        DIV 7       WEEKS    90H
```

RPG III supported a limited set of data types:

- Character
- Signed numeric
- Packed numeric (P)
- Binary (B)

RPG III did not directly support any of the following data types:

- Dates, times, timestamps
- Integers, unsigned integers
- Named indicators
- Pointers, objects

RPG III did let programmers define one variable "like" another, but in the absence of Definition specifications this feature was implemented using a Calculation specification. *LIKE was the Factor 1 value, DEFN was the operation, the reference field was Factor 2, and the field being defined was the result. The following code illustrates this RPG III feature.

```
*.. 1 ...+... 2 ...+... 3 ...+... 4 ...+... 5 ...+... 6 ...+... 7 ...
CLØN01NØ2NØ3Factor1+++OpcodFactor2+++ResultLenDHHiLoEqComment........
 * Older method of defining one field like another
C           *LIKE      DEFN OLDFLD    NEWFLD
```

RPG III used Input specifications to define data structures and named constants:

```
*.. 1 ...+... 2 ...+... 3 ...+... 4 ...+... 5 ...+... 6 ...+... 7 ...
IFilenameSqNORiPos1NCCPos2NCCPos3NCC.............................
I...............................PFromTo++DField+L1M1FrP1MnZr....
 * DATA STRUCTURE
IMYDATA   DS
I                                          1  10 FNAME
I                                         11  20 LNAME
I                                         21 300PHONE
 * NAMED CONSTANT
I              .0751                 C           FICA
I              'MY COMPANY NAME'      C           CPYNAM
```

To define arrays and tables, RPG III had a separate specification, the Extension specification (E-spec) which appeared just after File specifications:

```
*.. 1 ...+... 2 ...+... 3 ...+... 4 ...+... 5 ...+... 6 ...+... 7 ...
E....FromfileTofile++Name++PrcDim+LenPDSAltnamLenPDS.................
 * RUNTIME ARRAY (12 ELEMENTS, 10 DIGITS, 2 DECIMALS)
E               SAL          12 10 2
 * COMPILE TIME ARRAY (50 ELEMENTS, 25 PER RECORD, 2 BYTES EACH)
E               STA    25 50 2
```

Instead of indicating the beginning of compile time data with a **CTDATA specification, RPG III used ** without any other notation. Because this older delimiter gives no indication of which array or table follows it, programs with multiple compile time arrays or tables must define the arrays or tables in the same order as the data appears at the program's end.

RPG III used a comma to code an array index, instead of parentheses. So the third element of the Sta array would be reference by Sta,3 instead of Sta(3). You'll also undoubtedly find that array names are usually limited to three or four characters, to allow for an index notation.

Converting to RPG IV

To let RPG shops migrate code as effortlessly as possible to RPG IV, IBM supplies a CL command, CVTRPGSRC (Convert RPG Source), that converts RPG III source code to RPG IV syntax. This conversion utility automatically rearranges fixed-position entries to new locations, changes obsolete positional entries to appropriate keywords, creates Definition specifications for tables and arrays to replace the eliminated Extension specifications, substitutes new six-character operation codes for their obsolete five-character equivalents (e.g., LOOKUP for LOKUP, EXCEPT for EXCPT), and so on.

In general, companies using AS/400s traditionally store RPG programs within source file QRPGSRC. As companies use command CVTRPGSRC to convert their old programs to RPG IV syntax, many choose to store the converted source code in the default source file QRPGLESRC. Depending on a company's approach to program migration, the business may have converted all its source code shortly after adopting RPG IV, or it may have taken a more leisurely approach, converting code on a member-by-member basis only as program maintenance needs required it. CVTRPGSRC modifies only those syntactical variants that are no longer valid under RPG IV. In converted RPG IV source code, you can still find many coding styles and syntactical usage once necessary and/or appropriate for earlier versions of RPG.

RPG II: A Blast from the Past

Because some RPG shops may be in a transitional stage between RPG III and RPG IV, you might find that some programmers still use the features discussed so far in this appendix. You will also frequently encounter these features in any maintenance programming you do. However, you may wonder, "Why bother with RPG II, a language version that IBM officially retired two decades ago?" The primary reason why you should be at least conversationally familiar with RPG II is that you may be asked to maintain programs that have been based in part, or perhaps entirely, on features from this version of the language. Some of the programs may be old, written before RPG III existed; others may be more recent but written by programmers who had not entirely embraced more modern styles of programming.

RPG II resembles RPG III in many respects. But, because it appears early in RPG's evolutionary past, RPG II does not support many of the features found in RPG III. RPG II does not have any structured operation codes; it depends entirely upon "Go to" logic using a GOTO operation code to branch to another program line, indicated by a TAG operation. Lacking structured operation codes, RPG II also makes heavy use of conditional indicators. RPG II is limited to program-described files; it does not support externally described files.

The major difference, however, between RPG II and RPG III is RPG II's heavy reliance on a built-in "read-process-write" cycle that automates many of the processing requirements for typical batch programs (especially report programs), eliminating the need to explicitly code much of the input/output processing in the Calculation specifications. At its most basic level, the RPG cycle followed these steps:

1. Read a record from a primary input file
2. Using that record, execute the operations in the Calculation specifications
3. Write any relevant output
4. Repeat, starting with Step 1, until end of file

There were many more steps, but the basic "read-process-write" cycle repeated until the program read the last record from the primary input file. Figure E.1 illustrates a few more details about the basic RPG cycle. The RPG cycle was especially useful for programming solutions that required control level break logic (discussed in Chapter 8), because it could automatically detect those breaks using special indicators call level break indicators—without requiring explicit code to detect them.

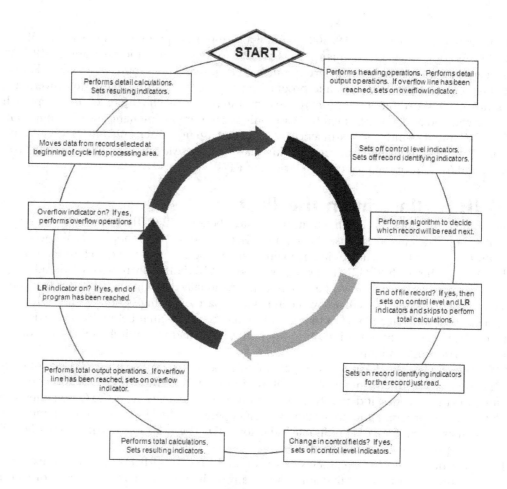

Figure E.1
RPG Cycle Summary

All versions of RPG (including RPG IV's main procedure) have the RPG cycle built into them, but use of this cycle fell out of favor with the adoption of RPG III. RPG's cycle still underlies every RPG program written, but, more and more, today's programmers are ignoring its automatic features in favor of taking complete procedural control over program logic. Rather than "riding" the basic process loop built into RPG, contemporary RPG programmers structure their own loops that are executed repeatedly during the first (and only) pass through RPG's cycle.

The RPG cycle truly is worthless for interactive applications because the cycle presupposes that you have a primary data file that you want to sequentially process from beginning to end. On the other hand, when all you require is a straightforward report of a data file's contents—with or without subtotals—using RPG's cycle may result in somewhat shorter programs, perhaps more quickly developed than if you coded full procedural programs. Because very few programmers today understand the cycle, however, you'll probably find that procedural programs are easier to maintain. Most of the RPG programs written recently are full procedural programs, reflecting a structured, modular approach to program design.

Appendix F

Data Files

This appendix contains definitions of the data files used in the Programming Assignments throughout the book. Most of the assignments focus on three companies to provide a sense of the work involved in developing a company's application system. An application system is a series of programs that use the same set of data files to record and maintain data important to some facet of the company's business, process that data, permit online queries of the data, and produce needed reports. Depending on which programs your instructor assigns, you will be working with several of the data files described below. An overview of each company precedes the descriptions of the files to provide the context needed to understand each company's data and program needs.

On the System i the programmer will find numeric date fields and native date fields. To allow students the greatest learning opportunity, the files in this text will contain both field types.

1. Numeric date fields are represented using an eight-digit number in *ccyymmdd* format.

2. Native date fields are noted as such in the Notes column.

3. A number of files contain both numeric and native dates: these are duplicate fields. An example of this is the GTCSTP file. There are two date fields in this file: PAYDAT, which is stored as a numeric date, and PAYDATL, which is stored as a native date.

The key fields of each file are preceded by an asterisk (*), and if the key is unique, "UNIQUE" is displayed in the notes field. A UNIQUE key field will not allow duplicates of the key to be written to the file. The Notes column in each file description table shows additional information about a field that is helpful to the student.

Case 1: CompuSell

CompuSell is a small mail-order company specializing in computers and computer supplies. The company needs an integrated system of programs to handle its orders and inventory, as well as to generate needed reports for management. An analyst has already done the preliminary design work and determined the files needed as part of the system. The files, and their record layouts, are described below.

CSCHST: CompuSell's Merchandise Sales History File

This file stores information about the yearly sales of a specific part number. The character field PSALES contains the sales information. This field consists of 12 sets (fields) of 5 bytes each, containing the part number sales for a year. The first 5 bytes of a field might be 52000, which when processed would equal $520.00 for a specific month. The elements of this field will need to be converted to a numeric value before processing.

Record Layout of CSCHST
Record Format SLSHREC

Field	Description	Length/Type	(Decimal positions)	Notes
*PART#	Part number	6S	--	UNIQUE
*YEAR	Sales year	4S	--	--
PSALES	Sales by month	60A	--	--

CSCFINP: CompuSell's Customer Finance File

This file contains information about customers who are financing purchases. The CDATE field contains the date of the first payment.

Record Layout of CSCFINP
Record Format FINREC

Field	Description	Length/Type	(Decimal positions)	Notes
*FINNO	Finance number	6S	(0)	UNIQUE
CUSTNO	Customer number	6S	(0)	
FINAMT	Finance amount	7S	(2)	--
DWNPAY	Down payment	7S	(2)	--
CDATE	Commencement date	8	--	ccyymmdd
REMIT	Remittance period	1	--	M (Monthly) or Q (Quarterly)
TERM	Term	3S	--	--
BALDUE	Balance due	7S	(2)	--

CSCSTP: CompuSell's Customer Master File

This file stores basic information about CompuSell's customers. A unique customer number assigned to each new customer serves as that customer's identifier. In addition to storing name, address, and telephone information, this file tracks date of last order (for marketing purposes) and balance owed (for billing purposes). (Although most customers are cash customers, occasionally a customer will under- or overpay on an order.)

Record Layout of CSCSTP
Record Format CUSTREC

Field	Description	Length/Type	(Decimal positions)	Notes
*CUSTNO	Customer number	6S	(0)	UNIQUE
CFNAME	First name	10	--	--
CLNAME	Last name	15	--	--
CSTREET	Street address	20	--	--
CCITY	City	15	--	--
CSTATE	State	2	--	--
CZIP	Zip+4	9	(0)	--
CPHONE	Phone	10S	(0)	--
CALPHONE	Alternate phone	10S	(0)	--
CEMAIL	Customer email	35	--	--
ORDDAT	Last order date	8S	(0)	--
BALDUE	Balance due	6S	(2)	--

CSINVP: CompuSell's Inventory Master File

This file is used to maintain inventory records. When a company adds a new product to its line, the information is recorded in this file. Each item carried has a unique product number. As items are sold, they are subtracted from inventory; as stock comes in from suppliers, the stock is added to inventory. When quantity on hand drops to the reorder quantity, the item is reordered from the appropriate supplier using the reorder quantity field to decide the number to order. The reorder code field is used to prevent the same item from accidentally being reordered more than once. Supplier code is a supplier identification number assigned by CompuSell; supplier product ID is the supplier's identifier for that product. Current cost reflects the most recent cost paid for the item, and average cost is the average cost of the items in inventory. Selling price is what CompuSell currently charges for the item.

Record Layout of CSINVP
Record Format INVREC

Field	Description	Length/Type	(Decimal positions)	Notes
*PRODNO	Product number	6S	(0)	UNIQUE
PACT	Product active	1	-	-
DESCRP	Description	25	--	--
SELLPR	Selling price	6S	(2)	--
SHIPWT	Shipping weight	5	--	1st 3 positions are pounds; last 2 are ounces
QTYOH	Quantity on hand	4P	(0)	--
RORPNT	Reorder point	4P	(0)	--
RORQTY	Reorder quantity	4P	(0)	--
RORCOD	Reorder code	1	--	Blank or R
SUPCOD	Supplier code	3	--	--
CURCST	Current cost	6S	(2)	--
AVGCST	Average cost	6S	(2)	--

CSORDP: CompuSell's Orders File

This file contains "header" information about each order placed with CompuSell. The detailed information about items ordered is stored in file CSORDPRP.

Record Layout of CSORDP
Record Format ORDRREC

Field	Description	Length/Type	(Decimal positions)	Notes
*ORDNBR	Order number	5S	(0)	UNIQUE
ODATE	Date ordered	8S	(0)	yyyymmdd
CUST#	Customer number	6S	(0)	--
PAYMNT	Payment included	7S	(2)	--
ORDTOT	Total cost of order	7S	(2)	--
OSTS	Order status	1	--	SH – Shipped BO - Backordered

CSORDPRP: CompuSell's Order/Products File

This file, in conjunction with file CSORDP, contains information about customer orders.

Record Layout of CSORDPRP
Record Format ORDERREC

Field	Description	Length/Type	(Decimal positions)	Notes
*ORD#	Order number	5S	(0)	UNIQUE
*PRODNO	Product number	6S	(0)	--
QTYORD	Quantity ordered	4S	(0)	--
QTYHOLD	Quantity on hold	4S	(0)	--
COSEQ#	Line item number	3S	(0)	--
TRACK	Tracking number	7A	(0)	UPS or FedEx Tracking number
STS	Product status	2A	(0)	SH – Shipped BO - Backordered

CSSUPP: CompuSell's Supplier File

This file stores information about the suppliers of CompuSell's products. It is used for validation purposes for a number of files.

Record Layout of CSSUPP
Record Format SUPREC

Field	Description	Length/Type	(Decimal positions)	Notes
*SUPCOD	Supplier code	3	--	--
SNAME	Supplier name	25	--	--
CONTAC	Contact person	30	--	--
SSTRET	Street address	20	--	--
SCITY	City	15	--	--
SSTAT	State	2	--	--
SZIP	Zip	9	(0)	--
SPHONE	Phone	10	(0)	--
SEMAIL	Email	30	–	–

CSZPZNP: CompuSell's Zip/Zone Table File

In addition to the above files, CompuSell will need two "table" files to help it determine what to charge its customers for shipping. The first table file, CSZPZNP, will be used to determine the correct shipping zone based on the first three digits of a customer's zip code. Zones range from 2 to 7, depending on zip code. CSZPZNP is a range table file, such that each zip-code record represents the highest of a range of zip codes.

Record Layout of CSZPZNP
Record Format ZIPREC

Field	Description	Length/Type	(Decimal positions)	Notes
*TZIP	Three zip digits	3	(0)	UNIQUE
TZONE	Related shipping zone	1	(0)	--

CSCHGP: CompuSell's Charges Table File

This second table file contains shipping charges based on weight and zone. Each record contains a weight and six charges (one each for zones 2–7).

Record Layout of CSCHGP
Record Format CHGREC

Field	Description	Length/Type	(Decimal positions)	Notes
*TWGT	Weight in pounds	3S	(0)	UNIQUE
TCHG2	Charge zone 2	4S	(2)	--
TCHG3	Charge zone 3	4S	(2)	--
TCHG4	Charge zone 4	4S	(2)	--
TCHG5	Charge zone 5	4S	(2)	--
TCHG6	Charge zone 6	4S	(2)	--
TCHG7	Charge zone 7	4S	(2)	--

CSORDSTS: CompuSell's Order Status File

This table is used to validate entries in the Status code fields in the CSPO and CSPOD tables.

Record Layout of ORDSTS
Record Format STSREC

Field	Description	Length/Type	(Decimal positions)	Notes
*STSCOD	Product status	1	(0)	--
*STS	Order status	1	(0)	--

CSPO: CompuSell's Purchase Order File

This is the Purchase Order Header file for CompuSell. It is parent of the Purchase Order Detail file (CSPOD). The data in the field STSCOD is validated against the Order Status file (CSORDSTS). The data in the field SUPCOD is validated against the Supplier file (CSSUPP).

Record Layout of CSPO
Record Format CSPOREC

Field	Description	Length/Type	(Decimal positions)	Notes
PONBR	Purchase order	5S	(0)	--
PODATE	PO date	L	--	Native date
SUPCOD	Supplier code	3S	(0)	Refer file description
STSCOD	Status code	3A	--	Refer file description
AGENT	Purchasing agent	25A	--	--

CSPOD: CompuSell's Purchase Order Detail File

This is the Purchase Order Detail file for CompuSell. It is a child of the Purchase Order Header file (CSPO). The POSEQ number allows a purchase order to have multiple line items. The data in the field SUPPID is validated against the Supplier file (CSSUPP).

Record Layout of CSPOD
Record Format CSPODREC

Field	Description	Length/Type	(Decimal positions)	Notes
*PO#	Purchase order #	5S	(0)	UNIQUE
*POSEQ#	Sequence number	3S	(0)	UNIQUE
SUPPID	Supplier ID	3S	(0)	--
PARTNO	Part number	6S	(0)	--
QTYORD	Quantity ordered	4S	(0)	--
QTYHOLD	Quantity on hold	4S	(0)	--
STSCOD	Status code	3A	(0)	Refer file description
POTRACK	Tracking number	7A	(0)	--
QYTRCV	Quantity received	4S	(0)	--
COST	Purchase price	6S	(2)	--

CSRCVP: CompuSell's Goods Received

This table is used to track the received goods when items are received from vendors and allows CompuSell to track parts as they are received. Each time goods are received from a supplier, the information is stored in this file until it can be processed in batch to update the inventory file. The data in the field RSUPCOD is validated against the Supplier file (CSSUPP).

Record Layout of CSRCVP
Record Format RCVREC

Field	Description	Length/Type	(Decimal positions)	Notes
*RPO#	PO number	5S	(0)	UNIQUE
*RLINE#	Line number	2S	(0)	UNIQUE
RDTRCV	Date received	L		Native Date
RSUPCOD	Supplier code	3S	(0)	Refer file description
RQTYRCV	Quantity received	4S	(0)	--

CSSEMP: CompuSell's Employee Master File

This table contains the demographic information for CompuSell employees.

Record Layout of CSSEMP
Record Format CEMPREC

Field	Description	Length/Type	(Decimal positions)	Notes
*CSEMPNO	Employee number	6S	(0)	UNIQUE
CSFNAME	First name	15		--
CSLNAME	Last name	20		--
CSSTRET	Street address	20		--
CSCITY	City	15		--
CSSTATE	State	2		--
CSZIP	Zip+4	9S	(0)	--
CSPHONE	Phone	10S	(0)	--
CSSOCSEC	Social Security number	9S		--
CSHIREDT	Hire date	L		Native Date
CSGRADE	Position	3A		--
CSEMAIL	Email address	35A		--

Case 2: Wexler University

Wexler University is a small Midwestern university that needs a system for student records and registration. The system will store information about departments, instructors, courses, sections, students, and enrollment. The files required as part of the system are described below.

WUCRDP: Wexler University Earned Credits File

This file contains a record for each course a student has completed.

Record Layout of WUCRDP
Record Format CRDTREC

Field	Description	Length/Type	(Decimal positions)	Notes
*CSTUNO	Student number	9S	(0)	UNIQUE
*CDEPT	Course department	3	--	--
*CCOURSE	Course number	3	--	--
CGRADE	Grade	2	--	--
CYEAR	Year taken	4S	(0)	ccyy
CTERM	Term code	1	--	1 = spring , 2 = fall , 3 = summer

WUCRSDSP: Wexler University Course Description File

Each course has a description of varying length; the description may include an overview of the course, prerequisites, and so on. One or more records in this file represent a description for a given course; the records for a given course are sequentially assigned a line number.

Record Layout of WUCRSDSP
Record Format CRSDREC

Field	Description	Length/Type	(Decimal positions)	Notes
*DEPT	Course department	3	--	UNIQUE
*COURSE	Course number	3	--	--
*LINE	Description line number	2S	(0)	--
CRSDSC	Description	50	--	--

WUCRSP: Wexler University Course File

Each record in this file represents a course the university offers. Each course is uniquely identified by a six-position identification of course department and course number (e.g., CIS264).

Record Layout of WUCRSP
Record Format CRSREC

Field	Description	Length/Type	(Decimal positions)	Notes
*DEPT	Course department	3	--	UNIQUE
*COURSE	Course number	3	--	--
CRSTTL	Course title	25	--	--
CREDIT	Credits	1S	(0)	--

WUDPTP: Wexler University Department File

This file contains information about each department of Wexler University.

Record Layout of WUDPTP
Record Format DEPTREC

Field	Description	Length/Type	(Decimal positions)	Notes
*DEPT	Department code	3	--	UNIQUE
DNAME	Department name	20	--	--
CHAIR	Name of chair	25	--	--
DOFFIC	Department office	10	--	--
DPHONE	Department phone	10S	(0)	--
DEMAIL	Department email	30	--	--

WUENRLP: Wexler University Current Enrollment File

A record is entered in this file for each student for each section in which he or she is enrolled. At the end of the semester, scanned grades are added to this file before preparing semester grade reports.

Record Layout of WUENRLP
Record Format ENRREC

Field	Description	Length/Type	(Decimal positions)	Notes
*SECT	Section number	5S	(0)	UNIQUE
*STUNO	Student number	9S	(0)	--
GRADE	Grade received	2	--	--

WUEXAMP: Wexler University Student Exam File

This file contains information about students in a class and includes five exam grades for each student.

Record Layout of WUEXAMP
Record Format EXAMREC

Field	Description	Length/Type	(Decimal positions)	Notes
*STUNO	Student Soc. Sec.	9S	(0)	UNIQUE
SFNAME	First name	10	--	--
SLNAME	Last name	15	--	--
EXAM1	Exam 1 grade	3S	(0)	--
EXAM2	Exam 2 grade	3S	(0)	--
EXAM3	Exam 3 grade	3S	(0)	--
EXAM4	Exam 4 grade	3S	(0)	--
EXAM5	Exam 5 grade	3S	(0)	--

WUHRLYP: Wexler University Hourly Employees File

This file contains information about hourly employees at Wexler University.

Record Layout of WUHRLYP
Record Format EMPREC

Field	Description	Length/Type	(Decimal positions)	Notes
*EMPNO	Social Security number	9S	(0)	UNIQUE
LNAME	Last name	15	--	--
FNAME	First name	10	--	--
REGHRS	Regular hours	3S	(1)	--
OTHRS	Overtime hours	3S	(1)	--
RATE	Regular pay rate	4S	(2)	--
PAYCODE	Pay code	1	--	--

WUINPAY: Wexler University Instructor Earnings History File

This file contains earnings history information for instructors at the university. The character field PMNTHS contains the earnings information. This character field is composed of 12 sets (fields) of 7 bytes containing the instructor's earnings for a year. The first 7 bytes of a field might be 0230000, which when processed would be equal to $2300.00 for a specific month. The elements of this field will need to be converted to a numeric value before processing.

Record Layout of WUINPAY
Record Format PAYHREC

Field	Description	Length/Type	(Decimal positions)	Notes
*PINST#	Instructor SSN	9S	--	UNIQUE
*PYEAR	Year	4S	--	--
PMNTHS	Pay by month	84A	--	--

WUINSTP: Wexler University Instructor File

This is the Instructor master file for Wexler University.

Record Layout of WUINSTP
Record Format INSTREC

Field	Description	Length/Type	(Decimal positions)	Notes
INSTNO	Instructor SSN	9S	(0)	UNIQUE
IFNAME	First name	10	--	--
ILNAME	Last name	15	--	--
DEPT	Department	3	--	--
SALARY	Salary	8S	(2)	--
RANK	Academic rank	1	--	1 = instructor; 2 = assistant professor; 3 = associate professor; 4 = full professor
SEX	Sex	1	--	M = male; F = female
HIRDAT	Date of hire	8S	(0)	ccyymmdd
MARSTS	Marital status	1	--	M = married; S = single
DEPEND	Number of dependents	2S	(0)	
TENURE	Tenured faculty	1	--	Y = yes; N = no
TITLE	Preferred title	1	--	1 = Dr.; 2 = Mr.; 3 = Mrs.; 4 = Ms.
STREET	Street address	20	--	--
CITY	City	15	--	--
STATE	State	2	--	--
ZIP	Zip	9S	(0)	--
IEMAIL	Instructor email	30	--	--

WUKEYP: Wexler University File of Keys to Tests in WUTSTP

This file contains the keys (answers) to the tests contained in file WUTSTP, the student test file. There is one answer key (record) for each test. The file is keyed on course ID and test number; these values match those in the student test file.

Record Layout of WUKEYP
Record Format KEYREC

Field	Description	Length/Type	(Decimal positions)	Notes
*TESTNO	Test number	4S	(0)	--
*CRSID	Course ID	6	--	--
ILNAM	Section number	15	--	--
KEY	Answer key	50	--	--

WULOANP: Wexler University Faculty Credit Union Loan File

This file contains records for loan applications to the credit union.

Record Layout of WULOANP
Record Format LOANREC

Field	Description	Length/Type	(Decimal positions)	Notes
*LOANNO	Loan number	5S	(0)	UNIQUE
INSTNO	Instructor number	9S	(0)	--
LAMT	Loan amount	9S	(2)	--
ANNRAT	Annual interest rate	4S	(4)	--
LYEARS	Years for loan	2S	(0)	--

WUSCTP: Wexler University Current Sections File

A record in this file represents every section of each course currently being offered. Each section has been assigned a unique number.

Record Layout of WUSCTP
Record Format SECREC

Field	Description	Length/Type	(Decimal positions)	Notes
*SECTION	Section number	5S	(0)	UNIQUE
DEPT	Course department	3	--	--
CRSNO	Course number	3S	(0)	--
SECTIM	Meeting time	4S	(0)	hhmm - Military Time
SECDAY	Meeting days	3	---	--
ROOM	Room	4	--	--
CAP	Maximum enroll.	3S	(0)	--
CURENL	Current enroll.	3S	(0)	--
INSTNO	Instructor SSN	9S	(0)	--

WUSTDP: Wexler University Student Master File

This file contains information about all Wexler University's students who are actively enrolled as well as those who have graduated within the past five years.

Record Layout of WUSTDP
Record Format STUDREC

Field	Description	Length/Type	(Decimal positions)	Notes
STUSSN	Student SSN	9S	(0)	--
SLNAME	Last name	15	--	--
SFNAME	First name	10	--	--
SMNAME	Middle name	10	--	--
STREET	Street address	20	--	--
CITY	City	15	--	--
STATE	State	2	--	--
ZIP	Zip+4	9S	(0)	--
PHONE	Phone	10S	(0)	--
CRDTOT	Tot. earned credits	3S	(0)	--
DCODE	District code	1	--	I = in-district; O = out-of-district; F = international
ADMDAT	Date admitted	8S	(0)	--
CLASS	Classification	1	--	--
GRDDAT	Date graduated	8	--	ccyymmdd
SDEPT	Dept. of major	3	--	U = undergraduate; G = graduate
GPA	Grade point avg.	3	(2)	--
DEGREE	Degree granted	3	--	Blanks, MS or BS
SEMAIL	Student email	30	--	--

WUTRANSP: Wexler University Transcript Request File

This file contains Social Security numbers for students requesting transcripts. When a student requests a transcript, this file is updated with the student's ID number, and a batch process produces a transcript and then deletes the Student ID from the file.

Record Layout of WUTRANSP
Record Format TRNSREC

Field	Description	Length/Type	(Decimal positions)	Notes
*STUDENT	Student number	9S	(0)	--

WUTSTP: Wexler University Student Test File

This file contains student answers to 50-question, multiple-choice tests and is used in conjunction with the Test Keys file (WUKEYP). This file is keyed on Section number, Test number, and Student ID. Each section has been assigned a unique number. The TESTDATE and GRADE fields are updated when the test is graded.

Record Layout of WUTSTP
Record Format TESTREC

Field	Description	Length/Type	(Decimal positions)	Notes
*TESTNO	Test number	4S	(0)	UNIQUE
*TSECTION	Section number	5S	(0)	--
TCOURSE	Course number	6	--	--
*TSTUDID	Student number	9S	(0)	--
TANS	Answers 1-50 to test	50	--	Values: A, B, C, D, E
TESTDATE	Test date	L	--	Native date
GRADE	Letter grade	1	--	Letter grade on test

Case 3: GTC, Inc.

GTC is a small regional telephone company that needs an application system to maintain customer accounts, bill for calls, process payments, generate management reports, and so on. Four main files will be needed as part of the system. The files, and their record layouts, are described below.

GTCLSP: Calls Transaction File

The telephone switching system generates records automatically in this file, and the CALLKEY field is assigned sequentially. Records accumulate in the file during the month; once a month, the file is processed to determine monthly billing. The file is then cleared at the beginning of each new billing period.

Record Layout of GTCLSP
Record Format CALREC

Field	Description	Length/Type	(Decimal positions)	Notes
*CALLKEY	Unique ID	10S	(0)	Unique key
CPHONE	Caller's number	10S	(0)	--
PHCALLED	Called number	10S	(0)	--
CALDATL	Date of call	L	--	Native date
CALDAT	Date of call	8S	(0)	--
CALLEN	Length of call	3S	(0)	--
CALTIMT	Time of call	T		Time field
CALTIM	Time of call	6S	(0)	--
CALCST	Call cost	5S	(2)	--

GTCSTP: Customer Master File

This file contains a record for each of GTC's customers.

Record Layout of GTCSTP
Record Format CUSREC

Field	Description	Length/Type	(Decimal positions)	Notes
*CPHONE	Customer phone number	10S	(0)	UNIQUE
CLNAME	Last name	15	--	--
CFNAME	First name	10	--	--
CSTRET	Street address	20	--	--
CCITY	City	15	--	--
CSTAT	State	2	--	--
CZIP	Zip	5S	(0)	--
CURBIL	Current billing amount	6S	(2)	--
AMTOWE	Amount owed	6S	(2)	--
PAYDATL	Date last payment	90–99	--	Native date
PAYDAT	Date last payment	90–97	(0)	ccyymmdd

GTCPAYP: Payments Transaction File

This file is generated through optical character recognition (OCR) and manual entry techniques. Records are used once to update the customer account figures and generate a payment report and then archived.

Record Layout of GTCPAYP
Record Format PAYREC

Field	Description	Length/Type	(Decimal positions)	Notes
CPHONE	Payer's phone number	10S	(0)	--
AMTPD	Amount paid	6S	(2)	--
DATRCVL	Date payment received	L		Native timestamp
DATRCV	Date payment received	8S	(0)	--

GTCRATP: Rates Table File

This is a sequential file, used as a table, to determine cost of calls to a given area code and exchange.

Record Layout of GTCRATP
Record Format RATEREC

Field	Description	Length/Type	(Decimal positions)
TAREA	Area code called	3S	(0)
TEXCH	Exchange called	3S	(0)
TCITY	City called	10	--
TSTATE	State called	2	--
CST1ST	Cost for first minute	3S	(2)
CSTADL	Cost for each additional minute	3S	(2)

Miscellaneous Files

The following files are not part of any of the above application systems. They represent "standalone" applications included as Programming Assignments to demonstrate certain programming concepts.

ACP001: Acme Work File

This is an Acme manufacturing company file used to represent one day's work for an employee. Records are accumulated for a week, so there will be several records per employee. This file is used in Chapter 8, Programming Assignment 4.

Record Layout of ACP001
Record Format ACMEREC

Field	Description	Length/Type	(Decimal positions)	Notes
*SOCSEC	Social Sec. number	9S	(0)	--
NAME	Name	16	--	--
WKDATE	Date worked	8S		mmddyyyy
HOURS	Hours worked	4S	(2)	--
QTY	Quantity produced	3S	(0)	--

BIDS: Bids File

Ida Lapeer, an Interior Decorator, owns a small interior design company and uses the data in this file to give estimates for painting rooms. This file is used in Chapter 5, Programming Assignment 5.

Record Layout for BIDS
Record Format BIDREC

Field	Description	Length/Type	(Decimal positions)	Notes
*JOBNO	Job number	4S	(0)	Unique
PCODE	Paint code	5S	(0)	--
PCOST	Per gallon cost	4S	(2)	--
COVRG	Coverage per gallon	3S	(0)	--
LENFT	Room length, feet	2S	(0)	--
LENIN	Room length, inches	2S	(0)	--
WIDFT	Room width, feet	2S	(0)	--
WIDIN	Room width, inches	2S	(0)	--
HTFT	Room height, feet	2S	(0)	--
HTIN	Room height, inches	2S	(0)	--
PCT	Percent windows, doors	2S	(2)	--

HJSLPP: Salesperson File

Honest John's Used Car's is a small used car dealership. Honest John's also sells used car parts. This is the salesperson master file for this company. This file is not used in this version of the book but your instructor might assign a programming assignment based on this file.

Record Layout for HJSLPP
Record Format SLSPREC

Field	Description	Length/Type	(Decimal positions)	Notes
*SLSMNO	Salesperson number	3S	(0)	Unique
SLNAME	Salesperson last name	15		--
SFNAME	Salesperson first name	10		--
BASPAY	Weekly base pay	6S	(2)	

HJSLSP: Honest John's Used Car's Sales File

Honest John's Used Car's is a small used car dealership. Honest John's also sells used car parts. This is the sales detail file for this company. This file is not used in this version of the book but your instructor might assign a programming assignment based on this file.

Record Layout for HJSLSP
Record Format SLSREC

Field	Description	Length/Type	(Decimal positions)	Notes
*INVNO	Invoice number	5S	(0)	Unique
SLSMNO	Salesperson number	3S	(0)	--
ORDDAT	Date of order	L		Date field
ORDTOT	Total cost of order	7S	(2)	--

HJSLDTP: Honest John's Used Car's Sales Order Detail File

Honest John's Used Car's is a small used car dealership. Honest John's also sells used car parts. This is the sales order detail file for this company. This file is not used in this version of the book but your instructor might assign a programming assignment based on this file.

Record Layout for HJSLDTP
Record Format SLLIREC

Field	Description	Length/Type	(Decimal positions)	Notes
*INVNO	Invoice number	5S	(0)	Unique
*LINE	Line number	4S	(0)	--
PRODNO	Product number	6S	(0)	--
QTYORD	Quantity ordered	4S	(0)	--

HJINVP: Honest John's Used Car's Inventory Master File

Honest John's Used Car's is a small used car dealership. Honest John's also sells used car parts. This is the inventory master file for this company. This file is not used in this version of the book but your instructor might assign a programming assignment based on this file.

Record Layout for HJINVP
Record Format INVREC

Field	Description	Length/Type	(Decimal positions)	Notes
*PRODNO	Product number	6S	(0)	UNIQUE
DESCRP	Description	25		--
SELLPR	Selling price	6S	(2)	--
SHIPWT	Shipping weight	5S	(0)	First 3 numbers are pounds and last 2 numbers are ounces
QTYOH	Quantity on hand	4S	(0)	--
RORPNT	Reorder point	4S	(0)	--
RORQTY	Reorder quantity	4S	(0)	--
RORCOD	Reorder code	1		Valid values are Blank or R
CURCST	Current cost	6S	(2)	--
AVGCST	Average cost	6S	(2)	--

MWC001P: Municipal Water Company Meter Reading File

The municipal water company uses this file to calculate monthly water charges. This file is used in Chapter 8, Programming Assignment 3.

Record Layout for MWC001P
Record Format MWREC

Field	Description	Length/Type	(Decimal positions)	Notes
*CUSTNO	Customer number	5S	(0)	UNIQUE
CNAME	Customer name	20	--	--
OLDMTR	Old meter reading	4S	(0)	--
NEWMTR	New meter reading	4S	(0)	--
RCODE	Residency code	1S	(0)	1 = city resident; 2 = non-city resident

PIPRESP: Airline Reservation File

This file is not used in this version of the book but your instructor might assign a programming assignment based on this file.

Record Layout for PIPRESP
Record Format PIPREC

Field	Description	Length/Type	(Decimal positions)	Notes
*DY	Day of week	1S	(0)	--
*FLIGHT	Flight number	1S	(0)	--
RESERV	Seats reserved	2S	(0)	--
FNAME	First name of reserver	10	--	--
LNAME	Last name of reserver	15	--	--
PHONE	Phone number of reserver	10S	(0)	--

PRDSLSP: Sales Volume File

This file is an example of storing a year's sales data for a specific product in one field of a record. This file is not used in this version of the book but your instructor might assign a programming assignment based on this file.

Record Layout for PRDSLSP
Record Format PRDREC

Field	Description	Length/Type	(Decimal positions)	Notes
*PRODNO	Product number	6	(0)	UNIQUE
SLS	12 monthly sales*	72	(0)	--

* Represents monthly total sales figures for that product, arranged sequentially from January to December; each sales figure is a six-digit integer.

Index